Political Quotations

Political Quotations

A Collection of Notable Sayings on Politics from Antiquity through 1989

Daniel B. Baker, Editor

Gale Research Inc. · DETROIT · NEW YORK · LONDON

Daniel B. Baker, *Editor*

Gale Research Inc. staff

Mary Beth Trimper, *Production Manager*
Marilyn Jackman, *External Production Assistant*

Arthur Chartow, *Art Director*
Kathleen A. Mouzakis, *Graphic Designer*
C.J. Jonik, *Keyliner*

Laura Bryant, *Production Supervisor*
Louise Gagné, *Internal Production Associate*

Theresa Rocklin, *Supervisor of Systems and Programming*
Kenneth J. Muth, *Manager of Computer Systems Administration*
Thomas Potts and Dan Bono, *Programmers*

Copyright © 1990
Gale Research Inc.
835 Penobscot Bldg.
Detroit, MI 48226-4094

ISBN: 0-8103-4920-5

Printed in the United States of America

Published simultaneously in the United Kingdom by Gale Research International Limited (An affiliated company of Gale Research Inc.)

To my mother

C O N T E N T S

P R E F A C E

This first edition of *Political Quotations* assembles a collection of specifically political statements, from the well-known to the lesser-known and from the past as well as more recent years. In fact, 36 percent of the quotations date from the end of World War II. In compiling this book, the editor discovered no limit on the potential number of relevant and "quotable" quotations, and every foray into a new source typically turned up several, rather than one or two, possibilities.

Highlights

- 4,000 quotations on specifically political subjects.
- Quotations have been selected from all eras but all are relevant to the modern world.
- Arranged by general subject headings, such as "Democracy," which cover a broad range of entries to provide a thorough overview of the topic.
- Arranged by date under each subject heading to make it possible to see the development of thinking over the centuries.
- Source citations within the text enable users to attribute quotations accurately.
- Keyword indexing serves as a quick way to access half-remembered statements or to gather appropriate quotes on a particular theme or idea.
- Author index allows all quotations by a specific person to be located.
- Birth/death dates and brief author descriptions in the Author Index help identify the person quoted and provide context for the quotation.
- Original language version of the quotation and reliable translations are provided.

Specifically Political Quotations Selected

The aim has been to limit the book to specifically political quotations, thus eliminating scores of other quotations on hundreds of subjects found in general quotation books. Moreover, these quotations were to be relevant to the modern world. This criterion does not eliminate historical quotations but, rather, involved searching out those with general and continuing application. Eliminated, then, were quotations that referred to one historical event ("Tippecanoe and Tyler too") and those that may have made sense to a classically-educated politician of the nineteenth century but would be meaningless to audiences today.

Subject Access Provides Overview

In order to make the book as useful as possible to a wide readership, the quotations are grouped by subject matter. These subject headings are general and include a broad range of citations in each category. The quotations are arranged by date under each heading to make it possible to read through each section as a narrative of the development of thinking over the centuries about a concept such as "Democracy."

Author and Keyword Indexes

The Author Index groups by subject heading all quotations by a specific person. If the reader knows of a quote by a specific author or is curious about who said what, the Author Index provides categories and entry numbers for the authors of interest. In addition, birth and death dates and brief background information help identify the authors and their accomplishments.

Special effort has been expended on supplying as many keywords as possible in this index as a way of accessing half-remembered statements or of finding a particularly pertinent reference. Under each keyword is an abbreviated form of the quotation followed by the quotation's entry number.

Original Language and Reliable Translations Provided

To the extent possible, the editor has tracked down the original quotations in languages other English. The English translations of these quotations can vary enormously. Typically, however, the variance is between a "literary" translation that reads well in English (and therefore is often best known) but has only a tenuous relationship to the original and a "literal" translation that faithfully reproduces the meaning of the original but is eminently "unquotable" in English. The editor has tried to steer a middle course in choosing a translation or, in some cases, making his own. In any case, the most honest method seemed to be to include the original language version so readers, in so far as their expertise allow, can make their own choices.

Source Material

In order to be sure to include all well-known political quotations, the editor initially turned to the following references:

Bartlett's Familiar Quotations, 15th edition (Boston: Little, Brown and Company, 1980)
Classical and Foreign Quotations (London: J. Whitaker & Sons, 1904)
Das Grosse Kruger Zitaten Buck (Frankfurt: Wolfgang Kruger Verlag)
Dictionary of Contemporary Quotations (John Gordon Burke Publisher, Inc. 1981)
A Dictionary of Political Quotations (London: Europa Publications, 1984)
Dictionnaire de citations francaises (Paris: Le Robert, 1978)
The Great Quotations (Secaucus, N. J.: Lyle Stuart Inc., 1983)
The International Thesaurus of Quotations (New York: Harper and Row, 1970)
The Oxford Dictionary of Quotations, 2nd edition (London, Oxford University Press, 1955)
The Quotable Woman (New York: Facts on File, 1982)
Quotations in Black (Westport, Conn.: Greenwood Press, 1981)
Respectfully Quoted (Washington, D.C.: Library of Congress, 1989)
Simpson's Contemporary Quotations (Boston: Houghton Mifflin Company, 1988)
Treasury of Presidential Quotations (Chicago: Follett Publishing Company, 1964)

For the initial legwork in tracking down and documenting famous quotations, the editor of the current volume is very grateful to those editors who have gone before.

Using these well-known references as a base, the editor turned to the original sources and verified, as much as possible, the accuracy of the quotations themselves as well as related data. This search then turned up numerous other potential quotations that have been sifted through and included or not. Occasionally, two sources differed and an adjudication between them had to be made. In addition, misquotes and other errors in citation were identified through this search, and these have been corrected.

The editor has provided (where possible) the original date of the quotation and the original source as opposed to, say, a recent edition of a work. While providing specific recent data may initially appear to be more helpful to the reader trying to track down a quotation, over the years—as editions follow each other— page numbers no longer have meaning and the 1967 edition becomes as difficult to track down as the 1767 edition.

To help researchers, however, the approach has been to give the most detailed information possible that is not likely to change over the years, e.g., chapter numbers and article titles. For classical works, this means supplying standard divisions that have become accepted over the years.

Suggestions Are Welcome

Comments are always welcome and can be addressed to: Editor, *Political Quotations,* Gale Research Inc., 835 Penobscot Building, Detroit, MI 48226-4094.

Political Quotations

BUREAUCRACY

1. It's all papers and forms, the entire Civil Service is like a fortress made of papers, forms, and red tape. —Alexander Ostrovsky, *The Diary of a Scoundrel*, 1868

2. The bureaucracy is what we all suffer from. [*Die Bürokratie ist es, an der wir alle kranken.*] —Prince Otto von Bismarck, comments in Friedrichsruh, Dec 12, 1891

3. I believe there are still some people who think that a democratic State is scarcely distinguishable from the people. This, however, is a delusion. The State is a collection of officials, different for different purposes, drawing comfortable incomes so long as the status quo is preserved. The only alteration they are likely to desire in the status quo is an increase of bureaucracy and of the power of the bureaucrats. —Bertrand Russell, Maurice Conaway lecture, 1922

4. A statesman is judged by results. If his policy fails he goes. It may be unfair, but there is a kind of rough justice about it. Mr. Montagu Norman (Governor of the Bank of England), on the other hand, is never called upon to explain, justify or defend his policies. And it is his policies which have been carried out for the past ten years. Governments may come and governments may go, but the Governor of the Bank of England goes on for ever. It is a classic example of power without responsibility. —Robert Baron Boothby, speech in the House of Commons, Apr 25, 1932

5. The power which a multiple millionaire, who may be my neighbor and perhaps my employer, has over me is very much less than that which the smallest fonctionnaire possesses who wields the coercive power of the state, and on whose discretion it depends whether and how I am to be allowed to live or to work. —Friedrich August von Hayek, *The Road to Serfdom*, 1944

6. The nearest approach to immortality on earth is a government bureau. —James F. Byrnes, *Speaking Frankly*, 1947

7. Bureaucracies are designed to perform public business. But as soon as a bureaucracy is established, it develops an autonomous spiritual life and comes to regard the public as its enemy. —Brooks Atkinson, "September 9", *Once Around the Sun*, 1951

8. The perfect bureaucrat everywhere is the man who manages to make no decisions and escape all responsibility. —Brooks Atkinson, "September 9", *Once Around the Sun*, 1951

9. Farming looks mighty easy when your plow is a pencil, and you're a thousand miles from the corn field. —Dwight D. Eisenhower, speech in Peoria, Illinois, Sep 25, 1956

10. Bureaucracy, the rule of no one, has become the modern form of despotism. —Mary McCarthy, "The Vita Activa", *New Yorker*, Oct 18, 1958

11. There is something about a bureaucrat that does not like a poem. —Gore Vidal, *Sex, Death and Money*, 1968

12. The only thing that saves us from the bureaucracy is inefficiency. An efficient bureaucracy is the greatest threat to liberty. —Eugene J. McCarthy, *Time*, Feb 12, 1979

13. Bureaucrats write memoranda both because they appear to be busy when they are writing and because the memos, once written, immediately become proof they were busy. —Charles Peters, *How Washington Really Works*, 1980

14. If you're going to sin, sin against God, not the bureaucracy, God will forgive you but the bureaucracy won't. —Hyman G. Rickover, quoted by William A. Clinkscales Jr., *The New York Times*, Nov 3, 1986

CITIZENSHIP

15. Citizens are not born, but made. [*Homines enim civiles non nascuntur, sed fiunt.*] —Baruch (Benedictus de) Spinoza, *Tractatus Politicus*, 1676

16. He who would not wish his own country to be bigger or smaller, richer or poorer, would be a citizen of the universe. [*Celui qui voudrait que sa patrie ne fût jamais ni plus grande ni plus petite, ni plus riche ni plus pauvre serait le citoyen de l'univers.*] —Voltaire, "Patrie", *Dictionnaire philosophique*, 1764

17. A strict observance of the written laws is doubtless one of the high virtues of a good citizen, but it is not the highest. The laws of necessity, of self-preservation, of saving our country when in danger, are of higher obligation. —Thomas Jefferson, letter to John B. Colvin, Sep 20, 1810

18. Whatever makes men good Christians, makes them good citizens. —Daniel Webster, speech in Plymouth, Massachusetts, Dec 22, 1820

19. Before Man made us citizens, great Nature made us men. —James Russell Lowell, "On the Capture of Fugitive Slaves near Washington", 1845

20. Everyone who receives the protection of society owes a return for the benefit. —John Stuart Mill, *On Liberty*, 1859

21. Without a home their can be no good citizen. With a home there can be no bad one. —Andrew Johnson, quoted by George L. Tappan, *Andrew Johnson, Not Guilty*, May, 1872

22. The first requisite of a good citizen in this republic of ours is that he shall be able and willing to pull his weight. —Theodore Roosevelt, speech in New York City, Nov 11, 1902

23. To acquire immunity to eloquence is of the utmost importance to the citizens of a democracy. —Bertrand Russell, *Power*, 1938

24. The Constitution does not provide for first and second class citizens. —Wendell Lewis Willkie, *An American Program*, 1944

25. It is the duty of every citizen according to his best capacities to give validity to his convictions in political affairs. —Albert Einstein, *Treasury for the Free World*, 1946

26. It is not the function of our Government to keep the citizen from falling into error; it is the function of the citizen to keep the Government from falling into error. —Robert H. Jackson, *American Communications Association v. Douds*, May, 1950

27. Politics ought to be the part-time profession of every citizen who would protect the rights and privileges of free people and who would preserve what is good and fruitful in our national heritage. —Dwight D. Eisenhower, broadcast speech, Jan 28, 1954

28. I deplore the need or the use of troops anywhere to get American citizens to obey the orders of constituted courts. —Dwight D. Eisenhower, on Arkansas' refusal to accept the Supreme Court's school desegregation ruling, May 14, 1958

29. The ignorance of one voter in a democracy impairs the security of all. —John F. Kennedy, speech at Vanderbilt Univ., Nashville, Tennessee, May 18, 1963

30. We will have to repent in this generation not merely for the vitriolic words and actions of the bad people, but for the appalling silence of the good people. —Martin Luther King Jr., "Letter from the Birmingham Jail", Jan 16, 1963

31. Because all Americans just must have the right to vote. And we are going to give them that right. All Americans must have the privileges of citizenship regardless of race. And they are going to have those privileges of citizenship regardless of race. —Lyndon Baines Johnson, speech to a joint session of U.S. Congress, Mar 15, 1965

32. The citizen who criticizes his country is paying it an implied tribute. —J. William Fulbright, speech to the American Newspaper Publishers Association, Apr 28, 1966

CLASS DIVISIONS

33. Oligarchy: A government resting on a valuation of property, in which the rich have power and the poor man is deprived of it. —Plato, *The Republic*, ca. 390 B.C.

34. The best political community is formed by citizens of the middle class. —Aristotle, *Politics*, 343 B.C.

35. When quarrels and complaints arise, it is when people who are equal have not got equal shares, or vice versa. —Aristotle, *Nicomachean Ethics*, ca. 325 B.C.

36. It is not easy for men to rise whose qualities are thwarted by poverty. [*Haud facile emergunt quorum virtutibus obstat.*] —Juvenal, (Decimus Junius Juvenalis), *Satires*, ca. 100

37. Excess of wealth is cause of covetousness. —Christopher Marlowe, *The Jew of Malta*, 1589

38. He whose belly is full believes not him whose is empty. —Thomas Fuller, *Gnomologia*, 1732

39. They (the rich) are led by an invisible hand to make nearly the same distribution of the necessaries of life, which would have been made, had the earth been divided into equal portions among all its inhabitants; and thus, without intending it, without knowing it, advance the interest of the society, and afford means to the multiplication of the species. —Adam Smith, *The Theory of Moral Sentiments*, 1759

40. All communities divide themselves into the few and the many. The first are the rich and wellborn, the other the mass of the people. ... The people are turbulent and changing; they seldom judge or determine right. Give therefore to the first class a distinct, permanent share in the government. They will check the unsteadiness of the second, and as they cannot receive any advantage by a change, they therefore will ever maintain good government. —Alexander Hamilton, debate at the Constitutional Convention, Jun 18, 1787

41. A true natural aristocracy is not a separate interest in the state, or separable from it. It is an essential integrant part of any large body rightly constituted. —Edmund Burke, *Appeal from the New to the Old Whigs*, 1791

42. The freest government, if it could exist, would not be long acceptable, if the tendency of the laws were to create a rapid accumulation of property in few hands, and to render the great mass of the population dependent and penniless. —Daniel Webster, speech at Plymouth, Massachusetts on 200th anniversary of landing of Pilgrims, Dec 22, 1820

43. Distinctions in society will always exist under every just government. Equality of talents, of education, or of wealth can not be produced by human institutions. —Andrew Jackson, veto message, Jul 10, 1832

44. Nobility, say the aristocracy, is the intermedium between the king and the people—true; just as a sporting dog is the intermedium between the sportsman and the hare. —Honore Gabriel, Comte de Mirabeau, "Apophthegms", *Mirabeau's Letters During His Residence in England*, 1832

45. Society is composed of two classes: they who have more dinners than appetite, and they who have more appetite than dinners. —Honore Gabriel, Comte de Mirabeau, "Apophthegms", *Mirabeau's Letters During His Residence in England*, 1832

46. Aristocracy as a predominant element in a government, whether it be aristocracy of skin, of race, of wealth, of nobility, or of priesthood, has been to my mind the greatest source of evil throughout the world, because it has been the most universal and the most enduring. —Thomas Arnold, letter to T. Coolidge, May 18, 1838

47. The American aristocracy can be found in the lawyer's bar and the judge's bench. [*L'aristocratie américaine est au banc des avocats et le siège des juges.*] —Alexis, Comte de Tocqueville, *Democracy in America*, 1835-39

48. The English laborer does not find his worst enemy in the nobility, but in the middling class. —Orestes Augustus Brownson, *Boston Quarterly Review*, 1840

49. I believe and I say it is true Democratic feeling, that all the measures of the government are directed to the purpose of making the rich richer and the poor poorer. —William Henry Harrison, speech, Oct 1, 1840

50. If trade unionists failed to register their protest by striking, their silence would be regarded as an admission that they acquiesced in the pre-eminence of economic forces over human welfare. Such acquiescence would be a recognition of the right of the middle classes to exploit the workers when business was flourishing and to let the workers go hungry when business was slack. —Friedrich Engels, *The Condition of the Working Class in England in 1844*, 1844

51. Two nations between whom there is no intercourse and no sympathy; who are as ignorant of each other's habits, thoughts and feelings, as if they were dwellers in different zones or inhabitants of different planets ... the rich and the poor. —Benjamin Disraeli, *Sybil*, 1845

52. I was told that the Privileged and the People formed two nations. —Benjamin Disraeli, *Sybil*, 1845

53. The ruling ideas of each age have ever been the ideas of its ruling class. —Karl Marx, *The Communist Manifesto*, 1848

54. In proportion as the antagonism between classes within the nation vanishes, the hostility of one nation to another will come to an end. —Karl Marx, *The Communist Manifesto*, 1848

55. The history of all hitherto existing society is the history of class struggles. —Karl Marx, *The Communist Manifesto*, 1848

56. The executive of the modern state is but a committee for managing the common affairs of the whole bourgeoisie. —Karl Marx, *The Communist Manifesto*, 1848

57. Of all the classes that stand face to face with the bourgeoisie to-day, the proletariat alone is a really revolutionary class. The other classes decay and finally disappear in the face of modern industry; the proletariat is its special essential product. —Karl Marx, *The Communist Manifesto*, 1848

58. What the bourgeoisie, therefore, produces, above all, is its own grave-diggers. Its fall and the victory of the proletariat are equally inevitable. —Karl Marx, *The Communist Manifesto*, 1848

59. Wherever there is excessive wealth, there is also in the train of it excessive poverty; as, where the sun is brightest, the shade is deepest. —Walter Savage Landor, "Aristoteles and Callisthenes", *Imaginary Conversations*, 1824-53

60. The people are the safest, the best, and the most reliable lodgement of power. ... Keep up the middle class; lop off an aristocracy on the one hand, and a rabble at the other; let the middle class ... have the power, and your government is always secure. —Andrew Johnson, speech in the U.S. Senate, May 20, 1858

61. The rich rob the poor and poor rob one another. —Sojourner Truth, attributed

62. You who have read the history of nations, from Moses down to our last election, where have you ever seen one class looking after the interests of another? —Elizabeth Cady Stanton, speech to the New York state legislature, Feb 18, 1860

63. Aristocracy is always cruel. —Wendell Phillips, speech on Toussaint L'Ouverture, 1861

64. There is always more misery among the lower classes than there is humanity in the higher. [*Il y a toujours encore plus de misère en bas que de fraternité en haut.*] —Victor Hugo, *Les Misérables*, 1862

65. The bourgeoisie of the whole world, which looks complacently upon the wholesale massacre after the battle, is convulsed by horror at the desecration of brick and mortar. —Karl Marx, *The Civil War in France*, 1871

66. Inequality has the natural and necessary effect, under the present circumstances, of materializing our upper class, vulgarizing our middle class, and brutalizing our lower class. —Matthew Arnold, "Equality", *Mixed Essays*, 1879

67. So long as all the increased wealth which modern progress brings goes but to build up great fortunes, to increase luxury and make sharper the contrast between the House of Have and the House of Want, progress is not real and cannot be permanent. —Henry George, *Progress and Povery*, 1879

68. Private ownership of land is the nether millstone. Material progress is the upper millstone. Between them, with increasing pressure, the working classes are being ground. —Henry George, *Progress and Poverty*, 1879

69. The danger is not that a particular class is unfit to govern. Every class is unfit to govern. —Lord Acton, letter to Mary Gladstone, Apr 24, 1881

70. There are three ways by which an individual can get wealth—by work, by gift, and by theft. And, clearly, the reasons why the workers get so little is that the beggars and thieves get so much. —Henry George, *Social Problems,* 1883

71. Capital is dead labor that, vampire-like, lives only by sucking living labor, and lives the more, the more labor it sucks. —Karl Marx, *Das Kapital*, 1867-83

72. The most grinding poverty is a trifling evil compared with the inequality of classes. —William Morris, letter to Andreas Scheu, Sep 5, 1883

73. It is enough political economy for me to know that the idle rich class is rich and the working class is poor, and that the rich are rich because they rob the poor. —William Morris, lecture in Glasgow in 1884, quoted by J.B. Glasier, *William Morris and the Early Days of the Socialist Movement*, 1921

74. It has become an article of the creed of modern morality that all labor is good in itself—a convenient belief to those who live on the labor of others. —William Morris, *Useful Work Versus Useless Toil*, 1884

75. Where justice is denied, where poverty is enforced, where ignorance prevails, and where any one class is made to feel that society is in an organized conspiracy to oppress, rob, and degrade them, neither persons nor property will be safe. —Frederick Douglass, speech on twenty-fourth anniversary of emancipation in the District of Columbia, Apr, 1886

76. He mocks the people who proposes that the Government shall protect the rich and that they in turn will care for the laboring poor. —Grover Cleveland, fourth annual message to Congress, Dec 3, 1888

77. The state is nothing but an instrument of oppression of one class by another—no less so in a democratic republic than in a monarchy. —Friedrich Engels, preface to the 1891 edition of Karl Marx, *The Civil War in France*, 1891

78. The great mistake made in regard to the matter now under consideration, is to take up the notion that class is naturally hostile to class, and that the wealthy and the working man are intended by nature to live in mutual conflict. So irrational and so false is this view, that the direct contrary is the truth. Just as the symmetry of the human frame is the result of the suitable arrangement of the different parts of the body, so in a state is it ordained by nature that these two classes should dwell in harmony and agreement, so as to maintain the balance of the body politic. —Leo XIII, encyclical, *Rerum Novarum*, 1891

79. It is a very curious fact that, with all our boasted "free and equal" superiority over the communities of the Old World, our people have the most enormous appetite for Old World titles of distinction. —Oliver Wendell Holmes Sr., *Over the Teacups*, 1891

80. For as true as that a house divided against itself cannot stand, and that a nation half-slave and half-free cannot permanently endure, it is true that a people who are slaves to market-tyrants will surely come to be their slaves in all else, that all liberty begins to be lost when one liberty is lost, that a people half democratic and half plutocratic cannot permanently endure. —Henry Demarest Lloyd, *Wealth Against Commonwealth*, 1894

81. Having behind us the producing masses of the nation and the world, supported by the commercial interests, the laboring interests and the toilers, everywhere, we will answer their demand for a gold standard by saying to them: You shall not press down upon the brow of labor this crown of thorns; you shall not crucify mankind upon a cross of gold. —William Jennings Bryan, "Cross of Gold" speech at the Democratic National Convention, Chicago, Illinois, Jul 8, 1896

82. For twenty-one years the Social Democratic Federation has based its propaganda on the class-war theory, and the result is dismal failure. How could it be otherwise? Mankind in the mass is not moved by hatred, but by love of what is right. —Keir Hardie, quoted by Iain McLean, *Keir Hardie*, 1975

83. To be a poor man is hard, but to be a poor race in a land of dollars is the very bottom of hardships. —W.E.B. Du Bois, *The Souls of Black Folk*, 1903

84. The oligarchic character of the modern English commonwealth does not rest, like many oligarchies, on the cruelty of the rich to the poor. It does not even rest on the kindness of the rich to the poor. It rests on the perennial and unfailing kindness of the poor to the rich. —G.K. Chesterton, *Heretics*, 1905

85. An aristocracy is like cheese; the older it is the higher it becomes. —David Lloyd George, speech at Mile End, London, Dec, 1910

86. All down History, nine-tenths of mankind have been grinding the corn for the remaining one-tenth, been paid with the husks—and bidden to thank God they had the husks. —David Lloyd George, quoted by Martin Gilbert in introduction, *Lloyd George*, 1968

87. Energy in a nation is like sap in a tree; it rises from bottom up. —Woodrow Wilson, speech, Oct 28, 1912

88. It's no disgrace t' be poor, but it might as well be. —"Kin" Hubbard, *Abe Martin's Sayings and Sketches*, 1915

89. If capital an' labor ever do git t'gether it's good night fer th' rest of us. —"Kin" Hubbard, saying

90. A society without an aristocracy, without an elite minority, is not a society. [*Una sociedad sin aristocracia, sin minoría egregia, no es una sociedad.*] —Jose Ortega y Gasset, *Invertebrate Spain*, 1922

91.　The government of the United States is a device for maintaining in perpetuity the rights of the people, with the ultimate extinction of all privileged classes. —Calvin Coolidge, speech in Philadelphia, Pennsylvania, Sep 25, 1924

92.　(Its object was) to make working-class bees without a sting, who were to gather honey for the rich, but be deprived of the right to defend themselves. —Sir Oswald Mosley, on policies of British government during 1926 General Strike, *The Star*, Dec 15, 1926

93.　Advocates of capitalism are very apt to appeal to the sacred principles of liberty, which are embodied in one maxim. The fortunate must not be restrained in the exercise of tyranny over the unfortunate. —Bertrand Russell, "Freedom in Society", *Skeptical Essays*, 1928

94.　The conflict between capitalism and democracy is inherent and continuous; it is often hidden by misleading proaganda and by the outward forms of democracy, such as parliaments, and the sops that the owning classes throw to the other classes to keep them more or less contented. —Jawaharlal Nehru, *Glimpses of World History*, 1933

95.　The defeats and victories of the fellows at the top aren't defeats and victories for the fellows at the bottom. [*Die Sieg und Niederlagen der Grossköpfigen oben und der von unten fallen nämlich nicht immer zusammen, durchaus nicht.*] —Bertolt Brecht, *Mother Courage*, 1939

96.　Civilization cannot survive if it rests upon a propertyless proletariat. —Ernest Bevin, speech to the annual conference of the Transport and General Workers' Union, Aug 18, 1941

97.　The century on which we are entering can be and must be the century of the common man. —Henry Wallace, speech in New York City, May 8, 1942

98.　A government which robs Peter to pay Paul can always depend on the support of Paul. —George Bernard Shaw, *Everybody's Political What's What?*, 1944

99.　We have two American flags always; one for the rich and one for the poor. When the rich fly it it means that things are under control; when the poor fly it it means danger, revolution. —Henry Miller, "Good News! God Is Love!", *The Air-Conditioned Nightmare*, 1945

100.　Numerous cross-divisions favour peace within a nation, by dispersing and confusing animosities; they favour peace between nations, by giving every man enough antagonism at home to exercise all his aggressiveness. ... A nation which has gradations of class seems to me, other things being equal, likely to be more tolerant and pacific than one which is not so organised. —T.S. Eliot, *Notes Towards the Definition of Culture*, 1948

101.　When the rich wage war it's the poor who die. —Jean-Paul Sartre, *The Devil and the Good Lord*, 1951

102.　An aristocracy in a republic is like a chicken whose head has been cut off: it may run about in a lively way, but in fact it is dead. —Nancy Mitford, *Noblesse Oblige*, 1956

103.　The forces of a capitalist society, if left unchecked, tend to make the rich richer and the poor poorer. —Jawaharlal Nehru, *The New York Times*, Sep 7, 1958

104.　If a free society cannot help the many who are poor, it cannot save the few who are rich. —John F. Kennedy, inaugural address, Jan 20, 1961

105.　For the urban poor the police are those who arrest you. In almost any slum there is a vast conspiracy against the forces of law and order. —Michael Harrington, *The Other America*, 1962

106.　People who are much too sensitive to demand of cripples that they run races ask of the poor that they get up and act just like everyone else in the society. —Michael Harrington, *The Other America*, 1962

107.　Clearly the most unfortunate people are those who must do the same thing over and over again, every minute, or perhaps twenty to the minute. They deserve the shortest hours and the highest pay. —John Kenneth Galbraith, *Made to Last*, 1964

108. A man's respect for law and order exists in precise relationship to the size of his paycheck. —Adam Clayton Powell Jr., "Black Power: A Form of Godly Power", *Keep the Faith, Baby!*, 1967

109. The poor in Resurrection City have come to Washington to show that the poor in America are sick, dirty, disorganized, and powerless—and they are criticized daily for being sick, dirty, disorganized, and powerless. —Calvin Trillin, "U.S. Journal: Resurrection City", *The New Yorker*, Jun 15, 1968

110. The whole paraphernalia of the criminal law and the criminal courts is based on the need of the upper class to keep the lower class in its place. —David Frost, and Anthony Jay, *The English*, 1968

111. Forgive us for pretending to care for the poor, when we do not like poor people and do not want them in our homes. —Church United Presbyterian, *Litany for Holy Communion*, 1968

112. There is no need to feel pessimistic about this country. It is only the upper echelons who are licked. —Anthony Wedgwood Benn, *Arguments for Socialism*, 1979

113. Anyone today who speaks of class in the context of politics runs the risk of excommunication and outlawry. —Anthony Wedgwood Benn, Marx Memorial Lecture in London, 1982

COMMUNISM

114. What is a communist? One who hath yearnings/ For equal division of unequal earnings. —Ebenezer Elliott, "Epigram", *Poetical Works*, 1840

115. From each according to his abilities, to each according to his needs. —Louis Blanc, *The Organization of Work*, 1840

116. Communism is inequality, but not as property is. Property is exploitation of the weak by the strong. Communism is exploitation of the strong by the weak. —Pierre Joseph Proudhon, *Qu'est-ce la propriété?*, 1840

117. The earth is the first condition of our existence. To make it an object of trade was the last step towards making human beings an object of trade. To buy and sell land is an immorality surpassed only by the immorality of selling oneself into slavery. —Friedrich Engels, *Outlines of a Critique of Political Economy*, 1844

118. It (Communism) is the solution of the riddle of history and knows itself to be the solution. —Karl Marx, "Private Property and Communism", *Economic and Philosophical Manuscripts*, 1844

119. In this sense, the theory of the communists may be summed up in the single sentence: Abolition of private property. —Karl Marx, *The Communist Manifesto*, 1848

120. The communists disdain to conceal their views and aims. They openly declare that their ends can be obtained only be forcible overthrow of all existing social conditions. —Karl Marx, *The Communist Manifesto*, 1848

121. A spectre is haunting Europe—the spectre of Communism. All the powers of old Europe have united in a holy alliance to exorcise this spectre. —Karl Marx, introduction, *The Communist Manifesto*, 1848

122. Let the ruling classes tremble at a communist revolution. The proletarians have nothing to lose but their chains. They have a world to win. Working men of all countries, unite! —Karl Marx, *The Communist Manifesto*, 1848

123. Communism is a Russian autocracy turned upside down. —Alexander Ivanovich Herzen, *The Development of Revolutionary Ideas in Russia*, 1851

124. What I did that was new was to demonstrate: (1) that the existence of classes is merely linked to particular phases in the development of production; (2) that class struggle necessarily leads to the dictatorship of the proletariat; (3) that this dictatorship itself constitutes the transition to the abolition of all classes and to a classless society. —Karl Marx, letter to J. Wedemeyer, 1852

125. History is the judge;—its executioner, the proletarian. —Karl Marx, speech to English Chartists, 1856

126. The first act by virtue of which the State really constitutes itself the representative of the whole of society—the taking possession of the means of production in the name of society—that is, at the same time, its last independent act as a State. State interference in social relations becomes, in one domain after another, superfluous, and then dies out of itself; the government of persons is replaced by the administration of things, and by the conduct of processes of production. The State is not "abolished." It dies out. —Friedrich Engels, *Socialism, Utopian and Scientific*, 1892

127. These two great discoveries, the materialistic conception of history and the revelation of the secret of capitalistic produciton through surplus-value, we owe to Marx. With these discoveries socialism becomes a science. —Friedrich Engels, *Socialism, Utopian and Scientific*, 1892

128. By its economic essence imperialism is monopolist capitalism. The fact alone determines the place of imperialism in history. —Vladimir Ilyich Lenin, *Imperialsm, The Highest Stage of Capitalism*, 1917

129. The working class is for a Lenin what ore is for a metal worker. —Maxim Gorky, *New Life*, Jan, 1918

130. I have been over into the future, and it works. —Lincoln Steffens, reported conversation with Bernard Baruch following visit to the Soviet Union, 1919

131. A Bolshevik as far as I can tell is nothing but a socialist who wants to do something about it. To the best of my knowledge I am a Bolshevik myself. —George Bernard Shaw, interview, *The Liberator*, 1919

132. Socialism is Soviet power plus the electrification of the whole country. —Vladimir Ilyich Lenin, Report to the Congress of Soviets, Dec 22, 1920

133. Marx's Capital is in essence a collection of atrocity stories designed to stimulate martial ardour against the enemy. Very naturally, it also stimulates the martial ardour of the enemy. It thus brings about the class-war which it prophesies. —Bertrand Russell, presidential address to the Students Union, London School of Economics, Oct 10, 1923

134. Print is the sharpest and the strongest weapon of our party. —Joseph Stalin, speech, Apr 19, 1923

135. The party in the last instance is always right, because it is the single historic instrument which the working class possesses for the solution of its fundamental problems. ... I know that one must not be right against the party. One can be right only with the party, and through the party, because history has created no other road for the realization of what is right. —Leon Trotsky, speech to the congress of the Communist Party of the Soviet Union, May, 1924

136. The dictatorship of the Communist Party is maintained by recourse to every form of violence. —Leon Trotsky, *Terrorism and Communism*, 1924

137. Marxian Socialism must always remain a portent to the historians of opinion—how a doctrine so illogical and so dull can have exercised so powerful and enduring an influence over the minds of men, and, through them, the events of history. —John Maynard Keynes, *The End of Laissez-Faire*, 1925

138. It is impossible to build a socialist paradise as an oasis amid the inferno of world capitalism. —Leon Trotsky, *Critique of the Programme of the Third International*, 1928

139. Whereas in Britain we are slaves to the past, in Russia they are slaves to the future. —Aneurin Bevan, remark on returning from the Soviet Union, 1930

140. Leninism is a combination of two things which Europeans have kept for some centuries in different compartments of their soul—religion and business. —John Maynard Keynes, "A Short View of Russia", *Essays in Persuasion*, 1933

141. The more Communism, the more civilization. —George Bernard Shaw, *The Intelligent Woman's Guide to Socialism, Capitalism, Sovietism and Fascism*, 1937

142. Every Communist must grasp the truth, "Political power grows out of the barrel of a gun." —Mao Tse-tung, "Problems of War and Strategy", Nov 6, 1938

143. Our principle is that the Party commands the gun, and the gun must never be allowed to command the Party. —Mao Tse-tung, "Problems of War and Strategy", Nov 6, 1938

144. The idea that a completely planned or directed economic system could and would be used to bring about distributive justice presupposes, in fact, the existence of something which does not exist and has never existed, a complete moral code in which the relative values of all human ends, the relative importance of all the needs of all the different people, are assigned a definite place and a definite quantitative significance. —Friedrich August von Hayek, *Freedom and the Economic System*, 1940

145. He who places his trust in the Marxian synthesis as a whole, in order to understand present situations and problems, is apt to be woefully wrong. —Joseph Schumpeter, *Capitalism, Socialism and Democracy*, 1942

146. There is little reason to believe that this socialism will mean the advent of the civilization of which orthodox socialists dream. It is much more likely to present fascist features. That would be a strange answer to Marx's prayer. But history sometimes indulges in jokes of questionable taste. —Joseph Schumpeter, *Capitalism, Socialism and Democracy*, 1942

147. Marxism is essentially a product of the bourgeois mind. —Joseph Schumpeter, *Capitalism, Socialism, and Democracy*, 1942

148. We Communists are like seeds and the people are like the soil. Wherever we go, we must unite with the people, take root and blossom among them. —Mao Tse-tung, "On the Chungking Negotiations", Oct 17, 1945

149. What is to happen about Russia? ... An iron curtain is drawn down upon their front. We do not know what is going on behind. —Sir Winston S. Churchill, telegram to President Truman, May 12, 1945

150. From Stettin in the Baltic to Trieste in the Adriatic an iron curtain has descended across the Continent. —Sir Winston S. Churchill, speech in Fulton, Missouri, Mar 6, 1946

151. Communism is like Prohibition, it's a good idea, but it won't work. —Will Rogers, *The Autobiography of Will Rogers*, 1949

152. Communism is not love. Communism is a hammer which we use to crush the enemy. —Mao Tse-tung, *Time*, Dec 18, 1950

153. Communism is the corruption of a dream of justice. —Adlai E. Stevenson Jr., speech in Urbana, Illinois, 1951

154. We must have faith in the masses and we must have faith in the Party. These are two cardinal principles. If we doubt these principles, we shall accomplish nothing. —Mao Tse-tung, *On the Question of Agricultural Co-operation*, Jul 31, 1955

155. The objection to a Communist always resolves itself into the fact that he is not a gentleman. —H.L. Mencken, *Minority Report*, 1956

156. Whether you like it or not, history is on our side. We will bury you. —Nikita S. Khrushchev, reported remark at the Polish embassy in Moscow, Nov 18, 1956

157. A Communist has no right to be a mere onlooker. —Nikita S. Khrushchev, report to the Central Committee of the Communist party, Feb 14, 1956

158. Comrades! The cult of the individual acquired such monstrous size chiefly because Stalin himself, using all conceivable methods, supported the glorification of his own person. —Nikita S. Khrushchev, speech to a secret session of the 20th Congress of Communist party, Feb 23, 1956

159. Comrades! We must abolish the cult of the individual decisively, once and for all. —Nikita S. Khrushchev, speech to a secret session of the 20th Congress of the Communist party, Feb 23, 1956

160. Power is an end in itself and the essence of contemporary Communism. —Milovan Djilas, *The New Class*, 1957

161. Letting a hundred flowers blossom and a hundred schools of thought contend is the policy for promoting the progress of the arts and the sciences and a flourishing socialist culture in our land. —Mao Tse-tung, speech at Beijing "On the Correct Handling of Contradictions Among the People", Feb 27, 1957

162. The only vital political difference between Marx and Lenin is that Lenin had a revolution to practice on and Marx had not. —Max Eastman, letter, 1958

163. Marxism is too uncertain of its grounds to be a science. I do not know a movement more self-centered and further removed from the facts than Marxism. —Boris Pasternak, *Doctor Zhivago*, 1958

164. A strange, a perverted creed that has a queer attraction both for the most primitive and for the most sophisticated societies. —Harold Macmillan, remarks on Communism, *New York Herald Tribune*, Oct 15, 1961

165. I am a good friend to Communists abroad but I do not like them at home. —Souvanna Phouma, on his country's attempt to remain neutral, *Life*, Nov 3, 1961

166. As an organized political group, the Communists have done nothing to damage our society a fraction as much as what their enemies have done in the name of defending us against subversion. —Murray Kempton, "What Harvey Did", *America Comes of Middle Age*, 1963

167. I once said, "We will bury you," and I got into trouble with it. Of course we will not bury you with a shovel. Your own working class will bury you. —Nikita S. Khrushchev, speaking of capitalists in a speech in Split, Yugoslavia, Aug 24, 1963

168. Far from being a classless society, Communism is governed by an elite as steadfast in its determination to maintain its prerogatives as any oligarchy known to history. —Robert F. Kennedy, "Berlin East and West", *The Pursuit of Justice*, 1964

169. Communists have committed great crimes, but at least they have not stood aside, like an established society, and been indifferent. I would rather have blood on my hands than water like Pilate. —Graham Greene, *The Comedians*, 1966

170. In dealing with the Communists, remember that in their mind what is secret is serious, and what is public is merely propaganda. —Charles E. Bohlen, *The New York Times*, Jan 2, 1966

171. There may be thousands of principles of Marxism, but in the final analysis they can be summed up in one sentence. Rebellion is justified. —Mao Tse-tung, quoted, "The Thoughts of Mao Tse-tung", *London Times*, Oct 31, 1966

172. They (communists) are not supermen at all. They are men with feet of clay which extend almost all the way up to their brains. —Edwin O. Reischauer, hearing before U.S. Senate Committee on Foreign Relations, Jan 31, 1967

173. Guerilla warfare is to peasant uprisings what Marx is to Sorel. —Régis Debray, *Revolution in the Revolution?*, 1967

174. When internal and external forces which are hostile to Socialism try to turn the development of any Socialist country towards the restoration of a capitalist regime ... it becomes not only a problem of the people concerned, but a common problem and concern of all Socialist countries. —Leonid Brezhnev, speech to the Congress of the Polish Communist Party, Nov 12, 1968

175. Give socialism back its human face. —Alexander Dubcek, frequently used slogan during the "Prague Spring", 1968

176. Stalinism is the essence of Communism. —Jean-François Ravel, *Time*, Feb 2, 1976

177. The confrontation between a man—any man— and Communism is always over in two rounds. Communism nearly always wins the first round, like a wild beast that leaps at its adversary and bowls him over. But, if there is a second round, Communism nearly always loses. The man's eyes open and he sees that he admired a bundle of cast-offs, a semblance, an optical illusion. Then he's immunized, and for ever. —Alexander Solzhenitsyn, interview with Georges Suffert, *Encounter*, Apr, 1976

178. Communist countries never expel correspondents for telling lies. —Ross H. Munro, *The New York Times*, Nov 27, 1977

179. I don't like Communism because it hands out wealth through rationing books. —Omar Torrijos Herrera, *The New York Times*, Sep 7, 1977

180. No communist country has solved the problem of succession. —Henry A. Kissinger, *Time*, Mar 12, 1979

181. The terrible thing is that one cannot be a Communist and not let oneself in for the shameful act of recantation. One cannot be a Communist and preserve an iota of one's personal integrity. —Milovan Djilas, interview with George Urban, *Encounter*, Dec, 1979

182. The dictatorship of the proletetariat is an historically regressive idea for it makes the individual a servant of the state, robs him of his power of decision, and is thus at odds with the aspirations of mankind. —W. Averell Harriman, *Encounter*, Nov, 1981

183. It depends on the way you measure the concept of good, bad, better, worse, because, if you choose the example of what we Polish have in our pockets and in our shops, then I answer that Communism has done very little for us. If you choose the example of what is in our souls, instead, I answer that Communism has done very much for us. In fact our souls contain exactly the contrary of what they wanted. They wanted us not to believe in God and our churches are full. They wanted us to be materialistic and incapable of sacrifices: we are anti-materialistic, capable of sacrifice. They wanted us to be afraid of the tanks, of the guns, and instead we don't fear them at all. —Lech Walesa, interview with Oriana Fallaci, *The Sunday Times*, Mar 22, 1981

184. It doesn't matter if a cat is black or white, so long as it catches mice. —Deng Xiaoping, quoted on liberalization of Communist Party rules, *Time*, Jan 6, 1986

185. Without glasnost there is not, and there cannot be, democratism, the political creativity of the masses and their participation in management. —Mikhail S. Gorbachev, speech to the Communist Party Congress, *The New York Times*, Nov 9, 1986

186. Isn't it strange that ... people build walls to keep an enemy out, and there's only one part of the world and one philosophy where they have to build walls to keep their people in? —Ronald Reagan, on the Berlin Wall, Aug 12, 1986

CONSERVATISM

187. When it is not necessary to change, it is necessary not to change. —2nd Viscount Falkland, (Lucius Cary), speech in the House of Commons, Nov 22, 1641

188. The sickly, weakly, timid man fears the people, and is a Tory by nature. —Thomas Jefferson, letter to the Marquis de Lafayette, Nov 4, 1823

189. I am a Conservative to preserve all that is good in our constitution, a Radical to remove all that is bad. I seek to preserve property and to respect order, and I equally decry the appeal to the passions of the many or the prejudices of the few. —Benjamin Disraeli, campaign speech at High Wycombe, England, Nov 27, 1832

190. The principle of Conservatism has always appeared to me to be not only foolish, but to be actually felo de se: it destroys what it loves, because it will not mend it. —Thomas Arnold, letter to James Marshall, Jan 23, 1840

191. This maxim, "to preserve is to act", has always served me as a line of conduct, while those who should have backed me up were confusing the duty of preservation with inactivity. —Prince Clemens von Metternich, *Autobiography*, 1880-83

192. There is always a certain meanness in the argument of conservatism, joined with a certain superiority in its fact. —Ralph Waldo Emerson, lecture on "The Conservative" in Boston, Massachusetts, Dec 9, 1841

193. "A sound Conservative government," said Taper, musingly. "I understand: Tory men and Whig measures." —Benjamin Disraeli, *Coningsby*, 1844

194. Conservatism discards Prescription, shrinks from Principle, disavows Progress; having rejected all respect for Antiquity, it offers no redress for the Present, and makes no preparation for the Future. —Benjamin Disraeli, *Coningsby*, 1844

195. Men are conservatives when they are least vigorous, or when they are most luxurious. They are conservatives after dinner. —Ralph Waldo Emerson, "New England Reformers", 1844

196. A conservative government is an organized hypocrisy. —Benjamin Disraeli, 1st Earl of Beaconsfield, speech in the House of Commons, Mar 3, 1845

197. The man for whom law exists—the man of forms, the conservative—is a tame man. —Henry David Thoreau, *Journal*, Mar 30, 1851

198. It is not the metier of a Tory to have a policy, any more than it is that of a king to be a democrat. A tory government may do very well without a policy, just as a country gentleman may sit at home and live upon his rents. —Sir William Harcourt, "Pot and Kettle", *Saturday Review*, Mar 21, 1857

199. What is conservatism? Is it not adherence to the old and tried against the new and untried? —Abraham Lincoln, speech at the Cooper Union, New York City, Feb 27, 1860

200. That man's the true Conservative/ Who lops the moulder'd branch away. —Alfred. Lord Tennyson, "Hands All Round", 1885

201. When a nation's young men are conservative, its funeral bell is already rung. —Henry Ward Beecher, *Proverbs from Plymouth Pulpit*, 1887

202. Conservatism, I believe, is mainly due to want of imagination. In saying this, I do not for a moment mean to deny the other and equally obvious truth that Conservatism, in a lump, is a euphemism for selfishness. —Charles Grant Allen, "Imagination and Radicals", *Westminister Gazette*, 1894

203. Clearly to realise the condition of the unfortunate is the beginning of philanthropy. Clearly to realise the rights of others is the beginning of justice. "Put yourself in his place" strikes the keynote of ethics. Stupid people can only see their own side to a question: they cannot even imagine any other side possible. So, as a rule, stupid people are Conservative. —Charles Grant Allen, "Imagination and Radicals", *Westminster Gazette*, 1894

204. Come, come, my conservative friend, wipe the dew off your spectacles, and see that the world is moving. —Elizabeth Cady Stanton, *The Woman's Bible*, 1895

205. The radical invents the views. When he has worn them out the conservative adopts them. —Mark Twain, *Notebook*, 1935

206. The radical of one century is the conservative of the next. —Mark Twain, *Notebook*, 1935

207. Conservative, n. A statesman who is enamored of existing evils, as distinguished from the Liberal, who wishes to replace them with others. —Ambrose Bierce, *The Devil's Dictionary*, 1906

208. The healthy stomach is nothing if not conservative. Few radicals have good digestions. —Samuel Butler, Mind and Matter: Indigestion, *Notebooks*, 1912

209. Do the day's work. If it be to protect the rights of the weak, whoever objects, do it. If it be to help a powerful corporation better to serve the people, do that. Expect to be called a standpatter, but don't be a standpatter. Expect to be called a demagogue, but don't be a demagogue. Don't hesitate to be as reactionary as the multiplication table. Don't expect to build up the weak by pulling down the strong. —Calvin Coolidge, speech to the Massachusetts State Senate, Jan 7, 1914

210. Success makes men rigid and they tend to exalt stability over all the other virtues; tired of the effort of willing they become fanatics about conversatism. —Walter Lippmann, "Routineer and Inventor", *A Preface to Politics*, 1914

211. Toryism ... like the serpent sheds its skin, but ever remains the same reptile. —Sir Wilfrid Laurier, letter to Sir Allen Aylesworth, May 15, 1917

212. All political and religious systems have their root and their strength in the innate conservatism of the human mind, and its intense fear of autonomy. —Suzanne LaFollette, "The Beginnings of Emancipation", *Concerning Women*, 1926

213. The true conservative is the man who has a real concern for injustices and takes thought against the day of reckoning. —Franklin D. Roosevelt, speech in Syracuse, New York, Sep 29, 1936

214. Wise and prudent men—intelligent conservatives—have long known that in a changing world worthy institutions can be conserved only by adjusting them to the changing time. —Franklin D. Roosevelt, speech in Syracuse, New York, Sep 29, 1936

215. I never dared to be radical when young/ For fear it would make me conservative when old. —Robert Frost, "Ten Mills", *A Further Range*, 1936

216. A conservative is a man with two perfectly good legs who, however, has never learned how to walk forward. —Franklin D. Roosevelt, radio address, Oct 26, 1939

217. A love for tradition has never weakened a nation, indeed it has strengthened nations in their hour of peril; but the new view must come, the world must roll forward. —Sir Winston S. Churchill, speech in the House of Commons, Nov 29, 1944

218. How can wealth persuade poverty to use its political freedom to keep wealth in power? Here lies the whole art of Conservative politics in the twentieth century. —Aneurin Bevan, *In Place of Fear*, 1952

219. Vote Labor and you build castles in the air. Vote Conservative and you can live in them. —David Frost, BBC-TV, *That Was The Year*, Dec 31, 1962

220. I am driven to grudging toleration of the Conservative Party because it is the party of non-politics, of resistance to politics. —Kingsley Amis, *Sunday Telegraph*, Jul 2, 1967

221. Somehow liberals have been unable to acquire from life what conservatives seem to be endowed with at birth: namely, a healthy skepticism of the powers of government agencies to do good. —Daniel P. Moynihan, *The New York Post*, May 14, 1969

222. They (conservatives) define themselves in terms of what they oppose. —George F. Will, *Newsweek*, Sep 30, 1974

223. A conservative is a liberal who was mugged the night before. —Frank L. Rizzo, *American Opinion*, Nov, 1975

224. I've got money so I'm a Conservative. —Roy Herbert Thomson, Lord Thomson of Fleet, recalled on his death, Aug 4, 1976

225. Inflation is a great conservatizing issue. —George F. Will, *Newsweek*, Nov 7, 1977

226. Conservatives do not worship democracy. For them majority rule is a device. ... And if it is leading to an end that is undesirable or is inconsistent with itself, then there is a theoretical case for ending it. —Sir Ian Gilmour, *Inside Right*, 1977

227. A sharp Right turn ... is likely to be followed by an even sharper Left turn. Hence Conservative moderation brings its own reward. The best way of safeguarding the future is by not trying to return to the past. —Sir Ian Gilmour, *Inside Right*, 1977

CONSTITUTION

228. An act against the Constitution is void; an act against natural equity is void. —James Otis, *Argument Against the Writs of Assistance*, 1761

229. Our chief danger arises from the democratic parts of our constitutions. —Edmund Jennings Randolph, attributed remark in debate at Constitutional Convention, May 29, 1787

230. Constitutions are the work of time, one cannot leave too large a space for improvements. [*Les constitutions sont l'ouvrage du temps, on ne saurait laisser une trop large voie aux améliorations.*] —Napoleon I, remarks in the Council of State, Dec 1, 1803

231. Constitutions should be short and vague. [*Il faut qu'une constitution soit courte et obscure.*] —Napoleon I, conference with the Swiss deputies, Jan 29, 1803

232. In questions of power ... let no more be heard of confidence in men, but bind him down from mischief by the chains of the Constitution. —Thomas Jefferson, "Resolutions", 1803

233. Some men look at constitutions with sanctimonious reverence, and deem them like the ark of the covenant, too sacred to be touched. —Thomas Jefferson, letter to Samuel Kercheval, Jul 12, 1816

234. The peculiar circumstances of the moment may render a measure more or less wise, but cannot render it more or less constitutional. —John Marshall, quoted, *New York Times Magazine*, Oct 9, 1977

235. There is a higher law than the Constitution. —William H. Seward, speech in the U.S. Senate, Mar 11, 1850

236. The Constitution of the United States was made not merely for the generation that then existed, but for posterity—unlimited, undefined, endless, perpetual posterity. —Henry Clay, speech in the U.S. Senate, Jan 29, 1850

237. Don't interfere with anything in the Constitution. That must be maintained, for it is the only safeguard of our liberties. —Abraham Lincoln, speech in Kalamazoo, Michigan, Aug 27, 1856

238. Your Constitution is all sail and no anchor. —Lord Macaulay, letter to Henry Randall, May 23, 1857

239. Amendments to the Constitution ought to not be too frequently made; ... (if) continually tinkered with it would lose all its prestige and dignity, and the old instrument would be lost sight of altogether in a short time. —Andrew Johnson, speech in Washington, D.C., Feb 22, 1866

240. We have seen that the American Constitution has changed, is changing, and by the laws of its existence must continue to change, in its substance and practical working even when its words remain the same. —James Bryce, Viscount Bryce, *The American Commonwealth*, 1888

241. The Constitution is the sole source and guaranty of national freedom. —Calvin Coolidge, acceptance speech as Republican nominee for president, Aug 4, 1924

242. What is constitutional may still be unwise. —Zechariah Chaffee Jr., *The Nation*, Jul 28, 1952

243. It must always be remembered that what the Constitution forbids is not all searches and seizures, but unreasonable searches and seizures. —Potter Stewart, majority opinion, *Elkins v. United States*, Jun 27, 1960

244. The basic guarantees of our Constitution are warrants for the here and now, and unless there is an overwhelmingly compelling reason, they are to be promptly fulfilled. —Arthur J. Goldberg, unanimous opinion, May 27, 1963

245. The Constitution is not a panacea for every blot upon the public welfare, nor should this court, ordained as a judicial body, be thought of as a general haven for reform movements. —John Marshall Harlan, dissenting opinion, *Reynolds, Judge et al. v. Sims et al.*, 1964

246. Can any of you seriously say the Bill of Rights could get through Congress today? It wouldn't even get out of committee. —F. Lee Bailey, *Newsweek*, Apr 17, 1967

247. Most faults are not in our Constitution, but in ourselves. —Ramsey Clark, *Washington Post*, Nov 12, 1970

248. It is indeed an odd business that it has taken this Court nearly two centuries to "discover" a constitutional mandate to have counsel at a preliminary hearing. —Warren E. Burger, dissenting opinion, *Coleman v. Alabama*, Jun 22, 1970

249. Our Constitution was not written in the sands to be washed away by each wave of new judges blown in by each successive political wind. —Hugo L. Black, dissenting opinion, Jan 20, 1970

250. Recalling that it is a Constitution intended to endure for ages to come we also remember that the Founders wisely provided the means for that endurance: Changes in the Constitution, when thought necessary, are to be proposed by Congress or conventions and ratified by the states. The Founders gave no such amending power to this Court. —Hugo L. Black, dissenting opinion, Jan 20, 1970

251. The layman's constitutional view is that what he likes is constitutional and that which he doesn't like is unconstitutional. —Hugo L. Black, *The New York Times*, Feb 26, 1971

252. Controversy over the meaning of our nation's most majestic guarantees frequently has been turbulent. ... Abortion raises moral and spiritual questions over which honorable persons can disagree sincerely and profoundly. But those disagreements did not then and do not now relieve us of our duty to apply the Constitution faithfully. —Harry A. Blackmun, majority opinion, *Roe v. Wade; Doe v. Bolton*, Jan 22, 1973

253. My faith in the constitution is whole. —Barbara Jordan, statement at the House Judiciary Committee on impeachment of Richard Nixon, Jul 25, 1974

254. Our constitution works. Our great republic is a government of laws, not of men. —Gerald R. Ford, on succeeding Richard Nixon as president, Aug 9, 1974

255. "We, the people." It is a very eloquent beginning. But when that document was completed on the seventeenth of September in 1787 I was not included in that "We, the people." I felt somehow for many years that George Washington and Alexander Hamilton, just left me out by mistake. But through the process of amendment, interpretation and court decision I have finally been included in "We, the people." —Barbara Jordan, statement at the House Judiciary Committee on impeachment of Richard Nixon, Jul 25, 1974

256. The Constitution is not neutral. It was designed to take the government off the backs of people. —William O. Douglas, *The Court Years 1939-75*, 1980

257. The Constitution requires that Congress treat similarly situated persons similarly, not that it engage in gestures of superficial equality. —William H. Rehnquist, majority opinion, *Rostker v. Goldberg*, Jun 25, 1981

258. We look to the history of the time of framing and to intervening history of interpretation. But the ultimate question must be, what do the words of the text mean in our time. —William J. Brennan Jr., speech at Georgetown University, *The New York Times*, Oct 13, 1985

259. We current justices read the Constitution in the only way that we can: as 20th-century Americans. —William J. Brennan Jr., speech at Georgetown University, *The New York Times*, Oct 13, 1985

260. (Constitutional law) a ship with a great deal of sail but a very shallow keel. —Robert H. Bork, *The New York Times*, Jan 4, 1985

261. The states' role in our system of government is a matter of constitutional law, not of legislative grace. —Lewis F. Powell Jr., dissenting opinion, Feb 19, 1985

262. There is nothing new in the realization that the Constitution sometimes insulates the criminality of a few in order to protect the privacy of us all. —Antonin Scalia, majority opinion, *Arizona v. Hicks*, Mar 3, 1987

DEMOCRACY

263. Democracy ... is a charming form of government, full of variety and disorder, and dispensing a sort of equality to equals and unequals alike. —Plato, *The Republic*, ca. 390 B.C.

264. If liberty and equality, as is thought by some, are chiefly to be found in democracy, they will be best attained when all persons alike share   in the government to the utmost. —Aristotle, *Politics*, 343 B.C.

265. Democracy is the form of government in which the free are rulers. —Aristotle, *Politics*, 343 B.C.

266. The basis of a democratic state is liberty. —Aristotle, *Politics*, 343 B.C.

267. A democracy exists whenever those who are free and are not well-off, being in the majority, are in sovereign control of government, an oligarchy when control lies with the rich and better-born, these being few. —Aristotle, *The Politics*, 343 B.C.

268. Nor should we listen to those who say, "The voice of the people is the voice of God" (vox populi, vox dei), for the turbulence of the mob is always close to insanity. —Alcuin, letter to Charlemagne, *Works*, 800

269. What touches all shall be approved by all. [*Quod omnes tangit ab omnibus approbetur.*] —Edward I, statement to the Model Parliament, 1295

270. Some to the common pulpits, and cry out,/ "Liberty, freedom, and enfranchisement."
—William Shakespeare, *Julius Caesar*, 1599

271. What is the city but the people? —William Shakespeare, *Coriolanus*, 1607-08

272. The power of Kings and Magistrates is nothing else, but what is only derivative, transferr'd and committed to them in trust from the People, to the Common good of them all, in whom the power yet remianes fundamentally, and cannot be tak'n from them, without a violation of their natural birthright. —John Milton, *The Tenure of Kings and Magistrates*, 1649

273. The majority is the best way, because it is visible, and has strength to make itself obeyed. Yet it is the opinion of the least able. [*La pluralité est la meilleure voie, parce qu'elle est visible et qu'elle a la force pour se faire obéir. Cependant c'est l'avis des moins habiles.*] —Blaise Pascal, *Pensées*, 1670

274. The most may err as grossly as the few. —John Dryden, *Absalom and Achitophel*, 1681

275. Any government is free to the people under it where the laws rule and the people are a party to the laws. —William Penn, *The Frame of Government of Pennsylvania*, 1682

276. Every Man, by consenting with others to make one Body Politick under one Government, puts himself under an obligation to every one of that Society, to submit to the determination of the majority, and to be concluded by it; or else this original Compact, whereby he and other incorporates into one Society, would signifie nothing. —John Locke, *The Second Treatise on Government*, 1690

277. Men being ... by Nature, all free, equal and independent, no one can be put out of this Estate, and subjected to the Political Power of another, without his own Consent. —John Locke, *The Second Treatise on Government*, 1690

278. The Liberty of Man, in Society, is to be under no other Legislative Power, but that established, by consent, in the Commonwealth, nor under the Dominion of any will, or Restraint of any Law, but what the Legislative shall enact, according to the Trust put in it. —John Locke, *The Second Treatise on Government*, 1690

279. Our supreme governors, the mob. —Horace Walpole, 4th Earl of Orford, letter to Horace Mann, Sep 7, 1743

280. Were there a people of gods, their government would be democratic. So perfect a government is not for men. [*S'il y avait un peuple de dieux, il se gouvernerait démocratiquement. Un gouvernement si parfait ne convient pas à des hommes.*] —Jean Jacques Rousseau, *The Social Contract*, 1762

281. In the strict sense of the term, a true democracy has never existed and never will exist. [*A prendre le terme dans la rigueur de l'acception, il n'a jamais existé de véritable démocratie, et il n'en existera jamais.*] —Jean Jacques Rousseau, *The Social Contract*, 1762

282. Governments will never be awed by the voice of the people, so long as it is a mere voice, without overt acts. —Joseph Priestly, *The First Principles of Government*, 1771

283. There is danger from all men. The only maxim of a free government ought to be to trust no man living with power to endanger the public liberty. —John Adams, handwritten notes for a speech in Braintree, Massachusetts, 1772

284. As the happiness of the people is the sole end of government, so the consent of the people is the only foundation of it. —John Adams, proclamation to the Massachusetts Bay Council, 1774

285. I cannot conceive a rank more honorable, than that which flows from the uncorrupted choice of a brave and free people, the purest source and original fountain of all power. —George Washington, letter to Lt. General Thomas Gage, Aug 20, 1775

286. That all men are by nature equally free and independent, and have certain inherent rights, of which, when they enter into a state of society, they cannot by any compact deprive or divest their posterity; namely, the enjoyment of life and liberty, with the means of acquiring and possessing property, and pursuing and obtaining happiness and safety. —George Mason, *Virginia Bill of Rights*, Jun 12, 1776

287. When, in the course of human events, it becomes necessary for one people to dissolve political bands which have connected them with another, and to assume among the powers of the earth the separate and equal station to which the Laws of Nature and of Nature's God entitle them, a decent respect to the opinions of mankind requires that they should declare the causes which impel them to the separation. —Thomas Jefferson, *Declaration Of Independence*, Jul 4, 1776

288. Governments ... deriv(e) their just powers from the consent of the governed. —Thomas Jefferson, *Declaration of Independence*, Jul 4, 1776

289. It is the greatest happiness of the greatest number that is the measure of right and wrong. —Jeremy Bentham, "A Fragment on Government", 1776

290. If any ask me what a free government is, I answer, that, for any practical purpose, it is what the people think so,—and that they, and not I, are the natural, lawful, and competent judges of this matter. —Edmund Burke, *Letter to the Sheriffs of Bristol*, Apr 3, 1777

291. I am persuaded there is among the mass of our people a fund of wisdom, integrity, and humanity which will preserve their happiness in a tolerable measure. —John Adams, letter to Abigail Adams, June 2, 1777

292. About things on which the public thinks long it commonly attains to think right. —Samuel Johnson, *The Lives of the Most Eminent English Poets: Addison*, 1779-81

293. Every government degenerates when trusted to the rulers of the people alone. The people themselves therefore are its only safe depositories. —Thomas Jefferson, *Notes on the State of Virginia*, 1782

294. The good sense of the people is the strongest army our government can ever have ... it will not fail them. —Thomas Jefferson, letter to William Carmichael, Dec 26, 1786

295. We are now forming a republican government. Real liberty is neither found in despotism or the extremes of democracy, but in moderate governments. —Alexander Hamilton, debate at the Constitutional Convention, Jun 26, 1787

296. Mobs will never do to govern states or command armies. —John Adams, letter to Benjamin Hichborn, Jan 27, 1787

297. Nothing but a permanent body can check the imprudence of democracy. —Alexander Hamilton, speech to the Constitutional Convention, Jun 18, 1787

298. We may define a republic ... as a government which derives all its powers directly or indirectly from the great body of the people, and is administered by persons holding their offices during pleasure, for a limited period, or during good behavior. It is essential to such a government that it be derived from the great body of the society, not from an inconsiderable proportion, or a favored class of it. —James Madison, *The Federalist*, Jan 16, 1788

299. The essence of a free government consists in an effectual control of rivalries. —John Adams, *Discourses on Davila*, 1789

300. What is the Third Estate? Everything. What has it hitherto been in the political order? Nothing. What does it ask? To be something. [*Qu'est-ce que le Tiers Etat? Tout. Qu'a-t-il été jusqu'à présent dans l'ordre politique? Rien. Que demande-t-il? A devenir quelque chose.*] —Abbé (Emmanuel) Siéyès, *Qu'est-ce que le Tiers Etat?*, 1789

301. The republican is the only form of government which is not eternally at open or secret war with the rights of mankind. —Thomas Jefferson, letter to William Hunter, Mar 11, 1790

302. If government be founded in the consent of the people, it can have no power over any individual by whom that consent is refused. —William Godwin, *An Enquiry Concerning Political Justice*, 1793

303. The basis of our political system is the right of the people to make and to alter their constitutions of government. —George Washington, *Farewell Address to the People of the United States*, Sep 17, 1796

304. The very idea of the power and the right of the people to establish Government, presupposes the duty of every individual to obey the established Government. —George Washington, *Farewell Address to the People of the United States*, Sep 19, 1796

305. No kingdom can be secure in its independence against a greater power that is not free in its spirit, as well as in its institutions. —William Hazlitt, *Free Thoughts in Public Affairs, or Advice to a Patriot*, 1806

306. That government is the strongest of which every man feels himself a part. —Thomas Jefferson, letter to Gov. H. D. Tiffin, Feb 2, 1807

307. There is but one element of government, and that is the people. From this element spring all governments. "For a nation to be free, it is only necessary that she will it." For a nation to be a slave, it is only necessary that she will it. —John Adams, letter to John Tyler, 1814

308. Sovereignty resides in the French People in the sense that everything, everything without exception, must be done in their interest, for their happiness, and for their glory. [*La souveraineté reside dans le Peuple français, en ce sens que tout, tout sans exception, doit être fait pour son intérêt, pour son bonheur et pour sa gloire.*] —Napoleon I, message to the Cour de Cassation, Mar 26, 1815

309. A state may prosper under any form of government, provided it is well administered. ... If political freedom is more advantageous for the development of wealth, it is indirectly because it is more favorable to learning. —Claude Henri, Comte de Saint-Simon, *Industry*, 1817

310. No government can continue good but under the control of the people. —Thomas Jefferson, letter to John Adams, Dec 10, 1819

311. The people made the Constitution, and the people can unmake it. It is the creature of their own will, and lives only by their will. —John Marshall, *Cohens v. Virginia*, 1821

312. The benefits of the Representative system are lost, in all cases in which the interests of the choosing body are not the same with those of the community. —James Mill, *Essay on Government*, 1821

313. I repeat ... that all power is a trust; that we are accountable for its exercise; that, from the people, and for the people, all springs, and all must exist. —Benjamin Disraeli, *Vivian Grey*, 1826

314. Not kings and lords, but nations!/ Not thrones and crowns, but men! —Ebenezer Elliott, *Corn Law Rhymes*, 1828

315. Government is a trust, and the officers of the government are trustees; and both the trust and the trustees are created for the benefit of the people. —Henry Clay, speech in Lexington, Kentucky, May 16, 1829

316. I now commend you, fellow-citizens, to the guidance of Almighty God, with a full reliance on His merciful providence for the maintenance of our free institutions, and with an earnest supplication that whatever errors it may be my lot to commit in discharging the arduous duties which have devolved on me will find a remedy in the harmony and wisdom of your counsels. —Andrew Jackson, first annual message to Congress, Dec 8, 1829

317.   The people's government, made for the people, made by the people, and answerable to the people. —Daniel Webster, second speech on Foote's Resolution, Jan 26, 1830

318.   Despotism accomplishes great things illegally; liberty doesn't even go to the trouble of accomplishing small things legally. [*Le despotisme fait illégalement de grandes choses, la liberté ne se donne même pas la peine d'en faire légalement de très-petites.*] —Honoré de Balzac, *La Peau de chagrin*, 1831

319.   Compact is the basis and essence of free government. ... No right to disregard it belongs to a party till released by causes of which the other parties have an equal right to judge. —James Madison, letter to Nicholas P. Trist, Jan 18, 1833

320.   Where the people possess no authority, their rights obtain no respect. —George Bancroft, "To the Workingmen of Northampton", *Boston Courier*, Oct 22, 1834

321.   The very essence of a free government consists in considering offices as public trusts, bestowed for the good of the country, and not for the benefit of an individual or a party. —John C. Calhoun, speech, Feb 13, 1835

322.   Democratic institutions generally give men a lofty notion of their country and themselves. [*Les institutions démocratiques donnent en général aux hommes une vaste idée de leur patrie et d'eux-mêmes.*] —Alexis, Comte de Tocqueville, *Democracy in America*, 1839

323.   One can change human institutions but not man. However energetically society in general may strive to make all citizens equal and alike, the personal pride of individuals will always seek to rise above the common level, and to form somewhere an inequality to their own advantage. [*On peut changer les institutions humaines, mais non l'homme: quel que soit l'effort général d'une société pour rendre les citoyens égaux et semblables, l'orgueil particulier des individus cherchera toujours à échapper au niveau, et voudra former quelque part une inégalité dont il profite.*] —Alexis, Comte de Tocqueville, *Democracy in America*, 1839

324.   The taste for well-being is the prominent and indelible feature of democratic times. [*Le goût du bien-être forme comme le trait saillant et indélébile des âges démocratiques.*] —Alexis, Comte de Tocqueville, *Democracy in America*, 1839

325.   Men living in democratic times have many passions, but most of their passions either end in the love of riches, or proceed from it. [*Les hommes qui vivent dans les temps démocratiques ont beaucoup de passions; mais la plupart de leurs passions aboutissent à l'amour de la richesse ou en sortent.*] —Alexis, Comte de Tocqueville, *Democracy in America*, 1839

326.   The only legitimate right to govern is an express grant of power from the governed. —William Henry Harrison, inaugural address, Mar 4, 1841

327.   Truth no more relies for success on ballot boxes than it does on cartridge boxes. ... Political action is not moral action, anymore than a box on the ear is an argument. —William Lloyd Garrison, *The Liberator*, Mar 13, 1846

328.   Democracy becomes a government of bullies tempered by editors. —Ralph Waldo Emerson, *Journals*, 1846

329.   A democratic constitution, not supported by democratic institutions in detail, but confined to the central government, not only is not political freedom, but often creates a spirit precisely the reverse, carrying down to the lowest grade in society the desire and ambition of political domination. —John Stuart Mill, *Principles of Political Economy*, 1848

330.   The American idea ... is a democracy, that is a government of all the people, by all the people, and for all the people. —Theodore Parker, speech in Boston, Massachusetts, May 29, 1850

331. Democracy is not possible except in a nation where there is so much property, and that so widely distributed, that the whole people can have considerable education—intellectual, moral, affectional, and religious. So much property, widely distributed, judiciously applied, is the indispensable material basis of a democracy. —Theodore Parker, quoted by Daniel Aaron, *Men of Good Hope*, 1951

332. The dangers of a concentration of all power in the general government of a confederacy so vast as ours are too obvious to be disregarded. —Franklin Pierce, inaugural address, Mar 4, 1853

333. No man is good enough to govern another man without that other's consent. —Abraham Lincoln, speech in Peoria, Illinois, Oct 16, 1854

334. Decision by majorities is as much an expedient as lighting by gas. —William Ewart Gladstone, speech in the House of Commons, 1858

335. As I would not be a slave, so I would not be a master. This expresses my idea of democracy. Whatever differs from this, to the extent of the difference, is no democracy. —Abraham Lincoln, written fragment, ca. Aug 1, 1858

336. The best form of Government (setting aside the question of morality) is one where the masses have little power, and seem to have a great deal. —3rd Marquess of Salisbury, "The Theories of Parliamentary Reform", *Oxford Essays*, 1858

337. The people—the people are the rightful masters of both congresses and courts—not to overthrow the Constitution, but to overthrow the men who pervert it. —Abraham Lincoln, notes for speeches in Ohio, Sep 16, 1859

338. The evils of popular government appear greater than they are; there is compensation for them in the spirit and energy it awakens. —Ralph Waldo Emerson, "Power", *Conduct of Life*, 1860

339. The instinct of the people is right. —Ralph Waldo Emerson, "Power", *The Conduct of Life*, 1860

340. This country, with its institutions, belongs to the people who inhabit it. Whenever they shall grow weary of the existing government, they can exercise their constitutional right of amending it, or their revolutionary right to dismember or overthrow it. —Abraham Lincoln, first inaugural address, Mar 4, 1861

341. Why should there not be a patient confidence in the ultimate justice of the people? Is there any better or equal hope in the world? —Abraham Lincoln, first inaugural address, Mar 4, 1861

342. While the people retain their virtue and vigilance, no administration, by any extreme of wickedness or folly, can very seriously injure the government in the short space of four years. —Abraham Lincoln, first inaugural address, Mar 4, 1861

343. Vox populi, vox humbug. —William Tecumseh Sherman, letter to his wife, Jun 2, 1863

344. We here highly resolve ... that this nation, under God, shall have a new birth of freedom, and that government of the people, by the people, and for the people, shall not perish from the earth. —Abraham Lincoln, from the Gettysburg address, Nov 19, 1863

345. The principle of our Government is that of equal laws and freedom of industry. —Andrew Johnson, first annual message to Congress, Dec 4, 1865

346. Our government springs from and was made for the people—not the people for the Government. To them it owes allegiance; from them it must derive its courage, strength, and wisdom. —Andrew Johnson, first annual message to Congress, Dec 4, 1865

347. It is the multiplication table which furnishes in the last resort the essential test that distinguishes right from wrong in the government of a nation. If one man imprisons you, that is tyranny ; if two men, or a number of men imprison you, that is freedom. —3rd Marquess of Salisbury, "Parliamentary Reform", *Quarterly Review*, Jul, 1865

348. All the world over, I will back the masses against the classes. —William Ewart Gladstone, speech in Liverpool, England, Jan 21, 1866

349. The mass of the English people are politically contented as well as politically deferential. —Walter Bagehot, *The English Constitution*, 1867

350. I shall on all subjects have a policy to recommend, but none to enforce against the will of the people. —Ulysses S. Grant, first inaugural address, Mar 4, 1869

351. Political democracy, as it exists and practically works in America, with all its threatening evils, supplies a training school for making first-class men. It is life's gymnasium, not of good only, but of all. —Walt Whitman, "Democratic Vistas", 1871

352. I have always been of the mind that in a democracy manners are the only effective weapons against the bowie-knife. —James Russell Lowell, letter to Miss Norton, Mar 4, 1873

353. In a pure democracy the ruling men will be the wirepullers and their friends. —Sir James Fitzjames Stephen, *Liberty, Equality, Fraternity*, 1873

354. Nations are not truly great solely because the individuals composing them are numerous, free, and active; but they are great when these numbers, this freedom, this activity are employed in the service of an ideal higher than that of an ordinary man, taken by himself. —Matthew Arnold, "Democracy", *Mixed Essays*, 1879

355. All free governments are managed by the combined wisdom and folly of the people. —James A. Garfield, letter, Apr 21, 1880

356. To fight against the government with any means is a basic right and sport of every German. [*Gegen die Regierung mit allen Mitteln zu kämpfen, ist ja ein Grundrecht und Sport eines jeden Deutschen.*] —Prince Otto von Bismarck, speech to the Reichstag, May 8, 1880

357. Macaulay's illustration of the man who would not go into the water until he had learned to swim is the type of all the objections raised to the extension of self-government amongst the people. —Joseph Chamberlain, on opposition to extending British suffrage to agricultural workers, Oct 18, 1882

358. We cannot safely leave politics to politicians, or political economy to college professors. The people themselves must think, because the people alone can act. —Henry George, *Social Problems*, 1883

359. Politics and law are (or rather, should be)—merely results, merely the expression of what the people wish. —Rutherford B. Hayes, letter, Nov 25, 1885

360. The real democratic American ideal is, not that every man shall be on a level with every other man, but that every man shall have liberty to be what god made him, without hindrance. —Henry Ward Beecher, *Proverbs from Plymouth Pulpit*, 1887

361. It is for men to choose whether they will govern themselves or be governed. —Henry Ward Beecher, *Proverbs from Plymouth Pulpit*, 1887

362. Democracy represents the disbelief in all great men and in all elite societies: everybody is everybody's equal. [*Die Demokratie repräsentirt den Unglauben an grosse Menschen und an Elite-Gesellschaft: Jeder ist jedem gleich.*] —Friedrich Nietzsche, *The Will to Power*, 1888

363. The bottom principle ... of our structure of government—is the principle of control by the majority. Everything else about our government is appendage, it is ornamentation. —Benjamin Harrison, speech in Detroit, Michigan, Feb 22, 1888

364. The majority voice should be controlling, but it must be after a full, fair, and candid expression. —William McKinley, speech to the House of Representatives, May 18, 1888

365. If this nation is not truly democratic, then she must die. —Alexander Crummell, speech to the Protestant Episcopal Church Congress, Buffalo, New York, Nov 20, 1888

366. Democratic institutions are never done—they are, like the living tissue, always a-making. It is a strenuous thing this of living the life of a free people: and we cannot escape the burden of our inheritance. —Woodrow Wilson, speech in Middletown, Connecticut, Apr 30, 1889

367. Democracy means simply the bludgeoning of the people by the people for the people. —Oscar Wilde, "The Soul of Man Under Socialism", *Fortnightly Review*, Feb, 1891

368. The Republican form of government is the highest form of government: but because of this it requires the highest type of human nature—a type nowhere at present existing. —Herbert Spencer, "The Americans", *Essays*, 1891

369. My plan cannot fail if the people are with us and we ought not to succeed unless we do have the people with us. —William Jennings Bryan, letter to Andrew Carnegie, Jan 13, 1899

370. I know of no better or safer human tribunal than the people. —William McKinley, speech in Boston, Massachusetts, Feb 16, 1899

371. Democracy is only an experiment in government, and it has the obvious disadvantage of merely counting votes instead of weighing them. —William Ralph Inge, *Possible Recovery?*

372. Democracy is not so much a form of government as a set of principles. —Woodrow Wilson, *Atlantic Monthly*, Mar, 1901

373. If Despotism failed only for want of a capable benevolent despot, what chance has Democracy, which requires a whole population of capable voters. —George Bernard Shaw, "Epistle Dedicatory", *Man and Superman*, 1902

374. Democracy substitutes election by the incompetent many for appointment by the corrupt few. —George Bernard Shaw, "Maxims for Revolutionists", *Man and Superman*, 1902

375. The government is us; we are the government, you and I. —Theodore Roosevelt, speech in Asheville, North Carolina, Sep 9, 1902

376. The noblest of all forms of government is self-government; but it is also the most difficult. —Theodore Roosevelt, fifth annual message to Congress, Dec 5, 1905

377. The danger to American democracy lies not in the least in the concentration of administrative power in responsible and accountable hands. It lies in having the power insufficiently concentrated, so that no one can be held responsible to the people for its use. Concentrated power is palpable, visible, responsible, easily reached, quickly held to account. —Theodore Roosevelt, eighth annual message to Congress, Dec 8, 1908

378. A great democracy must be progressive or it will soon cease to be great or a democracy. —Theodore Roosevelt, speech in Cleveland, Ohio, Nov 5, 1910

379. There is something to be said for government by a great aristocracy which has furnished leaders to the nation in peace and war for generations; even a democrat like myself must admit this. —Theodore Roosevelt, letter to Edward Grey, Nov 15, 1913

380. "The consent of the governed" is more than a safeguard against ignorant tyrants: it is an insurance against benevolent despots as well. —Walter Lippmann, "The Golden Rule and After", *A Preface to Politics*, 1914

381. Democracy is the most difficult form of government, because it is the form under which you have to persuade the largest number of persons to do anything in particular. —Woodrow Wilson, speech in Washington, D.C., Sep 28, 1915

382. A democracy is more than a form of government; it is primarily a mode of associated living, of conjoint communicated experience. —John Dewey, *Democracy and Education*, 1916

383. Only governments and not people initiate wars. ... Democracy, therefore, is the best preventive of such jealousies and suspicions and secret intrigues as produce wars among nations where small groups control rather than the great body of public opinion. —Woodrow Wilson, interview, Nov 5, 1916

384. Democracy is not a tearing-down; it is a building-up. ... It does not destroy; it fulfills. ... It is the alpha and omega of man's relation to man. ... Its foundation lays hold upon eternity. —Calvin Coolidge, speech in Springfield, Massachusetts, Jul 4, 1916

385. A democracy is a state which recognizes the subjection of the minority to the majority, that is, an organization for the systematic use of violence by one class against the other, by one part of the population against another. —Vladimir Ilyich Lenin, *The State and the Revolution*, 1917

386. The world must be made safe for democracy. Its peace must be planted on the tested foundations of political liberty. —Woodrow Wilson, speech to Congress, Apr 2, 1917

387. No democracy has ever long survived the failure of its adherents to be ready to die for it. ... My own conviction is this, the people must either go on or go under. —David Lloyd George, 1st Earl Lloyd-George, speech in London, Jan 18, 1918

388. In the last analysis, my fellow countrymen, as we in America would be the first to claim, a people are responsible for the acts of their government. —Woodrow Wilson, speech in Columbus, Ohio, Sep 4, 1919

389. Democracy is a form of government which may be rationally defended, not as being good, but as being less bad than any other. —William Ralph Inge, "Our Present Discontents", *Outspoken Essays: First Series*, 1919

390. It was the bitter experience of all public men from George Washington down that democracies are at least contemporarily fickle and heartless. —Herbert Hoover, in 1919 as quoted, *Memoirs*, 1952

391. Democracy is the theory that the common people know what they want, and deserve to get it good and hard. —H.L. Mencken, "Sententiae", *A Book of Burlesques*, 1920

392. The most valuable of all human possessions, next to a superior and disdainful air, is the reputation of being well to do. Nothing else so neatly eases one's way through life, especially in democratic countries. —H.L. Mencken, *Prejudices: Third Series*, 1922

393. It would be folly to argue that the people cannot make political mistakes. They can and do make mistakes. But compared with the mistakes which have been made by every kind of autocracy they are unimportant. —Calvin Coolidge, speech in Evanston, Illinois, Jan 21, 1923

394. Americans ought ever be asking themselves about their concept of the ideal republic. —Warren G. Harding, speech in Kansas City, Missouri, Jun 22, 1923

395. Whatever democracy may be theoretically, one is sometimes tempted to define it practically as standardized and commercial melodrama. —Irving Babbitt, *Democracy and Leadership*, 1924

396. There is one thing better than good government, and that is government in which all people have a part. —Walter Hines Page, *Life and Letters*, 1922-25

397. It is evident that our whole political machinery pre-supposes a people so fundamentally at one that they can safely afford to bicker; and so sure of their own moderation that they are not dangerously disturbed by the never-ending din of political conflict. May it always be so. —Arthur Balfour, 1st Earl of Balfour, introduction to Walter Bagehot, *The English Constitution*, Nov, 1927

398. We have not got democratic government today. We have never had it and I venture to suggest to Honourable Members opposite that we shall never have it. What we have done in all the progress of reform and evolution is to broaden the basis of oligarchy. —Anthony Eden, 1st Earl of Avon, speech in the House of Commons, Mar 29, 1928

399. The health of any democracy, no matter what its type or status, depends on a small technical detail: the conduct of elections. Everything else is secondary. [*La salud de las democracias, cualesquiera que sean su tipo y su grado, depende de un mísero detalle técnico: el procedimiento electoral. Todo lo demás es secundario.*] —Jose Ortega y Gasset, *The Revolt of the Masses*, 1930

400. I do not want the voice of the people shut out. —Huey P. Long, speech in the U.S. Senate, May 16, 1932

401. Even though counting heads is not an ideal way to govern, at least it is better than breaking them. —Learned Hand, speech to the Federal Bar Association, Mar 8, 1932

402. Democracy ... is a quest, a never-ending seeking for better things, and in the seeking ... and the striving for them there are many roads to follow. —Franklin D. Roosevelt, speech in San Francisco, California, Sep 23, 1932

403. All the ills of democracy can be cured by more democracy. —Alfred E. Smith, speech in Albany, New York, Jun 27, 1933

404. A democracy, the right kind of democracy, is bound together by the ties of neighborliness. —Franklin D. Roosevelt, speech to Conference of Catholic Charities, Oct 4, 1933

405. Democracy is not a static thing. It is an everlasting march. —Franklin D. Roosevelt, speech in Los Angeles, California, Oct 1, 1935

407. They realize that in thirty-four months we have built up new instruments of public power. In the hands of a people's Government this power is wholesome and proper. But in the hands of political puppets of an economic autocracy such power would provide   shackles for the liberties of the people. —Franklin D. Roosevelt, annual message to Congress, Jan 3, 1936

408. What the masses vote or do not vote for is not important—their opinion depends wholly on the extent to which they have been made conscious of their rights and potentialities. All the problems of society would have disappeared immediately if the masses really knew what was good for them. —Jayaprakash Narayan, *Why Socialism?*, 1936

409. My anchor is democracy—and more democracy. —Franklin D. Roosevelt, speech at Roanoke Island, North Carolina, Aug 18, 1937

410. The deeper purpose of democratic government is to assist as many of its citizens as possible ... to improve their conditions of life, to retain all personal liberty which does not adversely affect their neighbors, and to pursue the happiness which comes with security and an opportunity for recreation and culture. —Franklin D. Roosevelt, annual message to Congress, Jan 6, 1937

411. The continued maintenance and improvement of democracy constitute the most important guarantee of international peace. —Franklin D. Roosevelt, speech to the Pan-American Union, Washington, D.C., Apr 14, 1937

412. In the transition to political democracy, this country ... underwent ... no inner conversion. She accepted it as a convenience, like an improved system of telephones.... She changed her political garments, but not her heart. She carried into the democratic era, not only the institutions, but the social habits and mentality of the oldest and toughest plutocracy in the world. ... She went to the ballot-box touching her hat. —Richard Tawney, "The Realities of Democracy", *The Highway*, Jan, 1937

413. Democracy: a mockery that mouths the words and obstructs every effort of an honest people to establish a government for the welfare of the people. —Father Charles E. Coughlin, *Social Justice*, Aug 1, 1938

414. Let us never forget that government is ourselves and not an alien power over us. The ultimate rulers of our democracy are not a President and senators and congressmen and government officials, but the voters of this country. —Franklin D. Roosevelt, speech in Marietta, Ohio, Jul 8, 1938

415. In a social system in which power is open to all, the posts which confer power will, as a rule, be occupied by men who differ from the average in being exceptionally power-loving. —Bertrand Russell, *Power*, 1938

416. Democracy, the practice of self-government, is a covenant among free men to respect the rights and liberties of their fellows. —Franklin D. Roosevelt, State of the Union message, Jan 4, 1939

417. For democrats in troubled countries, the height of the art of governing seems to consist in accepting slaps so as to avoid kicks. ... The enemies of democracy take advantage of this and grow daily more insolent. [*Il colmo dell'arte di governo per i democratici dei paesi in crisi sembra consistere nell'incassare degli schiaffi per non ricevere dei calci. ... Gli avversari della democrazia ne approfittano e diventano sempre più insolenti.*] —Ignazio Silone, *The School for Dictatorships*, 1939

418. I'm tired of hearing it said that democracy doesn't work. Of course it doesn't work. It isn't supposed to work. We are supposed to work it. —Alexander Woollcott, quoted, *Kansas City Times*, Jan 4, 1977

419. Democracy is the superior form of government, because it is based on a respect for man as a reasonable being. —John F. Kennedy, *Why England Slept*, 1940

420. Democracy is not just a word, to be shouted at political rallies and then put back in the dictionary after election day. —Franklin D. Roosevelt, presidential campaign speech, Nov 4, 1940

421. It is one of the characteristics of a free and democratic nation that it have free and independent labor unions. —Franklin D. Roosevelt, speech to the Teamsters Union, Washington, D.C., Sep 11, 1940

422. The increasing discredit into which democratic government has fallen is due to democracy having been burdened with tasks for which it is not suited. —Friedrich August von Hayek, *Freedom and the Economic System*, 1940

423. If a democratic people comes under the sway of an anti-capitalistic creed, this means that democracy will inevitably destroy itself. —Friedrich August von Hayek, *Freedom and the Economic System*, 1940

424. The ultimate foundation of a free society is the binding tie of cohesive sentiment. —Felix Frankfurter, *Minersville School District v. Gobitis*, 1940

425. We can have democracy in this country or we can have great wealth concentrated in the hands of a few, but we can't have both. —Louis D. Brandeis, *Labor*, Oct 17, 1941

426. I am a child of the House of Commons. I was brought up in my father's house to believe in democracy. "Trust the people"—that was his message. —Sir Winston S. Churchill, speech to a joint session of U.S. Congress, Dec 26, 1941

427. It is the American vice, the democratic disease which expresses its tyranny by reducing everything unique to the level of the herd. —Henry Miller, "Raimu", *The Wisdom of the Heart*, 1941

428. The tragedy of modern democracies is that they have not yet succeeded in effecting democracy. —Jacques Maritain, "La Tragédie de la démocratie", *Christianisme et démocratie*, 1942

429. Democracy is a political method, that is to say, a certain type of institutional arrangement for arriving at political—legal and administrative—decisions and hence incapable of being an end in itself. —Joseph Schumpeter, *Capitalism, Socialism and Democracy*, 1942

430. In a democracy such as ours military policy is dependent on public opinion. —George C. Marshall, *Yank*, Jan 28, 1943

431. I swear to the Lord/ I still can't see/ Why Democracy means/ Everybody but me. —Langston Hughes, *The Black Man Speaks*, 1943

432. Nothing can be more abhorrent to democracy than to imprison a person or keep him in prison because he is unpopular. This is really the test of civilisation. —Sir Winston S. Churchill, letter to Herbert Morrison, Nov 21, 1943

433. The whole cornerstone of our democratic edifice was the principle that from the people and the people alone flows the authority of government. —Franklin D. Roosevelt, radio address, Feb 12, 1943

434. Man's capacity for justice makes democracy possible, but man's inclination to injustice makes democracy necessary. —Reinhold Niebuhr, foreword, *The Children of Light and the Children of Darkness*, 1944

435. Democracy is not tolerance. Democracy is a prescribed way of life erected on the premise that all men are created equal. —Chester Bomar Himes, *If You're Scared, Go Home!*, 1944

436. The blind lead the blind. It's the democratic way. —Henry Miller, "With Edgar Varese in the Gobi Desert", *The Air-Conditioned Nightmare*, 1945

437. To define democracy in one word, we must use the word "cooperation." —Dwight D. Eisenhower, speech in Abilene, Kansas, Jun, 1945

438. There is no indispensable man in a democracy. When a republic comes to a point where a man is indispensable, then we have a Caesar. —Harry S Truman, interview, ca. 1946

439. The constant danger to democracy lies in the tendency of the individual to hide himself in the crowd—to defend his own failure to act forthrightly according to conviction under the false excuse that the effort of one in one hundred forty million has no significance. —Dwight D. Eisenhower, speech in Northfield, Vermont, Jun 9, 1946

440. Democracy is the recurrent suspicion that more than half of the people are right more than half of the time. —E.B. White, *The Wild Flag*, 1946

441. Many forms of Government have been tried, and will be tried in this world of sin and woe. No one pretends that democracy is perfect or all-wise. Indeed, it has been said that democracy is the worst form of Government except all those other forms that have been tried from time to time. —Sir Winston S. Churchill, speech in the House of Commons, Nov 11, 1947

442. Human dignity, economic freedom, individual responsibility, these are the characteristics that distinguish democracy from all other forms devised by man. —Dwight D. Eisenhower, speech at the Univ. of West Virginia, Sep 24, 1947

443. Those who worry about radicalism in our schools and colleges are often either reactionaries who themselves do not bear allegiance to the traditional American principles, or defeatists who despair of the success of our own philosophy in an open competition. —James Bryant Conant, *Education in a Divided World*, 1948

444. My notion of democracy is that under it the weakest should have the same opportunity as the strongest. This can never happen except through non-violence. —Mohandas K. Gandhi, *Non-Violence in Peace and War*, 1948

445. I believe that the foundation of democratic liberty is a willingness to believe that other people may perhaps be wiser than oneself. —Clement Attlee, speech to the Labour Party annual conference, Oct, 1948

446. A democracy in which everybody had an equal responsibility in everything would be oppressive for the conscientious and licentious for the rest. —T.S. Eliot, *Notes Toward The Definition of Culture*, 1948

447. The taste of democracy becomes a bitter taste when the fullness of democracy is denied. —Max Lerner, "The Negroes and the Draft", *Actions and Passions*, 1949

448. One of the evils of democracy is, you have to put up with the man you elect whether you want him or not. —Will Rogers, *The Autobiography of Will Rogers*, 1949

449. It is not the armed forces which can protect our democracy. It is the moral strength of democracy which alone can give any meaning to the efforts at military security. —Max Lerner, "The Negroes and the Draft", *Actions and Passions*, 1949

450. Democracy is based on the conviction that man has the moral and intellectual capacity, as well as the inalienable right, to govern himself with reason and justice. —Harry S Truman, inaugural address, Jan 20, 1949

451. In a healthy nation there is a kind of balance between the will of the people and the government, which prevents its degeneration into tyranny. —Albert Einstein, *Out of My Later Years*, 1950

452. I am the people—the mob—the crowd—the mass./ Do you know that all the great work of the world is done through me? —Carl Sandburg, "I Am the People, the Mob", *Complete Poems*, 1950

453. Two Cheers for Democracy: one because it admits variety and two because it permits criticism. Two cheers are quite enough: there is no occasion to give three. Only Love, the Beloved Republic, deserves that. —E.M. Forster, *Two Cheers for Democracy*, 1951

454. A democracy can recover quickly from physical or economic disaster, but when its moral convictions weaken it becomes easy prey for the demagogue and the charlatan. Tyranny and oppression then become the order of the day. —J. William Fulbright, speech in the U.S. Senate, Mar 27, 1951

455. The essence of a republican government is not command. It is consent. —Adlai E. Stevenson Jr., speech in Springfield, Illinois, Aug 14, 1952

456. The issue ... in a capitalist democracy resolves itself into this: either poverty will use democracy to win the struggle against property, or property, in fear of poverty, will destroy democracy. —Aneurin Bevan, *In Place of Fear*, 1952

457. As citizens of this democracy, you are the rulers and the ruled, the lawgivers and the law-abiding, the beginning and the end. —Adlai E. Stevenson Jr., speech in Chicago, Illinois, Sep 29, 1952

458. The death of democracy is not likely to be an assassination from ambush. It will be a slow extinction from apathy, indifference, and undernourishment. —Robert Maynard Hutchins, *Great Books*, 1954

459. Democracy is clearly most appropriate for countries which enjoy an economic surplus and least appropriate for countries where there is an economic insufficiency. —David Morris Potter, *People of Plenty: Economic Abundance and the American Character*, 1954

460. The upward course of a nation's history is due in the long run to the soundness of heart of its average men and women. —Elizabeth II, Christmas address, Dec 25, 1954

461. A free society is one where it is safe to be unpopular. —Adlai E. Stevenson Jr., quoted, *Human Behavior*, May, 1978

462. Since the beginning of time, governments have been mainly engaged in kicking people around. The astonishing achievement of modern times in the Western world is the idea that the citizens should do the kicking. —Adlai E. Stevenson Jr., quoted, *Human Behavior*, May, 1978

463. Popular government has not yet been proved to guarantee, always and every where, good government. —Walter Lippmann, *The Public Philosophy*, 1955

464. Democracy cannot be saved by supermen, but only by the unswerving devotion and goodness of millions of little men. —Adlai E. Stevenson Jr., speech, 1955

465. If I were to attempt to put my political philosophy tonight into a single phrase, it would be this: Trust the people. —Adlai E. Stevenson Jr., speech in Harrisburg, Pennsylvania, Sep 13, 1956

466. The history of free men is never really written by chance but by choice—their choice. —Dwight D. Eisenhower, speech in Pittsburgh, Pennsylvania, Oct 9, 1956

467. The function of parliamentary democracy, under universal suffrage, historically considered, is to expose wealth-privilege to the attacks of the people. —Aneurin Bevan, *New York Times Magazine*, Oct 27, 1957

468. If one man offers you democracy and another offers you a bag of grain, at what stage of starvation will you prefer the grain to the vote? —Bertrand Russell, *Silhouettes in Satire*, 1958

469. We hold the view that the people make the best judgment in the long run. —John F. Kennedy, campaign speech, Greensboro, North Carolina, Sep 17, 1960

470. Democracy is good. I say this because other systems are worse. —Jawaharlal Nehru, *The New York Times*, Jan 25, 1961

471. We have no greater asset than the willingness of a free and determined people, through its elected officials, to face all problems frankly and meet all dangers free from panic or fear. —John F. Kennedy, State of the Union message, Jan 29, 1961

472. In these perilous hours, I fear that the American people are ahead of their leaders in realism and courage—but behind them in knowledge of the facts because the facts have not been given to them. —Margaret Chase Smith, speech in the U.S. Senate, Sep 21, 1961

473. In a democratic society like ours, relief must come through an aroused popular conscience that sears the conscience of the people's representatives. —Felix Frankfurter, *Baker v. Carr*, 1962

474. Democracy is never a final achievement. It is a call to untiring effort, to continual sacrifice and to the willingness, if necessary, to die in its defense. —John F. Kennedy, speech in San Jose, Costa Rica, Mar 19, 1963

475. We are inclined to confuse freedom and democracy, which we regard as moral principles, with the way in which these are practiced in America—with capitalism, federalism and the two-party system, which are not moral principles, but simply the accepted practices of the American people. —J. William Fulbright, speech in the U.S. Senate, Mar 27, 1964

476. Let no one think for a moment that national debate means national division. —Lyndon Baines Johnson, commencement address, National Cathedral School, Washington, D.C., Jun 1, 1965

477. You have the God-given right to kick the government around—don't hesitate to do so. —Edmund S. Muskie, speech in South Bend, Indiana, Sep 11, 1968

478. And so tonight—to you, the great silent majority of my fellow Americans—I ask for your support. —Richard M. Nixon, televised speech, Nov 3, 1969

479. Everyone else is represented in Washington by a rich and powerful lobby, it seems. But there is no lobby for the people. —Shirley Chisholm, *Unbought and Unbossed*, 1970

480. In a political sense, there is one problem that currently underlies all of the others. That problem is making Government sufficiently responsive to the people. If we don't make government responsive to the people, we don't make it believable. And we must make government believable if we are to have a functioning democracy. —Gerald R. Ford, address at Jacksonville Univ., Jacksonville, Florida, Dec 16, 1971

481. People are not an interruption of our business. People are our business. —Walter E. Washington, attributed, 1971

482. Divine right went out with the American Revolution and doesn't belong to the White House aides. What meat do they eat that makes them grow so great? —Sam Ervin, news conference during Watergate investigation, *Time*, Apr 16, 1973

483. Sovereignty remains at all times with the people and they do not forfeit through elections the rights to have the law construed against and applied to every citizen. —Court of Appeals United States, ruling that President Nixon had to turn over presidential tapes, *The New York Times*, Oct 14, 1973

484. Secrecy and a free, democratic government don't mix. —Harry S Truman, quoted by Merle Miller, *Plain Speaking: An Oral Biography of Harry S. Truman*, 1974

485. Television is democracy at its ugliest. —Paddy Chayefsky, *The New York Times*, Nov 14, 1976

486. That's what the American system is all about: to keep power divided, to prevent a small core from either pole suddenly thrusting its decisions on the country. —Charles M. Mathias Jr., *Time*, Aug 23, 1976

487. The stakes ... are too high for government to be a spectator sport. —Barbara Jordan, commencement address, Harvard Univ., Jun 16, 1977

488. I would rather trust twelve jurors with all their prejudices and biases than I would a judge. I think the reason democracy works is because as you multiply judgements, you reduce the incidence of errors. —Louis Nizer, *Chicago Tribune Magazine*, Feb 5, 1978

489. The experience of democracy is like the experience of life itself—always changing, infinite in its variety, sometimes turbulent and all the more valuable for having been tested by adversity. —Jimmy Carter, speech to the Indian Parliament, Jan 2, 1978

490. Most people's opinions are of no value at all. —A.L. Rowse, *The Observer*, Aug 26, 1979

491. (Our goal is) a society with a minimum of compulsion, a maximum of individual freedom and of voluntary association and the abolition of exploitation and poverty. —Roger N. Baldwin, recalled on his death, Aug 26, 1981

492. A government is not in power; it is in office, put there by the will of the people. —Stanley Baldwin, quoted by his daughter, Lorna Howard, in a letter, *The Times*, Jan 23, 1982

493. Democracy is not a fragile flower; still it needs cultivating. —Ronald Reagan, speech to British parliament, Jun 8, 1982

494. I don't run democracy. I train troops to defend democracy. —Lt. Gen. Alfred M. Gray, speech to new officers, *Newsweek*, Jul 9, 1984

495. The struggle is confused; our knight wins by no clean thrust of lance or sword, but the dragon somehow poops out, and decent democracy is victor. —Norman Thomas, quoted on the 30th anniversary of U.S. Senate's censure of Joseph McCarthy, *The New York Times*, Dec 2, 1984

496. Although only a few may originate a policy, we are all able to judge it. —Pericles, quoted by Sir Karl Popper, "Popper on Democracy", *The Economist*, Apr 23, 1988

497. Decisions arrived at democratically, and even the powers conveyed upon a government by a democratic vote, may be wrong. It is hard, if not impossible, to construct a constitution that safeguards against mistakes. —Sir Karl Popper, "Popper on Democracy", *The Economist*, Apr 23, 1988

498. How can we best avoid situations in which a bad ruler causes too much harm? When we say that the best solution known to us is a constitution that allows a majority vote to dismiss the government, then we do not say the majority vote will always be right. We do not even say that it will usually be right. We say only that this very imperfect procedure is the best so far invented. —Sir Karl Popper, "Popper on Democracy", *The Economist*, Apr 23, 1988

499. The moral way of government is the practical way of government. Democracy, the profoundly good, is also the profoundly productive. —Ronald Reagan, farewell address, Jan 11, 1989

500. "We the People" tell the government what to do, it doesn't tell us. "We the people" are the driver—the government is the car. And we decide where it should go, and by what route, and how fast. —Ronald Reagan, farewell address, Jan 11, 1989

DEMOCRATIC PARTY

501. The Democratic Party is like a mule. It has neither pride of ancestry nor hope of posterity. —Ignatius Donnelly, speech to the Minnesota state legislature, Sep 13, 1860

502. Th' dimmycratic party ain't on speakin' terms with itsilf. —Finley Peter Dunne, *Mr. Dooley's Opinions*, 1900

503. I love the Democratic Party; but I love America a great deal more. ... When the Democratic Party thinks that it is an end in itself, then I rise up and dissent. —Woodrow Wilson, speech in Indianapolis, Indiana, Jan 8, 1915

504. The Democrats today trust in the people, the plain, ordinary, everyday citizen, neither superlatively rich nor distressingly poor, not one of the "best minds" but the average mind. The Socialists believe in making the Government the people's master; the Republicans believe that the moneyed "aristocracy", the few great financial minds, should rule the Government; the Democrats believe that the whole people should govern. —Eleanor Roosevelt, "Jeffersonian Principles the Issue in 1928", *Current History*, Jun, 1928

505. We can make this thing into a Party, instead of a Memory. —Will Rogers, letter to Al Smith on the Democratic party, Jan 19, 1929

506. Let it be ... the task of our party to break with foolish traditions. —Franklin D. Roosevelt, quoted by Frank Kingdon, *As FDR Said*, 1932

507. You've got to be (an) optimist to be a Democrat, and you've got to be a humorist to stay one. —Will Rogers, Good Gulf radio show, Jun 24, 1934

508. I am not a member of any organized party—I am a Democrat. —Will Rogers, quoted by P.J. O'Brien, *Will Rogers, Ambassador of Good Will, Prince of Wit and Wisdom*, 1935

509. Every Harvard class should have one Democrat to rescue it from oblivion. —Will Rogers, *The Autobiography of Will Rogers*, 1949

510.   The Democratic Party at its worst is better for the country than the Republican Party at its best. —Lyndon Baines Johnson, speech, 1955

511.   Have you ever tried to split sawdust? —Eugene J. McCarthy, on accusation he had split Democratic Party, NBC-TV, Oct 23, 1969

512.   A new Government took office in Washington, not via bayonets and tanks as is the custom in some of the world's capitals (but) in the Democratic Way ... via hyperbole, sham, melodrama and public-spirited mendacity. —R. Emmett Tyrrell Jr., on Carter's inauguration, *Time*, Mar 7, 1977

513.   The Democratic Party is a party in name only, not in shared belief. —Ramsey Clark, *Time*, Aug 25, 1980

514.   There were so many candidates on the platform that there were not enough promises to go around. —Ronald Reagan, on Democratic presidential primary debate in New Hampshire, *Newsweek*, Feb 6, 1984

515.   In the pageant of unity (at the Democratic National Convention), one speaker after another recited a Whitmanesque litany of races and classes and minorities and interests and occupations—or unemployments. Some speakers, in fact, made the nation sound like an immense ingathering of victims—terrorized senior citizens, forsaken minorities, Dickensian children— warmed by the party's Frank Capra version of America: Say, it's a wonderful life! —Lance Morrow, "All Right, What Kind of People Are We?", *Time*, Jul 30, 1984

516.   (Democrats) can't get elected unless things get worse—and things won't get worse unless they get elected. —Jeane J. Kirkpatrick, *Time*, Jun 17, 1985

DICTATORSHIP/TYRANNY

517.   Any excuse will serve a tyrant. —Aesop, "The Wolf and the Lamb", *Fables*, ca. 550 B.C.

518.   This is a sickness rooted and inherent/ in the nature of a tyranny:/ that he that holds it does not trust his friends. —Aeschylus, *Prometheus Bound*, ca. 478 B.C.

519.   Death is better, a milder fate than tyranny. —Aeschylus, *Agamemnon*, 458 B.C.

520.   When the tyrant has disposed of foreign enemies by conquest or treaty, and there is nothing to fear from them, then he is always stirring up some war or other, in order that the people may require a leader. —Plato, *The Republic*, ca. 390 B.C.

521.   The people have always some champion whom they set over them and nurse into greatness. ... This and no other is the root from which a tyrant springs; when he first appears he is a protector. —Plato, *The Republic*, ca. 390 B.C.

522.   Let them hate me, so they but fear me. [*Oderint, dum metuant.*] —Lucius Accius, fragment from a lost tragedy

523.   The laws can't be enforced against the man who is the laws' master. —Benvenuto Cellini, *Autobiography*, 1558-66

524.   For how can tyrants safely govern home,/ Unless abroad they purchase great alliance? —William Shakespeare, *King Henry the Sixth, Part III*, 1591

525.   The abuse of greatness is when it disjoins/ Remorse from power. —William Shakespeare, *Julius Caesar*, 1599

526.   For the people, I desire their liberty and freedom as much as anybody whatever. But I must tell you that their liberty and freedom consists in having of government those laws by which their life and their goods may be most their own. It is not having a share in government; that is nothing pertaining to them. A subject and a sovereign are clean different things. —Charles I, speech on the scaffold, Jan 30, 1649

527. The face of tyranny / Is always mild at first. [*Toujours la tyrannie a d'heureuses prémices.*] —Jean Racine, *Britannicus*, 1669

528. Of all the tyrannies on humankind, / The worst is that which persecutes the mind. —John Dryden, *The Hind and the Panther*, 1687

529. You need neither art nor science to be a tyrant. [*Il ne faut ni art ni science pour exercer la tyrannie.*] —Jean de La Bruyère, "Du souverain ou de la république", *Les Caractères*, 1688

530. All men would be tyrants if they could. —Daniel Defoe, *The Kentish Petition*, 1712-13

531. The tyranny of the many would be when one body takes over the rights of the others, and then exercises its power to change the laws in its favor. ... One despot always has a few good moments, but an assembly of despots never does. [*Cette tyrannie de plusieurs serait celle d'un corps qui envahirait les droits des autres corps, et qui exercerait le despotisme à la faveur des lois corrompues par lui. ... Un despote a toujours quelques bons moments; une assemblée de despotes n'en a jamais.*] —Voltaire, "Tyrannie", *Dictionnaire philosophique*, 1764

532. We call a tyrant the leader whose only law is that of his own whim, who expropriates the property of his subjects, and then drafts them to go take that of their neighbors. [*On appelle tyran le souverain qui ne connaît de lois que son caprice, qui prend le bien de ses sujets, et qui ensuite les enrôle pour aller prendre celui des voisins.*] —Voltaire, "Tyrannie", *Dictionnaire philosophique*, 1764

533. Under which kind of tyranny would you rather live? Neither, but if a choice must be made I would prefer the tyranny of one to that of the many. [*Sous quelle tyrannie aimeriez-vous mieux vivre? Sous aucune; mais, s'il fallait choisir, je détesterais moins la tyrannie d'un seul que celle de plusieurs.*] —Voltaire, "Tyrannie", *Dictionnaire philosophique*, 1764

534. Whoever has power in his hands wants to be despotic; the craze for domination is an incurable disease. —Voltaire, letter to M. Damilaville, Oct 16, 1765

535. Pure despotism is the punishment for men's bad conduct. If a community of men is subdued by an individual or by a few, that is obviously because it has neither the courage nor the ability to govern itself. —Voltaire, *Republican Ideas*, 1765

536. Where law ends, tyranny begins. —William Pitt, 1st Earl of Chatham, speech in the House of Lords in defense of John Wilkes, Jan 9, 1770

537. The use of force alone is temporary. It may subdue for a moment, but it does not remove the necessity of subduing again: and a nation is not governed which is perpetually conquered. —Edmund Burke, speech, "On Conciliation with the American Colonies", Mar 22, 1775

538. Slavery they can have anywhere. It is a weed that grows in every soil. —Edmund Burke, speech, "On Conciliation with the American Colonies", Mar 22, 1775

539. Tyranny, like hell, is not easily conquered; yet we have this consolation with us, that the harder the conflict, the more glorious the triumph. What we obtain too cheap, we esteem too lightly: it is dearness only that gives everything its value. —Thomas Paine, *The American Crisis*, Dec. 23, 1776

540. A country governed by a despot is an inverted cone. —Samuel Johnson, quoted by James Boswell, *Life of Samuel Johnson*, Apr 14, 1778

541. Necessity is the plea for every infringement of human freedom. It is the argument of tyrants, it is the creed of slaves. —William Pitt, the Younger, speech in the House of Commons, Nov 18, 1783

543. When a people shall have become incapable of governing themselves, and fit for a master, it is of little consequence from what quarter he comes. —George Washington, letter to the Marquis de Lafayette, Apr 28, 1788

544. Kings will be tyrants from policy, when subjects are rebels from principle. —Edmund Burke, *Reflections on the Revolution in France*, 1790

545. Watch out for the fellow who talks about putting things in order! Putting things in order always means getting other people under your control. —Denis Diderot, *Supplement to Bougainville's "Voyage"*, 1796

546. Timid men who prefer the calm of despotism to the tempestuous sea of liberty. —Thomas Jefferson, letter to Philip Mazzei, Jan 1, 1797

547. I have sworn upon the altar of God, eternal hostility against every form of tyranny over the mind of man. —Thomas Jefferson, letter to Benjamin Rush, Sep 23, 1800

548. Force is the vital principle and immediate parent of despotism. —Thomas Jefferson, first inaugural address, Mar 4, 1801

549. Great ambition, unchecked by principle or the love of glory, is an unruly tyrant. —Alexander Hamilton, letter to James Bayard, Jan 16, 1801

550. What has always made the state a hell on earth has been precisely that man has tried to make it his heaven. —Friedrich Hölderlin, quoted by Friedrich von Hayek, *The Road to Serfdom*, 1944

551. The people are always in the wrong when they are faced by the armed forces. [*Le peuple a toujours tort, quand il s'oppose à la force armée.*] —Napoleon I, letter to Gen. Clarke, duc de Feltre, Oct 2, 1810

552. Power, like a desolating pestilence,/ Pollutes whate'er it touches; and obedience,/ Bane of all genius, virtue, freedom, truth,/ Makes slaves of men, and, of the human frame,/ A mechanized automaton. —Percy Bysshe Shelley, *Queen Mab*, 1813

553. Anarchy always brings about absolute power. [*L'anarchie ramène toujours au gouvernement absolu.*] —Napoleon I, speech at the opening of the legislature, Jun 7, 1815

554. Among the several cloudy appellatives which have been commonly employed as cloaks for misgovernment, there is none more conspicuous in this atmosphere of illusion than the word Order. —Jeremy Bentham, *The Book of Fallacies*, 1824

555. Whatever government is not a government of laws, is a despotism, let it be called what it may. —Daniel Webster, remarks in Bangor, Maine, Aug 25, 1835

556. Slavery always has, and always will, produce insurrections wherever it exists, because it is a violation of the natural order of things, and no human power can much longer perpetuate it. —Angelina Grimké, "Appeal to the Christian Women of the South", *The Anti-Slavery Examiner*, Sep, 1836

557. Our fathers waged a bloody conflict with England, because they were taxed without being represented. ... They were not willing to be governed by laws which they had no voice in making; but this is the way in which women are governed in this Republic. —Angelina Grimké, *Letters to Catherine Beecher*, 1836

558. France was long a despotism tempered by epigrams. —Thomas Carlyle, *History of the French Revolution*, 1837

559. Tyrants are but the spawn of Ignorance,/ Begotten by the slaves they trample on. —James Russell Lowell, "Prometheus", 1843

560. The nose of a mob is its imagination. By this, at any time, it can be quietly led. —Edgar Allan Poe, *Marginalia*, 1844-49

561.   Whoever puts his hand on me to govern me is a usurper and a tyrant; I declare him my enemy. —Pierre Joseph Proudhon, *Confessions of a Revolutionary*, 1849

562.   This is the negation of God erected into a system of Government. —William Ewart Gladstone, letter to the Earl of Aberdeen referring to the Kingdom of the Two Sicilies, 1851

563.   Oppression makes a wise man mad. —Frederick Douglass, speech on "The Meaning of July Fourth for the Negro" in Rochester, New York, Jul 5, 1852

564.   Tyrants never perish from tryanny, but always from folly. —Walter Savage Landor, "Anacreon and Polycrates", *Imaginary Conversations*, 1824-53

565.   When the white man governs himself, that is self-government; but when he governs himself and also governs another man, that is more than self-government—that is despotism. —Abraham Lincoln, speech in Peoria, Illinois, Oct 16, 1854

566.   As a nation, we began by declaring that all men are created equal. We now practically read it, all men are created equal except Negroes. When the know-nothings get control, it will read, all men are created equal except the negroes and foreigners and Catholics. When it comes to this I shall prefer emigrating to some country where they make no pretense of loving liberty—to Russia, for instance, where despotism can be pure, and without the base alloy of hypocrisy. —Abraham Lincoln, letter to Joshua Speed, Aug 24, 1855

567.   Whatever crushes individuality is despotism, by whatever name it may be called. —John Stuart Mill, *On Liberty*, 1859

568.   A State which dwarfs its men, in order that they may be more docile instruments in its hand even for beneficial purposes—will find that with small men no great thing can really be accomplished. —John Stuart Mill, *On Liberty*, 1859

569.   They who study mankind with a whip in their hands will always go wrong. —Frederick Douglass, speech in Geneva, New York, Aug 1, 1860

570.   Tyranny is a habit; it may develop, and it does develop at last, into a disease. —Fyodor Dostoevsky, *The House of The Dead*, 1862

571.   It is a fact attested in history that sometimes revolutions most disastrous to freedom are effected without the shedding of blood. The substance of your government may be taken away, while the form and the shadow remain to you. —Andrew Johnson, speech in Washington, D.C., Feb 22, 1866

572.   Was there ever any domination which did not appear natural to those who possessed it? —John Stuart Mill, *The Subjection of Women*, 1869

573.   You have not converted a man because you have silenced him. —John Morley, (1st Viscount Morley of Blackburn), *Rousseau*, 1876

574.   The more complete the despotism, the more smoothly all things move on the surface. —Elizabeth Cady Stanton, *History of Woman Suffrage*, 1881

575.   The prolonged slavery of women is the darkest page in human history. —Elizabeth Cady Stanton, *History of Woman Suffrage*, 1881

576.   Make men large and strong, and tyranny will bankrupt itself in making shackles for them. —Henry Ward Beecher, *Proverbs from Plymouth Pulpit*, 1887

577.   The Austrian government ... is a system of despotism tempered by casualness. —Victor Adler, speech to the International Socialist Congress in Paris, Jul 17, 1889

578.   There are three kinds of despots. There is the despot who tyrannizes over the body. There is the despot who tyrannizes over the soul. There is the despot who tyrannizes over soul and body alike. The first is called the Prince. The second is called the Pope. The third is called the People. —Oscar Wilde, "The Soul of Man Under Socialism", *Fortnightly Review*, Feb, 1891

579. A man may build himself a throne of bayonets, but he cannot sit on it. —William Ralph Inge, *Wit and Wisdom of Dean Inge*

580. The State is still, after individual despots have been largely modified or eliminated, a collective despot, mostly inexorable, almost irresponsible, and entirely inaccessible to those personal appeals which have sometimes moved the obsolete or obsolescent tyrants to pity. In its selfishness and meanness, it is largely the legislated and organized ideal of the lowest and stupidest of its citizens, whose daily life is nearest the level of barbarism. —William Dean Howells, quoted by Daniel Aaron, *Men of Good Hope*, 1951

581. The possession of unlimited power will make a despot of almost any man. There is a possible Nero in the gentlest human creature that walks. —Thomas Bailey Aldrich, "Leaves from a Notebook", *Ponkapog Papers*, 1903

582. No man is good enough to be another man's master. —George Bernard Shaw, *Major Barbara*, 1905

583. What can you do by killing? Nothing. You kill one dog, the master buys another—that's all there is to it. —Maxim Gorky, *Enemies*, 1906

584. People tolerate those they fear further than those they love. —Edgar Watson Howe, *Country Town Sayings*, 1911

585. The concentration of power is what always precedes the destruction of human initiative, and, therefore of human energy. —Woodrow Wilson, speech in New York City, Sep 4, 1912

586. Oppression costs the oppressor too much if the oppressed stand up and protest. The protest need not be merely physical—the throwing of stones and bullets—if it is mental, spiritual; if it expresses itself in silent, persistent dissatisfaction, the cost to the oppressor is terrific. —W.E.B. Du Bois, "Our Own Consent", *Crisis*, Jan, 1913

587. Excess of severity is not the path to order. On the contrary, it is the path to the bomb. —John Morley, *Recollections*, 1917

588. The one means that wins the easiest victory over reason: terror and force. [*Das freilich die Vernunft am leichtesten besiegt: der Terror, die Gewahlt.*] —Adolf Hitler, *Mein Kampf*, 1924

589. The great masses of the people ... will more easily fall victims to a big lie than to a small one. [*Die breite Masse eines Volkes ... einer grossen Lüge leichten zum Opfer fällt als einer kleinen.*] —Adolf Hitler, *Mein Kampf*, 1924

590. The man who is born to be a dictator is not compelled; he wills it. ... The man who feels called upon to govern a people has no right to say, If you want me or summon me, I will cooperate. No, it is his duty to step forward. —Adolf Hitler, speech at his trial for sedition in Munich, Mar 22, 1924

591. Fascism is Capitalism plus Murder. —Upton Sinclair, *Singing Jailbirds*, 1924

592. The willing sacrifice of the innocents is the most powerful retort to insolent tyranny that has yet been conceived by God or man. —Mohandas K. Gandhi, *Young India*, Feb 12, 1925

593. Whoever can conquer the street will one day conquer the state, for every form of power politics and any dictatorially-run state has its roots in the street. —Joseph Goebbels, speech to Nazi party congress, Nuremberg, Germany, Aug, 1927

594. We (the Nazi members) enter parliament in order to supply ourselves, in the arsenal of democracy, with its own weapons. ... If democracy is so stupid as to give us free tickets and salaries for this bear's work, that is its affair. —Joseph Goebbels, *Der Angriff*, Apr 30, 1928

595. Under the species of Syndicalism and Fascism there appears for the first time in Europe a type of man who does not want to give reasons or to be right, but simply shows himself resolved to impose his opinions. [*Bajo las especies de sindicalismo y fascismo aparece por primera vez en Europa un tipo de hombre que no quiere dar razones ni quiere tener razón, sino, sencillamente, se muestra resuelto a imponer sus opiniones.*] —Jose Ortega y Gasset, *The Revolt of the Masses*, 1930

596. We shall never secure emancipation from the tyranny of the white oppressor until we have achieved it in our own souls. —W.E.B. Du Bois, "Patient Asses", *Crisis*, Mar, 1930

597. If the nineteenth centruy was a century of individualism ... it may be expected that this will be the century of collectivism, and hence the century of the State. —Benito Mussolini, *The Political and Social Doctrine of Fascism*, 1932

598. Dictators ride to and fro upon tigers which they dare not dismount. And the tigers are getting hungry. —Sir Winston S. Churchill, *While England Slept*, 1936

599. So long as men worship the Caesars and Napoleons, Caesars and Napoleons will duly rise and make them miserable. —Aldous Huxley, *Ends and Means*, 1937

600. History proves that dictatorships do not grow out of strong and successful governments, but out of weak and helpless ones. —Franklin D. Roosevelt, fireside chat, Apr 14, 1938

601. You cannot organize civilization around the core of militarism and at the same time expect reason to control human destinies. —Franklin D. Roosevelt, radio address, Oct 26, 1938

602. The dictator, in all his pride, is held in the grip of his party machine. He can go forward; he cannot go back. He must blood his hounds and show them sport, or else, like Actaeon of old, be devoured by them. All strong without, he is all-weak within. —Sir Winston S. Churchill, radio address to the United States, Oct 16, 1938

603. A dictatorship is a regime in which people quote instead of thinking. [*Una dittatura è un regime in cui, invece di pensare, gli uomini citano.*] —Ignazio Silone, *The School for Dictatorships*, 1939

604. I suspect that in our loathing of totalitarianism, there is infused a good deal of admiration for its efficiency. —T.S. Eliot, "The Idea of a Christian Society", 1939

605. When a nation has al lowed itself to fall under a tyrannical regime, it cannot be absolved from the faults due to the guilt of the regime. —Sir Winston S. Churchill, message sent following a visit to Italy, Jul 28, 1944

606. True, it is evil that a single man should crush the herd, but see not there the worst form of slavery, which is when the herd crushes out the man. [*Il est certes mauvais que l'homme écrase le troupeau. Mais ne cherche point là le grand esclavage: il se montre quand le troupeau écrase l'homme.*] —Antoine de Saint-Exupéry, *Citadelle*, 1948

607. You cannot educate a man to be a trained technician inside a factory and ask him to accept the status of a political robot outside. ... A totalitarian state or a one-party state is a persistent contradiction with the needs of a thriving industrial community. —Aneurin Bevan, *Tribune*, Feb 3, 1950

608. The slave begins by demanding justice and ends by wanting to wear a crown. He must dominate in his turn. [*L'esclave commence par réclamer justice et finit par vouloir la royauté. Il lui faut dominer à son tour.*] —Albert Camus, "Metaphysical Rebellion", *The Rebel*, 1951

609. Fascism is not defined by the number of its victims, but by the way it kills them. —Jean-Paul Sartre, reported remarks on the execution of Julius and Ethel Rosenberg, Jun 22, 1953

610. From behind the Iron Curtain, there are signs that tyranny is in trouble and reminders that its structure is as brittle as its surf ace is hard. —Dwight D. Eisenhower, State of the Union address, Jan 7, 1954

611. Radicalism itself ceases to be radical when absorbed mainly in preserving its control over a society or an economy. —Eric Hoffer, *The Passionate State of Mind*, 1954

612. So efficient are the available instruments of slavery—fingerprints, lie detectors, brainwashings, gas chambers—that we shiver at the thought of political change which might put these instruments in the hands of men of hate. —Bernard Baruch, *A Philosphy of Time*, 1954

613. Man alone can enslave man. —Simone Weil, *Oppression and Liberty*, 1958

614. Whenever you have an efficient government you have a dictatorship. —Harry S Truman, speech at Columbia Univ., Apr 28, 1959

615. A police state finds it cannot command the grain to grow. —John F. Kennedy, State of the Union address, Jan 14, 1963

616. Nothing more exactly identifies the totalitarian or closed society than the rigid and, more often than not, brutish direction of labor at all levels. —John F. Kennedy, State of the Union address, Jan 14, 1963

617. The benevolent despot who sees himself as a shepherd of the people still demands from others the submissiveness of sheep. —Eric Hoffer, *The Ordeal of Change*, 1964

618. Totalitarianism spells simplification: an enormous reduction in the variety of aims, motives, interests, human types, and, above all, in the categories and units of power. —Eric Hoffer, *The Ordeal of Change*, 1964

619. When men are ruled by fear, they strive to prevent the very changes that will abate it. —Alan Paton, "The Challenge of Fear", *Saturday Review*, Sep 9, 1967

620. It is the common failing of totalitarian regimes that they cannot really understand the nature of our democracy. They mistake dissent for disloyalty. They mistake restlessness for a rejection of policy. They mistake a few committees for a country. They misjudge individual speeches for public policy. —Lyndon Baines Johnson, speech, Sep 29, 1967

621. The trouble with military rule is that every colonel or general is soon full of ambition. The navy takes over today and the army tomorrow. —Yakubu Gowon, *Chiacgo Daily News*, Aug 29, 1970

622. There are similarities between absolute power and absolute faith: a demand for absolute obedience, a readiness to attempt the impossible, a bias for simple solutions—to cut the knot rather than unravel it, the viewing of compromise as surrender. Both absolute power and absolute faith are instruments of dehumanization. Hence, absolute faith corrupts as absolutely as absolute power. —Eric Hoffer, "Thoughts of Eric Hoffer", *The New York Times Magazine*, Apr 25, 1971

623. The most potent weapon in the hands of the oppressor is the mind of the oppressed. —Steve Biko, speech in Cape Town, 1971

624. We are no longer interested in elections except as a means to reach our objectives. —Juan Peron, *The New York Times*, Jul 14, 1973

625. I don't mind dictatorships abroad provided they are pro-American. —George C. Wallace, *Time*, Oct 27, 1975

626. The totalitarian state is not power unchained it is truth chained. [*L'Etat totalitaire ... ce n'est pas la force déchaînée, c'est la vérité enchaînée.*] —Bernard-Henri Lévy, *La Barbarie à visage humain*, 1977

627. The more a regime claims to be the embodiment of liberty the more tyrannical it is likely to be. —Sir Ian Gilmour, *Inside Right*, 1977

628. Ours is not yet a totalitarian government, but it is an elitist democracy—and becoming more so every year. —Victor L. Marchetti, *Inquiry*, Feb 6, 1978

629. When you stop a dictator there are always risks. But there are greater risks in not stopping a dictator. —Margaret Thatcher, interview on BBC-TV during the Falklands War, Apr 5, 1982

630. Anybody who has ever lived ... under a dictatorship which cannot be removed without bloodshed will know that a democracy, imperfect though it is, is worth fighting for and, I believe, worth dying for. —Sir Karl Popper, "Popper on Democracy", *The Economist*, Apr 23, 1988

631. We do not base a choice on the goodness of democracy, which may be doubtful, but solely on the evilness of a dictatorship, which is certain. Not only because the dictator is bound to make bad use of his power, but because a dictator, even if he were benevolent, would rob all others of their responsibility, and thus of their human rights and duties. —Sir Karl Popper, "Popper on Democracy", *The Economist*, Apr 23, 1988

ECONOMICS/THE ECONOMY

632. Commerce, which has made the citizens of England rich, also helped to make them free, and this freedom has encouraged commerce even more. [*Le commerce, qui a enrichi les citoyens en Angleterre, a contribué à les rendre libres, et cette liberté a étendu le commerce à son tour.*] —Voltaire, *Lettres philosophiques*, 1734

633. Labour, therefore, it appears evidently, is the only universal, as well as the only accurate, measure of value, or the only standard by which we can compare the values of different commodities, at all times, and at all places. —Adam Smith, *An Inquiry Into the Nature and Causes of The Wealth of Nations*, 1776

634. No nation was ever ruined by trade. —Benjamin Franklin, *Thoughts on Commercial Subjects*, ca. 1780

635. If there ever existed a monarchy strong as granite, it would only take the ideas of the economists to reduce it to powder. [*S'il existait une monarchie de granit, il suffirait des idéalités des économistes pour la réduire en poudre.*] —Napoleon I, quoted by Emmanuel de Las Cases, *Mémorial de Ste. Hélène*, Jun 17, 1816

636. Free trade, one of the greatest blessings which a government can confer on a people, is in almost every country unpopular. —Lord Macaulay, "Essay on Mitford's History of Greece", 1824

637. Social prosperity means man happy, the citizen free, the nation great. [*Prospérité sociale, cela veut dire l'homme heureux, le citoyen libre, la nation grande.*] —Victor Hugo, *Les Misérables*, 1862

638. The very essence of competitive commerce is waste, the waste that comes from the anarchy of war. —William Morris, *Art Under Plutocracy*, 1883

639. Burn down your cities and leave our farms, and your cities will spring up again as if by magic; but destroy our farms and the grass will grow in the streets of every city in the country. —William Jennings Bryan, "Cross of Gold" speech at the Democratic National Convention, Chicago, Illinois, Jul 8, 1896

640. Commerce is the greatest of all political interests. —Joseph Chamberlain, speech in Birmingham, England, Nov 13, 1896

641. Political institutions are a superstructure resting on an economic foundation. —Vladimir Ilyich Lenin, *The Three Sources and Three Constituent Parts of Marxism*, 1913

642. There is no subtler, no surer means of overturning the existing basis of society than to debauch the currency. The process engages all the hidden forces of economic law on the side of destruction, and does it in a manner which not one man in a million is able to diagnose. —John Maynard Keynes, *The Economic Consequences of the Peace*, 1919

643. Unionism seldom, if ever, uses such power as it has to insure better work; almost always it devotes a large part of that power to safeguarding bad work. —H.L. Mencken, *Prejudices: Third Series*, 1922

644. When more and more people are thrown out of work, unemployment results. —Calvin Coolidge, attributed, *New York Herald Tribune*, Sep 29, 1954

645. The slogan of progress is changing from the full dinner pail to the full garage. —Herbert Hoover, *The New Day*, 1928

646. Prosperity is only an instrument to be used, not a deity to be worshiped. —Calvin Coolidge, speech, Jun 11, 1928

647. If the unemployed could eat plans and promises they would be able to spend the winter on the Riviera. —W.E.B. Du Bois, "As the Crow Flies", *Crisis*, Jan, 1931

648. True wealth is not a static thing. It is a living thing made out of the disposition of men to create and to distribute the good things of life and rising standards of living. —Franklin D. Roosevelt, speech in Washington, D.C., Oct 24, 1934

649. Practical men, who believe themselves to be quite exempt from any intellectual influences, are usually the slaves of some defunct economist. ... It is ideas, not vested interests, which are dangerous for good or evil. —John Maynard Keynes, *The General Theory of Employment, Interest and Money*, 1936

650. We have always known that heedless self-interest was bad morals; we know now that it is bad economics. —Franklin D. Roosevelt, second inaugural address, Jan 20, 1937

651. Economic progress, in capitalist society, means turmoil. —Joseph Schumpeter, *Capitalism, Socialism and Democracy*, 1942

652. There is inherent in the capitalist system a tendency toward self-destruction. —Joseph Schumpeter, *Capitalism, Socialism and Democracy*, 1942

653. True individual freedom cannot exist without economic security and independence. People who are hungry and out of a job are the stuff of which dictatorships are made. —Franklin D. Roosevelt, message to Congress, Jan 11, 1944

654. Nothing so weakens government as persistent inflation. —John Kenneth Galbraith, *The Affluent Society*, 1958

655. In a community where public services have failed to keep abreast of private consumption things are very different. Here, in an atmosphere of private opulence and public squalor, the private goods have full sway. —John Kenneth Galbraith, *The Affluent Society*, 1958

656. The farmer is the only man in our economy who buys everything at retail, sells everything he sells at wholesale, and pays the freight both ways. —John F. Kennedy, campaign speech in Sioux Falls, South Dakota, Sep 22, 1960

657. The Great Depression, like most other periods of severe unemployment, was produced by governmnet mismanagement rather than by any inherent instability of the private economy. —Milton Friedman, *Capitalism and Freedom*, 1962

658. If ignorance paid dividends, most Americans could make a fortune out of what they don't know about economics. —Luther H. Hodges, *Wall Street Journal*, Mar 14, 1962

659. You don't make the poor richer by making the rich poorer. —Sir Winston S. Churchill, quoted, *To the Point International*, Nov 1, 1976

660. The corrosive effects of inflation eat away at ties that bind us together as a people. —Jimmy Carter, (James Earl, Jr.), *Time*, Mar 26, 1979

661. The reality is that zero defects in products plus zero pollution plus zero risk on the job is equivalent to maximum growth of government plus zero economic growth plus runaway inflation. —Dixy Lee Ray, speech to Scientists and Engineers for Secure Energy, 1980

662. Recession is when your neighbor loses his job. Depression is when you lose yours. And recovery is when Jimmy Carter loses his. —Ronald Reagan, his recollection of a 1980 campaign remark, Oct 2, 1986

663. If you let me write $200 billion worth of hot checks every year, I could give you an illusion of prosperity, too. —Lloyd Bentsen, on Reagan administration's economic policies, televised campaign debate, Oct 5, 1988

EDUCATION

664. The people may be made to follow a path of action, but they may not be made to understand it. —Confucius, *The Analects*, ca. 480 B.C.

665. Liberty cannot be preserved without general knowledge among the people. —John Adams, "Dissertation on the Canon and the Feudal Law", Aug, 1765

666. It is an axiom in my mind that our liberty can never be safe but in the hands of the people themselves, and that, too, of the people with a certain degree of instruction. —Thomas Jefferson, letter to George Washington, Jan 4, 1786

667. Educate and inform the whole mass of people. Enable them to see that it is to their interest to preserve peace and order. ... They are the only sure reliance for the preservation of our liberty. —Thomas Jefferson, letter to James Madison, Dec 20, 1787

668. The project of a national education ought uniformly to be discouraged, on account of its obvious alliance with national government. This is an alliance of a more formidable nature than the old and much contested alliance of church and state. —William Godwin, *An Enquiry Concerning Political Justice*, 1793

669. Enlighten the people generally, and tyranny and oppressions of body and mind will vanish like the evil spirits at the dawn of day. —Thomas Jefferson, letter to Pierre S. du Pont de Nemours, Apr 24, 1816

670. If a nation expects to be ignorant and free, in a state of civilization, it expects what never was and never will be. —Thomas Jefferson, letter to Col. Charles Yancey, Jan 6, 1816

671. Let us by all wise and constitutional measures promote intelligence among the people as the best means of preserving our liberties. —James Monroe, first inaugural address, Mar 4, 1817

672. I know no safe depository of the ultimate powers of the society but the people themselves; and if we think them not enlightened enough to exercise their control with a wholesome discretion, the remedy is not to take it from them, but to inform their discretion by education. This is the true corrective of abuses of constitutional power. —Thomas Jefferson, letter to William Charles Jarvis, Sep 28, 1820

673. Learned Institutions ought to be favorite objects with every free people. They throw that light over the public mind which is the best security against crafty & dangerous encroachments on the public liberty. —James Madison, letter to W.T. Barry, Aug 4, 1822

674. What spectacle can be more edifying or more seasonable, than that of Liberty & Learning, each leaning on the other for their mutual & surest support? —James Madison, letter to W.T. Barry, Aug 4, 1822

675. A popular government without popular information or the means of acquiring it is but a prologue to a farce or a tragedy or perhaps both. —James Madison, letter to W.T. Barry, Aug 4, 1822

676. Education makes a people easy to lead, but difficult to drive; easy to govern, but impossible to enslave. —Henry Brougham, Baron Brougham, attributed

677. It is obvious that in democratic societies it is in the interest of the individual as well as that of the state that the education of the greatest number should be in scientific, commercial, and industrial subjects rather than literary ones. [*Il est évident que, dans les sociétés démocratiques, l'intérêt des individus, aussi bien que la sûreté de l'Etat, exigent que l'éducation du plus grand nombre soit scientifique, commerciale et industrielle plutôt que littéraire.*] —Alexis, Comte de Tocqueville, *Democracy in America*, 1839

678. Give a hungry man a stone and tell him what beautiful houses are made of it; give ice to a freezing man and tell him of its good properties in hot weather; throw a drowning man a dollar, as a mark of your good will; but do not mock the bondman in his misery by giving him a Bible when he cannot read it. —Frederick Douglass, "Bibles for the Slaves", Jun, 1847

679. Education, then, beyond all other devices of human origin, is the great equalizer of the conditions of men,—the balance-wheel of the social machinery. —Horace Mann, *Twelfth Annual Report to the Massachusetts State Board of Education*, 1848

680. I believe it will be absolutely necessary that you should prevail on our future masters to learn their letters. —Robert Lowe, speech in the House of Commons on grant of franchise to non-propertied men, Jul 15, 1867

681. Upon the education of the people of this country the fate of this country depends. —Benjamin Disraeli, speech in the House of Commons, Jun 15, 1874

682. Liberty can be safe only when Suffrage is illuminated by Education. —James A. Garfield, *Maxims*, 1880

683. A little learning, indeed, may be a dangerous thing, but the want of learning is a calamity to any people. —Frederick Douglass, speech at the Colored High School Commencement, Baltimore, Maryland, Jun 22, 1894

684. The free man cannot be long an ignorant man. —William McKinley, speech in Pittsburgh, Pennsylvania, Nov 3, 1897

685. We naturally associate democracy, to be sure, with freedom of action, but freedom of action without freed capacity of thought behind it is only chaos. —John Dewey, "Democracy in Education", *The Elementary School Teacher*, Dec, 1903

686. The highest result of education is tolerance. —Hellen Keller, *Optimism*, 1903

687. No amount of charters, direct primaries, or short ballots will make a democracy out of an illiterate people. —Walter Lippmann, "Revolution and Culture", *A Preface to Politics*, 1914

688. Human history becomes more and more a race between education and catastrophe. —H.G. Wells, *The Outline of History*, 1920

689. By educating the young generation along the right lines, the People's State will have to see to it that a generation of mankind is formed which will be adequate to this supreme combat that will decide the destinies of the world. —Adolf Hitler, *Mein Kampf*, 1924

690. Democracy has arrived at a gallop in England and I feel all the time that it is a race for life; can we educate them before the crash comes? —Stanley Baldwin, letter to Edward Wood, 1928

691. Knowledge—that is, education in its true sense—is our best protection against unreasoning prejudice and panic-making fear, whether engendered by special interest, illiberal minorities, or panic-stricken leaders. —Franklin D. Roosevelt, speech in Boston, Massachusetts, Oct 31, 1932

692. A democratic form of government, a democratic way of life, presupposes free public education over a long period; it presupposes also an education for personal responsibility that too often is neglected. —Eleanor Roosevelt, "Let Us Have Faith in Democracy", *Land Policy Review, Department of Agriculture*, Jan, 1942

693. If we value the pursuit of knowledge, we must be free to follow wherever that search may lead us. The free mind is no barking dog, to be tethered on a ten-foot chain. —Adlai E. Stevenson Jr., speech at the Univ. of Wisconsin, Madison, Oct 8, 1952

694. In history it is always those with little learning who overthrow those with much learning. ... When young people grasp a truth they are invincible and old people cannot compete with them. —Mao Tse-tung, address to the Chengtu conference, Mar 22, 1958

695. Liberty without learning is always in peril, and learning without liberty is always in vain. —John F. Kennedy, speech at Vanderbilt Univ., Nashville, Tennessee, May 18, 1963

696. Leadership and learning are indispensable to each other. —John F. Kennedy, speech prepared for delivery in Dallas the day of his assassination, Nov 22, 1963

697. Poverty has many roots, but the tap root is ignorance. —Lyndon Baines Johnson, message to Congress, Jan 12, 1965

ELECTIONS AND VOTING

698. The right of voting for representatives is the primary right by which other rights are protected. To take away this right is to reduce a man to slavery, for slavery consists in being subject to the will of another, and he that has not a vote in the election of representatives is in this case. —Thomas Paine, *Dissertation on First Principles of Government*, 1795

699. To request an honest man to vote according to his conscience is superfluous. To request him to vote against his conscience is an insult. The practice of canvassing is quite reasonable under a system in which men are sent to Parliament to serve themselves. It is the height of absurdity under a system in which men are sent to Parliament to serve the public. —Lord Macaulay, letter to an unnamed correspondent, Aug 3, 1832

700. A majority is always the best repartee. —Benjamin Disraeli, *Tancred*, 1847

701. All voting is a sort of gaming, like chequers of backgammon, with a slight moral tinge to it. —Henry David Thoreau, *Civil Disobedience*, 1849

702. The ballot is stronger than the bullet. —Abraham Lincoln, speech, May 19, 1856

703. "Vote early and vote often," the advice openly displayed on the election banners in one of our northern cities. —William Porcher Miles, speech in the House of Representatives, Mar 31, 1858

704. We cannot have free government without elections; and if the rebellion could force us to forego or postpone a national election, it might fairly claim to have already conquered and ruined us. —Abraham Lincoln, speech to his supporters following his re-election, Nov 10, 1864

705. An election is coming. Universal peace is declared, and the foxes have a sincere interest in prolonging the lives of the poultry. —George Eliot, (Mary Ann Evans), *Felix Holt, the Radical*, 1866

706. Our "pathway" is straight to the ballot box, with no variableness nor shadow of turning. ... We demand in the Reconstruction suffrage for all the citizens of the Republic. I would not talk of Negroes or women, but of citizens. —Elizabeth Cady Stanton, letter to Thomas Wentworth Higginson, Jan 13, 1868

707. I know nothing grander, better exercise, better digestion, more positive proof of the past, the triumphant result of faith in human kind, than a well-contested American national election. —Walt Whitman, "Democratic Vistas", 1871

708. If any intelligent and loyal company of American citizens were required to catalogue the essential human conditions of national life, I do not doubt that with absolute unanimity they would begin with "free and honest elections." —Benjamin Harrison, second annual address to Congress, Dec 1, 1890

709. Vote, n. The instrument and symbol of a freeman's power to make a fool of himself and a wreck of his country. —Ambrose Bierce, *The Devil's Dictionary*, 1906

710. A rayformer thinks he was ilicted because he was a rayformer, whin th' thruth iv th' matther is he was ilicted because no wan knew him. —Finley Peter Dunne, *Observations by Mr. Dooley*, 1906

711. We'd all like t'vote fer th'best man, but he's never a candidate. —"Kin" Hubbard, *The Best of Kin Hubbard*, 1984

712. Inside the polling booth every American man and woman stands as the equal of every other American man and woman. There they have no superiors. There they have no masters save their own minds and consciences. —Franklin D. Roosevelt, speech in Worcester, Massachusetts, Oct 21, 1936

713. Elections are won by men and women chiefly because most people vote against somebody, rather than for somebody. —Franklin P. Adams, *Nods and Becks*, 1944

714. I could not consent to the introduction into our national life of a device so alien to all our traditions as the referendum, which has only too often been the instrument of Nazism and Fascism. —Clement Attlee, 1st Earl Attlee, letter to Winston Churchill, May 21, 1945

715. Voting is merely a handy device; it is not to be identified with democracy, which is a mental and moral relation of man to man. —George Douglas Cole, *Essays in Social Theory*, 1950

716. Vote for the man who promises least; he'll be the least disappointing. —Bernard Baruch, quoted by Meyer Berger, *Meyer Berger's New York*, 1960

717. A whore's vote is just as good as a debutante's. —Sam Rayburn, quoted, *D Magazine*, Jun, 1979

718. The margin is narrow, but the responsibility is clear. —John F. Kennedy, press conference following a close congressional election, Nov 11, 1963

719. People only leave (Washington) by way of the box—ballot or coffin. —Claiborne Pell, *Vogue*, Aug 1, 1963

720. The vote is the most powerful instrument ever devised by man for breaking down injustice and destroying the terrible walls which imprison men because they are different from other men. —Lyndon Baines Johnson, speech on signing the Voting Rights Bill, Aug 6, 1965

721. The first step toward liberation for any group is to use the power in hand. ... And the power in hand is the vote. —Helen Gahagan Douglas, quoted by Lee Israel, *Ms.*, Oct, 1973

722. The voters are the people who have spoken—the bastards. —Morris K. Udall, anecdote about politician used to console campaign workers on defeat in primary, *Chicago Sun-Times*, Jul 14, 1976

723. Voters don't decide issues, they decide who will decide issues. —George F. Will, on conservatives, *Newsweek*, Mar 8, 1976

724. Voting is a civic sacrament. —Theodore M. Hesburgh, *Reader's Digest*, Oct, 1984

725. An election is a bet on the future, not a popularity test of the past. —James Reston, *The New York Times*, Oct 10, 1984

726. Bad politicians are sent to Washington by good people who don't vote. —William E. Simon, quoted, *A Guide to the 99th Congress*, 1985

727. This election is not about ideology; it's about competence. —Michael Dukakis, acceptance speech as Democratic nominee for president, Jul 21, 1988

ENVIRONMENT

728. The earth belongs always to the living generation: they may manage it, then and what proceeds from it, as they please, during their usufruct. —Thomas Jefferson, letter to James Madison, Sep 6, 1789

729. To waste, to destroy, our natural resources, to skin and exhaust the land instead of using it so as to increase its usefulness, will result in undermining in the days of our children the very prosperity which we ought by right to hand down to them amplified and developed. —Theodore Roosevelt, seventh annual message to Congress, Dec 3, 1907

730. The nation behaves well if it treats the natural resources as assets which it must turn over to the next generation increased, and not impaired, in value. —Theodore Roosevelt, speech to Colorado Live Stock Association, Aug 29, 1910

731. This policy (conservation) rests upon the fundamental law that neither man nor nation can prosper unless, in dealing with the present, thought is steadily taken for the future. —Theodore Roosevelt, *The Outlook*, Aug 27, 1910

732. Not one cent for scenery. —Joseph G. Cannon, attributed by Blair Bolles, *Tyrant from Illinois*, 1951

733. The greatest domestic problem facing our country is saving our soil and water. Our soil belongs also to unborn generations. —Sam Rayburn, quoted by Valton J. Young, *The Speaker's Agent*, 1956

734. It is our task in our time and in our generation to hand down undiminished to those who come after us, as was handed down to us by those who went before, the natural wealth and beauty which is ours. —John F. Kennedy, speech dedicating the National Wildlife Federation Building, Mar 3, 1961

735. Once you've seen one redwood, you've seen them all. —Ronald Reagan, *The New York Times Magazine*, Jul 4, 1976

736. For this generation, ours, life is nuclear survival, liberty is human rights, the pursuit of happiness is a planet whose resources are devoted to the physical and spiritual nourishment of its inhabitants. —Jimmy Carter, farewell address, Jan 14, 1981

EQUALITY

737. Democracy arises out of the notion that those who are equal in any respect are equal in all respects; because men are equally free, they claim to be absolutely equal. —Aristotle, *Politics*, 343 B.C.

738. For what people have always sought is equality before the law. For rights that were not open to all alike would be no rights. [*Ius enim semper est quaesitum aequabile; neque enim aliter esset ius.*] —Marcus Tullius Cicero, *De Officiis*, 44 B.C.

739. The poorest he that is in England hath a life to live as the greatest he. —Thomas Rainborowe, at the army debates at Putney, quoted by Thomas Love Peacock, *Life of Rainborowe*, Oct 29, 1647

740. It is better that some should be unhappy than that none should be happy, which would be the case in a general state of equality. —Samuel Johnson, quoted by James Boswell, *Life of Samuel Johnson*, Apr 7, 1776

741. The foundation on which all our constitutions are built is the natural equality of man. —Thomas Jefferson, letter to George Washington, Apr 16, 1784

742. There can be no truer principle than this—that every individual of the community at large has an equal right to the protection of government. —Alexander Hamilton, speech to the Constitutional Convention, Jun 29, 1787

743. Equal laws protecting equal rights ... the best guarantee of loyalty & love of country. —James Madison, letter to Jacob De La Motta, Aug, 1820

744. Under a pure despotism, a people may be contented, because all are slaves alike; but those who, under a free government, are refused equal participation, must be discontented. —3rd Viscount Palmerston, speech in the House of Commons on Catholic emancipation, Mar 18, 1829

745. It is to be regretted that the rich and powerful all too often bend the acts of government to their selfish purpose. ... In the full enjoyment of the gifts of Heaven and the fruits of superior industry, economy, and virtue, every man is equally entitled to protection by law. —Andrew Jackson, veto message, Jul 10, 1832

746. Democracy and socialism have nothing in common but one word: equality. But notice the difference: while democracy seeks equality in liberty, socialism seeks equality in restraint and servitude. —Alexis, Comte de Tocqueville, speech in the Constituent Assembly, Sep 12, 1848

747. We hold these truths to be self-evident, that all men and women are created equal. —Elizabeth Cady Stanton, First Women's Rights Convention, Seneca, New York, *Declaration of Sentiments*, Jul 19-20, 1848

748. It's a poor rule that won't work both ways. —Frederick Douglass, speech in Boston, Massachusetts, Jun 8, 1849

749. Be not deceived. Revolutions do not go backward. The founder of the Democratic party declared that all men were created equal. —Abraham Lincoln, speech in Bloomington, Illinois, May 19, 1856

750. I think the authors of that notable instrument (the Declaration of Independence) intended to include all men, but they did not intend to declare all men equal in all respects. They did not mean to say all were equal in color, size, intellect, moral developments, or social capacity. They defined with tolerable distinctness in what respects they did consider all men equal—equal with "certain inalienable rights, among which are life, liberty, and the pursuit of happiness." This they said, and this they meant. —Abraham Lincoln, speech in Springfield, Illinois, Jun 27, 1857

751. Let us discard all this quibbling about this man or the other man, this race or that race and the other race being inferior and therefore they must be placed in an inferior position— discarding our standard that we have left us! Let us discard all these things and unite as one people throughout this land until we shall once more stand up declaring that all men are created equal. —Abraham Lincoln, speech in Chicago, Illinois, Jul 10, 1858

752. Join the union, girls, and together say Equal Pay for Equal Work. —Susan B. Anthony, *The Revolution*, Mar 18, 1869

753. We wish, in a word, equality — equality in fact as corollary, or, rather, as primordial condition of liberty. From each according to his faculties, to each according to his needs; that is what we wish sincerely and energetically. —Michael Bakunin, *Anarchist Declaration*, 1870

754. Choose equality. —Matthew Arnold, "Equality", *Mixed Essays*, 1879

755. Equality—the informing soul of Freedom! —James A. Garfield, *Maxims*, 1880

756. The yearning after equality is the offspring of covetousness, and there is no possible plan for satisfying that yearning which can do aught else than rob A to give to B; consequently all such plans nourish some of the meanest vices of human nature, waste capital, and overthrow civilization. —William Graham Sumner, conclusion, *What Social Classes Owe to Each Other*, 1883

757. Emperors, kings, artisans, peasants, big people, little people—at the bottom we are all alike and all the same; all just alike on the inside, and when our clothes are off, nobody can tell which of us is which. —Mark Twain, "Does the Race of Man Love a Lord?", *North American Review*, Apr, 1902

758. Our aim is to recognize what Lincoln pointed out: The fact that there are some respects in which men are obviously not equal: but also insist that there should be an equality of self-respect and of mutual respect, an equality of rights before the law, and at least an approximate equality in the conditions under which each man obtains the chance to show the stuff that is in him when compared to his fellows. —Theodore Roosevelt, seventh annual message to Congress, Dec 3, 1907

759. Liberty without equality is a name of noble sound and squalid result. —Leonard Hobhouse, *Liberalism*, 1911

760. Couldn't we even argue that it is because men are unequal that they have that much more need to be brothers? —Charles Du Bos, *Journal*, Feb 27, 1918

761. All animals are equal/ But some animals are more equal than others. —George Orwell, *Animal Farm*, 1946

762. It is a wise man who said that there is no greater inequality than the equal treatment of unequals. —Felix Frankfurter, dissenting opinion, *Dennis v. United States*, 1949

763. We clamor for equality chiefly in matters in which we ourselves cannot hope to obtain excellence. —Eric Hoffer, *The Passionate State of Mind*, 1954

764. Legislation to apply the principle of equal pay for equal work without discrimination because of sex is a matter of simple justice. —Dwight D. Eisenhower, State of the Union message, Jan 5, 1956

765. There is always inequity in life. Some men are killed in war and some men are wounded, and some men are stationed in the Antarctic and some are stationed in San Francisco. It's very hard in military or personal life to assure complete equality. Life is unfair. —John F. Kennedy, letter to a reservist on active duty, Mar 21, 1962

766. All of us do not have equal talent, but all of us should have an equal opportunity to develop our talents. —John F. Kennedy, speech at San Diego State College, San Diego, California, Jun 6, 1963

767. A government conceived and dedicated to the purpose that all men are born free and equal cannot pervert its mission by rephrasing the purpose to suggest that men shall be free today—but shall be equal a little later. —Lyndon Baines Johnson, speech at Wayne State Univ., Detroit, Michigan, Jan 6, 1963

768. To live anywhere in the world today and be against equality because of race or color, is like living in Alaska and being against snow. —William Faulkner, "On Fear: Deep South in Labor: Mississippi", *Essays, Speeches & Public Letters*, 1965

769. The guarantee of equal protection cannot mean one thing when applied to one individual and something else when applied to a person of another color. If both are not accorded the same protection, then it is not equal. —Lewis F. Powell Jr., majority opinion, *Regents of the University of California v. Bakke*, Jun 28, 1978

ETHICS IN POLITICS

770. Righteousness exalteth a nation. —Bible, *1 Samuel*, ca. 800 B.C.

771. It is not always the same thing to be a good man and a good citizen. —Aristotle, *Nicomachean Ethics*, ca. 325 B.C.

772. A good man would prefer to be defeated than to defeat injustice by evil means. [*Sed bono vinci satius est quam malo more iniuriam vincere.*] —Sallust, *Jugurthine War*, ca. 41 B.C.

773. But who is to guard the guards themselves? [*Sed quis custodiet ipsos Custodes?*] —Juvenal, *Satires*, ca. 115

774. The prince must not mind incurring the scandal of those vices, without which it would be difficult to save the state, for if one considers well, it will be found that some things which seem virtues would, if followed, lead to one's ruin, and some others which appear vices result in one's greater security and wellbeing. [*Et etiam non si curi di incorrere nella infamia di quelli vizii, sanza quali e' possa difficilmente saluare lo stato; perché, se si considerrà bene tutto, si troverrà qualque cosa che parrà virtù, e seguendola sarebbe la ruina sua, e qualcuna altra che parrà vizio, e seguendola ne riesce la securtà e il bene essere suo.*] —Niccolò Machiavelli, *Il Principe*, 1532

776. Public life is a situation of power and energy; he trespasses against his duty who sleeps over his watch, as well as he that goes over to the enemy. —Edmund Burke, *Thoughts on the Cause of the Present Discontents*, 1770

777. The whole art of government consists in the art of being honest. —Thomas Jefferson, "Draft of Instructions to the Virginia Delegates in the Continental Congress", Aug, 1774

778. Conscience has no more to do with gallantry than it has with politics. —Richard Brinsley Sheridan, *The Duenna*, 1775

779. Corruption, the most infallible symptom of constitutional liberty. —Edward Gibbon, *The History of the Decline and Fall of the Roman Empire*, 1776-88

780. I have the consolation of having added nothing to my private fortune during my public service, and of retiring with hands as clean as they are empty. —Thomas Jefferson, letter to Count Diodati, 1807

781. He (Edward Livingston) is a man of splendid abilities, but utterly corrupt. He shines and stinks like rotten mackerel by moonlight. —John Randolph of Roanoke, quoted by W. Cabell Bruce, *John Randolph of Roanoke, 1773-1833*, 1922

782. A marciful Providunce fashioned us holler/ O' purpose thet we might our princerples swaller. —James Russell Lowell, *The Biglow Papers: First Series*, 1848

783. It is, when strictly judged, an act of public immorality to form and lead an opposition on a certain plea, to succeed, and then in office to abandon it. —William Ewart Gladstone, letter to Lord Aberdeen, Aug 5, 1852

784. Moral principle is a looser bond than pecuniary interest. —Abraham Lincoln, speech, Oct, 1856

785. Most of the great results of history are brought about by discreditable means. —Ralph Waldo Emerson, "Considerations by the Way", *The Conduct of Life*, 1860

786. I think I can say, and say with pride, that we have some legislatures that bring higher prices than any in the world. —Mark Twain, (Samuel L. Clemens), *Sketches, New and Old*, 1875

787. When I want to buy up any politician I always find the anti-monopolists the most purchasable—they don't come so high. —William Vanderbilt, interview, *Chicago Daily News*, Oct 9, 1882

788. The principles of public morality are as definite as those of the morality of private life; but they are not identical. —Lord Acton, letter to Bishop Mandell Creighton, Apr 5, 1887

789. There is nothing so bad or so good that you will not find Englishmen doing it; but you will never find an Englishman in the wrong. He does everything on principle. He fights you on patriotic principles; he robs you on business principles; he enslaves you on imperial principles. —George Bernard Shaw, *The Man of Destiny*, 1897

790. You tell me whar a man gits his corn pone, en I'll tell you what his 'pinions is. —Mark Twain, "Corn Pone Opinions", *Europe and Elsewhere*, 1925

791.   No man is justified in doing evil on the ground of expediency. —Theodore Roosevelt, "The Strenuous Life", *The Strenuous Life: Essays and Addresses*, 1900

792.   The men with the muck-rakes are often indispensable to the well-being of society, but only if they know when to stop raking the muck. —Theodore Roosevelt, on investigative journalists, in speech in Washington, D.C., Apr 14, 1906

793.   Corruption of politics has nothing to do with the morals, or the laxity of morals, of various political personalities. Its cause is altogether a material one. —Emma Goldman, "The Tragedy of Women's Emancipation", *Anarchism and Other Essays*, 1911

794.   The cure for bad politics is the same as the cure for tuberculosis. It is living in the open space. —Woodrow Wilson, speech in Minneapolis, Minnesota, Sep 18, 1912

795.   Publicity is one of the purifying elements of politics. ... Nothing checks all the bad practices of politics as public exposure. ... An Irishman, seen digging around the wall of a house, was asked what he was doing. He answered, "Faith, I am letting the dark out of the cellar." Now, that's exactly what we want to do. —Woodrow Wilson, quoted by William B. Hale, *The New Freedom*, 1913

796.   In my creed, waste of public money is like the sin against the Holy Ghost. —John Morley, *Recollections*, 1917

797.   But even a politician who is honest in the highest sense may be very harmful; one may take George III as an illustration. Stupidity and unconscious bias often work more damage than venality. —Bertrand Russell, presidential address to the Students Union, London School of Economics, Oct 10, 1923

798.   The conception of an "honest" politician is not altogether a simple one. The most tolerant definition is one whose political actions are not dictated by a desire to increase his own income. —Bertrand Russell, presidential address to the Students Union, London School of Economics, Oct 10, 1923

799.   The difference between a moral man and a man of honor is that the latter regrets a discreditable act, even when it has worked and he has not been caught. —H.L. Mencken, *Prejudices: Fourth Series*, 1924

800.   When a fellow says it hain't the money but the principle o' the thing, it's th' money. —"Kin" Hubbard, *Hoss Sense and Nonsense*, 1926

801.   You cannot adopt politics as a profession and remain honest. —Louis McHenry Howe, speech, Jan 17, 1933

802.   Shrewdness in Public Life all over the World is always honored, while honesty in Public Men is generally attributed to Dumbness and is seldom rewarded. —Will Rogers, *The Autobiography of Will Rogers*, 1949

803.   A lie is an abomination unto the Lord, and a very present help in trouble. —Adlai E. Stevenson Jr., speech in Springfield, Illinois, Jan, 1951

804.   I cannot and will not cut my conscience to fit this year's fashions. —Lillian Hellman, letter to Committee on Un-American Activities of the House of Representatives, May 19, 1952

805.   Those who corrupt the public mind are just as evil as those who steal from the public purse. —Adlai E. Stevenson Jr., speech in Albuquerque, New Mexico, Sep 12, 1952

806.   This Administration intends to be candid about its errors; for, as a wise man once said: "An error doesn't become a mistake until you refuse to correct it." We intend to accept full responsibility for our errors. —John F. Kennedy, speech in New York City, New York, Apr 27, 1961

807.　The basis of effective government is public confidence, and that confidence is endangered when ethical standards falter or appear to falter. —John F. Kennedy, message to Congress, Apr 27, 1961

808.　Congress—these, for the most part, illiterate hacks whose fancy vests are spotted with gravy and whose speeches, hypocritical, unctuous and slovenly, are spotted also with the gravy of political patronage. —Mary McCarthy, *On the Contrary*, 1961

809.　When there is a lack of honor in government, the morals of the whole people are poisoned. —Herbert Hoover, recalled on his 90th birthday, *The New York Times*, Aug 9, 1964

810.　The citizen is influenced by principle in direct proportion to his distance from the political situation. —Milton Rakove, *The Virginia Quarterly Review*, Summer, 1965

811.　Most of us are honest at all time, and all of us are honest most of the time. —Charles M. Mathias Jr., on ethics among congressmen and senators, *Time*, Mar 31, 1967

812.　There are plenty of recommendations on how to get out of trouble cheaply and fast. Most of them come down to this: Deny your responsibility. —Lyndon Baines Johnson, speech at a Democratic fundraising dinner, Sep 30, 1967

813.　When morality comes up against profit, it is seldom that profit loses. —Shirley Chisholm, *Unbought and Unbossed*, 1970

814.　Secrecy in government has become synonymous, in the public mind, with deception by the government. —Lawton M. Chiles Jr., *Christian Science Monitor*, Nov 4, 1975

815.　Washington is a place where the truth is not necessarily the best defense. It surely runs a poor second to the statute of limitations. —Peter Lisagor, *Time*, Dec 20, 1976

816.　Sunlight remains the world's best disinfectant. —William Proxmire, *The New York Times*, Sep 9, 1977

817.　I think that one of Nixon's great contributions to civil liberties was getting caught doing what the two presidents before him got away with. —William Safire, *Book Digest*, Jul, 1977

818.　It happens that intellectual honesty is not the coin of the realm in politics. —Edward I. Koch, *The New York Times*, Oct 23, 1979

819.　Certainly he (Richard Nixon) is not of the generation that regards honesty as the best policy. However, he does regard it as a policy. —Walter Lippmann, quoted, *Newsweek*, May 12, 1980

820.　The flood of money that gushes into politics today is a pollution of democracy. —Theodore H. White, *Time*, Nov 19, 1984

821.　If a person is an economic being and figures out the odds, then there is a very high incentive to cheat. That is, of course, putting aside honor, duty and patriotism. —Jerome Krutz, *Wall Street Journal*, Apr 10, 1984

822.　We do many things at the federal level that would be considered dishonest and illegal if done in the private sector. —Donald T. Regan, *The New York Times*, Aug 25, 1986

EXPRESSIONS AND PHRASES

823.　There is strength in the union even of very sorry men. —Homer, *Iliad*, ca. 700 B.C.

824.　Authority is never without hate. —Euripides, *Ion*, ca. 415 B.C.

825.　A sword never kills anybody; it's a tool in the killer's hand. [*Quemadmodum gladius neminem occidit; occidentis telum est.*] —Seneca (the Younger), *Letters to Lucilius*, ca. 63-65

826.　If a house be divided against itself, that house cannot stand. —Bible, *Mark*, ca. 70

827. Even on the highest throne in the world, we are still sitting on our ass. [*Et au plus eslevé throne du monde, si ne sommes assis que sus nostre cul.*] —Michel de Montaigne, "De l'experiénce", *Essais*, 1580-88

828. I will follow the right side even to the fire, but excluding the fire if I can. [*Je suivrai le bon parti jusques au feu, mais exclusivement si je puis.*] —Michel de Montaigne, "De l'utile et de l'honnête", *Essais*, 1580-88

829. To win without risk is to triumph without glory. [*A vaincre sans péril on triomphe sans gloire.*] —Pierre Corneille, *The Cid*, 1636

830. Many ... have too rashly charged the troops of error, and remain as trophies unto the enemies of truth. —Sir Thomas Browne, *Religio Medici*, 1642

831. If a donkey bray at you, don't bray at him. —George Herbert, *Jacula Prudentum*, 1651

832. Everyone complains about his memory, but no one complains about his judgement. [*Tout le monde se plaint de sa mémoire, et personne ne se plaint de son jugement.*] —Francois, Duc de La Rochefoucauld, *Réflexions, ou Sentences et maximes morales*, 1665

833. Nothing is as dangerous for the state as those who would govern kingdoms with maxims found in books. [*Il n'y a rien de plus dangereux pour l'Etat que ceux qui veulent gouverner les Royaumes par les maximes, qu'ils tirent de leurs livres.*] —Cardinal Richelieu, *Political Testament part I, chap. 8, sec. 2*, 1687

834. Changing Hands without changing Measures, is as if a Drunkard in a Dropsey should change his Doctors, and not his Dyet. —1st Marquess of Halifax, *Maxims of State*, 1700

835. The mob has many heads but no brains. —Thomas Fuller, *Gnomologia*, 1732

836. From fanaticism to barbarism is only one step. —Denis Diderot, *Essai sur le merite de la vertu*, 1745

837. The first man who, having enclosed a piece of ground, thought to himself to say, This is mine, and found people simple enough to believe him, was the true founder of civil society. —Jean Jacques Rousseau, *Discourse on the Origin of Inequality Among Men*, 1755

838. When bad men combine, the good must associate; else they will fall one by one, an unpitied sacrifice in a contemptible struggle. —Edmund Burke, *Thoughts on the Cause of the Present Discontents*, 1770

839. Facts are stubborn things; and whatever may be our wishes, our inclinations, or the dictates of our passions, they cannot alter the state of facts and evidence. —John Adams, "Argument in Defense of the Soldiers in the Boston Massacre Trials", Dec, 1770

840. The number of wise men will always be small. It is true that it has increased; but that is nothing compared with the fools, and unfortunately it is said that God is always on the side of the big battalions. —Voltaire, letter to M. le Riche, Feb 6, 1770

841. Force cannot give right. —Thomas Jefferson, "Draft of Instructions to the Virginia Delegates in the Continental Congress", Aug, 1774

842. I do not know the method of drawing up an indictment against a whole people. —Edmund Burke, speech, "On Conciliation with the American Colonies", Mar 22, 1775

843. We must all hang together, or assuredly we shall all hang separately. —Benjamin Franklin, at the signing of the Declaration of Independence, Jul 4, 1776

844. Whoever can surprize well must Conquer. —John Paul Jones, letter to the American commissioners in France, Feb 10, 1778

845. Good order is the foundation of all things. —Edmund Burke, *Reflections on the Revolution in France*, 1790

846. No man is prejudiced in favor of a thing knowing it to be wrong. He is attached to it on the belief of its being right. —Thomas Paine, *The Rights of Man*, 1791

847. Boldness, more boldness, and always boldness! [*De l'audace, et encore de l'audace, et toujours de l'audace!*] —Georges Jacques Danton, speech to the Legislative Committee of General Defence, Sep 2, 1792

848. Delay is preferable to error. —Thomas Jefferson, letter to George Washington, May 16, 1792

849. Every political good carried to the extreme must be productive of evil. —Mary Wollstonecraft, *The French Revolution*, 1794

850. The outcome of the greatest events is always determined by a trifle. —Napoleon I, letter to the foreign secretary, Oct 7, 1797

851. If our house be on fire, without inquiring whether it was fired from within or without, we must try to extinguish it. —Thomas Jefferson, letter to James Lewis, Jr., May 9, 1798

852. The state is the divine idea as it exists on earth. ... We must therefore worship the state as the manifestation of the divine on earth. ... The march of God in the world, that is what the state is. —Georg Wilhelm Friedrich Hegel, *The German Constitution*, 1802

853. It's worse than a crime, it's a blunder. [*C'est plus qu'un crime, c'est une faute.*] —Charles-Maurice de Talleyrand, attributed remark following the murder of the Duc d'Enghien by Napoleon's agents, Mar 21, 1804

854. This is the beginning of the end. [*Voilà le commencement de la fin.*] —Charles-Maurice de Talleyrand, attributed remark on the announcement of Napoleon's defeat at Borodino, 1812 Napoleon

855. My toast would be, may our country be always successful, but whether successful or otherwise, always right. —John Quincy Adams, letter to John Adams, Aug 1, 1816

856. Political truth is a libel—religious truth blasphemy. —William Hazlitt, "Commonplaces", *The Round Table*, 1817

857. Poets and philosophers are the unacknowledged legislators of the world. —Percy Bysshe Shelley, *A Philosophical View of Reform*, 1819-20

858. Any plan conceived in moderation must fail when the circumstances are set in extremes. —Prince Clemens von Metternich, letter to General de Vincent, Dec 2, 1822

859. We uniformly applaud what is right and condemn what is wrong, when it costs us nothing but the sentiment. —William Hazlitt, "Characteristics", *The Literary Examiner*, 1823

860. I called a New World into existence to redress the balance of the Old. —George Canning, speech in the House of Commons, Dec 12, 1826

861. In an age that is so full of dangers for the very foundations and safeguards of social order, the only good policy is to pursue no policy. —Prince Clemens von Metternich, letter to Count d'Apponyi, Jan 27, 1826

862. Nothing is so useless as a general maxim. —Lord Macaulay, "On Machiavelli", 1827

863. Our Union: It must be preserved. —Andrew Jackson, toast at a Jefferson Day dinner, Apr 13, 1830

864. My country is the world; my countrymen are mankind. —William Lloyd Garrison, prospectus, *The Liberator*, 1830

865. The Union, next to our liberty, most dear. May we all remember that it can only be preserved by respecting the rights of the States and by distributing equally the benefits and burdens of the Union. —John C. Calhoun, toast in reply to President Jackson's at Jefferson Day dinner, Apr 13, 1830

866. Liberty and Union, now and forever, one and inseparable. —Daniel Webster, second speech on Foote's Resolution, Jan 26, 1830

867. We know no spectacle so ridiculous as the British public in one of its periodical fits of morality. —Lord Macaulay, review of Moore's Life of Lord Byron, *Edinburgh Review*, Jun, 1831

868. Mere precedent is a dangerous source of authority. —Andrew Jackson, veto message, Jul 10, 1832

869. Amid the pressure of great events, a general principle gives no help. —Georg Wilhelm Friedrich Hegel, *Introduction to the Philosophy of History*, 1832

870. The body politic is like a tree; as it proceeds upwards, it stands as much in need of heaven as of earth. —Honore Gabriel, Comte de Mirabeau, "Apophthegms", *Mirabeau's Letters During His Residence in England*, 1832

871. It is the fashion to style the present moment an extraordinary crisis. —Benjamin Disraeli, speech at High Wycombe, England, Dec 16, 1834

872. Be always sure you are right—then go ahead. —David Crockett, *Autobiography*, 1834

873. Sometimes a scream is better than a thesis. —Ralph Waldo Emerson, *Journals*, 1836

874. One country, one constitution, one destiny. —Daniel Webster, speech, Mar 15, 1837

875. Nothing astonishes men so much as common sense and plain dealing. —Ralph Waldo Emerson, "Art", *Essays: First Series*, 1841

876. One must, if one can, kill one's opponent, but never rouse him by contempt and the whiplash. —Prince Clemens von Metternich, letter to Count d'Apponyi, Sep 10, 1842

877. The right hon. Gentleman caught the Whigs bathing, and walked away with their clothes. —Benjamin Disraeli, remarks in the House of Commons on the Tory government of Sir Robert Peel, Feb 28, 1845

878. I glory in conflict, that I may hereafter exult in victory. —Frederick Douglass, "Farewell Speech to the British People" in London, Mar 30, 1847

879. America cannot always sit as a queen in peace and repose. Prouder and stronger governments than hers have been shattered by the bolts of a just God. —Frederick Douglass, "Government and Its Subjects", *The North Star*, Nov 9, 1849

880. An invasion of armies can be resisted, but not an idea whose time has come. [*On résiste à l'invasion des armées; on ne résiste pas à l'invasion des idées.*] —Victor Hugo, *Histoire d'un crime*, 1852

881. The assailant is often in the right; the assailed is always. —Walter Savage Landor, "John of Gaunt and Joanna of Kent", *Imaginary Conversations*, 1824-53

882. The mass of men lead lives of quiet desperation. —Henry David Thoreau, "Economy", *Walden*, 1854

883. Better to abolish serfdom from above than to wait till it begins to abolish itself from below. —Alexander II, speech in Moscow, Mar 30, 1856

884. He said that he felt "like the boy that stumped his toe,—'it hurt too bad to laugh, and he was too big to cry.' " —Abraham Lincoln, attributed by John T. Morse, *Abraham Lincoln*, 1893

885. "A house divided against itself cannot stand." I believe this government cannot endure, permanently half slave and half free. I do not expect the Union to be dissolved—I do not expect the house to fall—but I do expect it will cease to be divided. It will become all one thing, or all the other. —Abraham Lincoln, speech at the Illinois Republican state convention, quoting Mark 3:25, Jun 16, 1858

886. You can fool some of the people all of the time, and all of the people some of the time, but you cannot fool all of the people all of the time. —Abraham Lincoln, attributed to a speech given at Clinton, Illinois, Sep 2, 1858

887. This regard for the liberties of Europe, this care at one time for the Protestant interest, this excessive love for the balance of power, is neither more nor less than a gigantic system of outdoor relief for the aristocracy of Great Britain. —John Bright, speech in Birmingham, England, Oct 29, 1858

888. Among the defects of the bill, which were numerous, one provision was conspicuous by its presence and another by its absence. —Lord John Russell, speech to the electors of the City of London, Apr, 1859

889. How much easier it is to be critical than to be correct. —Benjamin Disraeli, speech, Jan 24, 1860

890. Let us have faith that right makes might, and in that faith let us to the end do our duty as we understand it. —Abraham Lincoln, speech at the Cooper Union, New York City, Feb 27, 1860

891. The leap which the House of Commons is taking with such philosophic calmness is a leap absolutely in the dark. —3rd Marquess of Salisbury, "The Budget and the Reform Bill", *Quarterly Review*, Apr, 1860

892. All we ask is to be let alone. —Jefferson Davis, inaugural address as president of the Confederate States of America, Feb 18, 1861

893. I shall try to correct errors when shown to be errors, and I shall adopt new views so fast as they shall appear to be true views. —Abraham Lincoln, letter to Horace Greeley, Aug 22, 1862

894. Not by speech-making and the decisions of majorities will the great questions of the day be settled—that was the great mistake of 1848 and 1849—but by iron and blood. [*Nicht durch reden und Majoritätsbeschlüsse werden die grossen Fragen der Zeit entschieden—das ist der Fehler von 1848 und 1849 gewesen—sondern durch Eisen und Blut.*] —Prince Otto von Bismarck, speech to the Prussian House of Delegates, Sep 30, 1862

895. I could as easily bail out the Potomac River with a teaspoon as attend to all the details of the army. —Abraham Lincoln, attributed by General James B. Fry in Allen Thorndyke Rice, *Reminiscences of Abraham Lincoln*, 1886

896. It is not best to swap horses while crossing the river. —Abraham Lincoln, reply to National Union League, Jun 9, 1864

897. Truth is generally the best vindication against slander. —Abraham Lincoln, letter to Secretary of War Edwin Stanton, Jul 18, 1864

898. Fellow-citizens! God reigns and the government at Washington still lives. —James A. Garfield, speech in New York City following assassination of Abraham Lincoln, Apr 17, 1865

899. Assassination has never changed the history of the world. —Benjamin Disraeli, speech, May, 1865

900. As scarce as truth is, the supply has always been in excess of the demand. —Josh Billings, (Henry Wheeler Shaw), *Affurisms from Josh Billings: His Sayings*, 1865

901. England is the mother of parliaments. —John Bright, speech in Birmingham, England, Jan 18, 1865

902. No doubt we are making a great experiment and taking a leap in the dark. —14th Earl of Derby, speech on the Reform Act in the House of Lords, Aug 6, 1867

903. I have climbed to the top of the greasy pole. —Benjamin Disraeli, remarks on being made prime minister, 1868

904. Humanity is only I writ large, and love for Humanity generally means zeal for MY notions as to what men should be and how they should live. —Sir James Fitzjames Stephen, *Liberty, Equality, Fraternity,* 1873

905. I am grateful for even the sharpest criticism, as long as it sticks to the point. [*Ich bin dankbar fur die schärfste Kritik, wenn sie nur sachlich bleibt.*] —Prince Otto von Bismarck, speech to the Reichstag, Nov 30, 1874

906. The freethinking of one age is the common sense of the next. —Matthew Arnold, *God and the Bible,* 1875

907. Force is not a remedy. —John Bright, speech in Birmingham, England, Nov 16, 1880

908. Those who have given themselves the most concern about the happiness of peoples have made their neighbors very miserable. —Anatole France, *The Crime of Sylvestre Bonnard,* 1881

909. Error moves with quick feet ... and truth must never be lagging behind. —Alexander Crummell, speeech to the Freedmen's Aid Society, Ocean Grove, New Jersey, Aug 15, 1883

910. If money, according to Augier, "comes into the world with a congenital bloodstain on one cheek," capital comes dripping from head to foot, from every pore, with blood and dirt. —Karl Marx, *Das Kapital,* 1867-83

911. I will not accept if nominated and will not serve if elected. —William Tecumseh Sherman, message to the Republican National Convention, Jun 5, 1884

912. They love him most for the enemies he has made. —Edward Stuyvesant Bragg, speech seconding the Democratic nomination of Grover Cleveland for president, Jul 9, 1884

913. A man cannot be too careful in the choice of his enemies. —Oscar Wilde, *The Picture of Dorian Gray,* 1891

914. What is a cynic? A man who knows the price of everything, and the value of nothing. —Oscar Wilde, *Lady Windermere's Fan,* 1892

915. Experience is the name everyone gives to their mistakes. —Oscar Wilde, *Lady Windermere's Fan,* 1892

916. Nature is rich; but everywhere man, the heir of nature, is poor. —Henry Demarest Lloyd, *Wealth Against Commonwealth,* 1894

917. The humblest citizen of all the land, when clad in the armor of a righteous cause, is stronger than all the hosts of error. —William Jennings Bryan, "Cross of Gold" speech at the Democratic National Convention, Chicago, Illinois, Jul 8, 1896

918. After the war, and until the day of his death, his (Wendell Phillips) position on almost every public question was either mischievous or ridiculous, and usually both. —Theodore Roosevelt, *Thomas Hart Benton,* 1897

919. Stout hearts, my laddies! If the row comes, REMEMBER THE MAINE, and show the world how American sailors can fight. —Clifford K. Berryman, cartoon caption, *The Washington Post,* Apr 3, 1898

920. Half-heartedness never won a battle. —William McKinley, speech in New York City, Jan 27, 1898

921. Life'd not be worth livin' if we didn't keep our inimies. —Finley Peter Dunne, *Mr. Dooley in Peace and in War*, 1898

922. Among men, Hinnissy, wet eye manes dhry heart. —Finley Peter Dunne, "Casual Observations", *Mr. Dooley's Opinions*, 1900

923. Herein lies the tragedy of the age: not that men are poor—all men know something of poverty; not that men are wicked—who is good? Not that men are ignorant—what is truth? Nay, but that men know so little of men. —W.E.B. Du Bois, *The Souls of Black Folk*, 1903

924. The foes from whom we pray to be delivered are our own passions, appetites, and follies; and against these there is always need that we should war. —Theodore Roosevelt, proclamation, Nov 2, 1905

925. Compromise, n. Such an adjustment of conflicting interests as gives each adversary the satisfaction of thinking he has got what he ought not to have, and is deprived of nothing except what was unjustly his due. —Ambrose Bierce, *The Devil's Dictionary*, 1906

926. Abuse a man unjustly, and you will make friends for him. —Edgar Watson Howe, *Country Town Sayings*, 1911

927. There is nothing I love as much as a good fight. —Franklin D. Roosevelt, interview, *The New York Times*, Jan 22, 1911

928. The motto should not be: Forgive one another; rather, Understand one another. —Emma Goldman, "The Tragedy of Women's Emancipation", *Anarchism and Other Essays*, 1911

929. The Army will hear nothing of politics from me, and in return I expect to hear nothing of politics from the Army. —Herbert Asquith, speech at Ladybank, England, Apr 4, 1914

930. The lamps are going out all over Europe, we shall not see them lit again in our lifetime. —Edward Grey, 1st Viscount Grey of Fallodon, remark on the outbreak of World War I, *Twenty-Five Years*, Aug 3, 1914

931. To die for an idea is to place a pretty high price upon conjectures. —Anatole France, *The Revolt of the Angels*, 1914

932. Assassination is the extreme form of censorship. —George Bernard Shaw, *The Rejected Statement*, 1916

933. All dressed up, with nowhere to go. —William Allen White, referring to Progressive party in 1916, after Theodore Roosevelt declined to run, 1916

934. Capitalists are no more capable of self-sacrifice than a man is capable of lifting himself by his bootstraps. —Vladimir Ilyich Lenin, *Letter from Afar*, 1917

935. What is our task? To make Britain a fit country for heroes to live in. —David Lloyd George, speech at Wolverhampton, England, Nov 24, 1918

936. Instead of loving your enemy, treat your friend a little better. —Edgar Watson Howe, *Ventures in Common Sense*, 1919

937. Victory attained by violence is tantamount to a defeat, for it is momentary. —Mohandas K. Gandhi, *Satyagraha Leaflet No. 13*, May 3, 1919

938. Our true nationality is mankind. —H.G. Wells, *The Outline of History*, 1920

939. America's present need is not heroics, but healing; not nostrums, but normalcy; not revolution, but restoration. —Warren G. Harding, speech in Boston, Massachusetts, June, 1920

940. You see things; and you say, "Why?" But I dream things that never were; and I say "Why not?" —George Bernard Shaw, *Back to Methuselah*, 1921

941. A policy is a temporary creed liable to be changed, but while it holds good it has got to be pursued with apostolic zeal. —Mohandas K. Gandhi, letter to the general secretary of the Congress party, Mar 8, 1922

942. The pendulum will swing back. —Joseph G. Cannon, quoted on his retirement, *The Baltimore Sun*, Mar 4, 1923

943. I wish we might have less condemnation of error and more commendation of right. —Warren G. Harding, address at Arlington National Cemetery, May 30, 1923

944. If there is anybody in this land who thoroughly believes that the meek shall inherit the earth, they have not often let their presence be known. —W.E.B. Du Bois, *The Gift of Black Folk*, 1924

945. A little inaccuracy sometimes saves tons of explanation. —Hector Hugh Munro, (Saki), "The Comments of Moung Ka", *The Square Egg*, 1924

946. Rumor travels faster, but it don't say put as long as truth. —Will Rogers, "Politics Getting Ready to Jell", *The Illiterate Digest*, 1924

947. I do not choose to run. —Calvin Coolidge, public statement, Aug 2, 1927

948. A man always has two reasons for what he does—a good one, and the real one. —J.P. Morgan, attributed by Owen Wister, *Roosevelt: The Story of a Friendship*, 1930

949. Nothing is more dangerous than an idea, when it's the only one we have. [*Rien n'est plus dangereux qu'une idée quand on n'a qu'une idée.*] —Emile Auguste Chartier, *La Lumiere*, Jul 5, 1930

950. If you can't lick 'em, jine 'em. —James E. Watson, attributed, in article, "Senator James E. Watson", *The Atlantic Monthly*, Feb, 1932

951. I pledge you, I pledge myself, to a new deal for the American people. —Franklin D. Roosevelt, acceptance speech as Democratic nominee for president, Jul 2, 1932

952. People don't eat in the long run—they eat every day. —Harry L. Hopkins, attributed by Robert E. Sherwood, *Roosevelt and Hopkins: An Intimate History*, 1933

953. The only thing we have to fear is fear itself—nameless, unreasoning, unjustified terror which paralyzes needed efforts to convert retreat into advance. —Franklin D. Roosevelt, first inaugural address, Mar 4, 1933

954. (Hoover was the greatest engineer in the world since) he had drained, ditched, and damned the United States in three years. —Anonymous, attributed to a Kansas farmer by Roy Victor Peel, *The 1932 Campaign*, 1935

955. We have earned the hatred of entrenched greed. —Franklin D. Roosevelt, message to Congress, Jan 3, 1936

956. A poor man with nothing in his belly needs hope, illusion, more than bread. —Georges Bernanos, *The Diary of a Country Priest*, 1936

957. A technical objection is the first refuge of a scoundrel. —Heywood Broun, "'Jam-Tomorrow' Progressives", *New Republic*, Dec 15, 1937

958. Repetition does not transform a lie into a truth. —Franklin D. Roosevelt, radio address, Oct 26, 1939

959. I cannot forecast to you the action of Russia. It is a riddle wrapped in a mystery inside an enigma; but perhaps there is a key. That key is Russian national interest. —Sir Winston S. Churchill, BBC radio broadcast, Oct 1, 1939

960. Men are not prisoners of fate, but only prisoners of their own minds. —Franklin D. Roosevelt, Pan American Day address, Apr 15, 1939

961.　If you treat people right they will treat you right—90 percent of the time. —Franklin D. Roosevelt, quoted, *Kansas City Times*, Jan 14, 1977

962.　When you get to the end of your rope, tie a knot and hang on. —Franklin D. Roosevelt, quoted, *Kansas City Star*, Jun 5, 1977

963.　The core of our defense is the faith we have in the institutions we defend. —Franklin D. Roosevelt, speech in Dayton, Ohio, Oct 12, 1940

964.　We must be the great arsenal of democracy. —Franklin D. Roosevelt, fireside chat, Dec 29, 1940

965.　I have nothing to offer but blood, toil, tears and sweat. —Sir Winston S. Churchill, speech in the House of Commons, May 13, 1940

966.　We shall show mercy, but we shall not ask for it. —Sir Winston S. Churchill, speech in the House of Commons, Jul 14, 1940

967.　Let us ... brace ourselves to our duties, and so bear ourselves that if the British Empire and its Commonwealth last for a thousand years, men will still say: "This was their finest hour." —Sir Winston S. Churchill, speech in the House of Commons, Jun 18, 1940

968.　Eternal truths will be neither true nor eternal unless they have fresh meaning for every new social situation. —Franklin D. Roosevelt, speech at the Univ. of Pennsylvania, Sep 20, 1940

969.　We shall not fail or falter; we shall not weaken or tire. ... Give us the tools and we will finish the job. —Sir Winston S. Churchill, BBC radio broadcast, Feb 9, 1941

970.　When I warned them (the French government) that Britain would fight on alone whatever they did, their Generals told their Prime Minister and his divided Cabinet: "In three weeks England will have her neck wrung like a chicken." Some chicken! Some neck! —Sir Winston S. Churchill, speech to the Canadian parliament, Dec 30, 1941

971.　Never give in, never give in, never, never, never, never,—in nothing, great or small, large or petty—never give in except to convictions of honor and good sense. —Sir Winston S. Churchill, address at Harrow School, Oct 29, 1941

972.　This is one of those cases in which the imagination is baffled by the facts. —Sir Winston S. Churchill, remark in the House of Commons following the defection of Rudolf Hess, May 13, 1941

973.　This is not the end. It is not even the beginning of the end. But it is, perhaps, the end of the beginning. —Sir Winston S. Churchill, speech in London following Montgomery's victory in North Africa, Nov 10, 1942

974.　As always, victory finds a hundred fathers but defeat is an orphan. —Count Galeazzo Ciano, *The Ciano Diaries, 1939-1943*, Sep 9, 1942

975.　I always avoid prophesying beforehand, because it is a much better policy to prophesy after the event has already taken place. —Sir Winston S. Churchill, press conference in Cairo, Feb 1, 1943

976.　If this is a blessing, it is certainly very well disguised. —Sir Winston S. Churchill, remark to his wife following defeat in 1945 election, quoted, *Memoirs of Richard Nixon*, Jun 4, 1945

977.　Every segment of our population, and every individual, has a right to expect from his government a Fair Deal. —Harry S Truman, speech to Congress, Sep 6, 1945

978.　Any man's coward who won't die for what he believes. —Chester Bomar Himes, *If He Hollers Let Him Go*, 1945

979.　These proceedings are closed. —Douglas MacArthur, on the signing of the Japanese surrender in Tokyo Bay, Sep 2, 1945

980. The people, and the people alone, are the motive force in the making of world history. — Mao Tse-tung, "On Coalition Government", Apr 24, 1945

981. The only limit to our realization of tomorrow will be our doubts of today. —Franklin D. Roosevelt, message for Jefferson Day, Apr 13, 1945

982. All reactionaries are paper tigers. —Mao Tse-tung, "Talk with the American Correspondent Anna Louise Strong", Aug, 1946

983. Let us not be deceived—we are today in the midst of a cold war. —Bernard Baruch, speech in Columbia, South Carolina, Apr 16, 1947

984. Non-violence is not a garment to be put on and off at will. Its seat is in the heart, and it must be an inseparable part of our very being. —Mohandas K. Gandhi, *Non-Violence in Peace and War*, 1948

985. I never did give anybody hell. I just told the truth, and they thought it was hell. —Harry S Truman, quoted, *Time*, Jun 9, 1975

986. Neither a man nor a crowd nor a nation can be trusted to act humanely or to think sanely under the influence of a great fear. —Bertrand Russell, "An Outline of Intellectual Rubbish", *Unpopular Essays*, 1950

987. If Hitler invaded hell I would make at least a favorable reference to the devil in the House of Commons. —Sir Winston S. Churchill, *The Second World War*, 1950

988. A grievance is most poignant when almost redressed. —Eric Hoffer, *The True Believer*, 1951

989. The world has turned over many times since I took the oath on the plain at West Point, and the hopes and dreams have long since vanished; but I still remember the refrain of one of the most popular barracks ballads of that day which proclaimed most proudly that old soldiers never die; they just fade away. And like the old soldier in that ballad, I now close my military career and just fade away, an old soldier who tried to do his duty as God gave him the sight to see that duty. —Douglas MacArthur, address to Congress, Apr 19, 1951

990. A nation without dregs and malcontents, is orderly, decent, peaceful and pleasant, but perhaps without the seed of things to come. —Eric Hoffer, *The True Believer*, 1951

991. For it is often easier to fight for principles than to live up to them. —Adlai E. Stevenson Jr., speech in New York City, Aug 27, 1952

992. Words calculated to catch everyone may catch no one. —Adlai E. Stevenson Jr., speech to Democratic National Convention, Chicago, Illinois, Jul 21, 1952

993. Nature is neutral. Man has wrested from nature the power to make the world a desert or to make the deserts bloom. There is no evil in the atom; only in men's souls. —Adlai E. Stevenson Jr., speech in Hartford, Connecticut, Sep 18, 1952

994. The general has dedicated himself so many times, he must feel like the cornerstone of a public building. —Adlai E. Stevenson Jr., on Dwight D. Eisenhower, *The New York Times*, Nov, 1952

995. Let's talk sense to the American people. Let's tell them the truth, that there are no gains without pains. —Adlai E. Stevenson Jr., acceptance speech as Democratic nominee for president, Jul 26, 1952

996. No people on earth can be held, as a people, to be an enemy, for all humanity shares the common hunger for peace and fellowship and justice. —Dwight D. Eisenhower, address to the American Society of Newspaper Editors, Apr 16, 1953

997. For myself I am an optimist—it does not seem to be much use being anything else. —Sir Winston S. Churchill, speech at the Lord Mayor's banquet, London, Nov 9, 1954

998. A fanatic is one who can't change his mind and won't change the subject. —Sir Winston S. Churchill, quoted, *The New York Times*, Jul 5, 1954

999. You have a row of dominoes set up. You knock over the first one, and what will happen to the last one is a certainty that it will go over very quickly. —Dwight D. Eisenhower, on the strategic importance of Indochina, at a press conference, Apr 7, 1954

1000. This organization (the United Nations) is created to prevent you from going to hell. It isn't created to take you to heaven. —Henry Cabot Lodge Jr., *The New York Times*, Jan 28, 1954

1001. An editor is someone who separates the wheat from the chaff and then prints the chaff. —Adlai E. Stevenson Jr., quoted, *Texas Observer*, Dec 24, 1976

1002. Man does not live by words alone, despite the fact that sometimes he has to eat them. —Adlai E. Stevenson Jr., quoted, *Human Behavior*, May, 1978

1003. France cannot be France without greatness. [*La France ne peut être la France sans la grandeur.*] —Charles De Gaulle, *Mémoires de guerre: L'Appel*, 1955

1004. Everything will be all right—you know when? When people, just people, stop thinking of the United Nations as a weird Picasso abstraction and see it as a drawing they made themselves. —Dag Hammarskjold, *The New York Times*, Jun 27, 1955

1005. The first sign of corruption in a society that is still alive is that the end justifies the means. —Georges Bernanos, *Why Freedom?*, 1955

1006. There is no security on this earth; there is only opportunity. —Douglas MacArthur, quoted by Courtney Whitney, *MacArthur: His Rendez-Vous with History*, 1955

1007. Eggheads of the the world arise—I was even going to add that you have nothing to lose but your yolks. —Adlai E. Stevenson Jr., speech in Oakland, California, Feb 1, 1956

1008. The Last Hurrah. —Edwin O'Connor, title of novel, 1956

1009. The more I observed Washington, the more frequently I visited it, and the more people I interviewed there, the more I understood how prophetic L'Enfant was when he laid it out as a city that goes around in circles. —John Mason Brown, *Through These Men*, 1956

1010. What is there left for us to do? If we let things take their course the West would say we were either stupid or weak, and that's one and the same thing. —Nikita S. Khrushchev, on invasion of Hungary, quoted by Veljko Micunovich, *Moscow Diary*, Oct, 1956

1011. I am not sure I should have dared to start; but I am sure I should not have dared to stop. —Sir Winston S. Churchill, quoted by Hugh Thomas, *The Suez Affair*, 1967

1012. May we know unity - without conformity. —Dwight D. Eisenhower, second inaugural address, Jan 21, 1957

1013. Indeed let us be frank about it: most of our people have never had it so good. —Harold Macmillan, speech in Bedford, England, Jul 20, 1957

1014. Believe in life! Always human beings will live and progress to greater, broader, and fuller life. —W.E.B. Du Bois, last message to the world, 1957

1015. Support by United States rulers is rather in the nature of the support that the rope gives to a hanged man. —Nikita S. Khrushchev, interview in Egyptian newspaper, Nov 25, 1957

1016. What counts is not necessarily the size of the dog in the fight—it's the size of the fight in the dog. —Dwight D. Eisenhower, speech to the Republican National Committee, Jan 31, 1958

1017. He (Sen. Joseph McCarthy) stamped with his name a tendency, a whole cluster of tendencies in American life. The name survives. To many Americans, whatever is illiberal, anti-intellectual, repressive, reactionary, totalitarian or merely swinish will hereafter be McCarthyism. The word is imprecise, but it conveys a meaning and a powerful image. —Richard H. Rovere, "The Frivolous Demagogue", *Esquire*, Jun, 1958

1018. If you want to get along, go along. —Sam Rayburn, quoted, *Washingtonian*, Nov, 1978

1019. Son, always tell the truth. Then you'll never have to remember what you said the last time. —Sam Rayburn, quoted, *Chicago Sun-Times*, Jun 28, 1979

1020. The most striking of all the impressions I have formed since I left London a month ago is of the strength of African national consciousness.... The wind of change is blowing through the continent. Whether we like it or not, the growth of national consciousness is a political fact. —Harold Macmillan, speech to the South African parliament, Feb 3, 1960

1021. We stand today on the edge of a new frontier—the frontier of the 1960s—a frontier of unknown opportunities and perils—a frontier of unfulfilled hopes and threats. —John F. Kennedy, acceptance speech for the Democratic presidential nomination, Jul 15,1960

1022. The Assembly has witnessed over the last weeks how historical truth is established; once an allegation has been repeated a few times, it is no longer an allegation, it is an established fact, even if no evidence has been brought out in order to support it. —Dag Hammarskjold, on attacks by Soviet Premier Nikita S. Khrushchev in the U.N. General Assembly, *The New York Times*, Oct 4, 1960

1023. In battling evil, excess is good; for he who is moderate in announcing the truth is presenting half-truth. He conceals the other half out of fear of the people's wrath. —Kahlil Gibran, "Narcotics and Dissecting Knives", *Thoughts and Meditations*, 1960

1024. The opinions that are held with passion are always those for which no good ground exists; indeed the passion is the measure of the holder's lack of rational conviction. Opinions in politics and religion are almost always held passionately. —Bertrand Russell, introduction, *Sceptical Essays*, 1961

1025. Let the word go forth from this time and place, to friend and foe alike, that the torch has been passed to a new generation of Americans. —John F. Kennedy, inaugural address, Jan 20, 1961

1026. All this will not be finished in the first hundred days. Nor will it be finished in the first thousand days, nor in the life of this administration, nor even perhaps in our lifetime on this planet. But let us begin. —John F. Kennedy, inaugural address, Jan 20, 1961

1027. Khrushchev reminds me of the tiger hunter who has picked a place on the wall to hang the tiger's skin long before he has caught the tiger. This tiger has other ideas. —John F. Kennedy, *The New York Times*, Dec 24, 1961

1028. This is the first convention of the space age—where a candidate can promise the moon and mean it. —David Brinkley, on the 1960 Democratic National Convention, *Newsweek*, Mar 13, 1961

1029. There is no surer way to misread any document than to read it literally. —Learned Hand, recalled on his death, Aug 16, 1961

1030. With a good conscience our only sure reward, with history the final judge of our deeds, let us go forth to lead the land we love, asking His blessing and His help, but knowing that here on earth God's work must truly be our own. —John F. Kennedy, inaugural address, Jan 20, 1961

1031. When we got into office, the thing that surprised me most was to find that things were just as bad as we'd been saying they were. —John F. Kennedy, speech at a dinner on his 44th birthday, Washington D.C., May 27, 1961

1032. I think this is the most extraordinary collection of talent, of human knowledge, that has ever been gathered together at the White House, with the possible exception of when Thomas Jefferson dined alone. —John F. Kennedy, remarks at a dinner honoring American Nobel Prize winners, Apr 29, 1962

1033. We were eyeball-to-eyeball and the other fellow just blinked. —Dean Rusk, on the Cuban missile cirsis, *Saturday Evening Post*, Dec 8, 1962

1034. This is the first time I ever heard it said that the crime is not the burglary, but the discovery of the burglary. —Adlai E. Stevenson Jr., to Soviet ambassador Valerian Zorin at the United Nations, Oct 25, 1962

1035. Washington is a city of Southern efficiency and Northern charm. —John F. Kennedy, quoted by William Manchester, *Portrait of a President*, 1962

1036. And in bygone days, commanders were taught that, when in doubt, they should march their troops towards the sound of gunfire. I intend to march my trooper towards the sound of gunfire. —Jo Grimond, speech at the Liberal party annual conference, Sep 15, 1963

1037. I believe in the forgiveness of sin and the redemption of ignorance. —Adlai E. Stevenson Jr., retort to a heckler asking him to state his beliefs, *Time*, Nov 1, 1963

1038. All progress is precarious, and the solution of one problem brings us face to face with another problem. —Martin Luther King Jr., *Strength to Love*, 1963

1039. Our problems are man-made, therefore they may be solved by man. And man can be as big as he wants. No problem of human destiny is beyond human beings. —John F. Kennedy, speech at The American Univ., Washington, D.C., Jun 10, 1963

1040. The price of eternal vigilance is indifference. —Marshall McLuhan, *Understanding Media*, 1964

1041. What is objectionable, what is dangerous about extremists is not that they are extreme, but that they are intolerant. The evil is not what they say about their cause, but what they say about their opponents. —Robert F. Kennedy, "Extremism, Left and Right", *The Pursuit of Justice*, 1964

1042. I would remind you that extremism in the defense of liberty is no vice. And let me remind you also that moderation in the pursuit of justice is no virtue. —Barry Goldwater, speech accepting Republican nomination as president, Jul 16, 1964

1043. I just want to do God's will. And he's allowed me to go up to the mountain. And I've looked over, and I've seen the Promised Land. —Martin Luther King Jr., speech in Memphis, Tennessee, Apr 3, 1964

1044. A great writer is, so to speak, a second government in his country. And for that reason no regime has ever loved great writers, only minor ones. —Alexander Solzhenitsyn, *The First Circle*, 1964

1045. There are two problems in my life. The political ones are insoluble and the economic ones are incomprehensible. —Sir Alec Douglas-Home, *The New York Times*, Jan 9, 1964

1046. Where there are two PhDs in a developing country, one is head of state and the other is in exile. —Lord Samuel, *The New York Times*, Jul 5, 1964

1047. The Liberals talk about a stable government, but we don't know how bad the stable is going to smell. —Thomas Douglas, campaign speech, Oct, 1965

1048. You show me a black man who isn't an extremist and I'll show you one who needs psychiatric attention. —Malcolm X, introduction by Alex Haley, *Autobiography of Malcolm X*, 1965

1049. You may be sure that the Americans will commit all the stupidities they can think of, plus some that are beyond imagination. —Charles De Gaulle, *Time*, Dec 17, 1965

1050. I've got nothing against men wearing striped pants and black jackets if they want to, and they can wear Anthony Eden hats to their hearts' content. It's the wearing of striped pants in the soul that I object to, and having a Homburg hat where your heart ought to be. —George Brown, quoted, *Christian Science Monitor*, Aug 19, 1966

1051. Mix a conviction with a man and something happens. —Adam Clayton Powell Jr., "Minimum Living--Minimum Religion", *Keep the Faith, Baby!*, 1967

1052. Israel is not an aviary. —Abba Eban, on being asked if Israel's policy was hawkish or dovish, *The New York Post*, Jul 8, 1967

1053. We have produced a world of contented bodies and discontented minds. —Adam Clayton Powell Jr., "The Temptations of Modernity", *Keep the Faith, Baby!*, 1967

1054. I am not conscious of falling under any of those ornithological divisions. —Clark M. Clifford, on being asked if he was a hawk or a dove, *The New York Times*, Jan 2, 1968

1055. You're either part of the solution or part of the problem. —Eldridge Cleaver, attributed, 1968

1056. A spirit of national masochism prevails, encouraged by an effete corps of impudent snobs who characterize themselves as intellectuals. —Spiro T. Agnew, reported, *The New York Times*, Oct 20, 1969

1057. We're a sentimental people. We like a few kind words better than millions of dollars given in a humiliating way. —Gamal Abdel Nasser, on refusing Western economic assistance, *Réalités*, Jan 20, 1969

1058. In the United States today, we have more than our share of the nattering nabobs of negativism. —Spiro T. Agnew, speech in San Diego, California, Sep 11, 1970

1059. We have met the enemy and he is us. —Walt Kelly, cartoon strip, 1971

1060. It is not that we were so good, but those who followed us were so bad that they made us seem better than we were. —Juan Peron, *The New York Times*, Jul 14, 1973

1061. The experience may have been costly, but it was also priceless. —Peter G. Peterson, on his experience in the Nixon administration, *Quote*, Jan 18, 1973

1062. I think we ought to let him hang there, let him twist slowly, slowly in the wind. —John Ehrlichman, to presidential counsel John Dean, referring to FBI Director L. Patrick Gray, Mar 7, 1973

1063. Always give your best, never get discouraged, never be petty; always remember, others may hate you. Those who hate you don't win unless you hate them. And then you destroy yourself. —Richard M. Nixon, speech to members of his administration following his resignation, Aug 9, 1974

1064. My fellow Americans, our long national nightmare is over. —Gerald R. Ford, on succeeding Richard Nixon as president, Aug 9, 1974

1065. We are making remarkable progress toward an agreement—and toward a nervous breakdown. It's going to be a race to see which will be achieved first. —Henry A. Kissinger, on Middle East peace negotiations, *Time*, Sep 8, 1975

1066. We Americans are a peculiar people. We are for the underdog no matter how much of a dog he is. —A.B. Chandler, ("Happy"), *Reader's Digest*, Nov, 1975

1067. If this is a Great Society, I'd hate to see a bad one. —Fannie Lou Hamer, *The Worker*, Jul 13, 1975

1068. Totalitarianism is bad, gangsterism is worse, but capitulationism is the worst of all. —Daniel P. Moynihan, *Time*, Jan 26, 1976

1069. For God's sake, how many swan songs can a lame duck deliver? —Henry A. Kissinger, commenting on the number of his farewell ceremonies, *Rolling Stone*, Mar 10, 1977

1070. There cannot be a crisis next week. My schedule is already full. —Henry A. Kissinger, *Time*, Jan 24, 1977

1071. Our decision about energy will test the character of the American people and the ability of the President and the Congress to govern this Nation. This difficult effort will be the "moral equivalent of war," except that we will be uniting our efforts to build and not to destroy. —Jimmy Carter, televised address to the nation, Apr 18, 1977

1072. What the people want is very simple. They want an America as good as its promise. —Barbara Jordan, commencement address, Harvard Univ., Jun 16, 1977

1073. When do any of us ever do enough? —Barbara Jordan, interview, *Senior Scholastic*, Oct, 1977

1074. Welfare is hated by those who administer it, mistrusted by those who pay for it and held in contempt by those who receive it. —Peter C. Goldmark Jr., *The New York Times*, May 24, 1977

1075. It is easy enough to define what the Commonwealth is not. Indeed this is quite a popular pastime. —Elizabeth II, Silver Jubilee address, Jun 7, 1977

1076. Washington is the only town in the world where sound travels faster than light. —Wade Hampton McCree Jr., *Chicago Sun-Times*, Jun 20, 1978

1077. Military intelligence is a contradiction in terms. —Groucho Marx, *San Francisco Chronicle*, Jan 29, 1978

1078. (Watergate) was worse than a crime, it was a blunder. —Richard M. Nixon, *The Observer*, Dec 3, 1978

1079. It's a little like makin' love to a gorilla. You don't quit when you're tired—you quit when the gorilla's tired. —Robert S. Strauss, on being asked when he planned to quit as chairman of the Democratic Party, *Chicago Tribune*, Feb 5, 1978

1080. With our eyes fixed on the future, but recognizing the realities of today ... we will achieve our destiny to be as a shining city on a hill for all mankind to see. —Ronald Reagan, speech to Conservative Political Action Conference, Mar 17, 1978

1081. Each success only buys an admission ticket to a more difficult problem. —Henry A. Kissinger, *Wilson Library Bulletin*, Mar, 1979

1082. Winning isn't everything. It is the only thing. —Vince Lombardi, *Newsweek*, Nov 19, 1979

1083. The chief cause of problems is solutions. —Eric Sevareid, *Town & Country*, May, 1979

1084. History knows no resting places and no plateaus. —Henry A. Kissinger, *White House Years*, 1979

1085. One point has already been proved. Everything that happened once can happen again. —Jacobo Timerman, *Prisoner Without a Name, Cell Without a Number*, 1981

1086. Of course it's the same old story. Truth usually is the same old story. —Margaret Thatcher, *Time*, Feb 16, 1981

1087. You cannot shake hands with a clenched fist. —Indira Gandhi, quoted, *Christian Science Monitor*, May 17, 1982

1088. In crises the most daring course is often safest. —Henry A. Kissinger, *Years of Upheaval*, 1982

1089. Platitudes? Yes, there are platitudes. Platitudes are there because they are true. —Margaret Thatcher, *London Times*, Jun 1, 1984

1090. It is human nature that rules the world, not governments and regimes. —Svetlana Alliluyeva, *The New York Times*, Nov 3, 1984

1091. I cast my bread on the waters long ago. Now it's time for you to send it back to me—toasted and buttered on both sides. —Jesse Jackson, speech to African-American voters in New York City, Jan 30, 1984

1092. I'm not the type to get ulcers. I give them. —Edward I. Koch, *The New York Times*, Jan 20, 1984

1093. (Their) insatiable lust for power is only equaled by their incurable impotence in exercising it. —Sir Winston S. Churchill, on Labour Party, quoted by John Colville, *The Fringes of Power*, 1985

1094. Rarely have so many people been so wrong about so much. —Richard M. Nixon, on war in Vietnam, *No More Vietnams*, 1985

1095. If you don't like the president, it costs you 90 bucks to fly to Washington to picket. If you don't like the governor, it costs you 60 bucks to fly to Albany to picket. If you don't like me, 90 cents. —Edward I. Koch, *The New York Times*, Feb 28, 1985

1096. I think he is an entertainer. I would prefer if he were a performer. —Carol Bellamy, on New York City Mayor Edward Koch, *The New York Times*, Jan 31, 1985

1097. There are more secrets, but there is not more secrecy. —Steven Garfinkel, *The New York Times*, Apr 15, 1986

1098. I apologize for what was said even though I didn't say it. —Donald R. Manes, statement on radio on reports he called Mayor Koch a crook, Feb 3, 1986

1099. Do something. It it doesn't work, do something else. No idea is too crazy. —Jim Hightower, on instructions to his staff, speech to the Dallas Chamber of Commerce, *The New York Times*, Mar 9, 1986

1100. Don't fight the problem, decide it. —George C. Marshall, favorite advice, quoted by Walter Isaacson and Evan Thomas, *The Wise Men*, 1986

1101. To wear your heart on your sleeve isn't a very good plan; you should wear it inside, where it functions best. —Margaret Thatcher, interview with Barbara Walters on ABC-TV, Mar 18, 1987

1102. In that hearing, we didn't hear anything. —James A. McClure, on why there were no leaks from a closed Congressional hearing, *The New York Times*, Jan 24, 1987

1103. Keep hope alive. —Jesse Jackson, speech to the Democratic National Convention, Atlanta, Georgia, Jul 18, 1988

1104. We have more will than wallet; but will is what we need. —George Bush, inaugural address, Jan 20, 1989

1105. America is never wholly herself unless she is engaged in high moral principle. We as a people have such a purpose today. It is to make kinder the face of the nation and gentler the face of the world. —George Bush, inaugural address, Jan 20, 1989

FREEDOM OF SPEECH

1106. When law and order prevail in the land, a man may be bold in speech and bold in action; but when the land lacks law and order, though he may take bold action, he should lay restraint on his speech. —Confucius, *The Analects*, ca. 480 B.C.

1107. But this is slavery, not to speak one's thought. —Euripides, *The Phoenician Women*, 411-409 B.C.

1108. Reason and free inquiry are the only effectual agents against error. —Thomas Jefferson, *Notes on the State of Virginia*, 1782

1109. Opinions become dangerous to a state only when persecution makes it necessary for the people to communicate their ideas under the bond of secrecy. —Charles James Fox, speech in the House of Commons, May 1797

1110. When people talk of the freedom of writing, speaking or thinking I cannot choose but laugh. No such thing ever existed. No such thing now exists; but I hope it will exist. But it must be hundreds of years after you and I shall write and speak no more. —John Adams, letter to Thomas Jefferson, Jul 15, 1818

1111. Free Discussion is the only necessary Constitution—the only necessary Law of the Constitution. —Richard Carlile, *The Republican*, 1823

1112. Men are never so likely to settle a question rightly as when they discuss it freely. —Lord Macaulay, "Southey's Coloquies on Society", 1830

1113. When a country is tolerably quiet, it is better for a Government to be hard of hearing in respect of seditious language than to be very agile in prosecuting. —Sir Robert Peel, letter to Sir James Graham, Dec, 1841

1114. If all mankind, minus one, were of one opinion, and only one person were of the contrary opinion, mankind would be no more justified in silencing that one person, than he, if he had the power, would be justified in silencing mankind. —John Stuart Mill, *On Liberty*, 1859

1115. He who knows only his own side of the case, knows little of that. —John Stuart Mill, *On Liberty*, 1859

1116. We can never be sure that the opinion we are endeavoring to stifle is a false opinion; and if we are sure, stifling it would be an evil still. —John Stuart Mill, *On Liberty*, 1859

1117. The very aim and end of our institutions is just this: that we may think what we like and say what we think. —Oliver Wendell Holmes Sr., *The Professor at the Breakfast Table*, 1860

1118. Was Pilate right in crucifying Christ? I reply, Pilate's paramount duty was to preserve the peace in Palestine, to form the best judgment he could as to the means required for that purpose, and to act upon it when it was formed. Therefore, if and in so far as he believed, in good faith and on reasonable grounds, that what he did was necessary for the preservation of the peace of Palestine, he was right. It was his duty to run the risk of being mistaken, notwithstanding Mr. Mill's principle as to liberty, and particularly as to liberty in the expression of opinion. —Sir James Fitzjames Stephen, *Liberty, Equality, Fraternity*, 1873

1119. The wisest thing to do with a fool is to encourage him to hire a hall and discourse to his fellow-citizens. Nothing chills nonsense like exposure to the air. —Woodrow Wilson, *Constitutional Government*, 1908

1120. Where the people rule, discussion is necessary. —William Howard Taft, speech in Denver, Colorado, Sep 21, 1909

1121. Free speech, exercised both individually and through a free press, is a necessity in any country where people are themselves free. —Theodore Roosevelt, *Kiplinger Washington Letter*, Apr 23, 1918

1122.   But the character of every act depends upon the circumstances in which it is done. ... The most stringent protection of free speech would not protect a man in falsely shouting fire in a theatre and causing a panic. It does not even protect a man from an injunction against uttering words that may have all the effect of force. ... The question in every case is whether the words are used in such circumstances and are of such a nature as to create a clear and present danger that they will bring about the substantive evils that Congress has a right to prevent. It is a question of proximity and degree. —Oliver Wendell Holmes Jr., *Schenck v. United States; Baer v. United States*, 1919

1123.   It is said that this manifesto is more than a theory, that it was an incitement. Every idea is an incitement. —Oliver Wendell Holmes Jr., *Gitlow v. New York*, 1925

1124.   Free speech is about as good a cause as the world has ever known. But, like the poor, it is always with us and gets shoved aside in favor of things more vital. —Heywood Broun, "The Miracle of Debs", *New York World*, Oct 23, 1926

1125.   Almost nobody means precisely what he says when he makes the declaration, "I'm in favor of free speech." —Heywood Broun, "The Miracle of Debs", *New York World*, Oct 23, 1926

1126.   To think is to say no. —Emile Auguste Chartier, ("Alain"), *Le Citoyen contre les pouvoirs*, 1926

1127.   Fear of serious injury cannot alone justify suppression of free speech and assembly. Men feared witches and burned women. It is the function of speech to free men from the bondage of irrational fears. —Louis D. Brandeis, concurring opinion, *Whitney v. California*, 1927

1128.   If there is any principle of the constitution that more imperatively calls for attachment than any other it is the principle of free thought—not free thought for those who agree with us but freedom for the thought that we hate. —Oliver Wendell Holmes Jr., *United States v. Schwimmer*, 1928

1129.   Free speech does not live many hours after free industry and free commerce die. —Herbert Hoover, campaign speech in New York City, Oct 22, 1928

1130.   Freedom of expression is the matrix, the indispensable condition, of nearly every other form of freedom. —Benjamin N. Cardozo, *Palko v. Connecticut*, 1937

1131.   Everyone is in favour of free speech. Hardly a day passes without its being extolled, but some people's idea of it is that they are free to say what they like, but if anyone says anything back, that is an outrage. —Sir Winston S. Churchill, speech in the House of Commons, Oct 13, 1943

1132.   The problem of freedom in America is that of maintaining a competition of ideas, and you do not achieve that by silencing one brand of idea. —Max Lerner, "The Muzzling of the Movies", *Actions and Passions*, 1949

1133.   Laws alone cannot secure freedom of expression; in order that every man present his views without penalty there must be a spirit of tolerance in the entire population. —Albert Einstein, *Out of My Later Years*, 1950

1134.   Every man has the right to be heard; but no man has the right to strangle democracy with a single set of vocal cords. —Adlai E. Stevenson Jr., speech in New York City, Aug 28, 1952

1135.   Don't join the book burners. Don't think you are going to conceal faults by concealing evidence that they ever existed. —Dwight D. Eisenhower, speech at Dartmouth College, Jun 14, 1953

1136. Here in America we are descended in blood and in spirit from revolutionists and rebels— men and women who dared to dissent from accepted doctrine. As their heirs, we may never confuse honest dissent with disloyal subversion. —Dwight D. Eisenhower, speech at Columbia Univ. bicentennial dinner, May 31, 1954

1137. Free speech is not to be regulated like diseased cattle and impure butter. The audience ... that hissed yesterday may applaud today, even for the same performance. —William O. Douglas, dissenting opinion, *Roth v. United States*, Jun 24, 1957

1138. In the end it is worse to suppress dissent than to run the risk of heresy. —Learned Hand, Oliver Wendell Holmes lecture, Harvard Univ., 1958

1139. I am not so much concerned with the right of everyone to say anything he pleases as I am about our need as a self-governing people to hear everything relevant. —John F. Kennedy, speech to the National Civil Liberties Conference, Apr 16, 1959

1140. The censor's sword pierces deeply into the heart of free expression. —Earl Warren, dissenting opinion, *Times Film Corp. v. City of Chicago*, Jan 23, 1961

1141. Criticism of government finds sanctuary in several portions of the 1st Amendment. It is part of the right of free speech. It embraces freedom of the press. —Hugo L. Black, dissenting opinion, Feb 27, 1961

1142. The first principle of a free society is an untrammeled flow of words in an open forum. —Adlai E. Stevenson Jr., *The New York Times*, Jan 19, 1962

1143. Let other people speak out. The heavens will not fall and you will not be thrown out. If you do not let others speak, then the day will surely come when you will be thrown out. — Mao Tse-tung, speech to a Central Work Conference, Jan 30, 1962

1144. My view is, without deviation, without exception, without any ifs, buts, or whereases that freedom of speech means that you shall not do something to people either for the views they have or the views they express or the words they speak or write. —Hugo L. Black, at the American Jewish Congress, Apr 14, 1962

1145. An unconditional right to say what one pleases about public affairs is what I consider to be the minimum guarantee of the First Amendment. —Hugo L. Black, *New York Times Company v. Sullivan*, 1964

1146. Man's drive for self-expression, which over the centuries has built his monuments, does not stay within set bounds; the creations which yesterday were the detested and the obscene become the classics of today. —Matthew Tobriner, ruling that Henry Miller's Tropic of Cancer was not pornographic, *Wall Street Journal*, Feb 3, 1964

1147. The right to be heard does not automatically include the right to be taken seriously. —Hubert H. Humphrey, speech in Madison, Wisconsin, Aug 23, 1965

1148. If the 1st Amendment means anything, it means that a state has no business telling a man, sitting alone in his own house, what books he may read or what films he may watch. —Thurgood Marshall, unanimous opinion, *Stanley v. Georgia*, Apr 7, 1969

1149. The only way to make sure people you agree with can speak is to support the rights of people you don't agree with. —Eleanor Holmes Norton, *The New York Post*, Mar 28, 1970

1150. By placing discretion in the hands of an official to grant or deny a license, such a statute creates a threat of censorship that by its very existence chills free speech. —Harry A. Blackmun, majority opinion, *Roe v. Wade; Doe v. Bolton*, Jan 22, 1973

1151. There is no nation so poor that it cannot afford free speech, but there are few elites which will put up with the bother of it. —Daniel P. Moynihan, *Time*, Jan 26, 1976

1152. What we call the freedom of the individual is not just the luxury of one intellectual to write what he likes to write, but his being a voice which can speak for those who are silent. And if he permits his freedom of expression to be abolished, then he has abolished their freedom to find in his voice a voice for their wrongs. —Sir Stephen Spender, *The Thirties and After*, 1978

1153. One who comes to the Court must come to adore, not to protest. That's the new gloss on the 1st Amendment. —William O. Douglas, *The Court Years 1939-75*, 1980

1154. Free speech carries with it some freedom to listen. —Warren E. Burger, majority opinion, Jul 2, 1980

1155. (To restrict political spending) is much like allowing a speaker in a public hall to express his views while denying him the use of an amplifying system. —William H. Rehnquist, majority opinion, Jun 18, 1986

FREEDOM OF THE PRESS

1156. It is the characteristic of the most stringent censorships that they give credibility to the opinions they attack. [*C'est le propre des censures violentes d'accrediter les opinions qu'elles attaquent.*] —Voltaire, preface, "Poème sur le désastre de Lisbonne", 1758

1157. The abuses of the press are notorious. ... License of the press is no proof of liberty. When a people are corrupted, the press may be made an engine to complete their ruin. —John Adams, "Novanglus", *Boston Gazette*, Feb 6, 1775

1158. The freedom of the press is one of the great bulwarks of liberty, and can never be restrained but by despotic governments. —George Mason, *Virginia Bill of Rights*, Jun 12, 1776

1160. The basis of our government being the opinion of the people, the very first object should be to keep that right; and were it left to me to decide whether we should have a government without newspapers, or newspapers without a government, I should not hesitate a moment to prefer the latter. But I should mean that every man should receive those papers, and be capable of reading them. —Thomas Jefferson, letter to Col. Edward Carrington, Jan 16, 1787

1161. To the press alone, chequered as it is with abuses, the world is indebted for all the triumphs which have been gained by reason and humanity over error and oppression. —James Madison, "Report on the Resolutions" of the Virginia House of Delegates, 1799

1162. Let them say, if they want, that the sun revolves around the earth, that the melting of the ice causes the tides, and that we are charlatans: complete liberty must prevail. [*Qu'on dise, si l'on veut, que le soleil tourne, que c'est la fonte des glaces qui produit le flux et le reflux, et que nous sommes des charlatans; il doit régner la plus grande liberté.*] —Napoleon I, letter to the Consuls of the Republic, Jun 7, 1800

1163. I want a situation without censorship, because I do not want to be responsible for whatever they may say. [*Je voudrais une organisation sans censure, car je ne veux pas être responsable de tout ce qu'ils peuvent dire.*] —Napoleon I, letter to M. Fouché, Jun 1, 1805

1164. The man who never looks into a newspaper is better informed than he who reads them, inasmuch as he who knows nothing is nearer the truth than he whose mind is filled with falsehoods and errors. —Thomas Jefferson, letter to John Norvell, Jun 11, 1807

1165. Give them a corrupt House of Lords, give them a venal House of Commons, give them a tyrannical Prince, give them a truckling court, and let me have but an unfettered Press. I will defy them to encroach a hair's breadth upon the liberties of England. —Richard Brinsley Sheridan, speech in the House of Commons, Feb 6, 1810

1166. The functionaries of every government have propensities to command at will the liberty and property of their constituents. There is no safe deposit for these but with the people themselves; nor can they be safe with them without information. Where the press is free, and every man able to read, all is safe. —Thomas Jefferson, letter to Col. Charles Yancey, Jan 6, 1816

1167.   In order to enjoy the inestimable benefits that the liberty of the press ensures, it is necessary to submit to the inevitable evils that it creates. [*Pour recueillir les biens inestimables qu'assure la liberté de la presse, il faut savoir se soumettre aux maux inévitables qu'elle fait naître.*] —Alexis, Comte de Tocqueville, *Democracy in America*, 1835

1168.   Sovereignty of the people and freedom of the press are each necessary to the other while censorship and universal suffrage are contradictory. [*La souveraineté du peuple et la liberté de la presse sont donc deux choses entièrement correlatives: la censure et le vote universel sont au contraire deux choses qui se contredisent.*] —Alexis, Comte de Tocqueville, *Democracy in America*, 1835

1169.   Burke said there were Three Estates in Parliament; but, in the Reporters' Gallery yonder, there sat a Fourth Estate, more important by far than they all. —Thomas Carlyle, *On Heros, Hero-Worship, and the Heroic in History*, 1841

1170.   We live under a government of men and morning newspapers. —Wendell Phillips, speech, Jan 28, 1852

1171.   The chief danger which threatens the influence and honor of the press is the tendency of its liberty to degenerate into license. —James A. Garfield, speech to the Ohio Editorial Association, Jul 11, 1878

1172.   We have all of us at times suffered from the liberty of the press, but we have to take the good with the bad. —Theodore Roosevelt, speech to the New York state assembly, Mar 27, 1883

1173.   In old days men had the rack. Now they have the press. —Oscar Wilde, "The Soul of Man Under Socialism", *Fortnightly Review*, Feb, 1891

1174.   The more I see of the Czar, Kaiser, and the Mikado, the better I am content with democracy, even if we have to include the American newspapers as one of its assets—liability would be a better term. —Theodore Roosevelt, letter to Henry Cabot Lodge, Jun 16, 1905

1175.   The liberty of the press is most generally approved when it takes liberties with the other fellow, and leaves us alone. —Edgar Watson Howe, *Country Town Sayings*, 1911

1176.   The papers conducted by Lord Rothermere and Lord Beaverbrook are not newspapers in the ordinary acceptance of the term. They are engines of propaganda, for the constantly changing policies, desires, personal wishes, personal likes and dislikes of two men. ... What the proprietorship of these papers is aiming at is power, and power without responsibility—the prerogative of the harlot throughout the ages. —Stanley Baldwin, speech in London, Mar 18, 1931

1177.   A free press stands as one of the great interpreters between the government and the people. To allow it to be fettered is to be fettered ourselves. —George Sutherland, *Grosjean v. American Press Co.*, 1935

1178.   Freedom of conscience, of education, of speech, of assembly are among the very fundamentals of democracy and all of them would be nullified should freedom of the press ever be successfully challenged. —Franklin D. Roosevelt, letter to W.N. Hardy, Sep 4, 1940

1179.   The hand that rules the press, the radio, the screen and the far-spread magazine, rules the country. —Learned Hand, memorial address for Justice Brandeis, Dec 21, 1942

1180.   I ... will die for the freedom of the press, even for the freedom of newspapers that call me everything that is a good deal less than ... a gentleman. —Dwight D. Eisenhower, press conference in Moscow, Aug 14, 1945

1181.   It is very difficult to have a free, fair and honest press anywhere in the world. In the first place, as a rule, papers are largely supported by advertising, and that immediately gives the advertisers a certain hold over the medium which they use. —Eleanor Roosevelt, *If You Ask Me*, 1946

1182. Freedom from something is not enough. It should also be freedom for something. Freedom is not safety but opportunity. Freedom ought to be a means to enable the press to serve the proper functions of communication in a free society. —Zechariah Chaffee Jr., "The Press Under Pressure", *Nieman Reports*, Apr, 1948

1183. A politician wouldn't dream of being allowed to call a columnist the things a columnist is allowed to call a politician. —Max Lerner, "Love and Hate in Politics", *Actions and Passions*, 1949

1184. Freedom of the press is not an end in itself but a means to the end of a free society. —Felix Frankfurter, *The New York Times*, Nov 28, 1954

1185. Whenever the press quits abusing me I know I'm in the wrong pew. I don't mind it because when they throw bricks at me—I'm a pretty good shot myself and I usually throw 'em back at 'em. —Harry S Truman, speech in Washington, D.C., Feb 22, 1958

1186. A free press can of course be good or bad, but, most certainly, without freedom it will never be anything but bad. ... Freedom is nothing else but a chance to be better, whereas enslavement is a certainty of the worse. —Albert Camus, *Resistance, Rebellion, and Death*, 1960

1187. Responsible journalism is journalism responsible in the last analysis to the editor's own conviction of what, whether interesting or only important, is in the public interest. —Walter Lippmann, speech at the International Press Institute Assemby, London, May 27, 1965

1188. Without criticism and reliable and intelligent reporting, the government cannot govern. —Walter Lippmann, speech at the International Press Institute Assembly, London, May 24, 1965

1189. Paramount among the responsibilities of a free press is the duty to prevent any part of the government from deceiving the people and sending them off to distant lands to die of foreign fevers and foreign shot and shell. —Hugo L. Black, concurring opinion, Pentagon Papers case, *New York Times Co. v. U.S.; U.S. v. The Washington Post*, Jun 30, 1971

1190. In revealing the workings of government that led to the Vietnam War, the newspapers nobly did precisely that which the Founders hoped and trusted they would do. —Hugo L. Black, concurring opinion, Pentagon Papers case, *New York Times Co. v. U.S.; U.S. v. The Washington Post*, Jun 30, 1971

1191. In my view, far from deserving condemnation for their courageous reporting, the New York Times, the Washington Post and other newspapers should be commended for serving the purpose that the Founding Fathers saw so clearly. —Hugo L. Black, concurring opinion, Pentagon Papers case, *New York Times Co. v. U.S.; U.S. v. The Washington Post*, Jun 30, 1971

1192. I'm convinced that if reporters should ever lose the right to protect the confidentiality of their sources then serious investigative reporting will simply dry up. The kind of resourceful, probing journalism that first exposed most of the serious scandals, corruption and injustice in our nation's history would simply disappear. —Nelson A. Rockefeller, speech in Syracuse, New York, Nov 29, 1972

1193. When a person goes to a country and finds their newspapers filled with nothing but good news, he can bet there are good men in jail. —Daniel P. Moynihan, *University Daily Kansan*, Feb 16, 1977

1194. Freedom of the press belongs to those who own one. —A.J. Liebling, *American Film*, Jul/Aug, 1978

1195. The First Amendment gives newspapermen a status and a mandate, an honored place in society, that cannot be matched in England, much less on the European continent. It is peculiarly American. I feel as though I survived an Ice Age and helped to keep this heritage intact. —I.F. Stone, *Chicago Tribune*, Jan 26, 1978

1196. Vietnam was the first war ever fought without any censorship. Without censorship, things can get terribly confused in the public mind. —Gen. William C. Westmoreland, *Time,* Apr 5, 1982

1197. If you can manipulate news, a judge can manipulate the law. A smart lawyer can keep a killer out of jail, a smart accountant can keep a thief from paying taxes, a smart reporter could ruin your reputation—unfairly. —Mario Cuomo, NBC-TV, Aug 21, 1986

FREEDOM/LIBERTY

1198. Proclaim liberty throughout all the land unto all the inhabitants thereof. —Bible, inscribed on the Liberty Bell, Philadelphia, Pennsylvania, ca. 500 B.C.

1199. Freedom suppressed and again regained bites with keener fangs than freedom never endangered. [*Acriores autem morsus sunt intermissae libertatis quam retentae.*] —Marcus Tullius Cicero, *De Officiis,* 44 B.C.

1200. Freedom can't be kept for nothing. If you set a high value on liberty, you must set a low value on everything else. [*Non potest gratis constare libertas. Hanc si magno aestimas, omnia parvo aestimanda sunt.*] —Lucius Annaeus Seneca (the Younger), *Letters to Lucilius,* ca. 63-65

1201. Every subject's duty is the king's; but every subject's soul is his own. —William Shakespeare, *Henry V,* 1599

1202. I confess it cannot be thought, but that men should fly from oppression, but disorder will give them but an incommodious sanctuary. —John Locke, preface, *First Tract on Government,* 1660

1203. A man cannot part with his liberty and have it too, convey it by compact to the magistrate, and retain it himself. —John Locke, *First Tract on Government,* 1660

1204. He that complies against his will is of his opinion still. —Samuel Butler (1), *Hudibras,* 1664

1205. Without Freedom of Thought, there can be no such Thing as Wisdom; and no such Thing as publick Liberty, without Freedom of Speech. —Benjamin Franklin, *The New England Courant,* Jul 9, 1722

1206. Liberty of thought is the life of the soul. —Voltaire, *Essay on Epic Poetry,* 1727

1207. Lean liberty is better than fat slavery. —Thomas Fuller, *Gnomologia,* 1732

1208. One of the greatest blessings a people, my Lords, can enjoy is liberty; but every good in this life has its alloy of evil. ... Like a changeable silk, we cannot easily discover where the one ends, or where the other begins. —4th Earl of Chesterfield, speech in the House of Lords, Jun 2, 1737

1209. Liberty is the right of doing whatever the laws permit. [*La liberté est le droit de faire tout ce que les lois permettent.*] —Charles Louis de Montesquieu, *De l'Esprit des lois,* 1748

1210. Those who would give up essential Liberty, to purchase a little temporary Safety, deserve neither Liberty nor Safety. —Benjamin Franklin, reply of the Pennsylvania Assembly to the governor, Nov 11, 1755

1211. What man loses by the social contract is his natural liberty and an unlimited right to everything he tries to get and succeeds in getting; what he gains is civil liberty and the proprietorship of all he possesses. [*Ce que l'homme perd par le contrat social, c'est sa liberté naturelle et un droit illimité à tout ce qui le tente et qu'il peut atteindre; ce qu'il gagne, c'est la liberté civile et la propriété de tout ce qu'il possède.*] —Jean Jacques Rousseau, *The Social Contract,* 1762

1212. Man is born free; and everywhere he is in chains. [*L'homme est né libre, et partout il est dans les fers.*] —Jean Jacques Rousseau, *The Social Contract*, 1762

1213. To renounce liberty is to renounce being a man, to surrender the rights of humanity and even its duties. [*Renoncer à sa liberté c'est renoncer à sa qualite d'homme, aux droits de l'humanité, même a ses devoirs.*] —Jean Jacques Rousseau, *The Social Contract*, 1762

1214. The jaws of power are always open to devour, and her arm is always stretched out, if possible, to destroy the freedom of thinking, speaking, and writing. —John Adams, "Dissertation on the Canon and the Feudal Law", Aug, 1765

1215. I rejoice that America has resisted. Three millions of people, so dead to all the feelings of liberty, as voluntarily to submit to be slaves, would have been fit instruments to make slaves of the rest. —William Pitt, 1st Earl of Chatham, speech in the House of Commons, Jan 14, 1766

1216. The cause of Liberty is a cause of too much dignity to be sullied by turbulence and tumult. It ought to be maintained in a manner suitable to her nature. —John Dickinson, *Letters from a Farmer in Pennsylvania*, 1768

1217. It is an universal maxim, that the more liberty is given to everything which is in a state of growth, the more perfect it will become. —Joseph Priestly, *Essay on Government*, 1768

1218. The God who gave us life, gave us liberty at the same time. —Thomas Jefferson, "Draft of Instructions to the Virginia Delegates in the Continental Congress", Aug, 1774

1219. Is life so dear, or peace so sweet, as to be purchased at the price of chains and slavery? Forbid it, Almighty God!—I know not what course others may take, but as for me, give me liberty, or give me death! —Patrick Henry, speech to the Virginia Convention, Mar 23, 1775

1220. Liberty can no more exist without virtue and independence, than the body can live and move without a soul. —John Adams, "Novanglus", *Boston Gazette*, Feb 6, 1775

1221. Abstract liberty, like other mere abstractions, is not to be found. —Edmund Burke, speech, "On Conciliation with the American Colonies", Mar 22, 1775

1222. Freedom and not servitude is the cure of anarchy; as religion, and not atheism, is the true remedy for superstition. —Edmund Burke, speech, "On Conciliation with the American Colonies", Mar 22, 1775

1223. The arms we have been compelled by our enemies to assume we will, in defiance of every hazard, with unabating firmness and perseverance, employ for the preservation of our liberties; being with one mind resolved to die free rather than live slaves. —Thomas Jefferson, "Declaration of the Causes of Taking Up Arms", Jul 6, 1775

1224. Nip the shoots of arbitrary power in the bud, is the only maxim which can ever preserve the liberties of any people. —John Adams, "Novanglus", *Boston Gazette*, Feb 6, 1775

1225. How is it that we hear the loudest yelps for liberty among the drivers of negroes. —Samuel Johnson, "On the American Revolutionaries", *Taxation No Tyranny*, 1775

1226. Those who expect to reap the blessing of freedom must, like men, undergo the fatigue of supporting it. —Thomas Paine, *The American Crisis*, Dec 23, 1776

1227. Though the flame of liberty may sometimes cease to shine, the coal can never expire. —Thomas Paine, *The American Crisis*, Dec 23, 1776

1228. For the support of this Declaration, with a firm reliance on the protection of Divine Providence, we mutually pledge to each other our Lives, our Fortunes, and our sacred Honor. —Thomas Jefferson, closing lines, *Declaration of Independence*, 1776

1229. Liberty must be limited in order to be possessed. —Edmund Burke, *Letter to the Sheriffs of Bristol*, Apr 3, 1777

1230. The true danger is when liberty is nibbled away, for expedients, and by parts. —Edmund Burke, *Letter to the Sheriffs of Bristol*, Apr 3, 1777

1231. Posterity! You will never know how much it cost the present generation to preserve your freedom! I hope you will make good use of it! If you do not, I shall repent it in Heaven that I ever took half the pains to preserve it! —John Adams, letter to Abigail Adams, Apr 26, 1777

1232. The people never give up their liberties but under some delusion. —Edmund Burke, speech in Buckinghamshire, England, 1784

1233. I am tired of ruling over slaves. —Frederick the Great, on his deathbed, Apr 1, 1786

1234. The tree of liberty must be refreshed from time to time with the blood of patriots and tyrants. It is its natural manure. —Thomas Jefferson, letter to William Stephens Smith, Nov 13, 1787

1235. What country can preserve its liberties, if its rulers are not warned from time to time, that this people preserve the spirt of resistance? —Thomas Jefferson, letter to Col. William S. Smith, Nov 13, 1787

1236. Since the general civilization of mankind, I believe there are more instances of the abridgment of freedom of the people, by gradual and silent encroachments of those in power, than by violent and sudden usurpations. —James Madison, speech to the Virginia Convention on adoption of the U.S. Constitution, Jun 6, 1788

1237. The natural progress of things is for liberty to yield and government to gain ground. —Thomas Jefferson, letter to Edward Carrington, May 27, 1788

1238. No human government has a right to enquire into private opinions, to presume that it knows them, or to act on that presumption. Men are the best judges of the consequences of their own opinions, and how far they are likely to influence their actions; and it is most unnatural and tyrannical to say, "As you think, so must you act. I will collect the evidence of your future conduct from what I know to be your opinions." —Charles James Fox, speech in the House of Commons, May 8, 1789

1239. We are not to expect to be translated from despotism to liberty in a feather bed. —Thomas Jefferson, letter to the Marquis de Lafayette, Apr 2, 1790

1240. The ground of liberty is to be gained in inches. —Thomas Jefferson, letter to Rev. Charles Clay, Jan 27, 1790

1241. The condition upon which God hath given liberty to men is eternal vigilance. —John Philpot Curran, speech in Dublin, Ireland, Jul 10, 1790

1242. To erect and concentrate and perpetuate a large monied interest ... must in the course of human events produce one or other of two evils, the prostration of agriculture at the feet of commerce, or a change in the present form of federal government, fatal to the existence of American liberty. —Patrick Henry, speech to the Virginia House of Representatives, Dec, 23, 1790

1243. I would rather be exposed to the inconveniencies attending too much liberty than those attending too small a degree of it. —Thomas Jefferson, letter to Archibald Stuart, Dec 23, 1791

1244. It is ordained in the eternal constitution of things that men of intemperate minds cannot be free. Their passions forge their fetters. —Edmund Burke, *Letter to a Member of the French National Assembly*, 1791

1245. It is not because we have been free, but because we have a right to be free, that we ought to demand freedom. Justice and liberty have neither birth nor race, youth nor age. It would be the same absurdity to assert, that we have a right to freedom, because the Englishmen of Alfred's reign were free, as that three and three are six, because they were so in the camps of Genghis Khan. —Sir James Mackintosh, *Vindicae Gallicae*, 1791

1246. O liberty! O liberty! what crimes are committed in thy name! [*O liberté! O liberté! que de crimes on commet en ton nom!*] —Mme. Roland, (Marie-Jeanne), quoted by Alphonse de Lamartine, *Histoire des Girondins*, 1847

1247. As for me, I think anyone, whoever he may be, who has done nothing for liberty, or has not done all he could deserves to be counted as an enemy to it. —Joseph-Pierre Fayau, speech to the National Convention, Nov 26, 1793

1248. He that would make his own liberty secure, must guard even his enemy from oppression; for if he violates this duty, he establishes a precedent that will reach to himself. —Thomas Paine, *Dissertation on First Principles of Government*, 1795

1249. A people are free in proportion as they form their own opinions. —Samuel Taylor Coleridge, Prospectus, *The Watchman*, 1796

1250. With what deep worship I have still adored/ The spirit of divinest Liberty. —Samuel Taylor Coleridge, "France: An Ode", 1798

1251. Freedom of religion, freedom of the press, freedom of person under the protection of habeas corpus; and trial by juries impartially selected,—these principles form the bright constellation which has gone before us. —Thomas Jefferson, first inaugural address, Mar 4, 1801

1252. The love of liberty is the love of others; the love of power is the love of ourselves. —William Hazlitt, "The Times Newspaper", *Political Essays*, 1819

1253. The boisterous sea of liberty is never without a wave. —Thomas Jefferson, letter to Richard Rush, Oct 20, 1820

1254. Individual liberty is individual power, and as the power of a community is a mass compounded of individual powers, the nation which enjoys the most freedom must necessarily be in proportion to its numbers the most powerful nation. —John Quincy Adams, letter to James Lloyd, Oct 1, 1822

1255. There is only one cure for the evils which newly acquired freedom produces, and that cure is freedom. —Lord Macaulay, "On Milton", 1825

1256. Tell a man whose house is on fire, to give a moderate alarm; tell him to moderately rescue his wife from the hands of the ravisher; tell the mother to gradually extricate her babe from the fire into which it has fallen; but urge me not to use moderation in a cause like the present. I am in earnest—I will not equivocate —I will not excuse—I will not retreat a single inch—AND I WILL BE HEARD. —William Lloyd Garrison, prospectus, *The Liberator*, Jan 1, 1831

1257. The history of the world is none other than the progress of the consciousness of freedom. [*Die Weltgeschichte ist der Fortschritt im Bewusstsein der Freiheit.*] —Georg Wilhelm Friedrich Hegel, *Introduction to the Philosophy of History*, 1832

1258. The contest, for ages, has been to rescue Liberty from the grasp of executive power. —Daniel Webster, speech in the U.S. Senate, May 27, 1834

1259. God grants liberty only to those who love it, and are always ready to guard and defend it. —Daniel Webster, speech in the U.S. Senate, Jun 3, 1834

1260. In America, a glorious fire has been lighted upon the alter of liberty. ... Keep it burning, and let the sparks that continually go up from it fall on other altars, and light up in distant lands the fire of freedom. —William Henry Harrison, speech in Dayton, Ohio, Sep 10, 1840

1261. See to the government. See that the government does not acquire too much power. Keep a check upon your rulers. Do this, and liberty is safe. —William Henry Harrison, speech during presidential campaign, 1840

1262. At the moment that man inquires into the motives which govern the will of his sovereign—at that moment man revolts. If he obeys, no longer because the king commands, but because the king demonstrates the wisdom of his commands, it may be said that henceforth he will recognize no authority, and that he has become his own king. —Pierre Joseph Proudhon, *Qu'est-ce la propriéte?*, 1840

1263. True freedom is to share/ All the chains our brothers wear,/ And, with heart and hand, to be/ Earnest to make others free! —James Russell Lowell, "Stanzas on Freedom", 1843

1264. Let your motto be resistance, resistance, RESISTANCE! No oppressed people have ever secured their liberty without resistance. —Henry Highland Garnet, "Address to the Slaves of the United States", 1843

1265. They are slaves who dare not be/ In the right with two or three. —James Russell Lowell, "Stanzas on Freedom", 1843

1266. I didn't know I was a slave until I found out I couldn't do the things I wanted. —Frederick Douglass, *Narrative of the Life of Frederick Douglass*, 1845

1267. Liberty exists in proportion to wholesome restraint. —Daniel Webster, speech at the Charleston Bar, May 10, 1847

1268. It is harder to preserve than to obtain liberty. —John C. Calhoun, speech in the U.S. Senate, Jan, 1848

1269. The liberty of the individual is the greatest thing of all, it is on this and on this alone that the true will of the people can develop. —Alexander Ivanovich Herzen, introduction, "To My Son Alexander", *From The Other Shore*, 1848-49

1270. The word "liberty" in the mouth of Mr. Webster sounds like the word "love" in the mouth of a courtesan. —Ralph Waldo Emerson, *Journal*, Feb 12, 1851

1271. No one can be perfectly free till all are free; no one can be perfectly moral till all are moral; no one can be perfectly happy till all are happy. —Herbert Spencer, *Social Statics*, 1851

1272. Eternal vigilance is the price of liberty. —Wendell Phillips, speech, 1852

1273. Liberty unregulated by law degenerates into anarchy, which soon becomes the most horrid of all despotisms. —Millard Fillmore, third annual message to Congress, Dec 5, 1852

1274. Let us remember that revolutions do not always establish freedom. Our own free institutions were not the offspring of our Revolution. They existed before. —Millard Fillmore, third annual message to Congress, Dec 5, 1852

1275. True liberty acknowledges and defends the equal rights of all men, and all nations. —Gerrit Smith, speech in U.S. House of Representatives, Jun 27, 1854

1276. My faith in the proposition that each man should do precisely as he pleases with all which is exclusively his own lies at the foundation of the sense of justice there is in me. I extend the principle to communities of men as well as to individuals. —Abraham Lincoln, speech in Peoria, Illinois, Oct 16, 1854

1277. Let us readopt the Declaration of Independence, and with it the practices and policy which harmonize with it. Let North and South—let all Americans—let all lovers of liberty everywhere join in the great and good work. If we do this, we shall not only save the Union, but we shall have so saved it that the succeeding millions of free, happy people, the world over, shall rise up and call us blessed to the latest generations. —Abraham Lincoln, speech in Peoria, Illinois, Oct 16, 1854

1278. He who would be free must strike the first blow. —Frederick Douglass, *My Bondage and My Freedom*, 1855

1279. If there is no struggle there is no progress. Those who profess to favor freedom and yet deprecate agitation, are men who want crops without plowing up the ground, they want rain without thunder and lightning. They want the ocean without the awful roar of its many waters. This struggle may be a moral one, or it may be a physical one, and it may be both moral and physical, but it must be a struggle. Power concedes nothing without a demand. It never did and it never will. —Frederick Douglass, speech at Canandaigua, New York, Aug 4, 1857

1280. The whole history of the progress of human liberty shows that all concessions yet made to her august claims have been born of earnest struggle. —Frederick Douglass, speech in Canandaigua, New York, Aug 4, 1857

1281. The fight must go on. The cause of civil liberty must not be surrendered at the end of one or even one hundred defeats. —Abraham Lincoln, letter to H. Asbury, Nov 19, 1858

1282. The struggle between liberty and authority is the most conspicuous feature in the portions of history with which we are earliest familiar, particularly in that of Greece, Rome and England. —John Stuart Mill, *On Liberty*, 1859

1283. The only freedom which deserves the name, is that of pursuing our own good in our own way, so long as we do not attempt to deprive others of theirs, or impede their efforts to obtain it. —John Stuart Mill, *On Liberty*, 1859

1284. There is a limit to the legitimate interference of collective opinion with individual independence: and to find that limit, and maintain it against encroachment, is as indispensable to a good condition of human affairs, as protection against political despotism. —John Stuart Mill, *On Liberty*, 1859

1285. The sole end for which mankind are warranted, individually or collectively, in interfering with the liberty of action of any of their number is self-protection. —John Stuart Mill, *On Liberty*, 1859

1286. The individual is not accountable to society for his actions, insofar as these concern the interests of no person but himself. —John Stuart Mill, *On Liberty*, 1859

1287. The liberty of the individual must be thus far limited; he must not make himself a nuisance to other people. —John Stuart Mill, *On Liberty*, 1859

1288. Liberty consists in doing what one desires. —John Stuart Mill, *On Liberty*, 1859

1289. The only purpose for which power can be rightfully exercised over any member of a civilised community, against his will, is to prevent harm to others. His own good, either physical or moral, is not a sufficient warrant. —John Stuart Mill, *On Liberty*, 1859

1290. Whether in chains or in laurels, liberty knows nothing but victories. —Wendell Phillips, speech at Harper's Ferry, Virginia, Nov 1, 1859

1291. A person should be free to do as he likes in his own concerns; but he ought not to be free to do as he likes in acting for another, under the pretext that the affairs of the other are his own affairs. —John Stuart Mill, *On Liberty*, 1859

1292. The spirit of improvement is not always a spirit of liberty, for it may aim at forcing improvements on an unwilling people. —John Staurt Mill, *On Liberty*, 1859

1293. This is a world of compensation; and he who would be no slave must consent to have no slave. Those who deny freedom to others deserve it not for themselves, and under a just God, cannot long retain it. —Abraham Lincoln, letter to H.L. Pierce, Apr 6, 1859

1294. Mankind are greater gainers by suffering each other to live as seems good to themselves, than by compelling each to live as seems good to the rest. —John Stuart Mill, *On Liberty*, 1859

1295.   If this country cannot be saved without giving up the principle ... (of the Declaration of Independence), I would rather be assassinated on this spot than surrender it. —Abraham Lincoln, speech in Philadelphia, Pennsylvania, Feb 22, 1861

1296.   I am the son of Liberty and to her I owe all that I am. If it is necessary to veil her statue it is not for me to do it. —Camillo, Conte di Cavour, letter to the Countess of Circourt, Jan, 1861

1297.   Liberty, misunderstood by materialists as the right to do or not to do anything not directly injurious to others, we understand as the faculty of choosing, among the various modes of fulfilling duty, those most in harmony with our own tendencies. —Giuseppe Mazzini, *On the Unity of Italy*, 1861

1298.   A man who has nothing which he is willing to fight for, nothing which he cares more about than he does about his personal safety, is a miserable creature who has no chance of being free, unless made and kept so by the exertions of better men than himself. —John Stuart Mill, "The Contest in America", *Fraser's Magazine*, Feb, 1862

1299.   In giving freedom to the slave, we assure freedom to the free. ... We shall nobly save or meanly lose the last, best hope of earth. —Abraham Lincoln, message to Congress, Dec 1, 1862

1300.   Liberation is not deliverance. [*Libération n'est pas délivrance.*] —Victor Hugo, *Les Misérables*, 1862

1301.   Human liberty, the only true foundation of human government. —Ulysses S. Grant, message to the citizens of Memphis, Tennessee, 1863

1302.   Where Slavery is, there Liberty cannot be; and where Liberty is, there Slavery cannot be. —Charles Sumner, speech, "Slavery and the Rebellion" delivered at the Cooper Union, New York City, Nov 5, 1864

1303.   The shepherd drives the wolf from the sheep's throat, for which the sheep thanks the shepherd as his liberator, while the wolf denounces him for the same act, as the destroyer of liberty, especially as the sheep was a black one. —Abraham Lincoln, speech in Baltimore, Maryland, Apr 18, 1864

1304.   Whenever (I) hear any one, arguing for slavery I feel a strong impulse to see it tried on him personally. —Abraham Lincoln, speech to the 140th Indiana regiment, Mar 17, 1865

1305.   For what avail the plow or sail,/ Or land or life, if freedom fail? —Ralph Waldo Emerson, "Boston", *May-Day and Other Pieces*, 1867

1306.   Where the State begins, individual liberty ceases, and vice versa. —Michael Bakunin, *Federalism, Socialism and Anti-Theologism*, 1868

1307.   Intellectual slavery, of whatever nature it may be, will always have as a natural result both political and social slavery. —Michael Bakunin, *Federalism, Socialism and Anti-Theologism*, 1868

1308.   When I found I had crossed that line, I looked at my hands to see if I was the same person. There was such a glory over everything. —Harriet Tubman, quoted by Sarah H. Bradford, *Harriet, the Moses of Her People*, 1869

1309.   There was one of two things I had a right to, liberty or death. If I could not have one, I would have the other, for no man should take me alive. I should fight for my liberty as long as my strength lasted, and when the time came for me to go, the Lord would let them take me. —Harriet Tubman, quoted by Sarah H. Bradford, *Harriet, the Moses of Her People*, 1869

1310.   Liberty is not a means to a higher political end. It is itself the highest political end. —Lord Acton, lecture on "The History of Freedom in Antiquity" at Bridgnorth, England, Feb 26, 1877

1311.   The spirit of truth and the spirit of freedom—they are the pillars of society. [*Sandhedens og frihedens ånd,—det er samfundets stotter.*] —Henrik Ibsen, *Pillars of Society*, 1877

1312. Liberty, next to religion, has been the motive of good deeds and the common pretext of crime. —Lord Acton, lecture on "The History of Freedom in Antiquity" at Bridgnorth, England, Feb 26, 1877

1313. If the perpetual oscillation of nations between anarchy and despotism is to be replaced by the steady march of self-restraining freedom, it will be because men will gradually bring themselves to deal with political, as they now deal with scientific questions. —Thomas Henry Huxley, "Science and Culture", 1880

1314. The shallow consider liberty a release from all law, from every constraint. The wise see in it, on the contrary, the potent Law of Laws. —Walt Whitman, "Freedom", _Notes Left Over_, 1881

1315. Keep, ancient lands, your storied pomp! cries she/ With silent lips. Give me your tired, your poor,/ Your huddled masses yearning to breathe free,/ The wretched refuse of your teeming shore./ Send these, the homeless, tempest-tossed to me;/ I lift my lamp beside the golden door. —Emma Lazarus, _The New Colossus_, 1886

1316. Liberty cannot live apart from constitutional principle. —Woodrow Wilson, _Political Science Quarterly_, Jun, 1887

1317. When liberty becomes license, some form of one-man power is not far distant. —Theodore Roosevelt, _Works_, 1887

1318. Liberty is the soul's right to breathe, and, when it can not take a long breath, laws are girdled too tight. —Henry Ward Beecher, _Proverbs from Plymouth Pulpit_, 1887

1319. Then what is freedom? It is the will to be responsible to ourselves. [_Denn was ist Freiheit? Dasz man den Willen zur Selbstverantwortlichkeit hat._] —Friedrich Nietzsche, "Skirmishes in a War with the Age", _Twilight of the Idols_, 1888

1320. The demand of the Labour party is for economic freedom. It is the natural outcome of political enfranchisement. —Keir Hardie, speech to the inaugural conference of the Independent Labour party, Jan 13, 1893

1321. Liberty recast the old forms of government into the Republic, and it must remould our institutions of wealth into the Commonwealth. —Henry Demarest Lloyd, _Wealth Against Commonwealth_, 1894

1322. Liberty produces wealth and wealth destroys liberty. —Henry Demarest Lloyd, _Wealth Against Commonwealth_, 1894

1323. Liberty and monopoly cannot live together. —Henry Demarest Lloyd, _Wealth Against Commonwealth_, 1894

1324. It is by the goodness of God that in our country we have those three unspeakably precious things: freedom of speech, freedom of conscience, and the prudence never to practice either of them. —Mark Twain, _Following the Equator_, 1897

1325. It is a worthy thing to fight for one's freedom; it is another sight finer to fight for another man's. —Mark Twain, letter to the Reverend Joseph Twichell, 1898

1326. Freedom remains still the wisest cure for freedom's temporary inconveniences. —Prince Peter Kropotkin, _Memoirs of a Revolutionist_, 1899

1327. Irreverence is the champion of liberty and its only sure defense. —Mark Twain, _Notebook_, 1935

1328. Liberty is the most jealous and exacting mistress that can beguile the brain and soul of man. —Clarence S. Darrow, funeral oration for John P. Altgeld, Mar 14, 1902

1329. Liberty means responsibility. That is why most men dread it. —George Bernard Shaw, "Maxims for Revolutionists", _Man and Superman_, 1902

1331. Freedom, n. The distinction between freedom and liberty is not accurately known; naturalists have never been able to find a living specimen of either. —Ambrose Bierce, *The Devil's Dictionary*, 1906

1332. Liberty, n. One of Imagination's most precious possessions. —Ambrose Bierce, *The Devil's Dictionary*, 1906

1333. The ideals of liberty cannot be fixed from generation to generation; only its conception can be, the large image of what it is. Liberty fixed in unalterable law would be no liberty at all. —Woodrow Wilson, *Constitutional Government*, 1908

1334. Liberty is the means in the pursuit of happiness. —William Howard Taft, speech in Fresno, California, Oct 10, 1909

1335. Liberty trains for liberty. Responsibility is the first step in responsibility. —W.E.B. Du Bois, "The Legacy of John Brown", *John Brown*, 1909

1336. The cost of liberty is less than the price of repression. —W.E.B. Du Bois, "The Legacy of John Brown", *John Brown*, 1909

1337. No man can be just who is not free. —Woodrow Wilson, speech to the Democratic National Convention, Jul 7, 1912

1338. There will be no greater burden in our generation than to organize the forces of liberty on our time, in order to make conquest of a new freedom for America. —Woodrow Wilson, speech in Indianapolis, Indiana, Oct 3, 1912

1339. The only freedom consists in the people taking care of the government. —Woodrow Wilson, speech in New York City, Sep 4, 1912

1340. Liberty has never come from the government. Liberty has always come from the subjects of it. The history of liberty is a history of resistance. The history of liberty is a history of limitations of governmental power, not the increase in it. —Woodrow Wilson, speech at the New York Press Club, Sep 9, 1912

1341. Liberty is its own reward. —Woodrow Wilson, speech, Sep 12, 1912

1342. You cannot tear up ancient rootages and safely plant the tree of liberty in soil that is not native to it. —Woodrow Wilson, speech, Sep 25, 1912

1343. I would rather belong to a poor nation that was free than to a rich nation that had ceased to be in love with liberty. —Woodrow Wilson, speech in Mobile, Alabama, Oct 27, 1913

1344. Most men, after a little freedom, have preferred authority with the consoling assurances and the economy of effort which it brings. —Walter Lippmann, *A Preface to Morals*, 1913

1345. A thing that stands demonstrable is that nationhood is not achieved otherwise than in arms. ... We may make mistakes in the beginning and shoot the wrong people; but bloodshed is a cleansing and a sanctifying thing, and the nation which regards it as the final horror has lost its manhood. There are many things more horrible than bloodshed; and slavery is one of them. —Padraic Pearse, *The Coming Revolution*, 1913

1346. Liberty does not consist ... in mere general declarations of the rights of man. It consists in the translation of those declarations into definite action. —Woodrow Wilson, speech in Philadelphia, Pennsylvania, Jul 4, 1914

1347. Those men and women are fortunate who are born at a time when a great struggle for human freedom is in progress. —Emmeline Pankhurst, *My Own Story*, 1914

1348. There are two good things in life—freedom of thought and freedom of action. —W. Somerset Maugham, *Of Human Bondage*, 1915

1349. Liberty is often a fierce and intractable thing, to which no bounds can be set, and to which no bounds of a few men's choosing ought ever be set. —Woodrow Wilson, third annual message to Congress, Dec 7, 1915

1350. While the state exists there is no freedom; when there is freedom there will be no state. —Vladimir Ilyich Lenin, *The State and the Revolution*, 1917

1351. While there is a lower class I am in it, while there is a criminal class I am of it; while there is a soul in prison, I am not free. —Eugene V. Debs, speech in Cleveland, Ohio, Sep 9, 1917

1352. Only free peoples can hold their purpose and their honor steady to a common end, and prefer the interests of mankind to any narrow interest of their own. —Woodrow Wilson, speech to Congress, Apr 2, 1917

1353. We do not profess to be the champions of liberty, and then consent to see liberty destroyed. —Woodrow Wilson, speech in Indianapolis, Indiana, Sep 4, 1919

1354. There is no substitute for a militant freedom. —Calvin Coolidge, speech in Washington, D.C., Apr 27, 1922

1355. Radicalism is a label that is always applied to people who are endeavoring to get freedom. —Marcus Moziah Garvey, *Philosophy and Opinions*, 1923

1356. Liberty is not collective, it is personal. All liberty is individual liberty. —Calvin Coolidge, speech in Washington, D.C., Sep 21, 1924

1357. When we lose the right to be different, we lose the privilege to be free. —Charles Evans Hughes, speech in Faneuil Hall, Boston, Massachusetts, Jun 17, 1925

1358. It is necessary to grow accustomed to freedom before one may walk in it sure-footedly. —Suzanne LaFollette, "Women and Marriage", *Concerning Women*, 1926

1359. Those who won our independence believed that the final end of the State was to make men free to develop their faculties; and that in its government the deliberative forces should prevail over the arbitrary. They valued liberty both as an end and as a means. They believed liberty to be the secret of happiness and courage to be the secret of liberty. —Louis D. Brandeis, concurring opinion, *Whitney v. California*, 1927

1360. Liberty don't work as good in practice as it does in Speech. —Will Rogers, *There's Not a Bathing Suit in Russia*, 1927

1361. Men born to freedom are naturally alert to repel invasion of their liberty by evil-minded rulers. The greatest dangers to liberty lurk in insidious encroachment by men of zeal, well-meaning but without understanding. —Louis D. Brandeis, dissenting opinion, *Olmstead v. United States*, 1928

1363. Freedom is a very great reality. But it means, above all things, freedom from lies. —D.H. Lawrence, *Pornography and Obscenity*, 1930

1364. Liberty is so much latitude as the powerful choose to accord to the weak. —Learned Hand, speech, Univ. of Pennsylvania Law School, Jun 1930

1365. It must be admitted that liberty is the hardest test that one can inflict on a people. To know how to be free is not given equally to all men and all nations. —Paul Valéry, "On the Subject of Dictatorship", *Reflections on the World Today*, 1931

1366. It is a good thing to demand liberty for ourselves and for those who agree with us, but it is a better thing and a rarer thing to give liberty to others who do not agree with us. —Franklin D. Roosevelt, radio address, Nov 22, 1933

1367. Liberty is not just an idea, an abstract principle. It is power, effective power to do specific things. There is no such thing as liberty in general; liberty, so to speak, at large. —John Dewey, "Liberty and Social Control", *The Social Frontier*, Nov, 1935

1368. Freedom belongs to the strong. —Richard Wright, *Long Black Song*, 1936

1369. The truth is found when men are free to pursue it. —Franklin D. Roosevelt, speech at Temple Univ., Philadelphia, Feb 22, 1936

1370. The hungry and the homeless don't care about liberty any more than they care about cultural heritage. To pretend that they do care is cant. —E.M. Forster, "Liberty in England", *Abinger Harvest*, 1936

1371. The greater the importance of safeguarding the community from incitements to the overthrow of our institutions by force and violence, the more imperative is the need to preserve inviolate the constitutional rights of free speech, free press and free assembly in order to maintain the opportunity for free political discussion, to the end that government may be responsive to the will of the people and that changes, if desired, may be obtained by peaceful means. Therein lies the security of the Republic, the very foundation of constitutional government. —Charles Evans Hughes, *DeJonge v. Oregon*, 1937

1372. We hear about constitutional rights, free speech and the free press. Every time I hear these words I say to myself, "That man is a Red, that man is a Communist". You never hear a real American talk like that. —Frank Hague, *New York World-Telegram*, Apr 2, 1938

1373. For the saddest epitaph which can be carved in memory of a vanished liberty is that it was lost because its possessors failed to stretch forth a saving hand while yet there was time. —George Sutherland, dissenting opinion, *Associated Press v. National Labor Relations Board*, 1938

1374. Freedom to learn is the first necessity of guaranteeing that man himself shall be self-reliant enough to be free. —Franklin D. Roosevelt, speech in New York City, Jun 30, 1938

1375. Freedom is not worth fighting for if it means no more than license for everyone to get as much as he can for himself. —Dorothy Canfield Fisher, *Seasoned Timber*, 1939

1376. Morality, and the ideal of freedom which is the political expression of morality, are not the property of a given party or group, but a value that is fundamentally and universally human, to diffuse and enhance which all of us must devote our efforts and good will. ... No people will be truly free till all are free. —Benedetto Croce, *Freedom*, 1940

1377. Human kindness has never weakened the stamina or softened the fiber of a free people. A nation does not have to be cruel to be tough. —Franklin D. Roosevelt, radio address, Oct 13, 1940

1378. We have learned that freedom in itself is not enough. Freedom of speech is of no use to a man who has nothing to say. Freedom of worship is of no use to a man who has lost his God. —Franklin D. Roosevelt, campaign speech in Cleveland, Ohio, Nov 2, 1940

1379. We believe that the only whole man is a free man. —Franklin D. Roosevelt, speech at the dedication of the Great Smokey Mts. National Park, Sep 2, 1940

1380. Do not worry about what it costs. ... You can easily rebuild wealth, but you cannot create liberty when it has gone. Once a nation is put under another, it takes years and generations of struggle to get liberty back. —Ernest Bevin, speech in Cardiff, Wales, urging maximum war production, Nov, 1940

1381. If a nation values anything more than freedom, it will lose its freedom; and the irony of it is that if it is comfort or money that it values more, it will lose that too. —W. Somerset Maugham, *Strictly Personal*, 1941

1382. The dagger plunged in the name of Freedom is plunged into the breast of Freedom. —Jose Martí, *Granos de oro: pensamientos seleccionados en las Obras de Jose Martí,* 1942

1383. If liberty has any meaning it means freedom to improve. —Philip Wylie, introduction, *Generation of Vipers,* 1942

1384. The history of liberty has largely been the history of the observance of procedural safeguards. —Felix Frankfurter, *McNabb v. United States,* 1943

1385. Freedom is an indivisible word. If we want to enjoy it, and fight for it, we must be prepared to extend it to everyone, whether they are rich or poor, whether they agree with us or not, no matter what their race or the color of their skin. —Wendell Lewis Willkie, *One World,* 1943

1386. None who have always been free can understand the terrible fascinating power of the hope of freedom to those who are not free. —Pearl S. Buck, *What America Means to Me,* 1943

1387. Men would rather be starving and free than fed in bonds. —Pearl S. Buck, *What America Means to Me,* 1943

1388. A nation which makes the final sacrifice for life and freedom does not get beaten. —Kemal Atatürk, quoted by M.M. Mousharrafa, *Ataturk,* 1944

1389. Liberty lies in the hearts of men and women; when it dies there, no constitution, no law, no court can save it; no constitution, no law, no court can even do much to help it. —Learned Hand, speech in New York City, May 21, 1944

1390. The winning of freedom is not to be compared to the winning of a game—with the victory recorded forever in history. Freedom has its life in the hearts, the actions, the spirits of men and so it must be daily earned and refreshed—else like a flower cut from its life-giving roots, it will wither and die. —Dwight D. Eisenhower, speech to the English Speaking Union, London, England, 1944

1391. The ruling class or race must share their freedom with everyone in order to preserve it; or they must give it up. —Chester Bomar Himes, "Negro Martyrs are Needed", *Crisis,* May, 1944

1392. The system of private property is the most important guaranty of freedom, not only for those who own property, but scarcely less for those who do not. —Friedrich August von Hayek, *The Road to Serfdom,* 1944

1393. The spirit of liberty is the spirit which is not too sure it is right. —Learned Hand, speech in New York City, May 21, 1944

1394. I wish that every human life might be pure transparent freedom. —Simone de Beauvoir, *The Blood of Others,* 1946

1395. Political liberty is nothing else but the diffusion of power. —Lord Hailsham, (Quinton Hogg), *The Case for Conversatism,* 1947

1396. When poems stop talking about the moon and begin to mention poverty, trade unions, color, color lines and colonies, somebody tells the police. —Langston Hughes, *My Adventures as a Social Poet,* 1947

1397. No man is entitled to the blessings of freedom unless he be vigilant in its preservation. —Douglas MacArthur, title of a speech to the Japanese people, May 3, 1948

1398. The moment the slave resolves that he will no longer be a slave, his fetters fall. He frees himself and shows the way to others. Freedom and slavery are mental states. —Mohandas K. Gandhi, *Non-Violence in Peace and War,* 1948

1399. It is not enough merely to realize how freedom has been won. Essential also is it that we be ever alert to all threats to that freedom. ... One danger arises from too great a concentration of power in the hands of any individual or group: The power of concentrated finance, the power of selfish pressure groups, the power of any class organized in opposition to the whole—any one of these, when allowed to dominate, is fully capable of destroying individual freedom as is power concentrated in the political head of state. —Dwight D. Eisenhower, speech at Columbia Univ., Oct 12, 1948

1400. Diversity of opinion within the framework of loyalty to our free society is not only basic to a university but to the entire nation. —James Bryant Conant, *Education in a Divided World*, 1948

1401. The cause of liberty becomes a mockery if the price to be paid is the wholesale destruction of those who are to enjoy liberty. —Mohandas K. Gandhi, *Non-Violence in Peace and War*, 1948

1402. Freedom always entails danger. —W.E.B. Du Bois, "Freedom to Learn", *Midwest Journal*, Winter, 1949

1403. Too little liberty brings stagnation, and too much brings chaos. —Bertrand Russell, "The Role of Individuality", *Authority and the Individual*, 1949

1404. A Country can get more real joy out of just Hollering for their Freedom than they can if they get it. —Will Rogers, *The Autobiography of Will Rogers*, 1949

1405. While it is true that an inherently free and scrupulous person may be destroyed, such an individual can never be enslaved or used as a blind tool. —Albert Einstein, *Impact*, 1950

1406. Men are created different; they lose their social freedom and their individual autonomy in seeking to become like each other. —David Riesman, *The Lonely Crowd*, 1950

1407. The American feels so rich in his opportunities for free expression that he often no longer knows what he is free from. Neither does he know where he is not free; he does not recognize his native autocrats when he sees them. —Erik H. Erikson, *Childhood and Society*, 1950

1408. Everything that is really great and inspiring is created by the individual who can labor in freedom. —Albert Einstein, *Out of My Later Years*, 1950

1409. Man in Society is not free where there is no law; he is most free where he cooperates best with his equals in the making of laws. —George Douglas Cole, *Essays in Social Theory*, 1950

1410. ˙ Liberty is the possibility of doubting, the possibility of making a mistake, the possibility of searching and experimenting, the possibility of saying "No" to any authority—literary, artistic, philosophic, religious, social, and even political. —Ignazio Silone, *The God That Failed*, 1950

1411. A hungry man is not a free man. —Adlai E. Stevenson Jr., speech in Kasson, Minnesota, Sep 6, 1952

1412. The mind is the expression of the soul, which belongs to God and must be let alone by government. —Adlai E. Stevenson Jr., speech in Salt Lake City, Utah, Oct 14, 1952

1413. Carelessness about our security is dangerous; carelessness about our freedom is also dangerous. —Adlai E. Stevenson Jr., speech in Detroit, Michigan, Oct 7, 1952

1414. The right to be let alone is indeed the beginning of all freedoms. —William O. Douglas, dissenting opinion, *Public Utilities Commission v. Pollak*, May 26, 1952

1415. We can afford no liberties with liberty itself. —Robert H. Jackson, dissenting opinion, *Zorach v. Clausor*, Apr 7, 1952

1416. Shouting is not a substitute for thinking and reason is not the subversion but the salvation of freedom. —Adlai E. Stevenson Jr., Godkin Lectures, Harvard Univ., Mar, 1954

1417. The 5th Amendment is an old friend and a good friend ... one of the great landmarks in men's struggle to be free of tyranny, to be decent and civilized. —William O. Douglas, *An Almanac of Liberty*, 1954

1418. Not for the flag/ Of any land because myself was born there/ Will I give up my life./ But I will love that land where man is free,/ And that will I defend. —Edna St. Vincent Millay, "Not for a Nation", *Mine the Harvest*, 1954

1419. The real guarantee of freedom is an equilibrium of social forces in conflict, not the triumph of any one force. —Max Eastman, *Reflections on the Failure of Socialism*, 1955

1420. It has been well said that a hungry man is more interested in four sandwiches than four freedoms. —Henry Cabot Lodge Jr., *The New York Times*, Mar 29, 1955

1421. Civilization exists precisely so that there may be no masses but rather men alert enough never to constitute masses. —Georges Bernanos, *Why Freedom?*, 1955

1422. Liberty is always unfinished business. —(American Civil Liberties Union) ACLU, title, *Annual Report, 1955-56*

1423. We cannot choose freedom established on a hierarchy of degrees of freedom, on a caste system of equality like military rank. We must be free not because we claim freedom, but because we practice it. —William Faulkner, *Harper's Magazine*, Jun, 1956

1424. He is free ... who knows how to keep in his own hands the power to decide, at each step, the course of his life, and who lives in a society which does not block the exercise of that power. —Salvador de Madariaga, *The New York Times*, Jan 29, 1957

1425. The most powerful single force in the world today is neither Communism nor capitalism, neither the H-bomb nor the guided missile—it is man's eternal desire to be free and independent. —John F. Kennedy, speech in Washington, D.C., Jul 2, 1957

1426. Freedom has been defined as the opportunity for self-discipline. ... Should we persistently fail to discipline ourselves, eventually there will be increasing pressure on government to redress the failure. By that process freedom will step by step disappear. —Dwight D. Eisenhower, fifth annual message to Congress, Jan 10, 1957

1427. In my opinion, you can't take freedom and allow freedom finally to be pushed back to the shores of the United States and maintain it in the United States. It can't be done. There's too much interdependence in the world. —Dwight D. Eisenhower, remarks in Washington, D.C., May 1, 1957

1428. Freedom is a hard-bought thing. —Paul Robeson, *Here I Stand*, 1958

1429. Freedom is not worth having if it does not connote freedom to err. —Mohandas K. Gandhi, quoted, *Saturday Review*, Mar 1, 1959

1430. If men and women are in chains, anywhere in the world, then freedom is endangered everywhere. —John F. Kennedy, campaign speech in Washington, D.C., Oct 2, 1960

1431. We have confused the free with the free and easy. —Adlai E. Stevenson Jr., *Putting First Things First*, 1960

1432. Liberty is never out of bounds or off limits; it spreads wherever it can capture the imagination of men. —E.B. White, "Letter from the West", *The Points of My Compass*, 1960

1433. In the long history of the world, only a few generations have been granted the role of defending freedom in its hour of maximum danger. I do not shrink from this responsibility—I welcome it. —John F. Kennedy, inaugural address, Jan 20, 1961

1434. Conformity is the jailer of freedom and the enemy of growth. —John F. Kennedy, speech to the United Nations General Assembly, Sep 25, 1961

1435. Freedom is not something that anybody can be given; freedom is something people take and people are as free as they want to be. —James Baldwin, "Notes for a Hypothetical Novel", *Nobody Knows My Name*, 1961

1436. We stand for freedom. That is our conviction for ourselves; that is our only commitment to others. —John F. Kennedy, message to Congress, May 25, 1961

1437. If the self-discipline of the free cannot match the iron discipline of the mailed fist, in economic, political, scientific, and all the other kinds of struggles, as well as the military, then the peril to freedom will continue to rise. —John F. Kennedy, speech to the American Society of Newspaper Editors, Apr 20, .1961

1438. The best road to progress is freedom's road. —John F. Kennedy, message to Congress, Mar 14, 1961

1439. The cost of freedom is always high, but Americans have always paid it. —John F. Kennedy, radio and television address, Oct 12, 1962

1440. History suggests that capitalism is a necessary condition for political freedom. Clearly it is not a sufficient condition. —Milton Friedman, *Capitalism and Freedom*, 1962

1441. The kind of economic organization that provides economic freedom directly, namely, competitive capitalism, also promotes political freedom because it separates economic power from political power and in this way enables the one to offset the other. —Milton Friedman, *Capitalism and Freedom*, 1962

1442. Freedom in economic arrangements is itself a component of freedom broadly understood, so economic freedom is an end in itself ... Economic freedom is also an indispensable means toward the achievement of political freedom. —Milton Friedman, *Capitalism and Freedom*, 1962

1443. The wave of the future is not the conquest of the world by a single dogmatic creed but the liberation of the diverse energies of free nations and free men. —John F. Kennedy, speech at the Univ. of California, Berkeley, Mar 23, 1962

1444. Two thousand years ago the proudest boast was "Civis Romanus sum". Today, in the world of freedom, the proudest boast is "Ich bin ein Berliner." ... All free man, wherever they may live, are citizens of Berlin, and, therefore, as a free man, I take pride in the words, "Ich bin ein Berliner." —John F. Kennedy, speech in West Berlin, Jun 26, 1963

1445. Oppressed people cannot remain oppressed forever. —Martin Luther King Jr., "Letter from the Birmingham Jail", Jan 16, 1963

1446. No cause is left but the most ancient of all, the one, in fact, that from the beginning of our history has determined the very existence of politics, the cause of freedom versus tyranny. —Hannah Arendt, "Introduction", *On Revolution*, 1963

1447. Freedom is indivisible, and when one man is enslaved, all are not free. —John F. Kennedy, speech in West Berlin, Jun 26, 1963

1448. The free way of life proposes ends, but it does not prescribe means. —Robert F. Kennedy, "Berlin East and West", *The Pursuit of Justice*, 1964

1449. There can be no real freedom without the freedom to fail. —Eric Hoffer, *The Ordeal of Change*, 1964

1450. We must dare to think about "unthinkable things", because when things become "unthinkable," thinking stops and action becomes mindless. If we are to disabuse ourselves of old myths and to act wisely and creatively upon the new realities of our time, we must think about our problems with perfect freedom. —J. William Fulbright, speech in the U.S. Senate, Mar 25, 1964

1451. Freedom is the understanding of necessity and the transformation of necessity. —Mao Tse-tung, reported remarks, Aug 18, 1964

1452. Truth is on the side of the oppressed. —Malcolm X, speech at the Militant Labor Forum Symposium in New York City, May 29, 1964

1453. After you get your freedom, your enemy will respect you. —Malcolm X, speech in New York City, Dec 31, 1964

1454. Freedom to many means immediate betterment, as if by magic. ... Unless I can meet at least some of these aspirations, my support will wane and my head will roll just as surely as the tickbird follows the rhino. —Julius K. Nyerere, *Time*, Apr 9, 1964

1455. The suppression of civil liberties is to many less a matter of horror than the curtailment of the freedom to profit. —Marya Mannes, "A Time for Change", *But Will It Sell?*, 1964

1456. You can't separate peace from freedom because no one can be at peace unless he has his freedom. —Malcolm X, speech to the Militant Labor Forum Symposium in New York City, Jan 7, 1965

1457. Freedom is sweet, on the beat/ Freedom is sweet to the reet complete/ It's got zestness and bestness/ Sugar and cream on the blessedness,/ No more pains, no more chains,/ To keep free from being free./ Freedom is sweet fat, and that's for me. —Edward Kennedy Ellington, "Duke", "Sacred Concert", 1965

1458. Time is on the side of the oppressed today, it's against the oppressor. Truth is on the side of the oppressed today, it's against the oppressor. You don't need anything else. —Malcolm X, *Malcolm X Speaks*, 1965

1459. In a democracy dissent is an act of faith. Like medicine, the test of its value is not in its taste, but its effects. —J. William Fulbright, speech in the U.S. Senate, Apr 21, 1966

1460. Freedom is an internal achievement rather than an external judgment. —Adam Clayton Powell Jr., "Man's Debt to God", *Keep the Faith, Baby!*, 1967

1461. In the act of resistance the rudiments of freedom are already present. —Angela Yvonne Davis, *Lectures on Liberation, I*, 1968

1462. May God prevent us from becoming "right-thinking men"—that is to say men who agree perfectly with their own police. —Thomas Merton, quoted in his obituary, *The New York Times*, Dec 11, 1968

1463. We have to talk about liberating minds as well as liberating society. —Angela Yvonne Davis, open forum discussion with Herbert Marcuse at the University of California, Oct 24, 1969

1464. There are men—now in power in this country—who do not respect dissent, who cannot cope with turmoil, and who believe that the people of America are ready to support repression as long as it is done with a quiet voice and a business suit. And it is up to us to prove they are wrong. —John V. Lindsay, speech at the Univ. of California, Berkeley, Apr 2, 1970

1465. Yet we can maintain a free society only if we recognize that in a free society no one can win all the time. No one can have his own way all the time, and no one is right all the time. —Richard M. Nixon, Alfred M. Landon lecture at Kansas State Univ., Sep 16, 1970

1466. If you use words for political purposes, they soon lose whatever meaning they may have had. If you are tempted to brandish the word "free", remember that over the gates of Auschwitz there stretched—and still stretches—the inscription "Arbeit Macht Frei". —C.P. Snow, Baron Snow, speech at Loyola Univ., Chicago, 1970

1467. We know that the road to freedom has always been stalked by death. —Angela Yvonne Davis, "Tribute to George Jackson", *Daily World*, Aug 25, 1971

1468. The essence of a free life is being able to choose the style of living you prefer free from exclusion and without the compulsion of conformity or law. —Eleanor Holmes Norton, commencement address at Barnard College, New York City, Jun 6, 1972

1469. Since when have we Americans been expected to bow submissively to authority and speak with awe and reverence to those who represent us? —William O. Douglas, recalled on his retirement, concerning unjust arrests for disorderly conduct, Nov 12, 1975

1470. The biggest menace to American freedom is the intelligence community. —I.F. Stone, *Wilson Library Bulletin*, Sep, 1976

1471. There is no "slippery slope" toward loss of liberties, only a long staircase where each step downward must first be tolerated by the American people and their leaders. —Alan K. Simpson, *The New York Times*, Sep 26, 1982

1472. Only free men can negotiate; prisoners cannot enter into contracts. —Nelson Mandela, *Time*, Feb 25, 1985

1473. (American liberty) is premised on the accountability of free men and women for what they have done, not for what they may do. —Jon Newman, *The New York Times*, Nov 29, 1986

1474. We know what works: Freedom works. We know what's right: Freedom is right. We know how to secure a more just and prosperous life for man on earth: through free markets, free speech, free elections and the exercise of free will unhampered by the state. —George Bush, inaugural address, Jan 20, 1989

1475. I hope we have once again reminded people that man is not free unless government is limited. There's a clear cause and effect here that is as neat and predictable as a law of physics: as government expands, liberty contracts. —Ronald Reagan, farewell address, Jan 11, 1989

GOVERNMENT

1476. Good government obtains when those who are near are made happy, and those who are far off are attracted. —Confucius, *The Analects*, ca 480 B.C.

1477. Tzu-kung asked about government. The Master said, "Give them enough food, give them enough arms, and the common people will have trust in you." —Confucius, *The Analects*, ca. 480 B.C.

1478. The Master said, "Guide them by edicts, keep them in line with punishments, and the common people will stay out of trouble but will have no sense of shame. Guide them by virtue, keep them in line with the rites, and they will, besides having a sense of shame, reform themselves." —Confucius, *The Analects*, ca. 480 B.C.

1479. In a change of government, the poor change nothing beyond the change of their master. [*In principatu commutando saepius/ nil praeter domini nomen mutant pauperes.*] —Phaedrus, "The Ass and the Old Shepherd", *Fables*, 1st cent. A.D.

1480. It is very easy to accuse a government of imperfection, for all mortal things are full of it. [*Il est bien aisé d'accuser d'imperfection une police, car toutes choses mortelles en sont pleines.*] —Michel de Montaigne, "De la présomption", *Essais*, 1580-88

1481. Governments, like clocks, go from the motions men give them, and as governments are made and moved by men, so by them are they ruined too. Wherefore governments rather depend upon men than men upon governments. —William Penn, "Preface", *The Frame of Government of Pennsylvania*, 1682

1482. Let the people think they govern and they will be governed. —William Penn, *Some Fruits of Solitude in Reflections and Maxims*, 1693

1483. I speak of this incontestable truth: the social world is certainly the work of man. —Giovanni Battista Vico, *Scienza Nuova*, 1725

1484. Governments must be conformable to the nature of the governed; governments are even a result of that nature. —Giovanni Battista Vico, *Scienza Nuova*, 1725

1485. For forms of government let fools contest;/ Whate'er is best administer'd is best. —Alexander Pope, *Essay on Man*, 1733

1486. If it's true that you can't abolish vice, the science of those who govern is to at least see that it competes with the public good. [*S'il est vrai qu'on ne peut anéantir le vice, la science du ceux qui gouvernent est de le faire concourir au bien public.*] —Marquis de Vauvenargues, *Réflexions et maximes*, 1746

1487. For a state to be strong either the people must have freedom based on law or the sovereign must be all-powerful without any contradiction. [*Il faut, pour qu'un Etat soit puissant, ou que le peuple ait une liberté fondée sur les lois, ou que l'autorité souveraine soit affermie sans contradiction.*] —Voltaire, *Le Siècle de Louis XIV*, 1751

1488. Lawful and settled authority is very seldom resisted when it is well employed. —Samuel Johnson, *The Rambler*, 1750-52

1489. The body politic, as well as the human body, begins to die as soon as it is born, and carries in itself the causes of its destruction. [*Le corps politique, aussi bien que le corps de l'homme, commence à mourir dès sa naissance et porte en lui-même les causes de sa déstruction.*] —Jean Jacques Rousseau, *The Social Contract*, 1762

1490. In several countries it is maintained that citizens do not have the right to leave the country where they happened to have been born. What this says is clear: "This country is so bad and so misgoverned that we can't let anyone leave or everyone would want to." How much better to make it so the citizens want to stay and foreigners want to come. [*On a prétendu dans plusieurs pays qu'il n'était pas permis à un citoyen de sortir de la contrée ou le hasard l'a fait naître; le sens de cette loi est visiblement: "Ce pays est si mauvais et si mal gouverné que nous défendons à chaque individu d'en sortir, de peur que tout le monde n'en sorte." Faites mieux: donnez à tous vos sujets envie de demeurer chez vous, et aux étrangers d'y venir.*] —Voltaire, "Egalité", *Dictionnaire philosophique*, 1764

1491. A wise government knows how to enforce with temper or to conciliate with dignity. —George Grenville, speech during the Wilkes debate in the House of Commons, 1769

1492. I would not give half a guinea to live under one form of government rather than another. It is of no moment to the happiness of an individual. —Samuel Johnson, quoted by James Boswell, *Life of Samuel Johnson*, Mar 31, 1772

1493. A government of laws, and not of men. —John Adams, "Novanglus", *Boston Gazette*, 1774

1494. All government,—indeed, every human benefit and enjoyment, every virtue and every prudent act,—is founded on compromise and barter. —Edmund Burke, speech, "On Conciliation with the American Colonies", Mar 22, 1775

1495. Refined policy ever had been the parent of confusion, and ever will be so long as the world endures. Plain good intention, which is as easily discovered at the first view as fraud is surely detected at last, is, let me say, of no mean force in the government of mankind. —Edmund Burke, speech, "On Conciliation with the American Colonies", Mar 22, 1775

1496. All government is ultimately and essentially absolute. —Samuel Johnson, "On the American Revolutionaries", *Taxation No Tyranny*, 1775

1497. Society in every state is a blessing, but government, even in its best state is but a necessary evil; in its worst state, an intolerable one. —Thomas Paine, "Of the Origin and Design of Government in General", *Common Sense*, 1776

1498. Society is produced by our wants, and government by our wickedness; the former promotes our happiness positively by uniting our affections, the latter negatively by restraining our vices. —Thomas Paine, "Of the Origin and Design of Government in General", *Common Sense*, 1776

1499. It is error alone which needs the support of government. Truth can stand by itself. —Thomas Jefferson, *Notes on the State of Virginia*, 1782

1500. Experience has taught us that men will not adopt and carry into execution measures the best calculated for their own good without the intervention of a coercive power. —George Washington, letter to John Jay, Aug 1, 1786

1501. Why has government been instituted at all? Because the passions of men will not conform to the dictates of reason and justice, without constraint. —Alexander Hamilton, *The Federalist*, Dec 1, 1787

1502. It is not by consolidation, or concentration of powers, but by their distribution, that good government is effected. —Thomas Jefferson, *Autobiography*, 1787

1503. No man is a warmer advocate for proper restraints and wholesome checks in every department of government than I am; but I have never yet been able to discover the propriety of placing it absolutely out of the power of men to render essential services, because a possibility remains of their doing ill. —George Washington, letter to Bushrod Washington, Nov 10. 1787

1504. But what is government itself, but the greatest of all reflections on human nature? If men were angels, no government would be necessary. If angels were to govern men, neither external nor internal controls on government would be necessary. —James Madison, *The Federalist*, Feb 6, 1788

1505. Energy in government is essential to that security against external and internal danger, and to that prompt and salutary execution of the laws which enter into the very definition of good government. —James Madison, *Federalist*, Jan. 11, 1788

1506. Governments destitute of energy, will ever produce anarchy. —James Madison, speech to the Virginia Convention on adoption of the U.S. Constitution, Jun 7, 1788

1507. To model our political system upon speculations of lasting tranquility, is to calculate on the weaker springs of the human character. —Alexander Hamilton, *The Federalist*, Jan 5, 1788

1509. Governments arise either out of the people or over the people. —Thomas Paine, *The Rights of Man*, 1791

1510. The circumstances of the world are continually changing, and the opinions of men change also; and as Government is for the living, and not for the dead, it is the living only that have any right in it. —Thomas Paine, *The Rights of Man*, 1791

1511. Since government, even in its best state is an evil, the object principally to be aimed at is that we should have as little of it as the general peace of human society will permit. —William Godwin, *An Enquiry Concerning Political Justice*, 1793

1512. (Liberty) is indeed little less than a name, where the Government is too feeble to withstand the enterprises of faction, to confine each member of society within the limits prescribed by the law, and to maintain all in the secure and tranquil enjoyment of the rights of persons and property. —George Washington, *Farewell Address to the People of the United States*, Sep 19, 1796

1513. Without an army, authority, and discipline there is no political independence or civil liberty. [*Sans armée, sans force, sans discipline, il n'est ni indépendance politique ni liberté civil.*] —Napoleon I, speech to the National Guard of the Cisalpine Republic, May 14, 1797

1514. Governments are more the effect than the cause of that which we are. —Samuel Taylor Coleridge, letter to George Coleridge, Apr, 1798

1515. Don't forget that weakness produces civil wars, and that vigor maintains peace and prosperity in a state. [*N'oubliez pas que la faiblesse produit des guerres civiles, et que l'énergie maintient la tranquillité et la prospérité des Etats.*] —Napoleon I, letter to Gen. Commes, Mar 19, 1800

1516. It is in no one's interest to overturn a government in which everyone with ability can find a place. [*Personne n'a intérêt a renverser un gouvernement dans lequel tout ce qui a du mérite est placé.*] —Napoleon I, remarks quoted by Roederer, Aug 2, 1800

1517. A wise and frugal Government, which shall restrain men from injuring one another, shall leave them otherwise free to regulate their own pursuits of industry and improvement, and shall not take from the mouth of labor the bread it has earned—this is the sum of good government. —Thomas Jefferson, first inaugural address, Mar 4, 1801

1518. If we can prevent the government from wasting the labors of the people, under the pretence of taking care of them, they must become happy. —Thomas Jefferson, letter to Thomas Cooper, Nov 29, 1802

1519. See that government weighs as little as possible and does not unnecessarily burden the people. [*Veillez à ce que l'autorité se fasse sentir le moins possible et ne pèse pas inutilement sur les peuples.*] —Napoleon I, letter to Count Fouché, minister of police, Jan 1, 1809

1520. Every country has the government it deserves. [*Toute nation a le gouvernement qu'elle mérite.*] —Joseph de Maistre, *Lettres et opuscules inédits*, Aug 15, 1811

1521. Trust nothing to the enthusiasm of the people. Give them a strong and a just, and, if possible, a good, government; but, above all, a strong one. —1st Duke of Wellington, (Arthur Wellesley), letter to Lord William Bentinck, Dec 24, 1811

1522. Men are powerless to secure the future; institutions alone fix the destinies of nations. —Napoleon I, imperial séance, Jun 7, 1813

1523. No government can be maintained without the principle of fear as well as of duty. Good men will obey the last, but bad ones the former only. —Thomas Jefferson, letter to John Wayle Eppes, Sep 9, 1814

1524. The way to have good and safe government, is not to trust it all to one, but to divide it among the many, distributing to every one exactly the functions he is competent to (perform). —Thomas Jefferson, letter to Joseph C. Cabell, Feb 2, 1816

1525. Governments only keep their word when they are forced to, or when it is to their advantage. [*Les gouvernements ne tiennent leur parole que quand ils y sont forcés, ou que cela leur est avantageux.*] —Napoleon I, reported remarks, Feb 16, 1817

1526. Which is the best government? That which teaches us to govern ourselves. [*Welche Regierung die beste sei? Diejenige, die uns lehrt, uns selbst zu regieren.*] —Johann Wolfgang von Goethe, quoted by Bailey Saunders, *The Maxims and Reflections of Goethe*, 1893

1527. There are no necessary evils in government. Its evils exist only in its abuses. —Andrew Jackson, veto of Bank Bill, Jul 10, 1832

1528. Peoples and governments never have learned anything from history, or acted on principles deduced from it. —Georg Wilhelm Friedrich Hegel, *Introduction to the Philosophy of History*, 1832

1529. If the government would confine itself to equal protection, and, as Heaven does its rains, shower its favors alike on the high and the low, the rich and the poor, it would be an unqualified blessing. —Andrew Jackson, veto message, Jul 10, 1832

1530. What would happen if only the middle classes were involved in making the laws? One could be sure that they would not be extravagant with taxes, because there is nothing so disastrous for a small fortune as a large tax. ... Therefore, government by the middle classes would seem to be the most economical. [*Admettez, au contraire, que ce soient les classes moyennes qui seules fassent la loi. L'on peut compter qu'elles ne prodigueront pas les impôts, parce qu'il n'y a rien de si désastreux qu'une grosse taxe venant à frapper une petite fortune. ... Le gouvernement des classes moyennes me semble devoir être ... le plus economique.*] —Alexis, Comte de Tocqueville, *Democracy in America*, 1835

1531. Every central government worships uniformity: uniformity relieves it from inquiry into an infinity of details, which must be attended to if rules have to be adapted to different men, instead of indiscriminately subjecting all men to the same rule. [*Tout gouvernement central adore l'uniformité; l'uniformité lui évite l'examen d'une infinité de détails dont il devrait s'occuper, s'il fallait faire la règle pour les hommes, au lieu de faire passer indistinctement tous les hommes sous la meme règle.*] —Alexis, Comte de Tocqueville, *Democracy in America*, 1839

1532. A decent and manly examination of the acts of Government should be not only tolerated, but encouraged. —William Henry Harrison, inaugural address, Mar 4, 1841

1533. The greatest need a people have is for government; their greatest happiness is having good government. [*Le plus grand besoin d'un peuple est d'être gouverné; son plus grand bonheur, d'etre bien gouverné.*] —Joseph Joubert, *Pensées*, 1842

1534. In the long-run every Government is the exact symbol of its People, with their wisdom and unwisdom; we have to say, Like People like Government. —Thomas Carlyle, *Past and Present*, 1843

1535. Government is at best but an expedient; but most governments are usually, and all governments are sometimes, inexpedient. —Henry David Thoreau, *Civil Disobedience*, 1849

1536. The objections which have been brought against a standing army, and they are many and weighty, and deserve to prevail, may also at last be brought against a standing government. —Henry David Thoreau, *Civil Disobedience*, 1849

1537. To be governed is to be watched over, inspected, spied on, directed, legislated at, regulated, docketed, indoctrinated, preached at, controlled, assessed, weighed, censored, ordered about, by men who have neither the right nor the knowledge nor the virtue. —Pierre Joseph Proudhon, *Idée Générale de la Révolution au XIXe Siècle*, 1851

1538. The test of every religious, political, or educational system, is the man which it forms. If a system injures the intelligence it is bad. If it injures the character it is vicious, if it injures the conscience it is criminal. —Henri Frederic Amiel, *Journal*, Jun 17, 1852

1539. It is safe to assert that no government proper ever had a provision in its organic law for its own termination. —Abraham Lincoln, first inaugural address, Mar 4, 1861

1540. Perpetuity is implied, if not expressed, in the fundamental law of all national governments. —Abraham Lincoln, first inaugural address, Mar 4, 1861

1541. Government and co-operation are in all things the laws of life; anarchy and competition the laws of death. —John Ruskin, *Unto This Last*, 1862

1542. It has long been a grave question whether any government not too strong for the liberties of its people, can be strong enough to maintain its own existence? —Abraham Lincoln, "Response to a Serenade", Nov 10, 1864

1543. The test of political institutions is the condition of the country whose future they regulate. —Benjamin Disraeli, speech on "Conservative Principles", Apr 3, 1872

1544. Man is about the same, in the main, whether with despotism, or whether with freedom. —Walt Whitman, "Democracy in the New World", *Notes Left Over*, 1881

1545. There are times when one must govern liberally and times when one must be dictatorial; everything changes, there is no eternity here. [*Es gibt Zeiten, wo man liberal regieren muss, und Zeiten, wo man diktatorisch regieren muss; es wechselt alles, hier gibt es keine Ewigkeit.*] —Prince Otto von Bismarck, speech in the Reichstag, Feb 24, 1881

1546. The worst thing in this world, next to anarchy, is government. —Henry Ward Beecher, *Proverbs from Plymouth Pulpit*, 1887

1547. The purification of politics is an iridescent dream. Government is force. —John James Ingalls, *The New York World*, 1890

1548. The government's like a mule, it's slow and it's sure; it's slow to turn, and it's sure to turn the way you don't want it. —Ellen Glasgow, *The Voice of the People*, 1900

1549. Government is a matter of insight and of sympathy. If you don't know what the great body of men are up against how are you going to help them? —Woodrow Wilson, speech in Buffalo, New York, Sep 2, 1912

1550. What is a Government for except to dictate! If it does not dictate, then it is not a Government. —David Lloyd George, *War Memoirs*, 1933-36

1551. In anarchy it's not just the king who loses his rights but the worker as well. [*Wo nichts ist, da hat nicht nur der Kaiser, sondern auch der Proletarier sein Recht verloren.*] —Max Weber, *Politik als Beruf*, 1918-19

1552. Government is a very natural thing and in most instances ought to be a very normal and deliberate proceeding. —Warren G. Harding, speech in Marion, Ohio, Jul 5, 1920

1553. A good government remains the greatest of human blessings, and no nation has ever enjoyed it. —William Ralph Inge, "The State, Visible and Invisible", *Outspoken Essays: Second Series*, 1922

1554. The experience of Russia, more than any theories, has demonstrated that all government, whatever its forms or pretenses, is a dead weight that paralyzes the free spirit and activities of the masses. —Emma Goldman, *My Disillusionment in Russia*, 1923

1555. Order is not pressure which is imposed on society from without, but an equilibrium which is set up from within. [*Orden no es una presión que desde fuera se ejerce sobre la sociedad, sino un equilibro que se suscita en su interior.*] —Jose Ortega y Gasset, *Mirabeau o el político*, 1927

1556. We get the fundamental confusion that government, since it can correct much abuse, can also create righteousness. —Herbert Hoover, letter to William O. Thompson, Dec 30, 1929

1557. Governments are best classified by considering who are the "somebodies" they are in fact endeavoring to satisfy. —Alfred North Whitehead, *Adventures in Ideas*, 1933

1558. That government which thinks in terms of humanity will continue. —Franklin D. Roosevelt, campaign speech in Rochester, New York, Oct 17, 1936

1559. Mankind needs government, but in regions where anarchy has prevailed they will, at first, submit only to despotism. We must therefore seek first to secure government, even though despotic, and only when government has become habitual can we hope successfully to make it democratic. —Bertrand Russell, *Power*, 1938

1560. Any system of government will work when everything is going well. It's the system that functions in the pinches that survives. —John F. Kennedy, *Why England Slept*, 1940

1561. Government is more than the sum of all the interests; it is the paramount interest, the public interest. It must be the efficient, effective agent of a responsible citizenry, not the shelter of the incompetent and the corrupt. —Adlai E. Stevenson Jr., speech in Bloomington, Illinois, 1948

1562. In our complex world, there cannot be fruitful initiative without government, but unfortunately there can be government without initiative. —Bertrand Russell, "Control and Initiative", *Authority and the Individual*, 1949

1563. The really basic thing in government is policy. Bad administration, to be sure, can destroy good policy, but good administration can never save bad policy. —Adlai E. Stevenson Jr., speech in Los Angeles, California, Sep 11, 1952

1564. Government cannot be stronger or more tough-minded than its people. It cannot be more inflexibly committed to the task than they. —Adlai E. Stevenson Jr., speech in Chicago, Illinois, Sep 29, 1952

1565. No matter how noble the objectives of a government, if it blurs decency and kindness, cheapens human life, and breeds ill will and suspicion—it is an evil government. —Eric Hoffer, *The Passionate State of Mind*, 1954

1566. The basis of effective government is public confidence. —John F. Kennedy, message to Congress, Apr 27, 1961

1567. I think the inherent right of the Government to lie to save itself when faced with nuclear disaster is basic. —Arthur Sylvester, speech in New York City, Dec 6, 1962

1568. It is a function of government to invent philosophies to explain the demands of its own convenience. —Murray Kempton, "Academic Pride", *America Comes of Middle Age*, 1963

1569. You talk about capitalism and communism and all that sort of thing, but the important thing is the struggle everybody is engaged in to get better living conditions, and they are not interested too much in the form of government. —Bernard Baruch, press conference in New York City, Aug 18, 1964

1570. Government is like a big baby—an alimentary canal with a big appetite at one end and no sense of responsibility at the other. —Ronald Reagan, quoted, *The New York Times Magazine*, Nov 14, 1965

1571. To govern is always to choose among disadvantages. —Charles De Gaulle, *The New York Times*, Nov 14, 1965

1572. The single most exciting thing you encounter in government is competence, because it's so rare. —Daniel P. Moynihan, *The New York Times*, Mar 2, 1976

1573. I believe that government is the problem, not the answer. —Ronald Reagan, *Washington Post*, Apr 20, 1976

1574. The problem isn't a shortage of fuel, it's a surplus of government. —Ronald Reagan, *Newsweek*, Oct 1, 1979

1575. A government is not legitimate merely because it exists. —Jeane J. Kirkpatrick, on Sandinista government in Nicaragua, *Time*, Jun 17, 1985

1576. The nine most terrifying words in the English language are, "I'm from the government and I'm here to help." —Ronald Reagan, speech, Aug 12, 1986

1577. An entirely new problem should be recognised as the fundamental problem of a rational political theory: how is the state to be constituted so that bad rulers can be got rid of without bloodshed, without violence? —Sir Karl Popper, "Popper on Democracy", *The Economist*, Apr 23, 1988

GOVERNMENT AND BUSINESS

1578. Money is, with propriety, considered as the vital principle of the body politic; as that which sustains its life and motion, and enables it to perform its most essential functions. —Alexander Hamilton, *The Federalist*, Dec 28, 1787

1579. It is in the interests of those who govern and those who are governed to extend the political importance of the industrialists, since, on the one hand, they are always inclined to support the existing government and, on the other, they work ceaselessly to limit power and to decrease taxation. —Claude Henri, Comte de Saint-Simon, *Industry*, 1817

1580. In democracies, nothing is more great or more brilliant than commerce. [*Dans les démocraties, il n'y a rien de plus grand ni de plus brillant que le commerce.*] —Alexis, Comte de Tocqueville, *Democracy in America*, 1839

1581. Trade and commerce, if they were not made of Indian rubber, would never manage to bounce over the obstacles which legislators are continually putting in their way. —Henry David Thoreau, *Civil Disobedience*, 1849

1582. Property is a god. This god already has its theology (called state politics and juridical right) and also its morality, the most adequate expression of which is summed up in the phrase: "That man is worth so much!" —Michael Bakunin, *The Knouto-Germanic Empire and the Social Revolution*, 1871

1583. Glory be, whin business gets above sellin' tinpinny nails in a brown paper cornucopy, 't is hard to tell it fr'm murther. —Finley Peter Dunne, "On Wall Street", *Mr. Dooley's Opinions*, 1900

1584. The biggest corporation, like the humblest private citizen, must be held to strict compliance with the will of the people as expressed in the fundamental law. —Theodore Roosevelt, speech in Cincinnati, Ohio, 1902

1585. The man who wrongly holds that every human right is secondary to his profit must now give way to the advocate of human welfare, who rightly maintains that every man holds his property subject to the general right of the community to regulate its use to whatever degree the public welfare may require it. —Theodore Roosevelt, speech at Osawatomie, Kansas, Aug 31, 1910

1586. Politics is the reflex of the business and industrial world. —Emma Goldman, "The Tragedy of Women's Emancipation", *Anarchism and Other Essays*, 1911

1587. Sound business need have no fear of progressive government. It is only the business that thrives on special privilege that is in danger. —Woodrow Wilson, speech in Chicago, Illinois, Feb 12, 1912

1588. We demand that big business give the people a square deal; in return we must insist that when anyone engaged in big business honestly endeavors to do right he shall himself be given a square deal. —Theodore Roosevelt, *Autobiography*, 1913

1589. Civilization and profits go hand in hand. —Calvin Coolidge, speech in New York City, Nov 20, 1920

1590. We want wealth, but there are many other things we want very much more. Among them are peace, honor, charity, and idealism. —Calvin Coolidge, speech in Washington, D.C., Jan 17, 1924

1591. The chief business of the American people is business. —Calvin Coolidge, speech to the American Society of Newspaper Editors, Jan 17, 1925

1592. An organised money market has many advantages. But it is not a school of social ethics or of political responsibility. —Richard Tawney, *Religion and The Rise of Capitalism*, 1926

1593. If you are going to try to go to war, or to prepare for war, in a capitalist country, you have got to let business make money out of the process or business won't work. —Henry Stimson, *Diary*, Aug 26, 1940

1594. What is good for the country is good for General Motors, and vice versa. —Charles E. Wilson, remarks to the press, Jan 23, 1953

1595. My father always told me that all business men were sons of bitches, but I never believed it till now. —John F. Kennedy, reported remarks on steel industry executives who increased prices, Apr 11, 1962

1596. No political party can be a friend of the American people which is not a friend of American business. —Lyndon Baines Johnson, speech to the Houston Chamber of Commerce, Aug 12, 1963

1597. Nothing is illegal if one hundred businessmen decide to do it, and that's true anywhere in the world. —Andrew Young, *Rolling Stone*, Mar 24, 1977

1598. I learned in business that you had to be very careful when you told somebody that's working for you to do something, because the chances are very high he'd do it. In government, you don't have to worry about that. —George P. Shultz, *The New York Times*, Oct 14, 1984

1599. Little ol'boy in the Panhandle told me the other day you can still make a small fortune in agriculture. Problem is, you got to start with a large one. —Jim Hightower, speech to the Dallas Chamber of Commerce, *The New York Times*, Mar 9, 1986

1600. The only difference between a pigeon and the American farmer today is that a pigeon can still make a deposit on a John Deere. —Jim Hightower, speech to the Dallas Chamber of Commerce, *The New York Times*, Mar 9, 1986

INTERNATIONAL AFFAIRS/DIPLOMACY

1601. The rulers of the state are the only ones who should have the privilege of lying, either at home or abroad; they may be allowed to lie for the good of the state. —Plato, *The Republic*, ca. 390 B.C.

1602. Wisdom is better than weapons of war. —Bible, *Ecclesiates*, ca. 180 B.C.

1603. An ambassador is an honest man sent to lie abroad for the good of his country. —Sir Henry Wotton, written in the autograph album of Christopher Fleckmore, 1604

1604. If a man be gracious and courteous to strangers, it shows he is a citizen of the world, and that his heart is no island cut off from other lands, but a continent that joins to them. —Sir Francis Bacon, "Of Goodness and Goodness of Nature", *Essays*, 1625

1605. The problem of establishing a perfect civil constitution is subordinate to the problem of a law-governed external relationship with other states, and cannot be solved unless the latter is also solved. —Immanuel Kant, *Idea for a Universal History with a Cosmopolitan Purpose*, 1784

1606. Even to observe neutrality you must have a strong government. —Alexander Hamilton, speech to the Constitutional Convention, Jun 29, 1787

1607. I think every nation has a right to establish that form of government, under which it conceives it may live most happy; provided it infracts no right, or is not dangerous to others; and that no governments ought to interfere with the internal concerns of another, except for the security of what is due to themselves. —George Washington, letter to the Marquis de Lafayette, Dec 25, 1789

1608. Peace with all nations, and the right which that gives us with respect to all nations, are our object. —Thomas Jefferson, letter to Mr. Dumas, Mar 24, 1793

1609. It is our true policy to steer clear of permanent alliance with any portion of the foreign world. —George Washington, *Farewell Address to the People of the United States*, Sep 17, 1796

1610. There can be no greater error than to expect or calculate upon real favors from nation to nation. —George Washington, *Farewell Address to the People of the United States*, Sep 17, 1796

1611. I have always given it as my decided opinion that no nation had a right to intermeddle in the internal concerns of another; that every one had a right to form and adopt whatever government they liked best to live under themselves; and that, if this country could, consistently with its engagements, maintain a strict neutrality and thereby preserve peace, it was bound to do so by motives of policy, interest, and every other considerations. —George Washington, letter to James Monroe, Aug 25, 1796

1612. Peace, commerce, and honest friendship with all nations—entangling alliances with none. —Thomas Jefferson, first inaugural address, Mar 4, 1801

1613. It is but seldom that any one overt act produces hostilities between two nations; there exists, more commonly, a previous jealousy and ill will, a predisposition to take offense. —Washington Irving, "English Writers on America", *The Sketch Book of Geoffrey Crayon, Gent.*, 1819-20

1614. The foreign policy adopted by our government is to do justice to all, and to submit to wrong by none. —Andrew Jackson, second inaugural address, Mar 4, 1833

1615. Our institutions are essentially pacific. Peace and friendly intercourse with all nations are as much the desire of our Government as they are the interest of the people. —Andrew Jackson, sixth annual message to Congress, Dec 1, 1834

1616. A faithful observance in the management of our foreign relations of the practice of speaking plainly, dealing justly, and requiring truth and justice in return (are) the best conservatives of the peace of nations. —Martin Van Buren, fourth annual message to Congress, Dec 5, 1840

1617. The sun never sets upon the interests of this country. —3rd Viscount Palmerston, speech in the House of Commons, Mar 1, 1843

1618. In the management of our foreign relations it will be my aim to observe a careful respect for the rights of other nations, while our own will be the subject of constant watchfulness. Equal and exact justice should characterize all our intercourse with foreign countries. —James K. Polk, inaugural address, Mar 4, 1845

1619. We have no eternal allies, and we have no perpetual enemies. Our interests are eternal and perpetual, and those interests it is our duty to follow. —3rd Viscount Palmerston, (Henry John Temple), speech in the House of Commons, Mar 1, 1848

1620. Tranquility at home and peaceful relations abroad constitute the true permanent policy of our country. —James K. Polk, fourth annual message to Congress, Dec 5, 1848

1621. As the Roman in days of old held himself free from indignity when he could say Civis Romanus sum, so also a British subject, in whatever land he may be, shall feel confident that the watchful eye and the strong arm of England will protect him against injustice and wrong. —3rd Viscount Palmerston, speech in the House of Commons, Jun 25, 1850

1622. In ninety-nine cases out of a hundred, when there is a quarrel between two states, it is generally occasioned by some blunder of a ministry. —Benjamin Disraeli, speech in the House of Commons, Feb 19, 1858

1623. Colonies do not cease to be colonies because they are independent. —Benjamin Disraeli, speech in the House of Commons, Feb 5, 1863

1624. The foreign policy of the noble Earl (Russell, foreign secretary) ... may be summed up in two short homely but expressive words, "meddle" and "muddle". —14th Earl of Derby, speech in the House of Lords, Feb, 1864

1625. The old-world diplomacy of Europe was largely carried on in drawing rooms, and, to a great extent, of necessity still is so. Nations touch at their summits. —Walter Bagehot, *The English Constitution*, 1867

1626.   If we are to negotiate peace ... I imagine an essentially modest role ... that of an honest broker who means to do business. —Prince Otto von Bismarck, speech to the Reichstag, 19 Feb, 1878

1627.   Lord Salisbury and myself have brought you back peace—but a peace, I hope, with honour. —Benjamin Disraeli, speech in the House of Lords, Jul 16, 1878

1628.   Vacillation and inconsistency are as incompatible with successful diplomacy as they are with the national dignity. —Benjamin Harrison, speech in Indianapolis, Indiana, Sep 11, 1888

1629.   We Americans have no commission from God to police the world. —Benjamin Harrison, campaign speech, 1888

1630.   I asked Tom if countries always apologized when they had done wrong, and he says: "Yes; the little ones does." —Mark Twain, *Tom Sawyer Abroad*, 1894

1631.   Will it not be wise to allow the friendship between nations to rest upon deep and permanent things? ... Irritations of the cuticle must not be confounded with heart failure. —Benjamin Harrison, *North American Review*, Mar, 1901

1632.   There is a homely old adage which runs: "Speak softly and carry a big stick; you will go far." If the American Nation will speak softly, and yet build, and keep at a pitch of the highest training, a thoroughly efficient navy, the Monroe Doctrine will go far. —Theodore Roosevelt, speech in Chicago, Illinois, Apr 2, 1903

1633.   Courtesy, moderation, and self-restraint should mark international, no less than private, intercourse. —Theodore Roosevelt, directive to government officials, Mar 10, 1904

1634.   Diplomacy, n. The patriotic art of lying for one's country. —Ambrose Bierce, *The Devil's Dictionary*, 1906

1635.   Consul, n. In American politics, a person who having failed to secure an office from the people is given one by the Administration on condition that he leave the country. —Ambrose Bierce, *The Devil's Dictionary*, 1906

1636.   We can afford to exercise the self-restraint of a really great nation which realizes its own strength and scorns to misuse it. —Woodrow Wilson, message to Congress, Aug 27, 1913

1637.   When I have made a promise as a man I try to keep it, and I know no other rule permissible to a nation. —Woodrow Wilson, speech in Philadelphia, Pennsylvania, Jul 4, 1914

1638.   The United States must be neutral in fact as well as in name. We must be impartial in thought as well as in action. —Woodrow Wilson, "Proclamation", Aug 19, 1914

1639.   There is such a thing as man being too proud to fight. There is such a thing as a nation being so right that it does not need to convince others by force that it is right. —Woodrow Wilson, speech in Philadelphia, Pennsylvania, May 10, 1915

1640.   There must be, not a balance of power, but a community of power; not organized rivalries, but an organized common peace. —Woodrow Wilson, speech to the U.S. Senate, Jan 22, 1917

1641.   Open covenants of peace, openly arrived at, after which there shall be no private international understandings of any kind but diplomacy shall proceed always frankly and in the public view. —Woodrow Wilson, first of the "Fourteen Points" given in a speech to Congress, Jan 18, 1918

1642.   Whenever our policy in the West has run aground, it has always been wise to try something in the East. [*In Zeiten, in denen unsere Politik im Westen festgefahren war, ist es immer richtig gewesen, aktiv im Osten zu werden.*] —Hans von Seeckt, at the Rapallo Conference, quoted by Erich Eyck, *Geschichte der Weimarer Republik*, Apr, 1922

1643. The friendships of nations, built on common interests, cannot survive the mutability of those interests. —Agnes Repplier, "Allies", *Under Dispute*, 1924

1644. The foreign policy of America can best be described by one word—peace. —Calvin Coolidge, acceptance speech as Republican nominee for president, Aug 14, 1924

1645. Our foreign policy has one primary object, and that is peace. —Herbert Hoover, speech at Palo Alto, California, Aug 11, 1928

1646. We never lost a war and we never won a conference in our lives. I believe that we could without any degree of egotism, single-handed lick any nation in the world. But we can't confer with Costa Rica and come home with our shirts on. —Will Rogers, quoted by Paula McSpadden Love, *The Will Rogers Book*, 1972

1647. Diplomacy is to do and say the nastiest thing in the nicest way. —Isaac Goldberg, *The Reflex*, 1930

1648. If our civilization is to be perpetuated, the great causes of world peace, world disarmament and world recovery must prevail. They cannot prevail until a path to their attainment is built upon honest friendship, mutual confidence, and proper co-operation among the nations. —Herbert Hoover, statement to the press, Nov 23, 1932

1649. In the field of foreign policy I would dedicate this nation to the policy of the good neighbor. —Franklin D. Roosevelt, acceptance speech as the Democratic nominee for president, Jul 2, 1932

1650. I have always said that a conference was held for one reason only, to give everybody a chance to get sore at everybody else. Sometimes it takes two or three conferences to scare up a war, but generally one will do it. —Will Rogers, syndicated column, *The New York Times*, Jul 6, 1933

1651. Time is the very material commodity which the Foreign Office is expected to provide in the same way as other departments provide other war material. —Robert, 1st Baron Vansittart, memorandum, Dec 31, 1936

1652. Outside the kingdom of the Lord there is no nation which is greater than any other. God and history will remember your judgment. —Haile Selassie, speech at the League of Nations, 1936

1653. Much of what Mr. Wallace calls his global thinking is, no matter how you slice it, still globaloney. Mr. Wallace's warp of sense and his woof of nonsense is very tricky cloth out of which to cut the pattern of a postwar world. —Clare Boothe Luce, speech to the House of Representatives, Feb, 1943

1654. In foreign relations, as in all other relations, a policy has been formed only when commitments and power have been brought into balance. —Walter Lippmann, *U.S. Foreign Policy*, 1943

1655. There is nothing more likely to start disagreement among people or countries than an agreement. —E.B. White, "My Day", *One Man's Meat*, 1944

1656. When Kansas and Colorado have a quarrel over the water in the Arkansas River they don't call out the National Guard in each state and go to war over it. They bring a suit in the Supreme Court of the United States and abide by the decision. There isn't a reason in the world why we cannot do that internationally. —Harry S Truman, speech in Kansas City, Missouri, Apr, 1945

1657. My (foreign) policy is to be able to take a ticket at Victoria Station and go anywhere I damn well please. —Ernest Bevin, *The Spectator*, Apr 20, 1951

1658. Foreign policy must be clear, consistent and confident. —Dwight D. Eisenhower, State of the Union message, Feb 2, 1953

1659. Whatever America hopes to bring to pass in the world must first come to pass in the heart of America. —Dwight D. Eisenhower, first inaugural address, Jan 20, 1953

1660. By this I mean that a political society does not live to conduct foreign policy; it would be more correct to say that it conducts foreign policy in order to live. —George F. Kennan, Stafford Little Lectures, Princeton Univ., Mar, 1954

1661. For the nation's purposes always exceed its means, and it is finding a balance between means and ends that is the heart of foreign policy and that makes it such a speculative, uncertain business. —Adlai E. Stevenson Jr., *Call to Greatness*, 1954

1662. All diplomacy is a continuation of war by other means. —Chou En-lai, *Saturday Evening Post*, Mar 27, 1954

1663. A Foreign Secretary ... is always faced with this cruel dilemma. Nothing he can say can do very much good, and almost anything he may say may do a great deal of harm. Anything he says that is not obvious is dangerous; whatever is not trite is risky. He is forever poised between the cliche and the indiscretion. —Harold Macmillan, speech in the House of Commons, Jul 27, 1955

1664. I never discuss discussions. —Dag Hammarskjold, after talks with Soviet leaders, *Look*, Sep 19, 1956

1665. A foreign policy is not difficult to state. We are for peace, first, last and always, for very simple reasons. We know that it is only in a peaceful atmosphere, a peace with justice, one in which we can be confident, that America can prosper as we have known prosperity in the past. —Dwight D. Eisenhower, remarks to League of Women Voters, Washington. D.C., May 1, 1957

1666. You don't promote the cause of peace by talking only to people with whom you agree. —Dwight D. Eisenhower, news conference, Jan 30, 1957

1667. Until we stop pushing the Kremlin against a closed door, we shall never learn whether it would be prepared to go through an open one. —George F. Kennan, Reith Lectures on BBC radio, 1957

1668. The true end of political action is, after all, to affect the deeper convictions of men; this the atomic bomb cannot do. The suicidal nature of this weapon renders it unsuitable both as a sanction of diplomacy and as the basis of an alliance. —George F. Kennan, Reith Lectures on BBC radio, 1957

1669. What we call foreign affairs is no longer foreign affairs. It's a local affair. Whatever happens in Indonesia is important to Indiana. ... We must understand people. As long as any ... cannot enjoy the blessings of peace with justice, then indeed there is no peace anywhere. —Dwight D. Eisenhower, speech in Arlington, Virginia, Jun 12, 1959

1670. Let every nation know, whether it wishes us well or ill, that we shall pay any price, bear any burden, meet any hardship, support any friend, oppose any foe, to assure the survival and the success of liberty. —John F. Kennedy, inaugural address, Jan 20, 1961

1671. Diplomacy and defense are not substitutes for one another. Either alone would fail. —John F. Kennedy, speech at Univ. of Washington, Seattle, Nov 16, 1961

1672. So let us begin anew—remembering on both sides (Soviet and American) that civility is not a sign of weakness, and sincerity is always subject to proof. Let us never negotiate out of fear, but let us never fear to negotiate. —John F. Kennedy, inaugural address, Jan 20, 1961

1673. Every government is in some respects a problem for every other government, and it will always be this way so long as the sovereign state, with its supremely self-centered rationale, remains the basis of international life. —George F. Kennan, *Russia and the West under Lenin and Stalin*, 1961

1674. The freedom of the city is not negotiable. We cannot negotiate with those who say, "What's mine is mine and what's yours is negotiable." —John F. Kennedy, televised speech, Jul 25, 1961

1675. A state worthy of the name has no friends—only interests. —Charles De Gaulle, quoted by former aide Constantin Melnick, *Newsweek*, Oct 1, 1962

1676. Great Britain has lost an Empire and has not yet found a role. —Dean Acheson, speech at the U.S. Military Academy, West Point, New York, Dec 5, 1962

1677. Diplomats are useful only in fair weather. As soon as it rains they drown in every drop. —Charles De Gaulle, quoted by former aide Constantin Melnick, *Newsweek*, Oct 1, 1962

1678. The purpose of foreign policy is not to provide an outlet for our own sentiments of hope or indignation; it is to shape real events in a real world. —John F. Kennedy, speech at the Mormon Tabernacle, Salt Lake City, Sep 26, 1963

1679. We shall be judged more by what we do at home than what we preach abroad. —John F. Kennedy, State of the Union address, Jan 14, 1963

1680. Any man and any nation that seeks peace—and hates war—and is willing to fight the good fight against hunger, and disease and ignorance and misery will find the United States of America by their side, willing to walk with them—walk with them every step of the way. —Lyndon Baines Johnson, speech to the United Nations General Assembly, Dec 17, 1963

1681. We keep a vigil of peace around the world. —Lyndon Baines Johnson, speech in Gettysburg, Pennsylvania, May 30, 1963

1682. We must recognize that every nation determines its policies in terms of its own interests. —John F. Kennedy, speech at the Mormon Tabernacle, Salt Lake City, Sep 26, 1963

1683. A nation can be no stronger abroad than she is at home. Only an America which practices what it preaches about equal rights and social justice will be respected by those whose choice affects our future. —John F. Kennedy, speech prepared for delivery in Dallas the day of his assassination, Nov 22, 1963

1684. This is the devilish thing about foreign affairs: they are foreign and will not always conform to our whim. —James Reston, *The New York Times*, Dec 16, 1964

1685. You can always survive a mistake in domestic affairs but you can get killed by one made in foreign policy. —John F. Kennedy, quoted, *Saturday Review*, Mar 7, 1964

1686. Our ultimate goal is a world without war. A world made safe for diversity, in which all good men, goods and ideas can freely move across every border and every boundary. —Lyndon Baines Johnson, State of the Union address, Jan 8, 1964

1687. We are handicapped by (foreign) policies based on old myths rather than current realities. —J. William Fulbright, speech in the U.S. Senate, Mar 27, 1964

1688. Small nations are like indecently dressed women. They tempt the evil-minded. —Julius K. Nyerere, *Reporter*, Apr 9, 1964

1689. After four years at the United Nations I sometimes yearn for the peace and tranquility of a political convention. —Adlai E. Stevenson Jr., *The New York Times*, Aug 14, 1964

1690. Diplomacy is letting someone else have your way. —Lester B. Pearson, *Vancouver Sun*, Mar 18, 1965

1691. There is now a balance of terror. —Alex Quaison-Sackey, *Quote*, Jun 27, 1965

1692. Men and nations do behave wisely, once all other alternatives have been exhausted. —Abba Eban, *Vogue*, Aug 1, 1967

1693. Foreign relations are like human relations. They are endless. The solution of one problem usually leads to another. —James Reston, *Sketches in the Sand*, 1967

1694. Men may be linked in friendship. Nations are linked only by interests. —Rolf Hochhuth, *The Soldiers*, 1967

1695. Nations, like individuals, have to limit their objectives, or take the consequences. —James Reston, *Sketches in the Sand*, 1967

1696. If there ever was in the history of humanity an enemy who was truly universal, an enemy whose acts and moves trouble the entire world, threaten the entire world, attack the entire world in any way or another, that real and really universal enemy is precisely Yankee imperialism. —Fidel Castro, speech to the International Cultural Congress in Havana, Jan 12, 1968

1697. I report to you that our country is challenged at home and abroad: that it is our will that is being tried and not our strength; our sense of purpose and not our ability to achieve a better America. —Lyndon Baines Johnson, State of the Union address, Jan 17, 1968

1698. Why employ intelligent and highly paid ambassadors and then go and do their work for them? You don't buy a canary and sing yourself. —Sir Alec Douglas-Home, *The New York Times*, Apr 21, 1969

1699. If, when the chips are down, the world's most powerful nation, the United States of America, acts like a pitiful, helpless giant, the forces of totalitarianism and anarchy will threaten free nations and free institutions throughout the world. —Richard M. Nixon, televised speech, Apr 30, 1970

1700. Diplomacy...means the art of nearly deceiving all your friends, but not quite deceiving all your enemies. —Kofi Busia, interview, Feb 2, 1970

1701. I don't like hypocrisy—even in international relations. —Kofi Busia, interview, Feb 2, 1970

1702. Our idea is to create a situation in which those lands to which we have obligations or in which we have interests, if they are ready to fight a fire, should be able to count on us to furnish the hose and water. —Richard M. Nixon, *The New York Times*, Mar 10, 1971

1703. No foreign policy—no matter how ingenious—has any chance of success if it is born in the minds of a few and carried in the hearts of none. —Henry A. Kissinger, speech to the International Platform Association, Aug 2, 1973

1704. Making foreign policy is a little bit like making pornographic movies. It's more fun doing it than watching it. —William P. Rogers, *Chicago Sun-Times*, Jun 29, 1976

1705. Our greatest foreign policy problem is our divisions at home. Our greatest foreign policy need is national cohesion and a return to the awareness that in foreign policy we are all engaged in a common national endeavor. —Henry A. Kissinger, speech to the Boston World Affairs Council, Mar 11, 1976

1706. The (Carter) administration doesn't know the difference between being a diplomat and a doormat. —Ronald Reagan, *U.S. News & World Report*, May 7, 1979

1707. He who tugs Uncle Sam's beard too hard risks reprisal from the mightiest nation on the face of this earth. —George S. McGovern, *The Observer*, Nov 25, 1979

1708. The management of a balance of power is a permanent undertaking, not an exertion that has a foreseeable end. —Henry A. Kissinger, *White House Years*, 1979

1709. It was ... a Foreign Office joke that I could never make a speech of any length without using the word "mankind"; it seems to me a good word for a Foreign Secretary to have firmly fixed in his head. —Michael Stewart, *Life and Labour*, 1980

1710. The ultimate determinant in the struggle now going on for the world will not be bombs and rockets but a test of wills and ideas—a trial of spiritual resolve; the values we hold, the beliefs we cherish and the ideas to which we are dedicated. —Ronald Reagan, speech to British parliament, Jun 8, 1982

1711. What has happened to the dreams of the United Nations's founders? What has happened to the spirit which created the United Nations? The answer is clear: Governments got in the way of the dreams of the people. —Ronald Reagan, speech to the United Nations General Assembly, Sep 26, 1983

1712. I have a habit of comparing the phraseology of communiques, one with another across the years, and noting a certain similarity of words, a certain similarity of optimism in the reports which followed the summit meetings and a certain similarity in the lack of practical results during the ensuing years. —Margaret Thatcher, *London Times*, Jun 1, 1984

1713. (The) American temptation (is) to believe that foreign policy is a subdivision of psychiatry. —Henry A. Kissinger, commencement address at Univ. of South Carolina, *Time*, Jun 17, 1985

1714. We didn't have to do the minuets of diplomacy. We got down to business. —Margaret Thatcher, discussing talks with Mikhail Gorbachev, CBS-TV, Mar 11, 1985

1715. The fidelity of the United States to security treaties is not just an empty matter. It is a pillar of peace in the world. —Dean Rusk, on 10th anniversary of fall of Saigon, *The New York Times*, Apr 30, 1985

1716. You can safely appeal to the United Nations in the comfortable certainty that it will let you down. —Conor Cruise O'Brien, *New Republic*, Nov 4, 1985

1717. If the United Nations is a country unto itself, then the commodity it exports most is words. —Esther B. Fein, *The New York Times*, Oct 14, 1985

1718. Can you imagine a policeman being required to secure the assent of parties to a street fight before breaking up the conflict? —Carlos P. Romulo, on the role of the United Nations, recalled on his death, Dec 15, 1985

1719. We said nonsense but it was important nonsense. —Nora Astorga, on conversations at the United Nations with the U.S. ambassador, *The New York Times*, Sep 28, 1986

1720. It it better to discuss things, to argue and engage in polemics than make perfidious plans of mutual destruction. —Mikhail S. Gorbachev, following discussions with U.S. Secretary of State George Shultz, *The New York Times*, Apr 19, 1987

1721. A world without nuclear weapons would be less stable and more dangerous for all of us. —Margaret Thatcher, reported remarks to Mikhail Gorbachev, *Time*, Apr 27, 1987

1722. Watching foreign affairs is sometimes like watching a magician; the eye is drawn to the hand performing the dramatic flourishes, leaving the other hand—the one doing the important job—unnoticed. —David K. Shipler, "For Israel and U.S., A Growing Military Partnership", *The New York Times*, Mar 15, 1987

JUDICIARY AND JUDGES

1723. Judges must beware of hard constructions and strained inferences, for there is no worse torture than the torture of laws. —Sir Francis Bacon, "Of Judicature", *Essays*, 1625

1724. The duty of judges is to render justice; their profession is to discern it. There are some who know their duty and who practice their profession. [*Le devoir des juges est de rendre justice; leur métier de la différer: Quelques-uns savent leur devoir, et font leur métier.*] —Jean de La Bruyère, "De quelques usages", *Les Caractères*, 1688

1725. We must not regard political consequences, however formidable they may be; if rebellion was the certain consequence, we are bound to say, "Justitia fiat, ruat coelum" ("Let justice be done, though the sky falls"). —1st Earl of Mansfield, (William Murray), trial of John Wilkes to appeal his earlier conviction for non-appearance, 1768

1726. It is emphatically the province and duty of the judicial department to say what the law is. ... If two laws conflict with each other, the courts must decide on the operation of each. ... This is the very essence of judicial duty. —John Marshall, *Marbury v. Madison*, 1803

1727. The judiciary of the United States is the subtle corps of sappers and miners constantly working under ground to undermine the founda tions of our confederated fabric. ... A judiciary independent of a king or executive alone, is a good thing; but independent of the will of the nation is a solecism, at least in a republican government. —Thomas Jefferson, letter to Thomas Ritchie, Dec 25, 1820

1728. It is a very dangerous doctrine to consider the judges as the ultimate arbiters of all constitutional questions. It is one which would place us under the despotism of an oligarchy. —Thomas Jefferson, letter to W.C. Jarvis, Sep 28, 1820

1729. There is hardly a political question in the United States which does not sooner or later turn into a judicial one. [*Il n'est presque pas de question politique, aux Etats-Unis, qui ne se résolve tôt ou tard en question judiciaire.*] —Alexis, Comte de Tocqueville, *Democracy in America*, 1835

1730. No matter whether th' constitution follows th' flag or not, th' supreme coort follows th' iliction returns. —Finley Peter Dunne, "The Supreme Court's Decisions", *Mr. Dooley's Opinions*, 1901

1731. We are under a Constitution, but the Constitution is what the judges say it is, and the judiciary is the safeguard of our liberty and of our property under the Constitution. —Charles Evans Hughes, speech to the Elmira, New York, Chamber of Commerce, May 3, 1907

1732. But even judges sometimes progress. —Emma Goldman, "The Social Aspects of Birth Control", *Mother Earth*, Apr, 1916

1733. What five members of the Supreme Court say the law is may be something vastly different from what Congress intended the law to be. —Benjamin F. Fairless, speech in Boston, Massachusetts, May 18, 1950

1734. We do not sit as a superlegislature to weigh the wisdom of legislation. —William O. Douglas, majority opinion, *Day-Brite Lighting, Inc. v. Missouri*, Mar 3, 1952

1735. We are not unaware that we are not final because we are infallible; we know that we are infallible only because we are final. —Robert H. Jackson, concurring opinion, Feb 9, 1953

1736. Whenever you put a man on the Supreme Court he ceases to be your friend. —Harry S Truman, recalled on his 75th birthday, *The New York Times*, May 8, 1959

1737. As a member of this court I am not justified in writing my private notions of policy into the Constitution, no matter how deeply I may cherish them or how mischievous I may deem their disregard. —Felix Frankfurter, *The New York Times*, Aug 9, 1964

1738. Our chief justices have probably had more profound and lasting influence on their times and on the direction of the nation than most presidents. —Richard M. Nixon, on appointment of chief justice Warren Burger, May 21, 1969

1739. You sit up there, and you see the whole gamut of human nature. Even if the case being argued involves only a little fellow and $50, it involves justice. That's what is important. —Earl Warren, recalled on his death, *Time*, Jul 22, 1974

1740. The judicial system is the most expensive machine ever invented for finding out what happened and what to do about it. —Irving R. Kaufman, quoted, *San Francisco Chronicle*, Apr 17, 1977

1741. Presidents come and go, but the Supreme Court, through its decisions, goes on forever. —Richard M. Nixon, *Playboy*, Apr, 1979

1742. At the constitutional level where we work, 90 percent of any decision is emotional. The rational part of us supplies the reasons for supporting our predilections. —William O. Douglas, *The Court Years 1939-75*, 1980

1743. It is not our job to apply laws that have not yet been written. —John Paul Stevens, majority opinion, *Sony v. Universal City Studios*, Jan 17, 1984

1744. (The judiciary is) the least dangerous branch of our government. —Alexander M. Bickel, quoted, *Christian Science Monitor*, Feb 11, 1986

1745. Somewhere "out there," beyond the walls of the courthouse, run currents and tides of public opinion which lap at the courtroom door. —William H. Rehnquist, speech at the Suffolk University Law School, Boston, Massachusetts, Apr 17, 1986

1746. The Court is most vulnerable and comes nearest to illegitimacy when it deals with judge-made constitutional law having little or no cognizable roots in the language or design of the Constitution. —Byron R. White, majority opinion, *Bowers v. Hardwick*, Jun 30, 1986

JUSTICE

1747. If a man destroy the eye of another man, they shall destroy his eye. —Hammurabi, *Code of Hammurabi*, ca. 1760 B.C.

1748. Mankind censures injustice, fearing that they may be victims of it and not because they shrink from committing it. —Plato, *The Republic*, ca. 390 B.C.

1749. Everywhere there is one principle of justice, which is the interest of the stronger. —Plato, *The Republic*, ca. 390 B.C.

1750. All virtue is summed up in dealing justly. —Aristotle, *Nicomachean Ethics*, ca. 325 B.C.

1751. There is no such thing as justice in the abstract; it is merely a compact between men. — Epicurus, *Principal Doctrines*, ca. 300 B.C.

1752. Let the punishment match the offense. [*Noxiae poena par esto.*] —Marcus Tullius Cicero, *De Legibus*, ca. 52 B.C.

1753. More law, less justice. [*Summum ius summa iniuria.*] —Marcus Tullius Cicero, *De Officiis*, 44 B.C.

1754. If you study the history and records of the world you must admit that the source of justice was the fear of injustice. [*Iura inventa metu iniusti fateare necesse est, tempora si fastosque velis evolvere mundi.*] —Horace, *Satires*, 38 B.C.

1755. Justice is that virtue that assigns to every man his due. [*Quae igitur iustitia est hominis quae ipsum hominem.*] —Saint Augustine, *De Civitate Dei*, 413-426

1756. Consequently, if the republic is the weal of the people, and there is no people if it be not associated by a common acknowledgment of right, and if there is no right where there is no justice, then most certainly it follows that there is no republic where there is no justice. [*Ac per hoc, si res publica est populi et populus non est qui consensu non sociatus est iuris, non est autem ius ubi nulla iustitia est, procul dubio colligitur, ubi iustitia non est, non esse rem publicam.*] —Saint Augustine, *De Civitate Dei*, 413-426

1757.   One of the uses of our system of justice is to warn others. ... We are reforming, not the hanged man, but everyone else. [*C'est un usage de notre justice d'en condamner aucuns pour l'avertissement des autres. ... On ne corrige pas celui qu'on pend, on corrige les autres par lui.*] —Michel de Montaigne, "De l'art de conférer", *Essais*, 1580-88

1758.   Even the laws of justice themselves cannot subsist without mixture of injustice. [*Les lois mêmes de la justice ne peuvent subsister sans quelque mélange d'injustice.*] —Michel de Montaigne, "Nous ne goûtons rien de pur", *Essais*, 1580-88

1759.   There are in nature certain fountains of justice, whence all civil laws are derived but as streams. —Sir Francis Bacon, 1st Viscount St. Albans, *Advancement of Learning*, 1605

1760.   Extreme justice is often unjust. [*Une extrême justice est souvent une injure.*] —Jean Racine, *The Thebaid*, 1664

1761.   The love of justice in most men is simply the fear of suffering injustice. [*L'amour de la justice n'est, en la plupart des hommes, que la crainte de souffrir l'injustice.*] —Francois, Duc de La Rochefoucauld, *Réflexions, ou Sentences et maximes morales*, 1665

1762.   Justice without strength is powerless, strength without justice is tyrannical. ... Therefore, unable to make what is just strong, we have made what is strong just. [*La justice sans la force est impuissante. La force sans la justice est tyrannique. ... Et ainsi ne pouvant faire que ce qui est juste fût fort, on a fait que ce qui est fort fût juste.*] —Blaise Pascal, *Pensées*, 1670

1763.   A guilty man punished is an example for the mob; an innocent man convicted is the business of every honest person. [*Un coupable puni est un exemple pour la canaille; un innocent condamné est l'affaire de tous les honnêtes gens.*] —Jean de La Bruyère, "De quelques usages", *Les Caractères*, 1688

1764.   They have a Right to censure, that have a Heart to help: the rest is Cruelty, not Justice. —William Penn, *Some Fruits of Solitude in Reflections & Maxims*, 1693

1765.   Rigid justice is the greatest injustice. —Thomas Fuller, *Gnomologia*, 1732

1766.   One can't be just if one is not human at the same time. [*On ne peut être juste si on n'est pas humain.*] —Marquis de Vauvenargues, (Luc de Clapier), *Réflexions et maximes*, 1746

1767.   Be just before you're generous. —Richard Brinsley Sheridan, *The School for Scandal*, 1777

1768.   For the law holds, that it is better that ten guilty persons escape, than that one innocent suffer. —Sir William Blackstone, *Commentaries on the Laws of England*, 1783

1769.   The greatest problem for the human species, the solution of which nature compels him to seek, is that of attaining a civil society which can administer justice univers;ally. —Immanuel Kant, *Idea for a Universal History with a Cosmopolitan Purpose*, 1784

1770.   That it is better 100 guilty Persons should escape than that one innocent Person should suffer, is a Maxim that has been long and generally approved. —Benjamin Franklin, letter to Benjamin Vaughan, Mar 14, 1785

1771.   The administration of justice is the firmest pillar of Government. —George Washington, letter to Edmund Randolph, Sep 27, 1789

1772.   All punishment is mischief. All punishment in itself is evil. —Jeremy Bentham, *Introduction to the Principles of Morals and Legislation*, 1789

1773.   Justice is itself the great standing policy of civil society; and any eminent departure from it, under any circumstances, lies under the suspicion of being no policy at all. —Edmund Burke, *Reflections on the Revolution in France*, 1790

1774.   It is justice, not charity, that is wanting in the world. —Mary Wollstonecraft, *A Vindication of the Rights of Women*, 1792

1775. Equal and exact justice to all men of whatever state or persuasion, religious or political. —Thomas Jefferson, first inaugural address, Mar 4, 1801

1776. To be just is not simply doing right, the governed must be convinced that it is right. [*Il ne suffit pas pour être juste de faire le bien, il faut encore que les administres soient convaincus.*] —Napoleon I, remarks in the Council of State, Mar 12, 1803

1777. There is no authority without justice. [*Il n'y a point de force sans justice.*] —Napoleon I, remarks in the Council of State, Mar 12, 1803

1778. The art of policing is, in order not to punish often, to punish severely. [*L'art de la police, afin de ne pas punir souvent, est de punir sévèrement.*] —Napoleon I, letter to M. Fouché, Jun 20, 1805

1779. In matters of government, justice means force as well as virtue. [*En fait de gouvernement, justice veut dire force comme vertu.*] —Napoleon I, letter to M. Lebrun, quoted by Thibaudeau, *Le Consulat et l'Empire*, 1834

1780. I believe that justice is instinct and innate, that the moral sense is as much a part of our constitution as that of feeling, seeing, or hearing. —Thomas Jefferson, letter to John Adams, Oct 14, 1816

1781. It is the feeling of injustice that is insupportable to all men. —Thomas Carlyle, *Chartism*, 1839

1782. When I refuse to obey an unjust law, I do not contest the right of the majority to command, but I simply appeal from the sovereignty of the people to the sovereignty of mankind. [*Quand donc je réfuse d'obéir à une loi injuste, je ne dénie point à la majorité le droit de commander; j'en appelle seulement de la souveraineté du peuple à la souveraineté du genre humain.*] —Alexis, Comte de Tocqueville, *Democracy in America*, 1835-39

1783. Justice is truth in action. [*La justice est la vérité en action.*] —Joseph Joubert, *Pensées*, 1842

1784. Justice is the great interest of man on earth. —Daniel Webster, speaking on Supreme Court justice Joseph Story, Sep 12, 1845

1785. Sir, I say that justice is truth in action. —Benjamin Disraeli, speech in the House of Commons, Feb 11, 1851

1786. As long as justice and injustice have not terminated their ever-renewing fight for ascendancy in the affairs of mankind, human beings must be willing, when need is, to do battle for the one against the other. —John Stuart Mill, "The Contest in America", *Fraser's Magazine*, Feb, 1862

1787. The severest justice may not always be the best policy. —Abraham Lincoln, message to Congress, Jul 17, 1862

1788. "No, no!" said the Queen. "Sentence first—verdict afterwards." —Lewis Carroll, (Charles L. Dodgson), *Alice in Wonderland*, 1865

1789. I have always found that mercy bears richer fruits than strict justice. —Abraham Lincoln, speech in Washington, D.C., 1865

1790. National injustice is the surest road to national downfall. —William Ewart Gladstone, speech in Plumstead, England, 1878

1791. Justice and good will will outlast passion. —James A. Garfield, letter accepting the Republican nomination for president, Jul 12, 1880

1792. Justice should remove the bandage from her eyes long enough to distinguish between the vicious and the unfortunate. —Robert G. Ingersoll, *Prose-Poems and Selections*, 1884

1793. Once the laws are just, then men will be just. [*Quand les lois seront justes, les hommes seront justes.*] —Anatole France, *Monsieur Bergeret à Paris*, 1900

1794. I tell ye Hogan's r-right whin he says: "Justice is blind." Blind she is, an' deef an' dumb an' has a wooden leg! —Finley Peter Dunne, "Cross-Examinations", *Mr. Dooley's Opinions*, 1901

1795. Justice is the sanction used to support established injustices. [*La justice est la sanction des injustices établies.*] —Anatole France, "Crainquebille", 1905

1796. This home iv opporchunity where ivry man is th' equal iv ivry other man befure th' law if he isn't careful. —Finley Peter Dunne, "The Food We Eat", *Dissertations by Mr. Dooley*, 1906

1797. Justice is my being allowed to do whatever I like. Injustice is whatever prevents my doing so. —Samuel Butler, *Notebooks*, 1912

1798. The firm basis of government is justice, not pity. —Woodrow Wilson, first inaugural address, Mar 4, 1913

1799. The only kinds of courage and honesty which are permanently useful to good institutions anywhere are those shown by men who decide all cases with impartial justice on grounds of conduct and not on grounds of class. —Theodore Roosevelt, *Autobiography*, 1913

1800. I was transfixed with horror, and over me there swept the sudden conviction that hanging was a mistake—worse, a crime. It was my awakening to one of the most terrible facts of life—that justice and judgment lie often a world apart. —Emmeline Pankhurst, *My Own Story*, 1914

1801. Somehow, our sense of justice never turns in its sleep till long after the sense of injustice in others has been thoroughly aroused. —Sir Max Beerbohm, "Servants", *And Even Now*, 1920

1802. Injustice is relatively easy to bear; what stings is justice. —H.L. Mencken, *Prejudices: Third Series*, 1922

1803. For my part I think it a less evil that some criminals should escape, than that the government should play an ignoble part. —Oliver Wendell Holmes Jr., *Olmstead v. United States*, 1928

1804. If we are to keep our democracy, there must be one commandment: Thou shall not ration justice. —Learned Hand, speech to the New York Legal Aide Society, Feb 16, 1951

1805. Peace and justice are two sides of the same coin. —Dwight D. Eisenhower, radio and television address, Feb 20, 1957

1806. Fairness is what justice really is. —Potter Stewart, *Time*, Oct 20, 1958

1807. Swift justice demands more than just swiftness. —Potter Stewart, *Time*, Oct 20, 1958

1808. We will not be satisfied until justice rolls down like waters and righteousness like a mighty stream. —Martin Luther King Jr., speech in Washington, D.C., Jun 15, 1963

1809. Justice is like a train that's nearly always late. —Yevgeny Yevtushenko, *A Precocious Autobiography*, 1963

1810. We will demonstrate anew that the strong can be just in the use of strength—and the just can be strong in the defense of justice. —Lyndon Baines Johnson, speech to Congress, Nov 27, 1963

1811. Injustice anywhere is a threat to justice everywhere. —Martin Luther King Jr., "Letter from the Birmingham Jail", Jan 16, 1963

1812. Justice delayed is democracy denied.—Robert F. Kennedy, "To Secure These Rights", *The Pursuit of Justice*, 1964

1813. Get out of the way of Justice. She is blind. —Stanislaw Lec, *More Unkempt thoughts*, 1968

1814. White folks don't want peace; they want quiet. The price you pay for peace is justice. Until there is justice, there will be no peace and quiet. —Jesse Jackson, interview, *Playboy*, Nov, 1969

1815. We have accumulated a wealth of historical experience which confirms our belief that the scales of American justice are out of balance. —Angela Yvonne Davis, statement to the court, Marin County, California, Jan 5, 1971

1816. The criminal justice system is breaking down because we, as a nation, have for too long neglected to nourish its heart—the court systems of our country. —G. Gordon Liddy, *Connecticut*, Feb, 1977

1817. Before going to prison I believed that criticism of the criminal justice system for its treatment of the poor was so much liberal bleating and bunk. I was wrong. —G. Gordon Liddy, *Connecticut*, Feb, 1977

LAW

1818. Wrong must not win by technicalities. —Aeschylus, *The Eumenides*, 458 B.C.

1819. Law is order, and good law is good order. —Aristotle, *Politics*, 343 B.C.

1820. Even when laws have been written down, they ought not always to remain unaltered. —Aristotle, *Politics*, 343 B.C.

1821. Whereas the law is passionless, passion must ever sway the heart of man. —Aristotle, *Politics*, 343 B.C.

1822. Good laws if they are not obeyed, do not constitute good government. —Aristotle, *Politics*, 343 B.C.

1823. Extreme law is often extreme injustice. [*Ius summum saepe summa est malitia.*] —Terence, *Heauton Timoroumenos*, ca. 163 B.C.

1824. The good of the people is the supreme law. [*Salus populi suprema est lex.*] —Marcus Tullius Cicero, *De Legibus*, ca. 52 B.C.

1825. No law is quite appropriate for all. [*Nulla lex satis commoda omnibus est.*] —Livy, *Ab Urbe Condita*, ca. 29 B.C.

1826. Certain laws have not been written, but they are more fixed than all the written laws. [*Quaedam iura non scripta, sed omnibus scriptis certiora sunt.*] —Lucius Annaeus Seneca (the Elder), *Controversiae*, ca. 40

1827. The law is good, if a man use it lawfully. —Bible, *1 Timothy*, ca. 100

1828. Laws are like spider's webs which, if anything small falls into them they ensnare it, but large things break through and escape. —Solon, quoted by Diogenes Laërtius, *Lives and Opinions of Eminent Philosophers*, 3rd cent. A.D.

1829. No freeman shall be taken, or imprisoned, or outlawed, or exiled, or in any way harmed, nor will we go upon him nor will we send upon him, except by the legal judgment of his peers or by the law of the land. —Magna Carta, Clause 39, 1215

1830. To none will we sell, to none deny or delay, right or justice. —Magna Carta, Clause 40, 1215

1831. Law: an ordinance of reason for the common good, made by him who has care of the community. [*Legis, quae nihil est aliud quam quaedam rationis ordinatio ad bonum commune, ab eo qui curam communitatis habet, promulgata.*] —St. Thomas Aquinas, *Summa Theologiae*, 1273

1832. The highest and ultimate instrument of political power is capital punishment. [*Nervus potestatis politicae praecipuus et summus est supplicium capitale.*] —Philip Melanchthon, *Philosophiae Moralis Epitomes*, ca. 1530

1833. Whoever desires to found a state and give it laws, must start with assuming that all men are bad and ever ready to display their vicious nature, whenever they may find occasion for it. [*E necessario a chi dispone una republica e ordina leggi in quella, presupporre tutti gli uomini rei, e che li abbiano sempre a usare la malignità dello animo loro qualunque volta ne abbiano libera occasione.*] —Niccolò Machiavelli, *Discourses on the First Ten Books of Titus Livius*, 1531

1834. When it is a question of saving the fatherland, one should not stop for a moment to consider whether something is lawful or unlawful, gentle or cruel, laudable or shameful; but, putting aside every other consideration, one ought to follow to the end whatever resolve will save the life of the state and preserve the freedom of one's country. [*La quale cosa merita de essere notata et osservata da qualunque cittadino si truova a consigliare la patria sua; perché dove si dilibera al tutto della salute della patria, non vi debbe cadere alcuna considerazione né di giusto né d'ingiusto, né di piatoso né di crudele, né di laudabile né d'ignominioso; anzi, posposto ogni altre rispetto, seguire al tutto quel partito che le salvi la vita e mantenghile la libertà.*] —Niccolò Machiavelli, *Discourses on the First Ten Books of Titus Livius*, 1531

1835. Because just as good morals, if they are to be maintained, have need of the laws, so the laws, if they are to be observed, have need of good morals. [*Perché così come gli buoni costumi per mantenersi hanno bisogno delle leggi, così le leggi per osservarsi hanno bisogno de' buoni costumi.*] —Niccolò Machiavelli, *Discourses on the First Ten Books of Titus Livius*, 1531

1836. The chief foundations of all states, new as well as old or composite, are good laws and good arms; and as there cannot be good laws where the state is not well armed, it follows that where they are well armed they have good laws. [*E principali fondamenti che abbino tutti li stati, così nuovi, comme vecchi o misti, sono le buone legge e le buone arme. E perché non può essere buone legge dove non sono buone arme, e dove sono buone arme conviene sieno buone legge.*] —Niccolò Machiavelli, *Il Principe*, 1532

1837. If we insist, however, that sovereign power means exemption from all law whatsoever, there is no prince who can be regarded as sovereign, since all the princes of the earth are subject to the laws of God and of nature, and even to certain human laws common to all nations. —Jean Bodin, *Six Books of the Commonwealth*, 1576

1838. Nothing is more subject to change than the laws. [*Il n'est rien sujet à plus continuelle agitation que les lois.*] —Michel de Montaigne, "Apologie de Raimond Sebond", *Essais*, 1580-88

1839. The first thing we do, let's kill all the lawyers. —William Shakespeare, *Henry VI, Part II*, 1591

1840. In law, what plea so tainted and corrupt/ But, being seasoned with a gracious voice,/ Obscures the show of evil? —William Shakespeare, *The Merchant of Venice*, 1595

1841. We must not make a scarecrow of the law,/ Setting it up to fear the birds of prey,/ And let it keep one shape, till custom make it/ Their perch, and not their terror. —William Shakespeare, *Measure for Measure*, 1604-05

1842. Laws that only threaten, and are not kept, become like the log that was given to the frogs to be their king, which they feared at first, but soon scorned and trampled on. [*Las leyes que atemorizan y no se ejecutan, vienen á ser como la viga, rey de las ranas: que al principio las espantó, y con el tiempo, la menospreciaron y se subieron sobre ella.*] —Miguel de Cervantes, *Don Quixote*, 1605-15

1843. No rule is so general, which admits not some exception. —Robert Burton, *The Anatomy of Melancholy*, 1621

1844. A man's house is his castle. —Sir Edward Coke, *Institutes: Commentary upon Littleton*, 1628

1845. Where-ever Law ends, Tyranny begins. —John Locke, *The Second Treatise on Government*, 1690

1846. No prince is so Great, as not to think fit, for his own Credit at least, to give an outward, when he refuseth a real, worship to the laws. —1st Marquess of Halifax, (George Savile), *The Character of a Trimmer*, 1700

1847. Men are not hanged for stealing Horses, but that Horses may not be stolen. —1st Marquess of Halifax, *Political Thoughts and Reflections*, 1750

1848. Good and evil, reward and punishment, are the only motives to a rational creature; these are the spur and reins whereby all mankind are set on work and guided. —John Locke, *Some Thoughts Concerning Education*, 1693

1849. Laws are like cobwebs, which may catch small flies, but let wasps and hornets break through. —Jonathan Swift, *A Critical Essay upon the Faculties of the Mind*, 1707

1850. The more laws, the more offenders. —Thomas Fuller, *Gnomologia*, 1732

1851. Law cannot persuade where it cannot punish. —Thomas Fuller, *Gnomologia*, 1732

1852. It is better to risk saving a guilty man than to condemn an innocent one. [*Il vaut mieux hasarder de sauver un coupable que de condamner un innocent.*] —Voltaire, *Zadig*, 1747

1853. The wording of laws should mean the same thing to all men. [*Il est essentiel que les paroles des lois réveillent chez tous les hommes les mêmes idées.*] —Charles Louis de Montesquieu, *De l'Esprit des lois*, 1748

1854. Care must be taken that laws do not offend against nature. [*Il faut prendre garde que les lois soient concus de manière qu'elles ne choquent point la nature des choses.*] —Charles Louis de Montesquieu, *De l'Esprit des lois*, 1748

1855. Laws should not be changed without good reason. [*Il ne faut point faire de changement dans une loi sans une raison suffisante.*] —Charles Louis de Montesquieu, *De l'Esprit des lois*, 1748

1856. The language of laws should be simple; directness is always better than elaborate wording. [*Le style des lois doit être simple; l'expression directe s'entend toujours mieux que l'expression réfléchie.*] —Charles Louis de Montesquieu, *De l'Esprit des lois*, 1748

1857. Laws should not be subtle; they are designed for people of average understanding: they are not exercises in the art of logic but the simple reasoning of the head of the house. [*Les lois ne doivent point être subtiles; elles sont faites pour des gens de médiocre entendement: elles ne sont point un art de logique, mais la raison simple d'un père de famille.*] —Charles Louis de Montesquieu, *De l'Esprit des lois*, 1748

1858. Just as useless laws weaken necessary ones, those that can be evaded weaken all legislation. [*Comme les lois inutiles affaiblissent les lois nécessaires, celles qu'on peut éluder affaiblissent la législation.*] —Charles Louis de Montesquieu, *De l'Esprit des lois*, 1748

1859. Laws too gentle are seldom obeyed; too severe, seldom executed. —Benjamin Franklin, *Poor Richard's Almanack*, 1732-57

1860. The first of all laws is to respect the laws: the severity of penalties is only a vain resource, invented by little minds in order to substitute terror for that respect which they have no means of obtaining. —Jean Jacques Rousseau, *A Discourse on Political Economy*, 1758

1861. Good laws lead to the making of better ones; bad ones bring about worse. [*Les bonnes lois en font faire de meilleures, les mauvaises en amènent de pires.*] —Jean Jacques Rousseau, *The Social Contract*, 1762

1862. Laws grind the poor, and rich men rule the law. —Oliver Goldsmith, *The Traveller*, 1765

1863. Whatever is contra bonos mores et decorum the principles of our laws prohibit and the King's Court as the general censor and guardian of the public morals is bound to restrain and punish. —1st Earl of Mansfield, *Jones v. Randall*, 1774

1864. It is not, what a lawyer tells me I may do; but what humanity, reason, and justice tell me I ought to do. —Edmund Burke, speech, "On Conciliation with the American Colonies", Mar 22, 1775

1865. Laws made by common consent must not be trampled on by individuals. —George Washington, letter to Colonel Vanneter, 1781

1866. There is, therefore, only one categorical imperative. It is: Act only according to that maxim by which you can at the same time will that it should become a universal law. —Immanuel Kant, *Grundlagen zur Metaphysik der Sitten*, 1785

1867. The law is the last result of human wisdom acting upon human experience for the benefit of the public. —Samuel Johnson, quoted by Hester Lynch Piozzi, *Anecdotes of Samuel Johnson*, 1786

1868. Government implies the power of making laws. It is essential to the idea of a law, that it be attended with a sanction; or, in other words, a penalty or punishment for disobedience. —Alexander Hamilton, *The Federalist*, Dec 1, 1787

1869. Ignorance of the law is no excuse in any country. If it were, the laws would lose their effect, because it can be always pretended. —Thomas Jefferson, letter to M. Limozin, Dec 22, 1787

1870. It is more dangerous that even a guilty person should be punished without the forms of law than that he should escape. —Thomas Jefferson, letter to William Carmichael, May 27, 1788

1871. The execution of the laws is more important than the making of them. —Thomas Jefferson, letter to Abbé Arnond, May 27, 1789

1872. There is but one law for all, namely, that law which governs all law, the law of our Creator, the law of humanity, justice, equity—the law of nature, and of nations. —Edmund Burke, debate in the House of Commons on the impeachment of Warren Hastings, May 28, 1794

1873. The mass of the people have nothing to do with the laws but to obey them. —Samuel Horsley, speech in the House of Lords, 1795

1874. Anyone who takes it upon himself, on his private authority, to break a bad law, thereby authorizes everyone else to break the good ones. —Denis Diderot, *Supplement to Bougainville's "Voyage"*, 1796

1875. Men have feelings but the law does not. [*L'homme a des entrailles et la loi n'en a pas.*] —Napoleon I, attributed remark in the Council of State by Pelet de la Lozère, *Opinions de a sur divers sujets de politique et d'administration*, 1833

1876. Laws and institutions must go hand in hand with the progress of the human mind. —Thomas Jefferson, letter to Samuel Kercheval, Jul 12, 1816

1877. Laws are made for men of ordinary understanding, and should therefore be construed by the ordinary rules of common sense. Their meaning is not to be sought for in metaphysical subtleties, which may make anything mean everything or nothing, at pleasure. —Thomas Jefferson, letter to Judge William Johnson, Jun 12, 1823

1878. The victim to too severe a law is considered as a martyr rather than a criminal. —Charles Caleb Colton, *Lacön*, 1825

1879. I will not say with Lord Hale, that "The Law will admit of no rival" ... but I will say that it is a jealous mistress, and requires a long and constant courtship. It is not to be won by trifling favors, but by lavish homage. —Joseph Story, speech, "The Value and Importance of Legal Studies", Aug 5, 1829

1880. If a law commands me to sin I will break it; if it calls me to suffer, I will let it take its course unresistingly. The doctrine of blind obedience and unqualified submission to any human power, whether civil or ecclesiastical, is the doctrine of despotism, and ought to have no place among Republicans and Christians. —Angelina Grimké, "Appeal to the Christian Women of the South", *The Anti-Slavery Examiner*, Sep, 1836

1881. "If the law supposes that," said Mr. Bumble, ... "the law is a ass—a idiot. If that's the eye of the law, the law is a bachelor; and the worst I wish the law is that his eye may be opened by experience—by experience." —Charles Dickens, *Oliver Twist*, 1837-39

1882. Our written law is often difficult to understand, but anyone can read it. There is nothing, on the other hand, more obscure for the ordinary person and less in his grasp than a legal system based on precedent. The need for the student of the law in England and the United States, the high esteem in which his talent is held, separates him more and more from the people, and finally puts him in a class apart. [*Nos lois écrites sont souvent difficiles à comprendre, mais chacun peut y lire; il n'y a rien, au contraire, de plus obscur pour le vulgaire et de moins à sa portée qu'une législation fondée sur des précédents. Ce besoin qu'on a du légiste en Angleterre et aux Etats-Unis, cette haute idée qu'on se forme de ses lumières, le sépare de plus en plus du peuple, et achève de le mettre dans une classe à part.*] —Alexis, Comte de Tocqueville, *Democracy in America*, 1835-39

1883. Good men must not obey the laws too well. —Ralph Waldo Emerson, "Politics", *Essays: Second Series*, 1844

1884. The form of government which prevails is the expression of what cultivation exists in the population which permits it. The law is only a memorandum. —Ralph Waldo Emerson, "Politics", *Essays: Second Series*, 1844

1885. I think that we should be men first, and subjects afterward. It is not desirable to cultivate a respect for the law, so much as for the right. —Henry David Thoreau, *Civil Disobedience*, 1849

1886. The lawyer's truth is not Truth, but consistency or a consistent expediency. —Henry David Thoreau, *Civil Disobedience*, 1849

1887. The best use of good laws is to teach men to trample bad laws under their feet. —Wendell Phillips, speech, Apr 12, 1852

1888. Many laws as certainly make bad men, as bad men make many laws. —Walter Savage Landor, "Diogenes and Plato", *Imaginary Conversations*, 1824-53

1889. I know no method to secure the repeal of bad or obnoxious laws so effective as their stringent execution. —Ulysses S. Grant, first inaugural address, Mar 4, 1869

1890. Laws are like medicine; they generally cure an evil by a lesser or a passing evil. [*Gesetze sind wie Arzeneien, sie sind gewöhnlich nur Heilung einer Krankheit durch eine geringere oder vorübergehende Krankheit.*] —Prince Otto von Bismarck, speech in the Prussian Chamber of Deputies, Mar 6, 1872

1891. Coercion is the basis of every law in the universe—Human or Divine. A law is no law without coercion behind it. —James A. Garfield, *Maxims*, 1880

1892. The law embodies the story of a nation's development through many centuries, and it cannot be dealt with as if it contained only the axioms and corollaries of a book of mathematics. —Oliver Wendell Holmes Jr., *The Common Law*, 1881

1893. It usually takes a hundred years to make a law, and then, after it has done its work, it usually takes a hundred years to get rid of it. —Henry Ward Beecher, *Proverbs from Plymouth Pulpit*, 1887

1894. Riches without law are more dangerous than is poverty without law. —Henry Ward Beecher, *Proverbs from Plymouth Pulpit*, 1887

1895. Law will never be strong or respected unless it has the sentiment of the people behind it. If the people of a state make bad laws, they will suffer for it. They will be the first to suffer. Suffering, and nothing else, will implant that sentiment of responsibility which is the first step to reform. —James Bryce, *The American Commonwealth*, 1888

1896. To the law we bow with reverence. It is the one king that commands our allegiance. We will change our king when his rule is oppressive. —Benjamin Harrison, speech in Indianapolis, Indiana, Jul 12, 1888

1897. No good cause can be promoted upon the lines of lawlessness. Mobs do not discriminate, and the punishments inflicted by them have no repressive or salutary influence. —Benjamin Harrison, acceptance of renomination for presidency, Sep 3, 1892

1898. Liberty, my fellow citizens, is responsibilty, and responsibilty is duty, and that duty is to preserve the exceptional liberty we enjoy within the law and for the law and by the law. —William McKinley, speech in Cleveland, Ohio, Jul 4, 1894

1899. Law is merely the expression of the will of the strongest for the time being, and therefore laws have no fixity, but shift from generation to generation. —Brooks Adams, *The Law of Civilization and Decay*, 1895

1900. Law is largely crystallized custom, largely a mass of remedies which have been slowly evolved to meet the wrongs with which humanity has become thoroughly familiar. —Theodore Roosevelt, annual message as governor, Albany, New York, Jan 3, 1900

1901. So long as governments set the example of killing their enemies, private individuals will occasionally kill theirs. —Elbert G. Hubbard, *Contemplations*, 1902

1902. Every new time will give its law. —Maxim Gorky, *The Lower Depths*, 1903

1903. Today there's law and order in everything. You can't beat anybody for nothing. If you do beat anyone, it's got to be for the sake of order. —Maxim Gorky, *The Lower Depths*, 1903

1904. No man is above the law and no man is below it; nor do we ask any man's permission when we ask him to obey it. —Theodore Roosevelt, speech, Jan, 1904

1905. Great cases like hard cases make bad law. —Oliver Wendell Holmes Jr., *Northern Securities Company v. United States*, 1904

1906. Laws are sand, customs are rock. Laws can be evaded and punishment escaped, but an openly transgressed custom brings sure punishment. —Mark Twain, *The Gorkey Incident*, 1906

1907. It cannot be helped, it is as it should be, that the law is behind the times. —Oliver Wendell Holmes Jr., speech in New York City, Feb 15, 1913

1908. After all, that is what laws are for, to be made and unmade. —Emma Goldman, "The Social Aspects of Birth Control", *Mother Earth*, Apr, 1916

1909. The common law is not a brooding omnipresence in the sky but the articulate voice of some sovereign or quasi sovereign that can be identified. —Oliver Wendell Holmes Jr., *Southern Pacific Co. v. Jensen*, 1917

1910. As in law so in war, the longest purse finally wins. —Mohandas K. Gandhi, lecture to the Bombay Provincial Cooperative Conference, Sep 17, 1917

1911. Those who are too lazy and comfortable to think for themselves and be their own judges obey the laws. They have it easy. Others sense their own laws within them. [*Wer zu bequem ist, um selber zu denken und selber sein Richter zu sein, der fügt sich eben in die Verbote, wie sie nun einmal sind. Er hat es leicht. Andere spüren selber Gebote in sich.*] —Hermann Hesse, *Demian*, 1919

1912. One with the law is a majority. —Calvin Coolidge, acceptance speech as Republican vice-presidental nominee, Jul 27, 1920

1913. The law must be stable, but it must not stand still. —Roscoe Pound, *Introduction to the Philosophy of Law*, 1922

1914. Decency, security and liberty alike demand that government officials shall be subjected to the same rules of conduct that are commands to the citizen. In a government of laws, existence of the government will be imperilled if it fails to observe the law scrupulously. —Louis D. Brandeis, dissenting opinion, *Olmstead v. United States*, 1928

1915. The law is simply and solely made for the exploitation of those who do not understand it or of those, who out of naked need, cannot obey it. [*Das Gesetz ist einzig und allein gemacht zur Ausbeutung derer, die es nicht verstehen oder die es aus nackter Not nicht befolgen konnen.*] —Bertolt Brecht, *The Threepenny Opera*, 1928

1916. The language of the law must not be foreign to the ears of those who are to obey it. —Learned Hand, speech in Washington, D.C., May 11, 1929

1917. It will be of little avail to the people, that the laws are made by men of their own choice, if the laws be so voluminous that they cannot be read, or so incoherent that they cannot be understood. —James Truslow Adams, *The Adams Family*, 1930

1918. Nobody has a more sacred obligation to obey the law than those who make the law. —Jean Anouilh, *Antigone*, 1942

1919. If one man can be allowed to determine for himself what is law, every man can. That means first chaos, then tyranny. Legal process is an essential part of the democratic process. —Felix Frankfurter, concurring opinion, *United States v. Mine Workers*, 1946

1920. An unjust law is itself a species of violence. Arrest for its breach is more so. —Mohandas K. Gandhi, *Non-Violence in Peace and War*, 1948

1921. Government can easily exist without law, but law cannot exist without government. —Bertrand Russell, "Ideas That Have Helped Mankind", *Unpopular Essays*, 1950

1922. Every so often, we pass laws repealing human nature. —Howard Lindsay, quoted by John Crosby, *New York Herald Tribune*, Nov 21, 1954

1923. Time and again a number of people—I, among them—have argued that you cannot change people's hearts merely by laws. Laws presumably express the conscience of a nation and its determination or will to do something. —Dwight D. Eisenhower, news conference, Sep 3, 1957

1924. We are going to have to decide what kind of people we are—whether we obey the law only when we approve of it or whether we obey it no matter how distastful we may find it. —Harry Ashmore, on integration of Little Rock High School, *Arkansas Gazette*, Sep 4, 1957

1925. Common sense often makes good law. —William O. Douglas, in court ruling, Mar 25, 1957

1926. There is no person in this room whose basic rights are not involved in any successful defiance to the carrying out of court orders. —Dwight D. Eisenhower, on Arkansas' refusal to accept the Supreme Court's school desegregation ruling, May 14, 1958

1927. We have never stopped sin by passing laws; and in the same way, we are not going to take a great moral ideal and achieve it merely by law. —Dwight D. Eisenhower, news conference, May 13, 1959

1928. The police must obey the law while enforcing the law. —Earl Warren, unanimous opinion, Jun 22, 1959

1929. Life and liberty can be as much endangered from illegal methods used to convict those thought to be criminals as from the actual criminals themselves. —Earl Warren, unanimous opinion, Jun 22, 1959

1930. Fragile as reason is and limited as law is as the institutionalized medium of reason, that's all we have standing between us and the tyranny of mere will and the cruelty of unbridled, undisciplined feeling. —Felix Frankfurter, *Felix Frankfurter Reminisces*, 1960

1931. The law is a causeway upon which, so long as he keeps to it, a citizen may walk safely. —Robert Bolt, *A Man for All Seasons*, 1962

1932. Our nation is founded on the principle that observance of the law is the eternal safeguard of liberty and defiance of the law is the surest road to tyranny. —John F. Kennedy, televised speech, Sep 30, 1962

1933. In civilized life, law floats in a sea of ethics. —Earl Warren, *The New York Times*, Nov 12, 1962

1934. It may be true that the law cannot make man love me, but it can keep him from lynching me, and I think that's pretty important. —Martin Luther King Jr., *Wall Street Journal*, Nov 13, 1962

1935. Morality cannot be legislated, but behavior can be regulated. Judicial decrees may not change the heart, but they can restrain the heartless. —Martin Luther King Jr., *Strength to Love*, 1963

1936. Law alone cannot make men see right. —John F. Kennedy, televised speech, Jun 11, 1963

1937. Law is experience developed by reason and applied continually to further experience. —Roscoe Pound, *Christian Science Monitor*, Apr 24, 1963

1938. An individual who breaks a law that conscience tells him is unjust, and who willingly accepts the penalty of imprisonment in order to arouse the conscience of the community over its injustice, is in reality expressing the highest respect for the law. —Martin Luther King Jr., *Why We Can't Wait*, 1964

1939. I shall not today attempt further to define the kinds of material ... but I know it when I see it. —Potter Stewart, concurring opinion, *Jacobellis v. Ohio*, Jun 22, 1964

1940. There are not enough jails, not enough policemen, not enough courts to enforce a law not supported by the people. —Hubert H. Humphrey, speech in Williamsburg, Virginia, May 1, 1965

1941. Prior to any questioning, the person must be warned that he has a right to remain silent, that any statement he does make may be used as evidence against him and that he has a right to the presence of an attorney, either retained or appointed. —Earl Warren, majority opinion, *Miranda v. Arizona*, Jun 13, 1966

1942. One can always legislate against specific acts of human wickedness; but one can never legislate against the irrational itself. —Morton Irving Seiden, *The Paradox of Hate: A Study in Ritual Murder*, 1967

1943. If there isn't a law, there will be. —Harold Faber, *The New York Times Magazine*, Mar 17, 1968

1944. This is what has to be remembered about the law: Beneath that cold, harsh, impersonal exterior there beats a cold, harsh, impersonal heart. —David Frost, and Anthony Jay, *The English*, 1968

1945. The rule of law can be wiped out in one misguided, however well-intentioned, generation. —William T. Gossett, speech, Aug 11, 1969

1946. Law is a reflection and a source of prejudice. It both enforces and suggests forms of bias. —Diane B. Schulder, "Does the Law Oppress Women?", *Sisterhood is Powerful*, 1970

1947. Through the centuries, men of law have been persistently concerned with the resolution of disputes ... in ways that enable society to achieve its goals with a minimum of force and maximum of reason. —Archibald Cox, *The New York Times*, Dec 30, 1973

1948. The states are not free, under the guise of protecting maternal health or potential life, to intimidate women into continuing pregnancies. —Harry A. Blackmun, majority opinion, *Roe v. Wade; Doe v. Bolton*, Jan 22, 1973

1949. All laws are an attempt to domesticate the natural ferocity of the species. —John W. Gardner, *San Francisco Chronicle*, Jul 3, 1974

1950. It is quite obvious that there are certain inherently governmental actions which, if undertaken by the sovereign in protection of ... the nation's security, are lawful, but which if undertaken by private citizens are not. —Richard M. Nixon, *Wall Street Journal*, Mar 12, 1976

1951. There are times when national interest is more important than the law. —Henry A. Kissinger, *New York Times Magazine*, Oct 31, 1976

1952. (I am) appalled at the ethical bankruptcy of those who preach a right to life that means a bare existence in utter misery for so many. —Thurgood Marshall, *Time*, Jul 4, 1977

1953. I have spent all my life under a Communist regime, and I will tell you that a society without any objective legal scale is a terrible one indeed. But a society with no other scale but the legal one is not quite worthy of man either. —Alexander Solzhenitsyn, commencement address at Harvard Univ. on "The Exhausted West", Jun 8, 1978

1954. Things in law tend to be black and white. But we all know that some people are a little bit guilty, while other people are guilty as hell. —Donald R. Cressey, *Center Magazine*, May/ Jun, 1978

1955. Abortion is inherently different from other medical procedures because no other procedure involves the purposeful termination of a potential life. —Potter Stewart, majority opinion, *Harris v. McRae*, Jun 30, 1980

1956. We have the means to change the laws we find unjust or onerous. We cannot, as citizens, pick and choose the laws we will or will not obey. —Ronald Reagan, speech to the United Brotherhood of Carpenters and Joiners, Sep 3, 1981

1957. There is far too much law for those who can afford it and far too little for those cannot. —Derek Bok, report to the Board of Overseers of Harvard Univ., Apr 21, 1983

1958. (Law is) vulnerable to the winds of intellectual or moral fashion, which it then validates as the commands of our most basic concept. —Robert H. Bork, *The New York Times*, Jan 4, 1985

1959. In Germany, under the law everything is prohibited except that which is permitted. In France, under the law everything is permitted except that which is prohibited. In the Soviet Union, everything is prohibited, including that which is permitted. And in Italy, under the law everything is permitted, especially that which is prohibited. —Newton Minow, *Time*, Mar 18, 1985

1960. Law's empire is defined by attitude, not territory or power or process. —Ronald D. Dworkin, *Law's Empire*, 1986

1961. Moral principle is the foundation of law. —Ronald D. Dworkin, *Law's Empire*, 1986

1962. The law ... is constantly based on notions of morality, and if all laws representing essentially moral choices are to be invalidated under the due process clause, the courts will be very busy indeed. —Byron R. White, majority opinion, *Bowers v. Hardwick*, Jun 30, 1986

1963. Judges ... rule on the basis of law, not public opinion, and they should be totally indifferent to pressures of the times. —Warren E. Burger, quoted by Charlotte Saikowski, "The Power of Judicial Review", *Christian Science Monitor*, Feb 11, 1987

1964. A taxpaying public that doesn't understand the law is a taxpaying public that can't comply with the law. —Lawrence Gibbs, *Wall Street Journal*, Mar 3, 1987

1965. A law can be both economic folly and constitutional. —Antonin Scalia, concurring opinion, Apr 21, 1987

LEADERSHIP/STATESMANSHIP

1966. To be both a speaker of words and a doer of deeds. —Homer, *Iliad*, ca. 700 B.C.

1967. It is not possible to fight beyond your strength, even if you strive. —Homer, *Iliad*, ca. 700 B.C.

1968. He who exercises government by means of his virtue may be compared to the north polar star, which keeps its place and all the stars turn towards it. —Confucius, *The Analects*, ca. 480 B.C.

1969. Every ruler is harsh whose rule is new. —Aeschylus, *Prometheus Bound*, ca. 478 B.C.

1970. They should rule who are able to rule best. —Aristotle, *Politics*, 343 B.C.

1971. The man who commands efficiently must have obeyed others in the past, and the man who obeys dutifully is worthy of being some day a commander. [*Nam et quit bene imperat, paruerit aliquando necesse est, et qui modeste paret, videtur, qui aliquando imperet, dignus esse.*] —Marcus Tullius Cicero, *De Legibus*, ca. 52 B.C.

1972. But the actions of those who hold great power, and pass their lives in a lofty status, are known to all men. Therefore, in the highest position there is the least freedom of action. [*Qui magno imperio praediti in excelso aetatem agunt, eorum facta cuncti mortales novere. Ita in maxima fortuna minima licentia est.*] —Sallust, (Gaius Sallustius Crispus), *The War with Catiline*, ca. 40 B.C.

1973. The foremost art of kings is the power to endure hatred. [*Ars prima regni est posse invidiam pati.*] —Seneca (the Younger), *Hercules Furens*, ca. 50

1974. From this arises the question whether it is better to be loved rather than feared, or feared rather than loved. It might perhaps be answered that we should wish to be both: but since love and fear can hardly exist together, if we must choose between them, it is far safer to be feared than loved. [*Nasce da questo una disputa: s'elli è meglio essere amato che temuto, o e converso. Respondesi, che si vorebbe essere l'uno e l'altro; ma, perché elli è difficile accozzarli insieme, è molto più sicuro essere temuto che amato, quando si abbia a mancare del'uno de' dua.*] —Niccolò Machiavelli, *Il Principe*, 1532

1975. He will act like prudent archers, who, seeing that the mark they plan to hit is too far away and knowing what space can be covered by the power of their bows, take an aim much higher than their mark, not in order to reach with their arrows so great a height, but to be able, with the aid of so high an aim, to attain their purpose. [*Fare come gli arcieri prudenti, a' quali, parendo el loco dove disegnano ferire troppo lontano, e conoscendo fino a quanto va la virtù del loro arco, pongono la mira assai più alta che il loco destinato, non per aggiugnere con la loro freccia a tanta altezza, ma per potere con l'aiuto di sì alta mira pervenire al disegno loro.*] —Niccolò Machiavelli, *Il Principe*, 1532

1976. There is nothing more difficult to take in hand, more perilous to conduct, or more uncertain in its success, than to take the lead in the introduction of a new order of things. [*E debbasi considerare, come non è cosa più difficile a trattare, né più dubia a riuscire, né più periculosa a maneggiare, che farsi capo a introdurre nuovi ordini.*] —Niccolò Machiavelli, *Il Principe*, 1532

1977. A prince being thus obliged to know well how to act as a beast must imitate the fox and the lion, for the lion cannot protect himself from traps, and the fox cannot defend himself from wolves. One must therefore be a fox to recognize traps, and a lion to frighten wolves. [*Essendo adunque un principe necessitato sapere bene usare la bestia, debbe di quella pigliare la volpe ed il lione: perché il lione non si difenda da' lacci; la volpe non se difende da' lupi. Bisogna adunque essere volpe a conoscere i lacci, e lione a sbigottire i lupi.*] —Niccolò Machiavelli, *Il Principe*, 1532

1978. A man who wishes to act virtuously in every way necessarily comes to grief among so many who are not virtuous. Therefore if a prince wishes to maintain his rule he must learn how not to be virtuous, and to make use of this knowledge or not according to his need. [*Perché uno uomo, che voglia fare in tutte le parte professione di buono, conviene ruini infra tanti che non sono buoni. Onde è necessario a uno principe, volendosi mantenere, imparare a potere essere non buono, e usarlo e non l'usare secondo la necessità.*] —Niccolò Machiavelli, *Il Principe*, 1532

1979. We owe subjection and obedience to all our kings, whether good or bad, alike, for that has respect unto their office; but as to esteem and affection, these are only due to their virtue. [*Nous devons la sujétion et l'obéissance également à tous Rois, car elle regarde leur office; mais l'estimation, non plus que l'affection, nous ne la devons qu'à leur vertu.*] —Michel de Montaigne, "Nos affections s'emportent au-delà de nous", *Essais*, 1580-88

1980. Ill can he rule the great that cannot reach the small. —Edmund Spenser, *The Faerie Queene*, 1596

1981. Though God hath raised me high, yet this I count the glory of my crown: that I have reigned with your loves. —Elizabeth I, *The Golden Speech*, 1601

1982. Be not afraid of greatness: some are born great, some achieve greatness, and some have greatness thrust upon them —William Shakespeare, *Twelfth Night*, 1601

1983. Whom hatred frights,/ Let him not dream on sovereignty. —Ben Jonson, *Sejanus*, 1603

1984. No ceremony that to great ones 'longs,/ Not the king's crown, nor the deputed sword,/ The marshal's truncheon, nor the judge's robe,/ Become them with one half so good a grace/ As mercy does. —William Shakespeare, *Measure for Measure*, 1604-05

1985. We cannot all be masters, nor all masters / Cannot be truly followed. —William Shakespeare, *Othello*, 1604-05

1986. Ay, every inch a king. —William Shakespeare, *King Lear*, 1605-06

1987. If chance will have me king, why, chance may crown me,/ Without my stir. —William Shakespeare, *Macbeth*, 1605-06

1988. I would not be a queen/ For all the world. —William Shakespeare, *King Henry the Eighth*, 1613

1989. Nothing doth more hurt in a state than that cunning men pass for wise. —Sir Francis Bacon, "Of Cunning", *Essays*, 1625

1990. Men in great places are thrice servants: servants of the sovereign or state, servants of fame, and servants of business. —Sir Francis Bacon, "Of Great Place", *Essays*, 1625

1991. All rising to great place is by a winding stair. —Sir Francis Bacon, "Of Great Place", *Essays*, 1625

1992. He that would govern others, first should be/ Master of himself. —Philip Massinger, *The Bondman*, 1629

1993. Many punishments sometimes, and in some cases, as much discredit a prince as many funerals a physician. —Ben Jonson, "Of Statecraft", *Timber; or Discoveries*, 1640

1994. I am one of those whose heart God hath drawn out to wait for some extraordinary dispensations, according to those promises that He hath held forth of things to be accomplished in the later time, and I cannot but think that God is beginning of them. —Oliver Cromwell, the army debates at Putney, England, Nov 1, 1647

1995. The renown of great men should always be measured by the means which they have used to acquire it. [*La gloire des grands hommes se doit toujours mesurer aux moyens dont ils se sont servis pour l'acquérir.*] —Francois, Duc de La Rochefoucauld, *Réflexions, ou Sentences et maximes morales*, 1665

1996. The world usually rewards the appearance of ability rather than ability itself. [*Le monde récompense plus souvent les apparences du mérite que le mérite même.*] —Francois, Duc de La Rochefoucauld, *Réflexions, ou Sentences et maximes morales*, 1665

1997. The mercy of princes is often just a way of gaining the affection of the people. [*La clémence des princes n'est souvent qu'une politique pour gagner l'affection des peuples.*] —Francois, Duc de La Rochefoucauld, *Réflexions, ou Sentences et maximes morales*, 1665

1998. Those who spend their time on small things usually become incapable of large ones. [*Ceux qui s'appliquent trop aux petites choses deviennent ordinairement incapables de grandes.*] —Francois, Duc de La Rochefoucauld, *Réflexions, ou Sentences et maximes morales*, 1665

1999. Even though men usually flatter themselves on their great deeds, but they are not often the results of a great design, but simply the results of chance. [*Quoique les hommes se flattent de leurs grandes actions, elles ne sont pas souvent les effets d'un grand dessein, mais les effets du hasard.*] —Francois, Duc de La Rochefoucauld, *Réflexions, ou Sentences et maximes morales*, 1665

2000. The captain of a ship is not chosen from those of the passengers who comes from the best family. [*On ne choisit pas pour gouverner un vaisseau celui des voyageurs qui est de la meilleure maison.*] —Blaise Pascal, *Pensées*, 1670

2001. Not the least of the qualities that go into the making of a great ruler is the ability of letting others serve him. [*Etre capable de se laisser servir n'est pas une des moindres qualités, que puisse avoir un grand Roi.*] —Cardinal Richelieu, *Political Testament part I, chap. 6*, 1687

2002. The slave has only one master; the ambitious man has as many as there those who can help his career. [*L'esclave n'a qu'un maître; l'ambitieux en a autant qu'il y a des gens utiles à sa fortune.*] —Jean de La Bruyère, "De la cour", *Les Caractères*, 1688

2003. Ambition often puts Men upon doing the meanest offices; so climbing is performed in the same position with creeping. —Jonathan Swift, *Thoughts on Various Subjects*, 1706

2004. If men of eminence are exposed to censure on one hand, they are as much liable to flattery on the other. If they receive reproaches which are not due to them, they likewise receive praises which they do not deserve. —Joseph Addison, *The Spectator*, 1711

2005. Great and good are seldom the same man. —Thomas Fuller, *Gnomologia*, 1732

2006. If you command wisely, you'll be obeyed cheerfully. —Thomas Fuller, *Gnomologia*, 1732

2007. The subject's love is the king's best guard. —Thomas Fuller, *Gnomologia*, 1732

2008. One is not born for glory unless he is aware of the pace of time. [*On n'est pas né pour la gloire lorsqu'on ne connaît pas le pas du temps.*] —Marquis de Vauvenargues, *Réflexions et maximes*, 1746

2009. Those who see and observe kings, heroes, and statesmen, discover that they have headaches, indigestion, humors and passions, just like other people; every one which in their turns determine their wills in defiance of their reason. —4th Earl of Chesterfield, *Letters to His Son*, Dec 5, 1749

2010. The history of the world's great leaders is often the story of human folly. [*L'histoire des plus grands princes est souvent le récit des fautes des hommes.*] —Voltaire, *Le Siècle de Louis XIV*, 1751

2011. While taking his leave of the king to go off and command the army, Marshall Villars said so that all the court could hear: "Sire, I am going to fight Your Majesty's enemies, and I leave you here in the midst of mine." [*Le maréchal de Villars dit un jour au roi devant toute la cour, lorsqu'il prenait congé pour aller commander l'armée: "Sire, je vais combattre les ennemis de Votre Majesté, et je vous laisse au milieu des miens."*] —Voltaire, *Le Siècle de Louis XIV*, 1751

2012. I know that I can save this country and that no one else can. —William Pitt, 1st Earl of Chatham, reported remarks to the Duke of Devonshire, quoted by Peter Douglas Brown, *William Pitt, Earl of Chatham*, 1978

2013. No man was ever great by imitation. —Samuel Johnson, *Rasselas*, 1759

2014. The strongest is never strong enough to be always the master, unless he transforms strength into right, and obedience into duty. [*Le plus fort n'est jamais assez fort pour être toujours le maître, s'il ne transforme sa force en droit et l'obéissance en devoir.*] —Jean Jacques Rousseau, *The Social Contract*, 1762

2015. Men may be popular without being ambitious; but there is rarely an ambitious man who does not try to be popular. —Frederick North, 8th Baron North, speech in the House of Commons, March, 1769

2016. My rule, in which I have always found satisfaction, is, never to turn aside in public affairs through views of private interest; but to go straight forward in doing what appears to me right at the time, leaving the consequences with Providence. —Benjamin Franklin, letter to Mrs. Jane Mecom, Dec 30, 1770

2017. We must not in the course of public life expect immediate approbation and immediate grateful acknowlegment of our services. But let us persevere through abuse and even injury. The internal satisfaction of a good conscience is always present, and time will do us justice in the minds of the people, even those at present the most prejudiced against us. —Benjamin Franklin, letter to Joseph Galloway, Dec 2, 1772

2018. Great men are the guide-posts and landmarks in the state. —Edmund Burke, speech in the House of Commons, Apr 19, 1774

2019. If we do not lay out ourselves in the service of mankind whom should we serve? —Abigail Adams, *letter to John Thaxter*, Sep 29, 1778

2020. Great offices will have great talents. —William Cowper, "The Winter Evening", *The Task*, 1785

2021. A disposition to preserve, and an ability to improve, taken together, would be my standard of a statesman. —Edmund Burke, *Reflections on the Revolution in France*, 1790

2022. One can't reign and be innocent. [*On ne peut régner innocemment.*] —Louis Antoine Léon de Saint-Just, speech to the National Convention, Nov 13, 1792

2023. No one can rule guiltlessly. —Louis Antoine Léon de Saint-Just, speech to the National Convention, Nov 13, 1792

2024. It is undoubtedly the business of ministers very much to consult the inclinations of the people, but they ought to take great care that they do not receive that inclination from the few persons who may happen to approach them. —Edmund Burke, *Letters on a Regicide Peace*, 1796-97

2025. Herein lies political genius, in the identification of an individual with a principle. —Georg Wilhelm Friedrich Hegel, *The German Constitution*, 1802

2026. In a narrow sphere great men are blunderers. [*Dans une sphère étroite, les grands hommes sont des brouillons.*] —Napoleon I, reported remark

2027. You cannot accomplish good for the people unless you face up to the weak and the foolish. [*On ne fait le bien des peuples qu'en bravant l'opinion des faibles et des ignorants.*] —Napoleon I, letter to Louis a, King of Holland, Dec 15, 1806

2028. You do not inspire confidence, you are too good. [*Vous n'inspirez pas de confiance; vous êtes trop bon.*] —Napoleon I, letter to his brother, the King of Naples, Jul 30, 1806

2029. A leader of whom it is said, "he's a nice man," is lost. [*Un prince dont on dit, c'est un bon homme, est un roi perdu.*] —Napoleon I, letter to the King of Holland, Apr 19, 1807

2030. Were we to act but in cases where no contrary opinion of a lawyer can be had, we should never act. —Thomas Jefferson, letter to Albert Gallatin, Sep 20, 1808

2031. It is not by whining that one carries out the job of king. [*Ce n'est pas en se plaignant qu'on fait le métier de roi.*] —Napoleon I, letter to Louis a, King of Holland, Aug 13, 1809

2032. It is not with the words and explanations of theory that nations are governed. [*Ce n'est point avec des mots et des exposés de principes qu'on gouverne les nations.*] —Napoleon I, letter to M. Champagny, duc de Cadore, Jan 9, 1810

2033. There is a natural aristocracy among men. The grounds of this are virtue and talent. —Thomas Jefferson, letter to John Adams, Oct 28, 1813

2034. The heart of a statesman must be in his head. [*Le coeur d'un homme d'Etat doit être dans sa tête.*] —Napoleon I, quoted by Emmanuel de Las Cases, *Mémorial de Ste. Hélène*, Nov 18-19, 1816

2035. To know nor faith, nor love, nor law; to be/ Omnipotent but friendless is to reign. —Percy Bysshe Shelley, *Prometheus Unbound*, 1818-19

2036. In the council, there were men possessed of much more eloquence than I was: I always defeated them by this simple argument—two and two make four. —Napoleon I, attributed by Count Charles-Tristan de Montholon, *History of the Captivity of a at St. Helena*, 1847

2037. To govern you do not follow any more or less good theory, you build with the materials you have at hand; you have to do what is necessary and make the best of it. [*Il ne s'agit pas, pour gouverner, de suivre une théorie plus ou moins bonne, mais de bâtir avec les matériaux qu'on a sous la main; il faut savoir subir les necessités et en profiter.*] —Napoleon I, quoted by Count Charles-Tristan de Montholon, *Histoire de la captivité de Ste. Hélène*, 1846

2038. No man is truly great who is great only in his lifetime. The test of greatness is the page of history. —William Hazlitt, "The Indian Jugglers", *Table Talk*, 1821-22

2039. He (Martin Van Buren) rowed to his object with muffled oars. —John Randolph of Roanoke, quoted by W. Cabell Bruce, *John Randolph of Roanoke, 1773-1833*, 1922

2040. I consider myself stronger than most of my contemporaries, because I have an invincible hatred of words and empty phrases and my instinct is always towards action. —Prince Clemens von Metternich, letter to Friedrich von Gentz, Aug 5, 1825

2041. He who comes up to his own idea of greatness must always have had a very low standard of it in his mind. —William Hazlitt, "Whether Genius Is Conscious of Its Powers?", *The Plain Speaker*, 1826

2042. It was the boast of Augustus that he found Rome of brick and left it of marble. But how much nobler will be the sovereign's boast when he shall have it to say that he found law dear and left it cheap; found it a sealed book and left it a living letter; found it the patrimony of the rich and left it the inheritance of the poor; found it the two-edged sword of craft and oppression and left it the staff of honesty and the shield of innocence. —Henry Brougham, speech "On the Present State of the Law", Feb 7, 1828

2043. One must be something, in order to do something. [*Mann muss etwas sein, um etwas zu machen.*] —Johann Wolfgang von Goethe, quoted by Johann Peter Eckermann, *Conversations with Goethe*, Oct 20, 1828

2044. A statesman should be possessed of good sense, a primary political quality; and its fortunate possessor needs a second quality—the courage to show that he has it. —(Louis) Adolphe Thiers, speech to the Chamber of Deputies, May 6, 1834

2045. If you think you can win, you can win. Faith is necessary to victory. —William Hazlitt, "On Great and Little Things", *Literary Remains*, 1836

2046. A man who raises himself by degrees to wealth and power, contracts, in the course of this protracted labor, habits of prudence and restraint which he cannot afterwards shake off. A man cannot gradually enlarge his mind as he does his house. [*Un homme qui s'élève par degrés vers la richesse et le pouvoir, contracte, dans ce long travail, des habitudes de prudence et de retenue dont il ne peut ensuite se départir. On n'élargit pas graduellement son âme comme sa maison.*] —Alexis, Comte de Tocqueville, *Democracy in America*, 1839

2047. It is easy in the world to live after the world's opinion; it is easy in solitude to live after our own; but the great man is he who in the midst of the crowd keeps with perfect sweetness the independence of solitude. —Ralph Waldo Emerson, "Self-Reliance", *Essays: First Series*, 1841

2048. A foolish consistency is the hobgoblin of little minds, adored by little statesmen and philosophers and divines. ... Speak what you think today in hard words and tomorrow speak what tomorrow thinks in hard words again, though it contradicts everything you said today. —Ralph Waldo Emerson, "Self-Reliance", *Essays: First Series*, 1841

2049. To be great is to be misunderstood. —Ralph Waldo Emerson, "Self-Reliance", *Essays: First Series*, 1841

2050. No great man lives in vain. The history of the world is but the biography of great men. —Thomas Carlyle, *On Heroes, Hero-Worship, and the Heroic in History*, 1841

2051. You have to be like the pebble in the stream, keeping the grain, and rolling along without being dissolved or dissolving anything else. [*Il faut etre caillou dans le torrent, garder ses veines, et rouler sans être ni dissous, ni dissolvant.*] —Joseph Joubert, *Pensées*, 1842

2052. Princes are more sensitive to any offense that tends to diminish their authority than to any service that tends to reinforce it. [*Les princes sont plus sensibles aux offenses qui tendent à leur ôter l'autorité qu'aux services qui la leur donnent.*] —Joseph Joubert, *Pensées*, 1842

2053. Man is only truly great when he acts from the passions. —Benjamin Disraeli, *Coningsby*, 1844

2054. Mr. Emerson visited Thoreau at the jail, and the meeting between the two philosophers must have been interesting and somewhat dramatic. The account of the meeting was told me by (Thoreau's aunt)—"Henry, why are you here?" "Waldo, why are you not here?" —Henry David Thoreau, attributed by Arthur Samuel Jones, *Thoreau's Incarceration As Told by His Jailer*, Jul 23/24, 1846

2055. The philosophers have only interpreted the world differently, the point is to change it. —Karl Marx, *The German Ideology*, 1846

2056. Great events make me quiet and calm; it is only trifles that irritate my nerves. —Victoria, letter to King Leopold I of Belgium, Apr 4, 1848

2057. Any man more right than his neighbors constitutes a majority of one. —Henry David Thoreau, *Civil Disobedience*, 1849

2058. The difference between a politician and a statesman is: a politician thinks of the next election and a statesman thinks of the next generation. —James Freeman Clarke

2059. Every step of progress the world has made has been from scaffold to scaffold, and from stake to stake. —Wendell Phillips, speech in Worcester, Massachusetts, Oct 15, 1851

2060. There are a thousand hacking at the branches of evil to one who is striking at the root. —Henry David Thoreau, "Economy", *Walden*, 1854

2061. The rarity of great political oratory arises in great measure from this circumstance. Only those engaged in the jar of life have the material for it; only those withdrawn into a brooding imagination have the faculty for it. —Walter Bagehot, "Mr. Gladstone", *National Review*, Jul, 1857

2062. A constitutional statesman is in general a man of common opinions and uncommon abilities. —Walter Bagehot, "The Character of Sir Robert Peel", *National Review*, Jul, 1857

2063. With public sentiment, nothing can fail; without it, nothing can succeed. Consequently he who molds public sentiment goes deeper than he who enacts statutes or pronounces decisions. —Abraham Lincoln, speech at Ottawa, Illinois, Jul 31, 1858

2064. Fame usually comes to those who are thinking about something else. —Oliver Wendell Holmes Sr., *The Autocrat of the Breakfast Table*, 1858

2065. I hear many condemn these men because they were so few. When were the good and the brave ever in a majority? —Henry David Thoreau, *A Plea for Captain John Brown*, 1859

2066. Be ashamed to die until you have won some victory for humanity. —Horace Mann, commencement address at Antioch College, 1859

2067. There are men, who, by their sympathetic attractions, carry nations with them, and lead the activity of the human race. —Ralph Waldo Emerson, "Power", *The Conduct of Life*, 1860

2068. A great statesman is he who knows when to depart from traditions, as well as when to adhere to them. —John Stuart Mill, *Considerations on Representative Government*, 1861

2069. One person with a belief is a social power equal to ninety-nine who have only interests. —John Stuart Mill, *Considerations on Representative Government*, 1861

2070. I hope to "stand firm" enough not to go backward, and yet not go forward fast enough to wreck the country's cause. —Abraham Lincoln, letter to Zachariah Chandler, Nov 20, 1863

2071. I desire so to conduct the affairs of this administration that if at the end, when I come to lay down the reins of power, I have lost every friend on earth, I shall at least have one friend left, and that friend shall be down inside me. —Abraham Lincoln, reply to the Missouri Committee of Seventy, 1864

2072. I claim not to have controlled events, but confess plainly that events have controlled me. —Abraham Lincoln, letter to A.G. Hodges, Apr 4, 1864

2073. Important principles may and must be inflexible. —Abraham Lincoln, speech in Washington, D.C., Apr 11, 1865

2074. When I wish to estimate the danger that is likely to accrue to me from any adversary, I first of all subtract the man's vanity from his other qualities. —Prince Otto von Bismarck, quoted by Charles Lowe, *Bismarck's Table Talk*, 1895

2075. The secret of success is constancy to purpose. —Benjamin Disraeli, speech, Jun 24, 1872

2076. Reason may be the lever, but sentiment gives you the fulcrum and the place to stand on if you want to move the world. —Oliver Wendell Holmes Sr., *The Poet at the Breakfast Table*, 1872

2077. What makes a man minister? Debating power. And what makes a man Premier? Debating power. And what good is debating power to you? What has it ever done for you or for England? It bears the same relation to governing that tournaments did to fighting. —Frederic Harrison, *Order and Progress*, 1875

2078. To be a leader of men one must turn one's back on men. —Havelock Ellis, introduction to Joris Karl Huysman, *Against the Grain*, 1884

2079. To do great things is difficult; but to command great things is more difficult. [*Grosses vollführen ist schwer: aber das Schwerere ist, Grosses befehlen.*] —Friedrich Nietzsche, "The Stillest Hour", *Thus Spoke Zarathustra*, 1883-85

2080. Whoever fights monsters should see to it that in the process he does not become a monster. [*Wer mit Ungeheuern kämpft, mag zusehn, dasz er nicht dabei zum Ungeheuer wird.*] —Friedrich Nietzsche, *Beyond Good and Evil*, 1886

2081. Public men are bees working in a glass hive; and curious spectators enjoy themselves in watching every secret movement, as if it were a study in natural history. —Henry Ward Beecher, *Proverbs from Plymouth Pulpit*, 1887

2082. What is the use of being elected or re-elected unless you stand for something? —Grover Cleveland, reported remarks to a political adviser, 1887

2083. We are all in the gutter, but some of us are looking at the stars. —Oscar Wilde, *Lady Windermere's Fan*, 1892

2084. In statesmanship get formalities right, never mind about the moralities. —Mark Twain, *Following the Equator*, 1897

2085. We do not admire a man of timid peace. —Theodore Roosevelt, speech in Chicago, Illinois, Apr 10, 1899

2086. If a had been as intelligent as Spinoza, he would have written four volumes in an attic. [*Si a avait été aussi intelligent que Spinoza, il aurait écrit quatre volumes dans une mansarde.*] —Anatole France, *Monsieur Bergeret à Paris*, 1900

2087. Some men owe most of their greatness to the ability of detecting in those they destine for their tools the exact quality of strength that matters for their work. —Joseph Conrad, *Lord Jim*, 1900

2088. I sometimes think that great men are like great mountains: one cannot realize their greatness till one stands at some distance from them. —Joseph Chamberlain, quoted by Austen Chamberlain, *Down the Years*, 1935

2089. For the present, at any rate, I must proceed alone. I must plough my own furrow alone, but before I get to the end of that furrow it is possible that I may not find myself alone. —5th Earl of Rosebery, speech to the City of London Liberal Club on being out of government, Jul 19, 1901

2090. A great man's failures to understand define him. [*On peut même dire que ses incompréhensions font la définition du grand homme.*] —Andre Gide, "Concerning Influence in Literature", *Pretexts*, 1903

2091. It is at night that faith in light is admirable. [*C'est la nuit qu'il est beau de croire a la lumière.*] —Edmond Rostand, *Chantecler*, 1907

2092. If we believe a thing to be bad, and if we have a right to prevent it, it is our duty to try to prevent it, and to damn the consequences. —Alfred, 1st Viscount Milner, speech in Glasgow, Scotland, Nov 26, 1909

2093. If I am a great man, then a good many great men must have been frauds. —Andrew Bonar Law, reported conversation on becoming leader of Conservative party, Nov 13, 1911

2094. All ambitions are lawful except those which climb upward on the miseries or credulities of mankind. —Joseph Conrad, *A Personal Record*, 1912

2095. There is no cause half so sacred as the cause of a people. There is no idea so uplifting as the idea of the service of humanity. —Woodrow Wilson, campaign speech in New York City, Oct 31, 1912

2096. A man is not as big as his belief in himself; he is as big as the number of persons who believe in him. —Woodrow Wilson, speech, Oct 3, 1912

2097. It is harder for a leader to be born in a palace than to be born in a cabin. —Woodrow Wilson, speech in Denver, Colorado, Oct 7, 1912

2098. Every country is renewed out of the unknown ranks and not out of the ranks of those already famous and powerful and in control. —Woodrow Wilson, speech in Chester, Pennsylvania, Oct 28, 1912

2099. The unforgivable crime is soft hitting. Do not hit at all if it can be avoided. —Theodore Roosevelt, *Autobiography*, 1913

2100. If you think too much about being re-elected, it is very difficult to be worth re-electing. —Woodrow Wilson, speech in Philadelphia, Pennsylvania, Oct 25, 1913

2101. The man who is swimming against the stream knows the strength of it. —Woodrow Wilson, speech on "The New Freedom", 1913

2102. The greatest height of heroism to which an individual, like a people, can attain is to know how to face ridicule. [*El mas alto heroísmo para un individuo, como para un pueblo, es saber afrontar el ridículo*] —Miguel de Unamuno, "Don Quixote Today", *Tragic Sense of Life in Men and Nations*, 1913

2103. In public politics as in private life, character is better than brains, and loyalty more valuable then either; but, I shall have to work with the material that has been given to me. —Herbert Asquith, 1st Earl of Oxford, in conversation with his wife, Jul 31, 1914

2104. Like all weak men he laid an exaggerated stress on not changing one's mind. —W. Somerset Maugham, *Of Human Bondage*, 1915

2105. One cool judgment is worth a thousand hasty counsels. The thing to be supplied is light, not heat. —Woodrow Wilson, speech in Pittsburgh, Pennsylvania, Jan 29, 1916

2106. Blessed is he whose fame does not outshine his truth. —Sir Rabindranath Tagore, *Stray Birds*, 1916

2107. Great political and social changes begin to be possible as soon as men are not afraid to risk their lives. —Thomas Masaryk, letter to R. Seton-Watson, Mar 16, 1917

2108. It is unfortunate, considering that enthusiasm moves the world, that so few enthusiasts can be trusted to speak the truth. —Arthur Balfour, letter to Mrs. Drew, 1918

2109. There is something better, if possible, that a man can give than his life. That is his living spirit to a service that is not easy, to resist counsels that are hard to resist, to stand against purposes that are diffcult to stand against. —Woodrow Wilson, speech, May 30, 1919

2110. Great men are but life-sized. Most of them, indeed, are rather short. —Sir Max Beerbohm, "A Point to Be Remembered by Very Eminent Men", *And Even Now*, 1920

2111. To rule over oneself is the first condition for one who would rule over others. [*Ser emperador de sí mismo es la primera condición para imperar a los demás.*] —Jose Ortega y Gasset, *Invertebrate Spain*, 1922

2112. The tragedy of life is not that man loses but that he almost wins. —Heywood Broun, "Sport for Art's Sake", *Pieces of Hate, and Other Enthusiasms*, 1922

2113. The efficiency of the truly national leader consists primarily in preventing the division of the attention of a people, and always in concentrating it on a single enemy. [*Überhaupt besteht die Kunst aller wahrhaft grossen Volksführer zu allen Zeiten in erster Linie mit darin, die Aufmerksamkeit eines Volkes nicht zu zersplittern, sondern immer auf einen einzigen Gegner zu konzentrieren.*] —Adolf Hitler, *Mein Kampf*, 1924

2114. You cannot choose your battlefield,/ The gods do that for you,/ But you can plant a standard/ Where a standard never flew. —Nathalia Crane, *The Colors*, ca. 1925

2115. Statesmen must learn to live with scientists as the Medici once lived with artists. —Sir Oswald Mosley, quoted by Robert Skidelsky, *Oswald Mosley*, 1975

2116. Some men succeed by what they know; some by what they do; and a few by what they are. —Elbert G. Hubbard, *The Note Book*, 1927

2117. An ounce of loyalty is worth a pound of cleverness. —Elbert G. Hubbard, *The Note Book*, 1927

2118. Those who believe that they are exclusively in the right are generally those who achieve something. —Aldous Huxley, *Proper Studies*, 1927

2119. You show me a good and gracious loser, and I'll show you a failure! —Knut Rockne, quoted, *Argosy*, Nov, 1976

2120. If God were to come to me and say, "Ramsay, would you rather be a country gentleman than a Prime Minister?", I should reply, "Please, God, a country gentleman." —(James) Ramsay MacDonald, reported conversation with Harold Nicolson and Vita Sackville-West, Oct, 1930

2121. The truth is that you don't rule with the fist. And ruling is not the act of taking power, but exercising power in tranquillity. Actually, ruling is staying seated. [*La verdad es que no se manda con los jenízaros. ... Y mandar no es gesto de arrebatar el poder, sino tranquilo ejercicio de él. En suma: mandar es sentarse.*] —Jose Ortega y Gasset, *The Revolt of the Masses*, 1930

2122. One who brandishes a pistol must be prepared to shoot. —Herbert Hoover, in 1931, as quoted, *Memoirs*, 1952

2123. Government includes the art of formulating a policy, and using the political technique to attain so much of that policy as will receive general support; persuading, leading, sacrificing, teaching always, because the greatest duty of any statesman is to educate. —Franklin D. Roosevelt, speech in San Francisco, California, Sep 23, 1932

2124. The fate of America cannot depend on any one man. The greatness of America is grounded in principles and not on any single personally. —Franklin D. Roosevelt, speech in New York City, Nov 5, 1932

2125. Authority must be accompanied by prestige and prestige comes only from distance. [*L'autorité ne va pas sans prestige, ni le prestige sans l'éloignement.*] —Charles De Gaulle, *Le Fil de l'épée*, 1934

2126. The great leaders have always stage-managed their effects. —Charles De Gaulle, *Le fil de l'epée*, 1934

2127. The privilege of the great is to see catastrophes from the terrace. —Jean Giraudoux, *Tiger at the Gates*, 1935

2128. The king presupposes subjects; the leader, followers. [*Il re presuppone i sudditi, il dirigente i seguaci.*] —Ignazio Silone, *The School for Dictatorships*, 1939

2129. The future lies with those wise political leaders who realize that the great public is interested more in government than in politics. —Franklin D. Roosevelt, speech in Washington, D.C., Jan 8, 1940

2130. I am fighting, as I have always fought, for the rights of the little man as well as for the big man—for the weak as well as the strong. ... I am fighting to defend them against the power and might of those who rise up to challenge them. And I will not stop fighting. —Franklin D. Roosevelt, speech in Brooklyn, New York, 1940

2131. Glory is only given to those who have always dreamed of it. [*La gloire se donne seulement à ceux qui l'ont toujours rêvée.*] —Charles De Gaulle, *Vers l'armée de métier*, 1940

2132. The only guide to a man is his conscience; the only shield to his memory is the rectitude and sincerity of his actions. It is very imprudent to walk through life without this shield, because we are so often mocked by the failure of our hopes and the upsetting of our calculations; but with this shield, however the fates may play, we march always in the ranks of honor. —Sir Winston S. Churchill, tribute in the House of Commons to Neville Chamberlain, following his death, Nov 12, 1940

2133. I do not resent criticism, even when, for the sake of emphasis, it parts for the time with reality. —Sir Winston S. Churchill, speech in the House of Commons, Jan 22, 1941

2134. No man is great enough or wise enough for any of us to surrender our destiny to. The only way in which anyone can lead us is to restore to us the belief in our own guidance. —Henry Miller, "The Alcoholic Veteran with the Washboard Cranium", *The Wisdom of the Heart*, 1941

2135. The real leader has no need to lead—he is content to point the way. —Henry Miller, "The Wisdom of the Heart", *The Wisdom of the Heart*, 1941

2136. I have not become the King's First Minister in order to preside over the liquidation of the British Empire. —Sir Winston S. Churchill, speech at the Lord Mayor's luncheon, London, Nov 10, 1942

2137. A chief is a man who assumes responsibility. He says, "I was beaten." He does not say, "My men were beaten." Thus speaks a real man. [*Le chef est celui qui prend tout en charge. Il dit: J'ai été battu. Il ne dit pas: Mes soldats ont été battus. L'homme véritable parle ainsi.*] —Antoine de Saint-Exupéry, *Pilote de guerre*, 1942

2138. Heroes are created by popular demand, sometimes out of the scantiest materials, or none at all. —Gerald White Johnson, *American Heroes and Hero-Worship*, 1943

2139. Unlucky the country that needs a hero. [*Unglucklich das Land, das Helden nötig hat.*] —Bertolt Brecht, *Leben des Galilei*, 1943

2140. Take calculated risks. That is quite different from being rash. —George S. Patton, letter to Cadet George S. Patton, Jr., Jun 6, 1944

2141. We may make mistakes—but they must never be mistakes which result from faintness of heart or abandonment of moral principle. —Franklin D. Roosevelt, fourth inaugural address, Jan 20, 1945

2142. The final test of a leader is that he leaves behind him in other men the conviction and the will to carry on. —Walter Lippmann, "Roosevelt Has Gone", *New York Herald Tribune*, Apr 14, 1945

2143. Men prominent in life are mostly hard to converse with. They lack small-talk, and at the same time one doesn't like to confront them with their own great themes. —Sir Max Beerbohm, "T. Fenning Dodworth", *Mainly on the Air*, 1946

2144. You know, the greatest epitaph in the country is here in Arizona. It's in Tombstone, Ariz., and this epitaph says, "Here lies Jack Williams. He done his damndest." I think that is the greatest epitaph a man could have. Whenever a man does the best he can, then that is all he can do; and that is what your President has been trying to do for the last 3 years for this country. —Harry S Truman, remarks in Winslow, Arizona, Jun 15, 1948

2145. We believe in equal opportunity for all, but we know that this includes the opportunity to rise to leadership, to be uncommon! The great human advances have not been brought about by mediocre men and women. —Herbert Hoover, remarks, Nov 11, 1948

2146. You know what makes leadership? It is the ability to get men to do what they don't want to do, and like it. —Harry S Truman, quoted, *Time*, Nov 8, 1976

2147. We need supermen to rule us—the job is so vast and the need for wise judgment is so urgent. But, alas, there are no supermen. —Brooks Atkinson, "January 27", *Once Around the Sun*, 1951

2148. I distrust Great Men. They produce a desert of uniformity around them and often a pool of blood too, and I always feel a little man's pleasure when they come a cropper. —E.M. Forster, "What I Believe", *Two Cheers for Democracy*, 1951

2149. The first function of a political leader is advocacy. It is he who must make articulate the wants, the frustration, and the aspiration of the masses. —Aneurin Bevan, *In Place of Fear*, 1952

2150. There is nothing more agreeable in this life than to make peace with the Establishment—and nothing more corrupting. —A.J.P. Taylor, "William Cobbett", *New Statesman*, 1953

2151. This Republic was not established by cowards; and cowards will not preserve it. —Elmer Davis, *But We Were Born Free*, 1954

2152. A great man's greatest good luck is to die at the right time. —Eric Hoffer, *The Passionate State of Mind*, 1954

2153. We will not be driven by fear into an age of unreason if we ... remember that we are not descended from fearful men, not from men who feared to write, to speak, to associate and to defend causes which were, for the moment unpopular. —Edward R. Murrow, "See It Now" television broadcast, Mar 7, 1954

2154. In the face of great danger, salvation can only come through greatness. [*Face aux grands périls, le salut n'est que la grandeur.*] —Charles De Gaulle, *Mémoires de guerre: L'Appel*, 1955

2155. The leader is always alone in times of doom. [*Toujours, le Chef est seul en face du mauvais destin.*] —Charles De Gaulle, *Mémoires de guerre: L'Appel*, 1955

2156. Old age is a shipwreck. [*La vieillesse est un naufrage.*] —Charles De Gaulle, *Mémoires de guerre: L'Appel*, 1955

2157. I spoke. I had to. It is action that puts fervor to work. But it is words that create it. [*Je parle. Il le faut bien. L'action met les ardeurs en oeuvre. Mais c'est la parole qui les suscite.*] —Charles De Gaulle, *Mémoires de guerre: L'Appel*, 1955

2158. To act coolly, intelligently and prudently in perilous circumstances is the test of a man— and also a nation. —Adlai E. Stevenson Jr., *The New York Times*, Apr 11, 1955

2159. A decision is the action an executive must take when he has information so incomplete that the answer does not suggest itself. —Adm. Arthur W. Radford, *Time*, Feb 25, 1957

2160. The difference between being an elder statesman/ And posing successfully as an elder statesman/ Is practically negligible. —T.S. Eliot, *The Elder Statesman*, 1958

2161. At home, you always have to be a politician; when you're abroad, you almost feel yourself a statesman. —Harold Macmillan, *Look*, Apr 15, 1958

2162. Difficulty is the excuse history never accepts. —Edward R. Murrow, on President John F. Kennedy's inaugural address, Oct 19, 1959

2163. No one has a finer command of language than the person who keeps his mouth shut. —Sam Rayburn, quoted, *Lawrence Daily Journal-World*, Aug 29, 1978

2164. Some men can make decisions and some cannot. Some men fret and delay under criticism. I used to have a saying that applies here, and I note that some people have picked it up, "If you can't stand the heat, get out of the kitchen." —Harry S Truman, *Mr. Citizen*, 1960

2165. Few great men could pass Personnel. —Paul Goodman, *Growing Up Absurd*, 1960

2166. As for me, I know only too well my limits and weaknesses, and I also know that no man can take the place of a whole people. That is why I wanted to inspire their souls with the conviction that filled me. [*Quant à moi, qui ne connais que trop mes limites et mon infirmité et qui sais bien qu'aucun homme ne peut se substituer à un peuple, comme je voudrais faire entrer dans les âmes la conviction qui m'anime!*] —Charles De Gaulle, *Mémoires de guerre: Le Salut*, 1960

2167. Keep strong, if possible. In any case, keep cool. Have unlimited patience. Never corner an opponent, and always assist him to save his face. Put yourself in his shoes—so as to see things through his eyes. Avoid self-righteousness like the devil— nothing so self-blinding. —Sir Basil Liddell Hart, *Deterrent or Defense: Advice to Statesmen*, 1960

2168. To say he (John F. Kennedy) would not make mistakes would be silly. Anyone would make mistakes with the problems that lie ahead of us. —Eleanor Roosevelt, letter to Peter Kamitchis, Oct 21, 1960

2169. You cannot be a leader, and ask other people to follow you, unless you know how to follow, too. —Sam Rayburn, attributed, *The Leadership of Sam Rayburn, Collected Tributes of His Colleagues*, 1961

2170. The modern world is not given to uncritical admiration. It expects its idols to have feet of clay, and can be reasonably sure that press and camera will report their exact dimensions. —Barbara Ward, *Saturday Review*, Sep 30, 1961

2171. If we are to regard ourselves as a grown-up nation—and anything else will henceforth be mortally dangerous—then we must, as the Biblical phrase goes, put away childish things; and among these childish things the first to go, in my opinion, should be self-idealization and the search for absolutes in world affairs: for absolute security, absolute amity, absolute harmony. —George F. Kennan, *Russia and the West under Lenin and Stalin*, 1961

2172. I am certain that after the dust of centuries has passed over our cities, we, too, will be remembered not for victories or defeats in battle or politics, but for our contribution to the human spirit. —John F. Kennedy, closed-circuit television broadcast, Nov 29, 1962

2173. As I leave you I want you to know—just think how much you're going to be missing. You won't have Nixon to kick around anymore because, gentlemen, this is my last press conference. —Richard M. Nixon, press conference following defeat in California gubernatorial election, Nov 7, 1962

2174. I know of no higher fortitude than stubbornness in the face of overwhelming odds. —Louis Nizer, *My Life in Court*, 1962

2175. If a man hasn't discovered something that he will die for, he isn't fit to live. —Martin Luther King Jr., speech in Detroit, Michigan, Jun 23, 1963

2176. A nation reveals itself not only by the men it produces but also by the men it honors, the men it remembers. —John F. Kennedy, speech at Amherst College, Amherst, Massachusetts, Oct 26, 1963

2177. There are things a man must not do even to save a nation. —Murray Kempton, "To Save a Nation", *America Comes of Middle Age*, 1963

2178. I like to operate like a submarine on sonar. When I am picking up noise from both the left and right, I know my course is correct. —Gustavo Diaz Ordaz, while campaigning for presidency of Mexico, *US News & World Report*, Jul 13, 1964

2179. The leader must know, must know he knows, and must be able to make it abundantly clear to those about him that he knows. —Clarence B. Randall, *Making Good in Management*, 1964

2180. A political leader must keep looking over his shoulder all the time to see if the boys are still there. If they aren't still there, he's no longer a political leader. —Bernard Baruch, quoted, *The New York Times*, Jun 21, 1965

2181. Only he deserves power who every day justifies it. —Dag Hammarskjold, "1951", *Markings*, 1965

2182. When I want to know what France thinks, I ask myself. —Charles De Gaulle, *Time*, Dec 17, 1965

2183. I have against me the bourgeois, the military and the diplomats, and for me, only the people who take the Metro. —Charles De Gaulle, *The New York Times*, Dec 17, 1965

2184. It's never the right time to take a particular stand. —Adam Clayton Powell Jr., "One Must Die for Many", *Keep the Faith, Baby*, 1967

2185. I respect only those who resist me, but I cannot tolerate them. —Charles De Gaulle, quoted, *The New York Times Magazine*, May 12, 1968

2186. When statesmen forsake their own private conscience for the sake of their public duties ... they lead their country by a short route to chaos. —Robert Bolt, *A Man for All Seasons*, 1968

2187. There are some people, you know, they think the way to be a big man is to shout and stomp and raise hell—and then nothing ever really happens. I'm not like that ... I never shoot blanks. —Richard M. Nixon, *Look*, Oct 19, 1971

2188. My strong point is not rhetoric, it isn't showmanship, it isn't big promises—those things that create the glamour and the excitement that people call charisma and warmth. My strong point, if I have a strong point, is performance. I always do more than I say. I always produce more than I promise. —Richard M. Nixon, CBS-TV, Jan 2, 1972

2189. It's no accident many accuse me of conducting public affairs with my heart instead of my head. Well, what if I do?. ... Those who don't know how to weep with their whole heart don't know how to laugh either. —Golda Meir, *Ms*, Apr, 1973

2190. We are not going around looking for opportunities to prove our manhood. —Henry A. Kissinger, *Ms.*, Oct, 1975

2191. People tend to want to follow the beaten path. The difficulty is that the beaten path doesn't seem to be leading anywhere. —Charles M. Mathias Jr., *Time*, Dec 8, 1975

2192. If I have anything special that makes me "influential" I simply don't know how to define it. If I knew the ingredients I would bottle them, package them and sell them, because I want everyone to be able to work together in a spirit of cooperation and compromise and accommodation without, you know, any caving in or anyone being woefully violated personally or in terms of his principles. —Barbara Jordan, quoted in "Barbara Jordan" by Charles L. Sanders, *Ebony*, Feb, 1975

2193. The most important thing is to be strong. With strength, one can conquer others, and to conquer others gives one virtue. —Mao Tse-tung, quoted, *Time*, Sep 20, 1976

2194. A statesman who too far outruns the experience of his people will fail in achieving a domestic consensus, however wise his policies. (On the other hand), a statesman who limits his policies to the experience of his people is doomed to sterility. —Henry A. Kissinger, *Time*, Nov 8, 1976

2195. I am alone with the masses. —Mao Tse-tung, quoted, *Time*, Sep 20, 1976

2196. Charismatic leadership is hungered for, but at the same time we fear it. —Kevin White, *Time*, Feb 9, 1976

2197. We lost the American colonies because we lacked the statesmanship to know the right time and the manner of yielding what is impossible to keep. —Elizabeth II, in Philadelphia, Pennsylvania, during American bicentennial celebrations, *Newsweek*, Jul 17, 1976

2198. I don't know the key to success, but the key to failure is trying to please everybody. —Bill Cosby, *Ebony*, Jun, 1977

2199. If an individual wants to be a leader and isn't controversial, that means he never stood for anything. —Richard M. Nixon, *Dallas Times-Herald*, Dec 10, 1978

2200. If you don't stand for something, you will stand for anything. —Ginger Rogers, *Parade*, Jun 18, 1978

2201. It's the orders you disobey that make you famous. —Douglas MacArthur, *Time*, Sep 11, 1978

2202. Too bad that all the people who know how to run the country are busy driving taxicabs and cutting hair. —George Burns, *Life*, Dec, 1979

2203. One had the sense that if (Charles De Gaulle) moved to a window, the center of gravity might shift, and the whole room might tilt everybody into the garden. —Henry A. Kissinger, *Time*, Oct 15, 1979

2204. Competing pressures tempt one to believe that an issue deferred is a problem avoided: more often it is a crisis invited. —Henry A. Kissinger, *Time*, Oct 15, 1979

2205. High office teaches decision making, not substance. It consumes intellectual capital; it does not create it. —Henry A. Kissinger, *Time*, Oct 15, 1979

2206. The world is divided into those who want to become someone and those who want to accomplish something. —Jean Monnet, *Time*, Mar 26, 1979

2207. A leader should not get too far in front of his troops or he will be shot in the ass. —Joseph Clark, *Washingtonian*, Nov, 1979

2208. Men of power have no time to read; yet the men who do not read are unfit for power. —Michael Foot, *Debts of Honour*, 1980

2209. To those waiting with bated breath for that favourite media catch-phrase, the U-turn, I have only one thing to say: you turn if you want to. The lady's not turning. —Margaret Thatcher, speech to the Conservative party annual conference, Oct, 1980

2210. The statesman's duty is to bridge the gap between his nation's experience and his vision. —Henry A. Kissinger, *Years of Upheaval*, 1982

2211. To have striven so hard, to have moulded a public personality out of so amorphous an identity, to have sustained that superhuman effort only to end with every weakness disclosed and every error compounding the downfall—that was a fate of biblical proportions. Evidently the Deity would not tolerate the presumption that all can be manipulated; an object lesson of the limits of human presumption was necessary. —Henry A. Kissinger, on the resignation of Richard Nixon, *Years of Upheaval*, 1982

2212. For some days, people thought that India was shaking. But there are always tremors when a great tree falls. —Rajiv Gandhi, speech following his mother's assassination, *The New York Times*, Nov 20, 1984

2213. If I die a violent death, as some fear and a few are plotting, I know that the violence will be in the thought and the action of the assassins, not in my dying. —Indira Gandhi, handwritten statement found after her death, Oct 31, 1984

2214. I am a leader by default, only because nature does not allow a vacuum. —Desmond Tutu, *Christian Science Monitor*, Dec 20, 1984

2215. If you lead a country like Britain, a strong country, a country which has taken a lead in world affairs in good times and in bad, a country that is always reliable, then you have to have a touch of iron about you. —Margaret Thatcher, on reference to her as the Iron Lady, *Daily Telegraph*, Mar 21, 1986

2216. I do not know anyone who has got to the top without hard work. That is the recipe. It will not always get you to the top, but should get you pretty near. —Margaret Thatcher, *Daily Telegraph*, Mar 21, 1986

2217. What is success? I think it is a mixture of having a flair for the thing that you are doing; knowing that it is not enough, that you have got to have hard work and a certain sense of purpose. —Margaret Thatcher, *Parade*, Jul 13, 1986

2218. It was sheer professionalism and inspiration and the fact that you really cannot have people marching into other people's territory and staying there. —Margaret Thatcher, on the Falklands War, *New Yorker*, Feb 10, 1986

2219. I have been underestimated for decades. I've done very well that way. —Helmut Kohl, *The New York Times*, Jan 25, 1987

2220. There's nothing wrong with having a big ego. It's all right to have a Rolls Royce ego so long as you don't have a bicycle brain. If they coordinate, you can work it out pretty well. —Jesse Jackson, "Meet the Press," NBC-TV, Jun 12, 1988

LEGISLATURES AND LEGISLATION

2221. Parliament is not a congress of ambassadors from different and hostile interests; which interests each must maintain, as an agent and advocate, against other agents and advocates; but parliament is a deliberative assembly of one nation, with one interest, that of the whole. —Edmund Burke, speech to the electors of Bristol, Nov 3, 1774

2222. To render it (legislation) agreeable to good policy, three things are requisite. First, that the necessity of the times requires it; secondly, that it be not the probable source of greater evils than those it pretends to remedy; and lastly, that it have a probability of success. —Alexander Hamilton, "A Full Vindication", Dec 15, 1774

2223. The Commons, faithful to their system, remained in a wise and masterly inactivity. —Sir James Mackintosh, *Vindiciae Gallicae*, 1791

2224. Take a single step beyond the boundaries ... specially drawn around the powers of Congress, is to take possession of a boundless field of power, no longer susceptible of any definition. —Thomas Jefferson, "Opinion on the Constitutionality of the Bill for Establishing a National Bank", Feb 15, 1791

2225. Only make wise and moderate laws. But have them carried out with force and vigor. [*Ne faites que les lois sages et modérées. Faites-les éxécuter avec force et énergie.*] —Napoleon I, letter to the provisional government of the Ligurian Republic, Nov 11, 1797

2226. Legislation is not changed every day. [*On ne change pas la législation tous les jours.*] — Napoleon I, decision, Sep 18, 1805

2227. All the public business in Congress now connects itself with intrigues, and there is great danger that the whole government will degenerate into a struggle of cabals. —John Quincy Adams, *Diary*, Jan, 1819

2228. When no limits are set to representative authority, the representatives of the people are not defenders of liberty but candidates for tyranny. —Benjamin Constant de Rebecque, *Course of Constitutional Politics*, 1817-20

2229. That 150 lawyers should do business together is not to be expected. —Thomas Jefferson, on the functioning of Congress, *Autobiography*, Jan 6, 1821

2230. The science of legislation is like that of medicine in one respect: that it is far more easy to point out what will do harm than what will do good. —Charles Caleb Colton, *Lacön*, 1825

2231. We ought to observe that practice which is the hardest of all—especially for young physicians—we ought to throw in no medicine at all—to abstain—to observe a wise and masterly inactivity. —John Randolph of Roanoke, speech in the U.S. Senate, Jan 25, 1828

2232. The great problem of legislation is, so to organize the civil government of a community ... that in the operation of human institutions upon social action, self-love and social may be made the same. —John Quincy Adams, "Society and Civilization", *American Review*, Jul, 1845

2233. That a Parliament, especially a Parliament with Newspaper Reporters firmly established in it, is an entity which by its very nature cannot do work, but can do talk only. —Thomas Carlyle, *Latter-Day Pamphlets*, 1850

2234. Parliament will train you to talk; and above all things to hear, with patience, unlimited quantities of foolish talk. —Thomas Carlyle, *Latter-Day Pamphlets*, 1850

2235. The House of Commons allows itself to be led, but does not like to be driven, and is apt to turn upon those who attempts to drive it. —3rd Viscount Palmerston, letter to William Gladstone, May 16, 1861

2236. No man's life, liberty or property are safe while the Legislature is in session. — Anonymous, quoted by Gideon J. Tucker, *New York Surrogate Reports*, 1866

2237. Let us give our Republic not the best possible laws but the best which they will bear. This is the essence of politics; all the rest is speculation. —Sir William Harcourt, letter to Charles Dilke, 1870

2238. Permissive legislation is the characteristic of a free people. —Benjamin Disraeli, speech in the House of Commons, Jun 18, 1875

2239. If there is a free contract, in open market, between capital and labour, it cannot be right that one of the two contracting parties should have the making of the laws. —Lord Acton, letter to Mary Gladstone, Apr 24, 1881

2240. It could probably be shown by facts and figures that there is no distinctly native American criminal class except Congress. —Mark Twain, *Following the Equator*, 1897

2241. It must be remembered that legislatures are ultimate guardians of the liberties and welfare of the people in quite as great a degree as the courts. —Oliver Wendell Holmes Jr., *Missouri, Kansas and Texas Railway Company v. May*, 1904

2242. It is his jooty to rigorously enforce th' rules iv th' Sinit. There ar're none. Th' Sinit is ruled be courtesy, like th' longshoreman's union. —Finley Peter Dunne, "The Vice-President", *Dissertations by Mr. Dooley*, 1906

2243. A little group of wilful men (filibustering senators) representing no opinion but their own have rendered the great government of the United States helpless and contemptible. —Woodrow Wilson, address to the nation, Mar 4, 1917

2244. Now and then an innocent man is sent to the legislature. —"Kin" Hubbard, saying

2245. Nearly all legislation is the result of compromise. —Joseph G. Cannon, quoted on his retirement, *The Baltimore Sun*, Mar 4, 1923

2246. I may have grown cynical from long service, but ... I sometimes think I'd rather be a dog and bay at the moon than stay in the Senate another six years and listen to it. —John Sharp Williams, retirement speech, Mar 4, 1923

2247. When not realities but words are to be discussed Parliament wakes up. Then we are back in the comfortable pre-war world of make-believe. Politics are safe again; hairs are to be split, not facts to be faced. Hush! Do not awaken the dreamers. Facts will waken them in time with a vengeance. —Sir Oswald Mosley, *Birmingham Town Crier*, Dec 23, 1929

2248. There is good news from Washington today. The Congress is deadlocked and can't act. —Will Rogers, quoted, *Newsweek*, Jun 9, 1975

2249. The legislature, like the executive, has ceased to be even the creature of the people: it is the creature of pressure groups, and most of them, it must be manifest, are of dubious wisdom and even more dubious honesty. —H.L. Mencken, "The Library", *The American Mercury*, May 1930

2250. If today our action employs among its different weapons that of parliament, that is not to say that parliamentary parties exist only for parliamentary ends. For us parliament is not an end in itself, but merely a means to an end. —Adolf Hitler, speech in Munich, Sep 23, 1930

2251. "Do you pray for the Senators, Dr. Hale?" someone asked the chaplain. "No, I look at the Senators and pray for the country." —Edward Everett Hale, quoted by Van Wyck Brooks, *New England: Indian Summer, 1865-1915*, 1940

2252. One thing the House will NEVER forgive and that is if a Minister misleads it. If you find you have given an answer that isn't true, acknowledge it at once and express your regret. —Stanley Baldwin, letter to Sir John Reith, Jan 31, 1940

2253. The only way to do anything in the American government is to bypass the Senate. —Franklin D. Roosevelt, quoted, on his return from the Yalta Conference, *Chicago Tribune*, May 29, 1977

2254. The great executives have given inspiration and push to the advancement of human society, but it is the legislator who has given stability and continuity to that slow and painful progress. —J. William Fulbright, speech at Univ. of Chicago, 1946

2255. In one sense the House of Commons is the most unrepresentative of representative assemblies. It is an elaborate conspiracy to prevent the real clash of opinion which exists outside from finding an appropriate echo within its walls. It is a social shock absorber placed between privilege and the pressure of popular discontent. —Aneurin Bevan, *In Place of Fear*, 1952

2256. Parliament has joined the monarchy as a dignified, not an effective, element in the Constitution. —Richard Crossman, *Diary*, Mar 19, 1959

2257. Legislators represent people, not trees or acres. Legislators are elected by voters, not farms or cities or economic interests. —Earl Warren, *Reynolds v. Sims*, Jun 15, 1964

2258. If Moses had gone to Harvard Law School and spent three years working on the Hill, he would have written the Ten Commandments with three exceptions and a savings clause. —Charles Morgan Jr., *Rolling Stone*, Jan 15, 1976

2259. If you love the law and you love good sausage, don't watch either of them being made. —Betty Talmadge, *The Reader*, Nov 25, 1977

2260. The Senate is a place filled with goodwill and good intentions, and if the road to hell is paved with them, then it's a pretty good detour. —Hubert H. Humphrey, quoted, *Newsweek*, Jan 23, 1978

2261. (Congress is) functioning the way the Founding Fathers intended—not very well. They understood that if you move too quickly, our democracy will be less responsible to the majority. —Barber B. Conable Jr., *Time*, Oct 22, 1984

2262. Exhaustion and exasperation are frequently the handmaidens of legislative decision. —Barber B. Conable Jr., *Time*, Oct 22, 1984

2263. I don't think it's the function of Congress to function well. It should drag its heels on the way to decision. —Barber B. Conable Jr., *Time*, Oct 22, 1984

2264. This bill is the legislative equivalent of crack. It yields a short-term high but does long-term damage to the system and it's expensive to boot. —Barney Frank, remarks on an anti-drug bill passed by the U.S. House of Representatives, *The New York Times*, Sep 12, 1986

2265. We're in the hands of the state legislature and God, but at the moment, the state legislature has more to say than God. —Edward I. Koch, on budget of New York City, *The New York Times*, Jun 27, 1986

LIBERALISM

2266. I am a moderate liberal, as all rational people are and ought to be, and it is in this spirit that I have tried to act throughout a long life. [*Ein gemässigter Liberale, wie es alle vernünftigen Leute sind und sein sollen, und wie ich selber es bin und in welchem Sinne zu wirken ich während eines langen Lebens micht bemüht habe.*] —Johann Wolfgang von Goethe, quoted by Johann Peter Eckermann, *Conversations with Goethe*, Feb 30, 1830

2267. Liberalism is trust of the people tempered by prudence; Conservatism is distrust of the people tempered by fear. —William Ewart Gladstone, speech in Plumstead, England, 1878

2268. Liberal institutions straightway cease from being liberal the moment they are soundly established. [*Die liberalen Institutionen hören alsbald auf, liberal zu sein, sobald sie erreicht sind.*] —Friedrich Nietzsche, "Skirmishes in a War with the Age", *Twilight of the Idols*, 1888

2269. The main principle and foundation of liberalism is the rejection of the divine law. ... It rejects and destroys all authority and divine law. —Leo XIII, letter to Archbishop of Bogotá, Apr 6, 1900

2270. A liberal mind is a mind that is able to imagine itself believing anything. —Max Eastman, *Masses*, Sep, 1917

2271. A Liberal is a man who uses his legs and his hands at the behest—at the command—of his head. —Franklin D. Roosevelt, radio address, Oct 26, 1939

2272. It is the duty of the liberal to protect and to extend the basic democratic freedoms. —Chester Bowles, *New Republic*, Jul 22, 1946

2273. Political liberalism should also be defined in terms of objectives. A major objective is the protection of the economic work and doing it within the framework of a private economy. The liberal, emphasizing the civil and property rights of the individual, insists that the individual must remain so supreme as to make the state his servant. —Wayne Lyman Morse, *New Republic*, Jul 22, 1946

2274. The essence of the Liberal outlook lies not in what opinions are held, but in how they are held: instead of being held dogmatically, they are held tentatively, and with a consciousness that new evidence may at any moment lead to their abandonment. —Bertrand Russell, "Philosophy and Politics", *Unpopular Essays*, 1950

2275. We who are liberal and progressive know that the poor are our equals in every sense except that of being equal to us. —Lionel Trilling, "The Princess Casamassima", *The Liberal Imagination*, 1950

2276. A rich man told me recently that a liberal is a man who tells other people what to do with their money. —LeRoi Jones, "Tokenism: 300 years for five cents", *Home*, 1966

2277. The liberals in the House strongly resemble liberals I have known through the last two decades in the civil rights conflict. When it comes time to show on which side they will be counted, they suddenly excuse themselves. —Shirley Chisholm, *Unbought and Unbossed*, 1970

2278. Politics without ideology, and with a strong tendency towards autobiography, equals Liberalism. —Sir Stephen Spender, postscript, *The Thirties and After*, 1978

2279. There are no more liberals. ... They've all been mugged. —James Q. Wilson, *Time*, Jan 21, 1985

MAJORITY AND MINORITIES

2280. There is no maxim, in my opinion, which is more liable to be misapplied, and which, therefore, more needs elucidation, than the current one, that the interest of the majority is the political standard of right and wrong. —James Madison, letter to James Monroe, Oct 5, 1786

2281. That the desires of the majority of the people are often for injustice and inhumanity against the minority, is demonstrated by every page of the history of the whole world. —John Adams, *A Defence of the Constitution of the Government of the United States*, 1787-88

2282. On a candid examination of history, we shall find the turbulence, violence, and abuse of power, by the majority, trampling on the rights of the minority, have produced factions and commotions which, in republics, have, more frequently than any other cause, produced despotism. —James Madison, speech to the Virginia Convention on the adoption of the U.S. Constitution, Jun 5, 1788

2283. Though the will of the majority is in all cases to prevail, that will, to be rightful, must be reasonable. ... The minority possess their equal rights, which equal laws must protect, and to violate which would be oppression. —Thomas Jefferson, first inaugural address, Mar 4, 1801

2284. In Republics, the great danger is, that the majority may not sufficiently respect the rights of the minority. —James Madison, speech to the Virginia constitutional convention, Richmond, Virginia, Dec 2, 1829

2285. The American people are too well schooled in the duty and practice of submitting to the will of the majority to permit any serious uneasiness on that account. —James Madison, letter to Martin Van Buren, Jul 5, 1830

2286. It is impossible that the whisper of a faction shall prevail against the voice of a nation. —Lord John Russell, speech in the House of Commons, Oct 12, 1831

2287. When a faction in a state attempts to nullify a constitutional law of congress, or to destroy the union, the balance of the people composing this union have a perfect right to coerce them to obedience. This is my creed. —Andrew Jackson, letter to Gen. John Coffee, Dec 14, 1832

2288. The tyranny of the majority. [*La tyrannie de la majorité.*] —Alexis, Comte de Tocqueville, sub-heading, *Democracy in America*, 1835

2289. The blessings of Liberty which our Constitution secures may be enjoyed alike by minorities and majorities. —James K. Polk, inaugural address, Mar 4, 1845

2290. No society in which eccentricity is a matter of reproach, can be in a wholesome state. —John Stuart Mill, *Principles of Political Economy*, 1848

2291. A wise man will not leave the right to the mercy of chance, nor wish it to prevail through the power of the majority. There is but little virtue in the action of masses of men. —Henry David Thoreau, *Civil Disobedience*, 1849

2292. It is quite plain that your government will never be able to restrain a distressed and discontented majority. For with you the majority is the government, and has the rich, who are always a minority, absolutely at its mercy. —Lord Macaulay, letter to Henry Stephens Randall, May 23, 1857

2293. Governments exist to protect the rights of minorities. The loved and the rich need no protection: they have many friends and few enemies. —Wendell Phillips, speech in Boston, Massachusetts, Dec 21, 1860

2294. If by the mere force of numbers a majority should deprive a minority of any clearly written constitutional right, it might, in a moral point of view, justify revolution—certainly would if such a right were a vital one. —Abraham Lincoln, first inaugural address, Mar 4, 1861

2295. The majority rules. If they want anything, they get it. If they want anything not right, they get it, too. —Sojourner Truth, speech in Rochester, New York, 1871

2296. Let us not fall into the ... pernicious error that multitude is divine because it is multitude. —James A. Garfield, speech at Hudson College, Jul 2, 1873

2297. The most certain test by which we judge whether a country is really free is the amount of security enjoyed by minorities. —Lord Acton, lecture on "The History of Freedom in Antiquity" at Bridgnorth, England, Feb 26, 1877

2298. The one pervading evil of democracy is the tyranny of the majority, or rather of that party, not always the majority, that succeeds, by force or fraud, in carrying elections. —Lord Acton, lecture on "The History of Freedom in Antiquity" at Bridgnorth, England, Feb 26, 1877

2299. The minority is always right. [*Minoriteten har altid retten.*] —Henrik Ibsen, *An Enemy of the People*, 1882

2300. In the majority beat many hearts, but it has no heart. [*Die Majorität hat viele Herzen, aber ein Herz hat sie nicht.*] —Prince Otto von Bismarck, speech in the Reichstag, Jun 12, 1882

2301. Desperate courage makes One a majority. —Andrew Jackson, quoted by James Parton, *The Life of Andrew Jackson*, 1888

2302. So long as a minority conforms to the majority, it is not even a minority. They must throw in their whole weight in the opposite direction. —Mohandas K. Gandhi, *Indian Opinion*, Sep 14, 1907

2303. You can not have a decent, popular government unless the majority exercise the self-restraint that men with great power ought to exercise. —William Howard Taft, speech in Fresno, California, Oct 10, 1909

2304. Constitutions are checks upon the hasty action of the majority. They are the self-imposed restraints of a whole people upon a majority of them to secure sober action and a respect for the rights of the minority. —William Howard Taft, veto of Arizona Enabling Act, Aug 22, 1911

2305. Government is everywhere to a great extent controlled by powerful minorities, with an interest distinct from that of the mass of the people. —Goldsworthy Lowes Dickinson, *The Choice Before Us*, 1917

2306. No one can expect a majority to be stirred by motives other than ignoble. —Norman Douglas, *South Wind*, 1917

2307. When great changes occur in history, when great principles are involved, as a rule the majority are wrong. —Eugene V. Debs, speech at his trial in Cleveland, Ohio, Sep 12, 1918

2308. A majority can do anything. —Joseph G. Cannon, quoted on his retirement, *The Baltimore Sun*, Mar 4, 1923

2309. Society is always a dynamic interaction of two factors: minorities and the masses. Minorities are individuals or groups of individuals especially qualified. The masses are the collection of people not specially qualified. [*La sociedad es siempre una unidad dinámica de dos factores: minorías y masas. Las minorías son individuos o grupos de individuos especialmente cualificados. La masa es el conjunto de personas no especialmente cualificadas.*] —Jose Ortega y Gasset, *The Revolt of the Masses*, 1930

2310. The moment a mere numerical superiority by either states or voters in this country proceeds to ignore the needs and desires of the minority, and for their own selfish purpose or advancement, hamper or oppress that minority, or debar them in any way from equal privileges and equal rights—that moment will mark the failure of our constitutional system. —Franklin D. Roosevelt, radio address, Mar 2, 1930

2311. A government is free in proportion to the rights it guarantees to the minority. —Alfred M. Landon, Kansas Day address, Oct, 1936

2312. It is hell to belong to a suppressed minority. —Claude McKay, *A Long Way From Home*, 1937

2313. No democracy can long survive which does not accept as fundamental to its very existence the recognition of the rights of minorities. —Franklin D. Roosevelt, letter to the National Association for the Advancement of Colored People, Jun 25, 1938

2314. A resolute minority has usually prevailed over an easygoing or wobbly majority whose prime purpose was to be left alone. —James Reston, *Sketches in the Sand*, 1967

2315. I hear that melting pot stuff a lot, and all I can say is that we haven't melted. —Jesse Jackson, interview, *Playboy*, Nov, 1969

2316. Being black has made me sensitive to any group who finds limitations put on it. —Eleanor Holmes Norton, *The New York Post*, Mar 28, 1970

2317. There can be no assumption that today's majority is "right" and the Amish and others like them are "wrong." A way of life that is odd or even erratic but interferes with no right or interests of others is not to be condemned because it is different. —Warren E. Burger, majority opinion, *Wisconsin v. Yoder*, May 15, 1972

2318. Looking around the House, one realises that we are all minorities now - indeed, some more than others. —Jeremy Thorpe, speech in House of Commons after 1974 election when no party gained majority, Mar 6, 1974

2319. We are of course a nation of differences. Those differences don't make us weak. They're the source of our strength. —Jimmy Carter, speech at Al Smith Dinner in New York City, Oct 21, 1976

2320. America is not like a blanket—one piece of unbroken cloth, the same color, the same texture, the same size. America is more like a quilt—many patches, many pieces, many colors, many sizes, all woven and held together by a common thread. —Jesse Jackson, speech to the Democratic National Convention in San Francisco, Jul 17, 1984

2321. Our flag is red, white and blue, but our nation is a rainbow—red, yellow, brown, black and white—and we're all precious in God's sight. —Jesse Jackson, speech to the Democratic National Convention in San Francisco, Jul 17, 1984

2322. It is precisely because the issue raised by this case touches the heart of what makes individuals what they are that we should be especially sensitive to the rights of those whose choices upset the majority. —Harry A. Blackmun, dissenting opinion, *Bowers v. Hardwick*, Jun 30, 1986

MONARCHY

2323. A multitude of rulers is not a good thing. Let there be one ruler, one king. —Homer, *Iliad*, ca. 700 B.C.

2324. The principal mark of a commonwealth, that is to say the existence of a sovereign power, can hardly be established except in a monarchy. —Jean Bodin, *Six Books of the Commonwealth*, 1576

2325. Not all the water in the rough rude sea/ Can wash the balm from an annointed king —William Shakespeare, *King Richard II*, 1595

2326. A good king will frame his actions to be according to the Law, yet he is not bound thereto but of his Good Will. —James I, *The True Law of Free Monarchies*, 1598

2327. Uneasy lies the head that wears a crown. —William Shakespeare, *Henry IV, Part II*, 1597-98

2328. Kings are justly called Gods, for that they exercise a manner or resemblance of Divine power upon earth. For if you will consider the attributes of God, you shall see how they agree in the person of a king. —James I, speech to Parliament, Mar 23, 1609

2329. I will govern according to the common weal, but not according to the common will. —James I, message to the House of Commons, 1621

2330. Princes are like to heavenly bodies, which cause good or evil times, and which have much veneration but no rest. —Sir Francis Bacon, "Of Empire", *Essays*, 1625

2331. Nor do men, as some fondly conceive, enjoy any greater share of this freedom in a pure commonwealth, if anywhere to be found, than in an absolute monarchy, the same arbitrary power being there in the assembly (which acts like one person) as in a monarch. —John Locke, *First Tract on Government*, 1660

2332. Here lies our sovereign lord the King,/ Whose promise none relies on;/ He never said a foolish thing,/ Nor ever did a wise one. —Earl of Rochester, (John Wilmot), written on the bedchamber door of Charles II, ca. 1670

2333. This is very true: for my words are my own, and my actions are my ministers! —Charles II, reply to Lord Rochester, ca. 1670

2334. Men are not born free, and therefore could never have the liberty to choose either Governors, or Forms of Government. Princes have their Power Absolute, and by Divine Right, for Slaves could never have a Right to Compact of Consent. Adam was an absolute Monarch, and so are all Princes ever since. —Sir Robert Filmer, *Patriarcha, Or the Natural Power of Kings Asserted*, 1680

2335. Kings are the publick Pillars of the State, Born to sustain and prop the Nations weight. —John Dryden, *Absalom and Achitophel*, 1681

2336. If it is too much to have to take care of a family, if it's enough just to have to worry about yourself, think of the weight, of the burden, of a whole kingdom. [*Si c'est trop de se trouver chargé d'une seule famille, si c'est assez d'avoir à répondre de soi seul, quel poids, quel accablement, que celui de tout un royaume.*] —Jean de La Bruyère, "Du Souverain ou de la république", *Les Caractères*, 1688

2337. What is a King?—a man condemn'd to bear/ The public burden of the nation's care. —Matthew Prior, *Solomon*

2338. When kings the sword of justice first lay down,/ They are no kings, though they possess the crown./ Titles are shadows, crowns are empty things,/ The good of subjects is the end of kings. —Daniel Defoe, *The True-Born Englishman*, 1701

2339. The Right Divine of Kings to govern wrong. —Alexander Pope, *The Dunciad*, 1728-43

2340. He was the king's friend. Therefore, the king was the only monarch on earth who had a friend. [*Il fut l'ami du roi, et le roi fut alors le seul monarque de la terre qui eût un ami.*] — Voltaire, (Francois Marie Arouet), "Les énigmes", *Zadig*, 1747

2341. The prince is the first servant of his state. [*Der Fürst ist der erste Diener seines Staates.*] —Frederick II, (the Great), *Memoirs of the House of Brandenburg*, 1758

2342. The king never dies. —Sir William Blackstone, *Commentaries on the Laws of England*, 1765

2343. That the king can do no wrong, is a necessary and fundamental principle of the English constitution. —Sir William Blackstone, *Commentaries on the Laws of England*, 1768

2344. There is not a single crowned head in Europe whose talents or merit would entitle him to be elected a vestryman by the people of any parish in America. —Thomas Jefferson, letter to George Washington, May 2, 1788

2345. A monarchy is a merchantman which sails well, but will sometimes strike on a rock, and go to the bottom; a republic is a raft which will never sink, but then your feet are always in the water. —Fisher Ames, speech in the House of Representatives, 1795

2346. Monarchy is only the string which ties the robbers' bundle. —Percy Bysshe Shelley, *A Philosophical View of Reform*, 1819-20

2347. Democracy is in every case a principle of dissolution, of decomposition. It tends to separate men, it loosens society. I am opposed to this because I am by nature and by habit constructive. That is why monarchy is the only government that suits my way of thinking. ... Monarchy alone tends to bring men together, to unite them in compact, efficient masses, and to make them capable by their combined efforts of the highest degree of culture and civilization. —Prince Clemens von Metternich, reported conversation with George Ticknor, 1835

2348. Every noble crown is, and on earth will forever be, a crown of thorns. —Thomas Carlyle, *Past and Present*, 1843

2349. It is the misfortune of kings that they will not listen to the truth. —Johann Jacoby, letter to Frederick William II, Nov 2, 1848

2350. Obedience to the laws and to the Sovereign, is obedience to a higher Power, divinely instituted for the good of the people, not of the Sovereign, who has equally duties & obligations. —Victoria, reported conversation with Lord John Russell, Aug 6, 1848

2351. In Prussia it is only kings who make revolutions. —Prince Otto von Bismarck, reported conversation with a III of France, 1862

2352. The sovereign has, under a constitutional monarchy such as ours, three rights - the right to be consulted, the right to encourage, the right to warn. —Walter Bagehot, *The English Constitution*, 1867

2353. So long as the human heart is strong and the human reason weak, Royalty will be strong because it appeals to diffused feeling, and the Republics weak because they appeal to the understanding. —Walter Bagehot, *The English Constitution*, 1867

2354. All kings is mostly rapscallions. —Mark Twain, *The Adventures of Huckleberry Finn*, 1884

2355. You're still the king—even in your underwear. [*Du bleibst der König—auch in Unterhosen.*] —Ludwig Fulda, *Der Talisman*, 1893

2356. A prince is a gr-reat man in th' ol' counthry, but he niver is as gr-reat over there as he is here (in America). —Finley Peter Dunne, "Prince Henry's Reception", *Observations by Mr. Dooley*, 1902

2357. Absolute, adj. An absolute monarchy is one in which the sovereign does as he pleases so long as he pleases the assassins. —Ambrose Bierce, *The Devil's Dictionary*, 1906

2358. That a peasant may become king does not render the kingdom democratic. —Woodrow Wilson, speech in Chattanooga, Tennessee, Aug 31, 1910

2359. A monarch frequently represents his subjects better than an elected assembly; and if he is a good judge of character he is likely to have more capable and loyal advisers. —William Ralph Inge, "Our Present Discontents", *Outspoken Essays: First Series*, 1919

2360. In a few years there will be only five kings in the world—the King of England and the four kings in a pack of cards. —Farouk I, *Life*, Apr 10, 1950

2361. I cannot lead you into battle. I do not give you laws or administer justice but I can do something else—I can give my heart and my devotion to these old islands and to all the peoples of our brotherhood of nations. —Elizabeth II, first televised Christmas address, Dec 25, 1957

2362. Let me tell you quite bluntly that this king business has given me personally nothing but headaches. —Mohammed Reza Pahlevi, *The New York Times*, Oct 27, 1967

2363. No medieval monarch in the whole of British history ever had such power as every modern British Prime Minister has in his or her hands. Nor does any American President have power approaching this. —Anthony Wedgwood Benn, *Arguments for Socialism*, 1979

2364. Something as curious as the monarchy won't survive unless you take account of people's attitudes. ... After all, if people don't want it, they won't have it. —Prince Charles, quoted by Anthony Sampson, *The Changing Anatomy of Britain*, 1983

2365. Most of the monarchies of Europe were really destroyed by their greatest and most ardent supporters. It was the most reactionary people who tried to hold onto something without letting it develop and change. —Prince Philip, quoted by John Pearson, *The Selling of the Royal Family*, 1986

NATIONALISM

2366. Altogether, national hatred is something peculiar. You will always find it strongest and most violent where there is the lowest degree of culture. —Johann Wolfgang von Goethe, quoted by Johann Peter Eckermann, *Conversations with Goethe*, Mar 14, 1830

2367. The worth of a State, in the long run, is the worth of the individuals composing it. —John Stuart Mill, *On Liberty*, 1859

2368. Individualities may form communities, but it is institutions alone that can create a nation. —Benjamin Disraeli, speech in Manchester, England, 1866

2369. Size is not grandeur, and territory does not make a nation. —Thomas Henry Huxley, "On University Education", 1876

2370. The life of the nation is secure only while the nation is honest, truthful, and virtuous. —Frederick Douglass, speech on twenty-third anniversary of emancipation in the District of Columbia, Apr, 1885

2371. The idea of a lawful separation between one nationality and the other ... is a reactionary idea. —Vladimir Ilyich Lenin, *Socialism and War*, 1915

2372. Loyalty is a sentiment, not a law. It rests on love, not on restraint. The government of Ireland by England rests on restraint and not on law; and since it demands no love, it can evoke no loyalty. —Sir Roger Casement, at his trial for treason, Jul, 1916

2373. There comes a time when it is good for a nation to know that it must sacrifice if need be everything that it has to vindicate the principles which it possesses. —Woodrow Wilson, speech in Washington, D.C., Jun 5, 1917

2374. Self-determinism is not a mere phrase. It is an imperative principle of action, which statesmen will henceforth ignore at their peril. —Woodrow Wilson, speech to Congress, Feb 11, 1918

2375. The nationalist has a broad hatred and a narrow love. He cannot stifle a predilection for dead cities. —Andre Gide, *Journals*, 1918

2376. There can be no fifty-fifty Americanism in this country. There is room here for only hundred per cent Americanism. —Theodore Roosevelt, speech in Saratoga, New York, Jul 19, 1918

2377. Nationalism is an infantile disease. It is the measles of mankind. —Albert Einstein, statement to G.S. Viereck, 1921

2378. Nations are formed and are kept alive by the fact that they have a program for tomorrow. [*Las naciones se forman y viven de tener un programa para el mañana.*] —Jose Ortega y Gasset, *Invertebrate Spain*, 1922

2379. There is a wind of nationalism and freedom blowing round the world, and blowing as strongly in Asia as elsewhere. —Stanley Baldwin, speech in London, Dec 4, 1934

2380. The driving force of a nation lies in its spiritual purpose, made effective by free, tolerant but unremitting national will. —Franklin D. Roosevelt, message to Congress, Apr 14, 1938

2381. We are under no illusion that they (the Russian people) are fighting for us (the Communist party). They are fighting for Mother Russia. —Joseph Stalin, reported conversation with Averell Harriman, Sep, 1941

2382. Nationalism has two fatal charms for its devotees: it presupposes local self-sufficiency, which is a pleasant and desirable condition, and it suggests, very subtly, a certain personal superiority by reason of one's belonging to a place which is definable and familiar, as against a place which is strange, remote. —E.B. White, "Intimations", *One Man's Meat*, 1944

2383. All my life I have held on to a certain idea of France. [*Toute ma vie je me suis fait une certaine idée de la France.*] —Charles De Gaulle, *Mémoires de guerre: L'Appel*, 1955

2384. Nationalism is our form of incest, is our idolatry, is our insanity. "Patriotism" is its cult. —Erich Fromm, *The Sane Society*, 1955

2385. All nations have present, or past, or future reasons for thinking themselves incomparable. —Paul Valéry, "Extraneous Remarks", *Selected Writings*, 1964

2386. Patriotism is when love of your own people comes first; nationalism, when the hate for people other than your own comes first. —Charles De Gaulle, recalled on leaving the presidency, *Life*, May 9, 1969

2387. To me the nation is the ultimate political reality. There is no political reality beyond it. But what it is cannot be determined scientifically; you cannot pick it up; you cannot measure it. —Enoch Powell, *The Listener*, May 28, 1981

PATRIOTISM

2388. The single best augury is to fight for one's country. —Homer, *Iliad*, ca. 700 B.C.

2389. What a pity is it / That we can die but once to save our country! —Joseph Addison, *Cato*, 1713

2390. A patriot is a fool in ev'ry age. —Alexander Pope, "Epilogue to the Satires", *Imitations of Horace*, 1733-38

2391. It is sad that being a good patriot often means being the enemy of the rest of mankind. [*Il est triste que souvent, pour être bon patriote, on soit l'ennemi du reste des hommes.*] — Voltaire, "Patrie", *Dictionnaire philosophique*, 1764

2392. Patriotism is the last refuge of the scoundrel. —Samuel Johnson, quoted by James Boswell, *Life of Samuel Johnson*, Apr 7, 1775

2393. I only regret that I have but one life to lose for my country. —Nathan Hale, last words before being hanged by British, Sep 22, 1776

2394. These are the times that try men's souls. The summer soldier and the sunshine patriot will, in this crisis, shrink from the service of his country; but he that stands it NOW deserves the love and thanks of man and woman. —Thomas Paine, *The American Crisis*, Sep 12, 1777

2395. Everything belongs to the fatherland when the fatherland is in danger. —Georges Jacques Danton, speech to the National Convention, Aug 28, 1792

2396. Breathes there the man, with soul so dead,/ Who never to himself hath said,/ This is my own, my native land!/ Whose heart hath ne'er within him burn'd,/ As home his footsteps he hath turn'd,/ From wandering on a foreign strand! —Sir Walter Scott, *The Lay of the Last Minstrel*, 1805

2397. The love of country is the first virtue in a civilised man. —Napoleon I, speech to Polish deputies, Jul 14, 1812

2398. Our country! In her intercourse with foreign nations may she always be in the right; but our country, right or wrong. —Stephen Decatur, toast at a dinner in Norfolk, Virginia, Apr, 1816

2399. Patriotism itself is a necessary link in the golden chains of our affections and virtues. —Samuel Taylor Coleridge, "Political Knowledge", *The Friend*, 1818

2400. When a whole nation is roaring Patriotism at the top of its voice, I am fain to explore the cleanness of its hands and purity of its heart. —Ralph Waldo Emerson, *Journals*, 1824

2401. I have heard something said about allegiance to the South. I know no South, no North, no East, no West, to which I owe any allegiance. ... The Union, sir, is my country. —Henry Clay, speech in the U.S. Senate, 1848

2402. God has given you your country as cradle, and humanity as mother; you cannot rightly love your brethren of the cradle if you love not the common mother. —Giuseppe Mazzini, speech in Milan, Jul 25, 1848

2403. Patriotism is in political life what faith is in religion. —Lord Acton, "Nationality", *The Home and Foreign Review*, Jul, 1862

2404. True patriotism sometimes requires of men to act exactly contrary, at one period, to that which it does at another, and the motive which impels them—the desire to do right— is precisely the same. —Robert E. Lee, letter to General P.G.T. Beauregard, Oct 3, 1865

2405. I think patriotism is like charity—it begins at home. —Henry James, *The Portrait of a Lady*, 1881

2406. The song that nerves a nation's heart / Is in itself a deed. —Alfred, Lord Tennyson, The Charge of the Heavy Brigade, 1885

2407. My kind of loyalty was loyalty to one's country, not to its institutions or its officeholders. —Mark Twain, *A Connecticut Yankee at King Arthur's Court*, 1889

2408. Our country, right or wrong. When right, to be kept right; when wrong, to be put right. —Carl Schurz, speech to the Anti-Imperialistic Conference in Chicago, Illinois, Oct 17, 1899

2409. Talking of patriotism, what humbug it is; it is a word which always commemorates a robbery. There isn't a foot of land in the world which doesn't represent the ousting and re-ousting of a long line of successive owners. —Mark Twain, *Notebook*, 1935

2410. In the beginning of a change, the patriot is a scarce man, and brave, and hated and scorned. When his cause succeeds, the timid join him, for then it costs nothing to be a patriot. —Mark Twain, *Notebook*, 1935

2411. I realize that patriotism is not enough. I must have no hatred or bitterness towards anyone. —Edith Cavell, last words before being executed, Oct 12, 1915

2412. The things that the flag stands for were created by the experiences of a great people. Everything that it stands for was written by their lives. The flag is the embodiment, not of sentiment, but of history. —Woodrow Wilson, speech, Jun 14, 1915

2413. He who loves not his home and country which he has seen, how shall he love humanity in general which he has not seen? —William Ralph Inge, "Patriotism", *Outspoken Essays: First Series*, 1919

2414. Patriotism is easy to understand in America. It means looking out for yourself by looking out for your country. —Calvin Coolidge, speech in Northampton, Massachusetts, May 30, 1923

2415. Patriotism is a lively sense of responsibility. Nationalism is a silly cock crowing on its own dunghill. —Richard Aldington, *The Colonel's Daughter*, 1931

2416. Martyred many times must be/ Who would keep his country free. —Edna St. Vincent Millay, "To the Maid of Orleans", *Make Bright the Arrows*, 1940

2417. Whenever you hear a man speak of his love for his country it is a sign that he expects to be paid for it. —H.L. Mencken, *A Mencken Chrestomathy*, 1949

2418. Patriotism is not a short and frenzied outburst of emotion but the tranquil and steady dedication of a lifetime. —Adlai E. Stevenson Jr., speech to the American Legion Convention, Aug 30, 1952

2419. To strike freedom of the mind with the fist of patriotism is an old and ugly subtlety. —Adlai E. Stevenson Jr., speech in New York City, Aug 30, 1952

2420. The military caste did not originate as a party of patriots, but as a party of bandits. —H.L. Mencken, *Minority Report*, 1956

2421. You're not supposed to be so blind with patriotism that you can't face reality. Wrong is wrong, no matter who does it or who says it. —Malcolm X, *Malcolm X Speaks*, 1965

2422. We will survive and become the stronger—not only because of a patriotism that stands for love of country, but a patriotism that stands for love of people. —Gerald R. Ford, speech in Grand Rapids, Michigan, Sep 7, 1968

2423. The person who wants to fight senses his solitude and is frightened. Whereupon the silence reverts to patriotism. Fear finds its great moral revelation in patriotism. —Jacobo Timerman, *Prisoner Without a Name, Cell Without a Number*, 1981

2424. I think there is one higher office than president and I would call that patriot. —Gary Hart, television interview on "Nightline" after withdrawing from presidential race, Sep 8, 1987

POLITICAL CAMPAIGNS

2425. Prosperity is necessarily the first theme of a political campaign. —Woodrow Wilson, campaign speech, Sep 4, 1912

2426. A Presidential campaign may easily degenerate into a mere personal contest, and so lose its real dignity. —Woodrow Wilson, acceptance at Sea Girt, New Jersey, of the nomination for presidency, Aug 7, 1912

2427. Football strategy does not originate in a scrimmage; it is useless to expect solutions in a political campaign. —Walter Lippmann, "The Changing Focus", *A Preface to Politics*, 1914

2428. Political campaigns are designedly made into emotional orgies which endeavor to distract attention from the real issues involved, and they actually paralyze what slight powers of cerebration man can normally muster. —James Harvey Robinson, *The Human Comedy*, 1937

2429. The best audience is intelligent, well-educated and a little drunk. —Alben W. Barkley, recalled on his death, Apr 30, 1956

2430. There may be some cynics who think that a Platform is just a list of platitudes to lure the naive voter—a sort of facade behind which candidates sneak into power and then do as they please. I am not one of those. —Dwight D. Eisenhower, speech in Washington, D.C., Jun 7, 1957

2431. In your heart, you know he's right. —Barry Goldwater, slogan for presidential campaign, 1964

2432. The best time to listen to a politician is when he's on a stump on a street corner in the rain late at night when he's exhausted. Then he doesn't lie. —Theodore H. White, *The New York Times*, Jan 5, 1969

2433. Handshaking is friendly until your hands bleed. Confetti looks festive until you're forced to spit out mouthfuls hurled directly into your face. Applause is wonderful until you can hardly hear yourself speak. A crush of screaming women is flattering until they tear your clothes. —Ralph G. Martin, *A Hero for Our Time*, 1983

2434. The Kennedy organization doesn't run, it purrs. —Rowland Evans Jr., quoted by Ralph G. Martin, *A Hero for Our Times*, 1983

2435. The problems seem so easy out there on the stump. Deficits shrink with a rhetorical flourish. —Hugh Sidey, "Now Comes the Hard Part", *Time*, Nov 5, 1984

2436. We love the blather and boast, the charge and countercharge of campaigning. Governing is a tougher deal. —Hugh Sidey, "Now Comes the Hard Part", *Time*, Nov 5, 1984

2437. You can campaign in poetry. You govern in prose. —Mario Cuomo, *New Republic*, Apr 8, 1985

2438. There is no excitement anywhere in the world, short of war, to match the excitement of an American presidential campaign. —Theodore H. White, interview, May 15, 1986

2439. We were told our campaign wasn't sufficiently slick. We regard that as a compliment. —Margaret Thatcher, *The New York Times*, Jun 12, 1987

2440. Our debates have been like the mating of pandas in the zoo—the expectations are high, there's a lot of fuss and commotion, but there's never any kind of result. —Bruce Babbitt, presidential primary campaign speech in Des Moines, Iowa, Jan 4, 1988

2441. Senator, I served with Jack Kennedy. I knew Jack Kennedy. Jack Kennedy was a friend of mine. Senator, you're no Jack Kennedy. —Lloyd Bentsen, on Senator Dan Quayle's self-comparison to John F. Kennedy; televised debate, Oct 5, 1988

POLITICAL PARTIES

2442. Those who think that all virtue is to be found in their own party principles push matters to extremes; they do not consider that disproportion destroys a state. —Aristotle, *Politics*, 343 B.C.

2443. Party loyalty lowers the greatest men to the petty level of the masses. [*L'esprit de parti abaisse les plus grands hommes jusques aux petitesses du peuple.*] —Jean de La Bruyère, "De l'homme", *Les Caractères*, 1688

2444. The best Party is but a kind of Conspiracy against the rest of the Nation. —1st Marquess of Halifax, *Political Thoughts and Reflections*, 1750

2445. There cannot be a greater Judgement befall a Country than such a dreadful Spirit of Division as rends a Government into two distinct People, and makes them greater Strangers and more averse to one another, than if they were actually two different Nations. —Joseph Addison, *Spectator*, Jul 24, 1711

2446. Party-spirit, which at best is but the madness of many for the gain of a few. —Alexander Pope, letter to E. Blount, Aug 27, 1714

2447. I find myself ... hoping a total end of all the unhappy divisions of mankind by party-spirit, which at best is but the madness of many for the gain of a few. —Alexander Pope, letter to E. Blount, Aug 27, 1714

2448. All political parties die at last of swallowing their own lies. —John Arbuthnot, epigram, ca. 1735

2449. Ninety men out of one hundred, when they talk of forming principles, mean no more than embracing parties, and, when they talk of supporting their party, mean serving their friends; and the service of their friends implies no more than consulting self-interest. By this gradation, principles are fitted to party, party degenerates into faction, and faction is reduced to self. —4th Earl of Chesterfield, (Philip Stanhope), *Old England, or the Constitutional Journal*, Feb 5, 1743

2450. Party divisions, whether on the whole operating for good or evil, are things inseparable from free government. —Edmund Burke, *Observations on the Present State of the Nation*, 1769

2451. Party is a body of men united, for promoting by their joint endeavours the national interest, upon some particular principle in which they are all agreed. —Edmund Burke, *Thoughts on the Cause of the Present Discontents*, 1770

2452. Parties must ever exist in a free country. —Edmund Burke, speech, "On Conciliation with the American Colonies", Mar 22, 1775

2453. The most common and durable source of faction has been the various and unequal distribution of property. —James Madison, *The Federalist*, Nov. 22, 1787

2454. By a faction, I understand a number of citizens, whether amounting to a majority or a minority of the whole, who are united and actuated by some common impulse of passion, or of interest, adverse to the rights of other citizens, or to the permanent and aggregate interests of the community. —James Madison, *The Federalist*, Nov. 22, 1787

2455. Liberty is to faction what air is to fire, an aliment without which it instantly expires. But it could not be less folly to abolish liberty, which is essential to political life, because it nourishes faction, than it would be to wish annihilation of air, which is essential to animal life, because it imparts to fire its destructive agency. —James Madison, *The Federalist*, Nov. 22, 1787

2456. No free Country has ever been without parties, which are a natural offspring of Freedom. —James Madison, note of ca. 1821 on a speech at the Constitutional Convention, 1787

2457. If I could not go to heaven but with a party, I would not go there at all. —Thomas Jefferson, letter to Francis Hopkinson, Mar 13, 1789

2458. Let me now ... warn you in the most solemn manner against the baneful effects of the spirit of party. —George Washington, *Farewell Address to the People of the United States*, Sep 17, 1796

2459. The spirit of party serves always to distract the public councils, and enfeeble the public administration. It agitates the community with ill-founded jealousies and false alarms; kindles the animosity of one part against another; foments occasional riot and insurrection. —George Washington, *Farewell Address to the People of the United States*, Sep 19, 1796

2460. Your party man, however excellent his intentions may be, is always opposed to any limitation of sovereignty. He regards himself as the next in succession, and handles gently the property that is to come to him, even while his opponents are its tenants. —Benjamin Constant de Rebecque, *Course in Constitutional Politics*, 1817-20

2461. Party is in England a stronger passion than love, avarice, or ambition; it is often compounded of them, but is stronger than any of them individually. —John Wilson Croker, *Diary*, Jun 22, 1821

2462. I am one of those who have always thought that party attachments and consistency are in the first class of a statesman's duties, because without them he must be incapable of performing any useful service to the country. —John Wilson Croker, letter to a friend, 1830

2463. A sect or party is an elegant incognito devised to save a man from the vexation of thinking. —Ralph Waldo Emerson, *Journals*, 1831

2464. There are two great antagonistic principles at the root of all government—stability and experiment. The former is Tory, and the latter Whig: and the human mind divides itself into these classes as naturally and as inconsiderately, as to personal objects, as it does into indolence and activity, obstinacy and indecision, temerity and versatility, or any other of the various different or contradictory moods of the mind. —John Wilson Croker, letter to Lord Brougham, Mar 14, 1839

2465. The two parties which divide the state, the party of Conservatism and that of Innovation, are very old, and have disputed the possession of the world ever since it was made. —Ralph Waldo Emerson, lecture on "The Conservative" in Boston, Massachusetts, Dec 9, 1841

2466. If parties in a republic are necessary to secure a degree of vigilance sufficient to keep the public functionaries within the bounds of law and duty, at that point their usefulness ends. —William Henry Harrison, inaugural address, Mar 4, 1841

2467. When I first came into parliament, Mr. Tierney, a great Whig authority, used always to say that the duty of an Opposition was very simple—it was, to oppose everything, and propose nothing. —14th Earl of Derby, (Edward Stanley), speech in the House of Commons, Jun 4, 1841

2468. Mr. Pulteney, afterwards Earl of Bath, is reported to have said that political parties were like snakes, guided not by their heads but by their tails. Lord Melbourne does not know whether this is true of the snake, but it is certainly so of the party. —2nd Viscount Melbourne, letter to Queen Victoria, Apr 6, 1842

2469. No government can be long secure without formidable opposition. —Benjamin Disraeli, *Coningsby*, 1844

2470. He (Peel) is so vain that he wants to figure in history as the settler of all the great questions; but a Parliamentary constitution is not favourable to such ambitions, things must be done by parties, not by persons using parties as tools. —Benjamin Disraeli, letter to Lord John Manners, Dec 17, 1845

2471. Above all, maintain the line of demarcation between parties; for it is only by maintaining the independence of party that you can maintain the integrity of public men, and the power and influence of Parliament itself. —Benjamin Disraeli, speech in the House of Commons, Jan 22, 1846

2472. I have invariably objected to all violent and extreme measures, which is not exactly the mode of acquiring influence in a political party in England, particularly one in opposition to Government. —1st Duke of Wellington, letter to Lord Stanley, 1846

2473. You cannot choose between party government and Parliamentary government. I say you can have no Parliamentary government if you have no party government; and therefore when gentlemen denounce party government, they strike at the scheme of government which, in my opinion, has made this country great, and which, I hope, will keep it great. —Benjamin Disraeli, speech in the House of Commons, Aug 30, 1848

2474. We have a country as well as a party to obey. —James K. Polk, *Diary*, Dec 12, 1848

2475. All parties, without exception, in so far as they seek power, are varieties of absolutism. —Pierre Joseph Proudhon, *Confessions of a Revolutionary*, 1849

2476. There can be but two great political parties in this country. —Stephen A. Douglas, speech in Bloomington, Illinois, Jul 16, 1858

2477. A party of order or stability, and a party of progress or reform, are both necessary elements of a healthy state of political life. —John Stuart Mill, *On Liberty*, 1859

2478. Party is organised opinion. —Benjamin Disraeli, speech in Oxford, England, Nov 25, 1864

2479. It is one of the misfortunes of our political system that parties are formed more with reference to controversies that are gone by, than to the controversies which these parties have actually to decide. —3rd Marquess of Salisbury, "The Coming Session", *Quarterly Review*, Jan, 1866

2480. I had to prepare the mind of the country, and to educate—if it be not arrogant to use such a phrase—to educate our Party. It is a large Party, and requires its attention to be called to questions of this kind with some pressure. —Benjamin Disraeli, speech in Edinburgh, Scotland on the Reform Act of 1867, Oct 29, 1867

2481. So long as we have government by party, the very notion of repose must be foreign to English politics. Agitation is, so to speak, endowed in this country. —3rd Marquess of Salisbury, "The Commune and the Internationale", *Quarterly Review*, Oct, 1871

2482. He serves his party best who serves his country best. —Rutherford B. Hayes, inaugural address, Mar 5, 1877

2483. All free governments are party government. —James A. Garfield, speech to the House of Representatives, Jan 18, 1878

2484. I have always believed that what was best for the entire country was going to help both political parties in the end; for we are citizens in common of one great nation. —Ulysses S. Grant, speech in Kansas City, Missouri, Jul 2, 1880

2485. In England, a real, democratic party is impossible unless it be a working man's party. —Friedrich Engels, "A Working Man's Party", *Labour Standard*, Jul 23, 1881

2486. I often think it's comical/ How Nature always does contrive/ That every boy and gal,/ That's born into the world alive,/ Is either a little Liberal/ Or else a little Conservative! —Sir W.S. Gilbert, *Iolanthe*, 1882

2487. You cannot influence a Political Party to do Right, if you stick to it when it does wrong. —John Bengough, *The Prohibition Aesop*, ca. 1896

2488. I wish that party battles could be fought with less personal passion and more passion for the common good. I am not interested in fighting persons ... but in fighting things. —Woodrow Wilson, speech in Atlantic City, New Jersey, Sep 10, 1912

2489. I thank God that we have lived to see a time when men are beginning to reason upon the facts and not upon party tradition. I believe in party tradition, but ... only as it is founded upon eternal principles of justice. —Woodrow Wilson, speech at Williams Grove, Pennsylvania, Aug 29, 1912

2490. The success of a party means little except when the Nation is using the party for a large and definite purpose. —Woodrow Wilson, first inaugural address, Mar 4, 1913

2491. What difference does party make when mankind is involved? —Woodrow Wilson, speech in Richmond, Indiana, Sep 4, 1919

2492. The more you read and observe about this Politics thing, you got to admit that each party is worse than the other. The one that's out always looks the best. —Will Rogers, "Breaking into the Writing Game", *The Illiterate Digest*, 1924

2493. It's a damned good thing to remember in politics to stick to your party and never attempt to buy the favor of your enemies at the expense of your friends. —Joseph G. Cannon, attributed by L. White Busby, *Uncle Joe Cannon*, 1927

2494. To prevent resentment, governments attribute misfortunes to natural causes; to create resentment oppositions attribute them to human causes. —Bertrand Russell, "Freedom in Society", *Skeptical Essays*, 1928

2495. Talk is nauseous without practice. Who will believe that the Labour Party means business so long as some of its stalwarts sit up and beg for sugar-plums, like poodles in a drawing-room. ... To kick over an idol, you must first get off your knees. —Richard Tawney, quoted, *The Guardian*, 1934

2496. This is the most important lesson that a man can learn, that opinions are nothing but the mere result of chance and temperament; that no party is on the whole better than another. —Stanley Baldwin, quoted by K. Middlemas and J. Barnes, *Baldwin*, 1970

2497. The American people are quite competent to judge a political party that works both sides of a street. —Franklin D. Roosevelt, campaign speech in Boston, Nov 4, 1944

2498. Political language—and with variations this is true of all political parties, from Conservatives to Anarchists—is designed to make lies sound truthful and murder respectable. —George Orwell, "Politics and the English Language", *Shooting an Elephant*, 1950

2499. Even more important than winning the election is governing the nation. That is the test of a political party—the acid, final test. —Adlai E. Stevenson Jr., acceptance speech as Democratic candidate for president, Jul 26, 1952

2500. Under democracy one party always devotes its chief energies to trying to prove that the other party is unfit to rule—and both commonly succeed, and are right. —H.L. Mencken, *Minority Report*, 1956

2501. When the Tories are in trouble, they bunch together and cogger up. When we (Labor) get into trouble, we start blaming each other and rushing to the press to tell them all the terrible things that somebody else has done. —Richard Crossman, *Diary*, May 8, 1956

2502. To me, party platforms are contracts with the people. —Harry S Truman, *Memoirs*, 1955-56

2503. In our (British) traditional cricket match the parties are strong and the best team wins; in the strip poker of American politics, the parties are weak and the best man wins. —Richard Crossman, "Roosevelt--Warts and All", *New Statesman*, 1957

2504. Let us not seek the Republican answer or the Democratic answer, but the right answer. —John F. Kennedy, speech in Baltimore, Maryland, Feb 18, 1958

2505. There is no Democratic or Republican way of cleaning the streets. —Fiorello LaGuardia, attributed by Murray W. Stand in Charles Garrett, *The LaGuardia Years*, 1961

2506. Sometimes party loyalty asks too much. —John F. Kennedy, attributed by Arthur M. Schlesinger, Jr., *A Thousand Days: John F. Kennedy in the White House*, 1979

2507. The role of a minority party is to hammer out a program that will solve the problems of America—not just obstruct the work of the majority party. —Lyndon Baines Johnson, quoted by Henry A. Zeiger, *Lyndon B. Johnson: Man and President*, 1963

2508. Honor is not the exclusive property of any political party. —Herbert Hoover, quoted, *Christian Science Monitor*, May 21, 1964

2509. There are enough mistakes of the Democrats for the Republicans to criticize constructively without resorting to political smears. —Margaret Chase Smith, *Declaration of Conscience*, 1972

2510. The two-party system has given this country the war of Lyndon Johnson, the Watergate of Nixon, and the incompetence of Carter. Saying we should keep the two-party system simply because it is working is like saying the Titanic voyage was a success because a few people survived on life rafts. —Eugene J. McCarthy, *Chicago Tribune*, Sep 10, 1978

2511. There is one thing you can be sure of with the Conservative Party,before anything else— they have a grand sense for where the votes are. —Enoch Powell, *The Listener*, May 28, 1981

2512. The Soviet Union would remain a one-party nation even if an opposition party were permitted—because everyone would join that party. —Ronald Reagan, speech to British Parliament, Jun 8, 1982

2513. While people and their opinions always deserve the greatest respect, the opinions adopted by parties (which are typically instruments of personal advancement and of power, with all the chances for intrigue which this implies) are not to be identifed with ordinary human opinions: they are ideologies. —Sir Karl Popper, "Popper on Democracy", *The Economist*, Apr 23, 1988

POLITICIANS AND PUBLIC OFFICIALS

2514. Nowadays, for the sake of the advantage which is to be gained from the public revenues and from office, men want to be always in office. —Aristotle, *Politics*, ca. 325 B.C.

2515. Persistence in one opinion has never been considered a merit in political leaders. [*Numquam enim in praestantibus in republica gubernanda viris laudata est in una sententia perpetua permansio.*] —Marcus Tullius Cicero, *Epistulae ad Familiares*, ca. 50 B.C.

2516. No man in public life thinks of the many he has outstripped; he thinks rather of those who have outstripped him. [*Quod nemo eorum, qui in re publica versantur, quot vincat, sed a quibus vincatur, aspicit.*] —Seneca (the Younger), *Letters to Lucilius*, ca. 50

2517. Get thee glass eyes;/ And, like a scurvy politician, seem/ To see the things thou dost not. —William Shakespeare, *King Lear*, 1605-06

2518. The State, in choosing men to serve it, takes no notice of their opinions. If they be willing faithfully to serve it, that satisfies. —Oliver Cromwell, speech before the battle of Marston Moor, Jul 2, 1644

2519. No man can be a politician, except he be first a historian or a traveller; for except he can see what must be, or what may be, he is no politician. —James Harrington, *Oceana*, 1656

2520. There is nothing so despicable and useless as someone at court who can't do anything to further your career; I'm surprised that they even dare to show their face. [*Il n'y a rien à la cour de si méprisable et de si indigne qu'un homme qui ne peut contribuer en rien à notre fortune: je m'étonne qu'il ose se montrer.*] —Jean de La Bruyère, "De la cour", *Les Caractères*, 1688

2521. A private Life is to be preferr'd; the Honour and Gain of publick Posts, bearing no proportion with the Comfort of it. —William Penn, *Some Fruits of Solitude in Reflections and Maxims*, 1693

2522. Censure is the tax a man pays to the public for being eminent. —Jonathan Swift, *Thoughts on Various Subjects*, 1711

2523. He that puts on a public gown must put off a private person. —Thomas Fuller, *Gnomologia*, 1732

2524. There are scarcely any men more sour than those who are forced to be nice out of interest. [*Il n'y a guère de gens plus aigres que ceux qui sont doux par intérêt.*] —Marquis de Vauvenargues, *Réflexions et maximes*, 1746

2525. The sad knowledge of human nature, that always comes too late, led the king to say: "Every time I fill a vacancy, I create a hundred malcontents and one ingrate." [*Cette connaissance malheureuse des hommes, qu'on acquiert trop tard, faisait dire le roi: "Toutes les fois que je donne une place vacante, je fais cent mécontents et un ingrat."*] —Voltaire, *Le Siècle de Louis XIV*, 1751

2526. It is easier for a camel to go through the eye of a needle, or for a rich man to enter the kingdom of heaven, than for a politician to lay aside disguise. —1st Earl of Charlemont, (James Caulfeild), letter to the Earl of Chatham, Jan, 1867

2527. Your representative owes you, not his industry only, but his judgment; and he betrays, instead of serving you, if he sacrifices it to your opinion. —Edmund Burke, speech to the electors of Bristol, Nov 3, 1774

2528. His crimes are the only great things about him, and these are contrasted by the littleness of his motives. —Richard Brinsley Sheridan, *The Duenna*, 1775

2529. Patience. Patience. Patience! the first, and last, and the middle virtue of a politician. —John Adams, letter to Benjamin Rush, Feb 8, 1778

2530. There never was a bad man that had ability for good service. —Edmund Burke, debate in the House of Commons on impeachment of Warren Hastings, Feb 15, 1788

2531. No man has a right to pry into his neighbour's private concerns; and the opinions of every man are his private concern, while he keeps them so. ... But when he makes those opinions public; when he once attempts to make converts, whether it be in religion, politics, or anything else; when he once comes forward as a candidate for public admiration, esteem or compassion, his opinions, his principles, his motives, every action of his life, public or private, becomes the fair subject of public discussion. —William Cobbett, "Observations on the Emigration of Dr. Priestley", 1794

2532. In the appointments to the great offices of the government, my aim has been to combine geographical situation, and sometimes other considerations, with abilities and fitness of known characters. —George Washington, letter to Edward Carrington, Oct 9, 1795

2533. The great art of governing consists in not letting men grow old in their jobs. [*Ne pas laisser vieillir les hommes doit être le grand art du gouvernement.*] —Napoleon I, (Napoleon Bonaparte), letter to Citizen Carnot, Aug 9, 1796

2534. Offices are as acceptable here as elsewhere, and whenever a man has cast a longing eye on them, a rottenness begins in his conduct. —Thomas Jefferson, letter to Tench Coxe, May 21, 1799

2535. When a man assumes a public trust, he should consider himself as public property. —Thomas Jefferson, remark to Baron von Humboldt, 1807

2536. An honest man can feel no pleasure in the exercise of power over his fellow citizens. —Thomas Jefferson, letter to John McLish, Jan 13, 1813

2537.   I never have and never will (I hope) do anything for the sake of popularity; he that steers by any other compass than his own sense of duty may be a popular, but cannot be an honest, and I think not a useful public servant. —John Wilson Croker, letter to Lord Exmouth, Oct 23, 1816

2538.   A man to be a sound politician and in any degree useful to his country must be governed by higher and steadier considerations than those of personal sympathy and private regard. —Martin Van Buren, letter to Dr. Graham A. Worth, Apr 22, 1819

2539.   Every man who has been in office a few years believes he has a life estate in it, a vested right. This is not the principle of our government. It is a rotation in office that will perpetuate our liberty. —Andrew Jackson, *Journal*, May-Jun, 1829

2540.   We are here to consult the interests and not to obey the will of the people. —Sir Robert Peel, speech in the House of Commons, 1831

2541.   The art of governing is a great metier, requiring the whole man, and it is therefore not well for a ruler to have too strong tendencies for other affairs. —Johann Wolfgang von Goethe, quoted by Johann Peter Eckermann, *Conversations with Goethe*, Feb 18, 1831

2542.   The conduct and opinions of public men at different periods of their careers must not be curiously contrasted in a free and aspiring society. —Benjamin Disraeli, speech at High Wycombe, England, Dec 16, 1834

2543.   On my arrival in the United States, I was struck by the degree of ability among the governed and the lack of it among the governing. [*A mon arrivee aux Etats-Unis, je fus frappe de surprise en decouvrant a quel point le merite etait commun parmi les gouvernes, et combien il etait peu chez les gouvernants.*] —Alexis, Comte de Tocqueville, *Democracy in America*, 1835

2544.   Never with my consent shall an officer of the people, compensated for his services out of their pockets, become the pliant instrument of the Executive will. —William Henry Harrison, inaugural address, Mar 4, 1841

2545.   Timid and interested politicians think much more about the security of their seats than about the security of their country. —Lord Macaulay, speech in the House of Commons, May, 1842

2546.   So long as the people of any country place their hopes of political salvation in leadership of any description, so long will disappointment attend them. —William Lovett, "Public Letter to Daniel O'Connell", 1843

2547.   A man ain't got no right to be a public man, unless he meets the public views. —Charles Dickens, *Martin Chuzzlewit*, 1844

2548.   The passion for office among members of Congress is very great, if not absolutely disreputable, and greatly embarrasses the operations of the Government. —James K. Polk, *Diary*, Jun 22, 1846

2549.   I'm not a politician and my other habits are good. I've no enemys to reward, nor friends to sponge. But I'm a Union man. —Artemus Ward, (Charles Farrar Browne), speech in Weathersfield, Connecticut, Jul 4, 1859

2550.   You can always get the truth from an American statesman after he has turned seventy, or given up all hope of the Presidency. —Wendell Phillips, speech, Nov 7, 1860

2551.   An honest politician is one who, when he is bought, will stay bought. —Simon Cameron, reported remark, 1860

2552.   Politicians are like the bones of a horse's fore-shoulder—not a straight one in it. —Wendell Phillips, speech, Jul, 1864

2553. A fellow once came to me to ask for an appointment as a minister abroad. Finding he could not get that, he came down to some more modest position. Finally, he asked to be made a tidewaiter. When he saw he could not get that, he asked me for an old pair of trousers. It is sometimes well to be humble. —Abraham Lincoln, quoted, *Everyday Life*, 1865

2554. I trust that the time may never come when the love of fame shall cease to be the sovereign passion of our public men. —Benjamin Disraeli, speech in the House of Commons, Feb, 1866

2555. Let appointments and removals be made on business principles, and by fixed rules. ... Let no man be put ... out or in merely because he is our friend. —Rutherford B. Hayes, letter to General E.A. Merritt, Feb 4, 1879

2556. Public officers are the servants and agents of the people, to execute the laws which the people have made. —Grover Cleveland, on acceptance of Democratic nomination for governor of New York, Oct, 1882

2557. If you have a weak candidate and a weak platform, wrap yourself up in the American flag and talk about the Constitution. —Matthew Stanley Quay, speech, 1886

2558. There is no worse heresy than that the office sanctifies the holder of it. —Lord Acton, letter to Bishop Mandell Creighton, Apr 5, 1887

2559. No public character has ever stood the revelation of private utterance and correspondence. —Lord Acton, letter to Bishop Mandell Creighton, Apr 5, 1887

2560. Men in political life must be ambitious. —Rutherford B. Hayes, letter to William McKinley, Jun 27, 1888

2561. He (John Tyler) has been called a mediocre man; but this is unwarranted flattery. He was a politician of monumental littleness. —Theodore Roosevelt, *Thomas Hart Benton*, 1897

2562. There are two supreme pleasures in life. One is ideal, the other real. The ideal is when a man receives the seals of office from his Sovereign. The real pleasure comes when he hands them back. —5th Earl of Rosebery, *Sir Robert Peel*, 1899

2563. Tinhorn politicians. —William Allen White, *Emporia Gazette*, Oct 25, 1901

2564. The politician who once had to learn to flatter Kings has now to learn how to fascinate, amuse, coax, humbug, frighten, or otherwise strike the fancy of the electorate. —George Bernard Shaw, "The Revolutionist's Handbook", *Man and Superman*, 1902

2565. He knows nothing and he thinks he knows everything. That points clearly to a political career. —George Bernard Shaw, *Major Barbara*, 1905

2566. Politician, n. An eel in the fundamental mud upon which the superstructure of organized society is reared. When he wriggles he mistakes the agitation of his tail for the trembling of the edifice. As compared with the statesman, he suffers the disadvantage of being alive. —Ambrose Bierce, *The Devil's Dictionary*, 1906

2567. Nominee, n. A modest gentleman shrinking from the distinction of private life and diligently seeking the honorable obscurity of public office. —Ambrose Bierce, *The Devil's Dictionary*, 1906

2568. I hear our countrymen abroad saying: "you mustn't judge us by our politicians." I always want to interrupt and answer: "you must judge us by our politicians." We pretend to be the masters—we, the people—and if we permit ourselves to be ill served, to be served by corrupt and incompetent and inefficient men, then on our own head must the blame rest. —Theodore Roosevelt, speech at the Pacific Lutheran Theological Seminary, 1911

2569. Politicians are to serve the people, not to direct them. —Woodrow Wilson, speech in Pittsburgh, Pennsylvania, Oct 18, 1912

2570. The perfection of Parliamentary style is to utter cruel platitudes with a grave and informing air; and, if a little pomposity be superadded, the House will instinctively recognize the speaker as a Statesman. —George William Erskine Russell, *One Look Back*, 1912

2571. Once you touch the biographies of human beings, the notion that political beliefs are logically determined collapses like a pricked ballon. —Walter Lippmann, *A Preface to Morals*, 1913

2572. Politicians tend to live "in character," and many a public figure has come to imitate the journalism which describes him. —Walter Lippmann, "The Changing Focus", *A Preface to Politics*, 1914

2573. Most of the errors of public life ... come, not because men are morally bad, but because they are afraid of somebody. —Woodrow Wilson, speech to the Princeton Univ. class of 1879, Jun 13, 1914

2574. The best servants of the people, like the best valets, must whisper unpleasant truths in the master's ear. It is the court fool, not the foolish courtier, whom the king can least afford to lose. —Walter Lippmann, "Some Necessary Iconoclasm", *A Preface to Politics*, 1914

2575. Every man who takes office in Washington either grows or swells. ... When I give a man an office, I watch him carefully to see whether he is swelling or growing. The mischief of it is when they swell they do not swell enough to burst. —Woodrow Wilson, speech in Washington, D.C., May 16, 1916

2576. The proper memory for a politician is one that knows what to remember and what to forget. —John Morley, *Recollections*, 1917

2577. The Trade Union Movement has become, like the hereditary peerage, an avenue to political power through which stupid untrained persons may pass up to the highest office if only they have secured the suffrages of the members of a large union. One wonders when able rascals will discover this open door to remunerative power. —Beatrice Webb, *Diary*, Jun 7, 1917

2578. I am a Virginian, so naturally I am a politician. —Nancy Astor, Viscountess Astor, speech in Plymouth, England, 1919

2579. A political career brings out the basest qualities in human nature. —James Bryce, remark to Owen Wister, 1921

2580. The nauseous sham goodfellowship our democratic public men get up for shop use. —George Bernard Shaw, *Back to Methuselah*, 1921

2581. The politician is an acrobat. He keeps his balance by saying the opposite of what he does. —Maurice Barrès, *Mes cahiers*, 1923

2582. Are all Cabinets congeries of little autocrats with a super-autocrat presiding over them? —Beatrice Webb, *Diary*, Apr 7, 1924

2583. The middle man governs, however extreme may seem to be the men who sit on the Front Bench, in their reactionary or revolutionary opinions. —Beatrice Webb, *Diary*, Nov 10, 1925

2584. The public always prefers to be reassured. There are those whose job this is. There are only too many. —Andre Gide, Second Notebook, *Journal of the Counterfeiters*, Mar 29, 1925

2585. Faced with the alternative of saying good-bye to the gold standard, and therefore to his own employment, and good-bye to other people's employment, Mr. Churchill characteristically selected the latter course. —Sir Oswald Mosley, quoted by Robert Skidelsky, *Oswald Mosley*, 1975

2586. Politicians, who have not time to become acquainted with human nature, are peculiarly ignorant of the desires that move ordinary men and women. Any political party whose leaders knew a little psychology could sweep the country. —Bertrand Russell, "Freedom in Society", *Skeptical Essays*, 1928

2587. What we need in appointive positions is men of knowledge and experience who have sufficient character to resist temptations. —Calvin Coolidge, *Autobiography*, 1929

2588. The trouble with practical jokes is that very often they get elected. —Will Rogers, quoted, *Rocky Mountain News*, May 28, 1980

2589. Public office is the last refuge of the scoundrel. —Boies Penrose, *Collier's Weekly*, Feb 14, 1931

2590. There is just one rule for politicians all over the world. Don't say in Power what you say in Opposition; if you do, you only have to carry out what the other fellows have found impossible. —John Galsworthy, *Maid in Waiting*, 1931

2591. The public official must pick his way nicely, must learn to placate though not to yield too much, to have the art of honeyed words but not to seem neutral, and above all to keep constantly audible, visible, likable, even kissable. —Learned Hand, speech in Washington, D.C., Mar 8, 1932

2592. did you ever/ notice that when/ a politician/ does get an idea/ he usually/ gets it all wrong. —Don Marquis, *Archy's Life of Mehitabel*, 1933

2593. A politician will do anything to keep his job—even become a patriot. —William Randolph Hearst, editorial, *San Francisco Examiner*, Aug 28, 1933

2594. In our democracy officers of the government are the servants, and never the masters of the people. —Franklin D. Roosevelt, speech in Hollywood, California, Feb 27, 1941

2595. How different the new order would be if we could consult the veteran instead of the politician. —Henry Miller, "The Alcoholic Veteran with the Washboard Cranium", *The Wisdom of the Heart*, 1941

2596. When the political columnists say "Every thinking man" they mean themselves, and when the candidates appeal to "Every intelligent voter" they mean everybody who is going to vote for them. —Franklin P. Adams, *Nods and Becks*, 1944

2597. The trouble with this country is that there are too many politicians who believe, with a conviction based on experience, that you can fool all the people all of the time. —Franklin P. Adams, *Nods and Becks*, 1944

2598. Politicians are ambitious not to make important decisions but to say important things. —Richard Crossman, "Amery and Fisher", *New Statesman*, 1947

2599. The necessary and wise subordination of the military to civil power will be best sustained when life-long professional soldiers abstain from seeking high political office. —Dwight D. Eisenhower, letter to Harry S Truman, Jan, 1948

2600. A Lobbyist is a person that is supposed to help a Politician to make up his mind, not only help him but pay him. —Will Rogers, *The Autobiography of Will Rogers*, 1949

2601. Politicians, after all, are not over a year behind Public Opinion. —Will Rogers, *The Autobiography of Will Rogers*, 1949

2602. A Congressman is never any better than his roads, and sometimes worse. —Will Rogers, *The Autobiography of Will Rogers*, 1949

2603. There is a hundred things to single you out for promotion in party politics besides ability. —Will Rogers, *The Autobiography of Will Rogers*, 1949

2604. The kind of thing I'm good at is knowing every politician in the state and remembering where he itches. —Earl Long, quoted, *New Yorker*, Jun 4, 1960

2605. One of the difficulties of politics is that politicians are shocked by those who are really prepared to let their thinking reach any conclusion. Political thinking consists in deciding upon the conclusion first and then finding good arguments for it. An open mind is considered irresponsible—and perhaps it really is. —Richard Crossman, *Diary*, Nov 13, 1951

2606. I will undoubtedly have to seek what is happily known as gainful employment, which I am glad to say does not describe holding public office. —Dean Acheson, on retiring to private life, *Time*, Dec 22, 1952

2607. Your public servants serve you right; indeed often they serve you better than your apathy and indifference deserve. —Adlai E. Stevenson Jr., speech in Los Angeles, California, Sep 11, 1952

2608. Successful democratic politicians are insecure and intimidated men. They advance politically only as they placate, appease, bribe, seduce, bamboozle, or otherwise manage to manipulate the demanding and threatening elements in their constituencies. —Walter Lippmann, *The Public Philosophy*, 1955

2609. There is no such thing as a nonpolitical speech by a politician. —Richard M. Nixon, speech in New York City, Sep 14, 1955

2610. In government offices which are sensitive to the vehemence and passion of mass sentiment public men have no sure tenure. They are in effect perpetual office seekers, always on trial for their political lives, always required to court their restless constitu ents. —Walter Lippmann, *The Public Philosophy*, 1955

2611. "Don't teach my boy poetry," an English mother recently wrote the Provost of Harrow. " Don't teach my boy poetry; he is going to stand for Parliament." Well, perhaps she was right— but if more politicians knew poetry, and more poets knew politics, I am convinced the world would be a little better place to live on this Commencement Day of 1956. —John F. Kennedy, speech to the Harvard Alumni Association, Jun 14, 1956

2612. When I hear a man applauded by the mob I always feel a pang of pity for him. All he has to do to be hissed is to live long enough. —H.L. Mencken, *Minority Report*, 1956

2613. A good politician with nerve and a program that is right can win in the face of the stiffest opposition. —Harry S Truman, *Memoirs*, 1955-56

2614. The distinction between a statesman and a politician is that the former imposes his will and his ideas on his environment while the latter adapts himself to it. —Richard Crossman, "Roosevelt--Warts and All", *New Statesman*, 1957

2615. A politician is a man who understands government, and it takes a politician to run a government. A statesman is a politician who's been dead 10 or 15 years. —Harry S Truman, *New York World Telegram & Sun*, Apr 12, 1958

2616. A candidate for office can have no greater advantage than muddled syntax; no greater liability than a command of language. —Marya Mannes, *More in Anger*, 1958

2617. McCarthy invented the multi Lie—the lie with so many tiny gears and fragile connecting rods that reason exhausted itself in the effort to combat it. —Richard H. Rovere, "The Frivolous Demagogue", *Esquire*, Jun, 1958

2618. The politician is ... trained in the art of inexactitude. His words tend to be blunt or rounded, because if they have a cutting edge they may later return to wound him. —Edward R. Murrow, speech at Guildhall in London, Oct 19, 1959

2619. The politician in my country seeks votes, affection and respect, in that order. ... With few notable exceptions, they are simply men who want to be loved. —Edward R. Murrow, speech at Guildhall in London, Oct 19, 1959

2620. Politicians are the same all over. They promise to build a bridge even where there is no river. —Nikita S. Khrushchev, comments to the press on visit to United States, Oct, 1960

2621. No government is better than the men who compose it. —John F. Kennedy, campaign speech at Wittenberg College, Springfield, Ohio, Oct 17, 1960

2622. Public officials are not a group apart. They inevitably reflect the moral tone of the society in which they live. —John F. Kennedy, message to Congress, Apr 27, 1961

2623. They may be just as intelligent as you say. But I'd feel a helluva lot better if just one of them had ever run for sheriff. —Sam Rayburn, to Lyndon Johnson on advisers to President Kennedy, quoted by David Halberstam, *The Best and the Brightest*, 1972

2624. Since a politician never believes what he says, he is surprised when others believe him. —Charles De Gaulle, quoted, *Newsweek*, Oct 1, 1962

2625. Idealism is the noble toga that political gentlemen drape over the will to power. —Aldous Huxley, recalled on his death, *New York Herald Tribune*, Nov 24, 1963

2626. As the master politician navigates the ship of state, he both creates and responds to public opinion. Adept at tacking with the wind, he also succeeds, at times, in generating breezes of his own. —Stewart L. Udall, *The Quiet Crisis*, 1963

2627. A professional politician's first duty is to appeal to the forces that unite us, and to channel the forces that divide us into paths where a democratic solution is possible. It is our obligation to resolve issues—not to create them. —Lyndon Baines Johnson, *Life*, Nov 29, 1963

2628. One has to be a lowbrow, a bit of a murderer, to be a politician, ready and willing to see people sacrificed, slaughtered, for the sake of an idea, whether a good one or a bad one. —Henry Miller, quoted by George Plimpton, *Writers at Work*, 1963

2629. The biggest danger for a politician is to shake hands with a man who is physically stronger, has been drinking and is voting for the other guy. —William Proxmire, *New York Herald Tribune*, Feb 16, 1964

2630. He (Richard Nixon) is the kind of politician who would cut down a redwood tree, then mount the stump and make a speech for conservation. —Adlai E. Stevenson Jr., recalled on his death, Jul 14, 1965

2631. I once said cynically of a politician, "He'll double-cross that bridge when he comes to it." —Oscar Levant, *The Memoirs of an Amnesiac*, 1965

2632. Hyperbole was to Lyndon Johnson what oxygen is to life. —Lance Morrow, *The New York Times*, Apr 3, 1966

2633. Probably the most distinctive characteristic of the successful politician is selective cowardice. —Richard Harris, "Annals of Legislation", *The New Yorker*, Dec 14, 1968

2634. He (Richard Nixon) is like a good prewar house—solidly built. They don't build them that way anymore. He's also been repainted several times. —Theodore H. White, on Richard M. Nixon's decision to run for president, *Time*, Feb 16, 1968

2635. If people want a sense of purpose they should get it from their archbishop. They should certainly not get it from their politicians. —Harold Macmillan, Earl of Stockton, quoted by Henry Fairlie, *The Life of Politics*, 1969

2636. Politicians trim and tack in their quest for power, but they do so in order to get the wind of votes in their sails. —Sir Ian Gilmour, *The Body Politic*, 1969

2637. In Pierre Elliott Trudeau Canada has at last produced a political leader worthy of assassination. —Irving Layton, "Obo II", *The Whole Bloody Bird*, 1969

2638. Some members of congress are the best actors in the world. —Shirley Chisholm, *Unbought and Unbossed*, 1970

2639. I remember when I first came to Washington. For the first six months you wonder how the hell you ever got here. For the next six months you wonder how the hell the rest of them ever got here. —Harry S Truman, recalled on his death, Dec 26, 1972

2640. Reading about one's failings in the daily papers is one of the privileges of high office in this free country of ours. —Nelson A. Rockefeller, speech in Syracuse, New York, Nov 29, 1972

2641. Before you can become a statesman you first have to get elected, and to get elected you have to be a politician pledging support for what the voters want. —Margaret Chase Smith, *Declaration of Conscience*, 1972

2642. A passion for politics stems usually from an insatiable need, either for power, or for friendship and adulation, or a combination of both. —Fawn M. Brodie, *Thomas Jefferson*, 1974

2643. A politician ought to be born a foundling and remain a bachelor. —Claudia ("Lady Bird") Johnson, *Time*, Dec 1, 1975

2644. Most politicians have a right to feel morally superior to their constituencies. —Daniel P. Moynihan, *Rolling Stone*, Aug 12, 1976

2645. A boss is a political leader who is on somebody else's side. —Morris K. Udall, "Issues and Answers," ABC-TV, Apr 25, 1976

2646. The main essentials of a successful prime minister (are) sleep and a sense of history. —Harold Wilson, *The Government of Britain*, 1977

2647. Every public official should be recycled occasionally. —John V. Lindsay, *Chicago Tribune*, Jan 22, 1978

2648. Everybody in government is like a bunch of ants on a log floating down a river. Each one thinks he is guiding the log, but it's really just going with the flow. —Robert S. Strauss, *Time*, Apr 17, 1978

2649. I'd rather keep my promises to other politicians than to God. God, at least, has a degree of forgiveness. —Anonymous, *Washington Post*, Jun 9, 1978

2650. Politicians fascinate because they constitute such a paradox: they are an elite that accomplishes mediocrity for the public good. —Garry Wills, *Time*, Apr 23, 1979

2651. The politician who will refuse the Foreign Office is not yet born. —Michael Stewart, *Life and Labour*, 1980

2652. A populist politician is a politician who says things because he believes them to be popular. At least that is my understanding of the term. I have never been that. My worst enemies couldn't say that. —Enoch Powell, *The Listener*, May 28, 1981

2653. Most politicians will not stick their necks out unless they sense grass-roots support. ... Neither you nor I should expect someone else to take our responsibility. If we remain passive, they will surely win. —Katharine Hepburn, fundraising letter for the Planned Parenthood Federation, Nov, 1981

2654. The curious fascination in this job is the illusion that either you are being useful or you could be - and that's so tempting. —Millicent Fenwick, "Sixty Minutes," CBS-TV, Feb 1, 1981

2655. The only people who say worse things about politicians than reporters do are other politicians. —Andy Rooney, "60 Minutes," CBS-TV, Oct 7, 1984

2656. If we insist that public life be reserved for those whose personal history is pristine, we are not going to get paragons of virtue running our affairs. We will get the very rich, who contract out the messy things of life; the very dull, who have nothing to hide and nothing to show; and the very devious, expert at covering their tracks and ambitious enough to risk their discovery. —Charles Krauthammer, "Pietygate: School for Scandal", *Time*, Sep 10, 1984

2657. I am not a perfect servant. I am a public servant doing my best against the odds. —Jesse Jackson, speech to the Democratic National Convention in San Francisco, Jul 17, 1984

2658. He loved politicians—even Republicans. —Margaret Truman, speech to joint session of Congress on 100th anniversary of her father's birth, May 8, 1984

2659. Give a member of Congress a junket and a mimeograph machine and he thinks he is secretary of state. —Dean Rusk, quoted, *The New York Times*, May 6, 1985

2660. Here is an animal (the rhinoceros) with a hide two feet thick, and no apparent interest in politics. What a waste. —James C. Wright Jr., *The New York Times*, Dec 9, 1986

2661. I've often wondered how some people in positions of this kind ... manage without having had any acting experience. —Ronald Reagan, interview with Barbara Walters, ABC-TV, Mar 24, 1986

2662. In Mexico an air conditioner is called a politician because it makes a lot of noise but doesn't work very well. —Len Deighton, *Mexico Set*, 1986

2663. The average politician goes through a sentence like a man exploring a disused mine shaft—blind, groping, timorous and in imminent danger of cracking his shins on a subordinate clause or a nasty bit of subjunctive. —Robertson Davies, *The Papers of Samuel Marchbanks*, 1986

2664. Politicians have the same occupational hazard as generals—focusing on the last battle and overreacting to that. —Ann F. Lewis, *The New York Times*, Sep 24, 1986

2665. I heard his library burned down and that both books were destroyed—and one of them hadn't even been colored in yet. —John Dawkins, quoted remarks on a political colleague, *Wall Street Journal*, Nov 14, 1986

2666. I'm a participant in the doctrine of constructive ambiguity. —Vernon A. Walters, *Christian Science Monitor*, Sep 18, 1986

2667. She (Gladys Kinnock) is said to be inclined to cough noisily when he goes on too long at the rostrum: but this is a traditional prerogative of the political wife, and rather more necessary in this instance than in most. —George Hill, *London Times*, Feb 19, 1987

2668. When things haven't gone well for you, call in a secretary or a staff man and chew him out. You will sleep better and they will appreciate the attention. —Lyndon Baines Johnson, quoted, *People*, Feb 2, 1987

2669. The CIA is made up of boys whose families sent them to Princeton but wouldn't let them into the family brokerage business. —Lyndon Baines Johnson, quoted, *People*, Feb 2, 1987

2670. We (non-candidates) don't have to do what the candidates do—talk about huge issues in 30 seconds in a field somewhere, trying to make sure cows don't urinate on our shoes. —Mario Cuomo, quoted by A.M. Rosenthal, *The New York Times*, Mar 18, 1988

2671. (The representative's) duty is to represent the interests of all those people whom he represents to the best of his ability. These interests will in almost all cases be identical with those of all the citizens of the country, of the nation. These are the interests he must pursue to the best of his knowledge. He is personally responsible to persons. —Sir Karl Popper, "Popper on Democracy", *The Economist*, Apr 23, 1988

POLITICS

2672. Man is by nature a political animal. —Aristotle, *Politics*, 343 B.C.

2673. Many have imagined republics and principalities which have never been seen or known to exist in reality; for how we live is so far removed from how we ought to live, that he who abandons what is done for what ought to be done, will rather bring about his own ruin than his preservation. [*E molti si sono imaginati republiche e principati che non si sono mai visti né conosciuti essere in vero: perché egli è tanto discosto da come si vive a come si doverebbe vivere, che colui che lascia quello che si fa per quello che si doverrebbe fare impara piuttosto la ruina che la preservazione sua.*] —Niccolò Machiavelli, *Il Principe*, 1532

2674. We are much beholden to Machiavel and others, that write what men do, and not what they ought to do. —Sir Francis Bacon, *Advancement of Learning*, 1605

2675. The favor of princes does not exclude merit, but then neither is it based on it. [*La faveur des princes n'exclut pas le mérite, et ne le suppose pas aussi.*] —Jean de La Bruyère, "Des jugements", *Les Caractères*, 1688

2676. The wicked are always surprised to find ability in the good. [*Les méchants sont toujours surpris de trouver de l'habileté dans les bons.*] —Marquis de Vauvenargues, *Réflexions et maximes*, 1746

2677. In our Parliamentary government, connections are absolutely necessary; and, if prudently formed, ably maintained, the success of them is infallible. —4th Earl of Chesterfield, *Letters to His Son*, Oct 22, 1750

2678. I borrowed the Duke of Newcastle's majority to carry on the public business. —William Pitt, 1st Earl of Chatham, quoted by John Morley, *Walpole*, 1909

2679. Those people who treat politics and morality separately will never understand either of them. —Jean Jacques Rousseau, *Emile*, 1762

2680. Politics are now nothing more than a means of rising in the world. —Samuel Johnson, reported conversation, Apr 18, 1775

2681. I agree with you that in politics the middle way is none at all. —John Adams, letter to Horatio Gates, Mar 23, 1776

2682. I have lived long enough, and have experience enough of the conduct of governments and people, nations, and courts, to be convinced that gratitude, friendship, and unsuspecting confidence, and all the amiable passions of human nature, are the most dangerous guides in politics. —John Adams, letter to Robert R. Livingston, Jan 23, 1783

2683. In politics nothing is just save what is honest; nothing is useful except what is just. —Maximilien Robespierre, speech to the National Assembly, May, 1791

2684. The agents that move politicks, are the popular passions; and those are ever, from the very nature of things, under the command of the disturbers of society. —Fisher Ames, "No Revolutions", *Palladium*, Nov, 1801

2685. It is indeed a law of politicks as well as of physicks, that a body in action must overcome an equal body at rest. —Fisher Ames, *The Dangers of American Liberty*, 1805

2686. What is right must unavoidably be politic. —Sir Robert Peel, letter to Henry Goulburn, Sep 23, 1822

2687. In politics as in religion, it so happens that we have less charity for those who believe the half of our creed, than for those that deny the whole of it. —Charles Caleb Colton, *Lacön*, 1825

2688. I find the remark, "'Tis distance lends enchantment to the view" is no less true of the political than of the natural world. —Franklin Pierce, letter, 1832

2689.   The pendulum swung furiously to the left, because it had been drawn too far to the right. —Lord Macaulay, "Sir James Mackintosh", *Edinburgh Review*, Jul, 1835

2690.   Gratitude is not an active sentiment in politics. It is a mistake to take account of it. —Prince Clemens von Metternich, letter to Esterhazy, Mar 18, 1841

2691.   Politics is the art of knowing and leading a multitude or a plurality; its glory is to lead them not where they want to go but where they should go. [*La politique est l'art de connaître et de mener la multitude ou la pluralité; sa gloire est de la mener, non pas ou elle veut, mais ou elle doit aller.*] —Joseph Joubert, *Pensées*, 1842

2692.   In politics you should always leave an old bone behind for the critics to chew on. [*En politique, il faut toujours laisser un os à rongé aux frondeurs.*] —Joseph Joubert, *Pensées*, 1842

2693.   There seem to me very few facts, at least ascertainable facts, in politics. —Sir Robert Peel, letter to Lord Brougham, 1846

2694.   Great public measures cannot be carried by the influence of mere reason. —Sir Robert Peel, letter to Lord Radnor, 1846

2695.   I have always considered politics in the presence of social dangers to be a luxury. —Prince Clemens von Metternich, letter to the Archduchess Sophie, Mar 31, 1848

2696.   I have always noticed in politics how often men are ruined by having too good a memory. —Alexis, Comte de Tocqueville, *Recollections*, 1893

2697.   He (Tom Brown) never wants anything but what's right and fair; only when you come to settle what's right and fair, it's everything he wants, and nothing you want. And that's his idea of a compromise. —Thomas Hughes, *Tom Brown's Schooldays*, 1856

2698.   Finality is not the language of politics. —Benjamin Disraeli, speech in the House of Commons, Feb 28, 1859

2699.   My pollertics, like my religion, being of an exceeding' accommodatin' character. —Artemus Ward, "The Crisis", *Artemus Ward, His Book*, 1862

2700.   Politics is not an exact science. [*Die Politik ist keine exakte Wissenschaft.*] —Prince Otto von Bismarck, speech to Prussian legislature, Dec 18, 1863

2701.   Let us learn to respect sincerity of conviction in our opponents. [*Lernen wir Überzeugungstreue an den Gegnern achten.*] —Prince Otto von Bismarck, speech in the Prussian House of Deputies, Dec 18, 1863

2702.   Politics is the art of the possible. [*Die Politik ist die Lehre von Möglichen.*] —Prince Otto von Bismarck, conversation with Meyer von Waldeck, Aug 11, 1867

2703.   The whole life of English politics is the action and reaction between the Ministry and the Parliament. —Walter Bagehot, *The English Constitution*, 1867

2704.   To rule with the help of one's enemies is ever the worst kind of policy. —Prince Otto von Bismarck, quoted by Charles Lowe, *Bismarck's Table Talk*, 1895

2705.   All political questions, all matters of right, are at bottom only questions of might. —August Bebel, speech to the Reichstag, Jul 3, 1871

2706.   Politics makes strange bed-fellows. —Charles Dudley Warner, "Fifteenth Week", *My Summer in a Garden*, 1871

2707.   Idealism is the despot of thought, just as politics is the despot of will. —Michael Bakunin, "A Circular Letter to My Friends in Italy", 1871

2708.   To exploit and to govern mean the same thing. ... Exploitation and government are two inseparable expressions of what is called politics. —Michael Bakunin, *The Knouto-Germanic Empire and the Social Revolution*, 1871

2709. The optimist view of politics assumes that there must be some remedy for every political ill, and rather than not find it, it will make two hardships to cure one. —3rd Marquess of Salisbury, "The Position of Parties", *Quarterly Review*, Oct, 1872

2710. We are apt to be deluded into false security by political catch-words, devised to flatter rather than instruct. —James A. Garfield, speech at Hudson College, Jul 2, 1873

2711. In politics one must take nothing tragically and everything seriously. —(Louis) Adolphe Thiers, speech to the Chamber of Deputies, May 24, 1873

2712. The political spirit is the great force in throwing love of truth and accurate reasoning into a secondary place. —John Morley, *On Compromise*, 1874

2713. Those who would treat politics and morality apart will never understand the one or the other. —John Morley, *Rousseau*, 1876

2714. The commonest error in politics is sticking to the carcass of dead policies. —3rd Marquess of Salisbury, letter to Bulwer-Lytton, 1878

2715. Nothing is so dull as political agitation. —William Ewart Gladstone, speech at Glasgow Univ., Dec 5, 1879

2716. Politics are vulgar when they are not liberalised by history, and history fades into mere literature when it loses sight of its relation to practical politics. —Sir John Seely, *The Expansion of England*, 1883

2717. Politics is not a science, as many professors imagine, but an art. [*Die Politik ist keine Wissenschaft, wie viele der Herren Professoren sich einbilden, sondern eine Kunst.*] —Prince Otto von Bismarck, speech in the Reichstag, Mar 15, 1884

2718. In politics there is no use looking beyond the next fortnight. —Joseph Chamberlain, conversation with Arthur Balfour, Mar 22, 1886

2719. It were not best that we should all think alike; it is difference of opinion that makes horse races. —Mark Twain, "Pudd'nhead Wilson's Calendar", *Pudd'nhead Wilson*, 1894

2720. I ain't never seen no head so level that it could bear the lettin' in of politics. It makes a fool of a man and a worse fool of a fool. —Ellen Glasgow, *The Voice of the People*, 1900

2721. The most practical kind of politics is the politics of decency. —Theodore Roosevelt, remarks in Oyster Bay, New York, Jun, 1901

2722. Beware of the man who does not return your blow: he neither forgives you nor allows you to forgive yourself. —George Bernard Shaw, "Maxims for Revolutionists", *Man and Superman*, 1902

2723. Politics, as a practice, whatever its professions, has always been the systematic organization of hatreds. —Henry Adams, *The Education of Henry Adams*, 1906

2724. Politics, n. A strife of interests masquerading as a contest of principles. —Ambrose Bierce, *The Devil's Dictionary*, 1906

2725. Administration, n. An ingenious abstraction in politics, designed to receive the kicks and cuffs due to the premier or president. —Ambrose Bierce, *The Devil's Dictionary*, 1906

2726. Knowledge of human nature is the beginning and end of political education. —Henry Adams, *The Education of Henry Adams*, 1906

2727. Practical politics consists in ignoring facts. —Henry Adams, *The Education of Henry Adams*, 1906

2728. Modern politics is, at bottom, a struggle not of men but of forces. —Henry Adams, *The Education of Henry Adams*, 1906

2729.   The field of politics always presents the same struggle. There are the Right and the Left, and in the middle is the Swamp. —August Bebel, speech to the annual congress of the German Social Democratic Party, 1906

2730.   Opposition, n. In politics the party that prevents the Government from running amuck by hamstringing it. —Ambrose Bierce, *The Devil's Dictionary*, 1906

2731.   The people of this country are a straightforward people. They like honesty and straightforwardness of purpose. They may laugh at it and they may be amused by it and they may in a sense admire it, but they do not like cleverness. You may be too clever by half. —Sir Henry Campbell-Bannerman, speech in Plymouth, England, Jun 7, 1907

2732.   Compromise used to mean that half a loaf was better than no bread. Among modern statesmen it really seems to mean that half a loaf is better than a whole loaf. —G.K. Chesterton, *What's Wrong with the World*, 1910

2733.   My hat's in the ring. The fight is on and I'm stripped to the buff. —Theodore Roosevelt, announcement of candidacy for president, 1912

2734.   When the Government of the day and the Opposition of the day take the same side, one can be almost sure that some great wrong is at hand. —George William Erskine Russell, *One Look Back*, 1912

2735.   In politics habits, and not only good ones, but bad ones just as well, rule humanity. —Thomas Masaryk, memorandum on an "Independent Bohemia", Apr, 1915

2736.   Politics are almost as exciting as war, and quite as dangerous. In war you can only be killed once, but in politics many times. —Sir Winston S. Churchill, Remark, ca. 1920

2737.   The whole aim of practical politics is to keep the populace alarmed (and hence clamorous to be led to safety) by menacing it with an endless series of hobgoblins, all of them imaginary. —H.L. Mencken, "Women as Outlaws", *The Smart Set*, Dec, 1921

2738.   The instinctive appeal of every successful political movement is to envy, rivalry or hate, never to the need for co-operation. —Bertrand Russell, presidential address to the Students Union, London School of Economics, Oct 10, 1923

2739.   Politics, which, the planet over, are the fly in the amber, the worm in the bud ... had, with great suddenness, deprived Wharton Cameron of a job. —Katherine Gerould, *Conquistador*, 1923

2740.   Politics, as hopeful men practice it in the world, consists mainly of the delusion that a change in form is a change in substance. —H.L. Mencken, *Prejudices: Fourth Series*, 1924

2741.   The friend of humanity cannot recognize a distinction between what is political and what is not. There is nothing that is not political. [*Der Menschenfreund kann den Unterschied von Politik und Nichtpolitik überhaupt nicht anerkennen. Es gibt keine Nichtpolitik. Alles ist politik.*] —Thomas Mann, *The Magic Mountain*, 1924

2742.   More men have been elected between Sundown and Sunup than ever were elected between Sunup and Sundown. —Will Rogers, "Mr. Ford and Other Political Self-Starters", *The Illiterate Digest*, 1924

2743.   Politics is not an art, but a means. It is not a product, but a process. —Calvin Coolidge, quoted by Edward E. Whiting, *Calvin Coolidge: His Ideals of Citizenship*, 1924

2744.   In the field of politics, force and consent are correlative terms, and one does not exist without the other. The objection will be raised that this is a "forced" consent. But every consent is more or less forced ... in the most liberal State as in the most oppressive tyranny there is always a consent, and it is always forced, conditioned, changeable. —Benedetto Croce, *Elements of Politics*, 1925

2745. The more cant there is in politics the better. Cant is nothing in itself; but attached to even the smallest quantity of sincerity, it serves like a nought after a numeral, to multiply whatever of geniune good-will may exist. —Aldous Huxley, *Jesting Pilate*, 1926

2746. Nobuddy ever fergits where he buried a hatchet. —"Kin" Hubbard, *Abe Martin's Broadcast*, 1930

2747. Political principles resemble military tactics; they are usually designed for a war which is over. —Richard Tawney, *Equality*, 1931

2748. Politics has got so expensive that it takes lots of money to even get beat with. —Will Rogers, syndicated newspaper article, Jun 28, 1931

2749. Our nation was not founded on the pork barrel, and it has not become great by political log-rolling. —Herbert Hoover, press conference, May 27, 1932

2750. Nothing just happens in politics. If something happens you can be sure it was planned that way. —Franklin D. Roosevelt, quoted, *Oui*, May, 1978

2751. The science of politics ... may properly be said to be in large part the science of the adjustment of conflicting group interests. —Franklin D. Roosevelt, speech in Winter Park, Florida, Mar 23, 1936

2752. Politics: Who Gets What, When, How. —Harold Lasswell, book title, 1936

2753. Politics is war without bloodshed while war is politics with bloodshed. —Mao Tse-tung, "On Protracted War", May, 1938

2754. The opposition is indispensable. A good statesman, like any other sensible human being, always learns more from his opponents than from his fervent supporters. —Walter Lippmann, "The Indispensable Opposition", *Atlantic Monthly*, Aug, 1939

2755. We should support whatever the enemy opposes and oppose whatever the enemy supports. —Mao Tse-tung, "Interview with Three Correspondents", Sep 16, 1939

2756. A declining political class has all the infirmities of old age, including deafness. [*Una classe politica in declino ha tutti gli acciacchi della vecchiaia, compresa la sordità.*] —Ignazio Silone, *The School for Dictatorships*, 1939

2757. Politics can be relatively fair in the breathing spaces of history; at its critical turning points there is no other rule possible than the old one, that the end justifies the means. —Arthur Koestler, *Darkness at Noon*, 1940

2758. By comparison with the greatest subjects of art ... all politics seem like provincial struggles for booty between dusky tribes. —Sir Stephen Spender, "A Look at the Worst", *Horizon*, Sep, 1940

2759. Politics, and the fate of mankind, are shaped by men without ideals and without greatness. —Albert Camus, *Cahiers, 1935-1942*, 1962

2760. Politics is the art of preventing people from taking part in affairs which properly concern them. —Paul Valéry, *Tel quel*, 1943

2761. You will find in politics that you are much exposed to the attribution of false motives. Never complain and never explain. —Stanley Baldwin, recorded in Harold Nicolson, *Diary*, Jul 21, 1943

2762. Politics is the science of who gets what, when, and why. —Sidney Hillman, *Political Primer for All Americans*, 1944

2763. In politics, as in other things, there is no such thing as one getting something for nothing. The payoff may involve compromises of various types that may strike at the ideals and principles one has held dear all his life. —A. Philip Randolph, "Why I Can't Run for Congress on the Old Party Ticket", *The Call*, Apr 28, 1944

2764. Power politics is the diplomatic name for the law of the jungle. —Ely Culbertson, *Must We Fight Russia?*, 1946

2765. When I am abroad, I always make it a rule never to criticize or attack the government of my own country. I make up for lost time when I come home. —Sir Winston S. Churchill, speech in the House of Commons, Apr, 1947

2766. If you ever injected truth into politics you have no politics. —Will Rogers, *The Autobiography of Will Rogers*, 1949

2767. In our time, political speech and writing are largely the defense of the indefensible. —George Orwell, "Politics and the English Language", *Shooting an Elephant*, 1950

2768. People who think the mighty in Washington can be persuaded, or corrupted, if you will, by anything less than votes just don't understand what it's all about and never will. They don't know what Washington juice is made of. —George E. Allen, *Presidents Who Have Known Me*, 1950

2769. Honest difference of views and honest debate are not disunity. They are the vital process of policy among free men. —Herbert Hoover, speech in New York City, Dec 20, 1950

2770. Power-worship blurs political judgment because it leads, almost unavoidably, to the belief that present trends will continue. Whoever is winning at the moment will always seem to be invincible. —George Orwell, "Second Thoughts on James Burnham", *Shooting an Elephant*, 1950

2771. What is politics but persuading the public to vote for this and support that and endure these for the promise of those? —Gilbert Highet, "The Art of Persuasion", *Vogue*, Jan 1951

2772. Why is it that when political ammunition runs low, inevitably the rusty artillery of abuse is always wheeled into action? —Adlai E. Stevenson Jr., speech in New York City, Sep 22, 1952

2773. Our American political situation is about the same from generation to generation. The main difficulty is that the rising generation never knows about the acts of the previous one—most people think it too much trouble to find out. —Harry S Truman, quoted by William Hillman, *Mr. President*, 1952

2774. "How can you think of voting for my opponent?" I exhorted. ... "Surely you remember all these things I have done for you?" "Yeah," he said, "I remember. But what in hell have you done for me lately?" —Alben W. Barkley, *That Reminds Me*, 1954

2775. Politics is perhaps the only profession for which no preparation is thought necessary. —Robert Louis Stevenson, quoted, *Rocky Mountain News*, Sep 3, 1979

2776. I don't think ideas are incompatible with political reality. —Adlai E. Stevenson III, *Time*, Feb 26, 1979

2777. Good government cannot exist side by side with bad politics: the best government is the best politics. —Adlai E. Stevenson Jr., quoted, *Kansas City Star*, Jan 30, 1977

2778. Defeat in itself was part and parcel of the great gambling game of politics. A man who could not accept it and try again was not of the stuff of which leaders are made. —Agnes Sligh Turnbull, *The Golden Journey*, 1955

2779. The older you get the more you realize that gray isn't such a bad color. And in politics you work with it or you don't work at all. —Agnes Sligh Turnbull, *The Golden Journey*, 1955

2780. Never lose your temper with the Press or the public is a major rule of political life. —Christabel Pankhurst, *Unshackled*, 1959

2781. The tragedy of all political action is that some problems have no solution; none of the alternatives are intellectually consistent or morally uncompromising; and whatever decision is taken will harm somebody. —James Joll, *Three Intellectuals in Politics*, 1960

2782. What we need is a synthesis of practical thoughts and idealistic aspirations. [*Was wir brauchen, ist die Synthese von praktischem Denken und idealistischem Streben.*] —Willy Brandt, *Mein Weg nach Berlin*, 1960

2783. Politics is a systematic effort to move other men in the pursuit of some design. —Bertrand de Jouvenel, *The Pure Theory of Politics*, 1963

2784. (I despise people who) go to the gutter on either the right or the left and hurl rocks at those in the center. —Dwight D. Eisenhower, *Time*, Oct 25, 1963

2785. I have never found, in a long experience of politics, that criticism is ever inhibited by ignorance. —Harold Macmillan, *Wall Street Journal*, Aug 13, 1963

2786. If you're in politics and you can't tell when you walk into a room who's for you and who's against you, then you're in the wrong line of work. —Lyndon Baines Johnson, quoted by Boothe Mooney, *The Lyndon Johnson Story*, 1964

2787. A rigged convention is one with the other man's delegates in control. An open convention is when your delegates are in control. —James A. Farley, quoted, *Convention and Election Almanac*, 1964

2788. Ideas are great arrows, but there has to be a bow. And politics is the bow of idealism. —Bill Moyers, *Time*, Oct 29, 1965

2789. Insofar as it represents a genuine reconciliation of differences, a consensus is a fine thing; insofar as it represents a concealment of differences, it is a miscarriage of democratic procedure. —J. William Fulbright, speech in the U.S. Senate, Oct 22, 1965

2790. I happen to think that American politics is one of the noblest arts of mankind; and I cannot do anything else but write about it. —Theodore H. White, *The New York Times*, Jun 22, 1965

2791. An independent is the guy who wants to take the politics out of politics. —Adlai E. Stevenson Jr., "The Art of Politics", *The Stevenson Wit*, 1966

2792. In politics, it seems, retreat is honorable if dictated by military considerations and shameful if even suggested for ethical reasons. —Mary McCarthy, "Solutions", *Vietnam*, 1967

2793. All politics are based on the indifference of the majority. —James Reston, *The New York Times*, Jun 12, 1968

2794. Experience suggests that the first rule of politics is never to say never. The ingenious human capacity for maneuver and compromise may make acceptable tomorrow what seems outrageous or impossible today. —William V. Shannon, *The New York Times*, Mar 3, 1968

2795. Political extremism involves two prime ingredients: an excessively simple diagnosis of the world's ills and a conviction that there are identifiable villains back of it all. —John W. Gardner, *No Easy Victories*, 1968

2796. Politics is not the art of the possible. It consists in choosing between the disastrous and the unpalatable. —John Kenneth Galbraith, *Ambassador's Journal*, 1969

2797. Never forget posterity when devising a policy. Never think of posterity when making a speech. —Sir Robert G. Menzies, *The Measure of the Years*, 1970

2798. It (politics) is a beautiful fraud that has been imposed on the people for years, whose practitioners exchange gilded promises for the most valuable thing their victims own, their votes. And who benefits most? The lawyers. —Shirley Chisholm, *Unbought and Unbossed*, 1970

2799. The whole art of politics consists in directing rationally the irrationalities of men. —Reinhold Niebuhr, quoted on his death, *The New York Times*, Jun 2, 1971

2800. Politics is the skilled use of blunt objects. —Lester B. Pearson, "The Tenth Decade", CBC-TV, 1972

2801. Truth is the glue that holds governments together. Compromise is the oil that makes governments go. —Gerald R. Ford, hearings in the House of Representatives on his nomination as vice-president, Nov 15, 1973

2802. There is one thing solid and fundamental in politics—the law of change. What's up today is down tomorrow. —Richard M. Nixon, *Time*, Aug 19, 1974

2803. We cannot cure the evils of politics with politics. ... Fifty years ago if we had gone the way of Freud (to study and tackle hostility within ourselves) instead of Marx, we might be closer to peace than we are. —Anaïs Nin, "Letter to Geismar", *The Diary of Anais Nin*, 1974

2804. The sad duty of politics is to establish justice in a sinful world. —Reinhold Niebuhr, quoted by Jimmy Carter, *Why Not the Best?*, 1975

2805. Politics, like music and golf, is best learned at an early age. —Lawrence Welk, *Time*, Apr 14, 1975

2806. In politics, guts is all. —Barbara Castle, *Castle Diaries*, Apr 18, 1975

2807. Politics is the art of looking for trouble, finding it everywhere, diagnosing it incorrectly and applying the wrong remedies. —Groucho Marx, recalled on his death, Aug 19, 1977

2808. It's a piece of cake until you get to the top. You find you can't stop playing the game the way you've always played it. So you are lean and mean and resourceful and you continue to walk on the edge of the precipice because over the years you have become fascinated by how close you can walk without losing your balance. —Richard M. Nixon, television interview with David Frost, May 4, 1977

2809. Politics I supposed to be the second-oldest profession. I have come to realize that it bears a very close resemblance to the first. —Ronald Reagan, *Los Angeles Herald-Examiner*, Mar 3, 1978

2810. If you're in politics, you're a whore anyhow. It doesn't make any difference who you sleep with. —Robert S. Strauss, *Texas Monthly*, Feb, 1978

2811. The choice in politics isn't usually between black and white. It's between two horrible shades of gray. —Peter Thorneycroft, Lord Thorneycroft, *London Sunday Telegraph*, Feb 11, 1979

2812. Washington has no memory. —James Reston, *The Observer*, Sep 9, 1979

2813. Politics is motion and excitement. —John Sears, *Time*, Nov 12, 1979

2814. The best politics is no politics. —Henry M. Jackson, speech to the American Bar Association, Feb 3, 1980

2815. You never really win anything in politics. All you get is a chance to play for higher stakes and perform at a higher level. —John Sears, *Time*, Jan 21, 1980

2816.   We are not a cynical people. The will to believe lingers on. We like to think that heroes can emerge from obscurity, as they sometimes do; that elections do matter, even though the process is at least part hokum: that through politics we can change our society and maybe even find a cause to believe in. —Ronald Steel, "The Vanishing Campaign Biography", *The New York Times*, Aug 5, 1984

2817.   He (Dwight Eisenhower) wasn't used to being criticized, and he never did get it through his head that's what politics is all about. He was used to getting his ass kissed. —Harry S Truman, quoted on President Dwight D. Eisenhower, *The New York Times*, Dec 2, 1984

2818.   In writing and politicking, it's best not to think about it, just do it. —Gore Vidal, quoted, *A Guide to the 99th Congress*, 1985

2819.   Nothing is so admirable in politics as a short memory. —John Kenneth Galbraith, quoted, *A Guide to the 99th Congress*, 1985

2820.   Die-hard conservatives thought that if I couldn't get everything I asked for, I would jump off the cliff with the flag flying—go down in flames. No, if I can get 70 or 80 percent of what it is I'm trying to get ... I'll take that and then continue to try to get the rest in the future. —Ronald Reagan, *The New York Times*, Oct 6, 1985

2821.   I seldom think of politics more than 18 hours a day. —Lyndon Baines Johnson, quoted, *A Guide to the 99th Congress*, 1985

2822.   Politics in America is the binding secular religion. —Theodore H. White, *Time*, Dec 29, 1986

2823.   I always cheer up immensely if an attack is particularly wounding because I think, well, if they attack one personally, it means they have not a single political argument left. —Margaret Thatcher, *Daily Telegraph*, Mar 21, 1986

2824.   Nothing ever gets settled in this town (Washington) ... a seething debating society in which the debate never stops, in which people never give up, including me. And so that's the atmosphere in which you administer. —George P. Shultz, *The New York Times*, Dec 9, 1986

2825.   Politics, where fat, bald, disagreeable men, unable to be candidates themselves, teach a president how to act on a public stage. —Jimmy Breslin, *Table Money*, 1986

2826.   The price of running for the Senate today is spending more time than you'd like to spend asking people for more money than they'd like to give. —Harriett Woods, quoted by Steven V. Roberts in "Politicking Goes High-Tech", *The New York Times*, Nov 2, 1986

2827.   Although he's regularly asked to do so, God does not take sides in American politics. —George J. Mitchell, at Iran-Contra hearings, Jul 13, 1987

2828.   My opponent called me a cream puff. ... Well, I rushed out and got the baker's union to endorse me. —Claiborne Pell, *The New York Times*, Feb 3, 1987

2829.   Decide on some imperfect Somebody and you will win, because the truest truism in politics is: You can't beat Somebody with Nobody. —William Safire, "The Perfect Candidate", *The New York Times*, Apr 16, 1987

2830.   A man can take a little bourbon without getting drunk, but if you hold his mouth open an pour in a quart, he's going to get sick on it. —Lyndon Baines Johnson, quoted, *People*, Feb 2, 1987

2831.   The American people didn't send us here (Washington, D.C.) to bicker. —George Bush, address to Congress, Feb 9, 1989

POWER

2832. This is the bitterest pain among men, to have much knowledge but no power. —Herodotus, *The Histories of Herodotus*, ca. 430 B.C.

2833. Knowledge is power. [*Nam et ipsa scientia potestas est.*] —Sir Francis Bacon, *Meditationes Sacrae*, 1597

2834. In the first place, I put for a generall inclination of all mankind, a perpetuall and restlesse desire of Power after Power, that ceaseth onely in Death. —Thomas Hobbes, *Leviathan*, 1651

2835. Power is so apt to be insolent, and Liberty to be saucy, that they are very seldom upon good Terms. —1st Marquess of Halifax, *Political Thoughts and Reflections*, 1750

2836. Power and Liberty are like Heat and Moisture; where they are well mixt, everything prospers; where they are single, they are destructive. —1st Marquess of Halifax, *Maxims of State*, 1700

2837. Unlimited power is apt to corrupt the minds of those who possess it. —William Pitt, 1st Earl of Chatham, speech in the House of Lords, Jan 9, 1770

2838. The greater the power, the more dangerous the abuse. —Edmund Burke, speech, "On the Middlesex Election", 1771

2839. As wealth is power, so all power will infallibly draw wealth to itself by some means or other. —Edmund Burke, speech in the House of Commons, Feb 11, 1780

2840. One precedent in favor of power is stronger than an hundred against it. —Thomas Jefferson, *Notes on the State of Virginia*, 1782

2841. Neither philosophy, nor religion, nor morality, nor wisdom, nor interest will ever govern nations or parties against their vanity, their pride, their resentment or revenge, or their avarice or ambition. Nothing but force and power and strength can restrain them. —John Adams, letter to Thomas Jefferson, Oct 9, 1787

2842. In the main it will be found that a power over a man's support is a power over his will. —Alexander Hamilton, *The Federalist*, Mar 21, 1788

2843. What a perversion of the normal order of things! ... to make power the primary and central object of the social system, and Liberty but its satellite. —James Madison, *National Gazette*, Dec 20, 1792

2844. Power is not happiness. —William Godwin, *An Enquiry Concerning Political Justice*, 1793

2845. History has taught me that rulers are much the same in all ages, and under all forms of government; that they are as bad as they dare to be. The vanity of ruin and the curse of blindness have clung to them like an hereditary leprosy. —Samuel Taylor Coleridge, letter to George Coleridge, Apr, 1798

2846. The love of fame is consistent with the steadiest attachment to principle and indeed strengthens and supports it; whereas the love of power, where this is the ruling passion, requires the sacrifice of principle at every turn, and is inconsistent even with the shadow of it. —William Hazlitt, "Character of Mr. Fox", 1807

2847. The worst thing that can be said of the most powerful is that they can take your life; but the same thing can be said of the most weak. —Charles Caleb Colton, *Lacön*, 1825

2848. To know the pains of power, we must go to those who have it; to know its pleasure, we must go to those who are seeking it. —Charles Caleb Colton, *Lacön*, 1825

2849. You cannot divorce property from power. You can only make them change hands. —John Randolph of Roanoke, speech to the U.S. Senate, 1826

2850. Power is pleasure; and pleasure sweetens pain. —William Hazlitt, "On Application to Study", *The Plain Speaker*, 1826

2851. The essence of Government is power; and power, lodged as it must be in human hands, will ever be liable to abuse. —James Madison, speech to Virginia constitutional convention, Richmond, Virginia, Dec 2, 1829

2852. The secret of power is the will. [*Il segreto della potenza è nella volontà.*] —Giuseppe Mazzini, letter to King Carlo Alberto of Savoy, 1831

2853. Co-operation is power; in proportion as people combine, they know their strength; civilization itself is but the effect of combining. —Edward George Bulwer-Lytton, *England and the English*, 1833

2854. The arts of power and its minions are the same in all countries and in all ages. It marks its victim: denounces it; and excites the public odium and the public hatred, to conceal its own abuses and encroachments. —Henry Clay, speech in the U.S. Senate, Mar 14, 1834

2855. When the reality of power has been surrendered, it's playing a dangerous game to seek to retain the appearance of it; the external aspect of vigor can sometimes support a debilitated body, but most often it manages to deal it the final blow. —Alexis, Comte de Tocqueville, *Etat social et politique de la France*, 1834

2856. Power is insinuating. Few men are satisfied with less power than they are able to procure. ... No lover is ever satisfied with the first smile of his mistress. —William Henry Harrison, speech during presidential campaign, 1840

2857. Power makes you attractive; it even makes women love old men. [*Le pouvoir est une beauté; il fait aimer aux femmes la veillesse meme.*] —Joseph Joubert, *Pensées*, 1842

2858. You shall have joy, or you shall have power, said God; you shall not have both. —Ralph Waldo Emerson, *Journal*, 1842

2859. The highest proof of virtue is to possess boundless power without abusing it. —Lord Macaulay, review of Lucy Aikin, *Life and Writings of Addison*, 1843

2860. Political power, properly so called, is merely the organized power of one class for oppressing another. —Karl Marx, *The Communist Manifesto*, 1848

2861. As a matter of fact and experience, the more power is divided the more irresponsible it becomes. —Woodrow Wilson, *Congressional Government*, 1885

2862. Power tends to corrupt and absolute power corrupts absolutely. —Lord Acton, (Sir John E.E. Dalberg, 1st Baron Acton), *Life of Mandell Creighton*, 1904

2863. Power when wielded by abnormal energy is the most serious of facts. —Henry Adams, *The Education of Henry Adams*, 1906

2864. Power consists in one's capacity to link his will with the purpose of others, to lead by reason and a gift of cooperation. —Woodrow Wilson, letter to Mary A. Hulbert, Sep 21, 1913

2865. The only prize much cared for by the powerful is power. The prize of the general is not a bigger tent, but command. —Oliver Wendell Holmes Jr., speech at the Harvard Law School Association of New York, Feb 15, 1913

2866. Power takes as ingratitude the writhing of its victims. —Sir Rabindranath Tagore, *Stray Birds*, 1916

2867. All political structures are based on power. [*Alle politischen Gebilde sind Gewaltgebilde.*] —Max Weber, *Wirtschaft und Gesellschaft*, 1922

2868. Next to enjoying ourselves, the next greatest pleasure consists in preventing others from enjoying themselves, or more generally, in the acquisition of power. —Bertrand Russell, "The Recrudescence of Puritanism", *Skeptical Essays*, 1928

2869. More power than any good man should want, and more power than any other kind of man ought to have. —Daniel O. Hastings, speech in U.S. Senate, Mar 23, 1935

2870. We thought, because we had power, we had wisdom. —Stephen Vincent Benét, *Litany for Dictatorships*, 1935

2871. As intricacies of human relationships increase, so power to govern them must increase— power to stop evil; power to do good. The essential democracy of our Nation and the safety of our people depend not upon the absence of power, but upon lodging it with those whom the people can change or continue at stated intervals through an honest and free system of elections. —Franklin D. Roosevelt, second inaugural address, Jan 20, 1937

2872. True liberation can be acquired and maintained only when the Negro people possess power: and power is the product and flower of organization ... of the masses. —A. Philip Randolph, speech at the National Negro Congress, Philadelphia, Pennsylvania, Oct 15-17, 1937

2873. The purpose of getting power is to be able to give it away. —Aneurin Bevan, quoted by Michael Foot, *Aneurin Bevan, 1945-1960*, 1962

2874. It is when power is wedded to chronic fear that it becomes formidable. —Eric Hoffer, *The Passionate State of Mind*, 1954

2875. Our sense of power is more vivid when we break a man's spirit than when we win his heart. —Eric Hoffer, *The Passionate State of Mind*, 1954

2876. The first principle of a civilized state is that power is legitimate only when it is under contract. —Walter Lippmann, *The Public Philosophy*, 1955

2877. The urge to save humanity is almost always only a false-face for the urge to rule it. —H.L. Mencken, *Minority Report*, 1956

2878. Give me the writing of a nation's advertising and propaganda, and I care not who governs its politics. —Hugh MacLennan, *MacLean's Magazine*, Nov 5, 1960

2879. When power corrupts, poetry cleanses, for art establishes the basic human truths which must serve as the touch-stone of our judgment. —John F. Kennedy, speech at Amherst College, Amherst, Massachusetts, Oct 26, 1963

2880. The problem of power is how to achieve its responsible use rather than its irresponsible and indulgent use—of how to get men of power to live for the public rather than off the public. —Robert F. Kennedy, "I Remember, I Believe", *The Pursuit of Justice*, 1964

2881. Power, whether exercised over matter or over man, is partial to simplification. —Eric Hoffer, *The Ordeal of Change*, 1964

2882. There is a strong moralistic strain in the civil rights movement that would remind us that power corrupts, forgetting that the absence of power also corrupts. —Bayard Rustin, "From Protest to Politics", *Commentary*, Feb, 1965

2883. Power in defense of freedom is greater than power in behalf of tyranny and oppression. —Malcolm X, speech on "Prospects for Freedom" in New York City, 1965

2884. Power never takes a back step—only in the face of more power. —Malcolm X, *Malcolm X Speaks*, 1965

2885. We have, I fear, confused power with greatness. —Stewart L. Udall, commencement address at Dartmouth College, Hanover, New Hampshire, Jun 13, 1965

2886. Power tends to confuse itself with virtue and a great nation is peculiarly susceptible to the idea that its power is a sign of God's favor. ... Once imbued with the idea of a mission, a great nation easily assumes that it has the means as well as the duty to do God's work. —J. William Fulbright, speech in the U.S. Senate, Apr 21, 1966

2887. Law not served by power is an illusion; but power not ruled by law is a menace which our nuclear age cannot afford. —Arthur J. Goldberg, commencement address at the Catholic University of America, *Time*, Jun 17, 1966

2888. Power is always charged with the impulse to eliminate human nature, the human variable, from the equation of action. Dictators do it by terror or by the inculcation of blind faith; the miltary do it by iron discipline; and the industrial masters think they can do it by automation. —Eric Hoffer, "Automation, Leisure, and the Masses", *The Temper of Our Time*, 1967

2889. Powerlessness frustrates; absolute powerlessness frustrates absolutely. Absolute frustration is a dangerous emotion to run a world with. —Russell Baker, *The New York Times*, May 1, 1969

2890. Power is the great aphrodisiac. —Henry A. Kissinger, *The New York Times*, Jan 19, 1971

2891. Power and violence are opposites; where the one rules absolutely, the other is absent. —Hannah Arendt, "On Violence", *Crisis of the Republic*, 1972

2892. Nobody can overthrow me—I have the power. —Mohammed Reza Pahlevi, *U.S. News & World Report*, Jun 26, 1978

2893. If power corrupts, being out of power corrupts absolutely. —Douglass Cater, *Book Digest*, Dec, 1979

2894. Some people draw a comforting distinction between "force" and "violence". ... I refuse to cloud the issue by such word-play. ... The power which establishes a state is violence; the power which maintains it is violence; the power which eventually overthrows it is violence. ... Call an elephant a rabbit only if it gives you comfort to feel that you are about to be trampled to death by a rabbit. —Kenneth Kaunda, *Kaunda on Violence*, 1980

PREJUDICE AND DISCRIMINATION

2895. There is no prejudice so strong as that which arises from a fancied exemption from all prejudice. —William Hazlitt, "On the Tendency of Sects", *The Round Table*, 1817

2896. Treat us like men, and there is no danger but we will all live in peace and happiness together. For we are not like you, hard hearted, unmerciful, and unforgiving. What a happy country this will be, if the whites will listen. —David Walker, "Walker's Appeal", Sep 28, 1829

2897. Prejudice is the child of ignorance. —William Hazlitt, "On Prejudice", *Sketches and Essays*, 1839

2898. Prejudice is never easy unless it can pass itself off for reason. —William Hazlitt, "On Prejudice", *Sketches and Essays*, 1839

2899. The white man's happiness cannot be purchased by the black man's misery. —Frederick Douglass, "The Destiny of Colored Americans", *The North Star*, Nov 16, 1849

2900. Having despised us, it is not strange that Americans should seek to render us despicable; having enslaved us, it is natural that they should strive to prove us unfit for freedom; having denounced us as indolent, it is not strange that they should cripple our enterprises. —Frederick Douglass, *Proceedings of the Colored National Convention*, July 6-8, 1853

2901. It is never too late to give up our prejudices. —Henry David Thoreau, "Economy", *Walden*, 1854

2902.   The prejudice against color, of which we hear so much, is no stronger than that against sex. It is produced by the same cause, and manifested very much in the same way. The Negro's skin and the woman's sex are both prima facie evidence that they were intended to be in subjection to the white Saxon man. —Elizabeth Cady Stanton, speech to the New York state legislature, Feb 18, 1860

2903.   In a republic where all are declared equal an ostracised class of half of the people, on the ground of a distinction founded in nature, is an anomalous position, as harassing to its victims as it is unjust, and as contradictory as it is unsafe to the fundamental principles of a free government. —Elizabeth Cady Stanton, *History of Woman Suffrage*, 1881

2904.   We still wonder at the stolid incapacity of all men to understand that woman feels the invidious distinctions of sex exactly as the black man does those of color, or the white man the more transient distinctions of wealth, family, position, place, and power; that she feels as keenly as man the injustice of disfranchisement. —Elizabeth Cady Stanton, *History of Woman Suffrage*, 1881

2905.   Labor in a white skin cannot be free so long as labor in a black skin is branded. —Karl Marx, *Das Kapital*, 1867-83

2906.   Anti-semitism is the socialism of fools. —August Bebel, *Anti-semitism and Social Democracy*, 1893

2907.   After all there is but one race—humanity. —George Moore, *The Bending of the Bough*, 1900

2908.   Cannot the nation that has absorbed ten million foreigners into its political life without catastrophe absorb ten million Negro Americans into that same political life at less cost than their unjust and illegal exclusion will involve? —W.E.B. Du Bois, "No Cowards or Trucklers", *In Their Own Words: 1865-1916*, 1966

2909.   Race prejudice decreases values both real estate and human; crime, ignorance and filth decrease values. —W.E.B. Du Bois, "What Would You Do?", *The Crisis*, Nov, 1925

2910.   Persecution was at least a sign of personal interest. Tolerance is composed of nine parts of apathy to one of brotherly love. —Frank Moore Colby, "Trials of an Encyclopedist", *The Colby Essays*, 1926

2911.   The tendency of the casual mind is to pick out or stumble upon a sample which supports or defies its prejudices, and then to make it the representative of a whole class. —Walter Lippmann, *Public Opinion*, 1929

2912.   No one can make you feel inferior without your consent. —Eleanor Roosevelt, *This Is My Story*, 1937

2913.   The (Fifteenth) Amendment nullifies sophisticated as well as simple-minded modes of discrimination. —Felix Frankfurter, *Lane v. Wilson*, 1939

2914.   Injustice which lasts for three long centuries and which exists among millions of people over thousands of square miles of territory, is injustice no longer; it is an accomplished fact of life. —Richard Wright, *Native Son*, 1940

2915.   It is not healthy when a nation lives within a nation, as colored Americans are living inside America. A nation cannot live confident of its tomorrow if its refugees are among its citizens. —Pearl S. Buck, *What America Means to Me*, 1943

2916.   Race prejudice is not only a shadow over the colored—it is a shadow over all of us, and the shadow is darkest over those who feel it least and allow its evil effects to go on. —Pearl S. Buck, *What America Means to Me*, 1943

2917.   In the end, as any successful teacher will tell you, you can only teach the things that you are. If we practice racism then it is racism that we teach. —Max Lerner, "We Teach What We Are", *Actions and Passions*, 1949

2918.   Conformities are called for much more eagerly today than yesterday; loyalties are tested far more severely; sceptics, liberals, individuals with a taste for private life and their own inner standards of behaviour, are objects of fear or derision and targets of persecution for either side, execrated or despised by all the embattled parties in the great ideological wars of our time. —Sir Isaiah Berlin, *Political Ideas in the Twentieth Century*, 1950

2919.   If tolerance of diversity involves an admitted element of risk to national unity, intolerance involves a certainty that unity will be destroyed. —Alan Barth, *The Loyalty of Free Men*, 1951

2920.   It is a measure of the Negro's circumstance that, in America, the smallest things usually take him so very long, and that, by the time he wins them, they are no longer little things: they are miracles. —Murray Kempton, "George", *Part of Our Time*, 1955

2921.   Everyone is a prisoner of his own experiences. No one can eliminate prejudices—just recognize them. —Edward R. Murrow, television broadcast, Dec 31, 1955

2922.   All provisions of federal, state or local law requiring or permitting discrimination in public education must yield. —Earl Warren, unanimous opinion, *"Brown II"*, May 31, 1955

2923.   There are only two ways to be quite unprejudiced and impartial. One is to be completely ignorant. The other is to be completely indifferent. Bias and prejudice are attitudes to be kept in hand, not attitudes to be avoided. —Charles P. Curtis, *A Commonplace Book*, 1957

2924.   Only in the case of the Negro has the melting pot failed to bring a minority into the full stream of American life. —John F. Kennedy, *A Nation of Immigrants*, 1958

2925.   To be a Negro is to participate in a culture of poverty and fear that goes far deeper than any law for or against discrimination. —Michael Harrington, *The Other America*, 1962

2926.   The American economy, the American society, the American unconscious are all racist. —Michael Harrington, *The Other America*, 1962

2927.   So, let us not be blind to our differences—but let us also direct attention to our common interests and to the means by which those differences can be resolved. And if we cannot end now our differences, at least we can help make the world safe for diversity. —John F. Kennedy, commencement address at The American Univ., Jun 10, 1963

2928.   One hundred years ago, the slave was freed. One hundred years later, the Negro remains in bondage to the color of his skin. —Lyndon Baines Johnson, speech in Gettysburg, Pennsylvania, May 30, 1963

2929.   No one has been barred on account of his race from fighting or dying for America—there are no "white" or "colored" signs on the foxholes or graveyards of battle. —John F. Kennedy, message to Congress on his proposed civil rights bill, Jun 19, 1963

2930.   The good neighbor looks beyond the external accidents and discerns those inner qualities that make all men human and, therefore, brothers. —Martin Luther King Jr., *Strength to Love*, 1963

2931.   To the average white man, a courthouse even in Mississippi is a place where justice is dispensed. To me, the black man, it is a place where justice is dispensed with. —John Oliver Killens, "Explanation of the Black Psyche", *The New York Times*, Jun 7, 1964

2932.   Unfortunately many Americans live on the outskirts of hope—some because of their poverty, some because of their color, and all too many because of both. Our task is to help replace their despair with opportunity. —Lyndon Baines Johnson, first State of the Union message, Jan 8, 1964

2933. It will be helpful in our mutual objective to allow every man in America to look his neighbor in the face and see a man—not a color. —Adlai E. Stevenson Jr., *The New York Times*, Jun 22, 1964

2934. For the white man to ask the black man if he hates him is just like the rapist asking the raped, or the wolf asking the sheep, "Do you hate me?" The white man is in no moral position to accuse anyone else of hate! —Malcolm X, *Autobiography of Malcolm X*, 1965

2935. If you are black the only roads into the mainland of American life are through subservience, cowardice, and loss of manhood. These are the white man's roads. —LeRoi Jones, "Black Is a Country", *Home*, 1966

2936. Unless man is committed to the belief that all of mankind are his brothers, then he labors in vain and hypocritically in the vineyards of equality. —Adam Clayton Powell Jr., "Black Power: A Form of Godly Power", *Keep the Faith, Baby!*, 1967

2937. Its birthplace is the sinister back room of the mind where plots and schemes are hatched for the persecution and oppression of other human beings. —Bayard Rustin, "The Premise of the Stereotype", *Amsterdam News*, Apr 8, 1967

2938. Discrimination is a hellhound that gnaws at Negroes in every waking moment of their lives to remind them that the lie of their inferiority is accepted as truth in the society dominating them. —Martin Luther King Jr., speech to the Southern Christian Leadership Conference, Aug 16, 1967

2939. Our nation is moving toward two societies, one black, one white—separate and unequal. —Otto Kerner Jr., *Report of the National Advisory Commission on Civil Disorders*, 1968

2940. I draw the line in the dust and toss the gauntlet before the feet of tyranny, and I say segregation now, segregation tomorrow, segregation forever. —George C. Wallace, 1963 inaugural address as governor of Alabama, *Life*, Dec 26, 1969

2941. The myth of integration as propounded under the banner of the liberal ideology must be cracked because it makes people believe that something is being achieved when in reality the artificially integrated circles are a soporific to the blacks while salving the consciences of the few guilt-stricken whites. —Steve Biko, speech in Cape Town, 1971

2942. I believe that the essence of government lies with unceasing concern for the welfare and dignity and decency and innate integrity of life for every individual. I don't like to say this and I wish I didn't have to add these words to make it clear but I will—regardless of color, creed, ancestry, sex or age. —Lyndon Baines Johnson, remarks at a civil rights symposium at the Univ. of Texas, Dec 12, 1972

2943. If discrimination based on race is constitutionally permissible when those who hold the reins can come up with "compelling" reasons to justify it, then constitutional guarantees acquire an accordionlike quality. —William O. Douglas, dissenting opinion, *DeFunis v. Odegaard*, Apr 23, 1974

2944. So as a prelude whites must be made to realize that they are only human, not superior. Same with blacks. They must be made to realize that they are also human, not inferior. —Steve Biko, quoted, *Boston Globe*, Oct 25, 1977

2945. The Ku Klux Klan never dies. They just stop wearing sheets because sheets cost too much. —Thurgood Marshall, *Time*, Dec 4, 1978

2946. We cannot ... let colorblindness become myopia which masks the reality that many "created equal" have been treated within our lifetimes as inferior both by law and by their fellow citizens. —William J. Brennan Jr., dissenting opinion, Jun 28, 1978

2947. This administration is totally colorblind. —Ronald Reagan, press conference, Mar 13, 1981

2948. For goodness sake, will they hear, will white people hear what we are trying to say? Please, all we are asking you to do is to recognize that we are humans, too. —Desmond Tutu, *The New York Times*, Jan 3, 1985

2949. All I was doing was trying to get home from work. —Rosa Parks, on refusing to move to the back of the bus, interview on NBC-TV, Dec 1, 1985

PRESIDENCY

2950. You are apprehensive of monarchy; I, of aristocracy. I would therefore have given more power to the President and less to the Senate. —John Adams, letter to Thomas Jefferson, Dec 6, 1787

2951. The process of election (by the electoral college) affords a moral certainty that the office of President will never fall to the lot of any man who is not in an eminent degree endowed with the requisite qualifications. —Alexander Hamilton, *The Federalist*, Mar 12, 1788

2952. In executing the duties of my present important station, I can promise nothing but purity of intentions, and, in carrying these into effect, fidelity and diligence. —George Washington, message to Congress, Jul 9, 1789

2953. My country has in its wisdom contrived for me the most insignificant office (the vice-presidency) that ever the invention of man contrived or his imagination conceived. —John Adams, letter to Abigail Adams, Dec 19, 1793

2954. No man will ever carry out of the Presidency the reputation which carried him into it. —Thomas Jefferson, letter to Edward Rutledge, 1796

2955. I am tired of an office where I can do no more good than many others, who would be glad to be employed in it. To myself, personally, it brings nothing but unceasing drudgery and daily loss of friends. —Thomas Jefferson, letter to John Dickenson, Jan 13, 1807

2956. I had rather be right than be President. —Henry Clay, letter to Senator Preston of South Carolina, 1839

2957. No candidate for the Presidency ought ever to remain in the Cabinet. He is an unsafe advisor. —James K. Polk, *Diary*, Feb 21, 1848

2958. You have heard the story, haven't you, about the man who was tarred and feathered and carried out of town on a rail? A man in the crowd asked him how he liked it. His reply was that if it was not for the honor of the thing, he would much rather walk. —Abraham Lincoln, response to a friend when asked how he liked being president, 1861

2959. As President, I have no eyes but constitutional eyes; I cannot see you. —Abraham Lincoln, reply to a South Carolina commission, ca. 1861

2960. Everything I say, you know, goes into print. If I make a mistake it doesn't merely affect me, or you, but the country. I, therefore, ought at least try not to make mistakes. —Abraham Lincoln, to a crowd gathered before the White House, Apr 10, 1865

2961. History shows that no Administration from the time of Washington to the present has been free from ... mistakes. But I leave comparisons to history, claiming only that I have acted in every instance from a conscientious desire to do what was right, constitutional, within the law, and for the very best interests of the whole people. —Ulysses S. Grant, annual message to Congress, Dec 5, 1876

2962. And still the question, "What shall be done with our ex-Presidents?" is not laid at rest; and I sometimes think (one) solution of it, "Take them out and shoot them," is worthy of attention. —Grover Cleveland, letter to William F. Vilas, Apr 19, 1889

2963. In America the President reigns for four years, and Journalism governs for ever and ever. —Oscar Wilde, "The Soul of Man Under Socialism", *Fortnightly Review*, Feb, 1891

2964. Presidency, n. The greased pig in the field game of American politics. —Ambrose Bierce, *The Devil's Dictionary*, 1906

2965. Th' prisidincy is th' highest office in th' gift iv th' people. Th' vice-prisidincy is th' next highest an' the lowest. It isn't a crime exactly. Ye can't be sint to jail f'r it, but it's a kind iv a disgrace. —Finley Peter Dunne, "The Vice-President", *Dissertations by Mr. Dooley*, 1906

2966. The President is at liberty, both in law and and conscience, to be as big a man as he can. —Woodrow Wilson, *Constitutional Government*, 1908

2967. They talk of my power: my power vanishes into thin air the instant that my fellow citizens who are straight and honest cease to believe that I represent them and fight for what is straight and honest; that is all the strength I have. —Theodore Roosevelt, speech in Binghamton, New York, Oct 24, 1910

2968. It is an old maxim that there are other ways of killing a cat than by choking it with butter, and it is a great deal easier ... to use one's influence with the legislators to prevent objectionable bills passing than it is to wait until they do pass and then veto them. —William Howard Taft, speech at the Univ. of Virginia, Charlottesville, Jan, 1915

2969. The President can exercise no power which cannot be fairly and reasonably traced to some specific grant of power ... in the Federal Constitution or in an act of Congress passed in pursuance thereof. There is no undefined residuum of power which he can exercise because it seems to be in the public interest. —William Howard Taft, *Our Chief Magistrate and His Powers*, 1916

2970. I think the American public wants a solemn ass as a President and I think I'll go along with them. —Calvin Coolidge, reported remark to Ethel Barrymore, *Time*, May 16, 1955

2971. You have to stand three or four hours a day of visitors (to the White House). Nine-tenths of them want something they ought not have. If you keep dead-still they will run down in three or four minutes. If you even cough or smile they will start up all over again. —Calvin Coolidge, reported remarks to Herbert Hoover, 1928

2972. An examination of the records of those Presidents who have served eight years will disclose in most every instance the latter part of their term has shown very little in the way of constructive accomplishment. —Calvin Coolidge, *Autobiography*, 1929

2973. The President cannot, with success, constantly appeal to the country. After a time he will get no response. —Calvin Coolidge, *Autobiography*, 1929

2974. The Presidency is not merely an administrative office. ... It is pre-eminently a place of moral leadership. All our great Presidents were leaders of thought at times when certain historic ideas in the life of the nation had to be clarified. —Franklin D. Roosevelt, *The New York Times*, Sep 11, 1932

2975. In the end the President has become increasingly the depository of all national ills, especially if things go wrong. —Herbert Hoover, in 1933, as quoted, *Memoirs*, 1952

2976. Theodore Roosevelt said, "sometimes I wish I could be President and Congress too." Well, I suppose if the truth were told, he is not the only President that has had that idea. —Franklin D. Roosevelt, remarks in Dallas, Texas, June 12, 1936

2977. I should like to have it said of my first Administration that in it the forces of selfishness and of lust for power met their match. I should like to have it said of my second Administration that in it these forces met their master. —Franklin D. Roosevelt, speech at Madison Square Garden in New York City, Oct 31, 1936

2978. I would dare to dispute the integrity of the President on any occasion my country's welfare demanded it. ... After all, the President of the United States is neither an absolute monarch or a descendant of a sun goddess. —Harold L. Ickes, *Time*, Mar 11, 1946

2979. My God, this is a hell of a job! I have no trouble with my enemies. I can take care of them right now. But my damn friends, my god-damn friends, White, they're the ones that keep me walking the floor nights! —Warren G. Harding, quoted by William Allen White, *Autiobiography*, 1946

2980. In America any boy may become President and I suppose it's just one of the risks he takes. —Adlai E. Stevenson Jr., speech in Indianapolis, Indiana, Sep 26, 1952

2981. You know how it is in an election year. They pick a president and then for four years they pick on him. —Adlai R. Stevenson Jr., speech, Aug 28, 1952

2982. Any man who has had the job I've had and didn't have a sense of humor wouldn't still be here. —Harry S Truman, *The New York Times*, Apr 19, 1955

2983. The President is the only lobbyist that one hundred and fifty million americans have. The other twenty million are able to employ people to represent them—and that's all right, it's the exercise of the right of petition—but someone has to look out after the interests of the one hundred and fifty million that are left. —Harry S Truman, speech in San Francisco, California, Oct 25, 1956

2984. Most of the problems a President has to face have their roots in the past. —Harry S Truman, *Memoirs*, 1955-56

2985. The official position of the United States ... is defined by decisions and declarations of the President. There can be only one voice in stating the position of this country in the field of foreign relations. This is of fundamental constitutional significance. —Harry S Truman, *Memoirs*, 1955-56

2986. To be President of the United States is to be lonely, very lonely at times of great decisions. —Harry S Truman, *Memoirs*, 1955-56

2987. Jefferson ... was a master politician, and this helped make him a great leader. A President has to be a politician in order to get the majority to go along with him on his program. —Harry S Truman, *Memoirs*, 1955-56

2988. A President needs political understanding to run the government, but he may be elected without it. —Harry S Truman, *Memoirs*, 1955-56

2989. A President cannot always be popular. —Harry S Truman, *Memoirs*, 1955-56

2990. This desk of mine is one at which a man may die, but from which he cannot resign. —Dwight D. Eisenhower, quoted by a friend, *Parade*, Feb 2, 1958

2991. Oh, that lovely title, ex-president. —Dwight D. Eisenhower, *The New York Post*, Oct 26, 1959

2992. The President is the representative of the whole nation and he's the only lobbyist that all the 160 million people in this country have. —Harry S Truman, lecture at Columbia Univ., Apr 27, 1959

2993. He'll (Dwight D. Eisenhower) sit here, and he'll say, "Do this! Do that!" And nothing will happen. Poor Ike—it won't be a bit like the Army. He'll find it very frustrating. —Harry S Truman, quoted by Richard E. Neustadt, *Presidential Power, the Politics of Leadership*, 1960

2994. The function and responsibility of the President is to set before the American people the unfinished business, the things we must do if we are going to succeed as a nation. —John F. Kennedy, campaign speech, Crestwood, Missouri, Oct 22, 1960

2995. Always be on time. Do as little talking as humanly possible. Remember to lean back in the parade car so everybody can see the president. Be sure not to get too fat, because you'll have to sit there in the back seat. —Eleanor Roosevelt, on campaign behavior for first ladies, *The New York Times*, Nov 11, 1962

2996. No easy problems ever come to the President of the United States. If they are easy to solve, somebody else has solved them. —Dwight D. Eisenhower, quoted by John F. Kennedy, *Parade*, Apr 8, 1962

2997. I know that when things don't go well they like to blame the Presidents, and that is one of the things which Presidents are paid for. —John F. Kennedy, news conference, Jun 14, 1962

2998. I will do my best. That is all I can do. I ask for your help—and God's. —Lyndon Baines Johnson, following assassination of John F. Kennedy, Nov 22, 1963

2999. In the White House, the future rapidly becomes the past; and delay is itself a decision. —Theodore Sorensen, *Nation's Business*, Jun, 1963

3000. Extremism in the pursuit of the Presidency is an unpardonable vice, Moderation in the affairs of the nation is the highest virtue. —Lyndon Baines Johnson, speech in New York in reply to Barry Goldwater, Oct 31, 1964

3001. A President's hardest task is not to do what is right, but to know what is right. —Lyndon Baines Johnson, State of the Union Message, Jan 4, 1965

3002. The American Presidency, it occurs to us, is merely a way station en route to the blessed condition of being an ex-President. —John Updike, "Eisenhower's Eloquence", *Assorted Prose*, 1965

3003. "Why would anyone want to be President today?" the answer is not one of glory, or fame; today the burdens of the office outweigh its privileges. It's not because the President offers a chance to be somebody, but because it offers the chance to do something. —Richard M. Nixon, television campaign speech, Sep 19, 1968

3004. What we won when all of our people united ... must not be lost in suspicion and distrust and selfishness and politics. ... Accordingly, I shall not seek, and I will not accept, the nomination of my party for another term as president. —Lyndon Baines Johnson, televised speech, Mar 31, 1968

3005. The first lady is, and always has been, an unpaid public servant elected by one person, her husband. —Claudia ("Lady Bird") Johnson, quoted, *US News & World Report*, Mar 9, 1987

3006. The presidency has made every man who occupied it, no matter how small, bigger than he was: and no matter how big, not big enough for its demands. —Lyndon Baines Johnson, *The New York Times*, Mar 26, 1972

3007. If I were to make public these tapes, containing blunt and candid remarks on many different subjects, the confidentiality of the office of the president would always be suspect. —Richard M. Nixon, televised speech, Aug 15, 1973

3008. I began by telling the president that there was a cancer growing on the presidency and that if the cancer was not removed ... the president himself would be killed by it. —John Dean, testimony to the Senate Watergate hearings, Jul 25, 1973

3009. Being president is like being a jackass in a hailstorm. There's nothing to do but stand there and take it. —Lyndon Baines Johnson, recalled on his death, Jan 22, 1973

3010. I believe in the battle—whether it's the battle of a campaign or the battle of this office, which is a continuing battle. —Richard M. Nixon, interview following his second inauguration, Jan 22, 1973

3011. The presidency has many problems, but boredom is the least of them. —Richard M. Nixon, 60th birthday interview, Jan 9, 1973

3012. There is nothing in the Constitution that authorizes or makes it the official duty of a president to have anything to do with criminal activities. —Sam Ervin, at Senate Watergate hearings, *Washington Post*, Jul 12, 1973

3013. When people ask if the United States can afford to place on trial the president, if the system can stand impeachment, my answer is, "Can we stand anything else?" —George S. McGovern, on impeachment of Richard Nixon, *San Francisco Examiner*, Nov 29, 1973

3014. Being first lady is the hardest unpaid job in the world. —Pat Nixon, interview in Monrovia, Liberia, Mar 15, 1972

3015. The central question is simply put: What did the president know and when did he know it? —Howard H. Baker Jr., question to presidential counsel John Dean at the Watergate hearings, Jun 28, 1973

3016. When you get to be President, there are all those things, the honors, the twenty-one gun salutes, all those things. You have to remember it isn't for you. It's for the Presidency. —Harry S Truman, quoted by Merle Miller, *Plain Speaking: Conversations with Harry S Truman*, 1974

3017. I am acutely aware that you have not elected me as your president by your ballots, so I ask you to confirm me with your prayers. —Gerald R. Ford, on succeeding Richard Nixon as president, Aug 9, 1974

3018. I have never been a quitter. To leave office before my term is completed is opposed to every instinct in my body. But as president I must put the interests of America first. ... Therefore, I shall resign the presidency effective at noon tomorrow. —Richard M. Nixon, televised speech, Aug 8, 1974

3019. In all candor, the Court fails to perceive any reason for suspending the power of courts to get evidence and rule on questions of privilege in criminal matters simply because it is the president of the United States who holds the evidence. —John J. Sirica, ruling on obtaining Watergate tapes from President Nixon, *Christian Science Monitor*, Sep 15, 1974

3020. The president's need for complete candor and objectivity from advisers calls for great deference from the courts. However, when the privilege depends solely on the broad, undifferentiated claim of public interest in the confidentiality of such conversations, a confrontation with other values arises. —Warren E. Burger, unanimous opinion, *U.S. v. Nixon*, Jul 24, 1974

3021. You really have to experience the feeling of being with the president in the Oval Office....It's a disease I came to call Ovalitis. —John Dean, after conviction for his role in the Watergate coverup, Jan 1, 1975

3022. The Presidency is no place for on-the-job training. I've always advocated the politics of substance, not the politics of style. —Frank Church, *Encore American & Worldwide News*, Jun, 1976

3023. I think the President is the only person who can change the direction or attitude of our nation. —Jimmy Carter, *Encore American & Worldwide News*, Jun 21, 1976

3024. There is no inherent Constitutional authority for the President or any intelligence agency to violate the law. —Select Committee on Intelligence Oper. U.S. Senate, *The New York Times*, May 2, 1976

3025. I am against vice in every form, including the Vice Presidency. —Morris K. Udall, on being asked if he would accept vice presidential nomination, *The New York Times*, Apr 1, 1976

3026. When the President does it, that means that it is not illegal. —Richard M. Nixon, television interview with David Frost, May 19, 1977

3027. It isn't wisdom or intelligence that influences a President, it's opportunity. —Bill Moyers, *Newsweek*, Apr 17, 1978

3028. Old men running for the Presidency of the United States are like old men who take young brides. It's an exciting idea for a while but it seldom works. —James Reston, "Scotty", *The New York Times*, Jan 26, 1979

3029. If Nixon is not forced to turn over tapes of his conversations with the ring of men who were conversing on their violations of the law, then liberty will soon be dead in this nation. —Earl Warren, quoted by William O. Douglas, *The Court Years, 1939-75*, 1980

3030. History buffs probably noted the reunion at a Washington party a few weeks ago of three ex-presidents; Carter, Ford and Nixon—See No Evil, Hear No Evil and Evil. —Robert J. Dole, to Washington Gridiron Club dinner, Mar 26, 1983

3031. The first ladyship is the only federal office in which the holder can neither be fired nor impeached. —William Safire, *The New York Times*, Aug 16, 1984

3032. Once a president gets to the White House, the only audience that is left that really matters is history. They all start competing against Lincoln as the greatest president. And the (library) building becomes the symbol, the memorial to that dream. —Doris Kearns Goodwin, on presidential libraries, *The New York Times*, Oct 13, 1985

3033. I said I didn't want to run for president. I didn't ask you to believe me. —Mario Cuomo, *The New York Times*, Feb 12, 1985

3034. The United States brags about its political system, but the president says one thing during the election, something else when he takes office, something else at midterm and something else when he leaves. —Deng Xiaoping, quoted by John F. Burns, *The New York Times*, Jan 2, 1985

3035. Frankly, I don't mind not being president. I just mind that someone else is. —Edward M. Kennedy, speech to Washington Gridiron Club, Mar 22, 1986

3036. I think the presidency is an institution over which you have temporary custody. —Ronald Reagan, interview with Hugh Sidey, *Time*, Apr 7, 1986

3037. I have come to the conclusion that the 22nd Amendment (limiting a president to two terms) was a mistake. Shouldn't the people have the right to vote for someone as many times as they want to vote for him? —Ronald Reagan, interview with Barbara Walters, ABC-TV, Mar 24, 1986

3038. Of all the inherent duties of an American President, the duty to say no on matters of principle is among the most important. —Donald T. Regan, *For the Record*, 1988

PUBLIC OPINION

3039. The basis of our government (is) the opinion of the people. —Thomas Jefferson, letter to Edward Carrington, Jan 16, 1787

3040. Public opinion sets bounds to every government, and is the real sovereign in every free one. —James Madison, *National Gazette*, Dec 19, 1791

3041. A government is based on public opinion and must keep in step with what public opinion decides, which considers and calculates everything. [*Un gouvernement se forme de l'opinion publique, et marche avec ce qu'impose l'opinion publique, qui raisonne et calcule tout.*] — Napoleon I, letter to Citizen Melzi, Nov 25, 1803

3042. Public opinion is the mixed result of the intellect of the community acting upon general feeling. —William Hazlitt, "Characteristics", *The Literary Examiner*, 1823

3043. No minister ever stood, or could stand, against public opinion. —John Wilson Croker, *Quarterly Review*, Feb, 1835

3044. In Democracies there is a besetting disposition to make publick opinion stronger than the law. This is the particular form in which tyranny exhibits itself in a popular government. —James Fenimore Cooper, *The American Democrat*, 1838

3045. The Government must always be in advance of public opinion. [_Die Regierung muss der Bewegung immer um einen Schritt voraus sein._] —Count Adolf Heinrich Arnim-Boytzenburg, speech to the United Landtag, April 2, 1848

3046. A universal feeling, whether well or ill founded, cannot be safely disregarded. —Abraham Lincoln, speech in Peoria, Illinois, Oct 16, 1854

3047. Public opinion is a weak tyrant compared with our own private opinion. What a man thinks of himself, that is which determines, or rather, indicates, his fate. —Henry David Thoreau, "Economy", _Walden_, 1854

3048. Our government rests in public opinion. Whoever can change public opinion can change the government practically just so much. —Abraham Lincoln, speech in Chicago, Illinois, Dec 10, 1856

3049. Public opinion in this country is everything. —Abraham Lincoln, speech in Columbus, Ohio, Sep 16, 1859

3050. The press is not public opinion. [_Die Presse ist nicht die öffentliche Meinung._] —Prince Otto von Bismarck, speech in the Prussian Chamber of Deputies, Sep 30, 1862

3051. In the modern world the intelligence of public opinion is the one indispensable condition of social progress. —Charles William Eliot, inaugural address as president of Harvard Univ., 1869

3052. Public opinion is stronger than the legislature, and nearly as strong as the ten commandments. —Charles Dudley Warner, "Sixteenth Week", _My Summer in a Garden_, 1871

3053. Public opinion, the fear of losing public confidence, apprehension of censure by the press make all men in power conservative and safe. —Rutherford B. Hayes, _Diary_, Oct 22, 1876

3054. What we call public opinion is generally public sentiment. —Benjamin Disraeli, speech, Aug 3, 1880

3055. Lincoln said in his homely way that he wanted "to take a bath in public opinion." I think I have a right to take a bath before I do much talking. —James A. Garfield, letter to Burke A. Hinsdale, Nov 17, 1880

3056. The nation is a power hard to rouse, but when roused harder still and more hopeless to resist. —William Ewart Gladstone, speech at East Calder, Scotland, Apr 2, 1880

3057. There is nothing that makes more cowards and feeble men than public opinion. —Henry Ward Beecher, _Proverbs from Plymouth Pulpit_, 1887

3058. Public sentiment is to public officers what water is to the wheel of the mill. —Henry Ward Beecher, _Proverbs from Plymouth Pulpit_, 1887

3059. Public opinion is the most potent monarch this world knows. —Benjamin Harrison, speech in Detroit, Michigan, Feb 22, 1888

3060. Its name is Public Opinion. It is held in reverence. It settles everything. Some think it is the voice of God. —Mark Twain, "Corn Pone Opinions", _Europe and Elsewhere_, 1925

3061. No written law has ever been more binding than unwritten custom supported by popular opinion. —Carrie Chapman Catt, testimony at U.S. Senate hearing, Feb 13, 1900

3062. There must be public opinion back of the laws or the laws themselves will be of no avail. —Theodore Roosevelt, seventh annual message to Congress, Dec 3, 1907

3063. A straw vote only shows which way the hot air blows. —O. Henry, (William Sydney Porter), "A Ruler of Men", _Rolling Stones_, 1912

3064. Social movements are at once the symptoms and the instruments of progress. Ignore them and statesmanship is irrelevant; fail to use them and it is weak. —Walter Lippmann, "Revolution and Culture", *A Preface to Politics*, 1914

3065. Where public opinion is free and uncontrolled, wealth has a wholesome respect for the law. —Robert M. LaFollette Sr., "Fooling the People as a Fine Art", *LaFollette's Magazine*, Apr, 1918

3066. Public opinion, a vulgar, impertinent, anonymous tyrant who deliberately makes life unpleasant for anyone who is not content to be the average man. —William Ralph Inge, "Our Present Discontents", *Outspoken Essays: First Series*, 1919

3067. We are ruled by Public Opinion, not by Statute-law. —Elbert G. Hubbard, *The Note Book*, 1927

3068. Government, in the last analysis, is organized opinion. Where there is little or no public opinion, there is likely to be bad government, which sooner or later becomes autocratic government. —William Lyon Mackenzie King, *Message of the Carillon*, 1927

3069. One should respect public opinion in so far as is necessary to avoid starvation and to keep out of prison, but anything that goes beyond this is voluntary submission to an unnecessary tyranny. —Bertrand Russell, 3rd Earl Russell, *The Conquest of Happiness*, 1930

3070. There is no group in America that can withstand the force of an aroused public opinion. —Franklin D. Roosevelt, on signing the National Industrial Recovery Act, Jun 16, 1933

3071. A government can be no better than the public opinion that sustains it. —Franklin D. Roosevelt, speech in Washington, D.C., Jan 8, 1936

3072. The whole structure of democracy rests on public opinion. —Franklin D. Roosevelt, speech to the Institute of Human Relations, Aug 20, 1937

3073. Nothing is more dangerous in wartime than to live in the temperamental atmosphere of a Gallup Poll, always feeling one's pulse and taking one's temperature. —Sir Winston S. Churchill, speech in the House of Commons, Sep 30, 1941

3074. I see that a speaker at the week-end said that this was a time when leaders should keep their ears to the ground. All I can say is that the British nation will find it very hard to look up to leaders who are detected in that somewhat ungainly posture. —Sir Winston S. Churchill, speech in the House of Commons, Sep 30, 1941

3075. People on the whole are very simple-minded, in whatever country one finds them. They are so simple as to take literally, more often than no, the things their leaders tell them. —Pearl S. Buck, *What America Means to Me*, 1943

3076. It isn't polls or public opinion alone of the moment that counts. It is right and wrong, and leadership—men with fortitude, honesty and a belief in the right that make epochs in the history of the world. —Harry S Truman, interview, 1946

3077. When distant and unfamiliar and complex things are communicated to great masses of people, the truth suffers a considerable and often a radical distortion. The complex is made over into the simple, the hypothetical into the dogmatic, and the relative into an absolute. —Walter Lippmann, *The Public Philosophy*, 1955

3078. What the lawmaker has to ascertain is not the true belief but the common belief. —Patrick Devlin, *The Enforcement of Morals*, 1965

3079. It is far more difficult to change the mentality of the people than it is to change a country's political order or even its economy. —Ilya Ehrenburg, "What I Have Learned", *Saturday Review*, Sep 30, 1967

3080. Polling is merely an instrument for gauging public opinion. When a president or any other leader pays attention to poll results, he is, in effect, paying attention to the views of the people. Any other interpretation is nonsense. —George H. Gallup, *The New York Times*, Dec 1, 1979

3081. We must get the American public to look past the glitter, beyond the showmanship, to the reality, the hard substance of things. And we'll do it ... not so much with speeches that will bring people to their feet as with speeches that bring people to their senses. —Mario Cuomo, keynote address to Democratic National Convention in San Francisco, Jul 16, 1984

REFORM

3082. To give moderate liberty for griefs and discontentments to evaporate ... is a safe way. For he that turneth the humours back, and maketh the wound bleed inwards, endangereth malign ulcers and pernicious impostumations. —Sir Francis Bacon, "Of Seditions and Troubles", *Essays*, 1625

3083. It is a folly second to none,/ To try to improve the world. [*Et c'est une folie à nulle autre seconde/ De vouloir se mêler de corriger le monde.*] —Molière, *The Misanthrope*, 1666

3084. The hole and the patch should be commensurate. —Thomas Jefferson, letter to James Madison, Jun 20, 1787

3085. A state without some means of change is without the means of its conservation. —Edmund Burke, *Reflections on the Revolution in France*, 1790

3086. Power vegetates with more vigour after these gentle prunings. A slender reform amuses and lulls the people: the popular enthusiasm subsides; and the moment of effectual reform is irretrievably lost. No important political improvement was ever obtained in a period of tranquility. —Sir James Mackintosh, *Vindicae Gallicae*, 1791

3087. When we reflect how difficult it is to move or deflect the great machine of society, how impossible to advance the notions of a whole people suddenly to ideal right, we see the wisdom of Solon's remark, that no more good must be attempted than the nation can bear. —Thomas Jefferson, letter to Walter Jones, Mar 31, 1801

3088. Politics, like religion, hold up torches of martyrdom to the reformers of error. —Thomas Jefferson, letter to James Ogilvie, Aug 4, 1811

3089. Every reform, however necessary, will by weak minds be carried to an excess, that itself will need reforming. —Samuel Taylor Coleridge, *Biographia Literaria*, 1817

3090. Know you not that, as in the case of the body natural, so in the case of the body politic, when motion ceases, the body dies? —Jeremy Bentham, *Plan of Parliamentary Reform*, 1817

3091. The population of this country with regard to some important improvement in their government may be compared to a vessel of water exposed to a temperature of 32°. Leave it perfectly still, and the water will remain uncongealed; shake it a little, and it shoots into ice immediately. All great changes are easily effected, when the time is come. Was it not an individual, without fortune, without name, and in fact without talents, who produced the reformation? —James Mill, letter to David Ricardo, Sep 23, 1818

3092. Attempts at reform, when they fail, strengthen despotism, as he that struggles tightens those cords he does not succeed in breaking. —Charles Caleb Colton, *Lacön*, 1825

3093. I was ... a great reformist; but never suspected that the people in power were against reform. I supposed they only wanted to know what was good in order to embrace it. —Jeremy Bentham, written fragment, Feb 2, 1827

3094. The voice of great events is proclaiming to us, Reform, that you may preserve. —Lord Macaulay, speech on parliamentary reform, Mar 2, 1831

3096. Conservatism goes for comfort, reform for truth. —Ralph Waldo Emerson, lecture on "The Conservative" in Boston, Massachusetts, Dec 9, 1841

3097. If anything ail a man, so that he does not perform his functions, if he have a pain in his bowels even,—for that is the seat of sympathy,—he forthwith sets about reforming the world. —Henry David Thoreau, "Economy", *Walden*, 1854

3098. Cautious, careful people, always casting about to preserve their reputation and social standing, never can bring about a reform. Those who are really in earnest must be willing to be anything or nothing in the world's estimation. —Susan B. Anthony, speaking on the need to reform divorce law, 1860

3099. Experience has two things to teach: the first is that we must correct a great deal; the second, that we must not correct too much. [*Il y a deux choses que l'expérience doit apprendre: la première, c'est qu'il faut beaucoup corriger; la seconde, c'est qu'il ne faut pas trop corriger.*] —Eugene Delacroix, *Journal*, Mar 8, 1860

3100. Reformers can be as bigoted and sectarian and as ready to malign each other, as the Church in its darkest periods has been to persecute its dissenters. —Elizabeth Cady Stanton, speech on "The Kansas Campaign of 1867", 1867

3101. I believe that the labour of those who would ameliorate the conditions of the working classes is slower and more imperceptible than that of the insect which raises the coral reef from the bed of the ocean. —5th Earl of Rosebery, (Archibald Primrose), speech to the Working Men's Club and Institute Union, Jul 17, 1875

3102. If we wish a change to be as radical as possible, we have to apply the remedy in small doses, but unremittingly, for long periods. Can a great action be accomplished all at once? [*Soll eine Veränderung möglichst in die Tiefe gehen, so gebe man das Mittel in den kleinsten Dosen, aber unablässig auf weite Zeitstrecken hin! Was ist Grosses auf einmal zu schaffen?*] —Friedrich Nietzsche, *The Dawn*, 1881

3103. You should never wear your best trousers when you go out to fight for freedom and truth. [*En skulde aldrig ha' sine bedste buxer på når en er ude og strider for frihed og sandhed.*] —Henrik Ibsen, *An Enemy of the People*, 1882

3104. What is said by great employers of labour against agitators is unquestionably true. Agitators are a set of interfering, meddling people, who come down to some perfectly contented class of the community, and sow the seeks of discontent amongst them. That is the reason why agitators are so absolutely necessary. —Oscar Wilde, "The Soul of Man Under Socialism", *Fortnightly Review*, Feb, 1891

3105. Nothing so needs reforming as other people's habits. —Mark Twain, "Pudd'nhead Wilson's Calendar", *Pudd'nhead Wilson*, 1894

3106. Reformers who are always compromising, have not yet grasped the idea that truth is the only safe ground to stand upon. —Elizabeth Cady Stanton, *The Woman's Bible*, 1895

3107. Kansas had better stop raising corn and begin raising hell. —Mary Elizabeth Lease, attributed

3108. A man that'd expict to thrain lobsters to fly in a year is called a loonytic; but a man that thinks men can be tu'rrned into angels be an iliction is called rayformer an' remains at large. —Finley Peter Dunne, "Casual Observations", *Mr. Dooley's Opinions*, 1900

3109. All reformers are bachelors. —George Moore, *The Bending of the Bough*, 1900

3110. (Th' rayformer) don't undherstand that people wud rather be wrong an' comfortable thin right in jail. —Finley Peter Dunne, "Reform Administration", *Observations by Mr. Dooley*, 1902

3111. Radicalism, n. The conservatism of to-morrow injected into the affairs of to-day. —Ambrose Bierce, *The Devil's Dictionary*, 1906

3112. Reform must come from within, not without. You cannot legislate for virtue. —James Cardinal Gibbons, speech in Baltimore, Maryland, Sep 13, 1909

3113. Every man is a reformer until reform tramps on his toes. —Edgar Watson Howe, *Country Town Sayings*, 1911

3114. Standpatism is just as impossible in modern conditions as it is impossible for a thin crust of the earth to keep its place above the force of a volcano. All the blood in this nation is now running into the vital courses of reform, and the men who stand against reform are standing against nature, standing against all the impulses, all the energies, all the hopes, all the ambitions of America. —Woodrow Wilson, speech in Burlington, New Jersey, Oct 30, 1912

3115. Every reform movement has a lunatic fringe. —Theodore Roosevelt, speech, 1913

3116. Unless the reformer can invent something which substitutes attractive virtues for attractive vices, he will fail. —Walter Lippmann, "The Taboo", *A Preface to Politics*, 1914

3117. Hunger does not breed reform; it breeds madness and all the angry distempers that make an ordered life impossible. —Woodrow Wilson, speech to Congress, Nov 11, 1918

3118. As soon as the people fix one Shame of the World, another turns up. —Edgar Watson Howe, *Ventures in Common Sense*, 1919

3119. Laws do not make reforms, reforms make laws. —Calvin Coolidge, quoted by Edward E. Whiting, *Calvin Coolidge: His Ideals of Citizenship*, 1924

3120. Nobody expects to find comfort and companionability in reformers. —Heywood Broun, "Whims", *New York World*, Feb 6, 1928

3121. The desire to understand the world and the desire to reform it are the two great engines of progress, without which human society would stand still or retrogress. —Bertrand Russell, "The Place of Sex Among Human Values", *Marriage and Morals*, 1929

3122. If you try to make a big reform you are told you are doing too much, and if you make a modest contribution you are told you are only tinkering with the problem. —A.P. (Sir Alan Patrick) Herbert, speech in the House of Commons, Feb 3, 1939

3123. The man who is forever disturbed about the condition of humanity either has no problems of his own or has refused to face them. —Henry Miller, *Sunday after the War*, 1944

3124. You sometimes find something good in the lunatic fringe. In fact, we have got as part of our social and economic government today a whole lot of things which in my boyhood were considered lunatic fringe, and yet they are now part of everyday life. —Franklin D. Roosevelt, press conference, May 30, 1944

3125. A mass movement attracts and holds a following not because it can satisfy the desire for self-advancement, but because it can satisfy the passion for self-renunciation. —Eric Hoffer, *The True Believer*, 1951

3126. Mass movements can rise and spread without belief in a God, but never without belief in a devil. —Eric Hoffer, *The True Believer*, 1951

3127. You can't move so fast that you try to change the mores faster than people can accept it. That doesn't mean you do nothing but it means that you do the things that need to be done according to priority. —Eleanor Roosevelt, *On My Own*, 1958

3128. Nonviolent action, the Negro saw, was the way to supplement, not replace, the process of change. It was the way to divest himself of passivity without arraying himself in vindictive force. —Martin Luther King Jr., *Why We Can't Wait*, 1964

3129. To give up the task of reforming society is to give up one's responsibility as a free man. —Alan Paton, "The Challenge of Fear", *Saturday Review*, Sep 9, 1967

3130. To achieve reforms, you have sometimes to try to make the revolution. —Anonymous, quoting a student at the University of Nanterre, France, following 1968 upheaval, *The Economist*, May 14, 1988

3131. Personally, I am not nonviolent, but I'm not a fool either. I can count. —Whitney Moore Young Jr., recalled on his death, Mar 11, 1971

3132. Should I ... stand on 125th Street cussing out Whitey to show I am tough? Or should I go downtown and talk to an executive of General Motors about 20,000 jobs for unemployed Negroes? —Whitney Moore Young Jr., recalled on his death, Mar 11, 1971

3133. Many middle-class reformers will find to their surprise, that the populace is going to be quick to bite the hand that aims to feed it. The populace doesn't want to be fed; it wants more freedom to graze on its own. —Irving Kristol, *Esquire*, May 23, 1978

3134. If you fear making anyone mad, then you ultimately probe for the lowest common denominator of human achievement. —Jimmy Carter, speech to the Future Farmers of America in Kansas City, Nov 9, 1978

RELIGION AND THE STATE

3135. If men think that a ruler is religious and has a reverence for the Gods, they are less afraid of suffering injustice at his hands. —Aristotle, *Politics*, 343 B.C.

3136. Render therefore unto Caesar the things which are Caesar's; and unto God the things that are God's. —Bible, *Matthew*, ca. 90

3137. The doctrine of persecution for cause of conscience is most evidently and lamentably contrary to the doctrine of Christ Jesus the Prince of Peace. —Roger Williams, *The Bloudy Tenant of Persecution for Cause of Conscience*, 1644

3138. A sanctimonious man is one who under an atheist king would be atheist. [*Un dévot est celui qui sous un roi athée serait athée.*] —Jean de La Bruyère, "De la mode", *Les Caractères*, 1688

3139. All religions must be tolerated...every man must go to heaven in his own way. [*Die Religionen müssen alle toleriert werden ... denn hier muss ein jeder nach seiner Fasson selig werden.*] —Frederick the Great, note to the Religious Department, Jun 22, 1740

3140. That religion, or the duty which we owe to our Creator, and the manner of discharging it, can be directed only by reason and conviction, not by force or violence; and therefore all men are equally entitled to the free exercise of religion, according to the dictates of conscience. —Patrick Henry, *Virginia Bill of Rights*, Jun 12, 1776

3141. That to compel a man to furnish contributions of money for the propagation of opinions which he disbelieves and abhors, is sinful and tyrannical. —Thomas Jefferson, "A Bill for Establishing Religious Freedom", 1779

3142. It does me no injury for my neighbor to say there are twenty gods, or no God. It neither picks my pocket nor breaks my leg. —Thomas Jefferson, *Notes on the State of Virginia*, 1782

3143. It behoves every man who values liberty of conscience for himself, to resist invasions of it in the case of others; or their case may, by change of circumstances, become his own. —Thomas Jefferson, letter to Benjamin Rush, Apr 21, 1803

3144.   Are not Religion & Politics the Same Thing? Brotherhood is Religion. —William Blake, *Jerusalem*, 1804

3145.   All religions united with government are more or less inimical to liberty. All separated from government, are compatible with liberty. —Henry Clay, speech in the House of Representatives, Mar 24, 1818

3146.   Civil liberty can be established on no foundation of human reason which will not at the same time demonstrate the right to religious freedom. —John Quincy Adams, letter to Richard Anderson, May 27, 1823

3147.   Religion, true or false, is and ever has been the centre of gravity in a realm, to which all other things must and will accommodate themselves. —Samuel Taylor Coleridge, *On the Constitution of the Church and State*, 1830

3148.   I recognize no rights but human rights—I know nothing of men's rights and women's rights; for in Christ Jesus there is neither male nor female. It is my solemn conviction that, until this principal of equality is recognized and embodied in practice, the church can do nothing effectual for the permanent reformation of the world. —Angelina Grimké, *Letters to Catherine Beecher*, 1836

3149.   Religion is the sigh of the oppressed creatures, the heart of a heartless world, just as it is the soul of soulless conditions. It is the opium of the people. [*Die Religion ist der Seufzer der bedrängten Kreatur, das Gemüt einer herzlosen Welt, wie sie der Geist geistloser Zustände ist. Sie ist das Opium des Volkes.*] —Karl Marx, *A Contribution to the Critique of Hegel's Philosophy of Right: Introduction*, 1844

3150.   Christian socialism is but the holy water with which the priest consecrates the heart-burnings of the aristocrat. —Karl Marx, *The Communist Manifesto*, 1848

3151.   Politics would become an utter blank to me were I to make the discovery that we were mistaken in maintaining their association with religion. —William Ewart Gladstone, letter to Cardinal Manning, Apr, 1850

3152.   The religions are obsolete when the reforms do not proceed from them. —Ralph Waldo Emerson, *Journals*, 1872

3153.   In all ages, hypocrites, called priests, have put crowns upon the heads of thieves, called kings. —Robert G. Ingersoll, *Prose-Poems and Selections*, 1884

3154.   The way in which, amid the political and social unrest of his time, Christ keeps aloof from politics, is truly sublime. —Thomas Masaryk, *The Spirit of Russia*, 1913

3155.   The Church should no longer be satisfied to represent only the Conservative Party at prayer. —Agnes Maude Royden, speech at the City Temple, London, 1917

3156.   If I were asked to state the great objective which Church and State are both demanding for the sake of every man and woman and child in this country, I would say that that great objective is "a more abundant life." —Franklin D. Roosevelt, speech to the Federal Council of Churches of Christ, Dec 6, 1933

3157.   The Pope! How many divisions has he got? —Joseph Stalin, reported conversation with Pierre Laval, May 13, 1935

3158.   I could not be leading a religious life unless I identified myself with the whole of mankind, and that I could not do unless I took part in politics. —Mohandas K. Gandhi, *Non-Violence in Peace and War*, 1948

3159.   The day that this country ceases to be free for irreligion, it will cease to be free for religion. —Robert H. Jackson, dissenting opinion, *Zorach v. Clausor*, Apr 7, 1952

3160. I hope that no American ... will waste his franchise and throw away his vote by voting either for me or against me solely on account of my religious affiliation. It is not relevant. —John F. Kennedy, *Time*, Jul 25, 1960

3161. Tolerance implies no lack of commitment to one's own beliefs. Rather it condemns the oppression or persecution of others. —John F. Kennedy, letter to the National Conference of Christians and Jews, Oct 10, 1960

3162. The church must be reminded that it is not the master or the servant of the state, but rather the conscience of the state. —Martin Luther King Jr., *Strength to Love*, 1963

3163. If we get the federal government out of the classroom, maybe we'll get God back in. —Ronald Reagan, *Washingtonian*, Jul, 1976

3164. I think the government ought to stay out of the prayer business. —Jimmy Carter, *The New York Times*, Apr 8, 1979

3165. The government must pursue a course of complete neutrality toward religion. —John Paul Stevens, majority opinion, *Wallace v. Jaffree*, Jun 4, 1985

REPUBLICAN PARTY

3166. I knew that however bad the Republican party was, the Democratic party was much worse. The elements of which the Republican party was composed gave better ground for the ultimate hope of the success of the colored man's cause than those of the Democratic party. —Frederick Douglass, *Life and Times of Frederick Douglass*, 1881

3167. I recognize the Republican party as the sheet anchor of the colored man's political hopes and the ark of his safety. —Frederick Douglass, letter to men of Petersburg, Virginia, Aug 15, 1888

3168. Th' raypublican party broke ye, but now that ye're down we'll not turn a cold shoulder to ye. come in an' we'll keep ye - broke. —Finley Peter Dunne, "Mr. Dooley Discusses", *Mr. Dooley's Opinion*, 1900

3169. The trouble with the Republican Party is that it has not had a new idea in 30 years. I am not speaking as a politician; I am speaking as an historian. —Woodrow Wilson, speech in Indianapolis, Indiana, Jan 8, 1915

3170. Indeed there are some Republicans I would trust with anything—anything, that is, except public office. —Adlai E. Stevenson Jr., campaign speech in Springfield, Illinois, Aug 14, 1952

3171. It (the Republican Party) is an ancient political vehicle, held together by soft soap and hunger and with front-seat drivers and back-seat drivers contradicting each other in a bedlam of voices, shouting "go right" and "go left" at the same time. —Adlai E. Stevenson Jr., *The New York Times*, Nov 15, 1952

3172. I have been tempted to make a proposal to our Republican friends: that if they stop telling lies about us, we would stop telling the truth about them. —Adlai E. Stevenson Jr., quoted, *Human Behavior*, May, 1978

3173. The elephant has a thick skin, a head full of ivory, and as everyone who has seen a circus parade knows, proceeds best by grasping the tail of his predecessor. —Adlai E. Stevenson Jr., "The Art of Politics", *The Stevenson Wit*, 1966

3174. Brains, you know, are suspect in the Republican Party. —Walter Lippmann, recalled on his death, Dec 14, 1974

3175. I think the Republican Party is only going to be an effective party if it reflects the best interests of the American people, and traditionally that is in the center. That is where our country has always been. That is where the Republican Party has won. —Nelson A. Rockefeller, *Time*, Nov 17, 1975

3176. For a workingman or woman to vote Republican this year is the same as a chicken voting for Colonel Sanders. —Walter F. Mondale, *Rolling Stone*, Nov 4, 1976

3177. My answer to why did I choose the Democratic Party is that I spent three years in Washington under a Republican administration. —Dixy Lee Ray, *Wall Street Journal*, Mar 15, 1976

3178. There's nothing wrong with the Republican Party that double-digit inflation won't cure. —Richard Scammon, *Guardian Weekly*, Nov 12, 1978

3179. (Republicans are) men of narrow vision who are afraid of the future and whose leaders are inclined to shoot from the hip. —Jimmy Carter, *Time*, Jul 28, 1980

3180. Thou shalt not criticize other Republicans. —Ronald Reagan, *Time*, Jul 28, 1980

3181. We're the party that wants to see an America in which people can still get rich. —Ronald Reagan, remarks at a Republican fundraising dinner in Washington, D.C., May 4, 1982

3182. Republicans believe every day is the Fourth of July, but Democrats believe every day is April 15. —Ronald Reagan, *The New York Times*, Oct 10, 1984

REVOLUTION

3183. Rebellion is as the sin of witchcraft. —Bible, *1 Samuel*, ca. 800 B.C.

3184. Is it not a simple fact that in any form of government revolution always starts from the outbreak of internal dissension in the ruling class? The constitution cannot be upset so long as that class is of one mind, however small it may be. —Plato, *The Republic*, ca. 390 B.C.

3185. A desperate disease requires a dangerous remedy. —Guy Fawkes, to James I, Nov 5, 1605

3186. The surest way to prevent seditions ... is to take away the matter of them. For if there be fuel prepared, it is hard to tell whence the spark shall come that shall set it on fire. —Sir Francis Bacon, "Of Seditions and Troubles", *Essays*, 1625

3187. When the people are in movement, it's not possible to see how calm will be restored; when they're quiet, you can't see how the calm will be destroyed. [*Quand le peuple est en mouvement, on ne comprend pas par où le calme peut y entrer; et quand il est paisible, on ne voit pas par où le calme peut en sortir.*] —Jean de La Bruyère, "Du souverain ou de la république", *Les Caractères*, 1688

3188. If the abuse be enormous, nature will rise up, and claiming her original rights, overturn a corrupt political system. —Samuel Johnson, quoted by James Boswell, *Life of Samuel Johnson*, Jul 6, 1763

3189. The spirit of resistance to government is so valuable on certain occasions, that I wish it to be always kept alive. It will often be exercised when wrong but better so than not be exercised at all. I like a little rebellion now and then. It is like a storm in the atmosphere. —Thomas Jefferson, letter to Abigail Adams, Feb 22, 1787

3190. I hold it, that a little rebellion now and then, is a good thing, and as necessary in the political world as storms in the physical. ... It is a medicine for the sound health of government. —Thomas Jefferson, letter to James Madison, Jan 30, 1787

3191. Insurrection is the most sacred of duties. —Marie Joseph, Marquis de Lafayette, speech to the National Assembly, Feb 20, 1790

3192. Every successful revolt is termed a revolution, and every unsuccessful one a rebellion. —Joseph Priestly, letter to Edmund Burke, 1791

3193. The tree of liberty grows only when watered by the blood of tyrants. [*L'arbre de la liberté ne croit qu'arrosé par le sang des tyrans.*] —Bertrand Barère de Vieuzac, speech to the National Assembly, 1792

3194. Let the law be ruthless and order will be restored. [*Que la loi soit terrible et tout rentrera dans l'ordre.*] —Georges Jacques Danton, speech to the National Convention, Sep 22, 1792

3195. Let us make terror the order of the day. —Bertrand Barère de Vieuzac, speech to the National Convention, 1793

3196. An oppressed people are authorized whenever they can to rise and break their fetters. —Henry Clay, speech in the House of Representatives, Mar 4, 1818

3197. A great revolution is never the fault of the people, but of the government. —Johann Wolfgang von Goethe, quoted by Johann Peter Eckermann, *Conversations with Goethe*, Jan 4, 1824

3198. If we trace the history of most revolutions, we shall find that the first inroads upon the laws have been made by the governors, as often as by the governed. —Charles Caleb Colton, *Lacön*, 1825

3199. When the ground shakes under governments it is no good their trying to sit still; nature will not allow it! —Prince Clemens von Metternich, letter to Count d'Apponyi, Oct 28, 1829

3200. The spirit of revolution, the spirit of insurrection, is a spirit radically opposed to liberty. —Francois Guizot, speech in Paris, Dec 29, 1830

3201. In revolutions those who want everything always get the better of those who want only a certain amount. —Prince Clemens von Metternich, letter to Esterhazy, Mar 17, 1831

3202. I always had a horror of revolutionising any country for a political object. I always said, if they rise of themselves, well and good, but do not stir them up—it is a fearful responsibility. —1st Duke of Wellington, reported conversation with Lord Mahon, Nov 2, 1831

3203. Great revolutions are the work rather of principles than of bayonets, and are achieved first in the moral, and afterwards in the material sphere. [*Le grandi rivoluzioni si compiono più coi principii, che colle baionette: dapprima nell'ordine morale, poi nel materiale.*] —Giuseppe Mazzini, *Manifesto of Young Italy*, 1831

3204. Insurrection—by means of guerrilla bands—is the true method of warfare for all nations desirous of emancipating themselves from a foreign yoke. [*La guerra d'insurrezione per bande è la guerra di tutte le Nazioni che s'emancipano da un conquistatore straniero.*] —Giuseppe Mazzini, *General Instructions for the Members of Young Italy*, 1831

3205. Secession, like any other revolutionary act, may be morally justified by the extremity of oppression; but to call it a constitutional right is confounding the meaning of the term. —Andrew Jackson, "Proclamation to the People of South Carolina", Dec 10, 1832

3206. Moderation is fatal to factions, just as it is the vital principle of established power. To ask malcontents to be moderate is like asking them to destroy the foundations of their existence. —Prince Clemens von Metternich, letter to Count d'Apponyi, Feb 6, 1834

3207. There is no grievance that is a fit object of redress by mob law. —Abraham Lincoln, speech in Springfeld, Illinois, Jan 27, 1838

3208. Every revolution was first a thought in one man's mind, and when the same thought occurs to another man, it is the key to that era. —Ralph Waldo Emerson, "History", *Essays: First Series*, 1841

3209. The world is always childish, and with each new gewgaw of a revolution or new constitution that it finds, thinks it shall never cry any more. —Ralph Waldo Emerson, *Journals*, 1847

3210. When a sixth of the population of a nation which has undertaken to be the refuge of liberty are slaves, and a whole country (Mexico) is unjustly overrun and conquered by a foreign army, and subjected to military law, I think that it is not too soon for honest men to rebel and revolutionize. What makes this duty the more urgent is the fact that the country so overrun is not our own, but ours is the invading army. —Henry David Thoreau, *Civil Disobedience*, 1849

3211. Better to perish with the revolution than to seek refuge in the almshouse of reaction. —Alexander Ivanovich Herzen, introduction, "To My Son Alexander", *From The Other Shore*, 1848-49

3212. All men recognize the right of revolution; that is, the right to refuse allegiance to, and to resist, the government, when its tyranny or its inefficiency are great and unendurable. But almost all say that such is not the case now. —Henry David Thoreau, *Civil Disobedience*, 1849

3213. If powerful men will not write justice with black ink, on white paper, ignorant and violent men will write it on the soil, in letters of blood, and illuminate their rude legislation with burning castles, palaces, and towns. —Theodore Parker, quoted by Daniel Aaron, *Men of Good Hope*, 1951

3214. Revolutions are not made; they come. A revolution is as natural a growth as an oak. It comes out of the past. Its foundations are laid far back. —Wendell Phillips, speech, Jan 8, 1852

3215. Revolutions never go backward. —Wendell Phillips, speech, Feb 17, 1861

3216. Old forms of government finally grow so oppressive that they must be thrown off even at the risk of reigns of terror. —Herbert Spencer, "On Manners and Fashion", *Essays on Education*, 1861

3218. Two forces which are the worst enemies of civil freedom are the absolute monarchy and the revolution. —Lord Acton, "Nationality", *The Home and Foreign Review*, Jul, 1862

3219. Would you realize what Revolution is, call it Progress; and would you realize what Progress is, call it Tomorrow. [*Voulez-vous vous rendre compte de ce que la révolution, appelez-la Progrès; et voulez-vous vous rendre compte de ce que c'est que le progrès, appelez-le Demain.*] —Victor Hugo, *Les Misérables*, 1862

3220. A reform is a correction of abuses; a revolution is a transfer of power. —Edward George Bulwer-Lytton, 1st Baron Lytton, speech, House of Commons, 1866

3221. There are only two great currents in the history of mankind: the baseness which makes conservatives and the envy which makes revolutionaries. [*Il n'y a que deux courants dans l'histoire de l'humanité: la bassesse qui fait les conservateurs et l'envie qui fait les révolutionnaires.*] —Edmond & Jules de Goncourt, *Journal*, Jul 12, 1867

3222. A revolutionary idea is revolutionary, vital, real and true only because it expresses and only so far as it forms popular instincts which are the result of history. —Michael Bakunin, letter to Nechayev, 1870

3223. It is impossible to arouse the people artificially. People's revolutions are born from the course of events. —Michael Bakunin, letter to Nechayev, 1870

3224. There are but three ways for the populace to escape its wretched lot. The first two are by the route of the wineshop or the church; the third is by that of the social revolution. —Michael Bakunin, *God and the State*, 1882

3225. To despise legitimate authority, in whomsoever vested, is unlawful, as a rebellion against the Divine Will; and whoever resists that rushes wilfully to destruction. —Leo XIII, encyclical, *Immortale Dei*, 1885

3226. Revolution or dictatorship can sometimes abolish bad things, but they can never create good and lasting ones. Impatience is fatal in politics. —Thomas Masaryk, *The Foundations of Marxist Theory*, 1899

3227. Without a revolutionary theory there can be no revolutionary movement. —Vladimir Ilyich Lenin, *What Is To Be Done?*, 1902

3228. Any person under the age of thirty who, having knowledge of the existing social order, is not a revolutionist, is an inferior. And yet Revolutions have never lightened the burden of tyranny, they have only shifted it to another shoulder. —George Bernard Shaw, *Man and Superman*, 1902

3229. Only on the bones of the oppressors can the people's freedom be founded—only the blood of the oppressors can fertilize the soil for the people's self-rule. —Joseph Stalin, appeal written for the Tbilisi Social Democratic Committee, 1905

3230. Revolution, n. In politics, an abrupt change in the form of misgovernment. —Ambrose Bierce, *The Devil's Dictionary*, 1906

3231. Insurrection, n. An unsuccessful revolution. Disaffection's failure to substitute misrule for bad government. —Ambrose Bierce, *The Devil's Dictionary*, 1906

3232. Rebel, n. A proponent of a new misrule who has failed to establish it. —Ambrose Bierce, *The Devil's Dictionary*, 1906

3233. We have learned that it is pent-up feelings that are dangerous, whispered purposes that are revolutionary, covert follies that warp and poison the mind. —Woodrow Wilson, *Consitutional Government*, 1908

3234. You can never have a revolution in order to establish a democracy. You must have a democracy in order to have a revolution. —G.K. Chesterton, *Tremendous Trifles*, 1909

3235. The right of revolution is the inherent right of a people to cast out their rulers, change their policy, or effect radical reforms in their system of government or institutions, by force or a general uprising, when the legal and constitutional methods of making such changes have proved inadequate, or are so obstructed as to be unavailable. —Henry Campbell Black, *Constitutional Law*, 1910

3236. Jefferson's Declaration of Independence is a practical document for the use of practical men. It is not a thesis for philosophers, but a whip for tyrants; it is not a theory of government, but a program of action. —Woodrow Wilson, speech in Indianapolis, Indiana, Apr 13, 1911

3237. There is something that governments care far more for than human life, and that is the security of property, and so it is through property that we shall strike the enemy. —Emmeline Pankhurst, speech, "I Incite This Meeting to Rebellion", Oct 17, 1912

3238. An agitation to attain a political or economic end must rest upon an implied willingness and ability to use force. Without that it is mere wind and attitudinizing. —James Connolly, *Forward*, Mar 14, 1914

3239. The revolution is incapable either of regretting or of burying its dead. —Joseph Stalin, quoted by Isaac Deutscher, *Stalin, A Political Biography*, 1967

3240. Thinkers prepare the revolution; bandits carry it out. —Mariano Azuela, *The Flies*, 1918

3241. The seed of revolution is repression. —Woodrow Wilson, seventh annual message to Congress, Dec 2, 1919

3242. If there is one safe generalisation in human affairs, it is that revolutions always destroy themselves. —William Ralph Inge, "Our Present Discontents", *Outspoken Essays: First Series*, 1919

3243. Revolutions are as a rule not made arbitrarily. If it were possible to map out the revolutionary road beforehand and in a rational way, then it would probably also be possible to avoid the revolution altogether. Revolution is an expression of the impossibility of reconstructing class society by rational methods. —Leon Trotsky, *Where is Britain Going?*, 1926

3244. People never move towards revolution; they are pushed towards it by intolerable injustices in the economic and social order under which they live. —Suzanne LaFollette, "The Beginnings of Emancipation", *Concerning Women*, 1926

3245. The revolutionists did not succeed in establishing human freedom; they poured the new wine of belief in equal rights for all men into the old bottle of privilege for some; and it soured. —Suzanne LaFollette, "The Beginning of Emancipation", *Concerning Women*, 1926

3246. Those who won our independence by revolution were not cowards. They did not fear political change. They did not exalt order at the cost of liberty. —Louis D. Brandeis, concurring opinion, *Whitney v. California*, 1927

3247. A revolution is not a dinner party, or writing an essay, or painting a picture, or doing embroidery; it cannot be so refined, so leisurely and gentle, so temperate, kind, courteous, restrained and magnanimous. —Mao Tse-tung, "Report on an Investigation of the Peasant Movement in Hunan", Mar, 1927

3248. In the last analysis, all revolutions must be social revolutions, based upon fundamental changes in society; otherwise it is not revolution, but merely a change of government..... —Madame Sun Yat-sen, (Sung Ching-ling), *People's Tribune*, Jul 14, 1927

3249. A revolution only lasts fifteen years, a period which coincides with the effectiveness of a generation. [*Una revolución no dura más de quince años, período que coincide con la vigencia de una generación.*] —Jose Ortega y Gasset, *Revolt of the Masses*, 1930

3250. The revolutionary war is a war of the masses; it can be waged only by mobilizing the masses and relying on them. —Mao Tse-tung, "Be Concerned with the Well-Being of the Masses ...", Jan 27, 1934

3251. Revolt and terror pay a price. / Order and law have a cost. —Carl Sandburg, *The People, Yes*, 1936

3252. Under fully developed Capitalism civilization is always on the verge of revolution. We live as in a villa on Vesuvius. —George Bernard Shaw, *The Intelligent Woman's Guide to Socialism, Capitalism, Sovietism and Fascism*, 1937

3253. If you rebel against high-heeled shoes, take care to do it in a very smart hat. —George Bernard Shaw, *The Intelligent Woman's Guide to Socialism, Capitalism, Sovietism and Fascism*, 1937

3254. A revolutionary party is a contradiction in terms. —Richard Crossman, "Mussolini and Coolidge", *New Statesman*, 1939

3255. Fascism was a counter-revolution against a revolution that never took place. [*Il fascismo è stata una controrivoluzione contro una rivoluzione che hon ha avuto luogo.*] —Ignazio Silone, *The School for Dictatorships*, 1939

3256. Though a revolution may call itself "national," it always marks the victory of a single party. —Andre Gide, *Journals*, Oct 17, 1941

3257. The successful revolutionary is a statesman, the unsuccessful one a criminal. —Erich Fromm, *Escape from Freedom*, 1941

3258. Martyrs are needed to create incidents. Incidents are needed to create revolutions. Revolutions are needed to create progress. —Chester Bomar Himes, "Negro Martyrs are Needed", *Crisis*, May, 1944

3259. Everything reactionary is the same; if you don't hit it, it won't fall. This is also like sweeping the floor; as a rule, where the broom does not reach, the dust will not vanish of itself. —Mao Tse-tung, "The Situation and Our Policy After the Victory in the War Against Japan", Aug 13, 1945

3260. The revolutionary wants to change the world; he transcends it and moves toward the future, towards an order of values which he himself invents. The rebel is careful to preserve the abuses from which he suffers so that he can go on rebelling against them. —Jean-Paul Sartre, *Baudelaire*, 1947

3261. A non-violent revolution is not a program of seizure of power. It is a program of transformation of relationships, ending in a peaceful transfer of power. —Mohandas K. Gandhi, *Non-Violence in Peace and War*, 1948

3262. Every revolutionary ends by becoming either an oppressor or a heretic. [*Tout révolutionnaire finit en oppresseur ou en hérétique.*] —Albert Camus, *The Rebel*, 1951

3263. When hopes and dreams are loose in the streets, it is well for the timid to lock doors, shutter windows and lie low until the wrath has passed. —Eric Hoffer, *The True Believer*, 1951

3264. The time to stop a revolution is at the beginning, not the end. —Adlai E. Stevenson Jr., speech in Los Angeles, California, Sep 9, 1952

3265. Every social war is a battle between the very few on both sides who care and who fire their shots across a crowd of spectators. —Murray Kempton, "Father and Sons", *Part of Our Time*, 1955

3266. As a dimension of man, rebellion actually defines him. —Robert Lindner, "The Instinct of Rebellion", *Must You Conform?*, 1956

3267. Revolutions are the locomotives of history. —Nikita S. Khrushchev, speech to the Supreme Soviet, *Pravda*, May 8, 1957

3268. A regime, an established order, is rarely overthrown by a revolutionary movement; usually a regime collapses of its own weakness and corruption and then a revolutionary movement enters among the ruins and takes over the powers that have become vacant. —Walter Lippmann, "For Charles De Gaulle", *From Today and Tomorrow*, Jun 5, 1958

3269. I began revolution with 82 men. If I had to do it again, I'd do it with 10 or 15 and absolute faith. It does not matter how small you are if you have faith and a plan of action. —Fidel Castro, *The New York Times*, Apr 22, 1959

3270. A revolution that does not continue to grow deeper is a revolution that is retreating. —Ernesto Guevara, "Che", *Guerrilla Warfare, A Method*, 1961

3271. Those who make peaceful revolution impossible will make violent revolution inevitable. —John F. Kennedy, speech to Latin American diplomats, Mar 12, 1962

3272. If violence is wrong in America, violence is wrong abroad. If it is wrong to be violent defending black women and black children and black babies and black men, then it is wrong for America to draft us, and make us violent abroad in defense of her. And if it is right for America to draft us, and teach us how to be violent in defense of her, then it is right for you and me to do whatever is necessary to defend our own people right here in this country. —Malcolm X, speech in New York City, Nov, 1963

3273. The Negro revolution is controlled by foxy white liberals, by the Government itself. But the Black Revolution is controlled only by God. —Malcolm X, speech in New York City, Dec 1, 1963

3274. Revolutions are never peaceful. —Malcolm X, speech in New York City, Dec, 1963

3275. Revolutions are never waged singing "We Shall Overcome". Revolutions are based upon bloodshed. —Malcolm X, speech in New York City, Apr, 1964

3276. Not actual suffering but the hope of better things incites people to revolt. —Eric Hoffer, *The Ordeal of Change*, 1964

3277. If you feed the people just with revolutionary slogans they will listen today, they will listen tomorrow, they will listen the day after tomorrow, but on the fourth day they will say, "To hell with you." —Nikita S. Khrushchev, quoted, *The New York Times*, Oct 4, 1964

3278. In a nonviolent movement there must be a latent threat of eruption, a dormant possibility of sudden and violent action if concessions are to be won, respect gained, and the established order altered. —George Jackson, letter to his mother from Soledad prison, Mar, 1967

3279. We used to think that revolutions are the cause of change. Actually it is the other way around: change prepares the ground for revolution. —Eric Hoffer, "A Time of Juveniles", *The Temper of Our Time*, 1967

3280. The duty of every revolutionary is to make a revolution. —Fidel Castro, quoted by Herbert Matthews, *Castro*, 1969

3281. The most radical revolutionary will become a conservative the day after the revolution. —Hannah Arendt, *New Yorker*, Sep 12, 1970

3282. We must realize that today's Establishment is the new George III. Whether it will continue to adhere to his tactics, we do not know. If it does, the redress, honored in tradition, is also revolution. —William O. Douglas, *Points of Rebellion*, 1970

3283. The surest guide to the correctness of the path that women take is joy in the struggle. Revolution is the festival of the oppressed. —Germaine Greer, "Revolution", *The Female Eunich*, 1970

3284. I suggested that we use the panther as our symbol and call our political vehicle the Black Panther Party. The panther is a fierce animal, but he will not attack until he is backed into a corner; then he will strike out. —Huey Newton, *Revolutionary Suicide*, 1973

3285. Revolution is a drama of passion. We did not win the People over by appealing to reason but by developing hope, trust, fraternity. —Mao Tse-tung, quoted, *Time*, Sep 20, 1976

3286. It takes a revolution to make a solution. —Bob Marley, *To the Point International*, Sep 12, 1977

3287. It is easier to run a revolution than a government. —Ferdinand E. Marcos, *Time*, Jun 6, 1977

3288. The only successful revolution of this century is totalitarianism. —Bernard-Henri Lévy, *Time*, Sep 12, 1977

RIGHTS/HUMAN RIGHTS

3290. We hold these truths to be self-evident, that all men are created equal, that they are endowed by their creator with certain inalienable Rights, that among these are Life, Liberty and the pursuit of happiness. —Thomas Jefferson, *Declaration of Independence*, Jul 4, 1776

3291. I tremble for my country when I reflect that God is just; that his justice cannot sleep forever. —Thomas Jefferson, referring to slavery, *Notes on the State of Virginia*, 1782

3292. The public good is in nothing more essentially interested, than in the protection of every individual's private rights. —Sir William Blackstone, *Commentaries on the Laws of England*, 1783

3293. If we cannot secure all our rights, let us secure what we can. —Thomas Jefferson, letter to James Madison, Mar 15, 1787

3294. A bill of rights is what the people are entitled to against every government on earth, general or particular, and what no just government hould refuse, or rest in inferences. —Thomas Jefferson, letter to James Madison, Dec 20, 1787

3295. Man did not enter into society to become worse than he was before, nor to have fewer rights than he had before, but to have those rights better secured. —Thomas Paine, *The Rights of Man*, 1791

3296. As a man is said to have a right to his property, he may be equally said to have a property in his rights. —James Madison, "Property", *National Gazette*, Mar 29, 1792

3297. If the abstract rights of man will bear discussion and explanation, those of woman, by a parity of reasoning, will not shrink from the same test: though a different opinion prevails in the country. —Mary Wollstonecraft, "Dedication", *A Vindication of the Rights of Woman*, 1792

3298. The personal right to acquire property, which is a natural right, gives to property, when acquired, a right to protection, as a social right. —James Madison, speech to the Virginia constitutional convention, Richmond, Virginia, Dec 2, 1829

3299. Rights! There are no rights whatever without corresponding duties ... you will find nowhere in our parliamentary records the miserable sophism of the Rights of Man. —Samuel Taylor Coleridge, *Table-Talk*, Nov 20, 1831

3300. We first crush people to the earth, and then claim the right of trampling on them forever, because they are prostrate. —Lydia Maria Child, *An Appeal on Behalf of That Class of Americans Called Africans*, 1833

3301. Human beings have rights, because they are moral beings: the rights of all men grow out of their moral nature; and as all men have the same moral nature, they have essentially the same rights. —Jeanne-Françoise Deroin, *Letters to Catherine Beecher*, 1836

3302. The people know their rights, and they are never slow to assert and maintain them, when they are invaded. —Abraham Lincoln, speech in Springfield, Illinois, Jan, 1837

3303. They have rights who dare maintain them. —James Russell Lowell, "The Present Crisis", 1844

3304. The true Republic: men: their rights and nothing more; women: their rights and nothing less. —Susan B. Anthony, motto of her newspaper, *The Revolution,* 1867

3305. That ... man ... says women can't have as much rights as man, cause Christ wasn't a woman. Where did your Christ come from? ... From God and a woman. Man had nothing to do with it. —Sojourner Truth, speech at the Women's Rights Convention in Akron, Ohio, 1851

3306. Many Abolitionists have yet to learn the ABC of woman's rights. —Susan B. Anthony, *Journal*, Jun, 1860

3307. The rights and interests of every or any person are only secure from being disregarded, when the person interested is himself able, and habitually disposed, to stand up for them. —John Stuart Mill, *Considerations on Representative Government*, 1861

3308. The destiny of the colored American ... is the destiny of America. —Frederick Douglass, speech at the Emancipation League, Boston, Massachusetts, Feb 12, 1862

3309. If slavery is not wrong, nothing is wrong. —Abraham Lincoln, letter to A.G. Hodges, Apr 4, 1864

3310. There is a great stir about colored men getting their rights, but not a word about colored women; and if colored men get their rights, and not colored women theirs, you see, the colored men will be masters over the women and it will be as bad as before. So I am for keeping the thing going while things are stirring, because if we wait till it is still, it will take a great while to get it going again. —Sojourner Truth, speech to the annual meeting of the Equal Rights Convention in New York City, May 9, 1867

3311. The simplest truths often meet the sternest resistance and are slowest in getting general acceptance. —Frederick Douglass, "The Women's Suffrage Movement", *The New National Era*, Oct 6, 1870

3312. Here, in the first paragraph of the Declaration (of Independence), is the assertion of the natural right of all to the ballot; for how can "the consent of the governed" be given, if the right to vote be denied? —Susan B. Anthony, speech at her trial for voting, 1873

3313. Yours for the unshackled exercise of every faculty by every human being. —Lydia Maria Child, message to supporters of women's suffrage, ca. 1875

3314. Like all disfranchised classes, they began by asking to have certain wrongs redressed, and not be asserting their own right to make laws for themselves. —Elizabeth Cady Stanton, *History of Woman Suffrage*, 1881

3315. No man can put a chain about the ankle of his fellow man without at last finding the other end fastened about his own neck. —Frederick Douglass, speech at Civil Rights Mass Meeting, Washington, D.C., Oct 22, 1883

3316. Human law may know no distinction among men in respect of rights, but human practice may. —Frederick Douglass, speech in Louisville, Kentucky, Sep, 1883

3317. I am the inferior of any man whose rights I trample under foot. —Robert G. Ingersoll, *Prose-Poems and Selections*, 1884

3318. The race problem is a moral one. ... Its solution will come especially from the domain of principles. Like all the other great battles of humanity, it is to be fought out with the weapons of truth. —Alexander Crummell, speech to the Protestant Episcopal Church Congress, Buffalo, New York, Nov 20, 1888

3319. This country should be agitated and even convulsed till the battle of liberty is won and every man in the land is guaranteed fully every civil and political right. —Alexander Crummell, speech to the Protestant Episcopal Church Congress, Buffalo, New York, Nov 20, 1888

3320. Wherever there is a human being, I see God-given rights inherent in that being whatever may be the sex or complexion. —William Lloyd Garrison, *Life*, 1885-89

3321. There is no security for the personal or political rights of any man in a community where any man is deprived of his personal or political rights. —Benjamin Harrison, acceptance of renomination for the Presidency, Sep 3, 1892

3322. Men have no special right because they belong to one race or another: the word man defines all rights. —Jose Martí, *Mi Raza*, 1893

3323. In view of the Constitution, in the eye of the law, there is in this country no superior, dominant, ruling class of citizens. There is no caste here. Our Constitution is color-blind, and neither knows nor tolerates classes among citizens. In respect of civil rights, all citizens are equal before the law. The humblest is the peer of the most powerful. —John Marshall Harlan, dissenting opinion, *Plessy v. Ferguson*, 1896

3324. In every civilized society property rights must be carefully safeguarded; ordinarily and in the great majority of cases, human rights and property rights are fundamentally and in the long run, identical; but when it clearly appears that there is a real conflict between them, human rights must have the upper hand; for property belongs to man and not man to property. —Theodore Roosevelt, speech at the Univ. of Paris, Apr 23, 1910

3325. There is in this world no such force as the force of a man determined to rise. The human soul cannot be permanently chained. —W.E.B. Du Bois, speech to the Republican Club of New York, Mar 5, 1910

3326. A right is worth fighting for only when it can be put into operation. —Woodrow Wilson, speech in Chattanooga, Tennessee, Aug 31, 1910

3327. When a just cause reaches its flood tide ... whatever stands in the way must fall before its overwhelming power. —Carrie Chapman Catt, speech, "Is Woman Suffrage Progressing?" in Stockholm, Sweden, 1911

3328. We are here to claim our rights as women, not only to be free, but to fight for freedom. It is our privilege, as well as our pride and our joy, to take some part in this militant movement, which, as we believe, means the regeneration of all humanity. Nothing but contempt is due to those people who ask us to submit to unmerited oppression. We shall not do it. —Christabel Pankhurst, speech, Mar 23, 1911

3329. What I am interested in is having the government of the United States more concerned about human rights than about property rights. Property is an instrument of humanity; humanity isn't an instrument of property. —Woodrow Wilson, speech in Minneapolis, Minnesota, Sep 18, 1912

3330. Next to the right of liberty, the right of property is the most important individual right guaranteed by the Constitution and the one which, united with that of personal liberty, has contributed more to the growth of civilization than any other institution established by the human race. —William Howard Taft, *Popular Government*, 1913

3331. The American people ... believe that peace should rest upon the rights of peoples, not the rights of governments—the rights of peoples great or small, weak or powerful. —Woodrow Wilson, reply to the peace proposal of Pope Benedict XV, Aug 27, 1917

3332. There is no right to strike against the public safety by anybody, anywhere, anytime. —Calvin Coolidge, telegram to the president of the American Federation of Labor, Sep 14, 1919

3333. Men speak of natural rights, but I challenge any one to show where in nature any rights existed or were recognized until there was established for their declaration and protection a duly promulgated body of corresponding laws. —Calvin Coolidge, acceptance speech as Republican vice-presidential nominee, Jul 27, 1920

3334. It is fair to judge peoples by the rights they will sacrifice most for. —Clarence Day, *This Simian World*, 1920

3335. Most people, no doubt, when they espouse human rights, make their own mental reservations about the proper application of the word "human." —Suzanne LaFollette, "The Beginnings of Emancipation", *Concerning Women*, 1926

3336. Rights that depend on the sufferance of the State are of uncertain tenure. —Suzanne LaFollette, "What Is to Be Done", *Concerning Women*, 1926

3337. Of course we expected a great deal from our enfranchisement. But so did men when they fought for theirs. It is the only way—to keep fighting, to believe that the miracle is going to happen. —Emmeline Pankhurst, press conference, 1926

3338. There is only one right in the world and that right is one's own strength. —Adolf Hitler, speech to Nazi party leaders in Munich, Sep, 1928

3339. They (the makers of the constitution) conferred, as against the Government, the right to be let alone—the most comprehensive of rights and the right most valued by civilized men. —Louis D. Brandeis, Olmstead v. United States, 1928

3340. Better to die on one's feet than to live on one's knees. [*Mejor morir a pie que vivir en rodillas.*] —Dolores Ibarruri, "La Pasionaria", speech in Valencia, Spain, 1936

3341. If Negroes secure their goals, immediate and remote, they must win them, and to win them they must fight, sacrifice, suffer, go to jail and, if need be, die for them. —A. Philip Randolph, speech at the National Negro Congress, Philadelphia, Pennsylvania, Oct 15-17, 1937

3342. In Germany they came first for the Communists, and I didn't speak up because I wasn't a Communist. Then they came for the Jews, and I didn't speak up because I wasn't a Jew. Then they came for the trade unionists, and I didn't speak up because I wasn't a trade unionist. then they came for the Catholics, and I didn't speak up because I was a Protestant. Then they came for me and by that time no one was left to speak up. —Martin Niemoeller, attributed

3343. It is not that you set the individual apart from society but that you recognize in any society that the individual must have rights that are guarded. —Eleanor Roosevelt, *The New York Times*, Feb 4, 1947

3344. I say the time has come to walk out of the shadow of states' rights and into the sunlight of human rights. —Hubert H. Humphrey, speech to the Democratic national convention, Aug, 1948

3345. Certain rights can never be granted to the government, but must be kept in the hands of the people. —Eleanor Roosevelt, *The New York Times*, May 3, 1948

3346. In these days, it is doubtful that any child may reasonably be expected to succeed in life if he is denied the opportunity of an education. Such an opportunity, where the state has undertaken to provide it, is a right which must be made available to all on equal terms. Separate educational facilities are inherently unequal. —Earl Warren, unanimous opinion, *Brown v. Board of Education of Topeka, Kansas*, May 17, 1954

3347. We conclude that in the field of public education the doctrine of "separate but equal" has no place. —Earl Warren, unanimous opinion, *Brown v. Board of Education of Topeka, Kansas*, May 17, 1954

3348. "Freedom from fear" could be said to sum up the whole philosophy of human rights. —Dag Hammarskjold, on the 180th anniversary of the Virginia Declaration of Human Rights, May 20, 1956

3349. What men value in this world is not rights but privileges. —H.L. Mencken, *Minority Report*, 1956

3350. It is my hope that as the Negro plunges deeper into the quest for freedom and justice he will plunge even deeper into the philosophy of non-violence. The Negro all over the South must come to the point that he can say to his white brother: "We will match your capacity to inflict suffering with our capacity to endure suffering. We will meet your physical force with soul force. We will not hate you, but we will not obey your evil laws. We will soon wear you down by pure capacity to suffer." —Martin Luther King Jr., letter to Chester Bowles, Oct 28, 1957

3351. Homosexual behavior between consenting adults in private should no longer be a criminal offense. —Sir John Frederick Wolfenden, *Wolfenden Report*, Sep 5, 1957

3352. Where, after all, do universal human rights begin? In small places close to home—so close and so small that they cannot be seen on any map of the world. Yet they are the world of the individual person: the neighborhood he lives in; the school or college he attends; the factory, farm or office where he works. Such are the places where every man, woman and child seeks equal justice, equal opportunity, equal dignity without discrimination. Unless these rights have meaning there, they have little meaning anywhere. —Eleanor Roosevelt, remarks at the United Nations Commission on Human Rights, Mar 27, 1958

3353. I want every American free to stand up for his rights, even if he has to sit down for them. —John F. Kennedy, campaign speech, Aug 3, 1960

3354. The 4th Amendment and the personal rights it secures have a long history. At the very core stands the right of a man to retreat into his own home and there be free from unreasonable governmental intrusion. —Potter Stewart, unanimous opinion, *Bartkus v. Illinois; Abbate v. U.S.*, Mar 5, 1961

3355. America stands for progress in human rights as well as economic affairs, and a strong America requires the assurance of full and equal rights to all its citizens, of any race of any color. —John F. Kennedy, speech to Congress, Jan 11, 1962

3356. It is my belief that there are "absolutes" in our Bill of Rights, and that they were put there on purpose by men who knew what words meant and meant their prohibitions to be "absolutes." —Hugo L. Black, at the American Jewish Congress, Apr 14, 1962

3357. In giving rights to others which belong to them, we give rights to ourselves and to our country. —John F. Kennedy, speech on the 100th anniversary of the Emancipation Proclamation, Sep 22, 1962

3358. This Nation was founded by men of many nations and backgrounds. It was founded on the principle that all men are created equal, and that the rights of every man are diminished when the rights of one man are threatened. —John F. Kennedy, address to the nation on civil rights, Jun 11, 1963

3359. We have talked long enough in this country about equal rights. We have talked for 100 years or more. Yet, it is time now to write the next chapter—and to write it in books of law. —Lyndon Baines Johnson, speech to Congress, Nov 27, 1963

3360. I urge you ... to enact a civil rights law so that we can move forward to eliminate from this country every trace of discrimination and oppression based upon race or color. There could be no greater source of strength to this nation both at home and abroad. —Lyndon Baines Johnson, address to Congress, Nov 27, 1963

3361. One hundred years of delay have passed since President Lincoln freed the slaves, yet their heirs, their grandsons, are not fully free. They are not yet freed from the bonds of injustice; they are not yet freed from social and economic oppression. And this nation, for all its hopes and all its boasts, will not be fully free until all its citizens are free. —John F. Kennedy, televised speech, Jun 11, 1963

3362. Until justice is blind to color, until education is unaware of race, until opportunity ceases to squint its eyes at pigmentation of human complexions, emancipation will be a proclamation— but it will not be a fact. —Lyndon Baines Johnson, speech at Wayne State Univ., Detroit, Michigan, Jan 6, 1963

3363. I say to you today even though we face the difficulties of today and tomorrow, I still have a dream. It is a dream that is deeply rooted in the American dream. I have a dream that one day this nation will rise up, live out the true meaning of its creed. We hold these truths to be self-evident, that all men are created equal. I have a dream that one day on the red hills of Georgia the sons of former slaves and the sons of former slave-owners will be able to sit down together at the table of brotherhood ... I have a dream that one day every valley shall be exalted, every hill and mountain shall be made low. The rough places will be made plain and the crooked places will be made straight. —Martin Luther King Jr., speech at the Civil Rights March on Washington, D.C., Aug 28, 1963

3364. Every American ought to have the right to be treated as he would wish to be treated, as one would wish his children to be treated. This is not the case. —John F. Kennedy, televised speech on civil rights, Jun 11, 1963

3365. I have a dream that my four little children will one day live in a nation where they will not be judged by the color of their skin, but by the content of their character. —Martin Luther King Jr., speech at the Civil Rights March on Washington, D.C., Aug 28, 1963

3366. We are not fighting for integration, nor are we fighting for separation. We are fighting for recognition as human beings. We are fighting for ... human rights. —Malcolm X, speech on "Black Revolution" in New York City, 1964

3367. The political philosophy of black nationalism means that the black man should control the politics and the politicians in his own community; no more. —Malcolm X, speech on "The Ballot or the Bullet", 1964

3368. The Negro was willing to risk martyrdom in order to move and stir the social conscience of his community and the nation. ... He would force his oppressor to commit his brutality openly, with the rest of the world looking on. ... Nonviolent resistance paralyzed and confused the power structures against which it was directed. —Martin Luther King Jr., *Why We Can't Wait*, 1964

3369. Nonviolence is the answer to the crucial political and moral questions of our time; the need for man to overcome oppression and violence without resorting to oppression and violence. —Martin Luther King Jr., speech accepting the Nobel Peace Prize, Dec 11, 1964

3370. A rioter with a Molotov cocktail in his hands is not fighting for civil rights any more than a Klansman with a sheet on his back and mask on his face. They are both more or less what the law declares them: lawbreakers, destroyers of constitutional rights and liberties and ultimately destroyers of a free America. —Lyndon Baines Johnson, remarks to a White House conference during riots in Los Angeles, Aug 20, 1965

3371. We deal with a right of privacy older than the Bill of Rights—older than our political parties, older than our school system. —William O. Douglas, majority opinion, *Griswold v. Connecticut*, Jun 7, 1965

3372. The Negro revolt is not aimed at winning friends but at winning freedom, not interpersonal warmth but institutional justice. —Harvey G. Cox Jr., *The Secular City*, 1966

3373. The greatest achievement of the civil rights movement is that it has restored the dignity of indignation. —Frederic Wertham, *A Sign for Cain: An Exploration in Human Violence*, 1966

3374. Every man should know that his conversations, his correspondence, and his personal life are private. I have urged Congress—except when the Nation's security is at stake—to take action to that end. —Lyndon Baines Johnson, remarks at swearing-in of Ramsey Clark as attorney general, Mar 10, 1967

3375. The man who walks alone is soon trailed by the F.B.I. —Wright Morris, *A Bill of Rites, A Bill of Wrongs, A Bill of Goods*, 1967

3376. This court will not deny the equal protection of the law to the unwashed, unshod, unkempt and uninhibited. —Herman Weinkrantz, ruling on harrassment of "hippies", *The New York Times*, Jul 1, 1968

3377. At the very least, the freedom that Congress is empowered to secure ... includes the freedom to buy whatever a white man can buy, the right to live wherever a white man can live. If Congress cannot say that being a freeman means at least this much, then the 13th Amendment made a promise it cannot keep. —Potter Stewart, majority opinion, Jun 17, 1968

3378. Abhorrence of apartheid is a normal attitude, not a policy. —Edward Heath, speech at the Lord Mayor's banquet, London, Nov 16, 1970

3379. There is no such thing as a moderate in the civil rights movement; everyone is a radical. The difference is whether or not one is all rhetoric or relevant. —Whitney Moore Young Jr., recalled on his death, Mar 11, 1971

3380. Salvation for a race, nation, or class must come from within. Freedom is never granted; it is won. Justice is never given; it is exacted. Freedom and justice must be struggled for by the oppressed of all lands and races, and the struggle must be continuous, for freedom is never a final fact, but a continuing evolving process to higher and higher levels of human, social, economic, political and religious relationships. —A. Philip Randolph, quoted by Jervis Anderson, *A. Philip Randolph, a Biographical Portrait*, 1972

3381. The dichotomy between personal liberties and property rights is a false one. Property does not have rights. People have rights. —Potter Stewart, majority opinion, *Lynch v. Household Finance Corp.*, Mar 23, 1972

3382. In fact, a fundamental interdependence exists between the personal right to liberty and the personal right in property. —Potter Stewart, majority opinion, *Lynch v. Household Finance Corp.*, Mar 23, 1972

3383. The freer that women become, the freer will men be. Because when you enslave someone—you are enslaved. —Louise Nevelson, quoted, *AFTRA*, 1974

3384. The basic tenet of black consciousness is that the black man must reject all value systems that seek to make him a foreigner in the country of his birth and reduce his basic human dignity. —Steve Biko, statement at trial, May 3, 1976

3385. It may be assumed that parents have a 1st Amendment right to send their children to educational institutions that promote the belief that racial segregation is desirable, and that the children have an equal right to attend such institutions. But it does not follow that the practice of excluding racial minorities from such institutions is also protected by the same principle. —Potter Stewart, majority opinion, *Runyon v. McCrary, Fairfax-Brewster School, Inc.*, Jun 25, 1976

3386. A right is not what someone gives you; it's what no one can take from you. —Ramsey Clark, *The New York Times*, Oct 2, 1977

3387. We talk a lot about human rights, but I don't know of any human right that is more important than a job. —William Norris, *Time*, Apr 3, 1978

3388. The rights of all persons are wrapped in the same constitutional bundle as those of the most hated member of the community. —Abraham Lincoln Wirin, *Time*, Feb 20, 1978

3389. Human rights is the soul of our foreign policy, because human rights is the very soul of our sense of nationhood. —Jimmy Carter, speech on the 30th anniversary of UN Declaration of Human Rights, Dec 6, 1978

3390. I loathe all manifestations of extremism and I believe we should strive, above all else, for the dignity and human rights of mankind, regardless of race, color and creed. —Lord Louis Mountbatten, recalled on his death, *Time*, Sep 10, 1979

3391. My decision to register women ... confirms what is already obvious throughout our society—that women are now providing all types of skills in every profession. The military should be no exception. —Jimmy Carter, on proposal to register women for the draft, Feb 8, 1980

3392. The 4th Amendment protects the individual's privacy in a variety of settings. In none is the zone of privacy more clearly defined than when bounded by the unambiguous physical dimensions of an individual's home—a zone that finds its roots in clear and specific constitutional terms: "the right of the people to be secure in their ... houses ... shall not be violated." —John Paul Stevens, majority opinion, *Peyton v. New York; Riddick v. New York*, Apr 15, 1980

3393. America did not invent human rights. In a very real sense ... human rights invented America. —Jimmy Carter, farewell address, Jan 14, 1981

3394. This is a celebration of individual freedom, not of homosexuality. No government has the right to tell its citizens when or whom to love. The only queer people are those who don't love anybody. —Rita Mae Brown, speech in San Francisco, California, Aug 28, 1982

3395. My belief has always been ... that wherever in this land any individual's constitutional rights are being unjustly denied, it is the obligation of the federal government—at point of bayonet if necessary—to restore that individual's constitutional rights. —Ronald Reagan, press conference, May 17, 1983

3396. A married woman has the same right to control her own body as does an unmarried woman. —Sol Wachtler, unanimous opinion, New York State Court of Appeals, Dec 20, 1984

3397. America's view of apartheid is simple and straightforward: We believe it is wrong. We condemn it. And we are united in hoping for the day when apartheid will be no more. —Ronald Reagan, on sanctions against South Africa, Sep 9, 1985

3398. I am not interested in picking up crumbs of compassion thrown from the table of someone who considers himself my master. I want the full menu of rights. —Desmond Tutu, "Today", NBC-TV, Jan 9, 1985

3399. Where sexual proclivity does not relate to job function, it seems clearly unconstitutional to penalize an individual in one of the most imperative of life's endeavors, the right to earn one's daily bread. —Sidney H. Asch, majority opinion barring discrimination on basis of sexual orientation, May 7, 1985

3400. You don't have to love them. You just have to respect their rights. —Edward I. Koch, on signing law barring discrimination on basis of sexual orientation, *US News & World Report*, Apr 14, 1986

3401. The right of an individual to conduct intimate relationships in the intimacy of his or her own home seems to me to be the heart of the Constitution's protection of privacy. —Harry A. Blackmun, dissenting opinion, *Bowers v. Hardwick*, Jun 30, 1986

3402. (Disapproval of homosexuality cannot justify) invading the houses, hearts and minds of citizens who choose to live their lives differently. —Harry A. Blackmun, dissenting opinion, *Bowers v. Hardwick*, Jun 30, 1986

3403. What the Court really has refused to recognize is the fundamental interest all individuals have in controlling the nature of their intimate associations. —Harry A. Blackmun, dissenting opinion, *Bowers v. Hardwick*, Jun 30, 1986

ROLE OF THE STATE/OF GOVERNMENT

3404. A state is not a mere society, having a common place, established for the prevention of mutual crime and for the sake of exchange. ... Political society exists for the sake of noble actions, and not of mere companionship. —Aristotle, *Politics*, 343 B.C.

3405. Two things only the poeple anxiously desire, bread and the circus games. [*Duas tantem res anxius optat,/ Panem et Circenses.*] —Juvenal, *Satires*, ca. 125

3406. When neither their property not their honor is touched, the majority of men live content. [*Qualunque volta alle universalità degli uomini non si toglie né roba né onore, vivono contenti.*] —Niccolò Machiavelli, *Il Principe*, 1532

3407. Man seeketh in society comfort, use, and protection. —Sir Francis Bacon, *Advancement of Learning*, 1605

3408. Above all things, good policy is to be used that the treasure and monies in a state be not gathered into a few hands. For otherwise a state may have a great stock and yet starve. And money is like muck, not good except it be spread. —Sir Francis Bacon, "Of Seditions and Troubles", *Essays*, 1625

3409. The true aim of government is liberty. [*Finis ergo reipublicae revera libertas est.*] —Baruch (Benedictus de) Spinoza, *Tractatus Theologico-Politicus*, 1670

3410. The ultimate aim of government is not to rule, or restrain, by fear, nor to exact obedience, but contrariwise, to free every man from fear, that he may live in all possible security; in other words, to strengthen his natural right to exist and work without injury to himself or others. [*Finem ejus (reipublica) ultimum non esse dominari, nec homines metu retinere et alterius juris facere, sed contra, unumquemque metu liberare ut secure quoad ejus fieri potest vivat, hoc est, ut jus suum naturale ad existendum et operandum absque suo et alterius damno optime retineat.*] —Baruch (Benedictus de) Spinoza, *Tractatus Theologico-Politicus*, 1670

3411. The best condition of a commonwealth is easily discovered from the purpose of political order: which is simply peace and security of life. [*Qualis autem cujuscunque imperii optimus sit status facile ex fine status civilis cognoscitur: qui scilicet nullus alius est quam pax vitaeque securitas.*] —Baruch (Benedictus de) Spinoza, *Tractatus Politicus*, 1676

3412. Government has no other end but the preservation of Property. —John Locke, *The Second Treatise on Government*, 1690

3413. The public must and will be served. —William Penn, *Some Fruits of Solitude in Reflections and Maxims*, 1693

3414. That action is best, which procures the greatest happiness for the greatest numbers. —Francis Hutcheson, *Inquiry into the Original of our Ideas of Beauty and Virtue*, 1725

3415. Whatever alms may be given to a beggar in the street, this does not fulfill the state's obligation, which owes to every citizen an assured subsistence, proper nourishment, suitable clothing, and a mode of life not incompatible with health. [*Quelques aumônes que l'on fait à un homme nu dans les rues, ne remplissent point les obligations de l'Etat, qui doit à tous les citoyens une subsistance assurée, la nourriture, un vêtement convenable, et un genre de vie qui ne soit point contraire à la santé.*] —Charles Louis de Montesquieu, *De l'Esprit des lois*, 1748

3416. It should be remembered that the foundation of the social contract is property; and its first condition, that every one should be maintained in the peaceful possession of what belongs to him. —Jean Jacques Rousseau, *A Discourse on Political Economy*, 1758

3417. The good and happiness of the members, that is the majority of the members of any state, is the great standard by which every thing relating to that state must finally be determined. —Joseph Priestly, *Essay on Government*, 1768

3418. Government is, or ought to be instituted for the common benefit, protection, and security of the people, nation, or community; of all the various modes and forms of government, that is best which is capable of producing the greatest degree of happiness and safety, and is most effectually secured against the danger of maladministration. —George Mason, *Virginia Bill of Rights*, Jun 12, 1776

3419. The primary cause of all our disorders lies in the different State Governments, and in the tenacity of that power which pervades the whole of their system. ... Incompatibility in the laws of different States, and disrespect to those of the general government must render the situation of this great Country weak, inefficient and disgraceful. —George Washington, letter to David Stuart, Jul 1, 1787

3420. The safety and happiness of society are the objects at which all political institutions aim, and to which all such institutions must be sacrificed. —James Madison, *The Federalist*, Jan 23, 1788

3421. A good government implies two things: fidelity to the object of government, which is the happiness of the people; secondly, a knowledge of the means by which that object can be best attained. —James Madison, *Federalist*, Feb 27, 1788

3422. Justice is the end of government. It is the end of society. —James Madison, *The Federalist*, Feb 6, 1788

3423. Government is instituted no less for protection of the property, than of the persons of individuals. —James Madison, *The Federalist*, Feb. 12, 1788

3424. The best frame of government is that which is most likely to prevent the greatest sum of evil. —James Monroe, "Observations of the Federal Government", 1789

3425. The aggregate happiness of society, which is best promoted by the practice of a virtuous policy, is, or ought to be, the end of all government. —George Washington, letter to the Count de Moustier, Nov 1, 1790

3426. We hold the moral obligation of providing for old age, helpless infancy, and poverty, is far superior to that of supplying the invented wants of courtly extravagance. —Thomas Paine, *Declaration of the Friends of Universal Peace and Liberty*, 1791

3427. Government is a contrivance of human wisdom to provide for human wants. Men have a right that these wants should be provided for by this wisdom. —Edmund Burke, *Reflections on the Revolution in France*, 1791

3428. Government is instituted to protect property of every sort; as well that which lies in the various rights of individuals, as that which the term particularly expresses. This being the end of government, that alone is a just government, which impartially secures to every man, whatever is his own. —James Madison, *National Gazette*, Mar 29, 1792

3429. Government was intended to suppress injustice, but its effect has been to embody and perpetuate it. —William Godwin, "Summary of Principles", *An Enquiry Concerning Political Justice*, 1793

3430. And having looked to the Government for bread, on the very first scarcity they will turn and bite the hand that fed them. —Edmund Burke, *Thoughts and Details on Scarcity*, 1800

3431. States do not prosper through ideology. [*Les Etats ne prospèrent point par l'idéologie.*] —Napoleon I, letter to M. Cambacérès, Apr 24, 1805

3432. Where the state is weak, the army rules. [*Là où le gouvernement est faible, l'armée gouverne.*] —Napoleon I, remarks in the Council of State, Jan 9, 1808

3433. The care of human life and happiness, and not their destruction, is the first and only legitimate object of good government. —Thomas Jefferson, letter to the Republican citizens of Maryland, Mar 31, 1809

3434. The main objects of all science, the freedom and happiness of man ... (are) the sole objects of all legitimate government. —Thomas Jefferson, letter to General Thaddeus Kosciusko, Feb 26, 1810

3435. Were we directed from Washington when to sow, & when to reap, we should soon want bread. —Thomas Jefferson, *Autobiography*, 1892

3436. It is high time, My Lord, that the subjects of Christian Governments should be taught that neither historically or morally, in fact or by right, have men made the State; but that the State, and that alone, makes them men. —Samuel Taylor Coleridge, letter to Lord Liverpool, 1817

3437. It is an easy and a vulgar thing to please the mob, and not a very arduous task to astonish them; but essentially to benefit and improve them is a work fraught with difficulty and teeming with danger. —Charles Caleb Colton, *Lacön*, 1825

3438. The office of government is not to confer happiness, but to give men opportunity to work out happiness for themselves. —William Ellery Channing, *Christian Examiner*, Sep/Oct, 1827

3439. The business of government is not directly to make the people rich, but to protect them in making themselves rich; and a government which attempts more than this is precisely the government which is likely to perform less. Governments do not and cannot support the people. —Lord Macaulay, (Thomas Babington, 1st Baron Macaulay), speech on parliamentary reform, Mar 2, 1831

3440. All communities are apt to look to government too much. ... The framers of our excellent Constitution ... wisely judged that the less government interferes with private pursuits the better for the general prosperity. —Martin Van Buren, message to special session of Congress, Sep 4, 1837

3441. Man exists for his own sake and not to add a laborer to the State. —Ralph Waldo Emerson, *Journals*, 1839

3442. The whole duty of government is to prevent crime and to preserve contracts. —2nd Viscount Melbourne, quoted by Lord David Cecil, *Lord M.*, 1954

3443. As man seeks justice in equality, so society seeks order in anarchy. —Pierre Joseph Proudhon, *Qu'est-ce la propriété?*, 1840

3444. What the proletarian lack is capital, and the duty of the state is to see that he gets it. Were I to define the state, I should prefer to think of it as the poor man's bank. —Louis Blanc, *The Organization of Work*, 1840

3445. The final end of government is not to exert restraint but to do good. —Rufus Choate, speech in the U.S. Senate, Jul 2, 1841

3446. A government never loses anything by mildness and forbearance to its own citizens, more especially when the consequences of an opposite course may be the shedding of blood. —John Tyler, letter to Gov. Rufus King of Rhode Island, May 9, 1842

3447. "A fair day's wages for a fair day's work": it is as just a demand as governed men ever made of governing. It is the everlasting right of man. —Thomas Carlyle, *Past and Present*, 1843

3448. The less government we have, the better—the fewer laws, and the less confided power. —Ralph Waldo Emerson, "Politics", *Essays: Second Series*, 1844

3449. It is only the novice in political economy who thinks it is the duty of government to make its citizens happy.—Government has no such office. To protect the weak and the minority from the impositions of the strong and the majority—to prevent any one from positively working to render the people unhappy ... to do the labor not of an officious inter-meddler in the affairs of men, but of a prudent watchman who prevents outrage—these are rather the proper duties of a government. —Walt Whitman, editorial, *Brooklyn Eagle*, Apr 4, 1846

3450. Inexorable as to principles, tolerant and impartial as to persons. —Giuseppe Mazzini, *Watchword for the Roman Republic*, 1849

3451. The mass of men serve the state thus, not as men mainly, but as machines, with their bodies. —Henry David Thoreau, *Civil Disobedience*, 1849

3452. The legitimate object of government, is to do for a community of people, whatever they need to have done, but can not do, at all, or can not, so well do, for themselves—in their separate, and individual capacities. In all that the people can individually do as well for themselves, government ought not to interfere. —Abraham Lincoln, written fragment, Jul 1, 1854

3453. I am for those means which will give the greatest good to the greatest number. —Abraham Lincoln, speech in Cincinnati, Ohio, Feb 12, 1861

3454. The State ... is the most flagrant negation, the most cynical and complete negation of humanity. —Michael Bakunin, *Federalism, Socialism and Anti-Theologism*, 1868

3455. A great scholar and a great wit, 300 years ago, said that, in his opinion, there was a great mistake in the Vulgate, which, as you all know, is the Latin translation of the Holy Scriptures, and that, instead of saying "Vanity of vanities, all is vanity"—Vanitas vanitatum, omnia vanitas—the wise and witty king really said, Sanitas sanitatum, omnia sanitas. Gentlemen, it is impossible to overrate the importance of the subject. After all, the first consideration of a Minister should be the health of the people. —Benjamin Disraeli, speech in Manchester, England, Apr 3, 1872

3456. It is an old saying that, after all, the great end and aim of the British Constitution is to get twelve honest men into a box. That is really a very sensible way of putting the theory, that the first end of government is to give security to life and property, and to make people keep their contracts. —John Morley, speech to the Midland Institute in Birmingham, England, Oct 5, 1876

3457. The health of the people is really the foundation upon which all their happiness and all their powers as a state depend. —Benjamin Disraeli, speech in the House of Commons, Jul 24, 1877

3458. Is it not rooted in our entire moral relationships that the individual who comes before his fellow citizens and says, "I am physically fit, ready for work, but can find no job", is entitled to say, "Give me a job!" and the state is obliged to find a job for him? —Prince Otto von Bismarck, speech to the Reichstag, May 9, 1884

3459. Good government ... has for its objects the protection of every person within its care in the greatest liberty consistent with the good order of society, and his perfect security in the enjoyment of his earnings with the least possible diminution for public needs. —Grover Cleveland, second annual message to Congress, Dec 6, 1886

3460. The government is not an almoner of gifts among the people, but an instumentality by which the people's affairs should be conducted upon business principles, regulated by the public needs. —Grover Cleveland, message to the House of Representatives, Feb 26, 1887

3461. Prepare for war in time of peace. Not by fortifications, by navies, or by standing armies. But by policies which will add to the happiness and the comfort of all our people and which will tend to the distribution of intelligence and wealth equally among all. Our strength is a contented and intelligent community. —Rutherford B. Hayes, *Diary*, Jun 25, 1887

3462. The state is like the human body. All of the functions it carries out are not noble ones. [*L'Etat est comme le corps humain. Toutes les fonctions qu'il accomplit ne sont pas nobles.*] —Anatole France, *Les Opinions de M. Jérôme Coignard*

3463. The lessons of paternalism ought to be unlearned and the better lesson taught that while the people should patriotically and cheerfully support their Government its functions do not include the support of the people. —Grover Cleveland, second inaugural address, Mar 4, 1893

3464. That government is not best which best secures mere life and property—there is a more valuable thing—manhood. —Mark Twain, *Notebook*, 1935

3465. If the state has the power to send the flower of its manhood to die in thousands for the sake of the lives of the whole community,it would be absurd to deny it the right to put criminals to death if they are a danger to the public weal. —Heinrich von Treitschke, *Politics*, 1897-1901

3466. A man who is good enough to shed his blood for his country is good enough to be given a square deal afterwards. More than that no man is entitled to, and less than that no man shall have. —Theodore Roosevelt, speech in Springfield, Illinois, Jul 4, 1903

3467. The administration of justice lies at the foundation of government. —William Howard Taft, acceptance of Republican nomination for president in Chicago, Illinois, Jul 28, 1908

3468. Government should not be made an end in itself; it is a means only,—a means to be freely adapted to advance the best interests of the social organism. The State exists for the sake of Society, not Society for the sake of the State. —Woodrow Wilson, *The State: Elements of Historical and Practical Politics*, 1911

3469. We used to say that the ideal of government was for every man to be left alone and not interfered with, except when he interfered with somebody else; and that the best government was the government that did as little governing as possible. ... But we are coming now to realize that life is so complicated that ... the law has to step in and create new conditions under which we may live, the conditions which will make it tolerable for us to live. —Woodrow Wilson, speech in Fall River, Massachusetts, Sep 26, 1912

3470. Our thought has been "Let every man look out for himself, let every generation look out for itself," while we reared giant machinery which made it impossible that any but those who stood at the levers of control should have a chance to look out for themselves. —Woodrow Wilson, first inaugural address, Mar 4, 1913

3471. The general rule, at least, is that while property may be regulated to a certain extent, if regulation goes too far it will be recognized as a taking. —Oliver Wendell Holmes Jr., *Pennsylvania Coal Company v. H.J. Mahon*, 1922

3472. But to many the superfluous is the necessary, and it seems to me that Government does not go beyond its sphere in attempting to make life livable for them. —Oliver Wendell Holmes Jr., *Tyson & Bro. v. Banton*, 1927

3473. To me the foundation of American life rests upon the home and the family. I read into these great economic forces, these intricate and delicate relations of the government with business and with our political and social life, but one supreme end ... that we strengthen the security, the happiness, and the independence of every home. —Herbert Hoover, speech at Palo Alto, California, Aug 11, 1928

3474. If the moral and physical fibre of its manhood and its womanhood is not a state concern, the question is, what is? —Benjamin N. Cardozo, *Adler v. Deegan*, 1929

3475. Progress is born of cooperation in the community—not from government restraints. —Herbert Hoover, inaugural address, Mar 4, 1929

3476. Nations have recently been led to borrow billions for war; no nation has ever borrowed largely for education. Probably, no nation is rich enough to pay for both war and civilization. We must make our choice; we cannot have both. —Abraham Flexner, *Universities*, 1930

3477. It is the purpose of the government to see that not only the legitimate interests of the few are protected but that the welfare and the rights of the many are conserved. —Franklin D. Roosevelt, speech in Portland, Oregon, Sep 21, 1932

3478. Government has the definite duty to use all its power and resources to meet new social problems with new social controls. —Franklin D. Roosevelt, quoted, *Newsweek*, Nov 27, 1978

3479. It is customary in democratic countries to deplore expenditure on armaments as conflicting with the requirements of the social services. There is a tendency to forget that the most important social service that a government can do for its people is to keep them alive and free. —Sir John Cotesworth Slessor, *Strategy for the West,* 1954

3480. The government must be the trustee for the little man, because no one else will be. The powerful can usually help themselves—and frequently do. —Adlai E. Stevenson Jr., quoted, *Human Behavior,* May, 1978

3481. Chaos and ineptitude are anti-human; but so too is a superlatively efficient government equipped with all the products of a highly developed technology. —Aldous Huxley, *Tomorrow and Tomorrow and Tomorrow,* 1956

3482. Government should be concerned with anti-social conduct, not with utterances. —William O. Douglas, dissenting opinion, *Roth v. United States,* Jun 24, 1957

3483. Too often our Washington reflex is to discover a problem and then throw money at it, hoping it will somehow go away. —Kenneth B. Keating, *The New York Times,* Dec 24, 1961

3484. The state is the servant of the citizen, and not his master. —John F. Kennedy, State of the Union address, Jan 11, 1962

3485. The business of government is the business of the people. —John F. Kennedy, speech in New York City, May 20, 1962

3486. Work for elimination of concrete evils rather than for the realisation of abstract goods. Do not aim at establishing happiness by political means. Rather, aim at the elimination of poverty by direct means. —Sir Karl Popper, "Utopia and Violence", *Conjecture and Refutation,* 1962

3487. Wealth is the means, and people are the ends. All our material riches will avail us little if we do not use them to expand the opportunities of our people. —John F. Kennedy, State of the Union message, Jan 11, 1962

3488. I look forward to ... a future in which our country will match its military strength with our moral restraint, its wealth with our wisdom, its power with our purpose. —John F. Kennedy, speech at Amherst College, Amherst, Massachusetts, Oct 26, 1963

3489. A government that is big enough to give you all you want is big enough to take it all away. —Barry Goldwater, speech in West Chester, Pennsylvania, Oct 21, 1964

3490. The great society is a place where men are more concerned with the quality of their goals than the quantity of their goods. —Lyndon Baines Johnson, speech at the Univ. of Michigan, May 22, 1964

3491. We are rapidly entering the age of no privacy, where everyone is open to surveillance at all times; where there are no secrets from government. —William O. Douglas, dissenting opinion, *Osborn v. United States,* 1966

3492. The state has no business in the bedrooms of the nation. —Pierre Eliot Trudeau, *The New York Times,* Jun 16, 1968

3493. Prolong human life only when you can shorten its miseries. —Stanislaw Lec, *More Unkempt Thoughts,* 1968

3494. If we take the route of the permanent handout, the American character will itself be impoverished. —Richard M. Nixon, televised speech on welfare reform, Aug 8, 1969

3495. The American wage earner and the American housewife are a lot better economists than most economists care to admit. They know that a government big enough to give you everything you want is a government big enough to take from you everything you have. —Gerald R. Ford, address to Congress, Aug 12, 1974

3496. We must resist the myth that government is a gigantic conspiracy. We cannot allow the intelligence services of the country to be dismantled. —Henry A. Kissinger, *Washington Post*, Nov 25, 1975

3497. I am skeptical about the ability of government to solve problems, and I have a healthy respect for the ability of people to solve problems on their own. —Richard B. Cheney, *Washington Post*, Nov 6, 1975

3498. World War II was the last government program that really worked. —George F. Will, speech to Association of American Publishers, *Washingtonian*, Jul, 1975

3499. All I want is the same thing you want. To have a nation with a government that is as good and honest and decent and competent and compassionate and as filled with love as are the American people. —Jimmy Carter, speech to the California State Senate in Sacramento, May 20, 1976

3500. Anything that the private sector can do, the government can do it worse. —Dixy Lee Ray, *Mother Jones*, May, 1977

3501. It was once said that the moral test of government is how that government treats those who are in the dawn of life, the children; those who are in the twilight of life, the elderly; and those who are in the shadows of life—the sick, the needy and the handicapped. —Hubert H. Humphrey, speech at dedication of Hubert H. Humphrey building, Washington, D.C., Nov 4, 1977

3502. Americans have always had an ambivalent attitude toward intelligence. When they feel threatened, they want a lot of it, and when they don't, they regard the whole thing as somewhat immoral. —Vernon A. Walters, *Silent Missions*, 1978

3503. I believe that we have an obligation to those in need, but that government should not be the provider of first resort for things that the private sector can produce better. —George Bush, address to Congress, Feb 9, 1989

SEPARATION OF POWERS

3504. A legislative, an executive, and a judicial power comprehend the whole of what is meant and understood by government. It is by balancing each of these powers against the other two, that the efforts in human nature towards tyranny can alone be checked and restrained, and any degree of freedom preserved in the constitution. —John Adams, letter to Richard Henry Lee, Nov 15, 1775

3505. In all tyrannical governments the supreme magistracy, or the right both of making and enforcing the laws, is vested in one and the same man, or one and the same body of men; and wherever these two powers are united together, there can be no public liberty. —Sir William Blackstone, *Commentaries on the Laws of England*, 1783

3506. The accumulation of all powers legislative, executive, and judiciary in the same hands, whether of one, a few or many, and whether hereditary, self-appointed, or elective, may justly be pronounced the very definition of tyranny. —James Madison, *The Federalist*, Jan 30, 1788

3507. With all the fanatical and preposterous theories about the rights of man (the theories, not the rights themselves, I speak of) there is nothing but power that can restrain power. —John Randolph of Roanoke, speech, as quoted, *Richmond Enquirer*, Jun 4, 1824

3508. Within these limits the power vested in the American courts of justice of pronouncing a statute to be unconstitutional forms one of the most powerful barriers that have ever been devised against the tyranny of political assemblies. [*Resserré dans ses limites, le pouvoir accordé aux tribunaux américains de prononcer sur l'inconstitutionnalité des lois, forme encore une des plus puissantes barrières qu'on ait jamais élevées contre la tyrannie des assemblées politiques.*] —Alexis, Comte de Tocqueville, *Democracy in America*, 1835

3509. The principles of a free constitution are irrevocably lost, when the legislative power is nominated by the executive. —Edward Gibbon, *The History of the Decline and Fall of the Roman Empire*, 1838

3510. The doctrine of the separation of powers was adopted by the Convention of 1787, not to promote efficency but to preclude the exercise of arbitrary power. The purpose was, not to avoid friction, but, by means of the inevitable friction incident to the distribution of the governmental powers among three departments, to save the people from autocracy. —Louis D. Brandeis, dissenting opinion, *Myers v. United States*, 1926

3511. It is the duty of the President to propose and it is the privilege of the Congress to dispose. —Franklin D. Roosevelt, press conference, Jul 23, 1937

3512. Under the doctrine of separation of powers, the manner in which the president personally exercises his assigned executive powers is not subject to questioning by another branch of government. —Richard M. Nixon, White House statement, Mar 12, 1973

3513. Man has discovered no technique for long preserving free government except that the executive be under the law. —Court of Appeals United States, ruling that President Nixon had to turn over presidential tapes, *The New York Times*, Oct 14, 1973

3514. If we are to preserve freedom and keep constitutional government alive in America, it cannot be left to a President and his agents alone to decide what must be kept secret. Congress, if it is to check the abuse of executive power, must retain its right to inquiry and independent judgement. —Frank Church, *Washington Post*, Feb 17, 1976

SOCIAL JUSTICE

3515. The gods sent not/ Corn for the rich men only. —William Shakespeare, *Coriolanus*, 1607-08

3516. Where there is no property there is no injustice. —John Locke, *An Essay Concerning Human Understanding*, 1690

3517. A decent provision for the poor is the true test of civilization. —Samuel Johnson, quoted by James Boswell, *Life of Samuel Johnson*, 1770

3518. Under a government which imprisons any unjustly, the true place for a just man is also a prison ... the only house in a slave State in which a free man can abide with honor. —Henry David Thoreau, *Civil Disobedience*, 1849

3519. So we defend ourselves and our henroosts, and maintain slavery. —Henry David Thoreau, *A Plea for Captain John Brown*, 1859

3520. The strongest bond of human sympathy outside the family relation should be one uniting all working people of all nations and tongues and kindreds. —Abraham Lincoln, letter to New York Workingmen's Association, Mar 21, 1864

3521. Property is the fruit of labor. Property is desirable, is a positive good in the world. Let not him who is homeless pull down the house of another, but let him work diligently and build one for himself, thus by example assuring that his own shall be safe from violence. —Abraham Lincoln, "Reply to New York Workingmen's Democratic Republican Association", Mar 21, 1864

3522. I am weary seeing our laboring classes so wretchedly housed, fed, and clothed, while thousands of dollars are wasted every year over unsightly statues. If these great men must have outdoor memorials let them be in the form of handsome blocks of buildings for the poor. —Elizabeth Cady Stanton, *Diary*, 1880

3523. When commerical capital occupies a position of unquestioned ascendancy, it everywhere constitutes a system of plunder. —Karl Marx, *Das Kapital*, 1867-83

3524. Lack of money is the root of all evil. —George Bernard Shaw, "Maxims for Revolutionists", *Man and Superman*, 1902

3525. Security, the chief pretence of civilization, cannot exist where the worst of dangers, the danger of poverty, hangs over everyone's head. —George Bernard Shaw, preface, *Major Barbara*, 1905

3526. It is significant that whenever the public mind is to be diverted from a great social wrong, a crusade is inaugurated against indecency, gambling, saloons, etc. —Emma Goldman, "The Tragedy of Women's Emancipation", *Anarchism and Other Essays*, 1911

3527. There never can be equality of awards or possessions so long as the human plan contains varied talents and differing degrees of industry and thrift, but ours ought to be a country free from the great blotches of distressed poverty. —Warren G. Harding, inaugural address, Mar 4, 1921

3528. In every truth, the beneficiaries of a system cannot be expected to destroy it. —A. Philip Randolph, *The Truth About Lynching*, ca. 1922

3529. Hungry men have no respect for law, authority or human life. —Marcus Moziah Garvey, *Philosophy and Opinions*, 1923

3530. The ultimate end of all revolutionary social change is to establish the sanctity of human life, the dignity of man, the right of every human being to liberty and well-being. —Emma Goldman, *My Further Disillusionment in Russia*, 1924

3531. A man may have strong humanitarian and democratic principles; but if he happens to have been brought up as a bath-taking, shirt-changing lover of fresh air, he will have to overcome certain physical repugnances before he can bring himself to put those principles into practice. —Aldous Huxley, *Jesting Pilate*, 1926

3532. I see one-third of a nation ill-housed, ill-clad, ill-nourished. ... The test of our progress is not whether we add more to the abundance of those who have much; it is whether we provide enough for those who have too little. —Franklin D. Roosevelt, second inaugural address, Jan 20, 1937

3533. Capitalism inevitably and by virtue of the very logic of its civilization creates, educates and subsidizes a vested interest in social unrest. —Joseph Schumpeter, *Capitalism, Socialism, and Democracy*, 1942

3534. The Lord so constituted everybody that no matter what color you are you require the same amount of nourishment. —Will Rogers, *The Autobiography of Will Rogers*, 1949

3535. I don't believe in government for special privilege. Our resources should be used for the benefit of all the people. —Harry S Truman, speech in San Francisco, California, Sep 4, 1951

3536. Understanding human needs is half the job of meeting them. —Adlai E. Stevenson Jr., speech in Columbus, Ohio, Oct 3, 1952

3537. Social imbalance reflects itself in inability to enforce laws, including significantly those which protect and advance basic social justice, and in failure to maintain and improve essential service. —John Kenneth Galbraith, *The Affluent Society*, 1958

3538. An unrectified case of injustice has a terrible way of lingering, restlessly, in the social atmosphere like an unfinished question. —Mary McCarthy, "My Confession", *On the Contrary*, 1961

3539. For every talent that poverty has stimulated it has blighted a hundred. —John W. Gardner, *Excellence*, 1961

3540. Political sovereignty is but a mockery without the means of meeting poverty and illiteracy and disease. Self-determination is but a slogan if the future holds no hope. —John F. Kennedy, speech to the United Nations General Assembly, Sep 25, 1961

3541. One cannot raise the bottom of a society without benefiting everyone above. —Michael Harrington, *The Other America*, 1962

3542. There is the fundamental paradox of the welfare state: that it is not built for the desperate, but for those who are already capable of helping themselves. —Michael Harrington, *The Other America*, 1962

3543. This administration today, here and now, declares unconditional war on poverty in America. I urge this Congress and all Americans to join with me in that effort. —Lyndon Baines Johnson, State of the Union address, Jan 8, 1964

3544. The challenge of the next half-century is whether we have the wisdom to use wealth to enrich and elevate our national life—and to advance the quality of American civilization—for in your time we have the opportunity to move not only toward the rich society and the powerful society, but upward to the Great Society. —Lyndon Baines Johnson, speech at the Univ. of Michigan, May 22, 1964

3545. Speaking like this doesn't mean that we're anti-white, but it does mean we're anti-exploitation, we're anti-degradation, we're anti-oppression. —Malcolm X, speech on "The Ballot or the Bullet", 1964

3546. If freedom makes social progress possible, so social progress strengthens and enlarges freedom. The two are inseparable partners in the great adventure of humanity. —Robert F. Kennedy, "Berlin East and West", *The Pursuit of Justice*, 1964

3547. Neither you nor I are willing to accept the tyranny of poverty, nor the dictatorship of ignorance, nor the despotism of ill health, nor the oppression of bias and prejudice and bigotry. We want change. We want progress. We want it both abroad and at home—and we aim to get it. —Lyndon Baines Johnson, speech to college students, Aug 4, 1965

3548. The landscape should belong to the people who see it all the time. —LeRoi Jones, *Home*, 1966

3549. No poor, rural, weak, or black person should ever again have to bear the additional burden of being deprived of the opportunity for an education, a job, or simple justice. —Jimmy Carter, inaugural address as governor of Georgia in Atlanta, Jan 12, 1971

3550. Senator, I am one of them. You do not seem to understand who I am. I am a black woman, the daughter of a dining-car worker. ... If my life has any meaning at all, it is that those who start out as outcasts can wind up as being part of the system. —Patricia Roberts Harris, in testimony to the U.S. Senate, *Newsweek*, Jan 24, 1977

3551. If you turn your back on these people, you yourself are an animal. You may be a well-dressed animal, but you are nevertheless an animal. —Edward I. Koch, calling for civic compassion for persons with AIDS, *The New York Times*, Jan 25, 1987

SOCIALISM

3552. Property is theft. [*La propriété, c'est le vol.*] —Pierre Joseph Proudhon, *Qu'est-ce la propriété?*, 1840

3553. All socialism involves slavery. ... That which fundamentally distinguishes the slave is that he labours under coercion to satisfy another's desires. —Herbert Spencer, "The Coming Slavery", *The Contemporary Review*, Apr, 1884

3554. What I mean by Socialism is a condition of society in which there should be neither rich nor poor, neither master nor master's man, neither idle nor overworked, neither brain-sick brain workers nor heart-sick hand workers, in a word, in which all men would be living in equality of condition, and would manage their affairs unwastefully, and with the full consciousness that harm to one would mean harm to all—the realization at last of the meaning of the word commonwealth. —William Morris, written for "Justice", 1884

3555. Labor may be likened to a man who as he carries home his earnings is waylaid by a series of robbers. One demands this much, and another that much, but last of all stands one who demands all that is left, save just enough to enable the victim to maintain life and come forth the next day to work. ... And the robber that takes all that is left, is private property in land. —Henry George, *Protection or Free Trade*, 1885

3556. The issue is Socialism versus Capitalism. I am for Socialism because I am for humanity. —Eugene V. Debs, speech, Jan 1, 1897

3557. Socialism must come down from the brain and reach the heart. —Jules Renard, *Journal*, Aug, 1905

3558. Objectively, Social Democracy is the moderate wing of fascism. —Joseph Stalin, quoted by Isaac Deutscher, *Stalin, A Political Biography*, 1924

3559. The revolutionary transformation of the regime of property and production is not an end in itself, but the necessary means and the indispensable condition of the liberation of the human being, which is an end in itself and is the final goal of socialism. [*La transformation révolutionnaire du régime de propriété et de la production n'est pas une fin en soi, mais le moyen nécessaire et la condition indispensable de la libération de la personne humaine, qui est, elle, une fin en soi et la dernière du socialisme.*] —Leon Blum, preface to French edition of James Burnham, *The Age of the Organisers*

3560. Socialism and laisser faire are like the north and south poles. They don't really exist. —Stanley Baldwin, 1st Earl Baldwin of Bewdley, quoted by K. Middlemas and J. Barnes, *Baldwin*

3561. Whether considered as a doctrine, or as an historical fact, or as a movement, socialism, if it really remains socialism, cannot be brought into harmony with the dogmas of the Catholic Church. ... Religious socialism, Christian socialism, are expressions implying a contradiction in terms. —Pius XI, encyclical, *Quadragesimo Anno*, 1931

3562. Socialism means equality of income or nothing. —George Bernard Shaw, appendix, *The Intelligent Woman's Guide to Socialism, Capitalism, Sovietism and Fascism*, 1937

3563. The aim of Socialism is to set up a universal society founded on equal justice for all men and equal peace for all nations. —Leon Blum, *For All Mankind*, 1941

3564. As a matter of practical necessity, socialist democracy may eventually turn out to be more of a sham than capitalist democracy ever was. —Joseph Schumpeter, *Capitalism, Socialism and Democracy*, 1942

3565. The great corruption of Socialism which threatens us at present ... calls itself Fascism in Italy, National Socialism (Nazi for short) in Germany, New Deal in the United States, and is clever enough to remain nameless in England; but everywhere it means the same thing: Socialist production and Unsocialist distribution. —George Bernard Shaw, *Everybody's Political What's What?*, 1944

3566. Unimaginative people disparage Socialism because it will, they fear, reduce life to a dead level. Never was an apprehension less plausible. Millions of well-fed bumptious citizens with plenty of leisure for argument will provide all the excitement the most restless spirits can desire. —George Bernard Shaw, *Everybody's Politcal What's What?*, 1944

3567. No socialist system can be established without a political police. ... They would have to fall back on some form of Gestapo. —Sir Winston S. Churchill, BBC radio broadcast, Jun 4, 1945

3568. Every reasonable human being should be a moderate Socialist. —Thomas Mann, *The New York Times*, Jun 18, 1950

3569. The inherent vice of capitalism is the unequal sharing of blessings; the inherent virtue of socialism is the equal sharing of miseries. —Sir Winston S. Churchill, saying

3570. I believe that for the past twenty years there has been a creeping socialism spreading in the United States. —Dwight D. Eisenhower, speech to Republican leaders, Custer State Park, South Dakota, Jun 11, 1953

3571. If the Labour Party is not going to be a Socialist Party, I don't want to lead it. ... When you join a team in the expectation that you are going to play rugger, you can't be expected to be enthusiastic if you are asked to play tiddly-winks. —Aneurin Bevan, speech in Manchester, England, Jan 26, 1956

3572. Total abstinence and a good filing-system are not now the right sign-posts to the socialist Utopia; or at least, if they are, some of us will fall by the wayside. —Anthony Crosland, *The Future of Socialism*, 1956

3573. The two most important emotions of the Labour Party are a doctrinaire faith in nationalization, without knowing what it means, and a doctrinaire faith in pacifism, without facing its consequences. —Richard Crossman, *Diary*, Oct 4, 1957

3574. The definition of the Left is a group of people who will never be happy unless they can convince themselves that they are about to be betrayed by their leaders. —Richard Crossman, *Diary*, Jul 3, 1959

3575. Between the barbarity of capitalism, which censures itself much of the time, and the barbarity of socialism, which does not, I guess I might choose capitalism. —Bernard-Henri Lévy, *Time*, Mar 13, 1978

TAXATION AND BUDGETS

3576. When there is an income tax, the just man will pay more and the unjust less on the same amount of income. —Plato, *The Republic*, ca. 390 B.C.

3577. The art of taxation consists in so plucking the goose as to obtain the largest possible amount of feathers with the smallest possible amount of hissing. —Jean Baptiste Colbert, attributed, ca. 1665

3578. The British Parliament has no right to tax the Americans. ... Taxation and representation are inseparably united. God hath joined them; no British Parliament can put them asunder. To endeavour to do so is to stab our very vitals. —Charles Pratt, Earl Camden, speech in the House of Lords, 1765

3579. It is inseparably essential to the freedom of a people that no taxes be imposed on them but with their own consent, given personally or by their representatives. —John Dickinson, *Resolutions of the Stamp Act Congress*, Oct 19, 1765

3580. To please universally was the object of his life; but to tax and to please, no more than to love and to be wise, is not given to men. —Edmund Burke, speech in the House of Commons, Apr 19, 1774

3581. A national debt, if it is not excessive, will be to us a national blessing. —Alexander Hamilton, letter to Robert Morris, Apr 30, 1781

3582. Another means of silently lessening the inequality of property is to exempt all from taxation below a certain point, and to tax the higher portions of property in geometric progression as they rise. —Thomas Jefferson, letter to James Madison, Oct 28, 1785

3583. Our Constitution is in actual operation; everything appears to promise that it will last; but nothing in this world is certain but death and taxes. —Benjamin Franklin, letter to David Hartley, Dec 4, 1789

3584. Mere parsimony is not economy. ... Expense, and great expense, may be an essential part of true economy. —Edmund Burke, *Letter to a Noble Lord*, 1796

3585. Sound principles will not justify our taxing the industry of our fellow citizens to accumulate treasure for wars to happen we know not when, and which might not perhaps happen but from the temptations offered by that treasure. —Thomas Jefferson, first annual message to Congress, Dec 8, 1801

3586. Not one cent should be raised unless it is in accord with the law. [*Il ne doit pas être levé un centime, si ce n'est en vertu d'une loi.*] —Napoleon I, decision, Nov 15, 1804

3587. And to preserve their independence, we must not let our rulers load us with perpetual debt. We must make our election between economy and liberty, or profusion and servitude. —Thomas Jefferson, letter to Samuel Kercheval, Jul 12, 1816

3588. I, however, place economy among the first and most important of republican virtues, and public debt as the greatest of the dangers to be feared. —Thomas Jefferson, letter to William Plumer, Jul 21, 1816

3589. That the power to tax involves the power to destroy ... is not to be denied. —John Marshall, *McCullough v. Maryland*, 1819

3590. The greatest, the most important power entrusted to the government is the right to tax the citizens; it is from this right that all the others flow. Today, therefore, political science consists essentially in being able to draw up a good budget. Now, the ability to do this is an administrative ability, from which it follows that administrative ability is the principal ability needed in politics. —Claude Henri, Comte de Saint-Simon, *Politics*, 1819

3591. I am one of those who do not believe that a national debt is a national blessing ... it is calculated to raise around the administraiton a moneyed aristocracy dangerous to the liberties of the country. —Andrew Jackson, letter to L.H. Colman, Apr 26, 1824

3592. That most delicious of all privileges—spending other people's money. —John Randolph of Roanoke, quoted by W. Cabell Bruce, *John Randolph of Roanoke, 1773-1833*, 1922

3593. The wisdom of man never yet contrived a system of taxation that would operate with perfect equality. —Andrew Jackson, "Proclamation to the People of South Carolina", Dec 10, 1832

3594. Countries, therefore, when lawmaking falls exclusively to the lot of the poor cannot hope for much economy in public expenditure. [*Les pays ou les pauvres seraient exclusivement chargés de faire la loi ne pourraient donc espérer une grande économie dans les dépenses publiques.*] —Alexis, Comte de Tocqueville, *Democracy in America*, 1835

3595. In other words, a democratic government is the only one in which those who vote for a tax can escape the obligation to pay it. [*En d'autre termes, le gouvernement de la démocratie est le seul ou celui qui vote l'impôt puisse échapper à l'obligation de le payer.*] —Alexis, Comte de Tocqueville, *Democracy in America*, 1835

3596. As an individual who undertakes to live by borrowing, soon finds his original means devoured by interest, and next no one left to borrow from—so must it be with a government. —Abraham Lincoln, campaign circular, Mar 4, 1843

3597. Of all debts men are least willing to pay the taxes. What a satire is this on government! Everywhere they think they get their money's worth, except for these. —Ralph Waldo Emerson, "Politics", *Essays: Second Series*, 1844

3598. To tax the community for the advantage of a class is not protection: it is plunder. —Benjamin Disraeli, speech in the House of Commons, May 14, 1850

3599. People are glad to be defended, but they are not glad about paying for it. [*Man lässt sich gern schützen, aber man zahlt nicht gern.*] —Prince Otto von Bismarck, speech in the Prussian Chamber of Deputies, Jun 1, 1865

3600. The life of a republic lies certainly in the energy, virtue, and intelligence of its citizens; but it is equally true that a good revenue system is the life of an organized government. —Andrew Johnson, first annual message to Congress, Dec 4, 1865

3601. No favored class should demand freedom from assessment, and the taxes should be so distributed as to not fall unduly on the poor, but rather on the accumulated wealth of the country. —Andrew Johnson, first annual message to Congress, Dec 4, 1865

3602. The thing generally raised on city land is taxes. —Charles Dudley Warner, "Sixteenth Week", *My Summer in a Garden*, 1870

3603. When more than the people's sustenance is exacted through the form of taxation than is necessary to meet the just obligations of Government and expenses of its economical administration, such exaction becomes ruthless extortion and a violation of the fundamental principles of a free Government. —Grover Cleveland, second annual message to Congress, Dec 6, 1886

3604. Taxes are what we pay for civilized society. —Oliver Wendell Holmes Jr., *Compañía de Tabacos v. Collector*, 1904

3605. Houseless, adj. Having paid all taxes on household goods. —Ambrose Bierce, *The Devil's Dictionary*, 1906

3606. The power to tax is the power to destroy. ... A government which lays taxes on the people not required by urgent public necessity and sound public policy is not a protector of liberty, but an instrument of tyranny. —Calvin Coolidge, speech in Washington, D.C., Jun 30, 1924

3607. The Income Tax has made more Liars out of the American people than golf has. —Will Rogers, "Helping the Girls with Their Income Taxes", *The Illiterate Digest*, 1924

3608. I favor the policy of economy, not because I wish to save money, but because I wish to save people. The men and women of this country who toil are the ones who bear the cost of the Government. Every dollar that we carelessly waste means that their life will be so much the more meager. Every dollar that we prudently saves means that their life will be so much the more abundant. Economy is idealism in its most practical form. —Calvin Coolidge, inaugural address, Mar 4, 1925

3609. The collection of any taxes which are not absolutely required, which do not ... contribute to the public welfare, is only a species of legalized larceny. —Calvin Coolidge, inaugural address, Mar 4, 1925

3610. The power to tax is not the power to destroy while this Court sits. —Oliver Wendell Holmes Jr., dissenting opinion, *Panhandle Oil Company v. Mississippi ex rel. Knox, Attorney General*, 1928

3611. Lord, the money we do spend on Government and it's not one bit better than the government we got for one-third the money twenty years ago. —Will Rogers, quoted by Paula McSpadden Love, *The Will Rogers Book*, 1972

3612. Too often in recent history liberal governments have been wrecked on rocks of loose fiscal policy. —Franklin D. Roosevelt, message to Congress, Mar 10, 1933

3613. Taxes, after all, are the dues that we pay for the privileges of membership in an organized society. —Franklin D. Roosevelt, speech in Worcester, Massachusetts, Oct 21, 1936

3614. Our national debt after all is an internal debt owed not only by the Nation but to the Nation. If our children have to pay interest on it they will pay that interest to themselves. A reasonable internal debt will not impoverish our children or put the Nation into bankruptcy. —Franklin D. Roosevelt, speech to the American Retail Federation, May 22, 1939

3615. Noah must have taken into the Ark two taxes, one male and one female, and did they multiply bountifully! Next to guinea pigs, taxes must have been the most prolific animals. —Will Rogers, *The Autobiography of Will Rogers*, 1949

3616. When everybody has got money they cut taxes, and when they're broke they raise 'em. That's statesmanship of the highest order. —Will Rogers, *The Autobiography of Will Rogers*, 1949

3617. It's a terribly hard job to spend a billion dollars and get your money's worth. —George M. Humphrey, *Look*, Feb 23, 1954

3618. The purpose is clear. It is safety with solvency. The country is entitled to both. —Dwight D. Eisenhower, on unification of the three military services, Apr 17, 1958

3619. There is one difference between a tax collector and a taxidermist—the taxidermist leaves the hide. —Mortimer Caplin, *Time*, Feb 1, 1963

3620. The Federal Government is the people and the budget is a reflection of their need. —John F. Kennedy, speech in Washington, D.C., Apr 19, 1963

3621. Government expands to absorb revenue and then some. —Tom Wicker, quoted by Harold Faber, *The New York Times Magazine*, Mar 17, 1968

3622. Man is not like other animals in the ways that are really significant: animals have instincts, we have taxes. —Erving Goffman, interview, *The New York Times*, Feb 12, 1969

3623. There is no doubt that many expensive national projects may add to our prestige or serve science. But none of them must take precedence over human needs. As long as Congress does not revise its priorities, our crisis is not just material, it is a crisis of the spirit. —Nelson A. Rockefeller, letter to John V. Lindsay, *The New York Times*, Apr 25, 1971

3624. Virtually everything is under federal control nowadays except the federal budget. —Herman E. Talmadge, *American Legion Magazine*, Aug, 1975

3625. Budgeting is a black art practiced by bureaucratic magicians. —David Muchow, *Chicago Sun-Times*, Nov 19, 1976

3626. Tax reform means "Don't tax you, don't tax me, tax that fellow behind the tree." —Russell B. Long, *The New York Times*, Dec 31, 1976

3627. There's only one place where inflation is made: that's in Washington ... in response to pressures from the people at large. ... The voting public ... ask their Congressmen to enact goodies in the form of spending, but they are unhappy about having taxes raised to pay for those goodies. —Milton Friedman, *U.S. News & World Report*, Mar 7, 1977

3628. Any jackass can draw up a balanced budget on paper. —Lane Kirkland, *U.S. News & World Report*, May 19, 1980

3629. None of us really understands what's going on with all these numbers. —David Stockman, "The Education of David Stockman," by William Greider, *The Atlantic Monthly*, Dec, 1981

3630. Someone must stand up to those who say, "Here's the key, there's the Treasury, just take as many of those hard-earned tax dollars as you want." —Ronald Reagan, *The New York Times*, Mar 18, 1985

3631. Most (tax revisions) didn't improve the system, they made it more like Washington itself; complicated, unfair, cluttered with gobbledygook and loopholes designed for those with the power and influence to hire high-priced legal and tax advisers. —Ronald Reagan, televised speech, May 28, 1985

3632. The current tax code is a daily mugging. —Ronald Reagan, speech in Independence, Missouri, Sep 2, 1985

3633. Before we give you billions more, we want to know what you've done with the trillion you've got. —Les Aspin, report on letter to the Secretary of Defense, *The New York Times*, Feb 5, 1985

3634. (A tax loophole is) something that benefits the other guy. If it benefits you, it is tax reform. —Russell B. Long, recalled on his retirement, *Time*, Nov 10, 1986

3635. Read my lips: no new taxes. —George Bush, acceptance speech as Republican nominee for preseident, Aug 18, 1988

TREASON

3636. Treason doth never prosper: what's the reason?/ For if it prosper, none dare call it treason. —Sir John Harington, "Of Treason", *Epigrams*

3637. Caesar had his Brutus, Charles the First, his Cromwell, and George the Third ("Treason!" cried the Speaker) may profit by their example. If this be treason, make the most of it. —Patrick Henry, speech to the Virginia House of Representatives, 1765

3638. Traters, I will here remark, are a onfortnit class of peple. If they wasn't, they wouldn't be traters. They conspire to bust up a country—they fail, and they're traters. They bust her, and they become statesmen and heroes. —Artemus Ward, "The Tower of London", *Artemus Ward in London*, 1872

3639. The fear of doing right is the grand treason in times of danger. —Henry Ward Beecher, *Proverbs from Plymouth Pulpit*, 1887

3640. They talk of a man betraying his country, his friends, his sweetheart. There must be a moral bond first. All a man can betray is his conscience. —Joseph Conrad, *Under Western Eyes*, 1911

3641. If I had to choose between betraying my country and betraying my friend, I hope I should have the guts to betray my country. —E.M. Forster, "What I Believe", *Two Cheers for Democracy*, 1951

3642. We are the first victims of America fascism. —Ethel and Julius Rosenberg, letter released by their attorney the day of execution for espionage, Jun 19, 1953

3643. To betray you must first belong. —Kim (Harold) Philby, *The New York Times*, Dec 19, 1967

WAR AND PEACE

3644. Victory shifts from man to man. —Homer, *Iliad*, ca. 700 B.C.

3645. Better beans and bacon in peace than cakes and ale in fear. —Aesop, "The Town Mouse and the Country Mouse", *Fables*, ca. 550 B.C.

3646. Stretch a bow to the very full,/ And you will wish you had stopped in time. —Lao-Tse, *The Way of the Tao*, 6th cent. B.C.

3647. To lead an uninstructed people to war is to throw them away. —Confucius, *The Analects*, ca. 480 B.C.

3648. Dead men have no victory. —Euripides, *The Phoenician Women*, ca. 411-409 B.C.

3649.   We make war that we may live in peace. —Aristotle, *Nicomachean Ethics*, ca. 325 B.C.

3650.   And he shall judge among the nations, and shall rebuke many people: and they shall beat their swords into plowshares, and their spears into pruninghooks: nation shall not lift up sword against nation, neither shall they learn war any more. —Bible, *Isaiah*, ca. 200 B.C.

3651.   He is wise who tries everything before arms. [*Omnia prius experiri quam armis sapietem decet.*] —Terence, *Eunuchus*, ca. 165 B.C.

3652.   Laws are silent in time of war. [*Silent enim leges inter arma.*] —Cicero, *Pro T. Annio Milone oratio*, 52 B.C.

3653.   Let arms yield to the toga, the laurel crown to praise. [*Cedant arma togae, concedat laurea laudi.*] —Marcus Tullius Cicero, *De Officiis*, 44 B.C.

3654.   Endless money forms the sinews of war. [*Primum nervos belli, pecuniam infinitam.*] —Marcus Tullius Cicero, *Philippics*, 44-43 B.C.

3655.   The name of peace is sweet and the thing itself good, but between peace and slavery there is the greatest difference. [*Et nomen pacis dulce est et ipsa res salutaris, sed inter pacem et servitutem plurimum interest.*] —Marcus Tullius Cicero, *Philippics*, 44-43 B.C.

3656.   Peace is liberty in tranquility; servitude the last of all evils, one to be repelled, not only by war but even by death. [*Pax est tranquilla libertas, servitus postremum malorum omnium non modo bello, sed morte etiam repellendum.*] —Marcus Tullius Cicero, *Philippics*, 44-43 B.C.

3657.   Certain peace is better and safer than anticipated victory. [*Melior tutiorque est certa pax quam sperata victoria.*] —Livy, *Ab Urbe Condita*, ca. 29 B.C.

3658.   It is sweet and honorable to die for your country. [*Dulce et decorum est pro patria mori.*] —Horace, (Quintus Horatius Flaccus), *Odes*, 23 B.C.

3659.   Of war men ask the outcome, not the cause. [*Quaeritur belli exitus, non causa.*] —Seneca (the Younger), *Hercules Furens*, ca. 50

3660.   Blessed are the peacemakers: for they shall be called the children of God. —Bible, *Matthew*, ca. 90

3661.   Where they make a desert, they call it peace. [*Atque ubi solitudinem faciunt, pacem appellant.*] —Cornelius Tacitus, *Agricola*, ca. 98

3662.   The gods are on the side of the stronger. [*Deos fortioribus adesse.*] —Cornelius Tacitus, *Historiae*, ca. 100

3663.   We are now suffering the evils of a long peace. Luxury, more deadly than war, broods over the city, and avenges a conquered world. [*Nunc patimur longae pacis mala, saevior armis/ Luxuria incubuit victumque ulciscitur orbem.*] —Juvenal, *Satires*, ca. 115

3664.   Let him who desires peace prepare for war. [*Qui desiderat pacem, praeparet bellum.*] — Vegetius, (Flavius Vegetius Renatus), *De Rei Militari*, ca. 375

3665.   In order for a war to be just, three things are necessary. First, the authority of the sovereign. ... Secondly, a just cause. ... Thirdly ... a rightful intention. [*Dicendum quod ad hoc quod aliquod bellum sit justum, tria requiruntur. Primo quidem, auctoritas principis, cujus mandato bellum est gerendum. ... Secundo, requiritur causa justa. ... Tertio, requiritur ut sit intentio bellantium recta.*] —St. Thomas Aquinas, *Summa Theologiae*, 1273

3666.   The most disadvantageous peace is better than the most just war. —Desiderius Erasmus, *Adagia*, 1515

3667. A prince should therefore have no other aim or thought, nor take up any other thing for his study, but war and its organization and discipline, for that is the only art that is necessary to one who commands. [*Debbe adunque uno principe non avere altro obietto né altro pensiero, né prendere cosa alcuna per sua arte, fuora della guerra e ordini e disciplina di essa; perché quella è sola arte che si espetta a chi comanda.*] —Niccolò Machiavelli, *Il Principe*, 1532

3668. Among other evils which being unarmed brings you, it causes you to be despised. [*Perché intra le altre cagioni che ti arreca di male lo essere disarmato, ti fa contennendo.*] —Niccolò Machiavelli, *Il Principe*, 1532

3669. Since the chief and ultimate end of human society is not that men should live together in peace, but that, living in peace, they should serve God, it is the function of the Magistrate to risk even this outward peace (if no otherwise may it be done) in order to secure and maintain in his land the true service of God in its purity. —Theodore Beza, *De Haereticis*, 1554

3670. Accurst be he that first invented war. —Christopher Marlowe, *Tamburlaine the Great*, 1587

3671. A foreign war is a lot milder than a civil war. [*Une guerre étrangère est un mal bien plus doux que la civile.*] —Michel de Montaigne, "Des mauvais moyens employés à bonne fin", *Essais*, 1580-88

3672. It's not victory if it doesn't end the war. [*Ce n'est pas victoire, si elle ne met fin à la guerre.*] —Michel de Montaigne, "De l'incertitude de notre jugement", *Essais*, 1580-88

3673. There is nothing so subject to the inconstancy of fortune as war. [*Las cosas de la guerra más que otras, están sujetas a continua mudanza.*] —Miguel de Cervantes, *Don Quixote*, 1605-15

3674. Nay, number itself in armies importeth not much, where the people is of weak courage; for as Virgil saith, "It never troubles the wolf how many the sheep be." —Sir Francis Bacon, "Of the True Greatness of Kingdoms and Estates", *Essays*, 1625

3675. He that commands the sea is at great liberty, and may take as much and as little of the war as he will. —Sir Francis Bacon, "Of the True Greatness of Kingdoms and Estates", *Essays*, 1625

3676. No body can be healthful without exercise, neither natural body or politic; and certainly to a kingdom or estate, a just and honourable war is the true exercise. —Sir Francis Bacon, "Of the True Greatness of Kingdoms and Estates", *Essays*, 1625

3677. A just fear of an imminent danger, though there be no blow given, is a lawful cause of war. —Sir Francis Bacon, "Of Empire", *Essays*, 1625

3678. One sword keeps another in the sheath. —George Herbert, *Jacula Prudentum*, 1651

3679. The condition of man ... is a condition of war of everyone against everyone. —Thomas Hobbes, *Leviathan*, 1651

3680. Peace hath her victories no less renowned than war. —John Milton, Sonnet 16, 1652

3681. Peace is not the mere absence of war, but a virtue based on strength of character. [*Pax enim non belli privatio, sed virtus est quae ex animi fortitudine oritur.*] —Baruch (Benedictus de) Spinoza, *Tractatus Politicus*, 1677

3682. Just as with the soldier who does not carry his sword at all times is subject to mishaps, so too the Kingdom that is not always prepared has much to fear. [*Comme il arrive beaucoup d'inconvénients au soldat qui ne porte pas toujours son epée, le Royaume qui n'est pas toujours sur ses gardes ... à beaucoup a craindre.*] —Cardinal Richelieu, *Political Testament*, 1687

3683. From hence, let fierce contending nations know/ What dire effects from civil discord flow. —Joseph Addison, *Cato*, 1713

3684. Ever since the invention of gunpowder ... I continually tremble lest men should, in the end, uncover some secret which would provide a short way of abolishing mankind, of annihilating peoples and nations in their entirety. —Charles Louis de Montesquieu, *Les Lettres persanes*, 1721

3685. Better a lean peace than a fat victory. —Thomas Fuller, *Gnomologia*, 1732

3686. They may ring their bells now, before long they will be wringing their hands. —Sir Robert Walpole, 1st Earl of Orford, speech in the House of Commons on celebrations at outbreak of war with Spain, Oct 19, 1739

3687. The possession of battle-ready troops, a well-filled state treasury and a lively disposition, these were the real reasons which moved me to war. —Frederick the Great, on the invasion of Silesia, *A History of My Times*, 1741

3688. A victorious general has no faults in the eye of the public, while a defeated general is always wrong no matter how wise his conduct may have been. [*Un général victorieux n'a point fait de fautes aux yeux du public, de même que le general battu a toujours tort, quelque sage conduit qu'il ait eue.*] —Voltaire, *Le Siècle de Louis XIV*, 1751

3689. Among the calamities of war, may be justly numbered the diminution of the love of truth, by the falsehoods which interest dictates, and credulity encourages. —Samuel Johnson, *The Idler*, Nov 11, 1758

3690. In this country it is considered wise to kill an admiral from time to time in order to encourage the others. [*Dans ce pays-ci il est bon de tuer de temps en temps un amiral pour encourager les autres.*] —Voltaire, *Candide*, 1759

3691. The right of conquest has no foundation other than the right of the strongest. [*A l'égard du droit de conquête, il n'a d'autre fondement que la loi du plus fort.*] —Jean Jacques Rousseau, *The Social Contract*, 1762

3692. There never was a good war or a bad peace. —Benjamin Franklin, letter to Josiah Quincy, Sep 11, 1773

3693. The battle, sir, is not to the strong alone; it is to the vigilant, the active, the brave. —Patrick Henry, speech to the Virginia Convention, Mar 23, 1775

3694. There is a time for all things, a time to preach and a time to pray, but those times have passed away. There is a time to fight, and that time has now come. —Peter Muhlenberg, sermon in Woodstock, Virginia, Jan, 1776

3695. Nothing can be more hurtful to the service, than the neglect of discipline; for that discipline, more than numbers, gives one army the superiority over another. —George Washington, general orders, Jul 6, 1777

3696. It is not a field of a few acres of ground, but a cause, that we are defending, and whether we defeat the enemy in one battle, or by degrees, the consequences will be the same. —Thomas Paine, *The American Crisis*, Sep 12, 1777

3697. It is the object only of war that makes it honorable. And if there was ever a just war since the world began, it is this in which America is now engaged. —Thomas Paine, *The American Crisis*, Mar 21, 1778

3698. He who is the author of a war lets loose the whole contagion of hell and opens a vein that bleeds a nation to death. —Thomas Paine, *The American Crisis*, 1776-83

3699. War involves in its progress such a train of unforeseen and unsupposed circumstances that no human wisdom can calculate the end. It has but one thing certain, and that is to increase taxes. —Thomas Paine, *Prospects on the Rubicon*, 1787

3700. To be prepared for War is one of the most effectual means of preserving peace. —George Washington, first annual address to Congress, Jan 8, 1790

3701. A free people ought not only to be armed, but disciplined; to which end a uniform and well-digested plan is requisite. —George Washington, fifth annual message to Congress, Jan 8, 1790

3702. Whatever enables us to go to war, secures our peace. —Thomas Jefferson, letter to James Monroe, Jul 11, 1790

3703. War contains so much folly, as well as wickedness, that much is to be hoped from the progress of reason; and if any thing is to be hoped, every thing ought to be tried. —James Madison, "Universal Peace", *National Gazette*, Feb 2, 1792

3704. Each generation should be made to bear the burden of its own wars, instead of carrying them on, at the expense of other generations. —James Madison, *National Gazette*, Feb 2, 1792

3705. To make war upon those who trade with us is like setting a bulldog upon a customer at the shop-door. —Thomas Paine, *The Age of Reason*, 1794

3706. Avoiding occasions of expense by cultivating peace, we should remember also that timely disbursements to prepare for danger frequently prevent much greater disbursements to repel it. —George Washington, *Farewell Address to the People of the United States*, Sep 19, 1796

3707. I venture to say no war can be long carried on against the will of the people. —Edmund Burke, *Letters on a Regicide Peace*, 1796-97

3708. If they want peace, nations should avoid the pinpricks that precede cannon shots. — Napoleon I, reported conversation with Czar Alexander I at Tilsit, Jun 22, 1807

3709. In war one sees one's own difficulties, and does not take into account those of the enemy; one must have confidence in oneself. —Napoleon I, letter to Eugene Beauharnais, Apr 30, 1809

3710. In times of peace the people look most to their representatives; but in war, to the executive solely. —Thomas Jefferson, letter to Caesar A. Rodney, Feb 10, 1810

3711. May the pens of the diplomats not ruin again what the people have attained with such exertions. —Gebhard Leberecht von Blücher, words following the Battle of Waterloo, 1813

3712. If ever there was a holy war, it was that which saved our liberties and gave us independence. —Thomas Jefferson, letter to John Wayles Eppes, Nov 6, 1813

3713. Nothing except a battle lost can be half so melancholy as a battle won. —1st Duke of Wellington, dispatch from Waterloo, Jun, 1815

3714. My views and feelings (are) in favor of the abolition of war ... and I hope it is practicable, by improving the mind and morals of society, to lessen the disposition to war; but of its abolition I despair. —Thomas Jefferson, letter to Noah Worchester, Nov 26, 1817

3715. War is a game in which princes seldom win, the people never. —Charles Caleb Colton, *Lacön*, 1825

3716. War is the province of chance. In no other sphere of human activity must such a margin be left for this intruder. It increases the uncertainty of every circumstance and deranges the course of events. —Karl von Clausewitz, *War, Politics and Power*, 1962

3717. War therefore is an act of violence intended to compel our opponents to fulfil our will. —Karl von Clausewitz, *On War*, 1832

3718. War is regarded as nothing but the continuation of state policy with other means. [*Der Krieg ist nichts anderes als die Fortsetzung der Politik mit anderen Mitteln.*] —Karl von Clausewitz, *On War*, 1833

3719. We shall more certainly preserve peace when it is well understood that we are prepared for war. —Andrew Jackson, farewell address, Mar 4, 1837

3720. A quarter of a century of peace does not pass over a nation in vain. —3rd Viscount Palmerston, letter to Lord Granville of France, Jun 10, 1839

3721. The sound of the drum drives out thought; for that very reason it is the most military of instruments. —Joseph Joubert, *Pensées*, 1842

3722. War is a blessing compared with national degradation. —Andrew Jackson, letter to James A. Polk, May 2, 1845

3723. Living, just as much as dying/ For one's fatherland, is sweet. [*Leben bleiben, wie das Sterben/ Für das Vaterland ist süss.*] —Heinrich Heine, "Zwei Ritter", *Romancero*, 1851

3724. If peace cannot be maintained with honor, it is no longer peace. —Lord John Russell, speech in Greenock, Scotland, Sep 19, 1853

3725. Peace hath higher tests of manhood/ Than battle ever knew. —John Greenleaf Whittier, "The Hero", 1853

3726. If this phrase of the "balance of Power?" is to be always an argument for war, the pretence for war will never be wanting, and peace can never be secure. —John Bright, speech in the House of Commons, Mar 31, 1854

3727. It is magnificent, but it is not war. [*C'est magnifique, mais ce n'est pas la guerre.*] —Pierre Bosquet, reported remark on the charge of the Light Brigade at the Battle of Balaclava, Oct 25, 1854

3728. A nation will not count the sacrifice it makes, if it supposes it is engaged in a struggle for its fame, its influence and its existence. —Benjamin Disraeli, speech on "Prosecution of the War", May 24, 1855

3729. Still a Union that can only be maintained by swords and bayonets, and in which strife and civil war are to take the place of brotherly love and kindness, has no charm for me. —Robert E. Lee, letter to his son, George Washington Custis Lee, Jan 23, 1861

3730. There are good points about all ... wars. People forget self. The virtues of magnanimity, courage, patiotism, etc., are called into life. People are more generous, more sympathetic, better, than when engaged in the more selfish pursuits of peace. —Rutherford B. Hayes, letter to S. Birchard, May 8, 1861

3731. It is well that war is so terrible—we should grow too fond of it. —Robert E. Lee, to James Longstreet, Dec 13, 1862

3732. War is an ugly thing, but not the ugliest of things: the decayed and degraded state of moral and patriotic feeling which thinks nothing worth a war, is worse. —John Stuart Mill, "The Contest in America", *Fraser's Magazine*, Feb, 1862

3733. No terms except an unconditional and immediate surrender can be accepted. I propose to move immediately upon your works. —Ulysses S. Grant, mesage to General S.B. Buckner, Fort Donelson, Feb 16, 1862

3734. You cannot qualify war in harsher terms than I will. War is cruelty, and you cannot refine it. —William Tecumseh Sherman, letter to James M. Calhoun, mayor of Atlanta, Jul 12, 1864

3735. I propose to fight it out on this line, if it takes all summer. —Ulysses S. Grant, dispatch from Spotsylvania Court House, Virginia, May 11, 1864

3736. With malice toward none; with charity for all; with firmness in the right, as God gives us to see the right, let us strive on to finish the work we are in; to bind up the nation's wounds; to care for him who shall have borne the battle, and for his widow, and his orphan—to do all which may achieve and cherish a just, and a lasting peace, among ourselves, and with all nations. —Abraham Lincoln, second inaugural address, Mar 4, 1865

3737. The legitimate object of war is a more perfect peace. —William Tecumseh Sherman, speech in St. Louis, Missouri, Jul 20, 1865

3738. All wars are boyish, and are fought by boys. —Herman Melville, "The March into Virginia", *Battlepieces and Aspects of the War*, 1866

3739. Every State must conquer or be conquered. —Michael Bakunin, *Federalism, Socialism and Anti-Theologism*, 1868

3740. In time of war the loudest patriots are the greatest profiteers. —August Bebel, speech to the Reichstag, Nov, 1870

3741. The first object of a treaty of peace should be to make future war improbable. —3rd Marquess of Salisbury, "The Terms of Peace", *Quarterly Review*, Oct, 1870

3742. He who has once gazed into the glazed eye of a dying warrior on the field of battle will think twice before beginning a war. —Prince Otto von Bismarck, quoted by Charles Lowe, *Bismarck's Table Talk*, 1895

3743. Against war it may be said that it makes the victor stupid and the vanquished revengeful. [*Zuungunsten des Krieges kann man sagen: er macht den Sieger dumm, den Besiegten boshaft.*] —Friedrich Nietzsche, *Human, All Too Human*, 1878

3744. There is many a boy here to-day who looks on war as all glory, but, boys, it is all hell. —William Tecumseh Sherman, speech in Columbus, Ohio, Aug 11, 1880

3745. A war, even the most victorious, is a national misfortune. —Helmut von Moltke, letter, 1880

3746. Rendering oneself unarmed when one had been the best-armed, out of a height of feeling—that is the means to real peace, which must always rest on a peace of mind. [*Sich wehrlos machen, während man der Wehrhafteste war, aus einer Höhe der Empfindung heraus, —das ist das Mittel zum wirklichen Frieden welcher immer auf einem Frieden der Gesinnung ruhen muss.*] —Friedrich Nietzsche, *The Wanderer and His Shadow*, 1880

3747. If we heed the teachings of history we shall not forget that in the life every nation emergencies may arise when a resort to arms can alone save it from dishonor. —Chester Alan Arthur, first annual message to Congress, Dec 6, 1881

3748. War is not the normal state of the human family in its higher development, but merely a feature of barbarism lasting on through the transition of the race, from the savage to the scholar. —Elizabeth Cady Stanton, *History of Woman Suffrage*, 1881

3749. The real war will never get into the books. —Walt Whitman, "The Real War", *Specimen Days*, 1882

3750. If you have a nation of men who have risen to that height of moral cultivation that they will not declare war or carry arms, for they have not so much madness left in their brains, you have a nation of lovers, of benefactors, of true, great, and able men. —Ralph Waldo Emerson, "War", *Miscellanies*, 1884

3751. War educates the senses, calls into action the will, perfects the physical constitution, brings men into such swift and close collision in critical moments that man measures man. —Ralph Waldo Emerson, "War", *Miscellanies*, 1884

3752. The word state is identical with the word war. —Prince Peter Kropotkin, *Paroles d'un révolté*, 1885

3753. It is not merely cruelty that leads men to love war, it is excitement. —Henry Ward Beecher, *Proverbs from Plymouth Pulpit*, 1887

3754. Let us ever remember that our interest is in concord not in conflict, and that our real eminence as a nation lies in the victories of peace, not those of war. —William McKinley, speech in Washington, D.C., 1890

3755. As long as war is regarded as wicked, it will always have its fascination. When it is looked upon as vulgar, it will cease to be popular. —Oscar Wilde, "Intentions", *The Critic as Artist*, 1891

3756. We are not interested in the possibilities of defeat. —Victoria, letter to Arthur J. Balfour, Dec, 1899

3757. The wars of the people will be more terrible than those of the kings. —Sir Winston S. Churchill, speech in the House of Commons, May 12, 1901

3758. Without war no state could exist. All those we know of arose through war. ... War, therefore, will endure to the end of history, as long as there is a multiplicity of states. —Heinrich von Treitschke, *Politics*, 1897-1901

3759. A good navy is not a provocative of war. It is the surest guaranty of peace. —Theodore Roosevelt, second annual message to Congress, Dec 2, 1902

3760. Capitalism carries within itself war, as clouds carry rain. —Jean Jaurès, *Studies in Socialism*, 1902

3761. Generally peace tells for righteousness; but if there is conflict between the two, then our fealty is due first to the cause of righteousness. —Theodore Roosevelt, fourth annual message to Congress, Dec 6, 1904

3762. War, n. A by-product of the arts of peace. —Ambrose Bierce, *The Devil's Dictionary*, 1906

3763. To call war the soil of courage and virtue is like calling debauchery the soil of love. —George Santayana, *The Life of Reason: Reason in Society*, 1905-06

3764. To delight in war is a merit in the soldier, a dangerous quality in the captain and a positive crime in the statesman. —George Santayana, *The Life of Reason: Reason in Society*, 1905-06

3765. Battle, n. A method of untying with the teeth a political knot that would not yield to the tongue. —Ambrose Bierce, *The Devil's Dictionary*, 1906

3766. A really great people, proud and high-spirited, would face all the disasters of war rather than purchase that base prosperity which is bought at the price of national honor. —Theodore Roosevelt, speech at Harvard Univ., Feb 23, 1907

3767. The day will come when a nation that lifts up the sword against a nation will be put in the same felon category as the man who strikes his brother in anger. —David Lloyd George, speech in Manchester, England, Apr 21, 1908

3768. War makes rattling good history; but Peace is poor reading. —Thomas Hardy, *The Dynasts*, 1904-08

3769. A modern navy can not be improvised. It must be built and in existence when the emergency arises. —William Howard Taft, inaugural address, Mar 4, 1909

3770. War is a dreadful thing, and unjust war is a crime against humanity. But it is such a crime because it is unjust, not because it is war. —Theodore Roosevelt, speech at the Univ. of Paris, Apr 23, 1910

3771. No man can sit down and withhold his hands from the warfare against wrong and get peace from his acquiescence. —Woodrow Wilson, speech in Denver, Colorado, May 7, 1911

3772. You cannot fight hard unless you think you are fighting to win. —Theodore Roosevelt, letter to Henry L. Stoddard, Jul, 1912

3773. The main enemy is at home (is in our own camp). [*Der Feind steht im eigenen Lager.*]
—Karl Liebknecht, speech at outbreak of World War I, 1914

3774. The navy of the United States is the right arm of the United States and is emphatically the peacemaker. —Theodore Roosevelt, *The New York Times*, Nov 22, 1914

3775. I find war detestable but those who praise it without participating in it even more so.
—Romain Rolland, "Inter arma caritas", *Journal de Genève*, Oct 30, 1914

3776. I am proud of the fact that I never invented weapons to kill. —Thomas Alva Edison, *The New York Times*, Jun 8, 1915

3777. There is a price which is too great to pay for peace, and that price can be put in one word. One cannot pay the price of self-respect. —Woodrow Wilson, speech in Des Moines, Iowa, Feb 1, 1916

3778. The belief that public opinion or international public opinion, unbacked by force, had the slightest effect in restraining a powerful military nation in any course of action ... has been shown to be a pathetic fallacy. —Theodore Roosevelt, *Metropolitan*, Feb, 1916

3779. Only a peace between equals can last. Only a peace the very principle of which is equality and a common participation in a common benefit. —Woodrow Wilson, speech to the U.S. Senate, Jan 22, 1917

3780. I want to stand by my country, but I cannot vote for war. I vote no. —Jeanette Rankin, casting her vote against declaration of war, Apr 6, 1917

3781. All wars are wars among thieves who are too cowardly to fight and who therefore induce the young manhood of the whole world to do the fighting for them. —Emma Goldman, "Address to the Jury", *Mother Earth*, Jul, 1917

3782. The government will ... go on in the highly democratic method of conscripting American manhood for European slaughter. —Emma Goldman, "Address to the Jury", *Mother Earth*, Jul, 1917

3783. The right is more precious than peace. —Woodrow Wilson, speech to Congress, Apr 2, 1917

3784. This may be safely turned down. No sane enemy, acquainted with our institutions, would destroy the War Office. —Sir George Murray, comment on a World War I defence memo, quoted by Austen Chamberlain, *Down the Years*, 1935

3785. War is much too serious a matter to be left to generals. [*La guerre est une chose beaucoup trop sérieuse pour ˆetre confiée à des généraux.*] —Georges Clemenceau, quoted, *New York Times*, Jul 14, 1944

3786. My home policy? I wage war. My foreign policy? I wage war. Always, everywhere, I wage war. —Georges Clemenceau, speech to the Chamber of Deputies, Mar 8, 1918

3787. It is far easier to make war than to make peace. —Georges Clemenceau, speech at Verdun, France, Jul 14, 1919

3788. Injustice, arrogance, displayed in the hour of triumph will never be forgotten or forgiven. —David Lloyd George, memorandum written during the Paris peace conference, 1919

3789. Make wars unprofitable and you make them impossible. —A. Philip Randolph, "The Cause and Remedy of Race Riots", *The Messenger*, 1919

3790. Victory or defeat? It is the slogan of all-powerful militarism in every belligerent nation. ... And yet, what can victory bring to the proletariat? —Rosa Luxemburg, *The Crisis in the German Social Democracy*, 1919

3791. Is there any man ... who does not know that the seed of war in the modern world is industrial and commercial rivalry? —Woodrow Wilson, speech to veterans in St. Louis, Missouri, Sep 5, 1919

3792. We want to get rid of the militarist not simply because he hurts and kills, but because he is an intolerable thick-voiced blockhead who stands hectoring and blustering in our way to achievement. —H.G. Wells, *The Outline of History*, 1920

3793. I once believed in armed preparedness. I advocated it. But I have come now to believe there is a better preparedness in a public mind and a world opinion made ready to grant justice precisely as it exacts it. And justice is better served in conferences of peace than in conflicts at arms. —Warren G. Harding, address to the International Armaments Conference in Washington, D.C., Feb 6, 1922

3794. Violence seldom accomplishes permanent and desired results. Herein lies the futility of war. —A. Philip Randolph, *The Truth About Lynching*, ca. 1922

3795. The only true and lasting peace (is) based on justice and right. —Calvin Coolidge, radio broadcast, Dec 10, 1923

3796. Peace must have other guarantees than constitutions and covenants.Laws and treaties may help, but peace and war are attitudes of mind. —Calvin Coolidge, speech in Baltimore, Maryland, Sep 6, 1924

3797. Mankind has grown strong in eternal struggles and it will only perish through eternal peace. [*Im ewigen Kämpfe ist die Menschheit gross geworden—im ewigen Frieden geht sie zugrunde.*] —Adolf Hitler, *Mein Kampf*, 1924

3798. If we are to promote peace on earth, we must have a great deal more than the power of the sword. We must call into action the spiritual and moral forces of mankind. —Calvin Coolidge, speech in Annapolis, Maryland, Jun 3, 1925

3799. Struggle is the father of all things. ... It is not by the principles of humanity that man lives or is able to preserve himself above the animal world but solely by means of the most brutal struggle. —Adolf Hitler, speech in Kulmbach, Germany, Feb, 1928

3800. Those who in principle oppose birth control are either incapable of arithmetic or else in favour of war, pestilence and famine as permanent features of human life. —Bertrand Russell, "Some Prospects: Cheerful and Otherwise", *Skeptical Essays*, 1928

3801. War is not the continuation of policy. It is the breakdown of policy. —Hans von Seeckt, *Thoughts of a Soldier*, 1929

3802. Who would prefer peace to the glory of hunger and thirst, of wading through mud, and dying in the service of one's country? —Jean Giraudoux, *Amphitryon 38*, 1929

3803. The enemy advances, we retreat; the enemy camps, we harass; the enemy tires, we attack; the enemy retreats, we pursue. —Mao Tse-tung, letter, Jan 5, 1930

3804. No soldier starts a war—they only give their lives to it. Wars are started by you and me, by bankers and politicians, excitable women, newspaper editors, clergymen who are ex-pacifists, and Congressmen with vertebrae of putty. The youngsters yelling in the streets, poor kids, are the ones who pay the price. —Father Francis P. Duffy, sermon, Marshall Joffre memorial service, New York City, Jan, 1931

3805. There could be real peace only if everyone were satisfied. That means there is not often a real peace. There are only actual states of peace which, like wars, are mere expedients. [*Il n'y aurait de paix véritable que si tout le monde était satisfait. C'est dire qu'il n'y a pas souvent de paix véritable. Il n'y a que des paix réelles, qui ne sont comme les guerres que les expédients.*] —Paul Valéry, "Greatness and Decadence of Europe", *Reflections on the World Today*, 1931

3806. The only treaties that ought to count are those which would effect a settlement between ulterior motives. [_Les seuls traités qui compteraient sont ceux qui conclueraient entre les arrière-pensées._] —Paul Valéry, "Greatness and Decadence of Europe", _Reflections on the World Today_, 1931

3807. Everyone knows that war can no longer be considered, even by the coldest calculator or the strongest nation, as a means of attaining, with any reasonable probability, a determined objective. [_Tout le monde, par exemple, sait bien que la guerre ne peut plus être considérée, même par le calculateur le plus froid et par la nation la plus puissante, comme un moyen d'atteindre, avec une probabilité suffisante, un but determiné._] —Paul Valéry, preface to a book by Mariano H. Carnejo, _La Lutte pour la paix_, Oct, 1933

3808. Wars may be fought with weapons, but they are won by men. It is the spirit of the men who follow and of the man who leads that gains the victory. —George S. Patton, _Cavalry Journal_, Sep, 1933

3809. Peace is indivisible. —Maxim Litvinov, speech to the League of Nations, 1934

3810. Everyone, when there's war in the air, learns to live in a new element: falsehood. —Jean Giraudoux, _Tiger at the Gates_, 1935

3811. During war we imprison the rights of man. —Jean Giraudoux, _Tiger at the Gates_, 1935

3812. Once blood is shed in a national quarrel reason and right are swept aside by the rage of angry men. —David Lloyd George, _War Memoirs_, 1933-36

3813. We can do without butter, but ... not without guns. One cannot shoot with butter, but with guns. —Joseph Goebbels, speech in Berlin, Jan 17, 1936

3814. Guns will make us powerful; butter will only make us fat. —Joseph Goebbels, radio broadcast, 1936

3815. War is not an instinct but an invention. [_La guerra no es un instinto, sino un invento._] —Jose Ortega y Gasset, "En cuanto al pacifismo", 1937

3816. The most shocking fact about war is that its victims and its instruments are individual human beings, and that these individual beings are condemned by the monstrous conventions of politics to murder or be murdered in quarrels not their own. —Aldous Huxley, _The Olive Tree_, 1937

3817. This is the second time that there has come back from Germany to Downing Street peace with honour. I believe it is peace for our time. —Neville Chamberlain, on his return from the Munich Conference, Sep 30, 1938

3818. How horrible, fantastic, incredible it is that we should be digging trenches and trying on gas-masks here because of a quarrel in a faraway country between people of whom we know nothing. —Neville Chamberlian, radio broadcast about Hitler's threatened invasion of Czechoslovakia, Sep 27, 1938

3819. England has been offered a choice between war and shame. She has chosen shame and will get war. —Sir Winston S. Churchill, speech in the House of Commons on the Munich agreement, Sep, 1938

3820. All is over. Silent, mournful, abandoned, broken, Czechoslovakia recedes into darkness. ... We have sustained a defeat without a war. —Sir Winston S. Churchill, speech in the House of Commons on the Munich agreement, Oct 5, 1938

3821. History shows that wars are divided into two kinds, just and unjust. All wars that are progressive are just, and all wars that impede progress are unjust. —Mao Tse-tung, "On Protracted War", May, 1938

3822. War can be abolished only through war, and in order to get rid of the gun it is necessary to take up the gun. —Mao Tse-tung, "Problems of War and Strategy", Nov 6, 1938

3823. Weapons are an important factor in war, but not the decisive one; it is man and not materials that counts. —Mao Tse-tung, "Problems of War and Strategy", Nov 6, 1938

3824. I tell you there's nothing to stop war from going on forever. ... A slight case of negligence, and it's bogged down up to the axles. And then it's a matter of hauling the war out of the mud again. But emperor and kings and popes will come to its rescue. [*Ich sag: dass der Krieg einmal aufhort, ist nicht gesagt. ... Vielleicht ein Ubersehn, und das Schlamassel ist da. Und dann kann man den Krieg wieder aus dem Dreck ziehn! Aber die Kaiser und Konige und der Papst wird ihm zu Hilf kommen in seiner Not.*] —Bertolt Brecht, *Mother Courage*, 1939

3825. I hear the same talk about "sanctity of treaties," "law and order," "resisting agression" and "enforcement of morality." Such phrases have always been the stock in trade of those who have vested interests which they want to preserve against those in revolt against a rigid system. —John Foster Dulles, speech opposing U.S. entry into World War II, Detroit, Michigan, Oct 29, 1939

3826. Victory at all costs, victory in spite of all terror, victory however long and hard the road may be; for without victory there is no survival. —Sir Winston S. Churchill, speech in the House of Commons, May 13, 1940

3827. Never in the field of human conflict was so much owed by so many to so few. —Sir Winston S. Churchill, speech in the House of Commons on role of the R.A.F. during Battle of Britain, Aug 20, 1940

3828. You ask, what is our policy? I will say, it is to wage war by sea, land, and air, with all our might and with all the strength that God can give us. —Sir Winston S. Churchill, speech in the House of Commons, May 13, 1940

3829. We shall not flag or fail. We shall go on to the end. We shall fight in France, we shall fight on the seas and oceans, we shall fight with growing confidence and growing strength in the air, we shall defend our island, whatever the cost may be, we shall fight on the beaches, we shall fight on the landing grounds, we shall fight in the fields and in the streets, we shall fight in the hills; we shall never surrender. —Sir Winston S. Churchill, speech in the House of Commons following the Dunkirk evacuation, Jun 4, 1940

3830. We cannot accept the doctrine that war must be forever a part of man's destiny. —Franklin D. Roosevelt, campaign speech in Cleveland, Ohio, Nov 2, 1940

3831. War challenges virtually every other institution of society—the justice and equity of its economy, the adequacy of its political systems, the energy of its productive plant, the bases, wisdom and purposes of its foreign policy. —Walter Millis, *The Faith of an American*, 1941

3832. In the Soviet Army it takes more courage to retreat than to advance. —Joseph Stalin, reported conversation with Averell Harriman, Sep, 1941

3833. We kill because we're afraid of our own shadow, afraid that if we used a little common sense we'd have to admit that our glorious principles were wrong. —Henry Miller, "The Alcoholic Veteran with the Washboard Cranium", *The Wisdom of the Heart*, 1941

3834. The problems of victory are more agreeable than those of defeat, but they are no less difficult. —Sir Winston S. Churchill, speech in the House of Commons, Nov 11, 1942

3835. The Prime Minister wins debate after debate and loses battle after battle. The country is beginning to say that he fights debates like a war and a war like a debate. —Aneurin Bevan, debate in the House of Commons, Jul 2, 1942

3836. There is no working middle course in wartime. —Sir Winston S. Churchill, speech in the House of Commons, Jul 2, 1942

3837. War is not an adventure. It is a disease. It is like typhus. [*La guerre n'est pas une aventure. La guerre est une maladie. Comme le typhus.*] —Antoine de Saint-Exupéry, *Pilote de guerre*, 1942

3838. We used to wonder where war lived, what it was that made it so vile. And now we realize that we know where it lives, that it is inside ourselves. —Albert Camus, *Cahiers, 1935-1942*, 1962

3839. It is better to have a war for justice than peace in injustice. —Charles Péguy, "The Rights of Man", *Basic Verities*, 1943

3840. Older men declare war. But it is youth that must fight and die. And it is youth who must inherit the tribulation, the sorrow, and the triumphs that are the aftermath of war. —Herbert Hoover, speech to the Republican national convention in Chicago, Illinois, Jun 27, 1944

3841. Peace, like war, can succeed only where there is a will to enforce it, and where there is available power to enforce it. —Franklin D. Roosevelt, speech at the Foreign Policy Association, New York City, Oct 21, 1944

3842. The eagle has ceased to scream, but the parrots will now begin to chatter. The war of the giants is over and the pigmies will now start to squabble. —Sir Winston S. Churchill, remarks to General Ismay on V-E day, May 7, 1945

3843. We are going to have peace even if we have to fight for it. —Dwight D. Eisenhower, speech in Frankfurt, Germany, Jun 10, 1945

3844. As long as there are sovereign nations possessing great power, war is inevitable. —Albert Einstein, "Einstein on the Atomic Bomb", *Atlantic Monthly*, Nov, 1945

3845. If man does find the solution for world peace it will be the most revolutionary reversal of his record we have ever known. —George C. Marshall, *Biennial Report of the Chief of Staff, United States Army*, Sep 1, 1945

3846. We live under a system by which the many are exploited by the few, and war is the ultimate sanction of that exploitation. —Harold Joseph Laski, *Plan or Perish*, 1945

3847. Since wars begin in the minds of men, it is in the minds of men that the defences of peace must be constructed. —UNESCO, *Constitution*, 1946

3848. I hate war as only a soldier who has lived it can, only as one who has seen its brutality, its futility, its stupidity. Yet there is one thing to say on its credit side—victory required a mighty manifestation of the most ennobling of the virtues of man— faith, courage, fortitude, sacrifice! —Dwight D. Eisenhower, speech in Ottawa, Canada, Jan 10, 1946

3849. I have never met anybody who wasn't against war. Even Hitler and Mussolini were, according to themselves. —David Low, *The New York Times*, Feb 10, 1946

3850. Wars occur because people prepare for conflict, rather than for peace. —Trygve Lie, *Labor*, Sep 6, 1947

3851. I do not approve the extermination of the enemy; the policy of exterminating or, as it is barbarously said, liquidating enemies, is one of the most alarming developments of modern war and peace, from the point of view of those who desire the survival of culture. One needs the enemy. —T.S. Eliot, *Notes Towards the Definition of Culture*, 1948

3852. In War: Resolution. In Defeat: Defiance. In Victory:Magnanimity. In Peace: Good Will. —Sir Winston S. Churchill, *The Second World War*, 1948

3853. Morality is contraband in war. —Mohandas K. Gandhi, *Non-Violence in Peace and War*, 1948

3854. What difference does it make to the dead, the orphans and the homeless, whether the mad destruction is wrought under the name of totalitarianism or the holy name of liberty or democracy? —Mohandas K. Gandhi, *Non-Violence in Peace and War*, 1948

3855. War is an unmitigated evil. But it certainly does one good thing. It drives away fear and brings bravery to the surface. —Mohandas K. Gandhi, *Non-Violence in Peace and War*, 1948

3856. No one can guarantee success in war, but only deserve it. —Sir Winston S. Churchill, *The Second World War*, 1949

3857. We Smiths want peace so bad we're prepared to kill every one of the Joneses to get it. —I.F. Stone, quoted, *The Truman Era*, Jan 24, 1949

3858. The way to prevent war is to bend every energy toward preventing it, not to proceed by the dubious indirection of preparing for it. —Max Lerner, "On Peacetime Military Training", *Actions and Passions*, 1949

3859. Diplomats are just as essential to starting a war as Soldiers are for finishing it. You take Diplomacy out of war and the thing would fall flat in a week. —Will Rogers, *The Autobiography of Will Rogers*, 1949

3860. Peace is more the product of our day-to-day living than of a spectacular program, intermittently executed. —Dwight D. Eisenhower, speech at Columbia Univ., Mar 23, 1950

3861. The pact of Munich was a greater blow to humanity than the atomic bomb at Hiroshima. —Dwight D. Eisenhower, speech at Columbia Univ., Mar 23, 1950

3862. In war there is no second prize for the runner-up. —Omar N. Bradley, *Military Review*, Feb, 1950

3863. People who are vigorous and brutal often find war enjoyable, provided that it is a victorious war and that there is not too much interference with rape and plunder. This is a great help in persuading people that wars are righteous. —Bertrand Russell, "Ideas That Have Harmed Mankind", *Unpopular Essays*, 1950

3864. The quickest way of ending a war is to lose it. —George Orwell, "Second Thoughts on James Burnham", *Shooting an Elephant*, 1950

3865. In war there is no substitute for victory. —Douglas MacArthur, address to Congress, Apr 19, 1951

3866. I do not hold that we should rearm in order to fight. I hold that we should rearm in order to parley. —Sir Winston S. Churchill, radio address, Oct 8, 1951

3867. When you put on a uniform, there are certain inhibitions that you accept. —Dwight D. Eisenhower, statement on learning that Pres. Truman had fired Gen. Douglas MacArthur, April 11, 1951

3868. For it isn't enough to talk about peace. One must believe in it. And it isn't enough to believe in it. One must work at it. —Eleanor Roosevelt, radio broadcast on the Voice of America, Nov 11, 1951

3869. After each war there is a little less democracy to save. —Brooks Atkinson, "January 7", *Once Around the Sun*, 1951

3870. War is both the product of an earlier corruption and a producer of new corruptions. —Lewis Mumford, "The Challenge to Renewal", *The Conduct of Life*, 1951

3871. To my mind, to kill in war is not a whit better than to commit ordinary murder. —Albert Einstein, speech in Tokyo, 1952

3872. The field of combat was a long, narrow, green-baize covered table. The weapons were words. —Adm. C. Turner Joy, commenting on truce talks with North Korea, *The New York Times*, Dec 31, 1952

3873. I hate war. War destroys individuals and whole generations. It throws civilization into the dark ages. But there is only one kind of war the American people have any stomach for and that is a war against hunger and pestilence and disease. —Harry S Truman, quoted by William Hillman, *Mr. President*, 1952

3874. It is fatal to enter any war without the will to win it. —Douglas MacArthur, speech to the Republican National Convention, Jul 7, 1952

3875. War is an invention of the human mind. The human mind can invent peace with justice. —Norman Cousins, *Who Speaks for Man?*, 1953

3876. History does not long entrust the care of freedom to the weak or the timid. We must acquire proficiency in defense and display stamina in purpose. —Dwight D. Eisenhower, first inaugural address, Jan 20, 1953

3877. Every gun that is fired, every warship launched, every rocket fired signifies, in the final sense, a theft from those who hunger and are not fed, those who are cold and are not clothed. The world in arms is not spending money alone. It is spending the sweat of its labourers, the genius of its scientists, the hopes of its children. —Dwight D. Eisenhower, speech to the American Society of Newspaper Editors, Apr 16, 1953

3878. If any foreign minister begins to defend to the death a "peace conference," you can be sure his government has already placed its orders for new battleships and airplanes. —Joseph Stalin, recalled on his death, Mar 5, 1953

3879. The hand that signed the treaty bred a fever,/ And famine grew, and locusts came;/ Great is the hand that holds dominion over/ Man by scribbled name. —Dylan Thomas, "The Hand That Signed the Paper", *Collected Poems*, 1953

3880. In the final choice a soldier's pack is not so heavy a burden as a prisoner's chains. —Dwight D. Eisenhower, first inaugural address, Jan 20, 1953

3881. To jaw-jaw always is better than to war-war. —Sir Winston S. Churchill, *The New York Times*, Jun 27, 1954

3882. I have never accepted what many people have kindly said—namely that I inspired the nation. Their will was resolute and remorseless, and as it proved, unconquerable. It fell to me to express it. It was the nation and the race dwelling all round the globe that had the lion's heart. I had the luck to be called upon to give the roar. I also hope that I sometimes suggested to the lion the right place to use his claws. —Sir Winston S. Churchill, 80th birthday address to Parliament, Nov 30, 1954

3883. The only alternative to coexistence is codestruction. —Jawaharlal Nehru, *London Observer*, Aug 29, 1954

3884. The most terrible warfare is to be a second lieutenant leading a platoon when you are on the battlefield. —Dwight D. Eisenhower, reported remarks, Mar 17, 1954

3885. The war has started incredibly badly. Therefore, it must be continued. [*La guerre commence infiniment mal. Il faut donc qu'elle continue.*] —Charles De Gaulle, *Mémoires de guerre: L'Appel*, 1955

3886. As the bomb fell over Hiroshima and exploded, we saw an entire city disappear. I wrote in my log the words: "My God, what have we done?" —Capt. Robert Lewis, comments on 10th anniversary of first nuclear bomb, *Enola Gay*, May 19, 1955

3887. Some day there is going to be a man sitting in my present chair who has not been raised in the military services and who will have little understanding of where slashes in their estimates can be made with little or no damage. If that should happen while we still have the state of tension that now exists in the world, I shudder to think of what could happen in this country. —Dwight D. Eisenhower, letter to Everett E. Hazlett, Aug 20, 1956

3888. You have to take chances for peace, just as you must take chances in war. Some say that we were brought to the verge of war. The ability to get to the verge of war without getting into the war is the necessary art. —John Foster Dulles, *Life*, Jan 11, 1956

3889. Warfare, no matter what weapons it employs, is a means to an end, and if that end can be achieved by negotiated settlements of conditional surrender, there is no need for war. —Harry S Truman, *Memoirs*, 1955-56

3890. If our air forces are never used, they have achieved their finest goal. —Gen. Nathan F. Twining, *The New York Times*, Mar 31, 1956

3891. Mr. Dulles has just frightened most of our allies to death with a statement that there is an art in actually threatening war and coming to the brink but retreating from the brink. —Eleanor Roosevelt, letter to Gus Ranis, Jan 23, 1956

3892. I have always been opposed even to the thought of fighting a "preventive war." There is nothing more foolish than to think that war can be stopped by war. You don't "prevent" anything by war except peace. —Harry S Truman, *Memoirs*, 1955-56

3893. If you live among dogs, keep a stick. After all, this is what a hound has teeth for—to bite when he feels like it! —Nikita S. Khrushchev, interview in Japanese newspaper, Jul 9, 1957

3894. The more bombers, the less room for doves of peace. —Nikita S. Khrushchev, speech on Moscow radio, Mar 14, 1958

3895. It is far more important to be able to hit the target than it is to haggle over who makes a weapon or who pulls a trigger. —Dwight D. Eisenhower, on unification of the three military services, Apr 17, 1958

3896. A general and a bit of shooting makes you forget your troubles ... it takes your mind off the cost of living. —Brendan Behan, *The Hostage*, 1958

3897. A government needs one hundred soldiers for every guerrilla it faces. —Fulgencio Batista, telephone interview, *El Caribe*, Jan 1, 1959

3898. I like to believe that people, in the long run, are going to do more to promote peace than our governments. Indeed, I think that people want peace so much that one of these days governments had better get out of the way and let them have it. —Dwight D. Eisenhower, radio and television broadcast, London, England, Aug 31, 1959

3899. The new and terrible dangers which man has created can only be controlled by man. —John F. Kennedy, speech at the Univ. of California, Nov 2, 1959

3900. Youth is the first victim of war; the first fruit of peace. It takes twenty years or more of peace to make a man; it takes only twenty seconds of war to destroy him. —Baudouin I, address to joint session of U.S. Congress, May 12, 1959

3901. It is an unfortunate fact that we can secure peace only by preparing for war. —John F. Kennedy, campaign speech in Seattle, Washington, Sep 6, 1960

3902. The major deterrent (to war) is in a man's mind. —Adm. Arleigh Burke, *US News & World Report*, Oct 3, 1960

3903. It would indeed be the ultimate tragedy if the history of the human race proved to be nothing more noble than the story of an ape playing with a box of matches on a petrol dump. —David Ormsby-Gore, *Christian Science Monitor*, Oct 25, 1960

3904. In the councils of government, we must guard against the acquisition of unwarranted influence, whether sought or unsought, by the military-industrial complex. The potential for the disastrous rise of misplaced power exists and will persist. —Dwight D. Eisenhower, farewell address, Jan 17, 1961

3905. Let us call a truce to terror. Let us invoke the blessings of peace. And, as we build an international capacity to keep peace, let us join in dismantling the national capacity to wage war. —John F. Kennedy, speech to the United Nations General Assembly, Sep 25, 1961

3906. Peace and freedom do not come cheap, and we are destined—all of us here today—to live out most if not all of our lives in uncertainty and challenge and peril. —John F. Kennedy, speech at the Univ. of North Carolina, Oct 12, 1961

3907. Unconditional war can no longer lead to unconditional victory. ... Mankind must put an end to war or war will put an end to mankind. —John F. Kennedy, speech to the United Nations General Assembly, Sep 25, 1961

3908. I hear it said that West Berlin is militarily untenable—and so was Bastogne, and so, in fact, was Stalingrad. Any danger spot is tenable if men—brave men—will make it so. —John F. Kennedy, televised speech, Jul 25, 1961

3909. There were two kinds of sanctions, effective and ineffective. To apply the latter was provocative and useless. If we were to apply the former, we ran the risk of war, and it would be dangerous to shut our eyes to the fact. —Anthony Eden, *Facing the Dictators*, 1962

3910. The soldier, above all other people, prays for peace, for he must suffer and bear the deepest wounds and scars of war. —Douglas MacArthur, speech at the U.S. Military Academy, West Point, New York, May 12, 1962

3911. Arms alone are not enough to keep peace. It must be kept by men. —John F. Kennedy, State of the Union message, Jan 11, 1962

3912. Aggressive conduct, if allowed to go unchecked and unchallenged, ultimately leads to war. —John F. Kennedy, televised speech, Oct 22, 1962

3913. Treaties are like roses and young girls. They last while they last. —Charles De Gaulle, *Time*, Jul 12, 1963

3914. World peace, like community peace, does not require that each man love his neighbor—it requires only that they live together with mutual tolerance, submitting their disputes to a just and peaceful settlement. —John F. Kennedy, commencement address at the American Univ., Jun 10, 1963

3915. In this age when there can be no losers in peace and no victors in war—we must recognize the obligation to match national strength with national restraint. —Lyndon Baines Johnson, speech to Congress, Nov 27, 1963

3916. The mere absence of war is not peace. —John F. Kennedy, State of the Union address, Jan 14, 1963

3917. Peace is a daily, a weekly, a monthly process, gradually changing opinions, slowly eroding old barriers, quietly building new structures. —John F. Kennedy, speech to the United Nations General Assembly, Sep 20, 1963

3918. That's the way it is in war. You win or lose, live or die—and the difference is just an eyelash. —Douglas MacArthur, *Reminiscences*, 1964

3919. We are not about to send American boys nine or ten thousand miles away from home to do what Asian boys ought to be doing for themselves. —Lyndon Baines Johnson, televised speech, Oct 21, 1964

3920. This is not a jungle war, but a struggle for freedom on every front of human activity. —Lyndon Baines Johnson, televised speech on the war in Vietnam, Aug 4, 1964

3921. They call upon us to supply American boys to do the job that Asian boys should do. —Lyndon Baines Johnson, reported remarks, Aug 12, 1964

3922. To insist on strength ... is not war-mongering. It is peace-mongering. —Barry Goldwater, *The New York Times*, Aug 11, 1964

3923. I was in the Victoria Library in Toronto in 1915, studying a Latin poet, and all of a sudden I thought, "War can't be this bad." So I walked out and enlisted. —Lester B. Pearson, quoted by Robinson Deal, *The Pearson Phenomenon*, 1964

3924. We did not choose to be the guardians of the gate, but there is no one else. —Lyndon Baines Johnson, televised speech, Jul 28, 1964

3925. Could I have but a line a century hence crediting a contribution to the advance of peace, I would yield every honor which has been accorded by war. —Douglas MacArthur, recalled on his death, Apr 5, 1964

3926. War is a poor chisel to carve out tomorrows. —Martin Luther King Jr., television documentary, Dec, 1965

3927. To tell you the truth, I thought of all the damned paperwork this was going to mean in the morning. —Gen. Walter Bedell Smith, on signing the armistice that ended World War II in Europe, *The New York Times*, May 8, 1965

3928. Past experience provides little basis for confidence that reason can prevail in an atmosphere of mounting war fever. In a contest between a hawk and a dove the hawk has a great advantage, not because it is a better bird, but because it is a bigger bird with lethal talons and a highly developed will to use them. —J. William Fulbright, speech in the U.S. Senate, Apr 21, 1966

3929. A riot is a spontaneous outburst. A war is subject to advance planning. —Richard M. Nixon, speech in New York City, Dec 8, 1967

3930. This is particularly true of those bellicose Republican "conservatives" and Dixiecrats who are more ready to lay down lives than prejudices and who can hear the most distant drum more clearly than the cry of a hungry child in the street. —Herbert Block, "Herblock", *Herblock Gallery*, 1968

3931. Peace is an unstable equilibrium, which can be preserved only by acknowledged supremacy or equal power. —Will Durant, *The Lessons of History*, 1968

3932. I say when you get into a war, you should win as quick as you can, because your losses become a function of the duration of the war. I believe when you get in a war, get everything you need and win it. —Dwight D. Eisenhower, news conference in Indio, California, Mar 15, 1968

3933. One cannot fashion a credible deterrent out of an incredible action. —Robert McNamara, on the utility of nuclear weapons, *The Essence of Security*, 1968

3934. I don't know what it will take out there—500 casualties maybe, maybe 500,000. It's the aughts that scare me. —Lyndon Baines Johnson, quoted, *Time*, Apr 15, 1985

3935. (President John F.) Kennedy said that if we had nuclear war we'd kill 300 million people in the first hour. (Secretary of Defense Robert) McNamara, who is a good businessman and likes to save, says it would be only 200 million. —Norman Thomas, recalled on his death, Dec 19, 1968

3936. It is always a strain when people are being killed. I don't think anybody has held this job who hasn't felt personally responsible for those being killed. —Lyndon Baines Johnson, quoted, *Time*, Apr 15, 1985

3937. No country without an atom bomb could properly consider itself independent. —Charles De Gaulle, quoted, *The New York Times Magazine*, May 12, 1968

3938. North Vietnam cannot defeat or humiliate the United States. Only Americans can do that. —Richard M. Nixon, televised speech, Nov 3, 1969

3939. The greatest honor history can bestow is the title of peacemaker. This honor now beckons America. ... This is our summons to greatness. —Richard M. Nixon, first inaugural address, Jan 20, 1969

3940. We have always said that in our war with the Arabs we had a secret weapon—no alternative. —Golda Meir, *Life*, Oct 3, 1969

3941. People do not want words—they want the sound of battle ... the battle of destiny. —Gamal Abdel Nasser, speech to the National Assembly, Jan 20, 1969

3942. We don't thrive on military acts. We do them because we have to, and thank God we are efficient. —Golda Meir, *Vogue*, Jul, 1969

3943. You will kill 10 of our men, and we will kill 1 of yours, and in the end it will be you who tire of it. —Ho Chi Minh, recalled on his death, Sep 3, 1969

3944. It is not enough just to be for peace. The point is, what can we do about it? —Richard M. Nixon, interview with C.L. Sulzberger, *The New York Times*, Mar 10, 1971

3945. That was the order of the day. —William L. Calley Jr., on killing Vietnamese civilians at My Lai in 1968, Feb 23, 1971

3946. They were all enemy. They were all to be destroyed. —William L. Calley Jr., on killing Vietnamese civilians at My Lai in 1968, Feb 23, 1971

3947. If there is any one lesson to be plainly derived from the experiences we have had with disarmament in the past half-century, it is that armaments are a function and not a cause of political tensions and that no limitation of armaments on a multilateral scale can be effected as long as the political problems are not tackled and regulated in some realistic way. —George F. Kennan, *Memoirs*, 1972

3948. The sergeant is the Army. —Dwight D. Eisenhower, *The New York Times*, Dec 24, 1972

3949. Not war but peace is the father of all things. [*Nicht der Krieg, der Friede ist der Vater aller Dinge.*] —Willy Brandt, *Über den Tag hinaus*, 1974

3950. If the Third World War is fought with nuclear weapons, the fourth will be fought with bows and arrows. —Lord Louis Mountbatten, *Maclean's*, Nov 17, 1975

3952. I don't think the contradictions between capitalism and socialism can be resolved by war. This is no longer the age of the bow and arrow. It's the nuclear age, and war can annihilate us all. The only way to achieve solutions seems to be for the different social systems to coexist. —Fidel Castro, *Seven Days*, Jun 20, 1977

3953. A war regarded as inevitable or even probable, and therefore much prepared for, has a very good chance of eventually being fought. —George F. Kennan, *The Cloud of Danger*, 1977

3954. The superpowers have the privilege of being able to destroy our planet several times in rapid succession, and yet there are still those who try to score political points by declaring that one or other of them is lagging dangerously behind the other in potential for obliteration. —Peter Ustinov, *Dear Me*, 1977

3955. Peace is much more precious than a piece of land. —Muhammad Anwar El- Sadat, speech in Cairo, Mar 8, 1978

3956. Of the four wars in my lifetime, none came about because the U.S. was too strong. —Ronald Reagan, *The Observer*, Jun 29, 1980

3957. Passive resistance is a sport for gentlemen (and ladies)—just like the pursuit of war, a heroic enterprise for the ruling classes but a grievous burden on the rest. —Kenneth Kaunda, *Kaunda on Violence*, 1980

3958. The drama can only be brought to its climax in one of two ways—through the selective brutality of terrorism or the impartial horrors of war. —Kenneth Kaunda, "On the State of South Africa", *Kaunda on Violence*, 1980

3959. War is just like bush-clearing—the moment you stop, the jungle comes back even thicker, but for a little while you can plant and grow a crop in the ground you have won at such a terrible cost. —Kenneth Kaunda, *Kaunda on Violence*, 1980

3960. Aggression unopposed becomes a contagious disease. —Jimmy Carter, televised address to the nation on the invasion of Afghanistan by the USSR, Jan 4, 1980

3961. Within the soul of each Vietnam veteran there is probably something that says "Bad war, good soldier." (It is time to) separate the war from the warrior. —Max Cleland, speech at the dedication of Vietnam Veterans Memorial, Washington D.C., *Time*, Nov 22, 1982

3962. If they've been put there to fight, there are far too few. If they've been put there to be killed, there are far too many. —Ernest F. Hollings, on U.S. Marines in Lebanon, *Time*, Dec 26, 1983

3963. The awful truth is that the use of violence for political gain has become more, not less widespread in the last decade. —Ronald Reagan, speech to the United Nations General Assembly, Sep 26, 1983

3964. Some of your countrymen were unable to distinguish between their native dislike for war and the stainless patriotism of those who suffered its scars. But there has been a rethinking (and) now we can say to you, and say as a nation, thank you for your courage. —Ronald Reagan, referring to veterans of the Vietnam War, at a press conference, Nov 11, 1984

3965. We pray for the wisdom that this hero be America's last unknown. —Ronald Reagan, on the Unknown Soldier of the Vietnam War, May 25, 1984

3966. (My job is) to give the president and secretary of defense military advice before they know they need it. —Gen. John W. Vessey Jr., *The New York Times*, Jul 15, 1984

3967. The fact that the talk may be boring or turgid or uninspiring should not cause us to forget the fact that it is preferable to war. —Henry Cabot Lodge Jr., on the United Nations, recalled on his death, Feb 27, 1985

3968. You're not here to die for your country. You're here to make those so-and-sos die for theirs. —Gen. John Michaelis, to troops fighting in Korea, recalled on his death, *Time*, Nov 11, 1985

3969. (This is) an era of violent peace. —Adm. James D. Watkins, quoted by Richard Halloran, "A Silent Battle Surfaces", *The New York Times*, Dec 7, 1986

3970. The more you sweat in peace, the less you bleed in war. —Hyman G. Rickover, 1983 retirement speech, recalled on his death, Jul 8, 1986

3971. Terrorism (takes) us back to ages we thought were long gone if we allow it a free hand to corrupt democratic societies and destroy the basic rules of international life. —Jacques Chirac, speech to the U.N. General Assembly, Sep 24, 1986

3972. Terrorism has become the systematic weapon of a war that knows no borders or seldom has a face. —Jacques Chirac, speech to the U.N. General Assembly, Sep 24, 1986

3973. The notion of a defense that will protect American cities is one that will not be achieved, but it is that goal that supplies the political magic, as it were, in the president's vision. —James R. Schlesinger, testimony to the Senate Foreign Relations Committee, *The New York Times*, Feb 7, 1987

WOMEN IN POLITICS

3974. There is no occupation concerned with the management of social affairs which belongs either to women or to men, as such ... and every occupation is open to both. —Plato, *The Republic*, ca. 390 B.C.

3975. To promote a Woman to bear rule, superiority, dominion, or empire, above any Realm, Nation, or City, is repugnant to Nature; contumely to God, a thing most contrarious to his revealed will and approved ordinance; and finally it is the subversion of good Order, of all equity and justice. —John Knox, *First Blast of the Trumpet Against the Monstrous Regiment of Women*, 1558

3976. Women have, or ought to have, but little liberty; they are apt to indulge themselves excessively in what is allowed them. —Jean Jacques Rousseau, *Emile*, 1762

3977. If particular care is not paid to the ladies, we are determined to foment a rebellion, and will not hold ourselves bound by any laws in which we have no voice, no representation. —Abigail Adams, letter to John Adams, Mar 31, 1776

3978. When man, governed by reasonable laws, enjoys his natural freedom,let him despise woman, if she do not share it with him. —Mary Wollstonecraft, *A Vindication of the Rights of Woman*, 1792

3979. His wife "ruled the roast," and in governing the governor, governed the province, which might thus be said to be under petticoat government. —Washington Irving, *Knickerbocker's History of New York*, 1809

3980. Resolved, That it is the duty of the women of this country to secure to themselves their sacred right to the elective franchise. —Elizabeth Cady Stanton, First Woman's Rights Convention, Seneca Falls, New York, Jul 19-20, 1848

3981. If the first woman God ever made was strong enough to turn the world upside down all alone, these together ought to be able to turn it back and get it right side up again, and now that they're asking to do it, the men better let them. —Sojourner Truth, speech to the Women's Rights Convention in Akron, Ohio, 1851

3982. Because the revolutionary tempest, in over-turning at the same time the throne and the scaffold, in breaking the chain of the black slave, forgot to break the chain of the most oppressed of all—of Woman, the pariah of humanity. —Jeanne-Françoise Deroin, letter from St. Lazare Prison, Jun 15, 1851

3983. We have, moreover, the profound conviction that only by the power of association based on solidarity—by the union of the working classes of both sexes to organize labor—can be acquired, completely and pacifically, the civil and political equality of women, and the social right for all. —Jeanne-Françoise Deroin, letter from St. Lazare Prison, Jun 15, 1851

3984. Women—one half the human race at least—care fifty times more for a marriage than a ministry. —Walter Bagehot, *The English Constitution*, 1867

3985. Women must not depend upon the protection of man, but must be taught to protect herself. —Susan B. Anthony, speech in San Francisco, California, Jul, 1871

3986. The ignorance and indifference of the majority of women, as to their status as citizens of a republic, is not remarkable, for history shows that the masses of all oppressed classes, in the most degraded conditions, have been stolid and apathetic until partial success had crowned the faith and enthusiasm of the few. —Elizabeth Cady Stanton, *History of Woman Suffrage*, 1881

3987. The queens in history compare favorably with the kings. —Elizabeth Cady Stanton, *History of Woman Suffrage*, 1881

3988. But when at last woman stands on an even platform with man, his acknowledged equal everywhere, with the same freedom to express herself in the religion and government of the country, then, and not until then,... will he be able to legislate as wisely and generously for her as for himself. —Elizabeth Cady Stanton, *History of Woman Suffrage*, 1881

3989. Give women the vote, and in five years there will be a crushing tax on bachelors. —George Bernard Shaw, preface, *Man and Superman*, 1902

3990. We are here, not because we are lawbreakers; we are here in our efforts to become lawmakers. —Emmeline Pankhurst, speech at her trial in London, Oct 21, 1908

3991. True, the movement for women's rights has broken many old fetters, but it has also forged new ones. —Emma Goldman, "The Tragedy of Women's Emancipation", *Anarchism and Other Essays*, 1911

3992. There is no hope even that woman, with her right to vote, will ever purify politics. —Emma Goldman, "The Tragedy of Women's Emancipation", *Anarchism and Other Essays*, 1911

3993. If we women are wrong in destroying private property in order that human values may be restored, then I say, in all reverence, that it was wrong for the Founder of Christianity to destroy private property, as He did when He lashed the money changers out the Temple and when He drove the Gadarene swine into the sea. —Emmeline Pankhurst, *My Own Story*, 1914

3994. The militancy of men, through all the centuries, has drenched the world with blood, and for these deeds of horror and destruction men have been rewarded with monuments, with great songs and epics. The militancy of women has harmed no human life save the lives of those who fought the battle of righteousness. —Emmeline Pankhurst, foreword, *My Own Story*, 1914

3995. I can conceive of nothing worse than a man-governed world— except a woman-governed world. —Nancy Astor, *My Two Countries*, 1923

3996. We're half the people; we should be half the Congress. —Jeanette Rankin, quoted, *Newsweek*, Feb 14, 1966

3997. A woman is a citizen who works for Mexico. We must not treat her differently from a man, except to honor her more. —Adolfo Lopez Mateos, *Time*, Oct 12, 1959

3998. I want to make a policy statement. I am unabashedly in favor of women. —Lyndon Baines Johnson, on appointing ten women to top government positions, Mar 4, 1964

3999. To conclude that women are unfitted to the task of our historic society seems to me the equivalent of closing male eyes to female facts. —Lyndon Baines Johnson, on swearing-in of women appointees, Apr 13, 1964

4000. Certainly in the next 50 years we shall see a woman president, perhaps sooner than you think. A woman can and should be able to do any political job that a man can do. —Richard M. Nixon, speech to the League of Women Voters, Washington, D.C., Apr 16, 1969

4001. Women's liberation, if it abolishes the patriarchal family, will abolish a necessary substructure of the authoritarian state, and once that withers away, Marx will have come true willy-nilly, so let's get on with it. —Germaine Greer, "Revolution", *The Female Eunich*, 1970

4002. Of my two "handicaps," being female put many more obstacles in my path than being black. —Shirley Chisholm, *Unbought and Unbossed*, 1970

4003. Women have been and are prejudiced, narrowminded, reactionary, even violent. Some women. They, of course, have a right to vote and a right to run for office. I will defend that right, but I will not support them or vote for them. —Bella Abzug, speech to the National Women's Political Caucus, Washington, D.C., Jul 10, 1971

4004. One of the things being in politics has taught me is that men are not a reasoned or reasonable sex. —Margaret Thatcher, BBC-radio, Jan 14, 1972

4005. I am working for the time when unqualified blacks, browns and women join the unqualified men in running our government. —Sissy Farenthold, quoted, *The Los Angeles Times*, Sep 18, 1974

4006. In politics women ... type the letters, lick the stamps, distribute the pamphlets and get out the vote. Men get elected. —Clare Boothe Luce, quoted, *Saturday Review/World*, Sep 15, 1974

4007. You can't have a Congress that responds to the needs of the workingman when there are practically no people here who represent him.. And you're not going to have a society that understands its humanity if you don't have more women in government. —Bella Abzug, quoted, "Impeachment?" by Claire Safran, *Redbook*, Apr, 1974

4008. In politics if you want anything said, ask a man. If you want anything done, ask a woman. —Margaret Thatcher, *People*, Sep 15, 1975

4009. If you had to work in the environment of Washington, D.C. as I do,and watch those men who are so imprisoned and so confined by their 18th-century thought patterns, you would know that if anybody is going to be liberated, it's men who must be liberated in this country. —Barbara Jordan, speech at the International Women's Year Conference, Austin, Texas, Nov 10, 1975

4010. There aren't many women now I'd like to see as President—but there are fewer men. —Clare Boothe Luce, *Newsweek*, Oct 22, 1979

4011. When men talk about defense, they always claim to be protecting women and children, but they never ask the women and children what they think. —Patricia Schroeder, *The New York Times Book Review*, Feb 17, 1980

4012. Party organization matters. When the door of a smoke-filled room is closed, there's hardly ever a woman inside. —Millicent Fenwick, "Sixty Minutes," CBS-TV, Feb 1, 1981

4013. Toughness doesn't have to come in a pinstripe suit. —Dianne Feinstein, *Time*, Jun 4, 1984

4014. What has the women's movement learned from (Geraldine Ferraro's) candidacy for vice president? Never get married. —Gloria Steinem, quoted, *Boston Globe*, May 14, 1987

Author Index

Numbers refer to entry numbers not page numbers.

245

Allen, Charles Grant, 1848-1899. English author
& philosopher.
  Conservatism   202, 203
Allen, George E.. American public official; head of
Reconstruction Finance Corporation, 1946-47.
  Politics   2768
Alliluyeva, Svetlana, 1926- . Russian author;
daughter of Joseph Stalin.
  Expressions and Phrases   1090
Ames, Fisher, 1758-1808. American politician;
congressman from Massachusetts, 1789-97.
  Monarchy   2345
  Politics   2684, 2685
Amiel, Henri Frederic, 1821-1881. Swiss poet &
philosopher.
  Government   1538
Amis, Kingsley, 1922- . English novelist.
  Conservatism   220
Anonymous
  Expressions and Phrases   954
  Legislatures and Legislation   2236
  Politicians and Public Officials   2649
  Reform   3130
Anouilh, Jean, 1910- . French dramatist.
  Law   1918
Anthony, Susan B., 1820-1906. American feminist
& social reformer.
  Equality   752
  Reform   3098
  Rights/Human Rights   3304, 3306, 3312
  Women in Politics   3985
Aquinas, St. Thomas, 1225-1274. Italian
theologian & philosopher.
  Law   1831
  War and Peace   3665
Arbuthnot, John, 1667-1735. Scottish physician &
author.
  Political Parties   2448
Arendt, Hannah, 1906-1975. Political philosopher.
  Freedom/Liberty   1446
  Power   2891
  Revolution   3281
Aristotle, 384-322 B.C. Greek philosopher.
  Class Divisions   34, 35
  Democracy   264, 265, 266, 267
  Equality   737
  Ethics in Politics   771
  Justice   1750
  Law   1819, 1820, 1821, 1822
  Leadership/Statesmanship   1970
  Political Parties   2442
  Politicians and Public Officials   2514
  Politics   2672
  Religion and the State   3135
  Role of the State/of Government   3404
  War and Peace   3649
**Arnim-Boytzenburg, Count Adolf
Heinrich**Prussian public official.
  Public Opinion   3045

Arnold, Matthew, 1822-1888. English poet &
critic.
  Class Divisions   66
  Democracy   354
  Equality   754
  Expressions and Phrases   906
Arnold, Thomas, 1795-1842. English historian &
classicist; headmaster of Rugby, 1828-41.
  Class Divisions   46
  Conservatism   190
Arthur, Chester Alan. American politician;
president of the United States, 1881-1885.
  War and Peace   3747
Asch, Sidney H.
  Rights/Human Rights   3399
Ashmore, Harry, 1916- . American editor &
author.
  Law   1924
Aspin, Les, 1938- . American politician;
congressman from Wisconsin, 1970-.
  Taxation and Budgets   3633
Asquith, Herbert, 1st Earl of Oxford, 1858-1928.
British politician; prime minister of the United
Kingdom, 1908-1916.
  Expressions and Phrases   929
  Leadership/Statesmanship   2103
Astor, Nancy, Viscountess Astor, 1879-1945.
British politician; member of parliament, 1919-45
(first woman member).
  Politicians and Public Officials   2578
  Women in Politics   3995
Astorga, Nora. Nicaraguan diplomat.
  International Affairs/Diplomacy   1719
Atatürk, Kemal, 1880-1938. Turkish general &
political leader; first president of Turkey, 1923-38.
  Freedom/Liberty   1388
Atkinson, Brooks, 1894-1984. American drama
critic & journalist.
  Bureaucracy   7, 8
  Leadership/Statesmanship   2147
  War and Peace   3869
Attlee, Clement, 1st Earl Attlee, 1883-1967.
British politician; prime minister of the United
Kingdom, 1945-51.
  Democracy   445
  Elections and Voting   714
Augustine, Saint, 354-430. religious figure &
philosopher.
  Justice   1755, 1756
Azuela, Mariano, 1873-1952. Mexican author.
  Revolution   3240
Babbitt, Bruce, 1938- . American politician;
governor of Arizona, 1978-87.
  Political Campaigns   2440
Babbitt, Irving, 1865-1933. American author &
critic.
  Democracy   395

Bacon, Sir Francis, 1st Viscount St. Albans, 1561-1626. English statesman & philosopher.
   International Affairs/Diplomacy   1604
   Judiciary and Judges   1723
   Justice   1759
   Leadership/Statesmanship   1989, 1990, 1991
   Monarchy   2330
   Politics   2674
   Power   2833
   Reform   3082
   Revolution   3186
   Role of the State/of Government   3407, 3408
   War and Peace   3674, 3675, 3676, 3677
Bagehot, Walter, 1826-1877. British banker, editor & economist.
   Democracy   349
   International Affairs/Diplomacy   1625
   Leadership/Statesmanship   2061, 2062
   Monarchy   2352, 2353
   Politics   2703
   Women in Politics   3984
Bailey, F. Lee, 1933- . American lawyer & author.
   Constitution   246
Baker, Howard H., Jr., 1925- . American politician; senator from Tennessee, 1966-85.
   Presidency   3015
Baker, Russell, 1925- . American journalist & author.
   Power   2889
Bakunin, Michael
   Equality   753
   Freedom/Liberty   1306, 1307
   Government and Business   1582
   Politics   2707, 2708
   Revolution   3222, 3223, 3224
   Role of the State/of Government   3454
   War and Peace   3739
Baldwin, James, 1924-1987. American author, dramatist, essayist.
   Freedom/Liberty   1435
Baldwin, Roger N., 1884-1981. American social reformer; a founder of the American Civil Liberties Union & director, 1920-50.
   Democracy   491
Baldwin, Stanley, 1st Earl Baldwin of Bewdley, 1867-1937. British politician; prime minister of the United Kingdom, 1923, 1924-29, 1935-37.
   Democracy   492
   Education   690
   Freedom of the Press   1176
   Legislatures and Legislation   2252
   Nationalism   2379
   Political Parties   2496
   Politics   2761
   Socialism   3560
Balfour, Arthur, 1st Earl of Balfour, 1848-1930. British politician; prime minister of the United Kingdom, 1902-06.
   Democracy   397
   Leadership/Statesmanship   2108

Balzac, Honoré de, 1799-1850. French novelist.
   Democracy   318
Bancroft, George, 1800-1891. American historian.
   Democracy   320
Barère de Vieuzac, Bertrand, 1755-1841. French revolutionary.
   Revolution   3193, 3195
Barkley, Alben W., 1877-1956. American politician; vice-president of the United States, 1948-52.
   Political Campaigns   2429
   Politics   2774
Barrès, Maurice, 1896-1923. French author.
   Politicians and Public Officials   2581
Barth, Alan, 1906- . American writer.
   Prejudice and Discrimination   2919
Baruch, Bernard, 1870-1965. American businessman; adviser to presidents.
   Dictatorship/Tyranny   612
   Elections and Voting   716
   Expressions and Phrases   983
   Government   1569
   Leadership/Statesmanship   2180
Batista, Fulgencio, 1901-1973. Dictator of Cuba, 1952-59.
   War and Peace   3897
Baudouin I, 1930- . king of the Belgians, 1951-.
   War and Peace   3900
Beauvoir, Simone de, 1908-1986. French feminist & author.
   Freedom/Liberty   1394
Bebel, August, 1840-1913. German socialist & writer.
   Politics   2705, 2729
   Prejudice and Discrimination   2906
   War and Peace   3740
Beecher, Henry Ward, 1813-1887. American clergyman & social reformer.
   Conservatism   201
   Democracy   360, 361
   Dictatorship/Tyranny   576
   Freedom/Liberty   1318
   Government   1546
   Law   1893, 1894
   Leadership/Statesmanship   2081
   Public Opinion   3057, 3058
   Treason   3639
   War and Peace   3753
Beerbohm, Sir Max, 1872-1956. English critic, essayist & novelist.
   Justice   1801
   Leadership/Statesmanship   2110, 2143
Behan, Brendan, 1923-1964. Irish dramatist & author.
   War and Peace   3896
Bellamy, Carol
   Expressions and Phrases   1096
Benét, Stephen Vincent, 1898-1943. American poet & author.
   Power   2870

Bengough, John, 1851-1923. Canadian poet & political cartoonist.
  Political Parties   2487
Benn, Anthony Wedgwood, 1925- . British politician; member of parliament, 1950-60, 1963-83, 1984-.
  Class Divisions   112, 113
  Monarchy   2363
Bentham, Jeremy, 1748-1832. British philosopher.
  Democracy   289
  Dictatorship/Tyranny   554
  Justice   1772
  Reform   3090, 3093
Bentsen, Lloyd, 1921- . American politician; senator from Texas, 1971-.
  Economics/The Economy   663
  Political Campaigns   2441
Berlin, Sir Isaiah, 1909- . British philosopher & historian.
  Prejudice and Discrimination   2918
Bernanos, Georges, 1888-1948. French novelist & essayist.
  Expressions and Phrases   956, 1005
  Freedom/Liberty   1421
Berryman, Clifford K., 1869-1949. American editorial cartoonist.
  Expressions and Phrases   919
Bevan, Aneurin, 1897-1960. British Labour Party leader.
  Communism   139
  Conservatism   218
  Democracy   456, 467
  Dictatorship/Tyranny   607
  Leadership/Statesmanship   2149
  Legislatures and Legislation   2255
  Power   2873
  Socialism   3571
  War and Peace   3835
Bevin, Ernest. British labor leader & politician; foreign secretary, 1945-51.
  Class Divisions   96
  Freedom/Liberty   1380
  International Affairs/Diplomacy   1657
Beza, Theodore, 1519-1605. French religious reformer.
  War and Peace   3669
Bible
  Ethics in Politics   770
  Expressions and Phrases   826
  Freedom/Liberty   1198
  International Affairs/Diplomacy   1602
  Law   1827
  Religion and the State   3136
  Revolution   3183
  War and Peace   3650, 3660
Bickel, Alexander M., 1924-1974. American lawyer & legal scholar.
  Judiciary and Judges   1744

Bierce, Ambrose, 1842-1914. American author & journalist.
  Conservatism   207
  Elections and Voting   709
  Expressions and Phrases   925
  Freedom/Liberty   1331, 1332
  International Affairs/Diplomacy   1634, 1635
  Monarchy   2357
  Politicians and Public Officials   2566, 2567
  Politics   2724, 2725, 2730
  Presidency   2964
  Reform   3111
  Revolution   3230, 3231, 3232
  Taxation and Budgets   3605
  War and Peace   3762, 3765
Biko, Steve, 1947-1977. South African black nationalist & activist.
  Dictatorship/Tyranny   623
  Prejudice and Discrimination   2941, 2944
  Rights/Human Rights   3384
Billings, Josh, (Henry Wheeler Shaw), 1818-1885. American humorist author.
  Expressions and Phrases   900
Bismarck, Prince Otto von, 1815-1898. German statesman; chancellor of Germany, 1870-90.
  Bureaucracy   2
  Democracy   356
  Expressions and Phrases   894, 905
  Government   1545
  International Affairs/Diplomacy   1626
  Law   1890
  Leadership/Statesmanship   2074
  Majority and Minorities   2300
  Monarchy   2351
  Politics   2700, 2701, 2702, 2704, 2717
  Public Opinion   3050
  Role of the State/of Government   3458
  Taxation and Budgets   3599
  War and Peace   3742
Black, Henry Campbell, 1860-1927. American legal author & editor.
  Revolution   3235
Black, Hugo L., 1886-1971. American jurist; justice of the Supreme Court, 1937-71.
  Constitution   249, 250, 251
  Freedom of Speech   1141, 1144, 1145
  Freedom of the Press   1189, 1190, 1191
  Rights/Human Rights   3356
Blackmun, Harry A., 1908- . American jurist; justice of the Supreme Court, 1970-.
  Constitution   252
  Freedom of Speech   1150
  Law   1948
  Majority and Minorities   2322
  Rights/Human Rights   3401, 3402, 3403
Blackstone, Sir William, 1723-1780. British judge & author.
  Justice   1768
  Monarchy   2342, 2343

Rights/Human Rights 3292
Separation of Powers 3505
Blake, William, 1757-1827. English poet & artist.
Religion and the State 3144
Blanc, Louis, 1811-1882. French socialist theorist & author.
Communism 115
Role of the State/of Government 3444
Block, Herbert, "Herblock", 1909- . American political cartoonist.
War and Peace 3930
Blücher, Gebhard Leberecht von, 1742-1819. Prussian general.
War and Peace 3711
Blum, Leon, 1872-1950. French politician; premier of France, 1936-38.
Socialism 3559, 3563
Bodin, Jean, 1530-1596. French political philosopher.
Law 1837
Monarchy 2324
Bohlen, Charles E., 1904-1974. American diplomat.
Communism 170
Bok, Derek, 1930. American educator; president of Harvard Univ., 1971-.
Law 1957
Bolt, Robert, 1924- . English dramatist.
Law 1931
Leadership/Statesmanship 2186
Boothby, Robert, Baron, 1900-1986. British politician; member of parliament, 1924-58.
Bureaucracy 4
Bork, Robert H., 1927- . American lawyer & judge.
Constitution 260
Law 1958
Bosquet, Pierre, 1810-1861. French general.
War and Peace 3727
Bowles, Chester, 1901-1986. American diplomat.
Liberalism 2272
Bradley, Omar N., 1893-1981. American military leader.
War and Peace 3862
Bragg, Edward Stuyvesant, 1827-1912. American politician.
Expressions and Phrases 912
Brandeis, Louis D., 1856-1941. American jurist; justice of Supreme Court, 1916-41.
Democracy 425
Freedom of Speech 1127
Freedom/Liberty 1359, 1361
Law 1914
Revolution 3246
Rights/Human Rights 3339
Separation of Powers 3510

Brandt, Willy, 1913- . German politician; mayor of West Berlin, 1957-66; chancellor of Fed. Rep. of Germany, 1969-74.
Politics 2782
War and Peace 3949
Brecht, Bertolt, 1898-1956. German dramatist & poet.
Class Divisions 95
Law 1915
Leadership/Statesmanship 2139
War and Peace 3824
Brennan, William J., Jr., 1906- . American jurist; justice of the Supreme Court, 1956-.
Constitution 259
Prejudice and Discrimination 2946
Brennan Jr., William J.
Constitution 258
Breslin, Jimmy, 1930- . American journalist.
Politics 2825
Brezhnev, Leonid, 1906-1982. Russian communist leader; general secretary of the Communist Party of the Soviet Union, 1906-1982.
Communism 174
Bright, John, 1811-1889. English public official & author.
Expressions and Phrases 887, 901, 907
War and Peace 3726
Brinkley, David, 1920- . American television journalist.
Expressions and Phrases 1028
Brodie, Fawn M., 1915-1981. American biographer.
Politicians and Public Officials 2642
Brougham, Henry, Baron Brougham, 1778-1868. British jurist & politician; chancellor of the exchequer, 1830-34.
Education 676
Leadership/Statesmanship 2042
Broun, Heywood, 1888-1939. American journalist & author.
Expressions and Phrases 957
Freedom of Speech 1124, 1125
Leadership/Statesmanship 2112
Reform 3120
Brown, George, 1914-1985. British politician; member of parliament, 1945-70; deputy leader of Labour party, 1960-70.
Expressions and Phrases 1050
Brown, John Mason, 1900-1969. American critic & lecturer.
Expressions and Phrases 1009
Brown, Rita Mae, 1944- . American author.
Rights/Human Rights 3394
Browne, Sir Thomas, 1605-1682. English physician & author.
Expressions and Phrases 830
Brownson, Orestes Augustus, 1803-1876. American author & editor.
Class Divisions 48

Bryan, William Jennings, 1860-1925. American politician & lawyer; secretary of state, 1913-15.
  Class Divisions   81
  Democracy   369
  Economics/The Economy   639
  Expressions and Phrases   917
Bryce, James, Viscount Bryce, 1838-1922. British diplomat & historian; ambassador to the United States, 1907-13.
  Constitution   240
  Law   1895
  Politicians and Public Officials   2579
Buck, Pearl S., 1892-1973. American novelist.
  Freedom/Liberty   1386, 1387
  Prejudice and Discrimination   2915, 2916
  Public Opinion   3075
Bulwer-Lytton, Edward George, 1st Baron Lytton, 1803-1873. English author.
  Power   2853
  Revolution   3220
Burger, Warren E., 1907- . American jurist; chief justice of the Supreme Court, 1969-86.
  Constitution   248
  Freedom of Speech   1154
  Law   1963
  Majority and Minorities   2317
  Presidency   3020
Burke, Adm. Arleigh, 1901- . American naval officer.
  War and Peace   3902
Burke, Edmund, 1729-1797. British orator, author & politician; member of parliament, 1765-94.
  Class Divisions   41
  Democracy   290
  Dictatorship/Tyranny   537, 538, 544
  Ethics in Politics   776
  Expressions and Phrases   838, 842, 845
  Freedom/Liberty   1221, 1222, 1229, 1230, 1232, 1244
  Government   1494, 1495
  Justice   1773
  Law   1864, 1872
  Leadership/Statesmanship   2018, 2021, 2024
  Legislatures and Legislation   2221
  Political Parties   2450, 2451, 2452
  Politicians and Public Officials   2527, 2530
  Power   2838, 2839
  Reform   3085
  Role of the State/of Government   3427, 3430
  Taxation and Budgets   3580, 3584
  War and Peace   3707
Burns, George, 1896- . American comedian.
  Leadership/Statesmanship   2202
Burton, Robert, 1577-1640. English author.
  Law   1843
Bush, George, 1924- . American politician; president of the United States, 1989-.
  Expressions and Phrases   1104, 1105
  Freedom/Liberty   1474

  Politics   2831
  Role of the State/of Government   3503
  Taxation and Budgets   3635
Busia, Kofi, 1913-1978. Ghanaian politician; prime minister of Ghana, 1969-72.
  International Affairs/Diplomacy   1700, 1701
Butler, Samuel, 1835-1902. English novelist.
  Conservatism   208
  Justice   1797
Butler (1), Samuel, 1612-1680. English satirist.
  Freedom/Liberty   1204
Byrnes, James F.. American public official; secretary of state, 1945-47.
  Bureaucracy   6
Calhoun, John C., 1782-1850. American politician; congressman, secretary of war, vice-president, senator, secretary of state.
  Democracy   321
  Expressions and Phrases   865
  Freedom/Liberty   1268
Calley, William L., Jr., 1943- . American army lieutenant during Vietnam War.
  War and Peace   3945, 3946
Cameron, Simon, 1799-1889. American politician; secretary of war, 1861-62.
  Politicians and Public Officials   2551
Campbell-Bannerman, Sir Henry, 1836-1908. British politician; prime minister of the United Kingdom, 1905-1908.
  Politics   2731
Camus, Albert, 1913-1960. French author & philosopher.
  Dictatorship/Tyranny   608
  Freedom of the Press   1186
  Politics   2759
  Revolution   3262
  War and Peace   3838
Canning, George, 1770-1827. English politician & orator; foreign secretary, 1807-09, 1822; prime minister, Apr, 1827.
  Expressions and Phrases   860
Cannon, Joseph G., 1836-1926. American politician; speaker of the House of Representatives, 1903-11.
  Environment   732
  Expressions and Phrases   942
  Legislatures and Legislation   2245
  Majority and Minorities   2308
  Political Parties   2493
Caplin, Mortimer. American civil servant; commissioner, Internal Revenue Service.
  Taxation and Budgets   3619
Cardozo, Benjamin N., 1870-1938. American jurist; justice of the Supreme Court, 1932-38.
  Freedom of Speech   1130
  Role of the State/of Government   3474
Carlile, Richard, 1790-1843. English journalist & reformer.
  Freedom of Speech   1111

Chiles, Lawton M., Jr., 1930- . American politician; senator from Florida, 1971-89.
  Ethics in Politics 814
Chirac, Jacques, 1932- . French politician; prime minister of France, 1974-76, 1986-88.
  War and Peace 3971, 3972
Chisholm, Shirley, 1924- . American politician; congresswoman from New York, 1968-82.
  Democracy 479
  Ethics in Politics 813
  Liberalism 2277
  Politicians and Public Officials 2638
  Politics 2798
  Women in Politics 4002
Choate, Rufus, 1799-1859. American lawyer & politician.
  Role of the State/of Government 3445
Chou En-lai, 1898-1976. Chinese communist leader; premier of China, 1949-76.
  International Affairs/Diplomacy 1662
Church, Frank, 1924-1984. American politician; senator from Idaho, 1956-81.
  Presidency 3022
  Separation of Powers 3514
Churchill, Sir Winston S., 1874-1965. British statesman; prime minister of the United Kingdom, 1940-45, 1952-54.
  Communism 149, 150
  Conservatism 217
  Democracy 426, 432, 441
  Dictatorship/Tyranny 598, 602, 605
  Economics/The Economy 659
  Expressions and Phrases 959, 965, 966, 967, 969, 970, 971, 972, 973, 975, 976, 987, 997, 998, 1011, 1093
  Freedom of Speech 1131
  Leadership/Statesmanship 2132, 2133, 2136
  Politics 2736, 2765
  Public Opinion 3073, 3074
  Socialism 3567, 3569
  War and Peace 3757, 3819, 3820, 3826, 3827, 3828, 3829, 3834, 3836, 3842, 3852, 3856, 3866, 3881, 3882
Ciano, Count Galeazzo, 1903-44. Italian politician; foreign minister, 1936-43.
  Expressions and Phrases 974
Cicero, Marcus Tullius, 106-43 B.C. Roman orator, statesman & philosopher.
  Equality 738
  Freedom/Liberty 1199
  Justice 1752, 1753
  Leadership/Statesmanship 1971
  Politicians and Public Officials 2515
  War and Peace 3652, 3653, 3654, 3655, 3656
  Law 1824
Clark, Joseph, 1901- . American politician; senator from Pennsylvania, 1956-69.
  Leadership/Statesmanship 2207

Clark, Ramsey, 1927- . American politician; Attorney General, 1967-69.
  Constitution 247
  Democratic Party 513
  Rights/Human Rights 3386
Clarke, James Freeman, 1810-1888. American clergyman & writer.
  Leadership/Statesmanship 2058
Clausewitz, Karl von, 1780-1831. Prussian military leader & author.
  War and Peace 3716, 3717, 3718
Clay, Henry, 1777-1852. American politician & orator.
  Constitution 236
  Democracy 315
  Patriotism 2401
  Power 2854
  Presidency 2956
  Religion and the State 3145
  Revolution 3196
Cleaver, Eldridge, 1935- . American author & political activist.
  Expressions and Phrases 1055
Cleland, Max American public official; head of the Veterans Administration, 1977-80.
  War and Peace 3961
Clemenceau, Georges, 1841-1929. French statesman; premier of France, 1917-20.
  War and Peace 3785, 3786, 3787
Cleveland, Grover, 1837-1908. American politician; president of the United States, 1885-89, 1893-97.
  Class Divisions 76
  Leadership/Statesmanship 2082
  Politicians and Public Officials 2556
  Presidency 2962
  Role of the State/of Government 3459, 3460, 3463
  Taxation and Budgets 3603
Clifford, Clark M., 1906- . American lawyer & public official.
  Expressions and Phrases 1054
Cobbett, William, 1762-1835. English journalist & author.
  Politicians and Public Officials 2531
Coke, Sir Edward, 1552-1634. English judge.
  Law 1844
Colbert, Jean Baptiste, 1619-1683. French public official.
  Taxation and Budgets 3577
Colby, Frank Moore, 1865-1925. American educator & essayist.
  Prejudice and Discrimination 2910
Cole, George Douglas, 1889-1959. English economist & historian.
  Elections and Voting 715
  Freedom/Liberty 1409

Coleridge, Samuel Taylor, 1772-1834. English author, poet & critic.
  Freedom/Liberty   1249, 1250
  Government   1514
  Patriotism   2399
  Power   2845
  Reform   3089
  Religion and the State   3147
  Rights/Human Rights   3299
  Role of the State/of Government   3436
Colton, Charles Caleb, 1780-1832. English clergyman, sportsman & author.
  Law   1878
  Legislatures and Legislation   2230
  Politics   2687
  Power   2847, 2848
  Reform   3092
  Revolution   3198
  Role of the State/of Government   3437
  War and Peace   3715
Conable, Barber B., Jr., 1922- . American politician & public official; New York congressman, 1964-84; president, World Bank 1986-.
  Legislatures and Legislation   2261, 2262, 2263
Conant, James Bryant, 1893-1978. American educator.
  Democracy   443
  Freedom/Liberty   1400
Confucius, 551-479 B.C. Chinese philosopher.
  Education   664
  Freedom of Speech   1106
  Government   1476, 1477, 1478
  Leadership/Statesmanship   1968
  War and Peace   3647
Connolly, James, 1870-1916. Irish labor leader.
  Revolution   3238
Conrad, Joseph, 1857-1924. English author.
  Leadership/Statesmanship   2087, 2094
  Treason   3640
Constant de Rebecque, Benjamin, 1767-1830. French author & politician.
  Legislatures and Legislation   2228
  Political Parties   2460
Coolidge, Calvin, 1872-1933. American politician; president of the United States, 1923-1929.
  Class Divisions   91
  Conservatism   209
  Constitution   241
  Democracy   384, 393
  Economics/The Economy   644, 646
  Expressions and Phrases   947
  Freedom/Liberty   1354, 1356
  Government and Business   1589, 1590, 1591
  International Affairs/Diplomacy   1644
  Law   1912
  Patriotism   2414
  Politicians and Public Officials   2587
  Politics   2743

  Presidency   2970, 2971, 2972, 2973
  Reform   3119
  Rights/Human Rights   3332, 3333
  Taxation and Budgets   3606, 3608, 3609
  War and Peace   3795, 3796, 3798
Cooper, James Fenimore, 1789-1851. American author.
  Public Opinion   3044
Corneille, Pierre, 1606-1684. French dramatist.
  Expressions and Phrases   829
Cosby, Bill, 1937- . American actor & comedian.
  Leadership/Statesmanship   2198
Coughlin, Father Charles E., 1891-1974. American priest & radio commentator.
  Democracy   413
Cousins, Norman, 1912- . American editor.
  War and Peace   3875
Cowper, William, 1731-1800. English poet.
  Leadership/Statesmanship   2020
Cox, Archibald, 1912- . American lawyer.
  Law   1947
Cox, Harvey G., Jr., 1929- . American theologian & social reformer.
  Rights/Human Rights   3372
Crane, Nathalia, 1913- . American poet.
  Leadership/Statesmanship   2114
Cressey, Donald R., 1919- . American criminologist & sociologist.
  Law   1954
Croce, Benedetto, 1866-1952. Italian philosopher.
  Freedom/Liberty   1376
  Politics   2744
Crockett, David, 1786-1836. American frontiersman & politician.
  Expressions and Phrases   872
Croker, John Wilson, 1780-1857. British politician.
  Political Parties   2461, 2462, 2464
  Politicians and Public Officials   2537
  Public Opinion   3043
Cromwell, Oliver, 1599-1658. English military & political leader; Lord Protector, 1653-58.
  Leadership/Statesmanship   1994
  Politicians and Public Officials   2518
Crosland, Anthony, 1918-1977. British politician; foreign secretary, 1976-77.
  Socialism   3572
Crossman, Richard, 1907-1974. British politician & author.
  Legislatures and Legislation   2256
  Political Parties   2501, 2503
  Politicians and Public Officials   2598, 2605, 2614
  Revolution   3254
  Socialism   3573, 3574
Crummell, Alexander, 1819-1898. American missionary.
  Democracy   365
  Expressions and Phrases   909
  Rights/Human Rights   3318, 3319

Culbertson, Ely, 1891-1955. American author & bridge player; invented contract bridge.
Politics 2764
Cuomo, Mario, 1932- . American politician; governor of New York, 1982-.
Freedom of the Press 1197
Political Campaigns 2437
Politicians and Public Officials 2670
Presidency 3033
Public Opinion 3081
Curran, John Philpot, 1750-1817. Irish politician & orator.
Freedom/Liberty 1241
Curtis, Charles P., 1891-1959. American lawyer, author & educator.
Prejudice and Discrimination 2923
Danton, Georges Jacques, 1759-1794. French revolutionary.
Expressions and Phrases 847
Patriotism 2395
Revolution 3194
Darrow, Clarence S., 1857-1938. American lawyer & writer.
Freedom/Liberty 1328
Davies, Robertson, 1913- . Canadian novelist.
Politicians and Public Officials 2663
Davis, Angela Yvonne, 1944- . American author & political activist.
Freedom/Liberty 1461, 1463, 1467
Justice 1815
Davis, Elmer, 1890-1958. American writer & commentator.
Leadership/Statesmanship 2151
Davis, Jefferson, 1808-1889. American politician; president of the Confederate States of America, 1861-65.
Expressions and Phrases 892
Dawkins, John, 1947- . Australian politician; member, House of Representatives, 1974-.
Politicians and Public Officials 2665
Day, Clarence, 1874-1935. American essayist & humorist.
Rights/Human Rights 3334
De Gaulle, Charles, 1890-1970. French military leader & statesman; president of France, 1959-69.
Expressions and Phrases 1003, 1049
Government 1571
International Affairs/Diplomacy 1675, 1677
Leadership/Statesmanship 2125, 2126, 2131, 2154, 2155, 2156, 2157, 2166, 2182, 2183, 2185
Nationalism 2383, 2386
Politicians and Public Officials 2624
War and Peace 3885, 3913, 3937
Dean, John, 1938- . American lawyer & public official; counsel to the president, 1971-73.
Presidency 3008, 3021
Debray, Régis, 1940- . French author & public official.
Communism 173

Debs, Eugene V., 1855-1926. American socialist leader.
Freedom/Liberty 1351
Majority and Minorities 2307
Socialism 3556
Decatur, Stephen, 1779-1820. American naval officer.
Patriotism 2398
Defoe, Daniel, 1661-1731. English author.
Dictatorship/Tyranny 530
Monarchy 2338
Deighton, Len, 1929- . English novelist.
Politicians and Public Officials 2662
Delacroix, Eugene, 1798-1863. French artist.
Reform 3099
Deng Xiaoping, 1904- . Chinese political leader.
Communism 184
Presidency 3034
Derby, 14th Earl of, (Edward Stanley), 1799-1869. British politician; prime minister of United Kingdom, 1852, 1858-59,1866-68.
Expressions and Phrases 902
International Affairs/Diplomacy 1624
Political Parties 2467
Deroin, Jeanne-Françoise, 1805-1894. French feminist.
Rights/Human Rights 3301
Women in Politics 3982, 3983
Devlin, Patrick, 1905- . British jurist.
Public Opinion 3078
Dewey, John, 1859-1952. American educator & philosopher.
Democracy 382
Education 685
Freedom/Liberty 1367
Diaz Ordaz, Gustavo, 1911-1979. Mexican politician; president of Mexico, 1964-70.
Leadership/Statesmanship 2178
Dickens, Charles, 1812-1870. English author.
Law 1881
Politicians and Public Officials 2547
Dickinson, Goldsworthy Lowes, 1862-1932. British essayist, pacifist & philosopher.
Majority and Minorities 2305
Dickinson, John, 1732-1808. American politician & revolutionary leader.
Freedom/Liberty 1216
Taxation and Budgets 3579
Diderot, Denis, 1713-1784. French philosopher & editor.
Dictatorship/Tyranny 545
Expressions and Phrases 836
Law 1874
Disraeli, Benjamin, 1st Earl of Beaconsfield, 1804-1881. British author & statesman; prime minister of the United Kingdom 1868,1874-80.
Class Divisions 51, 52
Conservatism 189, 193, 194, 196
Democracy 313

Education   681
Elections and Voting   700
Expressions and Phrases   871, 877, 889, 899, 903
Government   1543
International Affairs/Diplomacy   1622, 1623, 1627
Justice   1785
Leadership/Statesmanship   2053, 2075
Legislatures and Legislation   2238
Nationalism   2368
Political Parties   2469, 2470, 2471, 2473, 2478, 2480
Politicians and Public Officials   2542, 2554
Politics   2698
Public Opinion   3054
Role of the State/of Government   3455, 3457
Taxation and Budgets   3598
War and Peace   3728
Djilas, Milovan, 1911- . Yugoslav Communist leader & writer.
Communism   160, 181
Dole, Robert J., 1923- . American politician; senator from Kansas, 1968-.
Presidency   3030
Donnelly, Ignatius, 1831-1901. American politician & author.
Democratic Party   501
Dostoevsky, Fyodor, 1821-1881. Russian novelist.
Dictatorship/Tyranny   570
Douglas, Helen Gahagan, 1900-1980. American singer & politician; congresswoman from California, 1945-51.
Elections and Voting   721
Douglas, Norman, 1868-1952. Scottish author.
Majority and Minorities   2306
Douglas, Stephen A., 1813-1861. American politician; senator from Illinois, 1847-61.
Political Parties   2476
Douglas, Thomas, 1904-1986. Canadian clergyman & politician; premier of Saskatchewan, 1944-61;leader, New Democrats, 1961-71.
Expressions and Phrases   1047
Douglas, William O., 1898-1980. American jurist; justice of Supreme Court, 1939-75.
Constitution   256
Freedom of Speech   1137, 1153
Freedom/Liberty   1414, 1417, 1469
Judiciary and Judges   1734, 1742
Law   1925
Prejudice and Discrimination   2943
Revolution   3282
Rights/Human Rights   3371
Role of the State/of Government   3482, 3491
Douglas-Home, Sir Alec. British politician; prime minister of the United Kingdom, 1963-64.
Expressions and Phrases   1045
International Affairs/Diplomacy   1698

Douglass, Frederick, 1817-1895. American lecturer & author; a leading abolitionist.
Class Divisions   75
Dictatorship/Tyranny   563, 569
Education   678, 683
Equality   748
Expressions and Phrases   878, 879
Freedom/Liberty   1266, 1278, 1279, 1280
Nationalism   2370
Prejudice and Discrimination   2899, 2900
Republican Party   3167, 3166
Rights/Human Rights   3308, 3311, 3315, 3316
Dryden, John, 1631-1700. English poet & dramatist.
Democracy   274
Dictatorship/Tyranny   528
Monarchy   2335
Du Bois, W.E.B., 1868-1963. American author & social reformer.
Class Divisions   83
Dictatorship/Tyranny   586, 596
Economics/The Economy   647
Expressions and Phrases   923, 944, 1014
Freedom/Liberty   1335, 1336, 1402
Prejudice and Discrimination   2908, 2909
Rights/Human Rights   3325
Du Bos, Charles, 1882-1939. French critic.
Equality   760
Dubček, Alexander, 1921- . Czech political leader; leader of Czech Communist Party, 1968-69.
Communism   175
Duffy, Father Francis P., 1871-1932. American priest.
War and Peace   3804
Dukakis, Michael. American politician; governor of Massachusetts, 1975-79, 1983-.
Elections and Voting   727
Dulles, John Foster, 1888-1959. American lawyer & public official; secretary of state, 1953-59.
War and Peace   3825, 3888
Dunne, Finley Peter, 1867-1936. American humorist, author & editor.
Democratic Party   502
Elections and Voting   710
Expressions and Phrases   921, 922
Government and Business   1583
Judiciary and Judges   1730
Justice   1794, 1796
Legislatures and Legislation   2242
Monarchy   2356
Presidency   2965
Reform   3108, 3110
Republican Party   3168
Durant, Will, 1885-1981. American historian.
War and Peace   3931
Dworkin, Ronald D., 1931- . American author & legal scholar.
Law   1960, 1961

Eastman, Max, 1883-1969. American writer &
editor.
   Communism   162
   Freedom/Liberty   1419
   Liberalism   2270
Eban, Abba, 1915- . Israeli diplomat.
   Expressions and Phrases   1052
   International Affairs/Diplomacy   1692
Eden, Anthony, 1st Earl of Avon, 1897-1977.
British politician; foreign secretary, 1935-38, 1940-
45, 1951-55; prime minister, 1955-57.
   Democracy   398
   War and Peace   3909
Edison, Thomas Alva, 1847-1931. American
inventor.
   War and Peace   3776
Edward I, 1274-1307. king of England, 1239-1307.
   Democracy   269
Ehrenburg, Ilya, 1891-1967. Russian author.
   Public Opinion   3079
Ehrlichman, John, 1925. American public official
& author; assistant to the president, 1969-74.
   Expressions and Phrases   1062
Einstein, Albert, 1879-1955. American physicist.
   Citizenship   25
   Democracy   451
   Freedom of Speech   1133
   Freedom/Liberty   1405, 1408
   Nationalism   2377
   War and Peace   3844, 3871
Eisenhower, Dwight D., 1890-1969. American
military leader & politician; president of the
United States, 1953-61.
   Bureaucracy   9
   Citizenship   27, 28
   Democracy   437, 439, 442, 466
   Dictatorship/Tyranny   610
   Equality   764
   Expressions and Phrases   966, 999, 1012, 1016
   Freedom of Speech   1135, 1136
   Freedom of the Press   1180
   Freedom/Liberty   1390, 1399, 1426, 1427
   International Affairs/Diplomacy   1658, 1659,
1665, 1666, 1669
   Justice   1805
   Law   1923, 1926, 1927
   Political Campaigns   2430
   Politicians and Public Officials   2599
   Politics   2784
   Presidency   2990, 2991, 2996
   Socialism   3570
   Taxation and Budgets   3618
   War and Peace   3843, 3848, 3860, 3861, 3867,
3876, 3877, 3880, 3884, 3887, 3895, 3898, 3904,
3932, 3948
Eliot, Charles William, 1834-1926. American
educator; president of Harvard Univ., 1869-1909.
   Public Opinion   3051

Eliot, George, (Mary Ann Evans), 1819-1880.
English novelist.
   Elections and Voting   705
Eliot, T.S., 1888-1965. English poet & critic.
   Class Divisions   100
   Democracy   446
   Dictatorship/Tyranny   604
   Leadership/Statesmanship   2160
   War and Peace   3851
Elizabeth I, 1533-1603. queen of England, 1558-
1603.
   Leadership/Statesmanship   1981
Elizabeth II, 1926- . queen of United Kingdom,
1952-.
   Democracy   460
   Expressions and Phrases   1075
   Leadership/Statesmanship   2197
   Monarchy   2361
Ellington, Edward Kennedy, "Duke", 1899-1974.
American musician.
   Freedom/Liberty   1457
Elliott, Ebenezer, 1781-1849. English merchant &
poet.
   Communism   114
   Democracy   314
Ellis, Havelock, 1859-1939. English psychologist.
   Leadership/Statesmanship   2078
Emerson, Ralph Waldo, 1803-1882. American
essayist, poet & philosopher.
   Conservatism   192, 195
   Democracy   328, 338, 339
   Ethics in Politics   785
   Expressions and Phrases   873, 875
   Freedom/Liberty   1270, 1305
   Law   1883, 1884
   Leadership/Statesmanship   2047, 2048, 2049,
2067
   Patriotism   2400
   Political Parties   2463, 2465
   Power   2858
   Reform   3096
   Religion and the State   3152
   Revolution   3208, 3209
   Role of the State/of Government   3441, 3448
   Taxation and Budgets   3597
   War and Peace   3750, 3751
Engels, Friedrich, 1820-1895. German political
theorist.
   Class Divisions   50, 77
   Communism   117, 126, 127
   Political Parties   2485
Epicurus, 342-270 B.C. Greek philosopher.
   Justice   1751
Erasmus, Desiderius, 1469-1536. Dutch
philosopher & scholar.
   War and Peace   3666
Erikson, Erik H., 1902- . American psychoanalyst.
   Freedom/Liberty   1407

Ervin, Sam, 1896-1985. American politician; senator from North Carolina, 1954-74.
  Democracy   482
  Presidency   3012
Euripides, 480-406 B.C. Greek dramatist.
  Expressions and Phrases   824
  Freedom of Speech   1107
  War and Peace   3648
Evans, Rowland, Jr., 1921- . American journalist.
  Political Campaigns   2434
Faber, Harold, 1919- . American journalist & author.
  Law   1943
Fairless, Benjamin F., 1890-1962. American philanthropist.
  Judiciary and Judges   1733
Falkland, 2nd Viscount, (Lucius Cary), 1610-43. English author & politician; secretary of state, 1642-43.
  Conservatism   187
Farenthold, Sissy, 1926- . American educator & politician.
  Women in Politics   4005
Farley, James A., 1888-1976. American political leader & business executive.
  Politics   2787
Farouk I, 1920-1965. king of Egypt, 1936-52.
  Monarchy   2360
Faulkner, William, 1897-1962. American author.
  Equality   768
  Freedom/Liberty   1423
Fawkes, Guy, 1570-1606. English soldier & political conspirator.
  Revolution   3185
Fayau, Joseph-Pierre, 1766-1799. French revolutionary.
  Freedom/Liberty   1247
Fein, Esther B.. American journalist.
  International Affairs/Diplomacy   1717
Feinstein, Dianne, 1933- . American politician; mayor of San Francisco, 1978-86.
  Women in Politics   4013
Fenwick, Millicent American politician & diplomat; congresswoman from New Jersey, 1975-83; ambassador to FAO, 1983-87.
  Politicians and Public Officials   2654
  Women in Politics   4012
Fillmore, Millard, 1800-1874. American politician; president of the United States, 1850-52.
  Freedom/Liberty   1273, 1274
Filmer, Sir Robert, 1590-1653. English author & political theorist.
  Monarchy   2334
Fisher, Dorothy Canfield, 1879-1959. American author.
  Freedom/Liberty   1375
Flexner, Abraham, 1866-1959. American educator and author.
  Role of the State/of Government   3476

Foot, Michael, 1913- . British journalist & politician; leader of the Labour Party, 1890-83.
  Leadership/Statesmanship   2208
Ford, Gerald R., 1913- . American politician; President of the United States, 1974-76.
  Constitution   254
  Democracy   480
  Expressions and Phrases   1064
  Patriotism   2422
  Politics   2801
  Presidency   3017
  Role of the State/of Government   3495
Forster, E.M., 1879-1970. English novelist.
  Democracy   453
  Freedom/Liberty   1370
  Leadership/Statesmanship   2148
  Treason   3641
Fox, Charles James, 1749-1806. English politician & orator.
  Freedom of Speech   1109
  Freedom/Liberty   1238
France, Anatole, 1844-1924. French author & critic.
  Expressions and Phrases   908, 931
  Justice   1793, 1795
  Leadership/Statesmanship   2086
  Role of the State/of Government   3462
Frank, Barney, 1940- . American politician; congressman from Massachusetts, 1980-.
  Legislatures and Legislation   2264
Frankfurter, Felix, 1882-1965. American jurist; justice of the Supreme Court, 1939-62.
  Democracy   424, 473
  Equality   762
  Freedom of the Press   1184
  Freedom/Liberty   1384
  Judiciary and Judges   1737
  Law   1919, 1930
  Prejudice and Discrimination   2913
Franklin, Benjamin, 1706-1790. American writer, diplomat, statesman.
  Economics/The Economy   634
  Expressions and Phrases   843
  Freedom/Liberty   1205, 1210
  Justice   1770
  Law   1859
  Leadership/Statesmanship   2016, 2017
  Taxation and Budgets   3583
  War and Peace   3692
Frederick II, (the Great), 1712-1786. king of Prussia, 1740-86.
  Monarchy   2341
  Freedom/Liberty   1233
  Religion and the State   3139
  War and Peace   3687
Friedman, Milton, 1912- . American economist.
  Economics/The Economy   657
  Freedom/Liberty   1440, 1441, 1442
  Taxation and Budgets   3627

Fromm, Erich, 1900-1980. American
psychoanalyst.
  Nationalism   2384
  Revolution   3257
Frost, David, and Anthony Jay, 1939- .
British/American television commentator.
  Class Divisions   110
  Conservatism   219
  Law   1944
Frost, Robert, 1874-1963. American poet.
  Conservatism   215
Fulbright, J. William, 1905- . American politician;
senator from Arkansas, 1944-74.
  Citizenship   32
  Democracy   454, 475
  Freedom/Liberty   1450, 1459
  International Affairs/Diplomacy   1687
  Legislatures and Legislation   2254
  Politics   2789
  Power   2886
  War and Peace   3928
Fulda, Ludwig, 1862-1939. German author.
  Monarchy   2355
Fuller, Thomas, 1654-1734. English physician &
writer.
  Class Divisions   38
  Expressions and Phrases   835
  Freedom/Liberty   1207
  Justice   1765
  Law   1850, 1851
  Leadership/Statesmanship   2005, 2006, 2007
  Politicians and Public Officials   2523
  War and Peace   3685
Galbraith, John Kenneth, 1908- . American
economist, diplomat & author.
  Class Divisions   107
  Economics/The Economy   654, 655
  Politics   2796, 2819
  Social Justice   3537
Gallup, George H., 1901-1984. American pollster.
  Public Opinion   3080
Galsworthy, John, 1867-1933. English novelist &
dramatist.
  Politicians and Public Officials   2590
Gandhi, Indira, 1917-1984. Indian politician;
prime minister of India, 1966-77, 1980-84.
  Expressions and Phrases   1087
  Leadership/Statesmanship   2213
Gandhi, Mohandas K., 1869-1948. Indian religious
& political leader.
  Democracy   444
  Dictatorship/Tyranny   592
  Expressions and Phrases   937, 941, 984
  Freedom/Liberty   1398, 1401, 1429
  Law   1910, 1920
  Majority and Minorities   2302
  Religion and the State   3158
  Revolution   3261
  War and Peace   3853, 3854, 3855

Gandhi, Rajiv, 1944- . Indian politician; prime
minister of India, 1984-.
  Leadership/Statesmanship   2212
Gardner, John W., 1912- . American public
official.
  Law   1949
  Politics   2795
  Social Justice   3539
Garfield, James A., 1831-1881. American
politician; president of the United States, 1881.
  Democracy   355
  Education   682
  Equality   755
  Expressions and Phrases   898
  Freedom of the Press   1171
  Justice   1791
  Law   1891
  Majority and Minorities   2296
  Political Parties   2483
  Politics   2710
  Public Opinion   3055
Garfinkel, Steven
  Expressions and Phrases   1097
Garnet, Henry Highland, 1815-1882. American
clergyman & abolitionist.
  Freedom/Liberty   1264
Garrison, William Lloyd, 1805-1879. American
abolitionist & author.
  Democracy   327
  Expressions and Phrases   864
  Freedom/Liberty   1256
  Rights/Human Rights   3320
Garvey, Marcus Moziah, 1887-1940. Jamaican
nationalist leader.
  Freedom/Liberty   1355
  Social Justice   3529
George, Henry, 1839-1897. American economist,
author & social reformer.
  Class Divisions   67, 68, 70
  Democracy   358
  Socialism   3555
Gerould, Katherine, 1879-1944. American author.
  Politics   2739
Gibbon, Edward, 1737-1794. English historian.
  Ethics in Politics   779
  Separation of Powers   3509
Gibbons, James Cardinal, 1834-1921. American
religious leader.
  Reform   3112
Gibbs, Lawrence
  Law   1964
Gibran, Kahlil, 1883-1931. American poet &
artist.
  Expressions and Phrases   1023
Gide, Andre, 1869-1951. French author & critic.
  Leadership/Statesmanship   2090
  Nationalism   2375
  Politicians and Public Officials   2584
  Revolution   3256

Gilbert, Sir W.S., 1836-1911. English librettist & humorist.
   Political Parties   2486
Gilmour, Sir Ian. British Conservative Party leader.
   Conservatism   226, 227
   Dictatorship/Tyranny   627
   Politicians and Public Officials   2636
Giraudoux, Jean, 1882-1944. French dramatist & diplomat.
   Leadership/Statesmanship   2127
   War and Peace   3802, 3810, 3811
Gladstone, William Ewart, 1809-1898. British statesman; prime minister of the United Kingdom, 1868-74, 1880-85, 1886, 1892-94.
   Democracy   334, 348
   Dictatorship/Tyranny   562
   Ethics in Politics   783
   Justice   1790
   Liberalism   2267
   Politics   2715
   Public Opinion   3056
   Religion and the State   3151
Glasgow, Ellen, 1874-1945. American author.
   Government   1548
   Politics   2720
Godwin, William, 1756-1836. English novelist & philosopher.
   Democracy   302
   Education   668
   Government   1511
   Power   2844
   Role of the State/of Government   3429
Goebbels, Joseph, 1897-1945. German politician; minister of propaganda under Nazi regime.
   Dictatorship/Tyranny   593, 594
   War and Peace   3813, 3814
Goethe, Johann Wolfgang von, 1749-1832. German poet, dramatist & author.
   Government   1526
   Leadership/Statesmanship   2043
   Liberalism   2266
   Nationalism   2366
   Politicians and Public Officials   2541
   Revolution   3197
Goffman, Erving, 1922- . American anthropologist & educator.
   Taxation and Budgets   3622
Goldberg, Arthur J., 1908- . American lawyer, jurist & public official; justice of the Supreme Court, 1962-65.
   Constitution   244
   Power   2887
Goldberg, Isaac, 1887-1938. American author.
   International Affairs/Diplomacy   1647
Goldman, Emma, 1869-1940. American anarchist.
   Ethics in Politics   793
   Expressions and Phrases   928
   Government   1554

   Government and Business   1586
   Judiciary and Judges   1732
   Law   1908
   Social Justice   3526, 3530
   War and Peace   3781, 3782
   Women in Politics   3991, 3992
Goldmark, Peter C., Jr., 1906-1977. American engineer & inventor.
   Expressions and Phrases   1074
Goldsmith, Oliver, 1728-1774. British poet & dramatist.
   Law   1862
Goldwater, Barry, 1909- . American politician; senator from Arizona, 1952-86.
   Expressions and Phrases   1042
   Political Campaigns   2431
   Role of the State/of Government   3489
   War and Peace   3922
Goncourt, Edmond & Jules de, 1822-1896. French authors.
   Revolution   3221
Goodman, Paul, 1911-1972. American author & educator.
   Leadership/Statesmanship   2165
Goodwin, Doris Kearns, 1943- . American political scientist & biographer.
   Presidency   3032
Gorbachev, Mikhail S., 1931- . Russian communist leader; secretary general of Communist Party of the Soviet Union, 1985-.
   Communism   185
   International Affairs/Diplomacy   1720
Gorky, Maxim, 1868-1936. Russian dramatist.
   Communism   129
   Dictatorship/Tyranny   583
   Law   1902, 1903
Gossett, William T.
   Law   1945
Gowon, Yakubu, 1934- . Nigerian military & political leader; head of state, 1966-75.
   Dictatorship/Tyranny   621
Grant, Ulysses S., 1822-1885. American military leader & politician; president of the United States, 1869-77.
   Democracy   350
   Freedom/Liberty   1301
   Law   1889
   Political Parties   2484
   Presidency   2961
   War and Peace   3733, 3735
Gray, Lt. Gen. Alfred M.
   Democracy   494
Greene, Graham, 1904- . English author.
   Communism   169
Greer, Germaine, 1939- . Australian author & feminist.
   Revolution   3283
   Women in Politics   4001
Grenville, George, 1712-1770. British politician.
   Government   1491

Grey, Edward, 1st Viscount Grey of Fallodon, 1862-1933. British politician; foreign secretary, 1905-16.
   Expressions and Phrases   930
Grimké, Angelina, 1805-1879. American abolitionist & feminist.
   Dictatorship/Tyranny   556, 557
   Law   1880
   Religion and the State   3148
Grimond, Jo. British politician; leader of the Liberal Party, 1956-1967.
   Expressions and Phrases   1036
Guevara, Ernesto, "Che", 1928-1967. Argentine revolutionary.
   Revolution   3270
Guizot, Francois, 1787-1874. French historian & politician.
   Revolution   3200
Hague, Frank, 1896-1956. American politician; boss of Union County, New Jersey.
   Freedom/Liberty   1372
Haile Selassie, 1892-1975. emperor of Ethiopia, 1930-75.
   International Affairs/Diplomacy   1652
Hailsham, Lord, (Quinton Hogg), 1907- . British politician.
   Freedom/Liberty   1395
Hale, Edward Everett, 1822-1909. American clergyman and author; sometime chaplain of the United States Senate.
   Legislatures and Legislation   2251
Hale, Nathan, 1755-1776. American Revolutionary spy.
   Patriotism   2393
Halifax, 1st Marquess of, (George Savile), 1633-1695. English politician & author.
   Expressions and Phrases   834
   Law   1846, 1847
   Political Parties   2444
   Power   2835, 2836
Hamer, Fannie Lou, 1917-1977. American political activist.
   Expressions and Phrases   1067
Hamilton, Alexander, 1757-1804. American politician & author; secretary of the treasury, 1789-95.
   Class Divisions   40
   Democracy   295, 297
   Dictatorship/Tyranny   549
   Equality   742
   Government   1501, 1507
   Government and Business   1578
   International Affairs/Diplomacy   1606
   Law   1868
   Legislatures and Legislation   2222
   Power   2842
   Presidency   2951
   Taxation and Budgets   3581

Hammarskjold, Dag, 1905-1961. Swedish statesman; secretary general of the United Nations, 1953-61.
   Expressions and Phrases   1004, 1022
   International Affairs/Diplomacy   1664
   Leadership/Statesmanship   2181
   Rights/Human Rights   3348
Hammurabi, 1955-1913 B.C. Babylonian king.
   Justice   1747
Hand, Learned, 1872-1961. American jurist; judge, U.S. Court of Appeals, 1924-51.
   Democracy   401
   Expressions and Phrases   1029
   Freedom of Speech   1138
   Freedom of the Press   1179
   Freedom/Liberty   1364, 1389, 1393
   Justice   1804
   Law   1916
   Politicians and Public Officials   2591
Harcourt, Sir William, 1827-1904. British lawyer & politician; leader of the Liberal Party, 1893-98.
   Conservatism   198
   Legislatures and Legislation   2237
Hardie, Keir, 1856-1915. Scottish labor leader; a founder of the Labour Party and its first candidate for parliament.
   Class Divisions   82
   Freedom/Liberty   1320
Harding, Warren G., 1865-1923. American politician; president of the United States, 1920-23.
   Democracy   394
   Expressions and Phrases   939, 943
   Government   1552
   Presidency   2979
   Social Justice   3527
   War and Peace   3793
Hardy, Thomas, 1840-1928. English novelist & poet.
   War and Peace   3768
Harington, Sir John, 1561-1612. English courtier & writer.
   Treason   3636
Harlan, John Marshall, 1833-1911. American jurist; justice of the supreme court, 1877-1911.
   Constitution   245
   Rights/Human Rights   3323
Harriman, W. Averell, 1891-1986. American politician & public official; governor of New York, 1955-58.
   Communism   182
Harrington, James, 1611-1677. English political theorist.
   Politicians and Public Officials   2519
Harrington, Michael, 1928-1989. American author & social reformer.
   Class Divisions   105, 106
   Prejudice and Discrimination   2925, 2926
   Social Justice   3541, 3542

Harris, Patricia Roberts, 1924-1985. American public official.
  Social Justice   3550
Harris, Richard. American journalist.
  Politicians and Public Officials   2633
Harrison, Benjamin, 1833-1901. American politician; president of the United States, 1888-92.
  Democracy   363
  Elections and Voting   708
  International Affairs/Diplomacy   1628, 1629, 1631
  Law   1896, 1897
  Public Opinion   3059
  Rights/Human Rights   3321
Harrison, Frederic, 1831-1923. English philosopher & lawyer.
  Leadership/Statesmanship   2077
Harrison, William Henry, 1773-1841. American military leader & politician; president of the United States, 1841.
  Class Divisions   49
  Democracy   326
  Freedom/Liberty   1260, 1261
  Government   1532
  Political Parties   2466
  Politicians and Public Officials   2544
  Power   2856
Hart, Gary, 1936- . American politician; senator from Colorado, 1975-86.
  Patriotism   2424
Hastings, Daniel O., 1874-1966. American politician; senator from Delaware, 1928-37.
  Power   2869
Hayek, Friedrich August von, 1899- . British economist & author.
  Bureaucracy   5
  Communism   144
  Democracy   422, 423
  Freedom/Liberty   1392
Hayes, Rutherford B., 1822-1893. American politician; president of the United States, 1877-81.
  Democracy   359
  Political Parties   2482
  Politicians and Public Officials   2555, 2560
  Public Opinion   3053
  Role of the State/of Government   3461
  War and Peace   3730
Hazlitt, William, 1778-1830. English essayist and critic.
  Democracy   305
  Expressions and Phrases   856, 859
  Freedom/Liberty   1252
  Leadership/Statesmanship   2038, 2041, 2045
  Power   2846, 2850
  Prejudice and Discrimination   2895, 2897, 2898
  Public Opinion   3042
Hearst, William Randolph, 1863-1951. American press lord.
  Politicians and Public Officials   2593

Heath, Edward, 1916- . British politician; prime minister of the United Kingdom, 1970-74.
  Rights/Human Rights   3378
Hegel, Georg Wilhelm Friedrich, 1770-1831. German philosopher.
  Expressions and Phrases   852, 869
  Freedom/Liberty   1257
  Government   1528
  Leadership/Statesmanship   2025
Heine, Heinrich, 1797-1856. German poet & essayist.
  War and Peace   3723
Hellman, Lillian, 1905-1984. American dramatist.
  Ethics in Politics   804
Henry, O., (William Sydney Porter), 1862-1910. American journalist & author.
  Public Opinion   3063
Henry, Patrick, 1736-1799. American revolutionary leader & politician; governor of Virginia, 1776-1779, 1784-86.
  Freedom/Liberty   1219, 1242
  Religion and the State   3140
  Treason   3637
  War and Peace   3693
Hepburn, Katharine, 1907- . American actress.
  Politicians and Public Officials   2653
Herbert, A.P. (Sir Alan Patrick), 1890-1971. British politician & author; member of parliament, 1935-50.
  Reform   3122
Herbert, George, 1593-1633. English clergyman and poet.
  Expressions and Phrases   831
  War and Peace   3678
Herodotus, ca. 485-425 B.C Greek historian.
  Power   2832
Herzen, Alexander Ivanovich, 1812-1870. Russian author.
  Communism   123
  Freedom/Liberty   1269
  Revolution   3211
Hesburgh, Theodore M., 1917- . American author & educator; president of Notre Dame Univ., 1952-86.
  Elections and Voting   724
Hesse, Hermann, 1877-1962. Swiss author.
  Law   1911
Highet, Gilbert, 1906-1978. American author, educator & critic.
  Politics   2771
Hightower, Jim. American public official; Texas state commissioner of agriculture.
  Expressions and Phrases   1099
  Government and Business   1599, 1600
Hill, George. British journalist.
  Politicians and Public Officials   2667
Hillman, Sidney, 1887-1946. American labor leader.
  Politics   2762

Himes, Chester Bomar, 1909-1984. American author.
Democracy 435
Expressions and Phrases 978
Freedom/Liberty 1391
Revolution 3258
Hitler, Adolf, 1889-1945. German dictator; leader of Germany, 1933-45.
Dictatorship/Tyranny 588, 589, 590
Education 689
Leadership/Statesmanship 2113
Legislatures and Legislation 2250
Rights/Human Rights 3338
War and Peace 3797, 3799
Ho Chi Minh, 1890-1969. Vietnamese national leader.
War and Peace 3943
Hobbes, Thomas, 1588-1679. English philospher & writer.
Power 2834
War and Peace 3679
Hobhouse, Leonard, 1864-1929. British journalist & social reformer.
Equality 759
Hochhuth, Rolf, 1931- . German dramatist.
International Affairs/Diplomacy 1694
Hodges, Luther H., 1898-1974. American politician & public official.
Economics/The Economy 658
Hoffer, Eric, 1902-1983. American author & philosopher.
Dictatorship/Tyranny 611, 617, 618, 622
Equality 763
Expressions and Phrases 988, 990
Freedom/Liberty 1449
Government 1565
Leadership/Statesmanship 2152
Power 2874, 2875, 2881, 2888
Reform 3125, 3126
Revolution 3263, 3276, 3279
Hölderlin, Friedrich, 1770-1843. German poet.
Dictatorship/Tyranny 550
Hollings, Ernest F., 1922- . American politician; senator from South Carolina, 1966-.
War and Peace 3962
Holmes, Oliver Wendell, Sr., 1809-1894. American poet, author & essayist.
Freedom of Speech 1122, 1123, 1128
Justice 1803
Law 1892, 1905, 1907, 1909
Legislatures and Legislation 2241
Power 2865
Role of the State/of Government 3471, 3472
Taxation and Budgets 3604, 3610
Class Divisions 79
Freedom of Speech 1117
Leadership/Statesmanship 2064, 2076

Homer, ca. 700 B.C. Greek poet.
Expressions and Phrases 823
Leadership/Statesmanship 1966, 1967
Monarchy 2323
Patriotism 2388
War and Peace 3644
Hoover, Herbert, 1874-1964. American politician; president of the United States, 1929-1933.
Democracy 390
Economics/The Economy 645
Ethics in Politics 809
Freedom of Speech 1129
Government 1556
International Affairs/Diplomacy 1645, 1648
Leadership/Statesmanship 2122, 2145
Political Parties 2508
Politics 2749, 2769
Presidency 2975
Role of the State/of Government 3473, 3475
War and Peace 3840
Hopkins, Harry L., 1890-1946. American public official.
Expressions and Phrases 952
Horace, (Quintus Horatius Flaccus), 65-8 B.C. Roman poet & satirist.
Justice 1754
War and Peace 3658
Horsley, Samuel, 1733-1806. English bishop.
Law 1873
Howe, Edgar Watson, 1853-1937. American editor and author.
Dictatorship/Tyranny 584
Expressions and Phrases 926, 936
Freedom of the Press 1175
Reform 3113, 3118
Howe, Louis McHenry, 1871-1920. American journalist; secretary to F.D. Roosevelt.
Ethics in Politics 801
Howells, William Dean, 1837-1920. American novelist & editor.
Dictatorship/Tyranny 580
Hubbard, "Kin", 1868-1930. American journalist & humorist.
Class Divisions 88, 89
Elections and Voting 711
Ethics in Politics 800
Legislatures and Legislation 2244
Politics 2746
Hubbard, Elbert G., 1856-1915. American author, publisher & biographer.
Law 1901
Leadership/Statesmanship 2116, 2117
Public Opinion 3067
Hughes, Charles Evans, 1862-1948. American politician & jurist; chief justice of the Supreme Court, 1930-41.
Freedom/Liberty 1357, 1371
Judiciary and Judges 1731

Hughes, Langston, 1902-1967. American poet & author.
Democracy   431
Freedom/Liberty   1396
Hughes, Thomas, 1822-1896. English author & reformer.
Politics   2697
Hugo, Victor, 1802-1885. French author & dramatist.
Class Divisions   64
Economics/The Economy   637
Expressions and Phrases   880
Freedom/Liberty   1300
Revolution   3219
Humphrey, George M., 1890-1970. American politician.
Taxation and Budgets   3617
Humphrey, Hubert H., 1911-1978. American politician; senator from Minnesota, 1949-65,1971-78; vice president of the U.S., 1965-69.
Freedom of Speech   1147
Law   1940
Legislatures and Legislation   2260
Rights/Human Rights   3344
Role of the State/of Government   3501
Hutcheson, Francis, 1694-1746. Scottish philosopher.
Role of the State/of Government   3414
Hutchins, Robert Maynard, 1899-1977. American educator.
Democracy   458
Huxley, Aldous, 1894-1963. British author.
Dictatorship/Tyranny   599
Leadership/Statesmanship   2118
Politicians and Public Officials   2625
Politics   2745
Role of the State/of Government   3481
Social Justice   3531
War and Peace   3816
Huxley, Thomas Henry, 1825-1895. English biologist & author.
Freedom/Liberty   1313
Nationalism   2369
Ibarruri, Dolores, "La Pasionaria", 1895-1989. Spanish communist leader.
Rights/Human Rights   3340
Ibsen, Henrik, 1828-1906. Norwegian dramatist.
Freedom/Liberty   1311
Majority and Minorities   2299
Reform   3103
Ickes, Harold L., 1874-1952. American public official; secretary of the interior, 1933-46.
Presidency   2978
Ingalls, John James, 1833-1900. American politician.
Government   1547

Inge, William Ralph, 1860-1954. British religious leader & author; dean, St. Paul's Cathedral, London, 1911-1934.
Democracy   371, 389
Dictatorship/Tyranny   579
Government   1553
Monarchy   2359
Patriotism   2413
Public Opinion   3066
Revolution   3242
Ingersoll, Robert G., 1833-1899. American lawyer & politician.
Justice   1792
Religion and the State   3153
Rights/Human Rights   3317
Irving, Washington, 1783-1859. American author, diplomat & historian.
International Affairs/Diplomacy   1613
Women in Politics   3979
Jackson, Andrew, 1767-1845. American military leader & politician; president of the United States, 1828-36.
Class Divisions   43
Democracy   316
Equality   745
Expressions and Phrases   863, 868
Government   1527, 1529
International Affairs/Diplomacy   1614, 1615
Majority and Minorities   2287, 2301
Politicians and Public Officials   2539
Revolution   3205
Taxation and Budgets   3591, 3593
War and Peace   3719, 3722
Jackson, George, 1941-1971. American criminal & political activist.
Revolution   3278
Jackson, Henry M., 1912-1983. American politician; senator from Washington, 1953-83.
Politics   2814
Jackson, Jesse, 1941- . American religious & political leader.
Expressions and Phrases   1091, 1103
Justice   1814
Leadership/Statesmanship   2220
Majority and Minorities   2315, 2320, 2321
Politicians and Public Officials   2657
Jackson, Robert H., 1892-1954. American jurist; justice of the Supreme Court, 1941-1954.
Citizenship   26
Freedom/Liberty   1415
Judiciary and Judges   1735
Religion and the State   3159
Jacoby, Johann, 1805-1877. Prussian public official.
Monarchy   2349
James, Henry, 1843-1916. American novelist.
Patriotism   2405
James I, 1566-1625. king of England (1603-25) & Scotland (1567-1625).
Monarchy   2326, 2328, 2329

Jaurès, Jean, 1859-1914. French socialist leader.
War and Peace   3760
Jefferson, Thomas, 1743-1826. American
statesman; president of the United States, 1801-09.
Citizenship   17
Conservatism   188
Constitution   232, 233
Democracy   287, 288, 293, 294, 301, 306, 310
Dictatorship/Tyranny   546, 547, 548
Education   666, 667, 669, 670, 672
Environment   728
Equality   741
Ethics in Politics   777, 780
Expressions and Phrases   841, 848, 851
Freedom of Speech   1108
Freedom of the Press   1160, 1164, 1166
Freedom/Liberty   1218, 1223, 1228, 1234,
1235, 1237, 1239, 1240, 1243, 1251, 1253
Government   1499, 1502, 1517, 1518, 1523,
1524
International Affairs/Diplomacy   1608, 1612
Judiciary and Judges   1727, 1728
Justice   1775, 1780
Law   18769, 1870, 1871, 1876, 1877
Leadership/Statesmanship   2030, 2033
Legislatures and Legislation   2224, 2229
Majority and Minorities   2283
Monarchy   2344
Political Parties   2457
Politicians and Public Officials   2534, 2535,
2536
Power   2840
Presidency   2954, 2955
Public Opinion   3039
Reform   3084, 3087, 3088
Religion and the State   3141, 3142, 3143
Revolution   3189, 3190
Rights/Human Rights   3290, 3291, 3293, 3294
Role of the State/of Government   3433, 3434,
3435
Taxation and Budgets   3582, 3585, 3587, 3588
War and Peace   3702, 3710, 3712, 3714
Johnson, Andrew, 1808-1875. American politician;
president of the United States, 1865-69.
Citizenship   21
Class Divisions   60
Constitution   239
Democracy   345, 346
Dictatorship/Tyranny   571
Taxation and Budgets   3600, 3601
Johnson, Claudia ("Lady Bird"), 1912- . American
public figure; first lady of the United States, 1963-
69.
Politicians and Public Officials   2643
Presidency   3005
Johnson, Gerald White, 1890-1980. American
journalist.
Leadership/Statesmanship   2138

Johnson, Lyndon B., 1908-1973. American
politician; president of the United States, 1963-69.
Citizenship   31
Democracy   476
Democratic Party   510
Dictatorship/Tyranny   620
Education   697
Elections and Voting   720
Equality   767
Ethics in Politics   812
Government and Business   1596
International Affairs/Diplomacy   1680, 1681,
1686, 1697
Justice   1810
Political Parties   2507
Politicians and Public Officials   2627, 2668,
2669
Politics   2786, 2821, 2830
Prejudice and Discrimination   2928, 2932, 2942
Presidency   2998, 3000, 3001, 3004, 3006, 3009
Rights/Human Rights   3359, 3360, 3362, 3370,
3374
Role of the State/of Government   3490
Social Justice   3543, 3544, 3547
War and Peace   3915, 3919, 3920, 3921, 3924,
3934, 3936
Women in Politics   3998, 3999
Johnson, Samuel, 1709-1784. English
lexicographer & critic.
Democracy   292
Dictatorship/Tyranny   540
Equality   740
Freedom/Liberty   1225
Government   1488, 1492, 1496
Law   1867
Leadership/Statesmanship   2013
Patriotism   2392
Politics   2680
Revolution   3188
Social Justice   3517
War and Peace   3689
Joll, James, 1918- . American political analyst.
Politics   2781
Jones, John Paul, 1747-1792. American naval
officer.
Expressions and Phrases   844
Jones, LeRoi, 1934- . American poet & dramatist.
Liberalism   2276
Prejudice and Discrimination   2935
Social Justice   3548
Jonson, Ben, 1572-1637. English dramatist & poet.
Leadership/Statesmanship   1983, 1993
Jordan, Barbara, 1936- . American politician;
congresswoman from Texas, 1972-78.
Constitution   253, 255
Democracy   487
Expressions and Phrases   1072, 1073
Leadership/Statesmanship   2192
Women in Politics   4009

Joubert, Joseph, 1754-1824. French writer & moralist.
Government   1533
Justice   1783
Leadership/Statesmanship   2051, 2052
Politics   2691, 2692
Power   2857
War and Peace   3721
Jouvenel, Bertrand de, 1903- . French political theorist.
Politics   2783
Joy, Adm. C. Turner American naval officer.
War and Peace   3872
Juvenal, (Decimus Junius Juvenalis), 60-140. Roman satirist.
Class Divisions   36
Ethics in Politics   773
Role of the State/of Government   3405
War and Peace   3663
Kant, Immanuel, 1724-1804. German philosopher.
International Affairs/Diplomacy   1605
Justice   1769
Law   1866
Kaufman, Irving R., 1910- . American lawyer & jurist.
Judiciary and Judges   1740
Kaunda, Kenneth, 1924- . Zambian politician; president of Zambia, 1964-.
Power   2894
War and Peace   3957, 3958, 3959
Keating, Kenneth B., 1900-1975. American politician; senator from New York, 1959-64.
Role of the State/of Government   3483
Keller, Hellen, 1880-1968. American educator & author.
Education   686
Kelly, Walt, 1913-1973. American cartoonist.
Expressions and Phrases   1059
Kempton, Murray, 1918- . American journalist.
Communism   166
Government   1568
Leadership/Statesmanship   2177
Prejudice and Discrimination   2920
Revolution   3265
Kennan, George F., 1904- . American diplomat & historian.
International Affairs/Diplomacy   1660, 1667, 1668, 1673
Leadership/Statesmanship   2171
War and Peace   3947, 3953
Kennedy, Edward M., 1932- . American politician; senator from Massachusetts, 1962-.
Presidency   3035
Kennedy, John F., 1917-1963. American politician; president of the United States, 1961-63.
Citizenship   29
Class Divisions   104
Democracy   419, 469, 471, 474
Dictatorship/Tyranny   615, 616

Economics/The Economy   656
Education   695, 696
Elections and Voting   718
Environment   734
Equality   765, 766
Ethics in Politics   806, 807
Expressions and Phrases   1021, 1025, 1026, 1027, 1030, 1031, 1032, 1035, 1039
Freedom of Speech   1139
Freedom/Liberty   1425, 1430, 1433, 1434, 1436, 1437, 1438, 1439, 1443, 1444, 1447
Government   1560, 1566
Government and Business   1595
International Affairs/Diplomacy   1670, 1671, 1672, 1674, 1678, 1679, 1682, 1683, 1685
Law   1932, 1936
Leadership/Statesmanship   2172, 2176
Political Parties   2504, 2506
Politicians and Public Officials   2611, 2621, 2622
Power   2879
Prejudice and Discrimination   2924, 2927, 2929
Presidency   2994, 2997
Religion and the State   3160, 3161
Revolution   3271
Rights/Human Rights   3353, 3355, 3357, 3358, 3361, 3364
Role of the State/of Government   3484, 3485, 3487, 3488
Social Justice   3540
Taxation and Budgets   3620
War and Peace   3899, 3901, 3905, 3906, 3907, 3908, 3911, 3912, 3914, 3916, 3917
Kennedy, Robert F., 1925-1968. American politician; attorney general of the United States, 1961-64;senator from New York, 1964-68.
Communism   168
Expressions and Phrases   1041
Freedom/Liberty   1448
Justice   1812
Power   2880
Social Justice   3546
Kerner, Otto, Jr., 1908-1976. American jurist & politician; governor of Illinois, 1960-68.
Prejudice and Discrimination   2939
Keynes, John Maynard, 1883-1946. English economist.
Communism   137, 140
Economics/The Economy   642, 649
Khrushchev, Nikita S., 1894-1971. Russian political leader; premier of the Soviet Union, 1958-64.
Communism   156, 157, 158, 159, 167
Expressions and Phrases   1010, 1015
Politicians and Public Officials   2620
Revolution   3267, 3277
War and Peace   3893, 3894
Killens, John Oliver, 1916- . American novelist.
Prejudice and Discrimination   2931

King, Martin Luther, Jr., 1929-1958. American religious & civil rights leader.
  Citizenship 30
  Expressions and Phrases 1038, 1043
  Freedom/Liberty 1445
  Justice 1808, 1811
  Law 1934, 1935, 1938
  Leadership/Statesmanship 2175
  Prejudice and Discrimination 2930, 2938
  Reform 3128
  Religion and the State 3162
  Rights/Human Rights 3350, 3363, 3365, 3368, 3369
  War and Peace 3926

King, William Lyon Mackenzie, 1874-1950. Canadian politician; prime minister of Canada, 1921-30, 1935-48.
  Public Opinion 3068

Kirkland, Lane, 1922- . American labor union official; president, AFL-CIO, 1979-.
  Taxation and Budgets 3628

Kirkpatrick, Jeane J., 1926- . American diplomat.
  Democratic Party 516
  Government 1575

Kissinger, Henry A., 1923- . American diplomat; Secretary of State, 1973-76.
  Communism 180
  Expressions and Phrases 1065, 1069, 1070, 1081, 1084, 1088
  International Affairs/Diplomacy 1703, 1705, 1708, 1713
  Law 1951
  Leadership/Statesmanship 2190, 2194, 2203, 2204, 2205, 2210, 22011
  Power 2890
  Role of the State/of Government 3496

Knox, John, 1505-1572. Scottish religious leader & reformer.
  Women in Politics 3975

Koch, Edward I., 1924- . American politician; mayor of New York City, 1981-89.
  Ethics in Politics 818
  Expressions and Phrases 1092, 1095
  Legislatures and Legislation 2265
  Rights/Human Rights 3400
  Social Justice 3551

Koestler, Arthur, 1905-1983. Hungarian author.
  Politics 2757

Kohl, Helmut, 1930- . German politician; chancellor of Federal Republic of Germany, 1982-.
  Leadership/Statesmanship 2219

Krauthammer, Charles, 1950- . American psychiatrist, journalist & author.
  Politicians and Public Officials 2656

Kristol, Irving, 1920- . American editor & author.
  Reform 3133

Kropotkin, Prince Peter, 1842-1921. Russian geographer & anarchist.
  Freedom/Liberty 1326
  War and Peace 3752

Krutz, Jerome
  Ethics in Politics 821

La Bruyère, Jean de, 1645-1696. French author & philosopher.
  Dictatorship/Tyranny 529
  Judiciary and Judges 1724
  Justice 1763
  Leadership/Statesmanship 2002
  Monarchy 2336
  Political Parties 2443
  Politicians and Public Officials 2520
  Politics 2675
  Religion and the State 3138
  Revolution 3187

La Rochefoucauld, Francois, Duc de, 1613-180. French epigramist.
  Expressions and Phrases 832
  Justice 1761
  Leadership/Statesmanship 1995, 1996, 1997, 1998, 1999

Lafayette, Marie Joseph, Marquis de, 1757-1834. French military & political leader.
  Revolution 3191

LaFollette, Robert M., Sr., 1855-1925. American politician & reform leader; congressman from Wisconsin, 1885-1891; senator, 1906-1925.
  Public Opinion 3065

LaFollette, Suzanne, 1893- . American feminist & social reformer.
  Conservatism 212
  Freedom/Liberty 1358
  Revolution 3244, 3245
  Rights/Human Rights 3335, 3336

LaGuardia, Fiorello, 1882-1947. American politician; mayor of New York, 1934-45.
  Political Parties 2505

Landon, Alfred M., 1887- . American politician; Republican candidate for president, 1936.
  Majority and Minorities 2311

Landor, Walter Savage, 1775-1864. English author & poet.
  Class Divisions 59
  Dictatorship/Tyranny 564
  Expressions and Phrases 881
  Law 1888

Lao-Tse, 570-490 B.C. Chinese philosopher.
  War and Peace 3646

Laski, Harold Joseph, 1893-1950. British socialist theorist.
  War and Peace 3846

Lasswell, Harold, 1902- . American economist.
  Politics 2752

Laurier, Sir Wilfrid, 1841-1919. Canadian politician; prime minister of Canada, 1896-1911.
  Conservatism 211

Law, Andrew Bonar, 1858-1923. British politician; prime minister of the United Kingdom, 1922-23.
  Leadership/Statesmanship 2093

Lawrence, D.H., 1885-1930. English novelist & essayist.
  Freedom/Liberty 1363
Layton, Irving, 1916- . Canadian author.
  Politicians and Public Officials 2637
Lazarus, Emma, 1849-1887. American poet.
  Freedom/Liberty 1315
Lease, Mary Elizabeth, 1853-1933. American populist & social reformer.
  Reform 3107
Lec, Stanislaw, 1909-1966. Czech author.
  Justice 1813
  Role of the State/of Government 3493
Lee, Robert E., 1807-1870. American military leader.
  Patriotism 2404
  War and Peace 3729, 3731
Lenin, Vladimir Ilyich, 1870-1924. Russian revolutionary; head of U.S.S.R., 1917-24.
  Communism 128, 132
  Democracy 385
  Economics/The Economy 641
  Expressions and Phrases 934
  Freedom/Liberty 1350
  Nationalism 2371
  Revolution 3227
Leo XIII, 1810-1903. Pope, 1878-1903.
  Class Divisions 78
  Liberalism 2269
  Revolution 3225
Lerner, Max, 1902- . American author, lecturer & journalist.
  Democracy 447, 449
  Freedom of Speech 1132
  Freedom of the Press 1183
  Prejudice and Discrimination 2917
  War and Peace 3858
Levant, Oscar, 1906-1972. American composer, musician & wit.
  Politicians and Public Officials 2631
Lévy, Bernard-Henri, 1948- . French philosopher.
  Dictatorship/Tyranny 626
  Revolution 3288
  Socialism 3575
Lewis, Ann F. American journalist.
  Politicians and Public Officials 2664
Lewis, Capt. Robert American World War II military pilot.
  War and Peace 3886
Liddell Hart, Sir Basil, 1895-1970. British military theorist.
  Leadership/Statesmanship 2167
Liddy, G. Gordon, 1930- . American public official; participant in Watergate conspiracy.
  Justice 1816, 1817
Lie, Trygve, 1896-1968. Norwegian lawyer & diplomat; Secretary-General of the United Nations, 1946-53.
  War and Peace 3850

Liebknecht, Karl, 1871-1919. German socialist leader.
  War and Peace 3773
Liebling, A.J., 1904-1963. American journalist.
  Freedom of the Press 1194
Lincoln, Abraham, 1809-1865. American statesman; president of the United States, 1861-1865.
  Conservatism 199
  Constitution 237
  Democracy 333, 335, 337, 340, 341, 342, 344
  Dictatorship/Tyranny 565, 566
  Elections and Voting 702, 704
  Equality 749, 750, 751
  Ethics in Politics 784
  Expressions and Phrases 884, 885, 886, 890, 893, 895, 896, 897
  Freedom/Liberty 1276, 1277, 1281, 1293, 1295, 1299, 1303, 1304
  Government 1539, 1540, 1542
  Justice 1787, 1789
  Leadership/Statesmanship 2063, 2070, 2071, 2072, 2073
  Majority and Minorities 2294
  Politicians and Public Officials 2553
  Presidency 2958, 2959, 2960
  Public Opinion 3046, 3048, 3049
  Revolution 3207
  Rights/Human Rights 3302, 3309
  Role of the State/of Government 3452, 3453
  Social Justice 3520, 3521
  Taxation and Budgets 3596
  War and Peace 3736
Lindner, Robert, 1914-1956. American psychoanalyst.
  Revolution 3266
Lindsay, Howard, 1889-1968. American playwright.
  Law 1922
Lindsay, John V., 1921- . American politician; mayor of New York City, 1966-74.
  Freedom/Liberty 1464
  Politicians and Public Officials 2647
Lippmann, Walter, 1889-1974. American political commentator.
  Conservatism 210
  Democracy 380, 463
  Education 687
  Ethics in Politics 819
  Freedom of the Press 1187, 1188
  Freedom/Liberty 1344
  International Affairs/Diplomacy 1654
  Leadership/Statesmanship 2142
  Political Campaigns 2427
  Politicians and Public Officials 2571, 2672, 2574, 2608, 2610
  Politics 2754
  Power 2876
  Prejudice and Discrimination 2911

Public Opinion   3064, 3077
Reform   3116
Republican Party   3174
Revolution   3268
Lisagor, Peter, 1915-1976. American journalist.
Ethics in Politics   815
Litvinov, Maxim, 1876-1951. Soviet diplomat.
War and Peace   3809
Livy, 59 B.C.-17 A.D. Roman historian.
Law   1825
War and Peace   3657
Lloyd, Henry Demarest, 1847-1903. American author.
Class Divisions   80
Expressions and Phrases   916
Freedom/Liberty   1321, 1322, 1323
Lloyd George, David, 1st Earl Lloyd-George, 1863-1945. British politician; prime minister of the United Kingdom, 1916-22.
Class Divisions   85, 86
Democracy   387
Expressions and Phrases   935
Government   1550
War and Peace   3767, 3788, 3812
Locke, John, 1632-1704. English philosopher.
Democracy   276, 277, 278
Freedom/Liberty   1202, 1203
Law   1845, 1848
Monarchy   2331
Role of the State/of Government   3412
Social Justice   3516
Lodge, Henry Cabot, Jr., 1902-1985. American politician & diplomat.
Expressions and Phrases   1000
Freedom/Liberty   1420
War and Peace   3967
Lombardi, Vince, 1913-1970. American football coach.
Expressions and Phrases   1082
Long, Earl, 1895-1960. American politician; governor of Louisiana, 1939-40, 1948-52, 1956-60.
Politicians and Public Officials   2604
Long, Huey P., 1893-1935. American politician; governor of Louisiana, 1928-31; senator from Louisiana, 1932-35.
Democracy   400
Long, Russell B., 1918- . American politician; senator from Louisiana, 1951-86.
Taxation and Budgets   3626, 3634
Lopez Mateos, Adolfo, 1910-1969. Mexican politician; president of Mexico, 1958-64.
Women in Politics   3997
Lovett, William, 1800-1877. English political reformer.
Politicians and Public Officials   2546
Low, David, 1891-1963. British political cartoonist.
War and Peace   3849

Lowe, Robert, 1811-1892. British politician; chancellor of the exchequer, 1863-73.
Education   680
Lowell, James Russell, 1819-1891. American editor & essayist.
Citizenship   19
Democracy   352
Dictatorship/Tyranny   559
Ethics in Politics   782
Freedom/Liberty   1263, 1265
Rights/Human Rights   3303
Luce, Clare Boothe, 1903- . American author, politician & diplomat.
International Affairs/Diplomacy   1653
Women in Politics   4006, 4010
Luxemburg, Rosa, 1870-1919. German revolutionary & communist leader.
War and Peace   3790
MacArthur, Douglas, 1881-1964. American general.
Expressions and Phrases   979, 987, 1006
Freedom/Liberty   1397
Leadership/Statesmanship   2201
War and Peace   3865, 3874, 3910, 3918, 3925
Macaulay, Lord, (Thomas Babington, 1st Baron Macaulay), 1800-1859. English historian, essayist & politician.
Constitution   238
Economics/The Economy   636
Elections and Voting   699
Expressions and Phrases   862, 867
Freedom of Speech   1112
Freedom/Liberty   1255
Majority and Minorities   2292
Politicians and Public Officials   2545
Politics   2689
Power   2859
Reform   3094, 3095
Role of the State/of Government   3439
MacDonald, (James) Ramsay, 1866-1937. British politician; prime minister of the United Kingdom, 1924, 1929-35.
Leadership/Statesmanship   2120
Machiavelli, Niccolò, 1469-1527. Italian political philosopher.
Ethics in Politics   774
Law   1833, 1834, 1835, 1836
Leadership/Statesmanship   1974, 1975, 1976, 1977, 1978
Politics   2673
Role of the State/of Government   3406
War and Peace   3667, 3668
Mackintosh, Sir James, 1765-1832. Scottish lawyer & politician; member of parliament, 1812-32.
Freedom/Liberty   1245
Legislatures and Legislation   2223
Reform   3086
MacLennan, Hugh, 1907- . Canadian novelist.
Power   2878

Martin, Ralph G.
Political Campaigns 2433
Marx, Groucho, 1890-1977. American comedian.
Expressions and Phrases 1077
Politics 2807
Marx, Karl, 1818-1883. German philosopher.
Class Divisions 53, 54, 55, 56, 57, 58, 65, 71
Communism 118, 119, 120, 121, 122, 124, 125
Expressions and Phrases 910
Leadership/Statesmanship 2055
Power 2860
Prejudice and Discrimination 2905
Religion and the State 3149, 3150
Social Justice 3523
Masaryk, Thomas, 1850-1937. Czech national leader; president of Czechoslovakia, 1918-35.
Leadership/Statesmanship 2107
Politics 2735
Religion and the State 3154
Revolution 3226
Mason, George, 1725-1792. American political leader.
Democracy 286
Freedom of the Press 1158
Role of the State/of Government 3418
Massinger, Philip, 1583-1640. English dramatist.
Leadership/Statesmanship 1992
Mathias, Charles M., Jr., 1922- . American politician; congressman from Maryland, 1960-68; senator, 1969-87.
Democracy 486
Ethics in Politics 811
Leadership/Statesmanship 2191
Maugham, W. Somerset, 1874-1965. English author.
Freedom/Liberty 1348, 1381
Leadership/Statesmanship 2104
Mazzini, Giuseppe, 1805-1872. Italian political thinker & revolutionary leader.
Freedom/Liberty 1297
Patriotism 2402
Power 2852
Revolution 3203, 3204
Role of the State/of Government 3450
McCarthy, Eugene J., 1916. American politician; senator from Minnesota, 1958-70; presidential candidate, 1968.
Bureaucracy 12
Democratic Party 511
Political Parties 2510
McCarthy, Mary, 1912- . American author.
Bureaucracy 10
Ethics in Politics 808
Politics 2792
Social Justice 3538
McClure, James A., 1924- . American politician; congressman from Idaho, 1966-72; senator, 1973-.
Expressions and Phrases 1102

McCree, Wade Hampton, Jr., 1920- . American public official.
Expressions and Phrases 1076
McGovern, George S., 1922- . American politician; senator from South Dakota, 1963-81; presidential candidate,.
International Affairs/Diplomacy 1707
Presidency 3013
McKay, Claude, 1890-1948. American poet & novelist.
Majority and Minorities 2312
McKinley, William, 1843-1901. American politician; president of the United States, 1897-1901.
Democracy 364, 370
Education 684
Expressions and Phrases 920
Law 1898
War and Peace 3754
McLuhan, Marshall, 1911-1980. Canadian author & educator.
Expressions and Phrases 1040
McNamara, Robert. American public official; secretary of defense, 1961-68; president, World Bank, 1968-81.
War and Peace 3933
Meir, Golda, 1898-1978. Israeli political leader; prime minister of Israel, 1969-74.
Leadership/Statesmanship 2189
War and Peace 3940, 3942
Melanchthon, Philip, 1497-1560. German religious reformer.
Law 1832
Melbourne, 2nd Viscount, 1779-1848. British politician; prime minister of the United Kingdom, 1834, 1835-41.
Political Parties 2468
Role of the State/of Government 3442
Melville, Herman, 1819-1891. American novelist & essayist.
War and Peace 3738
Mencken, H.L., 1880-1956. American journalist, editor & satirist.
Communism 155
Democracy 391, 392
Economics/The Economy 643
Ethics in Politics 799
Justice 1802
Legislatures and Legislation 2249
Patriotism 2417, 2420
Political Parties 2500
Politicians and Public Officials 2612
Politics 2737, 2740
Power 2877
Rights/Human Rights 3349
Menzies, Sir Robert G., 1894-1978. Australian politician; prime minister of Australia, 1939-66.
Politics 2797

Merton, Thomas, 1915-1968. American poet &
author.
   Freedom/Liberty   1462
Metternich, Prince Clemens von, 1773-1859.
Austrian statesman; foreign minister, 1809-48.
   Conservatism   191
   Expressions and Phrases   858, 861, 876
   Leadership/Statesmanship   2040
   Monarchy   2347
   Politics   2690, 2695
   Revolution   3199, 3201, 3206
Michaelis, Gen. John. American Korean War
general.
   War and Peace   3968
Miles, William Porcher, 1822-1899. American
politician.
   Elections and Voting   703
Mill, James, 1773-1836. Scottish philosopher.
   Democracy   312
   Reform   3091
Mill, John Staurt
   Freedom/Liberty   1292
Mill, John Stuart, 1806-1873. English philosopher.
   Citizenship   20
   Democracy   329
   Dictatorship/Tyranny   567, 568, 572
   Freedom of Speech   1114, 1115, 1116
   Freedom/Liberty   1282, 1283, 1284, 1285,
1286, 1287, 1288, 1289, 1291, 1294, 1298
   Justice   1786
   Leadership/Statesmanship   2068, 2069
   Majority and Minorities   2290
   Nationalism   2367
   Political Parties   2477
   Rights/Human Rights   3307
   War and Peace   3732
Millay, Edna St. Vincent, 1892-1950. American
poet.
   Freedom/Liberty   1418
   Patriotism   2416
Miller, Henry, 1891-1980. American author.
   Class Divisions   99
   Democracy   427, 436
   Leadership/Statesmanship   2134, 2135
   Politicians and Public Officials   2595, 2628
   Reform   3123
   War and Peace   3833
Millis, Walter, 1899-1968. American author.
   War and Peace   3831
Milner, Alfred, 1st Viscount. British public
official; secretary for war, 1918-19; colonial
secretary, 1919-21.
   Leadership/Statesmanship   2092
Milton, John, 1608-1674. English poet &
philosopher.
   Democracy   272
   War and Peace   3680
Minow, Newton, 1926- . American lawyer &
public official.
   Law   1959

Mirabeau, Honore Gabriel, Comte de, 1749-1791.
French revolutionary.
   Class Divisions   44, 45
   Expressions and Phrases   870
Mitchell, George J., 1933- . American politician;
senator from Maine, 1974-.
   Politics   2827
Mitford, Nancy, 1904-1973. English author.
   Class Divisions   102
Molière, 1622-1673. French dramatist.
   Reform   3083
Moltke, Helmut von, 1800-1891. German general
& statesman.
   War and Peace   3745
Mondale, Walter F., 1928- . American politician;
senator from Minnesota, 1964-77; vice-president of
the United States, 1977-81.
   Republican Party   3176
Monnet, Jean, 1888-1979. French economist &
diplomat; a founder of European Community.
   Leadership/Statesmanship   2206
Monroe, James. American politician; president of
the United States, 1758-1831.
   Education   671
   Role of the State/of Government   3424
Montaigne, Michel de, 1533-1592. French essayist.
   Expressions and Phrases   827, 828
   Government   1480
   Justice   1757, 1758
   Law   1838
   Leadership/Statesmanship   1979
   War and Peace   3671, 3672
Montesquieu, Charles Louis de, 1689-1755.
French philosopher.
   Freedom/Liberty   1209
   Law   1853, 1854, 1855, 1856, 1857, 1858
   Role of the State/of Government   3415
   War and Peace   3684
Moore, George, 1873-1958. English philosopher.
   Prejudice and Discrimination   2907
   Reform   3109
Morgan, Charles, Jr., 1930- . American lawyer &
author.
   Legislatures and Legislation   2258
Morgan, J.P., 1837-1913. American financier.
   Expressions and Phrases   948
Morley, John, (1st Viscount Morley of
Blackburn), 1838-1923. English author &
politician.
   Dictatorship/Tyranny   573, 587
   Ethics in Politics   796
   Politicians and Public Officials   2576
   Politics   2712, 2713
   Role of the State/of Government   3456
Morris, William, 1834-1896. English poet, author
& craftsman.
   Class Divisions   72, 73, 74
   Economics/The Economy   638
   Socialism   3554

Morris, Wright, 1910- . American author.
Rights/Human Rights   3375
Morrow, Lance, 1939- . American journalist &
author.
Democratic Party   515
Politicians and Public Officials   2632
Morse, Wayne Lyman, 1900-1974. American
politician; senator from Oregon, 1945-69.
Liberalism   2273
Mosley, Sir Oswald, 1896-1980. British politician;
founder of Union of Fascists.
Class Divisions   92
Leadership/Statesmanship   2115
Legislatures and Legislation   2247
Politicians and Public Officials   2585
Mountbatten, Lord Louis, 1900-1979. British
naval officer & member of royal family.
Rights/Human Rights   3390
War and Peace   3950
Moyers, Bill, 1934- . American political
commentator.
Politics   2788
Presidency   3027
Moynihan, Daniel P., 1927- . American politician;
senator from New York, 1976-.
Conservatism   221
Expressions and Phrases   1068
Freedom of Speech   1151
Freedom of the Press   1193
Government   1572
Politicians and Public Officials   2644
Muchow, David
Taxation and Budgets   3625
Muhlenberg, Peter, 1746-1801. American religious
leader & politician; congressman from
Pennsylvania, 1789-91, 1793-95, 1799-1801.
War and Peace   3694
Mumford, Lewis, 1895- . American author &
architect.
War and Peace   3870
Munro, Hector Hugh, (Saki), 1870-1916. English
author.
Expressions and Phrases   945
Munro, Ross H.
Communism   178
Murray, Sir George, 1849-1938. British public
official.
War and Peace   3784
Murrow, Edward R., 1908-1965. American
broadcaster & political commentator.
Leadership/Statesmanship   2153, 2162
Politicians and Public Officials   2618, 2619
Prejudice and Discrimination   2921
Muskie, Edmund S., 1914- . American politician;
senator from Maine, 1959-80; secretary of state,
1980-81.
Democracy   477
Mussolini, Benito, 1883-1945. Italian political
leader; fascist dictator of Italy, 1922-43.
Dictatorship/Tyranny   597

Napoleon I, (Napoleon Bonaparte), 1769-1821.
French general & political leader; Emperor of
France, 1804-18814.
Constitution   230, 231
Democracy   308
Dictatorship/Tyranny   551, 553
Economics/The Economy   635
Expressions and Phrases   850
Freedom of the Press   1162, 1163
Government   1513, 1515, 1516, 1519, 1522,
1525
Justice   1776, 1777, 1778, 1779
Law   1875
Leadership/Statesmanship   2026, 2027, 2028,
2029, 2031, 2032, 2034, 2036, 2037
Legislatures and Legislation   2225, 2226
Patriotism   2397
Politicians and Public Officials   2533
Public Opinion   3041
Role of the State/of Government   3431, 3432
Taxation and Budgets   3586
War and Peace   3708, 3709
Narayan, Jayaprakash, 1902-1979. Indian socialist
political leader.
Democracy   408
Nasser, Gamal Abdel, 1918-1970. Egyptian
military & political leader; president of Egypt,
1956-70.
Expressions and Phrases   1057
War and Peace   3941
Nehru, Jawaharlal, 1889-1964. Indian political
leader; prime minister of India, 1947-64.
Class Divisions   94, 103
Democracy   470
War and Peace   3883
Nevelson, Louise, 1900-1988. American artist.
Rights/Human Rights   3383
Newman, Jon, 1932- . American lawyer & author.
Freedom/Liberty   1473
Newton, Huey, 1942-1989. American political
activist.
Revolution   3284
Niebuhr, Reinhold, 1892-1971. American
clergyman & author.
Democracy   434
Politics   2799, 2804
Niemoeller, Martin, 1892-1984. German religious
leader & theologian; leading anti-Nazi.
Rights/Human Rights   3342
Nietzsche, Friedrich, 1844-1900. German
philosopher.
Democracy   362
Freedom/Liberty   1319
Leadership/Statesmanship   2079, 2080
Liberalism   2268
Reform   3102
War and Peace   3743, 3746
Nin, Anaïs, 1903-1977. American novelist &
diarist.
Politics   2803

Nixon, Pat, 1912- . American public figure; first lady of the United States, 1969-74.
Presidency 3014
Nixon, Richard M., 1913- . American politician; president of the United States, 1969-1974.
Democracy 478
Expressions and Phrases 1063, 1078, 1094
Freedom/Liberty 1465
International Affairs/Diplomacy 1699, 1702
Judiciary and Judges 1738, 1741
Law 1950
Leadership/Statesmanship 2173, 2187, 2188, 2199
Politicians and Public Officials 2609
Politics 2802, 2808
Presidency 3003, 3007, 3010, 3011, 3018, 3026
Role of the State/of Government 3494
Separation of Powers 3512
War and Peace 3929, 3938, 3939, 3944
Women in Politics 4000
Nizer, Louis, 1902- . American lawyer & author.
Democracy 488
Leadership/Statesmanship 2174
Norris, William
Rights/Human Rights 3387
North, Frederick, 8th Baron North, 1732-1779. British politician; prime minister of Great Britain, 1770-82.
Leadership/Statesmanship 2015
Norton, Eleanor Holmes, 1937- . American lawyer & public official.
Freedom of Speech 1149
Freedom/Liberty 1468
Majority and Minorities 2316
Nyerere, Julius K., 1922- . Tanzanian national leader.
Freedom/Liberty 1454
International Affairs/Diplomacy 1688
O'Brien, Conor Cruise, 1917- . Irish author & diplomat.
International Affairs/Diplomacy 1716
O'Connor, Edwin, 1918-1968. American author.
Expressions and Phrases 1008
Ormsby-Gore, David. British diplomat; ambassador to the United States during Kennedy administration.
War and Peace 3903
Ortega y Gasset, Jose, 1883-1955. Spanish philosopher.
Class Divisions 90
Democracy 399
Dictatorship/Tyranny 595
Government 1555
Leadership/Statesmanship 2111, 2121
Majority and Minorities 2309
Nationalism 2378
Revolution 3249
War and Peace 3815

Orwell, George, 1903-1950. English author.
Equality 761
Political Parties 2498
Politics 2767, 2770
War and Peace 3864
Ostrovsky, Alexander, 1823-1886. Russian author.
Bureaucracy 1
Otis, James, 1725-1783. American revolutionary leader.
Constitution 228
Page, Walter Hines, 1855-1918. American journalist & diplomat.
Democracy 396
Pahlevi, Mohammed Reza, 1919-1980. Shah of Iran, 1941-79.
Monarchy 2362
Power 2892
Paine, Thomas, 1737-1809. American political writer.
Dictatorship/Tyranny 539
Elections and Voting 698
Expressions and Phrases 846
Freedom/Liberty 1226, 1227, 1248
Government 1497, 1498, 1509, 1510
Patriotism 2394
Rights/Human Rights 3295
Role of the State/of Government 3426
War and Peace 3696, 3697, 3698, 3699, 3705
Palmerston, 3rd Viscount, (Henry John Temple), 1784-65. British statesman & diplomat; prime minister of the United Kingdom, 1855-58, 1859-65.
Equality 744
International Affairs/Diplomacy 1617, 1619, 1621
Legislatures and Legislation 2235
War and Peace 3720
Pankhurst, Christabel, 1880-1958. English feminist.
Politics 2780
Rights/Human Rights 3328
Pankhurst, Emmeline, 1858-1928. English feminist; leader of the women's suffrage movement.
Freedom/Liberty 1347
Justice 1800
Revolution 3237
Rights/Human Rights 3337
Women in Politics 3990, 3993, 3994
Parker, Theodore, 1810-1860. American religious leader.
Democracy 330, 331
Revolution 3213
Parks, Rosa, 1913- . American civil rights leader.
Prejudice and Discrimination 2949
Pascal, Blaise, 1623-1662. French mathematician & theologian.
Democracy 273
Justice 1762
Leadership/Statesmanship 2000

Pound, Roscoe, 1870-1964. American educator; dean, Harvard Law School, 1916-37.
   Law   1913, 1937

Powell, Adam Clayton, Jr., 1908-1972. American politician; congressman from New York, 1945-67, 1969-70.
   Class Divisions   108
   Expressions and Phrases   1051, 1053
   Freedom/Liberty   1460
   Leadership/Statesmanship   2184
   Prejudice and Discrimination   2936

Powell, Enoch, 1912- . British classicist & right-wing politician.
   Nationalism   2387
   Political Parties   2511
   Politicians and Public Officials   2652

Powell, Lewis F., Jr., 1907- . American jurist; justice of the supreme court, 1971-88.
   Constitution   261
   Equality   769

Pratt, Charles, Earl Camden, 1714-1794. English jurist & political leader.
   Taxation and Budgets   3578

Priestly, Joseph, 1733-1804. English clergyman, chemist & philosopher.
   Democracy   282
   Freedom/Liberty   1217
   Revolution   3192
   Role of the State/of Government   3417

Prior, Matthew, 1664-1721. English poet and diplomat.
   Monarchy   2337

Proudhon, Pierre Joseph, 1809-1865. French socialist theorist.
   Communism   116
   Dictatorship/Tyranny   561
   Freedom/Liberty   1262
   Government   1537
   Political Parties   2475
   Role of the State/of Government   3443
   Socialism   3552

Proxmire, William, 1915. American politician; senator from Wisconsin, 1957-88.
   Ethics in Politics   816
   Politicians and Public Officials   2629

Quaison-Sackey, Alex, 1924- . Ghanaian diplomat.
   International Affairs/Diplomacy   1691

Quay, Matthew Stanley, 1833-1904. American political boss; senator from Pennsylvania, 1887-99; 1901-04.
   Politicians and Public Officials   2557

Racine, Jean, 1639-1699. French poet & dramatist.
   Dictatorship/Tyranny   527
   Justice   1760

Radford, Adm. Arthur W., 1896-1973. American admiral; chairman, joint chiefs of staff, 1953-57.
   Leadership/Statesmanship   2159

Rainborowe, Thomas, d. 1648. English politician & soldier under Cromwell.
   Equality   739

Rakove, Milton, 1918- . American political scientist & author.
   Ethics in Politics   810

Randall, Clarence B., 1891- . American businessman.
   Leadership/Statesmanship   2179

Randolph, A. Philip, 1889-1979. American labor union leader.
   Politics   2763
   Power   2872
   Rights/Human Rights   3341, 3380
   Social Justice   3528
   War and Peace   3789, 3794

Randolph, Edmund Jennings, 1753-1813. American politician; gov. of Virginia, 1786-88; attorney general, 1789-94; sec'ty of state, 1794-95.
   Constitution   229

Randolph of Roanoke, John, 1773-1833. American politician; congressman & senator from Virginia.
   Ethics in Politics   781
   Leadership/Statesmanship   2039
   Legislatures and Legislation   2231
   Power   2849
   Separation of Powers   3507
   Taxation and Budgets   3592

Rankin, Jeanette, 1880-1973. American politician; first woman in Congress; congresswoman from Montana, 1917-19, 1941-43.
   War and Peace   3780
   Women in Politics   3996

Ravel, Jean-François
   Communism   176

Ray, Dixy Lee, 1914- . American politician; governor of Washington, 1977-80.
   Economics/The Economy   661
   Republican Party   3177
   Role of the State/of Government   3500

Rayburn, Sam, 1882-1961. American politician; speaker of the House of Representatives at various times, 1940-61.
   Elections and Voting   717
   Environment   733
   Expressions and Phrases   1018, 1019
   Leadership/Statesmanship   2163, 2169
   Politicians and Public Officials   2623

Reagan, Ronald, 1911- . American politician; president of the United States, 1981-1989.
   Communism   186
   Democracy   493, 499, 500
   Democratic Party   514
   Economics/The Economy   662
   Environment   735
   Expressions and Phrases   1080
   Freedom/Liberty   1470
   Government   1573, 1574, 1575, 1576

International Affairs/Diplomacy 1706, 1710, 1711
Law 1956
Political Parties 2512
Politicians and Public Officials 2661
Politics 2809, 2820
Prejudice and Discrimination 2947
Presidency 3036, 3037
Religion and the State 3163
Republican Party 3180, 3181, 3182
Rights/Human Rights 3395, 3397
Taxation and Budgets 3630, 3631, 3632
War and Peace 3956, 3963, 3964, 3965
Regan, Donald T., 1918- . American public official; secretary of Treasury, 1981-85; White House chief of staff, 1985-87.
Ethics in Politics 822
Presidency 3038
Rehnquist, William H., 1924- . American jurist; justice of the Supreme Court, 1972-86; chief justice, 1986-.
Constitution 257
Freedom of Speech 1155
Judiciary and Judges 1745
Reischauer, Edwin O., 1910- . American scholar & diplomat; ambassador to Japan, 1961-66.
Communism 172
Renard, Jules, 1864-1910. French educator & author.
Socialism 3557
Repplier, Agnes, 1858-1950. American essayist.
International Affairs/Diplomacy 1643
Reston, James, "Scotty", 1909- . American journalist & political commentator.
Elections and Voting 725
International Affairs/Diplomacy 1684, 1693, 1695
Majority and Minorities 2314
Politics 2793, 2812
Presidency 3028
Richelieu, Cardinal, 1585-1642. French political leader; first minister to Louis XIII, 1624-42.
Expressions and Phrases 833
Leadership/Statesmanship 2001
War and Peace 3682
Rickover, Hyman G., 1900-1986. American admiral.
Bureaucracy 14
War and Peace 3970
Riesman, David, 1909- . American sociologist.
Freedom/Liberty 1406
Rizzo, Frank L., 1920- . American politician; mayor of Philadelphia, 1972-80.
Conservatism 223
Robeson, Paul, 1898-1976. American singer, actor & civil rights activist.
Freedom/Liberty 1428
Robespierre, Maximilien, 1758-1794. French revolutionary.
Politics 2683

Robinson, James Harvey, 1863-1936. American historian & educator.
Political Campaigns 2428
Rochester, Earl of, (John Wilmot), 1647-1680. English courtier, poet & author.
Monarchy 2332
Rockefeller, Nelson A., 1908-1979. American politician; governor of New York, 1959-73; vice president of the United States, 1974-76.
Freedom of the Press 1192
Politicians and Public Officials 2640
Republican Party 3175
Taxation and Budgets 3623
Rockne, Knut, 1888-1931. American football coach.
Leadership/Statesmanship 2119
Rogers, Ginger, 1911- . American dancer & movie star.
Leadership/Statesmanship 2200
Rogers, Will, 1879-1935. American humorist.
Communism 151
Democracy 448
Democratic Party 505, 507, 508, 509
Ethics in Politics 802
Expressions and Phrases 946
Freedom/Liberty 1360, 1404
International Affairs/Diplomacy 1646, 1650
Legislatures and Legislation 2248
Political Parties 2492
Politicians and Public Officials 2588, 2600, 2601, 2602, 2603
Politics 2742, 2748, 2766
Social Justice 3534
Taxation and Budgets 3607, 3611, 3615, 3616
War and Peace 3859
Rogers, William P., 1913- . American lawyer & public official; secretary of state, 1969-73.
International Affairs/Diplomacy 1704
Roland, Mme., (Marie-Jeanne), 1754-1793. French writer; held salon during revolutionary years; wife of Jean-Marie Roland, a girondist leader.
Freedom/Liberty 1246
Rolland, Romain, 1866-1944. French author & dramatist.
War and Peace 3775
Romulo, Carlos P., 1899-1985. Filipino journalist & national leader; foreign minister of the Philippines, 1952-53, 1968-84.
International Affairs/Diplomacy 1718
Rooney, Andy, 1919- . American author & television commentator.
Politicians and Public Officials 2655
Roosevelt, Eleanor, 1884-1962. American social reformer; first lady of the United States, 1933-45.
Democratic Party 504
Education 692
Freedom of the Press 1181
Leadership/Statesmanship 2168
Prejudice and Discrimination 2912

Solon, ca. 630-560 B.C Athenian statesman.
  Law   1828
Solzhenitsyn, Alexander, 1918- . Russian author.
  Communism   177
  Expressions and Phrases   1044
  Law   1953
Sorensen, Theodore, 1928- . American lawyer &
public official.
  Presidency   2999
Souvanna Phouma, 1901-1984. Laotian political
leader.
  Communism   165
Spencer, Herbert, 1820-1903. English philosopher.
  Democracy   368
  Freedom/Liberty   1271
  Revolution   3216
  Socialism   3553
Spender, Sir Stephen, 1909- . English journalist &
author.
  Freedom of Speech   1152
  Liberalism   2278
  Politics   2758
Spenser, Edmund, 1552-1599. English poet.
  Leadership/Statesmanship   1980
Spinoza, Baruch (Benedictus de), 1632-1677.
Dutch philosopher.
  Citizenship   15
  Role of the State/of Government   3409, 3411
  War and Peace   3681
  Role of the State/of Government   3410
Stalin, Joseph, 1879-1953. Soviet communist
leader; head of Soviet Union, 1929-53.
  Communism   134
  Nationalism   2381
  Religion and the State   3157
  Revolution   3229, 3239
  Socialism   3558
  War and Peace   3832, 3878
Stanton, Elizabeth Cady, 1815-1902. American
feminist & social reformer.
  Class Divisions   62
  Conservatism   204
  Dictatorship/Tyranny   574, 575
  Elections and Voting   706
  Equality   747
  Prejudice and Discrimination   2902, 2903, 2904
  Reform   3100, 3106
  Rights/Human Rights   3314
  Social Justice   3522
  War and Peace   3748
  Women in Politics   3980, 3986, 3987, 3988
Steel, Ronald, 1931- . American political scientist
& author.
  Politics   2816
Steffens, Lincoln, 1866-1936. American journalist
& social reformer.
  Communism   130
Steinem, Gloria, 1935- . American feminist.
  Women in Politics   4014

Stephen, Sir James Fitzjames, 1829-1894. British
jurist.
  Democracy   353
  Expressions and Phrases   904
  Freedom of Speech   1118
Stevens, John Paul, 1920- . American jurist;
justice of the Supreme Court, 1975-.
  Judiciary and Judges   1743
  Religion and the State   3165
  Rights/Human Rights   3392
Stevenson, Adlai E., Jr., 1900-1965. American
politician; Democratic candidate for president,
1952 & 1956.
  Politics   2776
  Communism   153
  Democracy   455, 457, 461, 462, 464, 465
  Education   693
  Ethics in Politics   803, 805
  Expressions and Phrases   991, 992, 993, 994,
  995, 1001, 1002, 1007, 1034, 1037
  Freedom of Speech   1134, 1142
  Freedom/Liberty   1411, 1412, 1413, 1416, 1431
  Government   1561, 1563, 1564
  International Affairs/Diplomacy   1661, 1689
  Leadership/Statesmanship   2158
  Patriotism   2418, 2419
  Political Parties   2499
  Politicians and Public Officials   2607, 2630
  Politics   2772, 2777, 2791
  Prejudice and Discrimination   2933
  Presidency   2980
  Republican Party   3170, 3171, 3172, 3173
  Revolution   3264
  Role of the State/of Government   3480
  Social Justice   3536
Stevenson, Adlai R., Jr.
  Presidency   2981
Stevenson, Robert Louis, 1850-1894. Scottish
author.
  Politics   2775
Stewart, Michael, 1906- . British politician;
foreign secretary, 1965-66, 1968-70.
  International Affairs/Diplomacy   1709
  Politicians and Public Officials   2651
Stewart, Potter, 1915-1985. American jurist;
justice of the Supreme Court, 1958-81.
  Constitution   243
  Justice   1806, 1807
  Law   1939, 1955
  Rights/Human Rights   3354, 3377, 3381, 3382,
  3385
Stimson, Henry, 1867-1950. American public
official; secretary of war, 1911-13, 1940-45;
secretary of state, 1929-33.
  Government and Business   1593
Stockman, David, 1946- . American public official;
director, Office of Management and Budget,1981-
85.
  Taxation and Budgets   3629

Thorneycroft, Peter, Lord Thorneycroft, 1909- . British politician; chancellor of the exchequer, 1957-58; chairman, Conservative Party, 1975-78.
  Politics 2811
Thorpe, Jeremy, 1929- . British politician; head of Liberal Party, 1967-76.
  Majority and Minorities 2318
Timerman, Jacobo, 1923- . Argentine author & journalist.
  Expressions and Phrases 1085
  Patriotism 2423
Tobriner, Matthew American jurist.
  Freedom of Speech 1146
Tocqueville, Alexis, Comte de
  Class Divisions 47
  Democracy 322, 323, 324
Tocqueville, Alexis de
  Democracy 325
Tocqueville, Alexis, Comte de
  Education 677
  Equality 746
  Freedom of the Press 1167, 1168
  Government 1530, 1531
  Government and Business 1580
Tocqueville, Alexis de
  Judiciary and Judges 1729
Tocqueville, Alexis, Comte de, 1805-1859. French political philosopher & author.
  Justice 1782
  Law 1882
  Leadership/Statesmanship 2046
  Majority and Minorities 2288
  Politicians and Public Officials 2543
  Politics 2696
  Power 2855
  Taxation and Budgets 3594, 3595
  Separation of Powers 3508
Torrijos Herrera, Omar, 1929-1981. Panamanian military & political leader.
  Communism 179
Treitschke, Heinrich von, 1834-1896. German historian.
  Role of the State/of Government 3465
  War and Peace 3758
Trillin, Calvin, 1935- . American journalist & author.
  Class Divisions 109
Trilling, Lionel, 1905-1975. American critic & author.
  Liberalism 2275
Trotsky, Leon, 1879-1940. Russian communist leader.
  Communism 135, 136, 138
  Revolution 3243
Trudeau, Pierre Eliot, 1919- . Canadian politician; prime minister of Canada, 1969-79, 1980-84.
  Role of the State/of Government 3492

Truman, Harry S, 1884-1972. American politician; president of the United States, 1945-1953.
  Democracy 438, 450, 484
  Dictatorship/Tyranny 614
  Expressions and Phrases 977, 985
  Freedom of the Press 1185
  International Affairs/Diplomacy 1656
  Judiciary and Judges 1736
  Leadership/Statesmanship 2144, 2146, 2164
  Political Parties 2502
  Politicians and Public Officials 2613, 2615, 2639
  Politics 2773, 2817
  Presidency 2982, 2983, 2984, 2985, 2986, 2987, 2988, 2989, 2992, 2993, 3016
  Public Opinion 3076
  Social Justice 3535
  War and Peace 3873, 3889, 3892
Truman, Margaret, 1924- . American author.
  Politicians and Public Officials 2658
Truth, Sojourner, 1797-1883. American feminist & abolitionist.
  Class Divisions 61
  Majority and Minorities 2295
  Rights/Human Rights 3305, 3310
  Women in Politics 3981
Tubman, Harriet, 1826-1913. American abolitionist; leader of Underground Railroad.
  Freedom/Liberty 1308, 1309
Turnbull, Agnes Sligh, 1888-1982. American author.
  Politics 2778, 2779
Tutu, Desmond, 1931- . South African religious & civil rights leader.
  Leadership/Statesmanship 2214
  Prejudice and Discrimination 2948
  Rights/Human Rights 3398
Twain, Mark, (Samuel L. Clemens), 1835-1910. American author.
  Conservatism 205, 206
  Equality 757
  Ethics in Politics 786, 790
  Freedom/Liberty 1324, 1325, 1327
  International Affairs/Diplomacy 1630
  Law 1906
  Leadership/Statesmanship 2084
  Legislatures and Legislation 2240
  Monarchy 2354
  Patriotism 2407, 2409, 2410
  Politics 2719
  Public Opinion 3060
  Reform 3105
  Role of the State/of Government 3464
Twining, Gen. Nathan F., 1897-1982. American air force general; chairman, joint chiefs of staff, 1957-60.
  War and Peace 3890
Tyler, John, 1790-1862. American politician; president of the United States, 1841-45.
  Role of the State/of Government 3446

Tyrrell, R. Emmett, Jr., 1943- . American author
& political commentator.
Democratic Party   512
U.S. Senate, Select Committee on Intelligence
Oper.
Presidency   3024
Udall, Morris K., 1922- . American politician;
congressman from Arizona, 1961-.
Elections and Voting   722
Politicians and Public Officials   2645
Presidency   3025
Udall, Stewart L., 1920- . American public
official; secretary of the interior, 1961-69.
Politicians and Public Officials   2626
Power   2885
Unamuno, Miguel de, 1864-1936. Spanish
philosopher & author.
Leadership/Statesmanship   2102
UNESCO
War and Peace   3847
United Presbyterian Church
Class Divisions   111
United States Court of Appeals
Democracy   483
Separation of Powers   3513
Updike, John, 1932- . American author.
Presidency   3002
Ustinov, Peter, 1921- . English actor & author.
War and Peace   3954
Valéry, Paul, 1871-1945. French poet & critic.
Freedom/Liberty   1365
Nationalism   2385
Politics   2760
War and Peace   3805, 3806, 3807
Van Buren, Martin, 1782-1862. American
politician; president of the United States, 1837-41.
International Affairs/Diplomacy   1616
Politicians and Public Officials   2538
Role of the State/of Government   3440
Vanderbilt, William, 1849-1920. American
railroad tycoon.
Ethics in Politics   787
Vansittart, Robert, 1st Baron, 1881-1957. British
diplomat.
International Affairs/Diplomacy   1651
Vauvenargues, Marquis de, (Luc de Clapier),
1715-1747. French soldier & moralist.
Government   1486
Justice   1766
Leadership/Statesmanship   2008
Politicians and Public Officials   2524
Politics   2676
Vegetius, (Flavius Vegetius Renatus), ca. 375.
Roman military writer.
War and Peace   3664
Vessey Jr., Gen. John W., 1922- . American
military leader; head, joint chiefs of staff, 1979-85.
War and Peace   3966

Vico, Giovanni Battista, 1668-1744. Italian
political philosopher.
Government   1483, 1484
Victoria, 1819-1901. queen of the United
Kingdom, 1837-1901; empress of India, 1876-1901.
Leadership/Statesmanship   2056
Monarchy   2350
War and Peace   3756
Vidal, Gore, 1925- . American author.
Bureaucracy   11
Politics   2818
Voltaire, (François Marie Arouet), 1694-1778.
French philosopher & author.
Citizenship   16
Dictatorship/Tyranny   531, 532, 533, 534, 535
Economics/The Economy   632
Expressions and Phrases   840
Freedom of the Press   1156
Freedom/Liberty   1206
Government   1487, 1490
Law   1852
Leadership/Statesmanship   2010, 2011
Monarchy   2340
Patriotism   2391
Politicians and Public Officials   2525
War and Peace   3688, 3690
Wachtler, Sol, 1930- . American jurist; chief
judge, New York State Court of Appeals, 1985-.
Rights/Human Rights   3396
Walesa, Lech, 1943- . Polish labor union leader;
founded Solidarity, 1980.
Communism   183
Walker, David, 1785-1830. American abolitionist.
Prejudice and Discrimination   2896
Wallace, George C., 1919- . American politician;
governor of Alabama, 1963-67, 1971-79, 1983-87.
Dictatorship/Tyranny   625
Prejudice and Discrimination   2940
Wallace, Henry American politician; vice-president
of the United States, 1941-45.
Class Divisions   97
Walpole, Horace, 4th Earl of Orford, 1717-1797.
English author.
Democracy   279
Walpole, Sir Robert, 1st Earl of Orford, 1676-
1745. English politician; first lord of the treasury,
1721-42.
War and Peace   3686
Walters, Vernon A., 1917- . American military
leader & diplomat; ambassador to the United
Nations, 1985-89.
Politicians and Public Officials   2666
Role of the State/of Government   3502
Ward, Artemus, (Charles Farrar Browne), 1834-
1867. American journalist, humorist & lecturer.
Politicians and Public Officials   2549
Politics   2699
Treason   3638

Ward, Barbara, 1914-1981. English economist & author.
  Leadership/Statesmanship 2170
Warner, Charles Dudley, 1829-1900. American editor & author.
  Politics 2706
  Public Opinion 3052
  Taxation and Budgets 3602
Warren, Earl, 1891-1974. American politician & jurist; chief justice of the Supreme Court, 1953-69.
  Freedom of Speech 1140
  Judiciary and Judges 1739
  Law 1928, 1929, 1933, 1941
  Legislatures and Legislation 2257
  Prejudice and Discrimination 2922
  Presidency 3029
  Rights/Human Rights 3346, 3347
Washington, George, 1732-1799. American general & statesman; president of the United States, 1789-97.
  Democracy 285, 303, 304
  Dictatorship/Tyranny 543
  Government 1500, 1503, 1512
  International Affairs/Diplomacy 1607, 1609, 1610, 1611
  Justice 1771
  Law 1865
  Political Parties 2458, 2459
  Politicians and Public Officials 2532
  Presidency 2952
  Role of the State/of Government 3419, 3425
  War and Peace 3695, 3700, 3701, 3706
Washington, Walter E., 1915- . American public official; mayor of Washington, D.C., 1967-74.
  Democracy 481
Watkins, Adm. James D., 1927- . American naval officer; Chief of Naval Operations, 1982-86; secretary of energy, 1989-.
  War and Peace 3969
Watson, James E., 1863-1948. American politician; congressman from Indiana, 1895-1909; senator, 1916-33.
  Expressions and Phrases 950
Webb, Beatrice, 1858-1943. British social economist & social reformer.
  Politicians and Public Officials 2577, 2582, 2583
Weber, Max, 1864-1920. German sociologist & political economist.
  Government 1551
  Power 2867
Webster, Daniel, 1782-1852. American politician; senator from Massachusetts, 1827-41, 1845-50; sec'ty of state, 1841-43, 1850-52.
  Citizenship 18
  Class Divisions 42
  Democracy 317
  Dictatorship/Tyranny 555
  Expressions and Phrases 866, 874

  Freedom/Liberty 1258, 1259, 1267
  Justice 1784
Weil, Simone, 1909-1943. French essayist & religious philosopher.
  Dictatorship/Tyranny 613
Weinkrantz, Herman. American jurist.
  Rights/Human Rights 3376
Welk, Lawrence, 1903- . American musician.
  Politics 2805
Wellington, 1st Duke of, (Arthur Wellesley), 1769-1852. British general & political leader; prime minister of the United Kingdom, 1828-30.
  Government 1521
  Political Parties 2472
  Revolution 3202
  War and Peace 3713
Wells, H.G., 1866-1946. English novelist & historian.
  Education 688
  Expressions and Phrases 938
  War and Peace 3792
Wertham, Frederic, 1895-1981. German author & psychiatrist.
  Rights/Human Rights 3373
Westmoreland, Gen. William C., 1914- . American military leader; commander of U.S. forces in Vietnam, 1964-68.
  Freedom of the Press 1196
White, Byron R., 1917- . American jurist; justice of the Supreme Court, 1962-.
  Judiciary and Judges 1746
  Law 1962
White, E.B., 1899-1985. American author, essayist & humorist.
  Democracy 440
  Freedom/Liberty 1432
  International Affairs/Diplomacy 1655
  Nationalism 2382
White, Kevin, 1929- . American politician; mayor of Boston, 1967-84.
  Leadership/Statesmanship 2196
White, Theodore H., 1915-1986. American author & political commentator.
  Ethics in Politics 820
  Political Campaigns 2432, 2438
  Politicians and Public Officials 2634
  Politics 2790, 2822
White, William Allen, 1868-1944. American journalist; editor & publisher of the Emporia Gazette, 1895-1944.
  Expressions and Phrases 933
  Politicians and Public Officials 2563
Whitehead, Alfred North, 1861-1947. English philosopher & mathematician.
  Government 1557
Whitman, Walt, 1819-1892. American poet, essayist & journalist.
  Democracy 351
  Elections and Voting 707

Young, Whitney Moore, Jr., 1921-1971. American
civil rights leader.
   Reform   3131, 3132
   Rights/Human Rights

Keyword Index

Numbers refer to entry numbers not page numbers.

ABILITY
from each according to his abilities   115

in which everyone with ability can find a place   1516

rewards the appearance of ability rather than ability itself   1996

the ability to get men to do what they don't want   2146

my aim has been to combine geographical situation ... with abilities   2532

the degree of ability among the governed   2543

a hundred things to single you out ... in party politics besides ability   2603

administrative ability is the principal ability needed in politics   3590

the ability to do this is an administrative ability   3590

ABOLISH
The State is not "abolished." It dies out.   126

better to abolish serfdom from above   883

if it's true that you can't abolish vice   1486

ABOLITION
abolition of private property   119

this dictatorship ... constitutes ... the abolition of all classes   124

the abolition of exploitation and poverty   491

my views ... (are) in favor of the abolition of war   3714

of its abolition I despair   3714

ABOLITIONIST
Many Abolitionists have yet to learn the ABC of woman's rights.   3306

ABOMINATION
a lie is an abomination unto the Lord   803

ABORTION
abortion raises moral and spiritual questions   252

abortion is inherently different from other medical procedures   1955

ABOVE
better to abolish serfdom from above   883

ABRIDGMENT
more instances of the abridgment of freedom   1236

ABROAD
I don't mind dictatorships abroad provided they are pro-American.   625

the privilege of lying, either at home or abroad   1601

judged more by what we do at home than what we preach abroad   1679

A nation can be no stronger abroad than she is at home.   1683

when you're abroad, you almost feel yourself a statesman   2161

when I am abroad, I always make it a rule never to criticize   2765

If violence is wrong in America, violence is wrong abroad.   3272

source of strength to this nation both at home and abroad   3360

ABSENCE
one provision was conspicuous by its ... absence   888

The mere absence of war is not peace.   3916

ABSOLUTE
Anarchy always brings about absolute power.   553

absolute faith corrupts as absolutely as absolute power   622

There are similarities between absolute power and absolute faith: 622

government is ultimately and essentially absolute   1496

for absolute security, absolute amity, absolute harmony   2171

the search for absolutes in world affairs   2171

nor do men ... enjoy any greater ... freedom than in an absolute monarchy   2331

Princes have their Power Absolute, and by Divine Right   2334

Adam was an absolute Monarch   2334

An absolute monarchy is one in which the sovereign ... pleases the assassins.   2357

absolute power corrupts absolutely   2862

Absolute frustration is a dangerous emotion to run a world with. 2889

absolute powerlessness frustrates absolutely 2889

If power corrupts, being out of power corrupts absolutely. 2893

the President of the United States is neither an absolute monarch 2978

worst enemies of civil freedom are the absolute monarchy 3218

It is my belief that there are "absolutes" in our Bill of Rights 3356

meant their prohibitions to be "absolutes" 3356

ABSOLUTISM

All parties ... are varieties of absolutism. 2475

ABSTAIN

to abstain—to observe a wise and masterly inactivity 2231

ABSTINENCE

abstinence ... not now the right sign-posts to the socialist Utopia 3572

ABSTRACT

Abstract liberty ... is not to be found 1221

Liberty is not just an idea, an abstract principle. 1367

no such thing as justice in the abstract 1751

the realisation of abstract goods 3486

ABUNDANCE

the abundance of those who have much 3532

ABUNDANT

"a more abundant life" 3156

ABUSE

The abuse of greatness is when it disjoins 525

Abuse a man unjustly, and you will make friends for him. 926

The abuses of the press are notorious. 1157

To the press alone, chequered as it is with abuses 1161

Its evils exist only in its abuses. 1527

But let us persevere through abuse and even injury. 2017

the rusty artillery of abuse 2772

The greater the power, the more dangerous the abuse. 2838

power ... will ever be liable to abuse 2851

to possess boundless power without abusing it 2859

If the abuse be enormous, nature will rise up 3188

ACCEPT

I will not accept if nominated 911

ACCEPTABLE

compromise may make acceptable tomorrow 2794

ACCEPTANCE

The simplest truths ... are slowest in getting general acceptance. 3311

ACCIDENT

The good neighbor looks beyond the external accidents 2930

ACCOMMODATE

My pollertics ... being of an exceeding' accommodatin' character 2699

ACCOMPLISH

You cannot accomplish good for the people 2027

those who want to accomplish something 2206

very little in the way of constructive accomplishment 2972

ACCOUNTABITY

(American liberty) is premised on the accountability of free men 1473

ACCOUNTABLE

individual is not accountable to society for his actions 1286

ACCUMULATION

The accumulation of all powers 3506

ACCURST

Accurst be he that first invented war. 3670

ACHIEVE

those who achieve something 2118

ACHIEVEMENT

The astonishing achievement of modern times 462

Democracy is never a final achievement. 474

who stands hectoring ... in our way to achievement 3792

ACID

That is the test of a political party—the acid, final test. 2499

ACQUIESCENCE

Such acquiescence would be a recognition 50

ACQUISITION

the next greatest pleasure consists ... in the acquisition of power 2868

ACROBAT

The politician is an acrobat. 2581

ACT

"to preserve is to act" 191

so long as it is a mere voice, without overt acts 282

manage without having had any acting experience 2661

ACTION

Political action is not moral action   327
freedom of action without freed capacity of
    thought   685
Justice is truth in action.   1783
Sir, I say that justice is truth in action.   1785
our action employs among its different weapons
    that of parliament   2250
my actions are my ministers'   2333
a body in action must overcome an equal body at
    rest   2685
The whole life of English politics is the
    action   2703
That action is best, which procures the greatest
    happiness   3414

ACTOR

Some members of congress are the best actors in
    the world.   2638

ADMINISTER

provided it is well administered   309
Welfare is hated by those who administer it   1074
Whate'er is best administer'd is best   1485
that's the atmosphere in which you
    administer   2824

ADMINISTRATION

This Administration intends to be candid about its
    errors;   806
Nor will it be finished ... in the life of this
    administration   1026
Bad administration ... can destroy good
    policy   1563
good administration can never save bad
    policy   1563
The ... administration doesn't know the
    difference   1706
administration of justice is the firmest pillar of
    Government   1771
Administration, n. An ingenious abstraction in
    politics   2725
no Administration ... has been free from ...
    mistakes   2961
administration of justice lies at the foundation of
    government   3467

ADMINISTRATIVE

The Presidency is not merely an administrative
    office.   2974

ADMIRABLE

Nothing is so admirable in politics as a short
    memory.   2819

ADMIRAL

to kill an admiral ... in order to encourage the
    others   3690

ADORE

One who comes to the Court must come to
    adore   1153

ADULATION

an insatiable need ... for friendship and
    adulation   2642

ADVANCE

They advance politically only as they
    placate   2608
The Government must always be in advance of
    public opinion.   3045

ADVANTAGE

Governments only keep their word when ... it is to
    their advantage.   1525
for the sake of the advantage which is to be
    gained   2514

ADVENTURE

War is not an adventure.   3837

ADVERSARY

the danger that is likely to accrue to me from any
    adversary   2074

ADVERSE

adverse to the rights of other citizens   2454

ADVERSITY

democracy is ... the more valuable for having been
    tested by adversity   489

ADVERTISING

papers are largely supported by advertising   1181
Give me the writing of a nation's advertising and
    propaganda   2878

ADVICE

to give ... military advice before they know they
    need it   3966

ADVISOR

He is an unsafe advisor.   2957

ADVOCACY

first function of a political leader is
    advocacy   2149

ADVOCATE

No man is a warmer advocate for proper
    restraints   1503

AFFAIRS

Politics is ... preventing people from taking part in
    affairs   2760

AFFECTION

as to esteem and affection, these are only due to
    their virtue   1979
The mercy of princes is often just a way of gaining
    the affection   1997
The politician ... seeks votes, affection and
    respect   2619

AFFORD

far too much law for those who can afford
    it   1957

AFRAID

as soon as men are not afraid to risk their lives   2107

not because men are morally bad, but because they are afraid of somebody   2573

AGES

a Constitution intended to endure for ages   250

AGGRESSION

Aggression unopposed becomes a contagious disease.   3960

AGGRESSIVE

giving every man enough antagonism ... to exercise all his aggressiveness   100

Aggressive conduct ... ultimately leads to war.   3912

AGITATE

Those who profess to favor freedom and yet deprecate agitation   1279

It agitates the community with ill-founded jealousies   2459

Agitation is, so to speak, endowed in this country.   2481

Nothing is so dull as political agitation.   2715

Agitators are a set of interfering, meddling people   3104

An agitation to attain a political or economic end   3238

AGITATOR

the reason why agitators are so absolutely necessary   3104

AGREE

to give liberty to others who do not agree with us   1366

talking only to people with whom you agree   1666

AGREEMENT

We are making remarkable progress toward an agreement   1065

nothing more likely to start disagreement ... than an agreement   1655

AGRICULTURE

you can still make a small fortune in agriculture   1599

AIL

If anything ail a man   3097

AIM

The very aim and end of our institutions   1117

take an aim much higher than their mark   1975

ultimate aim of government is not to rule ... by fear   3410

AIR CONDITIONER

an air conditioner is called a politician   2662

AIR FORCE

If our air forces are never used   3890

ALASKA

like living in Alaska and being against snow   768

ALIKE

we are all alike ... all just alike on the inside   757

ALIMENTARY CANAL

an alimentary canal with a big appetite at one end   1570

ALIVE

Keep hope alive.   1103

ALL

What touches all shall be approved by all.   269

All strong without, he is all-weak within.   602

It will become all one thing, or all the other.   885

All we ask is to be let alone.   892

no one can win all the time   1465

the sovereign must be all-powerful   1487

ALLEGATION

once an allegation has been repeated ... it is no longer an allegation   1022

ALLEGIANCE

heard something said about allegiance to the South   2401

the right to refuse allegiance to ... the government   3212

ALLIANCE

Unless abroad they purchase great alliance?   524

an alliance ... more formidable than the ... alliance of church and state   668

our true policy to steer clear of permanent alliance   1609

entangling alliances with none   1612

ALLY

We have no eternal allies   1619

Mr. Dulles has just frightened most of our allies to death   3891

ALMONER

government is not an almoner of gifts among the people   3460

ALMSHOUSE

to seek refuge in the almshouse of reaction   3211

ALONE

All we ask is to be let alone.   892

Britain would fight on alone whatever they did   970

right to be let alone is ... beginning of all freedoms   1414

For the present, at any rate, I must proceed alone.   2089

it is possible that I may not find myself
  alone   2089

The leader is always alone in times of
  doom.   2155

I am alone with the masses.   2195

The man who walks alone is soon trailed by the
  F.B.I.   3375

ALONG
If you want to get along, go along.   1018

ALPHA
It is the alpha and omega of man's relation to
  man.   384

ALTAR
I have sworn upon the altar of God   547

ALTER
the right of the people ... to alter their
  constitutions   303

ALTERNATIVE
once all other alternatives have been
  exhausted   1692

we had a secret weapon—no alternative   3940

AMBASSADOR
An ambassador is an honest man sent to lie
  abroad   1603

Why employ intelligent and highly paid
  ambassadors   1698

Parliament is not a congress of
  ambassadors   2221

AMBIGUITY
a participant in the doctrine of constructive
  ambiquity   2666

AMBITION
Great ambition ... is an unruly tyrant.   549

every colonel or general is soon full of
  ambition   621

Ambition often puts Men upon doing the meanest
  offices;   2003

All ambitions are lawful   2094

AMBITIOUS
The slave has only one master; the ambitious man
  ... many   2002

rarely an ambitious man who does not try to be
  popular   2015

Men may be popular without being
  ambitious;   2015

Men in political life must be ambitious.   2560

Politicians are ambitious not to make important
  decisions   2598

AMENDMENT
Amendments to the Constitution ought to not be
  too frequently made;   239

AMERICA
America cannot always sit as a queen in peace and
  repose.   879

I rejoice that America has resisted.   1215

Whatever America hopes to bring to pass in the
  world   1659

must first come to pass in the heart of
  America   1659

America is not like a blanket—one piece of
  unbroken cloth   2320

Politics in America is the binding secular
  religion.   2822

America did not invent human rights ... human
  rights invented America.   3393

If we are to preserve freedom ... in America   3514

AMERICAN
American aristocracy can be found in the lawyer's
  bar   47

Americans ought ever be asking themselves about
  .. the ideal republic.   394

reactionaries who ... do not bear allegiance to ...
  American principles   443

Divine right went out with the American
  Revolution   482

That's what the American system is all
  about   486

You may be sure that the Americans will commit
  all the stupidities   1049

My fellow Americans, our long national nightmare
  is over.   1064

Since when have we Americans been expected to
  bow submissively   1469

We Americans have no commission from God to
  police the world.   1629

The American people are quite competent to judge
  a political party   2497

The American economy ... society are all
  racist   2926

if it reflects the best interests of the American
  people   3175

The destiny of the colored American ... is the
  destiny of America.   3308

AMERICANISM
room here for only hundred per cent
  Americanism   2376

AMISH
can be no assumption that ...the Amish ... are
  "wrong"   2317

AMMUNITION
Why is it that when political ammunition runs
  low   2772

AMPLIFYING SYSTEM
denying him the use of an amplifying
  system   1155

AMUCK

the party that prevents the Government from running amuck 2730

ANARCHY

Anarchy always brings about absolute power. 553

Freedom and not servitude is the cure of anarchy; 1222

Liberty unregulated by law degenerates into anarchy 1273

perpetual oscillation of nations between anarchy and despotism 1313

Governments destitute of energy, will ever produce anarchy. 1506

anarchy and competition the laws of death 1541

The worst thing in this world, next to anarchy, is government. 1546

In anarchy it's not just the king who loses his rights 1551

so society seeks order in anarchy 3443

ANCHOR

Your Constitution is all sail and no anchor. 238

My anchor is democracy—and more democracy. 409

ANEW

So let us begin anew 1672

ANGEL

If men were angels, no government would be necessary. 1504

ANIMAL

All animals are equal/ But some animals are more equal than others. 761

Man is by nature a political animal. 2672

You may be a well-dressed animal, but you are nevertheless an animal. 3551

If you turn your back on these people, you yourself are an animal. 3551

Man is not like other animals ...: animals have instincts, we have taxes 3622

ANIMOSITY

Numerous cross-divisions favour peace ... by dispersing ... animosities; 100

spirit of party ... kindles the animosity of one part against another; 2459

ANKLE

No man can put a chain about the ankle of his fellow man 3315

ANNIHILATE

annihilating peoples and nations in their entirety 3684

It's the nuclear age, and war can annihilate us all. 3952

ANNIHILATION

to wish annihilation of air, which is essential to animal life 2455

ANOTHER

he ought not to be free to do as he likes in acting for another 1291

ANSWER

I believe that government is the problem, not the answer. 1573

information so incomplete that the answer does not suggest itself 2159

not ... the Republican answer or the Democratic answer, but the right answer 2504

ANT

like a bunch of ants on a log floating down a river 2648

ANTARCTIC

some men are stationed in the Antarctic and some ... in San Francisco 765

ANTI-

If a democratic people comes under the sway of an anti-capitalistic creed 423

whatever is ... anti-intellectual ... will hereafter be McCarthyism 1017

Anti-semitism is the socialism of fools. 2906

Chaos and ineptitude are anti-human; 3481

Government should be concerned with anti-social conduct 3482

Speaking like this doesn't mean that we're anti-white 3545

we're anti-oppression 3545

ANTICIPATED

Certain peace is better and safer than anticipated victory. 3657

APARTHEID

Abhorrence of apartheid is a normal attitude 3378

hoping for the day when apartheid will be no more 3397

America's view of apartheid is simple and straightforward: 3397

APATHY

It will be a slow extinction from apathy 458

APE

the story of an ape playing with a box of matches 3903

APHRODISIAC

Power is the great aphrodisiac. 2890

APOLOGIZE

I apologize for what was said even though I didn't say it. 1098

if countries always apologized when they had done wrong 1630

APPALLED
(I am) appalled at the ethical bankruptcy 1952

APPEAL
The instinctive appeal of every successful political
movement 2738

APPEARANCE
The world usually rewards the appearance of
ability 1996
playing a dangerous game to seek to retain the
appearance 2855

APPELLATIVE
several cloudy appellatives ... have been ... cloaks
for misgovernment 554

APPETITE
they who have more dinners than appetite, and
they who have more appetite 45
a big appetite at one end and no sense of
responsibility at the other 1570

APPLAUD
We uniformly applaud what is right 859
When I hear a man applauded by the mob I
always feel a pang of pity 2612

APPLAUSE
Applause is wonderful until you can hardly hear
yourself speak. 2433

APPOINTIVE
What we need in appointive positions is men of
knowledge 2587

APPOINTMENT
appointment by the corrupt few 374
In the appointments to the great offices of the
government 2532
A fellow once came to me to ask for an
appointment as a minister abroad. 2553
Let appointments and removals be made on
business principles 2555

APPREHENSION
Never was an apprehension less plausible. 3566

APPROPRIATE
No law is quite appropriate for all. 1825

APPROVED
What touches all shall be approved by all. 269

APRIL 15
Democrats believe every day is April 15 3182

ARAB
in our war with the Arabs we had a secret
weapon 3940

ARBITER
the judges as the ultimate arbiters of all
constitutional questions 1728

ARBITRARY
Nip the shoots of arbitrary power in the
bud 1224
the deliberative forces should prevail over the
arbitrary 1359
separation of powers .. to preclude the exercise of
arbitrary power 3510

ARCHBISHOP
they should get it from their archbishop 2635

ARCHER
He will act like prudent archers 1975

ARGUMENT
anymore than a box on the ear is an
argument 327
this simple argument—two and two make
four 2036

ARISTOCRACY
A true natural aristocracy is not a separate
interest 41
Aristocracy ... has been the greatest source of
evil 46
The American aristocracy can be found in the
lawyer's bar 47
Aristocracy is always cruel. 63
An aristocracy is like cheese 85
A society without an aristocracy ... is not a
society. 90
An aristocracy in a republic is like a chicken
whose head has been cut off 102
something to be said for government by a great
aristocracy 379
system of outdoor relief for the aristocracy of
Great Britain 887
There is a natural aristocracy among men. 2033
You are apprehensive of monarchy; I, of
aristocracy. 2950
a moneyed aristocracy dangerous to the
liberties 3591

ARISTOCRAT
the holy water which ... consecrates the heart-
burnings of the aristocrat 3150

ARMAMENTS
customary ... to deplore expenditure on
armaments 3479

ARMED FORCES
not the armed forces which can protect our
democracy 449
The people are always in the wrong when ... faced
by the armed forces. 551

ARMS
nationhood is not achieved otherwise than in
arms 1345
give them enough arms 1477

He is wise who tries everything before
arms. 3651

Let arms yield to the toga 3653

when a resort to arms can alone save ...
dishonor 3747

Arms alone are not enough to keep peace. 3911

ARMY

The good sense of the people is the strongest
army 294

Mobs will never do to govern states or command
armies. 296

attend to all the details of the army 895

The Army will hear nothing of politics from
me 929

Without an army ... there is no political
independence 1513

The objections which have been brought against a
standing army 1536

Poor Ike—it won't be a bit like the Army. 2993

Where the state is weak, the army rules. 3432

Nay, number itself in armies importeth not
much 3674

The sergeant is the Army. 3948

AROUSE

the sense of injustice in others has been
thoroughly aroused 1801

no group ... can withstand the force of an aroused
public opinion 3070

It is impossible to arouse the people
artificially. 3223

ARREST

Arrest for its breach is more so. 1920

ARROW

Ideas are great arrows, but there has to be a
bow. 2788

ARSENAL

We must be the great arsenal of democracy. 964

ART

You need neither art nor science to be a
tyrant. 529

The art of policing is ... to punish severely. 1778

art of governing ... not letting men grow old in
their jobs 2533

Politics is not a science ... but an art. 2717

Politics is not an art, but a means. 2743

By comparison with the greatest subjects of
art 2758

the only art that is necessary to one who
commands 3667

ARTICULATE

It is he who must make articulate the
wants 2149

ARTILLERY

the rusty artillery of abuse is always wheeled into
action 2772

ASCENDANCY

their ever-renewing fight for ascendancy in the
affairs of mankind 1786

ASHAMED

Be ashamed to die until you have won some
victory for humanity. 2066

ASIA

There is a wind of nationalism and freedom
blowing ... in Asia 2379

what Asian boys ought to be doing for
themselves 3919

the job that Asian boys should do 3921

ASK

All we ask is to be let alone. 892

ASPIRATION

a synthesis of practical thoughts and idealistic
aspirations 2782

ASS

Even on the highest throne in the world, we are
still sitting on our ass. 827

the law is a ass—a idiot 1881

A leader should not get too far in front ... or he
will be shot in the ass. 2207

He was used to getting his ass kissed. 2817

the American public wants a solemn ass as a
President 2970

ASSAIL

assailant is often in the right; the assailed is
always. 881

ASSASSIN

the violence will be in the thought and the action
of the assassins 2213

the sovereign does as he pleases so long as he
pleases the assassins 2357

ASSASSINATE

I would rather be assassinated on this spot than
surrender it 1295

ASSASSINATION

The death of democracy is not likely to be an
assassination from ambush. 458

Assassination has never changed the history of the
world. 899

Assassination is the extreme form of
censorship. 932

Canada has at last produced a political leader
worthy of assassination 2637

ASSEMBLY

but an assembly of despots never does 531

parliament is a deliberative assembly of one
nation 2221

the same arbitrary power being there in the
assembly 2331

A monarch frequently represents his subjects
better than an elected assembly; 2359

ASSERT
The people know their rights, and they are never slow to assert ... them   3302

ASSESSMENT
No favored class should demand freedom from assessment   3601

ASSET
no greater asset than the willingness ... to face all problems frankly   471

ASTONISH
Nothing astonishes men so much as common sense   875

ATHEIST
one who under an atheist king would be atheist   3138

ATOMIC BOMB
a greater blow to humanity than the atomic bomb at Hiroshima   3861
No country without an atom bomb could ... consider itself independent.   3937

ATROCITY
a collection of atrocity stories designed to stimulate martial ardour   133

ATTACK
I always cheer up immensely if an attack is particularly wounding   2823

ATTEMPTED
no more good must be attempted than the nation can bear   3087

ATTENTION
they will appreciate the attention   2668

ATTIC
he would have written four volumes in an attic   2086

ATTITUDE
Law's empire is defined by attitude, not territory   1960
Bias and prejudice are attitudes to be kept in hand   2923
Abhorrence of apartheid is a normal attitude   3378
peace and war are attitudes of mind   3796

ATTITUDINIZING
Without that it is mere wind and attitudinizing.   3238

ATTORNEY
he has a right to the presence of an attorney   1941

ATTRACTED
Good government obtains when those who are ... far off are attracted.   1476

ATTRACTION
a perverted creed that has a queer attraction   164
men, who, by their sympathetic attractions, carry nations   2067

ATTRACTIVE
Power makes you attractive;   2857
something which substitutes attractive virtues for attractive vices   3116

AUDIENCE
The audience ... that hissed yesterday may applaud today   1137
The best audience is intelligent, well-educated and a little drunk.   2429

AUGHT
It's the aughts that scare me.   3934

AUGURY
The single best augury is to fight for one's country.   2388

AUSCHWITZ
over the gates of Auschwitz there stretched ... "Arbeit Macht Frei"   1466

AUTHOR
the author of a war lets loose the whole contagion of hell   3698

AUTHORITY
Where the people possess no authority, their rights obtain no respect.   320
Authority is never without hate.   824
Mere precedent is a dangerous source of authority.   868
henceforth he will recognize no authority   1262
The struggle between liberty and authority is the most conspicuous feature   1282
Most men, after a little freedom, have preferred authority   1344
the possibility of saying "No" to any authority   1410
Since when have we Americans been expected to bow submissively to authority   1469
Lawful and settled authority is very seldom resisted   1488
There is no authority without justice.   1777
more sensitive to any offense that tends to diminish their authority   2052
Authority must be accompanied by prestige   2125
It rejects and destroys all authority and divine law.   2269
To despise legitimate authority ... is unlawful   3225

AUTOBIOGRAPHY
Politics ... with a strong tendency towards autobiography   2278

AUTOCRACY

Communism is a Russian autocracy turned upside down.   123

the mistakes which have been made by every kind of autocracy   393

in the hands of political puppets of an economic autocracy   407

to save the people from autocracy   3510

AUTOCRAT

he does not recognize his native autocrats   1407

Are all Cabinets congeries of little autocrats   2582

AUTOMATION

industrial masters think they can do it by automation   2888

AUTOMATON

A mechanized automaton.   552

AUTONOMY

the human mind, and its intense fear of autonomy   212

they lose ... their individual autonomy in seeking to become like each other   1406

AVAIL

For what avail the plow or sail   1305

AVERAGE

men who differ from the average in being exceptionally power-loving   415

The upward course of a nation's history is due ... to ...its average men   460

anyone who is not content to be the average man   3066

AVIARY

Israel is not an aviary.   1052

AXIOMS

the axioms and corollaries of a book of mathematics   1892

AXLE

it's bogged down up to the axles   3824

BABY

Government is like a big baby   1570

BACHELOR

If that's the eye of the law, the law is a bachelor;   1881

A politician ought to be born a foundling and remain a bachelor.   2643

All reformers are bachelors.   3109

in five years there will be a crushing tax on bachelors   3989

BACK

designed to take the government off the backs of people   256

To be a leader of men one must turn one's back on men.   2078

Its birthplace is the sinister back room of the mind   2937

Remember to lean back in the parade car   2995

If you turn your back on these people, you yourself are an animal.   3551

BACKWARD

Revolutions do not go backward.   749

I hope to "stand firm" enough not to go backward   2070

Revolutions never go backward.   3215

BAD

the vitriolic words and actions of the bad people   30

How ... best avoid situations in which a bad ruler causes too much harm?   498

There is nothing so bad or so good that you will not find Englishmen doing it;   789

When bad men combine, the good must associate;   838

those who followed us were so bad that they made us seem better than we were   1060

how is the state to be constituted so that bad rulers can be got rid of   1577

all men are bad and ever ready to display their vicious nature   1833

bad ones bring about worse   1861

Anyone who takes it upon himself ... to break a bad law   1874

teach men to trample bad laws under their feet   1887

Many laws as certainly make bad men, as bad men make many laws.   1888

Great cases like hard cases make bad law.   1905

If we believe a thing to be bad ... it is our duty to try to prevent it   2092

There never was a bad man that had ability for good service.   2530

not because men are morally bad, but because they are afraid of somebody   2573

they are as bad as they dare to be   2845

There never was a good war or a bad peace.   3692

BAKER'S UNION

I rushed out and got the baker's union to endorse me.   2828

BALANCE

so as to maintain the balance of the body politic   78

a kind of balance between the will of the people and the government   451

Education ... is ... the balance-wheel of the social machinery   679

not a balance of power, but a community of
power;   1640

when commitments and power have been brought
into balance   1654

a balance between means and ends that is the
heart of foreign policy   1661

There is now a balance of terror.   1691

The management of a balance of power is a
permanent undertaking   1708

the scales of American justice are out of
balance   1815

He keeps his balance by saying the opposite of
what he does.   2581

how close you can walk without losing your
balance   2808

by balancing each of these powers ... that ...
tyranny can alone be checked   3504

this phrase of the "balance of Power" is to be
always an argument for war   3726

BALLOON

that political beliefs are logically determined
collapses like a ... balloon   2571

BALLOT

Truth no more relies for success on ballot
boxes   327

The ballot is stronger than the bullet.   702

Our "pathway" is straight to the ballot box   706

People only leave (Washington) by way of the
box--ballot or coffin.   719

the assertion of the natural right of all to the
ballot   3312

BALM

Can wash the balm from an annointed king   2325

BANDAGE

Justice should remove the bandage from her
eyes   1792

BANDIT

military caste ... a party of bandits   2420

Thinkers prepare the revolution; bandits carry it
out.   3240

BANEFUL

the baneful effects of the spirit of party   2458

BANK

the Governor of the Bank of England goes on for
ever   4

prefer to think of it as the poor man's bank   3444

BANKRUPTCY

A reasonable internal debt will not ... put the
Nation into bankruptcy   3614

BARBARISM

From fanaticism to barbarism is only one
step.   836

War is ... a feature of barbarism   3748

BARBARITY

Between the barbarity of capitalism ... and the
barbarity of socialism   3575

BARREL

"Political power grows out of the barrel of a
gun."   142

BARRIER

Peace is ... slowly eroding old barriers   3917

BASENESS

the baseness which makes conservatives   3221

BASIC RIGHT

To fight against the government ... is a basic
right   356

no person ... whose basic rights are not
involved   1926

BASIS

The firm basis of government is justice, not
pity.   1798

BASTARD

The voters are the people who have spoken—the
bastards.   722

BATH

"to take a bath in public opinion"   3055

BATHING

The right hon. Gentleman caught the Whigs
bathing   877

BATTALION

God is always on the side of the big
battalions   840

BATTLE

Half-heartedness never won a battle.   920

human beings must be willing ... to do
battle   1786

I cannot lead you into battle.   2361

focusing on the last battle and overreacting to
that   2664

no "white" or "colored" signs on the foxholes ...
of battle   2929

the battle of this office, which is a continuing
battle   3010

I believe in the battle   3010

Like all the other great battles of humanity   3318

The battle, sir, is not to the strong alone;   3693

whether we defeat the enemy in one battle   3696

Nothing except a battle lost can be half so
melancholy as a battle won.   3713

glazed eye of a dying warrior on the field of
battle   3742

Battle, n. A method of untying with the
teeth   3765

they want the sound of battle ... the battle of
destiny   3941

BATTLEFIELD

You cannot choose your battlefield   2114
most terrible warfare is ... leading a platoon ... on the battlefield   3884

BAYONET

A new Government took office in Washington, not via bayonets and tanks   512
A man may build himself a throne of bayonets   579
revolutions are the work rather of principles than of bayonets   3203
at point of bayonet if necessary   3395

BEAR

no more good must be attempted than the nation can bear   3087

BEARD

He who tugs Uncle Sam's beard too hard   1707

BEATEN

A nation which makes the final sacrifice ... does not get beaten.   1388
He says, "I was beaten." He does not say, "My men were beaten."   2137

BEATEN PATH

People tend to want to follow the beaten path.   2191
the beaten path doesn't seem to be leading anywhere   2191

BED-FELLOWS

Politics makes strange bed-fellows.   2706

BEDLAM

drivers contradicting each other in a bedlam of voices   3171

BEDROOM

The state has no business in the bedrooms of the nation.   3492

BEE

Public men are bees working in a glass hive;   2081

BEGIN

But let us begin.   1026

BEGINNING

This is the beginning of the end.   854
But it is, perhaps, the end of the beginning.   973
In the beginning of a change, the patriot is a scarce man   2410

BEGUILE

most jealous and exacting mistress that can beguile ... man   1328

BEING

it must be an inseparable part of our very being   984

BELIEF

Democratic Party is a party ... not in shared belief   513
One person with a belief is a social power   2069
A man is not as big as his belief in himself;   2096
Mass movements can rise ... without belief in a God   3126

BELIEVABLE

we must make government believable   480

BELIEVE

a politician never believes what he says   2624
I didn't ask you to believe me.   3033
One must believe in it. And it isn't enough to believe in it.   3868

BELL

They may ring their bells now   3686

BELLY

He whose belly is full believes not him whose is empty.   38

BELONG

To betray you must first belong.   3643

BENEFICIARY

beneficiaries of a system cannot be expected to destroy it   3528

BENEFIT

who receives the protection of society owes a return for the benefit   20
the trust and the trustees are created for the benefit of the people   315
not for the benefit of an individual or a party   321
inestimable benefits that the liberty of the press ensures   1167
The law is ... for the benefit of the public   1867
Government is ... instituted for the common benefit   3418
One cannot raise the bottom of a society without benefiting everyone above.   3541
(A tax loophole is) something that benefits the other guy.   3634
If it benefits you, it is tax reform.   3634

BENEVOLENT

an insurance against benevolent despots as well   380
benevolent despot who sees himself as a shepherd of the people   617

BERLIN

said that West Berlin is militarily untenable   3908

BERLINER

"Ich bin ein Berliner."   1444

Keyword Index

BEST

The majority is the best way, because it is visible   273

best form of Government ... one where the masses have little power   336

like t'vote fer th'best man, but he's never a candidate.   711

Always give your best, never get discouraged   1063

not the best possible laws but the best ... they will bear   2237

serves his party best who serves his country best   2482

best for the ... country was ... to help both political parties   2484

It were not best that we should all think alike;   2719

The best politics is no politics.   2814

I will do my best. That is all I can do.   2998

if it reflects the best interests of the American people   3175

That government is not best which best secures mere life and property   3464

BETRAY

he betrays ... if he sacrifices it to your opinion   2527

convince themselves that they are about to be betrayed by their leaders   3574

They talk of a man betraying his country   3640

to choose between betraying my country and betraying my friend   3641

To betray you must first belong.   3643

BETTER

unless made ... by the exertions of better men than himself   1298

No government is better than the men who compose it.   2621

Better to die on one's feet than to live on one's knees.   3340

BEWARE

Beware of the man who does not return your blow   2722

BIAS

It both enforces and suggests forms of bias.   1946

BIBLE

do not mock the bondman ... by giving him a Bible when he cannot read it   678

BIBLICAL

that was a fate of biblical proportions   2211

BICKER

a people so fundamentally at one that they can safely afford to bicker;   397

The American people didn't send us ... to bicker.   2831

BIG

He who would not wish his own country to be bigger or smaller   16

more easily fall victims to a big lie   589

We demand that big business give the people a square deal;   1588

"Speak softly and carry a big stick; you will go far."   1632

A man is not as big as his belief in himself;   2096

as big as the number of persons who believe in him   2096

the way to be a big man is to shout and stomp and raise hell   2187

to be as big a man as he can   2966

presidency has made every man who occupied it ... bigger than he was   3006

A government ... big enough to give you all ... is big enough to take it   3489

BIGOTED

Reformers can be as bigoted and sectarian ... as the Church   3100

BILL

Among the defects of the bill, which were numerous   888

BILL OF RIGHTS

Can ... you ... say the Bill of Rights could get through Congress today?   246

A bill of rights is what the people are entitled to   3294

there are "absolutes" in our Bill of Rights   3356

a right of privacy older than the Bill of Rights   3371

BILLION

It's a terribly hard job to spend a billion dollars   3617

Before we give you billions more   3633

BIOGRAPHY

history of the world is but the biography of great men   2050

Once you touch the biographies of human beings   2571

BIRDS OF PREY

Setting it up to fear the birds of prey   1841

BIRTH

that this nation ... shall have a new birth of freedom   344

BIRTH CONTROL

Those who oppose ... birth control are ... incapable of arithmetic   3800

BIRTHPLACE

Its birthplace is the sinister back room of the mind   2937

BIRTHRIGHT
without a violation of their natural
   birthright   272

BITE
they will turn and bite the hand that fed
   them   3430

BITTERNESS
I must have no hatred or bitterness towards
   anyone.   2411

BLACK
You show me a black man who isn't an
   extremist   1048
Things in law tend to be black and white.   1954
Being black has made me sensitive to any
   group   2316
choice in politics isn't usually between black and
   white   2811
white man's happiness cannot be purchased by the
   black man's misery.   2899
woman feels ... distinctions of sex ... as the black
   man does those of color   2904
so long as labor in a black skin is branded   2905
For the white man to ask the black man if he
   hates him   2934
If you are black the only roads into the mainland
   of American life   2935
if it is wrong to be violent defending black
   women   3272
But the Black Revolution is controlled only by
   God.   3273
black nationalism means that the black man
   should control the politics   3367
The basic tenet of black consciousness is that the
   black man must reject   3384
I am a black woman, the daughter of a dining-car
   worker.   3550
Budgeting is a black art practiced by bureaucratic
   magicians.   3625
being female put many more obstacles in my path
   than being black   4002
I am working for the time when unqualified
   blacks   4005

BLAME
When we (Labor) get into trouble, we start
   blaming each other   2501
when things don't go well they like to blame the
   Presidents   2997

BLANK
I'm not like that ... I never shoot blanks.   2187
Politics would become an utter blank to me   3151

BLANKET
America is not like a blanket   2320

BLASPHEMY
Political truth is a libel—religious truth
   blasphemy.   856

BLATHER
We love the blather and boast ... of
   campaigning   2436

BLEED
The more you sweat in peace, the less you bleed in
   war.   3970

BLESSED
succeeding millions ... shall ... call us
   blessed   1277
Blessed is he whose fame does not outshine his
   truth.   2106
Blessed are the peacemakers   3660

BLESSING
Free trade, one of the greatest blessings   636
If this is a blessing, it is certainly very well
   disguised.   976
One of the greatest blessings a people ... can enjoy
   is liberty   1208
Those who expect to reap the blessing of
   freedom   1226
No man is entitled to the blessings of
   freedom   1397
it would be an unqualified blessing   1529
A good government remains the greatest of human
   blessings   1553
The blessings of Liberty which our Constitution
   secures   2289
A national debt ... will be to us a national
   blessing.   3581
I ... do not believe that a national debt is a
   national blessing   3591

BLIGHT
For every talent that poverty has stimulated it has
   blighted a hundred.   3539

BLIND
The blind lead the blind. It's the democratic
   way.   436
such an individual can never be ... used as a blind
   tool   1405
"Justice is blind." Blind she is, an' deef an'
   dumb   1794
Get out of the way of Justice. She is blind.   1813
You're not supposed to be so blind with
   patriotism   2421
Until justice is blind to color   3362

BLINK
We were eyeball-to-eyeball and the other fellow
   just blinked.   1033

BLOCK
a society which does not block the exercise of that
   power   1424

BLOCKHEAD
because he is an intolerable thick-voiced
   blockhead   3792

BLOOD

effected without the shedding of blood   571

He must blood his hounds and show them sport   602

by iron and blood   894

I have nothing to offer but blood, toil, tears and sweat.   965

The tree of liberty must be refreshed ... with the blood of patriots   1234

Great Men ... produce a ... pool of blood too   2148

The tree of liberty grows only when watered by the blood of tyrants.   3193

violent men will write it on the soil, in letters of blood   3213

when the consequences of an opposite course may be the shedding of blood   3446

A man who is good enough to shed his blood for his country   3466

Once blood is shed in a national quarrel   3812

BLOODSHED

under a dictatorship which cannot be removed without bloodshed   630

but bloodshed is a cleansing and a sanctifying thing   1345

so that bad rulers can be got rid of without bloodshed   1577

Politics is war without bloodshed while war is politics with bloodshed.   2753

Revolutions are based upon bloodshed.   3275

BLOODSTAIN

"comes into the world with a congenital bloodstain on one cheek"   910

BLOTCH

ours ought to be a country free from the great blotches of distressed poverty   3527

BLOW

Beware of the man who does not return your blow   2722

BLUDGEON

Democracy means simply the bludgeoning of the people by the people   367

BLUNDER

It's worse than a crime, it's a blunder.   853

(Watergate) was worse than a crime, it was a blunder.   1078

generally occasioned by some blunder of a ministry   1622

In a narrow sphere great men are blunderers.   2026

BLUNT

His words tend to be blunt or rounded   2618

Politics is the skilled use of blunt objects.   2800

BOAST

how much nobler ... the sovereign's boast ... that he found law dear   2042

boast ... that he found Rome of brick and left it of marble   2042

BODY

to make one Body Politick under one Government   276

government which derives all its powers ... from the great body of people   298

that it be derived from the great body of the society   298

The body politic is like a tree   870

We have produced a world of contented bodies and discontented minds.   1053

The body politic, as well as the human body, begins to die   1489

Money is ... considered as the vital principle of the body politic   1578

a body in action must overcome an equal body at rest   2685

in the case of the body politic, when motion ceases, the body dies   3090

A married woman has the same right to control her own body   3396

The mass of men serve the state ... with their bodies.   3451

No body can be healthful without exercise, neither natural body or politic   3676

BOLD

a man may be bold in speech and bold in action   1106

BOLDNESS

Boldness, more boldness, and always boldness!   847

BOLSHEVIK

A Bolshevik is ... a socialist who wants to do something about it.   131

To the best of my knowledge I am a Bolshevik myself.   131

BOMB

it is the path to the bomb   587

the struggle ... will not be bombs and rockets but a test of wills   1710

BOMBER

The more bombers, the less room for doves of peace.   3894

BOND

Men would rather be starving and free than fed in bonds.   1387

The strongest bond ... should be one uniting all working people   3520

BONDAGE

function of speech to free men from the bondage of ... fears   1127

BONDMAN

do not mock the bondman ... by giving him a
Bible when he cannot read it   678

BONE

Politicians are like the bones of a horse's fore-
shoulder   2552

leave an old bone behind for the critics to chew
on   2692

Only on the bones of the oppressors can the
people's freedom be founded   3229

BOOK

Don't join the book burners.   1135

a state has no business telling a man ... what
books he may read   1148

The real war will never get into the books.   3749

BOOTSTRAPS

than a man is capable of lifting himself by his
bootstraps   934

BORDER

where all good men ... can freely move across
every border   1686

BOREDOM

The presidency has many problems, but boredom
is the least of them.   3011

BORING

the fact that the talk may be boring   3967

BORN

Citizens are not born, but made.   15

The body politic ... begins to die as soon as it is
born   1489

That every boy and gal,/ That's born into the
world alive   2486

BORROW

Nations have recently been led to borrow billions
for war   3476

undertakes to live by borrowing, soon finds his ...
means devoured   3596

no one left to borrow from   3596

BOSS

A boss is a political leader who is on somebody
else's side.   2645

BOTHER

few elites which will put up with the bother of
it   1151

BOUGHT

An honest politician is one who, when he is
bought, will stay bought.   2551

BOUNDARY

a single step beyond the boundaries ... around the
powers of Congress   2224

BOUNDS

Man's drive for self-expression ... does not stay
within set bounds   1146

Liberty is ... a fierce and intractable thing, to
which no bounds can be set   1349

no bounds of a few men's choosing ought ever be
set   1349

BOURBON

A man can take a little bourbon without getting
drunk   2830

BOURGEOIS

Marxism is essentially a product of the bourgeois
mind.   147

I have against me the bourgeois   2183

BOURGEOISIE

a committee for managing the common affairs of
the whole bourgeoisie   56

the bourgeoisie ... produces ... its own grave-
diggers   58

The bourgeoisie ... is convulsed ... at the
desecration of brick and mortar   65

BOW

when have we ... been expected to bow
submissively to authority   1469

there has to be a bow ... politics is the bow of
idealism   2788

Stretch a bow to the very full   3646

the fourth will be fought with bows and
arrows   3950

BOWIE-KNIFE

manners are the only effective weapons against the
bowie-knife   352

BOX

People only leave by way of the box—ballot or
coffin.   719

BOY

A political leader must keep looking ...to see if the
boys are still there   2180

All wars are boyish, and are fought by
boys.   3738

We are not about to send American boys nine or
ten thousand miles away   3919

to do what Asian boys ought to be doing for
themselves   3919

American boys to do the job that Asian boys
should do   3921

BRAIN

men with feet of clay which extend ... up to their
brains   172

The mob has many heads but no brains.   835

In public politics as in private life, character is
better than brains   2103

so long as you don't have a bicycle brain   2220

Brains ... are suspect in the Republican
   Party   3174
Socialism must come down from the brain and
   reach the heart.   3557

BRANCH
Who lops the moulder'd branch away   200

BRAVE
When were the good and the brave ever in a
   majority?   2065
it is to the vigilant, the active, the brave   3693
Any danger spot is tenable if men—brave men—
   will make it so.   3908

BRAVERY
It drives away fear and brings bravery to the
   surface.   3855

BRAY
If a donkey bray at you, don't bray at him.   831

BREAD
A poor man ... needs hope, illusion, more than
   bread.   956
I cast my bread on the waters long ago.   1091
shall not take from the mouth of labor the bread it
   has earned   1517
Compromise used to mean that half a loaf was
   better than no bread.   2732
Two things only the poeple anxiously desire, bread
   and the circus games.   3405
having looked to the Government for bread   3430

BREAK
at least it is better than breaking them   401
to break a bad law, thereby authorizes everyone ...
   to break good ones   1874

BREAKDOWN
It is the breakdown of policy.   3801

BREATHE
Breathes there the man, with soul so dead   2396

BREEZE
he also succeeds ... in generating breezes of his
   own   2626

BRICK
convulsed by horror at the desecration of brick
   and mortar   65
when they throw bricks at me ... I usually throw
   'em back   1185

BRIDE
like old men who take young brides   3028

BRIDGE
"He'll double-cross that bridge when he comes to
   it."   2631

BRINK
threatening war and coming to the brink but
   retreating from the brink   3891

BRITAIN
To make Britain a fit country for heroes to live
   in   935
If you lead a country like Britain, a strong
   country,   2215

BRITISH
so bear ourselves that if the British Empire ... last
   for a thousand years   967
a British subject ... shall feel confident ... that
   England will protect him   1621
to preside over the liquidation of the British
   Empire   2136

BROKE
Th' raypublican party broke ye   3168

BROKERAGE
wouldn't let them into the family brokerage
   business   2669

BROOM
where the broom does not reach, the dust will not
   vanish of itself   3259

BROTHER
because men are unequal that they have that much
   more need to be brothers   760
All the chains our brothers wear   1263
those inner qualities that make all men ...
   brothers   2930
Unless man is committed to the belief that all of
   mankind are his brothers   2936
the same felon category as the man who strikes his
   brother in anger   3767

BROTHERHOOD
my devotion ... to all the peoples of our
   brotherhood of nations   2361
Brotherhood is Religion.   3144
will be able to sit down together at the table of
   brotherhood   3363

BRUTAL
People who are vigorous and brutal often find war
   enjoyable   3863

BRUTALITY
as one who has seen its brutality   3848
through the selective brutality of terrorism or the
   impartial horrors of war   3958

BRUTISH
brutish direction of labor at all levels   616

BUDGET
the budget is a reflection of their need   3620
everything is under federal control nowadays
   except the federal budget   3624
Budgeting is a black art practiced by bureaucratic
   magicians.   3625
Any jackass can draw up a balanced budget on
   paper.   3628

BUFF

The fight is on and I'm stripped to the buff.   2733

BUILDINGS

in the form of handsome blocks of buildings for the poor   3522

BULLDOG

like setting a bulldog upon a customer at the shop-door   3705

BULLET

The ballot is stronger than the bullet.   702

BULLY

a government of bullies tempered by editors   328

BUNK

so much liberal bleating and bunk   1817

BURDEN

democracy having been burdened with tasks for which it is not suited   422

There will be no greater burden in our generation   1338

See that government ... does not unnecessarily burden the people.   1519

we shall pay any price, bear any burden   1670

think of the weight, of the burden, of a whole kingdom   2336

The public burden of the nation's care   2337

the burdens of the office outweigh its privileges   3003

the additional burden of being deprived of ... an education   3549

BUREAU

The nearest approach to immortality on earth is a government bureau.   6

BUREAUCRACY

The bureaucracy is what we all suffer from.   2

likely to desire ... an increase of bureaucracy   3

as soon as a bureaucracy is established, it develops an autonomous ... life   7

Bureaucracies are designed to perform public business.   7

Bureaucracy ... has become the modern form of despotism.   10

The only thing that saves us from the bureaucracy is inefficiency.   12

An efficient bureaucracy is the greatest threat to liberty.   12

God will forgive you but the bureaucracy won't.   14

If you're going to sin, sin against God, not the bureaucracy   14

BUREAUCRAT

The perfect bureaucrat ... is the man who manages to make no decisions   8

There is something about a bureaucrat that does not like a poem.   11

Bureaucrats write memoranda ... because they appear to be busy   13

BUREAUCRATIC

Budgeting is a black art practiced by bureaucratic magicians.   3625

BURGLARY

the crime is not the burglary, but the discovery of the burglary   1034

BURN

Burn down your cities and leave our farms   639

illuminate their rude legislation with burning castles   3213

BURST

when they swell they do not swell enough to burst   2575

BURY

history is on our side. We will bury you.   156

I once said, "We will bury you"   167

Your own working class will bury you.   167

BUSH-CLEARING

War is just like bush-clearing   3959

BUSINESS

in different compartments of their soul—religion and business.   140

People are not an interruption of our business. People are our business.   481

ready to support repression as long as it is done with a ... business suit   1464

whin business gets above sellin' tinpinny nails   1583

Politics is the reflex of the business ... world   1586

Sound business need have no fear of progressive government.   1587

only the business that thrives on special privilege that is in danger   1587

The chief business of the American people is business.   1591

you have got to let business make money ... or business won't work   1593

My father always told me that all business men were sons of bitches   1595

which is not a friend of American business   1596

I learned in business that you had to be very careful   1598

Men in great places are ... servants of business.   1990

That 150 lawyers should do business together is not to be expected.   2229

when the candidates appeal to "Every intelligent voter" 2596

A candidate for office can have no greater advantage 2616

We (non-candidates) don't have to do what the candidates do 2670

fat, bald, disagreeable men, unable to be candidates themselves 2825

No candidate for the Presidency ought ever to remain in the Cabinet. 2957

CANT

The more cant there is in politics the better. Cant is nothing in itself; 2745

CANVASSING

The practice of canvassing is quite reasonable 699

CAPACITY

duty of every citizen according to his best capacities 25

the conviction that man has the ... capacity ... to govern himself 450

one's capacity to link his will with the purpose of others 2864

We will match your capacity to inflict suffering with our capacity to endure 3350

We will soon wear you down by pure capacity to suffer. 3350

let us join in dismantling the national capacity to wage war 3905

as we build an international capacity to keep peace 3905

CAPITAL

Capital is dead labor 71

If capital an' labor ever do git t'gether 89

Marx's Capital is ... a collection of atrocity stories 133

capital comes dripping from head to foot ... with blood and dirt 910

The highest ... instrument of political power is capital punishment. 1832

High office ... consumes intellectual capital; 2205

If there is a free contract ... between capital and labour 2239

What the proletarian lacks is capital 3444

When commerical capital occupies a position of unquestioned ascendancy 3523

CAPITALISM

Advocates of capitalism ... appeal to the sacred principles of liberty 93

By its economic essence imperialism is monopolist capitalism. 128

an oasis amid the inferno of world capitalism 138

Fascism is Capitalism plus Murder. 591

capitalism is a necessary condition for ... freedom 1440

You talk about capitalism and communism 1569

Under ... Capitalism civilization is always on the verge of revolution. 3252

Capitalism ... creates ... a vested interest in social unrest. 3533

The issue is Socialism versus Capitalism. 3556

capitalism is the unequal sharing of blessings; 3569

Between the barbarity of capitalism 3575

Capitalism carries within itself war 3760

CAPITALIST

The forces of a capitalist society ... tend to make the rich richer 103

Economic progress, in capitalist society, means turmoil. 651

inherent in the capitalist system a tendency toward self-destruction. 652

Capitalists are no more capable of self-sacrifice 934

in a capitalist country, you have got to let business make money 1593

CAPITULATIONISM

capitulationism is the worst of all 1068

CAR

"We the people" are the driver—the government is the car. 500

CARCASS

The commonest error ... is sticking to the carcass of dead policies. 2714

CARD

the four kings in a pack of cards 2360

CAREER

the ambitious man has as many as there those who can help his career 2002

someone ... who can't do anything to further your career; 2520

The conduct ... of public men at different periods of their careers 2542

A political career brings out the basest qualities in human nature. 2579

CARELESSNESS

carelessness about our freedom is also dangerous 1413

Carelessness about our security is dangerous; 1413

CASTE

The military caste did not originate as a party of patriots 2420

CASTLE

Vote Labor and you build castles in the air. 219

A man's house is his castle. 1844

CASUALNESS

a system of despotism tempered by casualness 577

CASUALTY

I don't know what it will take out there—500
casualties maybe   3934

CAT

It doesn't matter if a cat is black or white   184

CATASTROPHE

Human history ... a race between education and
catastrophe.   688

The privilege of the great is to see catastrophes
from the terrace.   2127

CATCH

Words calculated to catch everyone may catch no
one.   992

CATCH-PHRASE

that favourite media catch-phrase, the U-
turn   2209

CATCH-WORDS

apt to be deluded into false security by political
catch-words   2710

CATHOLIC CHURCH

cannot be brought into harmony with the dogmas
of the Catholic Church   3561

CAUGHT

one of Nixon's great contributions to civil liberties
was getting caught   817

CAUSE

clad in the armor of a righteous cause   917

The evil is not what they say about their
cause   1041

Free speech is about as good a cause as the world
has ever known.   1124

No cause is left but the most ancient of all   1446

Governments are more the effect than the
cause   1514

There is no cause half so sacred as the cause of a
people.   2095

When a just cause reaches its flood tide   3327

Of war men ask the outcome, not the
cause.   3659

not a field of a few acres of ground, but a
cause   3696

CAUSEWAY

The law is a causeway upon which ... a citizen
may walk safely.   1931

CAUTIOUS

Cautious ... always casting about to preserve their
reputation   3098

CELLAR

"Faith, I am letting the dark out of the
cellar."   795

CENSOR

The censor's sword pierces deeply   1140

the King's Court as the general censor   1863

CENSORSHIP

Assassination is the extreme form of
censorship.   932

such a statute creates a threat of censorship   1150

censorships ... give credibility to the opinions they
attack   1156

I want a situation without censorship   1163

censorship and universal suffrage are
contradictory   1168

without censorship, things can get terribly
confused   1196

the first war ever fought without any
censorship.   1196

CENSURE

They have a Right to censure, that have a Heart
to help: 1764

If men of eminence are exposed to censure on one
hand   2004

Censure is the tax a man pays to the public for
being eminent.   2522

Between the barbarity of capitalism, which
censures itself   3575

CENT

Not one cent for scenery.   732

Not one cent should be raised unless it is in
accord with the law.   3586

CENTER

hurl rocks at those in the center   2784

traditionally that is in the center   3175

CENTRAL

Every central government worships
uniformity   1531

CENTURY

The century ... must be the century of the
common man   97

The radical of one century is the conservative of
the next.   206

only successful revolution of this century is
totalitarianism   3288

CEREBRATION

what slight powers of cerebration man can
normally muster   2428

CEREMONY

No ceremony that to great ones 'longs   1984

CERTAIN

nothing in this world is certain but death and
taxes   3583

Certain peace is better and safer than anticipated
victory.   3657

CHAFF

someone who separates the wheat from the chaff and then prints the chaff   1001

CHAIN

proletarians have nothing to lose but their chains   122

The totalitarian state is not power unchained it is truth chained.   626

The free mind is no barking dog, to be tethered on a ten-foot chain.   693

Man is born free; and everywhere he is in chains.   1212

Whether in chains or in laurels, liberty knows nothing but victories.   1290

If men and women are in chains, anywhere in the world   1430

No man can put a chain about the ankle of his fellow man   3315

The human soul cannot be permanently chained.   3325

breaking the chain of the black slave, forgot to break the chain of ... Woman   3982

CHALLENGE

our country is challenged at home and abroad   1697

The challenge of the next half-century   3544

CHAMPION

The people have always some champion whom they set over them   521

Irreverence is the champion of liberty   1327

We do not profess to be the champions of liberty   1353

CHANCE

The history of free men is never really written by chance   466

the chances are very high he'd do it   1598

If chance will have me king, why, chance may crown me   1987

simply the results of chance   1999

War is the province of chance.   3716

You have to take chances for peace, just as you must take chances in war.   3888

CHANGE

When it is not necessary to change, it is necessary not to change.   187

institutions can be conserved only by adjusting to the changing time   214

in a changing world worthy institutions can be conserved   214

the ... Constitution has changed, is changing, and ... must continue to change   240

they strive to prevent the very changes   619

Changing Hands without changing Measures   834

A fanatic is one who can't change his mind and won't change the subject.   998

the poor change nothing beyond the change of their master   1479

circumstances ... are continually changing, and opinions of men change also   1510

Nothing is more subject to change than the laws.   1838

Laws should not be changed without good reason.   1855

the point is to change it   2055

Great political ... changes begin to be possible   2107

Legislation is not changed every day.   2226

the delusion that a change in form is a change in substance   2740

one thing solid and fundamental in politics—the law of change   2802

A state without ... means of change is without the means of conservation   3085

change prepares the ground for revolution   3279

We used to think that revolutions are the cause of change.   3279

We want change. We want progress.   3547

CHAOS

freedom of action without freed capacity of thought ... is only chaos   685

Too little liberty brings stagnation, and too much brings chaos.   1403

That means first chaos, then tyranny.   1919

they lead their country by a short route to chaos   2186

Chaos and ineptitude are anti-human;   3481

CHARACTER

character is better than brains   2103

if he is a good judge of character   2359

Politicians tend to live "in character"   2572

men of knowledge ... who have sufficient character   2587

be judged ... by the content of their character   3365

CHARACTERISTIC

the characteristics that distinguish democracy   442

the most distinctive characteristic of the successful politician   2633

CHARGE

the charge and countercharge of campaigning   2436

CHARISMATIC

Charismatic leadership is hungered for   2196

CHARITY

It is justice, not charity, that is wanting in the world.   1774

I think patriotism is like charity—it begins at home.   2405

we have less charity for those who believe the half
of our creed   2687

With malice toward none; with charity for
all;   3736

CHARLATAN
Let them say, if they want ... that we are
charlatans   1162

CHARM
a Union that can only be maintained by swords ...
has no charm for me   3729

CHEAT
If a person ... figures out the odds, there is a very
high incentive to cheat   821

CHECK
If you let me write $200 billion worth of hot
checks every year   663

advocate for ... wholesome checks in every
department of government   1503

CHEER
Two Cheers for Democracy: 453

I always cheer up immensely if an attack is
particularly wounding   2823

CHEESE
An aristocracy is like cheese;   85

CHEW
call in a secretary or a staff man and chew him
out   2668

leave an old bone behind for the critics to chew
on   2692

CHICKEN
An aristocracy in a republic is like a chicken
whose head has been cut off: 102

"England will have her neck wrung like a
chicken." Some chicken!   970

the same as a chicken voting for Colonel
Sanders   3176

CHIEF
A chief is a man who assumes
responsibility.   2137

CHILDISH
The world is always childish   3209

CHILDREN
I have a dream that my four little children will
one day live in a nation   3365

a reasonable internal debt will not impoverish our
children   3614

If our children have to pay interest on it they will
pay ... to themselves.   3614

they always claim to be protecting women and
children   4011

CHISEL
War is a poor chisel to carve out
tomorrows.   3926

CHOICE
history of free men is ...written ... but by ... their
choice   466

The choice in politics isn't usually between black
and white.   2811

CHOOSE
It is for men to choose whether they will govern
themselves   361

I do not choose to run.   947

CHRIST
Was Pilate right in crucifying Christ?   1118

The way ... Christ keeps aloof from politics, is
truly sublime.   3154

Where did your Christ come from?   3305

CHRISTIAN
Whatever makes men good Christians, makes
them good citizens.   18

Christian socialism is but the holy water   3150

CHRISTIANITY
wrong for the Founder of Christianity to destroy
private property   3993

CHURCH
as the Church in its darkest periods has been to
persecute its dissenters   3100

The Church should no longer ... represent ... the
Conservative Party at prayer   3155

the great objective which Church and State are
both demanding   3156

The church must be reminded that it is ... the
conscience of the state   3162

CHURCHILL
Mr. Churchill characteristically selected the latter
course   2585

CIA
The CIA is made up of boys whose families sent
them to Princeton   2669

CIRCLES
how prophetic ... when he laid out a city that goes
around in circles   1009

CIRCUMSTANCE
peculiar circumstances ... may render a measure
more or less wise   234

War involves in its progress such a train of
unforeseen ... circumstances   3699

CIRCUS
as everyone who has seen a circus parade
knows   3173

Two things only the poeple anxiously desire, bread
and the circus games.   3405

CITIZEN

Citizens are not born, but made. 15

would be a citizen of the universe 16

observance of the ... laws is ... one of the virtues of a good citizen 17

Whatever makes men good Christians, makes them good citizens. 18

Before Man made us citizens, great Nature made us men. 19

Without a home their can be no good citizen. 21

a good citizen in this republic ... shall be able ... to pull his weight 22

immunity to eloquence is of ... importance to the citizens of a democracy 23

The Constitution does not provide for first and second class citizens. 24

It is the duty of every citizen ... to give validity to his convictions 25

Politics ought to be the part-time profession of every citizen 27

citizen who criticizes his country is paying it an implied tribute 32

As citizens of this democracy, you are the rulers and the ruled 457

the idea that the citizens should do the kicking 462

the rights to have the law construed ... applied to every citizen 483

not always the same thing to be a good man and a good citizen 771

The citizen is influenced by principle 810

The humblest citizen ... clad in the armor of a righteous cause 917

All free man ... are citizens of Berlin 1444

maintained that citizens do not have the right to leave the country 1490

how much better to make it so the citizens want to stay 1490

it shows he is a citizen of the world 1604

We cannot, as citizens, pick and choose the laws we will ... obey 1956

for we are citizens in common of one great nation 2484

this nation ... will not be fully free until all its citizens are free 3361

the state's obligation, which owes to every citizen an assured subsistence 3415

A government never loses anything by ... forbearance to its own citizens 3446

A woman is a citizen who works for Mexico. 3997

CITIZENS

the use of troops ... to get American citizens to obey the ... courts 28

CITIZENSHIP

All Americans must have the privileges of citizenship regardless of race. 31

CITY

What is the city but the people? 271

the grass will grow in the streets of every city 639

Burn down your cities and leave our farms 639

a defense that will protect American cities is one that will not be achieved 3973

CIVIL FREEDOM

Two forces which are the worst enemies of civil freedom 3218

CIVIL LIBERTY

one of Nixon's great contributions to civil liberties 817

what he gains is civil liberty 1211

The cause of civil liberty must not be surrendered 1281

suppression of civil liberties is to many less a matter of horror 1455

Civil liberty can be established on no foundation of human reason 3146

CIVIL RIGHTS

liberals I have known ... in the civil rights conflict 2277

strong moralistic strain in the civil rights movement 2882

I urge you ... to enact a civil rights law 3360

greatest achievement of the civil rights movement 3373

no such thing as a moderate in the civil rights movement; 3379

CIVIL SERVICE

the entire Civil Service is like a fortress made of papers 1

CIVIL SOCIETY

the true founder of civil society 837

Justice is itself the great standing policy of civil society; 1773

CIVIL WAR

Don't forget that weakness produces civil wars 1515

A foreign war is a lot milder than a civil war. 3671

strife and civil war are to take the place of brotherly love and kindness 3729

CIVILITY

remembering on both sides ... that civility is not a sign of weakness 1672

CIVILIZATION

Civilization cannot survive if it rests upon a propertyless proletariat. 96

The more Communism, the more civilization. 141

little reason to believe that this socialism will mean ... the civilization 146

This is really the test of civilisation.　432

You cannot organize civilization around the core of militarism　601

If a nation expects to be ignorant and free, in a state of civilization　670

Civilization exists precisely so that there may be no masses　1421

Civilization and profits go hand in hand.　1589

If our civilization is to be perpetuated　1648

civilization itself is but the effect of combining　2853

Under ... Capitalism civilization is always on the verge of revolution　3252

contributed more to the growth of civilization　3330

no nation is rich enough to pay for both war and civilization　3476

A decent provision for the poor is the true test of civilization.　3517

Security, the chief pretence of civilization　3525

the very logic of its civilization ... creates ... social unrest　3533

CLASS

Society is composed of two classes　45

as the antagonism between classes within the nation vanishes　54

The history of ... society is the history of class struggles　55

the proletariat alone is a really revolutionary class　57

where have you ever seen one class looking after the interests of another　62

materializing our upper class, vulgarizing our middle class　66

between them ... the working classes are being ground　68

The danger is not that a particular class is unfit to govern.　69

Every class is unfit to govern.　69

a trifling evil compared with the inequality of classes　72

where any one class is made to feel that society is an organized conspiracy　75

an instrument of oppression of one class by another　77

the notion that class is naturally hostile to class　78

based its propaganda on the class-war theory　82

the sops that the owning classes throw to the other classes　94

Anyone today who speaks of class in the context of politics　113

abolition of all classes and to a classless society　124

class struggle necessarily leads to the dictatorship of the proletariat　124

classes ... linked to ... phases in the development of production　124

I will back the masses against the classes　348

justice on grounds of conduct and not on grounds of class　1799

the need for the student of the law ... finally puts him in a class apart　1882

the organized power of one class for oppressing another　2860

meddling people, who come down to some perfectly contented class　3104

the impossibility of reconstructing class society　3243

CLASS-WAR

It thus brings about the class-war which it prophesies.　133

CLASSICS

the obscene become the classics of today　1146

CLASSLESS

Far from being a classless society, Communism is governed by an elite　168

CLASSROOM

If we get the federal government out of the classroom　3163

CLAUSE

in imminent danger of cracking his shins on a subordinate clause　2663

CLAW

I sometimes suggested to the lion the right place to use his claws　3882

CLEAN

retiring with hands as clean as they are empty　780

CLENCHED

You cannot shake hands with a clenched fist.　1087

CLERGYMEN

clergymen who are ex-pacifists　3804

CLEVER

You may be too clever by half.　2731

CLEVERNESS

An ounce of loyalty is worth a pound of cleverness.　2117

They may laugh at it ... but they do not like cleverness　2731

CLICHE

He is forever poised between the cliche and the indiscretion.　1663

CLIMBING

climbing is performed in the same position with creeping　2003

CLOCK

Governments, like clocks, go from the motions men give them　1481

CLOSED
These proceedings are closed.   979
Until we stop pushing the Kremlin against a
   closed door   1667

CLOTH
very tricky cloth out of which to cut the pattern of
   a postwar world   1653

CLOTHES
when our clothes are off, nobody can tell which of
   us is which   757
The right hon. Gentleman ... walked away with
   their clothes.   877

CLOUDS
Capitalism carries within itself war, as clouds
   carry rain.   3760

COAL
the coal can never expire   1227

COBWEB
Laws are like cobwebs, which may catch small
   flies   1849

COCK
Nationalism is a silly cock crowing on its own
   dunghill.   2415

CODESTRUCTION
The only alternative to coexistence is
   codestruction.   3883

COERCION
Coercion is the basis of every law in the
   universe   1891
he labours under coercion to satisfy another's
   desires   3553

COERCIVE
without the intervention of a coercive
   power   1500

COEXIST
The only way ... seems to be for the different
   social systems to coexist.   3952

COEXISTENCE
The only alternative to coexistence is
   codestruction.   3883

COFFIN
People only leave (Washington) by way of the
   box--ballot or coffin.   719

COHESION
Our greatest foreign policy need is national
   cohesion   1705

COIN
intellectual honesty is not the coin of the
   realm   818
Peace and justice are two sides of the same
   coin.   1805

COLD
we are today in the midst of a cold war   983
beneath that cold, harsh, impersonal exterior there
   beats a cold ... heart   1944

COLLECTION
the most extraordinary collection of talent   1032

COLLECTIVE
a limit to the legitimate interference of collective
   opinion   1284
Liberty is not collective, it is personal.   1356

COLLECTIVISM
this will be the century of collectivism   597

COLONEL SANDERS
the same as a chicken voting for Colonel
   Sanders   3176

COLONY
Colonies do not cease to be colonies because they
   are independent.   1623

COLOR
something else when applied to a person of
   another color   769
the Negro remains in bondage to the color of his
   skin   2928
many Americans live on the outskirts of hope ...
   some because of their color   2932
to look his neighbor in the face and see a man--not
   a color   2933
eliminate ... every trace of discrimination ... based
   upon race or color   3360
where they will not be judged by the color of their
   skin   3365
no matter what color you are you require the
   same amount of nourishment   3534

COLORBLIND
We cannot ... let colorblindness become
   myopia   2946
This administration is totally colorblind.   2947
Our Constitution is color-blind   3323

COLORED
one of them hadn't even been colored in yet   2665
a nation lives within a nation, as colored
   Americans are living inside America   2915
gave better ground for the ultimate ... success of
   the colored man's cause   3166
the Republican party as the sheet anchor of the
   colored man's political hopes   3167
The destiny of the colored American ... is the
   destiny of America.   3308
There is a great stir about colored men getting
   their rights   3310
if colored men get their rights, and not colored
   women theirs   3310

COLUMNIST

A politician wouldn't dream of being allowed to call a columnist 1183

When the political columnists say "Every thinking man" 2596

COMBAT

adequate to this supreme combat that will decide the destinies of the world 689

The field of combat was a ... green-baize covered table 3872

COMFORT

the Honour ... of publick Posts, bearing no proportion with the Comfort of it 2521

Conservatism goes for comfort, reform for truth. 3096

Nobody expects to find comfort and companionability in reformers. 3120

COMMAND

The man who commands efficiently must have obeyed others 1971

If you command wisely, you'll be obeyed cheerfully. 2006

but to command great things is more difficult 2079

No one has a finer command of language 2163

A Liberal is a man who uses ... his hands at the ... command--of his head. 2271

The prize of the general is not a bigger tent, but command. 2865

He that commands the sea is at great liberty 3675

COMMANDER

commanders ... should march their troops towards the sound of gunfire 1036

COMMANDMENT

If we are to keep our democracy, there must be one commandment: 1804

COMMERCE

Commerce, which has made the citizens of England rich 632

this freedom has encouraged commerce even more 632

The very essence of competitive commerce is waste 638

Commerce is the greatest of all political interests. 640

nothing is more great or more brilliant than commerce 1580

COMMITMENT

that is our only commitment to others 1436

Tolerance implies no lack of commitment to one's own beliefs. 3161

COMMODITY

the commodity it exports most is words 1717

COMMON

the century of the common man 97

in trust from the People, to the Common good of them all 272

Democracy is the theory that the common people know what they want 391

Nothing astonishes men so much as common sense 875

The freethinking of one age is the common sense of the next. 906

the common people will stay out of trouble 1478

Law: an ordinance of reason for the common good 1831

Laws ... should ... be construed by the ordinary rules of common sense 1877

The common law is not a brooding omnipresence in the sky 1909

Common sense often makes good law. 1925

A constitutional statesman is in general a man of common opinions 2062

I will govern according to the common weal, but not ... the common will 2329

but let us also direct attention to our common interests 2927

not the true belief but the common belief 3078

COMMONS

The Commons ... remained in a wise and masterly inactivity 2223

COMMONWEALTH

It is easy enough to define what the Commonwealth is not. 1075

The principal mark of a commonwealth ... the existence of a sovereign power 2324

The best condition of a commonwealth is ... peace and security 3411

the realization at last of the meaning of the word commonwealth 3554

COMMUNICATE

necessary for the people to communicate their ideas under ... secrecy 1109

COMMUNISM

Communism is exploitation of the strong by the weak. 116

Communism is inequality, but not as property is. 116

A spectre is haunting Europe—the spectre of Communism. 121

Communism is a Russian autocracy turned upside down. 123

The more Communism, the more civilization. 141

Communism is like Prohibition, it's a good idea, but it won't work. 151

Communism is not love. 152

Communism is a hammer which we use to crush the enemy. 152

Communism is the corruption of a dream of justice. 153

Power is an end in itself and the essence of contemporary Communism. 160

Communism is governed by an elite 168

Stalinism is the essence of Communism. 176

The confrontation between a man ... and Communism is ... over in two rounds. 177

Communism nearly always loses. 177

Communism nearly always wins the first round 177

Communism ... hands out wealth through rationing books. 179

Communism has done very little for us. 183

Communism has done very much for us. 183

You talk about capitalism and communism and all that 1569

COMMUNIST

What is a communist? 114

the theory of the communists may be summed up in the single sentence 119

The communists disdain to conceal their views and aims. 120

The dictatorship of the Communist Party is maintained by ... violence. 136

Every Communist must grasp the truth 142

We Communists are like seeds and the people are like the soil. 148

The objection to a Communist ... that he is not a gentleman 155

A Communist has no right to be a mere onlooker. 157

I am a good friend to Communists abroad 165

the Communists have done nothing ... as much as what their enemies have done 166

Communists have committed great crimes 169

In dealing with the Communists, remember that ... what is secret is serious 170

They (communists) are not supermen at all. 172

Communist countries never expel correspondents for telling lies. 178

No communist country has solved the problem of succession. 180

one cannot be a Communist and not let oneself in for ... recantation 181

One cannot be a Communist and preserve an iota of one's personal integrity. 181

"That man is a Red, that man is a Communist". 1372

I have spent all my life under a Communist regime 1953

they came first for the Communists, and I didn't speak up 3342

COMMUNITY

the interests of the choosing body are not ... those of the community 312

the black man should control the politics ... in his own community; 3367

All communities are apt to look to government too much. 3440

to do for a community of people, whatever they need to have done 3452

To tax the community for the advantage of a class is not protection 3598

COMPACT

this original Compact ... would signifie nothing 276

they cannot by any compact deprive or divest their posterity; 286

Compact is the basis and essence of free government. 319

it is merely a compact between men 1751

COMPANIONABILITY

Nobody expects to find comfort and companionability in reformers. 3120

COMPASS

he that steers by any other compass than his own sense of duty 2537

COMPATIBLE

All separated from government, are compatible with liberty. 3145

COMPEL

to compel a man to furnish contributions for the propagation of opinions 3141

COMPENSATION

This is a world of compensation; 1293

COMPETE

at least see that it competes with the public good 1486

COMPETENCE

This election is not about ideology; it's about competence. 727

The single most exciting thing you encounter in government is competence 1572

COMPETITION

the success of our own philosophy in an open competition 443

The problem of freedom ... is that of maintaining a competition of ideas 1132

COMPLACENT

The bourgeoisie ... which looks complacently upon the wholesale massacre 65

COMPLAIN

Everyone complains about his memory, but no one complains about his judgement. 832

Never complain and never explain. 2761

COMPLEX

unwarranted influence ...by the military-industrial complex 3904

COMPLEXION

God-given rights inherent ... whatever may be the sex or complexion 3320

COMPLICATE

But we are coming now to realize that life is so complicated 3469

COMPLIMENT

We regard that as a compliment. 2439

COMPLY

He that complies against his will is of his opinion still. 1204

COMPROMISE

Compromise, n. ... an adjustment of conflicting interests 925

All government ... is founded on compromise and barter. 1494

Nearly all legislation is the result of compromise. 2245

And that's his idea of a compromise. 2697

Compromise used to mean that half a loaf was better than no bread. 2732

The payoff may involve compromises of various types 2763

Compromise is the oil that makes governments go. 2801

Reformers who are always compromising 3106

COMPULSION

without the compulsion of conformity or law 1468

CONCEAL

Don't think you are going to conceal faults by concealing evidence 1135

CONCENTRATE

we can have great wealth concentrated in the hands of a few 425

always in concentrating it on a single enemy 2113

CONCENTRATION

The dangers of a concentration of all power ... are too obvious 332

the concentration of administrative power in responsible ... hands 377

concentration of power is what ... precedes destruction of human initiative 585

One danger arises from too great a concentration of power 1399

CONCEPT

It depends on the way you measure the concept of good 183

then validates as the commands of our most basic concept 1958

CONCERN

a problem of the people concerned, but a ... concern of all Socialist countries 174

Those who have given ... the most concern about the happiness of peoples 908

CONCESSION

a dormant possibility of ... violent action if concessions are to be won 3278

CONCILIATE

A wise government knows how to ... conciliate with dignity. 1491

CONCLUSION

Political thinking consists in deciding upon the conclusion first 2605

CONCRETE

Work for elimination of concrete evils 3486

CONDEMNATION

I wish we might have less condemnation of error 943

far from deserving condemnation for their courageous reporting 1191

CONDEMNED

A way of life ... is not to be condemned because it is different 2317

CONDITION

The earth is the first condition of our existence. 117

Freedom of expression is the matrix, the indispensable condition 1130

Clearly it is not a sufficient condition. 1440

capitalism is a necessary condition for political freedom 1440

The test of political institutions is the condition of the country 1543

The man who is forever disturbed about the condition of humanity 3123

the law has to step in and create new conditions under which we may live 3469

The condition of man ... is a condition of war of everyone against everyone. 3679

CONDUCT

I desire so to conduct the affairs of this administration 2071

The conduct and opinions of public men ... must not be curiously contrasted 2542

have experience enough of the conduct of governments and people 2682

CONE

A country governed by a despot is an inverted cone. 540

CONFERENCE

We never lost a war and we never won a conference in our lives. 1646

I have always said that a conference was held for one reason only 1650

Sometimes it takes two or three conferences to scare up a war 1650

CONFETTI

Confetti looks festive until you're forced to spit out mouthfuls 2433

CONFIDENCE

Why should there not be a patient confidence in the ultimate justice 341

The basis of effective government is public confidence 807

confidence is endangered when ethical standards falter 807

The basis of effective government is public confidence. 1566

one must have confidence in oneself 3709

Past experience provides little basis for confidence 3928

CONFIDENTIALITY

if reporters should ever lose the right to protect ... confidentiality 1192

the confidentiality of the office of the president would always be suspect 3007

the ... claim of public interest in the confidentiality of such conversations 3020

CONFLICT

The conflict between capitalism and democracy is inherent 94

they are not ... disturbed by the never-ending din of political conflict 397

I glory in conflict, that I may hereafter exult in victory. 878

an equilibrium of social forces in conflict 1419

Never in the field of human conflict 3827

Wars occur because people prepare for conflict 3850

CONFORMITY

May we know unity - without conformity. 1012

Conformity is the jailer of freedom 1434

Conformities are called for much more eagerly today than yesterday; 2918

CONFRONT

one doesn't like to confront them with their own great themes 2143

CONFUSE

We are inclined to confuse freedom and democracy 475

CONFUSION

Refined policy ever had been the parent of confusion 1495

the fundamental confusion that government ... can also create righteousness 1556

CONGERIES

Are all Cabinets congeries of little autocrats 2582

CONGRESS

Can any of you seriously say the Bill of Rights could get through Congress 246

Changes in the Constitution ... are to be proposed by Congress 250

Congress—these, for the most part, illiterate hacks 808

something vastly different from what Congress intended the law to be 1733

Take a single step beyond the boundaries ... around the powers of Congress 2224

All the public business in Congress now connects itself with intrigues 2227

no distinctly native American criminal class except Congress 2240

The Congress is deadlocked and can't act. 2248

(Congress is) functioning the way the Founding Fathers intended 2261

I don't think it's the function of Congress to function well. 2263

The passion for office among members of Congress is very great 2548

Some members of congress are the best actors in the world. 2638

Give a member of Congress a junket and a mimeograph machine 2659

"sometimes I wish I could be President and Congress too." 2976

it is the privilege of the Congress to dispose 3511

Congress ... must retain its right to inquiry 3514

we should be half the Congress 3996

You can't have a Congress that responds to the needs of the workingman 4007

CONGRESSMAN

A Congressman is never any better than his roads 2602

Wars are started by ... Congressmen with vertebrae of putty. 3804

CONJECTURE

To die for an idea is to place a pretty high price upon conjectures. 931

CONJOINT

it is primarily a ... conjoint communicated experience. 382

CONNECTION

In our Parliamentary government, connections are absolutely necessary; 2677

CONQUER

a nation is not governed which is perpetually conquered 537

Tyranny, like hell, is not easily conquered; 539

Whoever can conquer the street will one day conquer the state 593

Whoever can surprize well must Conquer. 844

With strength, one can conquer others, and to conquer others gives one virtue. 2193

Every State must conquer or be conquered. 3739

CONQUEST

The right of conquest has no foundation 3691

CONSCIENCE

aroused popular conscience that sears the conscience of the ... representatives 473

To request an honest man to vote according to his conscience is superfluous. 699

To request him to vote against his conscience is an insult. 699

Conscience has no more to do with gallantry than it has with politics. 778

I cannot and will not cut my conscience to fit this year's fashions. 804

With a good conscience our only sure reward 1030

Laws presumably express the conscience of a nation 1923

An individual who breaks a law that conscience tells him is unjust 1938

The only guide to a man is his conscience; 2132

When statesmen forsake their own private conscience 2186

persecution for cause of conscience is ... contrary to the doctrine of Christ 3137

the free exercise of religion, according to the dictates of conscience 3140

It behoves every man who values liberty of conscience for himself 3143

The church must be reminded that it is ... the conscience of the state 3162

All a man can betray is his conscience. 3640

CONSCIOUSNESS

the strength of African national consciousness 1020

the growth of national consciousness is a political fact 1020

the progress of the consciousness of freedom 1257

with a consciousness that new evidence may ... lead to their abandonment 2274

CONSENSUS

who too far outruns ... his people will fail in achieving a domestic consensus 2194

CONSENT

subjected to the Political Power of another, without his own Consent 277

so the consent of the people is the only foundation 284

Governments ... deriv(e) their just powers from the consent of the governed. 288

No man is good enough to govern another man without that other's consent. 333

"The consent of the governed" 380

The essence of a republican government is ... consent 455

Laws made by common consent must not be trampled on by individuals. 1865

force and consent are correlative terms 2744

No one can make you feel inferior without your consent. 2912

CONSEQUENCE

We must not regard political consequences, however formidable they may be; 1725

CONSERVATION

then mount the stump and make a speech for conservation 2630

A state without some means of change is without the means of its conservation. 3085

CONSERVATISM

Conservatism has always appeared to me to be not only foolish 190

always a certain meanness in the argument of conservatism 192

Conservatism discards Prescription, shrinks from Principle 194

What is conservatism? 199

Conservatism ... is a euphemism for selfishness. 202

Conservatism ... is mainly due to want of imagination 202

tired of the effort of willing they become fanatics about conversatism 210

the innate conservatism of the human mind 212

Conservatism is distrust of the people tempered by fear. 2267

the party of Conservatism and that of Innovation 2465

Conservatism goes for comfort, reform for truth. 3096

Radicalism, n. The conservatism of to-morrow 3111

CONSERVATIVE

I am a Conservative to preserve all that is good 189

"A sound Conservative government" 193

Men are conservatives when they are least vigorous 195

They are conservatives after dinner. 195

A conservative government is an organized hypocrisy. 196

the man of forms, the conservative—is a tame
 man   197

That man's the true Conservative   200

When a nation's young men are conservative   201

So, as a rule, stupid people are Conservative.   203

come, my conservative friend, wipe the dew off
 your spectacles   204

When he has worn them out the conservative
 adopts them.   205

The radical of one century is the conservative of
 the next.   206

Conservative, n. A statesman who is enamored of
 existing evils   207

The healthy stomach is nothing if not
 conservative.   208

The true conservative is the man who has a real
 concern for injustices   213

Wise and prudent men—intelligent
 conservatives   214

For fear it would make me conservative when
 old   215

A conservative is a man with two perfectly good
 legs   216

Here lies the whole art of Conservative
 politics   218

Vote Conservative and you can live in them.   219

I am driven to grudging toleration of the
 Conservative Party   220

what conservatives seem to be endowed with at
 birth   221

(conservatives) define themselves in terms of what
 they oppose   222

A conservative is a liberal who was mugged the
 night before.   223

I've got money so I'm a Conservative.   224

Conservatives do not worship democracy.   226

Hence Conservative moderation brings its own
 reward.   227

Or else a little Conservative!   2486

There is one thing you can be sure of with the
 Conservative Party   2511

Die-hard conservatives thought that if I couldn't
 get everything I asked for   2820

Public opinion ... make all men in power
 conservative and safe   3053

the Conservative Party at prayer   3155

the baseness which makes conservatives   3221

The most radical revolutionary will become a
 conservative   3281

This is particularly true of those bellicose
 Republican "conservatives"   3930

CONSERVATIZING
Inflation is a great conservatizing issue.   225

CONSIDERATION
his country must be governed by higher and
 steadier considerations   2538

CONSISTENCY
A foolish consistency is the hobgoblin of little
 minds   2048

party attachments and consistency are in the first
 class   2462

CONSISTENT
Foreign policy must be clear, consistent and
 confident.   1658

CONSOLATION
the consolation of having added nothing to my
 private fortune   780

CONSOLIDATION
not by consolidation ... of powers ... that good
 government is effected   1502

CONSPICUOUS
one provision was conspicuous by its
 presence   888

CONSPIRACY
society is in an organized conspiracy to
 oppress   75

an elaborate conspiracy to prevent the real clash
 of opinion   2255

The best Party is but a kind of Conspiracy   2444

We must resist the myth that government is a
 gigantic conspiracy.   3496

CONSTANCY
The secret of success is constancy to
 purpose.   2075

CONSTELLATION
these principles form the bright
 constellation   1251

CONSTITUENCY
to manipulate the demanding ... elements in their
 constituencies   2608

politicians ... feel morally superior to their
 constituencies   2644

CONSTITUTION
The Constitution does not provide for first and
 second class citizens.   24

An act against the Constitution is void;   228

Our chief danger arises from the democratic parts
 of our constitutions.   229

Constitutions are the work of time   230

Constitutions should be short and vague.   231

bind him down from mischief by the chains of the
 Constitution   232

Some men look at constitutions with
 sanctimonious reverence   233

There is a higher law than the Constitution.   235

The Constitution of the United States was made ...
 for posterity   236

Don't interfere with anything in the
 Constitution.   237

Your Constitution is all sail and no anchor. 238

Amendments to the Constitution ought to not be too frequently made; 239

the American Constitution has changed 240

The Constitution is the sole source ... of national freedom 241

what the Constitution forbids is not all searches and seizures 243

basic guarantees of our Constitution are warrants for the here and now 244

The Constitution is not a panacea for every blot 245

Most faults are not in our Constitution 247

Our Constitution was not written in the sands 249

it is a Constitution intended to endure for ages 250

Changes in the Constitution, when thought necessary 250

disagreements ... do not now relieve us of our duty to apply the Constitution 252

My faith in the constitution is whole. 253

Our constitution works. 254

The Constitution is not neutral. 256

The Constitution requires that Congress treat similarly 257

We current justices read the Constitution in the only way that we can 259

the Constitution sometimes insulates the criminality of a few 262

the right of the people to make and to alter their constitutions of government 303

The people made the Constitution, and the people can unmake it. 311

a constitution that allows a majority vote to dismiss the government 498

The foundation on which all our constitutions are built 741

One country, one constitution, one destiny. 874

Free Discussion is the only necessary Constitution 1111

It is ordained in the eternal constitution of things 1244

no constitution, no law, no court can save it 1389

establishing a perfect civil constitution is subordinate 1605

whether th' constitution follows th' flag or not 1730

We are under a Constitution, but the Constitution is what the judges say 1731

I am not justified in writing my private notions ... into the Constitution 1737

judge-made ... law having ... no cognizable roots in the ... Constitution 1746

Parliament ... as a dignified, not an effective, element in the Constitution 2256

Constitutions are checks upon the hasty action of the majority. 2304

a necessary and fundamental principle of the English constitution 2343

but a Parliamentary constitution is not favourable to such ambitions 2470

wrap yourself up in the American flag and talk about the Constitution 2557

no power which cannot be ... traced to ... the Federal Constitution 2969

nothing in the Constitution that authorizes ... a president 3012

The constitution cannot be upset so long as that class is of one mind 3184

each new gewgaw of a revolution or new constitution 3209

In view of the Constitution ... there is ... no ... ruling class 3323

Our Constitution is color-blind 3323

The framers of our excellent Constitution 3440

any degree of freedom preserved in the constitution 3504

The principles of a free constitution are irrevocably lost 3509

Our Constitution is in actual operation; 3583

CONSTITUTIONAL

cannot render it more or less constitutional 234

What is constitutional may still be unwise. 242

layman's constitutional view that what he likes is constitutional 251

(Constitutional law) is a ship with a great deal of sail 260

The states' role in our system of government is a matter of constitutional law 261

they can exercise their constitutional right of amending it 340

At the constitutional level ... 90 percent of any decision is emotional. 1742

A law can be both economic folly and constitutional. 1965

If ... a majority should deprive a minority of any ...˙constitutional right 2294

The sovereign has, under a constitutional monarchy such as ours, three rights 2352

then constitutional guarantees acquire an accordionlike quality 2943

If discrimination based on race is constitutionally permissible 2943

As President, I have no eyes but constitutional eyes; 2959

no inherent Constitutional authority for the President ... to violate the law 3024

to call it a constitutional right is confounding the meaning of the term 3205

The rights of all persons are wrapped in the same constitutional bundle 3388

If we are to ... keep constitutional government alive in America 3514

CONSTRAINT

men will not conform to the dictates of reason and justice, without constraint 1501

CONSTRUCTED
in the minds of men that the defences of peace must be constructed   3847

CONSTRUCTION
Judges must beware of hard constructions and strained inferences   1723

CONSUL
Consul, n. ... a person who having failed to secure an office from the people   1635

CONSULT
undoubtedly the business of ministers ... much to consult ... the people   2024

CONSUMPTION
public services have failed to keep abreast of private consumption   655

CONTAGION
He who is the author of a war lets loose the whole contagion of hell   3698

CONTEMPT
Welfare is ... held in contempt by those who receive it   1074

CONTEMPTIBLE
an unpitied sacrifice in a contemptible struggle   838

have rendered the great government of the United States ... contemptible   2243

CONTENDING
From hence, let fierce contending nations know   3683

CONTENT
The mass of the English people are politically contented   349

the majority of men live content   3406

CONTEST
The contest, for ages, has been to rescue Liberty   1258

CONTINUATION
War is regarded as nothing but the continuation of state policy   3718

CONTINUE
Therefore, it must be continued.   3885

CONTRABAND
Morality is contraband in war.   3853

CONTRACT
one of the two contracting parties should have the making of the laws   2239

If there is a free contract ... between capital and labour   2239

party platforms are contracts with the people   2502

power is legitimate only when it is under contract   2876

The whole duty of government is to prevent crime and to preserve contracts.   3442

CONTRADICT
though it contradicts everything you said today   2048

CONTRADICTION
A totalitarian state ... is a persistent contradiction   607

Military intelligence is a contradiction in terms.   1077

A revolutionary party is a contradiction in terms.   3254

Religious socialism ... are expressions implying a contradiction in terms   3561

I don't think the contradictions ... can be resolved by war   3952

CONTRADICTORY
as contradictory as it is unsafe to the ... principles of a free government   2903

CONTRARY
True patriotism sometimes requires of men to act exactly contrary   2404

CONTRASTED
The conduct and opinions of public men at different periods   2542

CONTRIBUTION
one of Nixon's great contributions to civil liberties   817

to compel a man to furnish contributions ... for the propagation of opinions   3141

CONTRIVE
My country has in its wisdom contrived for me the most insignificant office   2953

CONTROL
getting other people under your control   545

ceases to be radical when absorbed mainly in preserving its control   611

I claim not to have controlled events, but ... events have controlled me.   2072

everything is under federal control ... except the federal budget   3624

CONTROVERSIAL
If an individual wants to be a leader and isn't controversial   2199

CONTROVERSY
parties are formed more with reference to controversies that are gone by   2479

CONVENTION

This is the first convention of the space age   1028

I sometimes yearn for the peace and tranquility of a political convention   1689

A rigged convention is one with the other man's delegates in control.   2787

An open convention is when your delegates are in control.   2787

CONVERSATION

If Nixon is not forced to turn over tapes of his conversations   3029

Every man should know that his conversations ... are private   3374

CONVERSION

this country ... underwent ... no inner conversion   412

CONVERT

You have not converted a man because you have silenced him.   573

when he once attempts to make converts   2531

CONVICT

an innocent man convicted is the business of every honest person   1763

liberty can be as much endangered from illegal methods used to convict   1929

CONVICTION

to give validity to his convictions in political affairs   25

Mix a conviction with a man and something happens.   1051

That is our conviction for ourselves;   1436

The true end of political action is ... to affect the ... convictions of men   1668

he leaves behind him in other men the conviction ... to carry on   2142

I wanted to inspire their souls with the conviction that filled me   2166

learn to respect sincerity of conviction in our opponents   2701

my ... conviction that, until this principal of equality is recognized   3148

CONVINCE

the governed must be convinced that it is right   1776

COOL

Keep strong, if possible. In any case, keep cool.   2167

COOLLY

To act coolly ... in perilous circumstances   2158

COOPERATION

To define democracy in one word, we must use the word "cooperation."   437

Government and co-operation are in all things the laws of life;   1541

I want everyone to be able to work together in a spirit of cooperation   2192

appeal of every successful political movement is ... never ... for co-operation   2738

Co-operation is power;   2853

Progress is born of cooperation in the community   3475

COORDINATE

If they coordinate, you can work it out pretty well.   2220

CORAL REEF

more imperceptible than that of the insect which raises the coral reef   3101

CORE

to prevent a small core ... suddenly thrusting its decisions on the country   486

CORN

you're a thousand miles from the corn field   9

nine-tenths of mankind have been grinding the corn for the remaining one-tenth   86

You tell me whar a man gits his corn pone   790

Kansas had better stop raising corn and begin raising hell.   3107

Corn for the rich men only   3515

CORNERSTONE

The whole cornerstone of our democratic edifice   433

CORPORATION

The biggest corporation, like the humblest private citizen   1584

CORRECT

How much easier it is to be critical than to be correct.   889

CORRECTIVE

the true corrective of abuses of constitutional power   672

CORROSIVE

corrosive effects of inflation eat away at ties that bind us   660

CORRUPT

He ... is a man of splendid abilities, but utterly corrupt.   781

Those who corrupt the public mind are just as evil as those who steal   805

Give them a corrupt House of Lords   1165

Unlimited power is apt to corrupt the minds of those who possess it.   2837

Power tends to corrupt and absolute power
corrupts absolutely. 2862

power corrupts, forgetting that the absence of
power also corrupts 2882

If power corrupts, being out of power corrupts
absolutely. 2893

nature will rise up, and ... overturn a corrupt
political system 3188

CORRUPTION

Communism is the corruption of a dream of
justice. 153

Corruption, the most infallible symptom of
constitutional liberty. 779

Corruption of politics has nothing to do with the
morals 793

first sign of corruption ... is that the end justifies
the means 1005

The great corruption of Socialism which threatens
us at present 3565

the product of an earlier corruption and a
producer of new corruptions 3870

COST

it costs you 90 bucks to fly to Washington to
picket 1095

The cost of liberty is less than the price of
repression. 1336

Do not worry about what it costs. 1380

The cost of freedom is always high 1439

Order and law have a cost. 3251

it takes your mind off the cost of living 3896

COSTA RICA

we can't confer with Costa Rica and come home
with our shirts on 1646

COUGH

She ... is said to be inclined to cough noisily when
he goes on too long 2667

If you even cough or smile they will start up all
over again. 2971

COUNCIL

In the council, there were men possessed of much
more eloquence 2036

COUNSEL

a constitutional mandate to have counsel at a
preliminary hearing 248

One cool judgment is worth a thousand hasty
counsels. 2105

COUNT

the obvious disadvantage of merely counting
votes 371

counting heads is not an ideal way to govern 401

but I'm not a fool either. I can count. 3131

COUNTER-REVOLUTION

Fascism was a counter-revolution against a
revolution that never took place. 3255

COUNTRY

He who would not wish his own country to be
bigger or smaller 16

This country, with its institutions, belongs to the
people 340

Democracy is ... appropriate for countries which
enjoy an economic surplus 459

may our country be always successful 855

My country is the world; 864

One country, one constitution, one destiny. 874

A Country can get more real joy out of just
hollering for their Freedom 1404

Every country has the government it
deserves. 1520

if countries always apologized when they had done
wrong 1630

is given ... on condition that he leave the
country 1635

I know that I can save this country 2012

"Please, God, a country gentleman." 2120

would you rather be a country gentleman than a
Prime Minister 2120

I look at the Senators and pray for the
country 2251

The single best augury is to fight for one's
country. 2388

That we can die but once to save our
country! 2389

that I have but one life to lose for my
country 2393

but our country, right or wrong 2398

Our country! ... may she always be in the
right; 2398

Our country, right or wrong. 2408

He who loves not his home and country which he
has seen 2413

looking out for yourself by looking out for your
country 2414

not only because of a patriotism that stands for
love of country 2422

We have a country as well as a party to
obey. 2474

He serves his party best who serves his country
best. 2482

If I make a mistake it doesn't merely affect me ...
but the country 2960

a whole country is unjustly overrun and conquered
by a foreign army 3210

This country should be agitated ... till the battle of
liberty is won 3319

They talk of a man betraying his country 3640

If I had to choose between betraying my country
and betraying my friend 3641

It is sweet and honorable to die for your
country. 3658

a quarrel in a faraway country between people of
whom we know nothing 3818

No country without an atom bomb 3937

COUNTRYMEN

my countrymen are mankind 864

I hear our countrymen abroad saying: 2568

COURAGE

the American people are ahead of their leaders in realism and courage 472

it has neither the courage nor the ability to govern itself 535

The only kinds of courage and honesty which are permanently useful 1799

the courage to show that he has it 2044

Desperate courage makes One a majority. 2301

thank you for your courage 3964

COURSE OF EVENTS

People's revolutions are born from the course of events. 3223

It ... deranges the course of events 3716

COURT

to get American citizens to obey the orders of constituted courts 28

nor should this court ... be thought of as a general haven for reform 245

One who comes to the Court must come to adore 1153

As a member of this court I am not justified in writing my private notions 1737

The Court is most vulnerable ... when it deals with judge-made ... law 1746

too long neglected to nourish its heart—the court systems 1816

any successful defiance to the carrying out of court orders 1926

legislatures are ... guardians ... in quite as great a degree as the courts 2241

useless as someone at court who can't do anything to further your career; 2520

It is the court fool ... whom the king can least afford to lose 2574

the Court fails to perceive any reason 3019

This court will not deny the equal protection of the law 3376

What the Court really has refused to recognize 3403

the power in the American courts ... of pronouncing a statute unconstitutional 3508

COURTESAN

sounds like the word "love" in the mouth of a courtesan 1270

COURTESY

Courtesy ... and self-restraint should mark international ... intercourse. 1633

Th' Sinit is ruled be courtesy, like th' longshoreman's union. 2242

COURTHOUSE

Somewhere "out there," beyond the walls of the courthouse 1745

a courthouse ... is a place where justice is dispensed 2931

COURTSHIP

it is a jealous mistress, and requires a long and constant courtship 1879

COVENANT

Open covenants of peace, openly arrived at 1641

COVETOUSNESS

Excess of wealth is cause of covetousness. 37

The yearning after equality is the offspring of covetousness 756

COWARD

Any man's coward who won't die for what he believes. 978

This Republic was not established by cowards; and cowards will not preserve it 2151

There is nothing that makes more cowards ... than public opinion. 3057

Those who won our independence by revolution were not cowards. 3246

COWARDICE

the most distinctive characteristic of the ... politician is ... cowardice 2633

CRACK

This bill is the legislative equivalent of crack. 2264

CRADLE

God has given you your country as cradle, and humanity as mother; 2402

CRAZY

No idea is too crazy. 1099

CREAM PUFF

My opponent called me a cream puff. 2828

CREATIVITY

the political creativity of the masses and their participation in management 185

CREATOR

the law of our Creator, the law of humanity 1872

CREDIBILITY

stringent censorships ... give credibility to the opinions they attack 1156

CREDULITY

except those which climb upward on the ... miseries or credulities of mankind 2094

CREED

A strange, a perverted creed that has a queer attraction 164

A policy is a temporary creed liable to be changed 941

less charity for those who believe the half of our creed 2687

CREEPING SOCIALISM

for the past twenty years there has been a creeping socialism 3570

CRICKET

In our traditional cricket match the parties are strong 2503

CRIME

Communists have committed great crimes 169

It's worse than a crime, it's a blunder. 853

the crime is not the burglary, but the discovery of the burglary 1034

(Watergate) was worse than a crime, it was a blunder. 1078

O liberty! what crimes are committed in thy name! 1246

the motive of good deeds and the common pretext of crime 1312

the sudden conviction that hanging was a mistake- -worse, a crime 1800

The unforgivable crime is soft hitting. 2099

His crimes are the only great things about him 2528

The whole duty of government is to prevent crime 3442

To delight in war is ... a positive crime in the statesman. 3764

it is such a crime because it is unjust 3770

unjust war is a crime against humanity 3770

CRIMINAL

The whole paraphernalia of the criminal law and the criminal courts 110

while there is a criminal class I am of it; 1351

I think it a less evil that some criminals should escape 1803

The criminal justice system is breaking down 1816

criticism of the criminal justice system ... was so much liberal bleating 1817

illegal methods ... to convict ... criminals as from the actual criminals 1929

no distinctly native American criminal class except Congress 2240

rule on questions of privilege in criminal matters 3019

the unsuccessful one a criminal 3257

Homosexual behavior ... should no longer be a criminal offense. 3351

absurd to deny it the right to put criminals to death 3465

CRIMINALITY

the Constitution sometimes insulates the criminality of a few 262

CRIPPLE

People who are much too sensitive to demand of cripples that they run races 106

CRISIS

the fashion to style the present moment an extraordinary crisis 871

There cannot be a crisis next week. 1070

In crises the most daring course is often safest. 1088

more often it is a crisis invited 2204

our crisis is not just material, it is a crisis of the spirit 3623

CRITIC

leave an old bone behind for the critics to chew on 2692

CRITICAL

How much easier it is to be critical than to be correct. 889

such swift and close collision in critical moments that man measures man 3751

CRITICISM

I am grateful for even the sharpest criticism 905

Criticism of government finds sanctuary in ... the 1st Amendment. 1141

Without criticism ... the government cannot govern. 1188

I do not resent criticism, even when ... it parts for the time with reality. 2133

I have never found ... that criticism is ever inhibited by ignorance. 2785

CRITICIZE

The citizen who criticizes his country is paying it an implied tribute. 32

abroad, I always make it a rule never to criticize ... the government 2765

He wasn't used to being criticized 2817

Thou shalt not criticize other Republicans. 3180

CROPPER

I always feel a little man's pleasure when they come a cropper 2148

CROSS-DIVISION

Numerous cross-divisions favour peace within a nation 100

CROSSING

It is not best to swap horses while crossing the river. 896

CROWD

the tendency of the individual to hide himself in the crowd 439

CROWN

You shall not press down upon the brow of labor this crown of thorns   81

The slave ... ends by wanting to wear a crown.   608

this I count the glory of my crown   1981

Not the king's crown, nor the deputed sword   1984

If chance will have me king, why, chance may crown me   1987

Uneasy lies the head that wears a crown.   2327

not a single crowned head in Europe   2344

Every noble crown is ... a crown of thorns.   2348

CRUCIFY

you shall not crucify mankind upon a cross of gold   81

CRUEL

Aristocracy is always cruel.   63

CRUELTY

the modern English commonwealth does not rest ... on the cruelty of the rich   84

the rest is Cruelty, not Justice   1764

War is cruelty, and you cannot refine it.   3734

It is not merely cruelty that leads men to love war   3753

CRUMB

I am not interested in picking up crumbs of compassion   3398

CRUSADE

a crusade is inaugurated against indecency   3526

CRUSH

We first crush people to the earth   3300

CRY

it hurt too bad to laugh, and he was too big to cry   884

more clearly than the cry of a hungry child in the street   3930

CULT

We must abolish the cult of the individual   159

CULTIVATION

the expression of what cultivation exists in the population   1884

CULTURE

strongest and most violent where there is the lowest degree of culture   2366

To be a Negro is to participate in a culture of poverty and fear   2925

CUNNING

Nothing doth more hurt ... than that cunning men pass for wise.   1989

CURE

ills of democracy can be cured by more democracy   403

The cure for bad politics is the same as the cure for tuberculosis.   794

one cure for the evils ... freedom produces, and that cure is freedom   1255

Freedom remains still the wisest cure for freedom's temporary inconveniences.   1326

they generally cure an evil by a lesser or a passing evil   1890

We cannot cure the evils of politics with politics.   2803

CURRENT

policies based on old myths rather than current realities   1687

only two great currents in the history of mankind   3221

CUSS

Should I ... stand on 125th Street cussing out Whitey   3132

CUSTODY

the presidency is an institution over which you have temporary custody   3036

CUSTOM

Law is largely crystallized custom   1900

Laws are sand, customs are rock.   1906

No written law has ever been more binding than unwritten custom   3061

CUT

I cannot and will not cut my conscience to fit this year's fashions.   804

CUTTING EDGE

if they have a cutting edge they may later return to wound him   2618

CYNIC

What is a cynic?   914

some cynics who think that a Platform is just a list of platitudes   2430

CYNICAL

I may have grown cynical from long service   2246

We are not a cynical people.   2816

CZECHOSLOVAKIA

Silent, mournful, abandoned, broken, Czechoslovakia recedes into darkness.   3820

DAGGER

The dagger plunged in the name of Freedom is plunged into the breast   1382

DAILY

Reading about one's failings in the daily papers   2640

the right to earn one's daily bread   3399

DAMAGE

the Communists have done nothing to damage our society 166

It yields a short-term high but does long-term damage to the system 2264

DAMN

he had drained, ditched, and damned the United States in three years 954

"Here lies Jack Williams. He done his damndest." 2144

DANGER

Our chief danger arises from the democratic parts of our constitutions. 229

There is danger from all men. 283

danger to American democracy lies not ... in the concentration of ... power 377

danger to democracy lies in the tendency of the individual to hide in the crowd 439

so full of dangers for the very foundations ... of social order 861

The question ... is whether the words ... create a clear and present danger 1122

chief danger which threatens the ... honor of the press 1171

The true danger is when liberty is nibbled away 1230

One danger arises from too great a concentration of power 1399

Freedom always entails danger. 1402

When I wish to estimate the danger that is likely to accrue to me 2074

In the face of great danger, salvation can only come through greatness. 2154

the great danger is, that the majority may not ... respect the rights 2284

Everything belongs to the fatherland when the fatherland is in danger. 2395

biggest danger for a politician is to shake hands with a man 2629

politics in the presence of social dangers to be a luxury 2695

to benefit and improve them is a work ... teeming with danger 3437

where the worst of dangers, the danger of poverty, hangs over everyone's head 3525

public debt as the greatest of the dangers to be feared 3588

A just fear of an imminent danger ...is a lawful cause of war. 3677

new and terrible dangers which man has created 3899

Any danger spot is tenable if men—brave men— will make it so. 3908

DANGEROUS

Nothing is as dangerous for the state as those who would govern ... with maxims 833

Nothing is more dangerous than an idea 949

Opinions become dangerous to a state 1109

(The judiciary is) the least dangerous branch of our government. 1744

Riches without law are more dangerous than is poverty without law. 1894

anything else will henceforth be mortally dangerous 2171

amiable passions of human nature are the most dangerous guides in politics 2682

A desperate disease requires a dangerous remedy. 3185

DARE

I am not sure I should have dared to start; 1011

They have rights who dare maintain them. 3303

For if it prosper, none dare call it treason 3636

DARING

In crises the most daring course is often safest. 1088

DARK

a leap absolutely in the dark 891

It throws civilization into the dark ages. 3873

DAWN

how that government treats those who are in the dawn of life 3501

DAY

Do the day's work. 209

The true conservative ... takes thought against the day of reckoning 213

I seldom think of politics more than 18 hours a day. 2821

Peace is more the product of our day-to-day living 3860

DEAD

all government ... is a dead weight that paralyzes the free spirit 1554

He cannot stifle a predilection for dead cities. 2375

A statesman is a politician who's been dead 10 or 15 years. 2615

The revolution is incapable either of regretting or of burying its dead. 3239

Dead men have no victory. 3648

DEADLOCK

The Congress is deadlocked and can't act. 2248

DEAFNESS

all the infirmities of old age, including deafness 2756

DEARNESS

it is dearness only that gives everything its value 539

DEATH

The death of democracy is not likely to be an assassination from ambush. 458

Death is better, a milder fate than tyranny. 519

but as for me, give me liberty, or give me death! 1219

There was one of two things I had a right to, liberty or death. 1309

We know that the road to freedom has always been stalked by death. 1467

anarchy and competition the laws of death 1541

absurd to deny it the right to put criminals to death 3465

nothing in this world is certain but death and taxes 3583

DEBATE

Let no one think for a moment that national debate means national division. 476

What makes a man minister? Debating power. 2077

Our debates have been like the mating of pandas in the zoo 2440

a seething debating society in which the debate never stops 2824

The Prime Minister wins debate after debate and loses battle after battle. 3835

he fights debates like a war and a war like a debate 3835

DEBAUCH

no surer means of overturning ... society than to debauch the currency 642

DEBAUCHERY

like calling debauchery the soil of love 3763

DEBT

we must not let our rulers load us with perpetual debt 3587

Of all debts men are least willing to pay the taxes. 3597

DEBUTANTE

A whore's vote is just as good as a debutante's. 717

DECEIVE

deceiving all your friends, but not quite deceiving all your enemies 1700

DECENCY

The most practical kind of politics is the politics of decency. 2721

DECEPTION

synonymous, in the public mind, with deception by the government 814

DECIDE

who knows how to keep ... the power to decide 1424

DECISION

The perfect bureaucrat ... manages to make no decisions 8

Decision by majorities is as much an expedient as lighting by gas. 334

A decision is the action an executive must take 2159

Some men can make decisions and some cannot. 2164

High office teaches decision making, not substance. 2205

very lonely at times of great decisions 2986

DECISIVE

Weapons are an important factor in war, but not the decisive one; 3823

DECLARATION

For the support of this Declaration 1228

in the first paragraph of the Declaration is the ... right ... to the ballot 3312

DEDICATED

The general has dedicated himself so many times 994

DEDICATION

the tranquil and steady dedication of a lifetime 2418

DEFEAT

The defeats ... of the fellows at the top aren't defeats ... at the bottom 95

A good man would prefer to be defeated than to defeat injustice by evil means. 772

Victory attained by violence is tantamount to a defeat 937

civil liberty must not be surrendered at ... even one hundred defeats 1281

Defeat in itself was part ... of the great gambling game of politics 2778

not interested in the possibilities of defeat 3756

Victory or defeat? 3790

We have sustained a defeat without a war. 3820

The problems of victory are more agreeable than those of defeat 3834

North Vietnam cannot defeat ... the United States 3938

DEFEATIST

defeatists who despair of the success of our own philosophy 443

DEFECT

Among the defects of the bill, which were numerous 888

DEFEND

working-class bees ... deprived of the right to defend themselves 92

Democracy is a form of government which may be rationally defended 389

God grants liberty only to those ... ready to ...
defend it　1259

only a few generations have been granted the role
of defending freedom　1433

So we defend ourselves and our henroosts, and
maintain slavery.　3519

People are glad to be defended, but they are not
glad about paying　3599

DEFENSE

Washington ... where the truth is not necessarily
the best defense　815

core of our defense is the faith we have in the
institutions　963

Irreverence is the champion of liberty and its only
sure defense.　1327

Diplomacy and defense are not substitutes　1671

political speech ... largely the defense of the
indefensible　2767

We must acquire proficiency in defense　3876

a defense that will protect American cities　3973

When men talk about defense, they ... claim to be
protecting women and children　4011

DEFERENTIAL

mass of the English people are ... politically
deferential　349

DEFIANCE

defiance of the law is the surest road to
tyranny　1932

DEFICIT

Deficits shrink with a rhetorical flourish.　2435

DEFINE

(conservatives) define themselves in terms of what
they oppose　222

not ... attempt further to define the kinds of
material　1939

A great man's failures to understand define
him.　2090

rebellion actually defines him　3266

DEFINITE

assigned a definite place and a definite quantitative
significance　144

DEGRADATION

War is a blessing compared with national
degradation.　3722

DEHUMANIZATION

absolute power and absolute faith are instruments
of dehumanization　622

DEITY

Prosperity is ... to be used, not a deity to be
worshiped　646

DELAY

Delay is preferable to error.　848

Justice delayed is democracy denied.　1812

delay is itself a decision　2999

DELEGATE

An open convention is when your delegates are in
control.　2787

DELICIOUS

most delicious of all privileges—spending other
people's money　3592

DELIGHT

To delight in war is a merit in the soldier　3764

DELIVERANCE

Liberation is not deliverance.　1300

DELUSION

The people never give up their liberties but under
some delusion.　1232

the delusion that a change in form is a change in
substance　2740

DEMAGOGUE

when its moral convictions weaken it becomes
easy prey for the demagogue　454

DEMAND

no matter how big, not big enough for its
demands　3006

DEMOCRACY

immunity to eloquence is of the utmost
importance to ... a democracy　23

Conservatives do not worship democracy.　226

Democracy ... is a charming form of
government　263

If liberty and equality ... are chiefly to be found in
democracy　264

Democracy is the form of government in which
the free are rulers.　265

A democracy exists whenever those who are free
and are not well-off　267

Real liberty is neither found in ... the extremes of
democracy　295

Democracy becomes a government of bullies
tempered by editors.　328

Democracy is not possible except in a nation
where there is so much property　331

to the extent of the difference, is no
democracy　335

This expresses my idea of democracy.　335

Political democracy ... supplies a training school
for making first-class men　351

in a democracy manners are the only effective
weapons against the bowie-knife　352

In a pure democracy the ruling men will be the
wirepullers　353

Democracy represents the disbelief in all great
men　362

Democracy means simply the bludgeoning of the
people　367

Democracy is not so much a form of government
as a set of principles.　372

Keyword Index

the reason democracy works is because as you multiply judgements 488

The experience of democracy is like the experience of life 489

Democracy is not a fragile flower; 493

I don't run democracy. I train troops to defend democracy. 494

Democracy, the profoundly good, is also the profoundly productive. 499

in order to supply ourselves, in the arsenal of democracy 594

if democracy is so stupid as to give us free tickets and salaries 594

Ours is not yet a totalitarian government, but it is an elitist democracy 628

a democracy, imperfect though it is, is worth fighting for 630

We do not base a choice on the goodness of democracy 631

We naturally associate democracy, to be sure, with freedom of action 685

No amount of charters ... will make a democracy out of an illiterate people 687

Democracy has arrived at a gallop in England 690

Voting is merely a handy device; it is not to be identified with democracy 715

Democracy ... those who are equal in any respect are equal in all respects 737

Democracy and socialism have nothing in common but one word: equality. 746

democracy seeks equality in liberty 746

The flood of money ... today is a pollution of democracy 820

We must be the great arsenal of democracy. 964

content with democracy, even if we have to include the American newspapers 1174

In a democracy dissent is an act of faith. 1459

In democracies, nothing is ... more brilliant than commerce 1580

If we are to keep our democracy, there must be one commandment: 1804

Justice delayed is democracy denied. 1812

our democracy will be less responsible to the majority 2261

No democracy can ... survive which does not accept ... the rights of minorities 2313

Democracy is in every case a principle of dissolution 2347

Under democracy one party always ... trying to prove that the other is unfit 2500

In our democracy officers of the government are the servants 2594

The essential democracy of our Nation ... depend not upon the absence of power 2871

In Democracies a ... disposition to make publick opinion stronger than the law 3044

You can never have a revolution in order to establish a democracy. 3234

You must have a democracy in order to have a revolution. 3234

socialist democracy may ... be more of a sham than capitalist democracy 3564

wrought under ... the holy name of liberty or democracy 3854

After each war there is a little less democracy to save. 3869

DEMOCRAT

even a democrat like myself must admit this 379

For democrats in troubled countries, the height of the art of governing 417

the Democrats believe that the whole people should govern 504

The Democrats today trust in the people 504

You've got to be (an) optimist to be a Democrat 507

I am not a member of any organized party—I am a Democrat. 508

Every Harvard class should have one Democrat 509

(Democrats) can't get elected unless things get worse 516

Democrats believe every day is April 15 3182

DEMOCRATIC

I believe and I say it is true Democratic feeling 49

Our chief danger arises from the democratic parts of our constitutions. 229

The basis of a democratic state is liberty. 266

Were there a people of gods, their government would be democratic. 280

Democratic institutions generally give men a lofty notion of their country 322

The taste for well-being is the ... indelible feature of democratic times. 324

Men living in democratic times have many passions 325

A democratic constitution, not supported by democratic institutions in detail 329

The real democratic American ideal 360

If this nation is not truly democratic, then she must die. 365

We have not got democratic government today. 398

The deeper purpose of democratic government 410

the democratic disease which expresses tyranny by reducing everything unique 427

The blind lead the blind. It's the democratic way. 436

In a democratic society ... relief must come through ... popular conscience 473

powers conveyed upon a government by a democratic vote 497

The Democratic Party is like a mule. 501

Th' dimmycratic party ain't on speakin' terms with itsilf. 502

I love the Democratic Party; but I love America a great deal more.   503

When the Democratic Party thinks that it is an end in itself   503

The Democratic Party at its worst is better for the country   510

the Democratic Way ... via hyperbole, sham   512

The Democratic Party is a party in name only   513

in democratic societies it is in the interest of the individual   677

A democratic form of government, a democratic way of life   692

That a peasant may become king does not render the kingdom democratic.   2358

In England, a real, democratic party is impossible   2485

Let us not seek the Republican answer or the Democratic answer   2504

no Democratic or Republican way of cleaning the streets   2505

however bad the Republican party was, the Democratic party was much worse   3166

My answer to why did I choose the Democratic Party   3177

customary in democratic countries to deplore expenditure on armaments   3479

A man may have strong humanitarian and democratic principles;   3531

a democratic government is the only one in which those who vote for a tax   3595

the highly democratic method of conscripting American manhood   3782

DEMOCRATISM
Without glasnost there is not, and there cannot be, democratism   185

DENOMINATOR
then you ultimately probe for the lowest common denominator   3134

DENY
Justice delayed is democracy denied.   1812

DEPEND
governments rather depend upon men than men upon governments   1481

DEPOSIT
a pigeon can still make a deposit on a John Deere   1600

DEPOSITORY
The people themselves therefore are its only safe depositories.   293

I know no safe depository of the ultimate powers of the society   672

DEPRESSION
The Great Depression was produced by government mismanagement   657

Depression is when you lose yours.   662

DEPRIVE
so long as we do not ... deprive others of theirs   1283

DERIVATIVE
The power of Kings and Magistrats ... is only derivative   272

DERIVE
Governments ... deriv(e) their just powers from the consent of the governed.   288

DESECRATION
convulsed by horror at the desecration of brick and mortar   65

DESERT
They produce a desert of uniformity around them   2148

Where they make a desert, they call it peace.   3661

DESERVE
They deserve the shortest hours and the highest pay.   107

Every country has the government it deserves.   1520

they likewise receive praises which they do not deserve   2004

No one can guarantee success in war, but only deserve it.   3856

DESIRE
I have acted ... from a conscientious desire to do what was right   2961

The desire to understand the world and the desire to reform it   3121

DESK
This desk of mine is one at which a man may die   2990

DESPERATE
A desperate disease requires a dangerous remedy.   3185

DESPERATION
The mass of men lead lives of quiet desperation.   882

DESPICABLE
nothing so despicable ... as someone ... who can't ... further your career;   2520

DESPISE
Having despised us, ... seek to render us despicable;   2900

being unarmed ... causes you to be despised   3668

DESPOSITORY
the President has become increasingly the depository of all national ills   2975

DESPOT

One despot always has a few good moments, but an assembly of despots never   531

A country governed by a despot is an inverted cone.   540

There are three kinds of despots.   578

There is the despot who tyrannizes over the body.   578

The State is still ... a collective despot   580

unlimited power will make a despot of almost any man   581

The benevolent despot ...still demands ... the submissiveness of sheep   617

Idealism is the despot of thought, just as politics is the despot of will.   2707

DESPOTIC

freedom of the press ... can never be restrained but by despotic governments   1158

DESPOTISM

Bureaucracy ... has become the modern form of despotism   10

Despotism accomplishes great things illegally;   318

If Despotism failed only for want of a capable benevolent despot   373

Pure despotism is the punishment for men's bad conduct.   535

Timid men who prefer the calm of despotism   546

Force is the vital principle ... of despotism   548

Whatever government is not a government of laws, is a despotism   555

France was long a despotism tempered by epigrams.   558

when he governs himself and also governs another man ... that is despotism   565

Whatever crushes individuality is despotism   567

The more complete the despotism, the more smoothly all things move   574

a system of despotism tempered by casualness   577

Under a pure despotism, a people may be contented   744

not to expect to be translated from despotism to liberty in a feather bed   1239

anarchy, which soon becomes the most horrid of all despotisms   1273

to find that limit ... as protection against political despotism   1284

Man is about the same ... whether with despotism   1544

where anarchy has prevailed they will ... submit only to despotism   1559

Attempts at reform, when they fail, strengthen despotism   3092

DESTINY

You cannot ... at the same time expect reason to control human destinies   601

this supreme combat that will decide the destinies of the world   689

One country, one constitution, one destiny.   874

institutions alone fix the destinies of nations   1522

No man is ... wise enough for any of us to surrender our destiny to.   2134

destiny of the colored American ... is the destiny of America.   3308

cannot accept the doctrine that war must be forever a part of man's destiny   3830

DESTROY

it destroys what it loves, because it will not mend it   190

And then you destroy yourself.   1063

then consent to see liberty destroyed   1353

it is true that an inherently free ... person may be destroyed   1405

you can't see how the calm will be destroyed   3187

revolutions always destroy themselves   3242

beneficiaries of a system cannot be expected to destroy it   3528

power to tax involves the power to destroy   3589

The power to tax is the power to destroy.   3606

The power to tax is not the power to destroy while this Court sits.   3610

They were all enemy. They were all to be destroyed.   3946

if we allow it a free hand to ... destroy the ... rules of international life   3971

DESTRUCTION

concentration of power ... precedes the destruction of human initiative   585

The process engages the ... forces of economic law on the side of destruction   642

if the price ... is the ... destruction of those who are to enjoy liberty   1401

The body politic ... carries in itself the causes of its destruction   1489

It is better ... to argue ...than make perfidious plans of mutual destruction   1720

whoever resists that rushes willfully to destruction   3225

whether the mad destruction is wrought under the name of totalitarianism   3854

DETAIL

The health of any democracy ... depends on a small technical detail   399

DETERMINANT

The ultimate determinant in the struggle now going on   1710

DETERMINATION

Laws ... express ... its determination ... to do something   1923

DETERRENT
The major deterrent (to war) is in a man's mind. 3902

One cannot fashion a credible deterrent out of an incredible action. 3933

DETESTABLE
I find war detestable but those who praise it ... even more so 3775

DETOUR
if the road to hell is paved with them, then it's a pretty good detour 2260

DEVELOPING COUNTRY
Where there are two PhDs in a developing country 1046

DEVIL
I would make at least a favorable reference to the devil in the House 987

but never without belief in a devil 3126

DEVILISH
This is the devilish thing about foreign affairs: 1684

DEVIOUS
the very devious, expert at covering their tracks 2656

DEVOTION
I can give my heart and my devotion to these old islands 2361

DEW
come, my conservative friend, wipe the dew off your spectacles 204

DIAGNOSE
Politics is the art of looking for trouble ... diagnosing it incorrectly 2807

DIAGNOSIS
excessively simple diagnosis of the world's ills 2795

DICHOTOMY
The dichotomy between personal liberties and property rights is a false one. 3381

DICTATE
What is a Government for except to dictate! 1550

DICTATOR
The man who is born to be a dictator is not compelled; 590

Dictators ride to and fro upon tigers which they dare not dismount. 598

The dictator, in all his pride, is held in the grip of his party machine. 602

When you stop a dictator there are always risks. 629

DICTATORIAL
times when one must govern liberally and times when one must be dictatorial; 1545

DICTATORSHIP
this dictatorship ... constitutes the transition to abolition of all classes 124

class struggle necessarily leads to the dictatorship of the proletariat 124

The dictatorship of the proletariat is an historically regressive idea 182

History proves that dictatorships do not grow out of strong ... governments 600

A dictatorship is a regime in which people quote instead of thinking. 603

Whenever you have an efficient government you have a dictatorship. 614

I don't mind dictatorships abroad provided they are pro-American. 625

Anybody who has ever lived ... under a dictatorship 630

solely on the evilness of a dictatorship, which is certain 631

People who are hungry ... are the stuff of which dictatorships are made 653

Revolution or dictatorship can sometimes abolish bad things 3226

DIE
The State is not "abolished." It dies out. 126

If this nation is not truly democratic, then she must die. 365

No democracy has ... survived the failure ... to be ready to die for it 387

It is a call to untiring effort ... if necessary, to die in its defense 474

To die for an idea is to place a pretty high price upon conjectures. 931

Any man's coward who won't die for what he believes. 978

old soldiers never die; they just fade away 989

The body politic ... begins to die as soon as it is born 1489

Be ashamed to die until you have won some victory for humanity. 2066

A great man's greatest good luck is to die at the right time. 2152

If a man hasn't discovered something that he will die for 2175

If I die a violent death, as some fear and a few are plotting 2213

The king never dies. 2342

That we can die but once to save our country! 2389

The Ku Klux Klan never dies. 2945

This desk of mine is one at which a man may die 2990

so in the case of the body politic, when motion ceases, the body dies 3090

to win them they must fight, sacrifice ... and, if
need be, die for them   3341

It is sweet and honorable to die for your
country.   3658

You're here to make those so-and-sos die for
theirs.   3968

You're not here to die for your country.   3968

DIFFERENCE

only vital political difference between Marx and
Lenin   162

difference between a moral man and a man of
honor   799

the difference between being a diplomat and a
doormat   1706

The difference between being an elder
statesman   2160

We are ... a nation of differences. Those
differences don't make us weak.   2319

it is difference of opinion that makes horse
races   2719

Honest difference of views and honest debate are
not disunity.   2769

insofar as it represents a concealment of
differences   2789

Insofar as it represents a genuine reconciliation of
differences   2789

and if we cannot end now our differences   2927

So, let us not be blind to our differences   2927

one difference between a tax collector and a
taxidermist   3619

but between peace and slavery there is the greatest
difference   3655

What difference does it make to the dead   3854

DIFFERENT

terrible walls which imprison men because they
are different   720

When we lose the right to be different, we lose the
privilege to be free.   1357

Men are created different;   1406

if rules have to be adapted to different men   1531

DIFFICULT

nothing more difficult ... than ... the introduction
of a new order of things   1976

To do great things is difficult; but to command
great things is more difficult.   2079

DIFFICULTY

Difficulty is the excuse history never
accepts.   2162

In war one sees one's own difficulties   3709

DIFFUSION

Political liberty is nothing else but the diffusion of
power.   1395

DIGESTION

Few radicals have good digestions.   208

DIGNITY

it has restored the dignity of indignation   3373

I believe we should strive ... for the dignity ... of
mankind   3390

revolutionary social change is to establish ... the
dignity of man   3530

DILEMMA

A Foreign Secretary ... is always faced with this
cruel dilemma.   1663

DIMINUTION

enjoyment of his earnings with the least possible
diminution for public needs   3459

DINNER

they who have more dinners than appetite   45

They are conservatives after dinner.   195

progress is changing from the full dinner pail to
the full garage   645

A revolution is not a dinner party   3247

DIPLOMACY

The old-world diplomacy of Europe was largely
carried on in drawing rooms   1625

Vacillation and inconsistency are as incompatible
with successful diplomacy   1628

Diplomacy, n. The patriotic art of lying for one's
country.   1634

Diplomacy is to do and say the nastiest thing in
the nicest way.   1647

diplomacy is a continuation of war by other
means   1662

Diplomacy and defense are not substitutes for one
another.   1671

Diplomacy is letting someone else have your
way.   1690

Diplomacy ... means the art of nearly deceiving all
your friends   1700

We didn't have to do the minuets of
diplomacy.   1714

DIPLOMAT

Diplomats are useful only in fair weather.   1677

the difference between being a diplomat and a
doormat   1706

May the pens of the diplomats not ruin again
what the people have attained   3711

Diplomats are just as essential to starting a war as
Soldiers   3859

DIRECTION

the President is the only person who can change
the direction   3023

DIRECTNESS

directness is always better than elaborate
wording   1856

DISADVANTAGE

To govern is always to choose among
disadvantages.   1571

DISINFECTANT

Sunlight remains the world's best
disinfectant. 816

DISOBEY

It's the orders you disobey that make you
famous. 2201

DISORDER

disorder will give them but an incommodious
sanctuary 1202

cause of all our disorders lies in the different State
Governments 3419

DISPENSATION

one of those ... God hath drawn out ... for some
extraordinary dispensations 1994

DISPENSE

a courthouse even in Mississippi is a place where
justice is dispensed 2931

DISPOSE

it is the privilege of the Congress to dispose 3511

DISPOSITION

by improving the mind ... of society, to lessen the
disposition to war 3714

DISPROPORTION

they do not consider that disproportion destroys a
state 2442

DISREGARD

A universal feeling ... cannot be safely
disregarded 3046

DISSATISFACTION

if it expresses itself in silent, persistent
dissatisfaction 586

DISSENT

then I rise up and dissent 503

They mistake dissent for disloyalty. 620

men and women who dared to dissent from
accepted doctrine 1136

we may never confuse honest dissent with disloyal
subversion 1136

In the end it is worse to suppress dissent 1138

In a democracy dissent is an act of faith. 1459

There are men—now in power in this country—
who do not respect dissent 1464

DISSOLUTION

Democracy is in every case a principle of
dissolution 2347

DISSOLVE

it becomes necessary for one people to dissolve
political bands 287

rolling along without being dissolved or dissolving
anything else 2051

DISTANCE

in direct proportion to his distance from the
political situation 810

one cannot realize their greatness till one stands at
some distance 2088

prestige comes only from distance 2125

" 'Tis distance lends enchantment to the
view" 2688

DISTANT

sending them off to distant lands to die of foreign
fevers 1189

who can hear the most distant drum ... than the
cry of a hungry child 3930

DISTINCTION

Distinctions in society will always exist under
every just government. 43

cannot recognize a distinction between what is
political and what is not 2741

DISTINGUISH

to distinguish between their native dislike for
war 3964

DISTRIBUTION

led by an invisible hand to make nearly the same
distribution 39

not by ... concentration of powers, but by their
distribution 1502

DISTRIBUTIVE

a ... directed economic system could ... bring about
distributive justice 144

DISTURBER

those are ever ... under the command of the
disturbers of society 2684

DISUNITY

Honest difference of views and honest debate are
not disunity. 2769

DIVERSE

liberation of the diverse energies of free
nations 1443

DIVERSITY

Diversity of opinion within the framework of
loyalty 1400

A world made safe for diversity 1686

If tolerance of diversity involves an admitted
element of risk 2919

at least we can help make the world safe for
diversity 2927

DIVIDE

If a house be divided against itself, that house
cannot stand. 826

the more power is divided the more irresponsible
it becomes 2861

DIVINE

Divine right went out with the American
Revolution 482

worship the state as the manifestation of the divine
on earth 852

The state is the divine idea as it exists on
earth. 852

The spirit of divinest Liberty 1250

main principle ... of liberalism is the rejection of
the divine law 2269

it rejects and destroys all authority and divine
law 2269

pernicious error that multitude is divine because it
is multitude 2296

Princes have their Power Absolute, and by Divine
Right 2334

The Right Divine of Kings to govern
wrong. 2339

To despise legitimate authority ... is a rebellion
against the Divine Will 3225

DIVISION

Let no one think ... that national debate means
national division 476

Our greatest foreign policy problem is our
divisions at home. 1705

a dreadful Spirit of Division as rends a
Government 2445

The Pope! How many divisions has he got? 3157

DIVORCE

You cannot divorce property from power. 2849

DIXIECRAT

Dixiecrats who are more ready to lay down
lives 3930

DOCTRINE

a doctrine so illogical and so dull 137

men and women who dared to dissent from
accepted doctrine 1136

a very dangerous doctrine to consider the judges
as the ultimate arbiters 1728

I'm a participant in the doctrine of constructive
ambiguity. 2666

DOER

To be both a speaker of words and a doer of
deeds. 1966

DOG

just as a sporting dog is the intermedium between
the sportsman and the hare 44

You kill one dog, the master buys another 583

The free mind is no barking dog, to be tethered on
a ten-foot chain. 693

it's the size of the fight in the dog 1016

for the underdog no matter how much of a dog he
is 1066

I'd rather be a dog and bay at the moon 2246

If you live among dogs, keep a stick. 3893

DOGMA

socialism ... cannot be brought into harmony with
the dogmas of the ... Church 3561

DOGMATIC

not the conquest of the world by a single dogmatic
creed 1443

DOLLAR

to be a poor race in a land of dollars is the very
bottom of hardships 83

DOMESTIC

The greatest domestic problem facing our country
is saving our soil and water. 733

You can always survive a mistake in domestic
affairs 1685

DOMESTICATE

All laws are an attempt to domesticate the natural
ferocity of the species. 1949

DOMINATION

carrying down to the lowest grade ... ambition of
political domination 329

the craze for domination is an incurable
disease 534

ever any domination which did not appear natural
to those who possessed it 572

DOMINO

You have a row of dominoes set up. 999

DONE

If you want anything done, ask a woman. 4008

DONKEY

If a donkey bray at you, don't bray at him. 831

DOOM

The leader is always alone in times of
doom. 2155

DOORMAT

difference between being a diplomat and a
doormat 1706

DOSE

we have to apply the remedy in small doses 3102

DOUBLE-CROSS

"He'll double-cross that bridge when he comes to
it." 2631

DOUBT

limit to our realization of tomorrow will be our
doubts of today 981

DOVE

between a hawk and a dove the hawk has a great
advantage 3928

DOWN

What's up today is down tomorrow. 2802

DOWNFALL

National injustice is the surest road to national downfall. 1790

DRAFT

drafts them to go take that of their neighbors 532

then it is wrong for America to draft us 3272

DRAGON

the dragon somehow poops out, and decent democracy is victor 495

DRAIN

he had drained, ditched, and damned the United States 954

DRAMA

Revolution is a drama of passion. 3285

The drama can only be brought to its climax in one of two ways 3958

DRAWING ROOM

The old-world diplomacy of Europe was largely carried on in drawing rooms 1625

DREAM

Governments got in the way of the dreams of the people. 1711

What has happened to the dreams of the United Nations's founders? 1711

Glory is only given to those who have always dreamed of it. 2131

When hopes and dreams are loose in the streets 3263

I still have a dream. 3363

I have a dream 3365

DREGS

A nation without dregs and malcontents 990

DRESSED UP

All dressed up, with nowhere to go. 933

DRIVE

The House of Commons ... does not like to be driven 2235

DRIVER

"We the people" are the driver—the government is the car. 500

with front-seat drivers and back-seat drivers contradicting each other 3171

DROWN

As soon as it rains they drown in every drop. 1677

DRUDGERY

it brings nothing but unceasing drudgery 2955

DRUM

The sound of the drum drives out thought; 3721

DRUNK

best audience is intelligent, well-educated and a little drunk. 2429

A man can take a little bourbon without getting drunk 2830

DRUNKARD

as if a Drunkard in a Dropsey should change his Doctors, and not his Dyet 834

DUBIOUS

most of them ... are of dubious wisdom and even more dubious honesty 2249

DUE

Justice is that virtue that assigns to every man his due. 1755

if laws representing ... moral choices are to be invalidated under due process 1962

DULL

how a doctrine ... so dull can have exercised so powerful ... an influence 137

the very dull, who have nothing to hide and nothing to show; 2656

Nothing is so dull as political agitation. 2715

DULLES

Mr. Dulles has just frightened most of our allies to death 3891

DUMBNESS

honesty in Public Men is generally attributed to Dumbness 802

DUTY

the duty of every citizen according to his best capacities 25

the duty of every individual to obey the established Government 304

No, it is his duty to step forward. 590

he trespasses against his duty who sleeps over his watch 776

let us to the end do our duty as we understand it 890

Let us ... brace ourselves to our duties, and so bear ourselves 967

who tried to do his duty as God gave him the sight to see that duty 989

Every subject's duty is the king's; 1201

the faculty of choosing, among the various modes of fulfilling duty 1297

No government can be maintained without ... fear as well as of duty 1523

duty of judges is to render justice ... some who know their duty 1724

This is the very essence of judicial duty. 1726

duty of the judicial department to say what the law is 1726

responsibility is duty, and that duty is to preserve the exceptional liberty 1898

it is our duty to try to prevent it 2092

economy among the first ... of republican
virtues 3588

Countries when lawmaking falls ... to the ... poor
cannot hope for much economy 3594

I favor the policy of economy, not because I wish
to save money 3608

Economy is idealism in its most practical
form. 3608

EDIFICE

The whole cornerstone of our democratic
edifice 433

EDITOR

Democracy becomes a government of bullies
tempered by editors. 328

An editor is someone who separates the wheat
from the chaff 1001

editor's own conviction of what ... is in the public
interest 1187

EDUCATE

You cannot educate a man to be a trained
technician 607

Educate and inform the whole mass of
people. 667

By educating the young generation along the right
lines 689

can we educate them before the crash
comes? 690

the greatest duty of any statesman is to
educate 2123

I had to prepare the mind of the country, and to
educate ... our Party 2480

EDUCATION

that the whole people can have considerable
education 331

project of a national education ought ... to be
discouraged 668

but to inform their discretion by education 672

Education makes a people easy to lead 676

education of the greatest number should be ...
scientific 677

Education ... beyond all other devices of human
origin 679

Upon the education of the people ... the fate of
this country depends 681

Liberty can be safe only when Suffrage is
illuminated by Education. 682

The highest result of education is tolerance. 686

Human history becomes ... a race between
education and catastrophe 688

A democratic form of government ... presupposes
free public education 692

Knowledge of human nature is the beginning and
end of political education. 2726

provisions of ... law requiring ... discrimination in
public education must yield 2922

to succeed in life if he is denied the opportunity of
an education 3346

in ... public education ... "separate but equal" has
no place 3347

EEL

Politician, n. An eel in the fundamental
mud 2566

EFFECT

Governments are more the effect than the
cause 1514

What dire effects from civil discord flow 3683

EFFECTIVE

basis of effective government is public
confidence 1566

EFFETE

an effete corps of impudent snobs 1056

EFFICIENCY

there is infused a good deal of admiration for its
efficiency 604

The efficiency of the truly national leader 2113

not to promote efficiency but to preclude the
exercise of arbitrary power 3510

EFFICIENT

An efficient bureaucracy is the greatest threat to
liberty. 12

Whenever you have an efficient government you
have a dictatorship. 614

so too is a superlatively efficient
government 3481

We do them because we have to, and thank God
we are efficient. 3942

EGGHEAD

Eggheads of the the world arise 1007

EGO

There's nothing wrong with having a big
ego. 2220

ELABORATE

directness is always better than elaborate
wording 1856

ELDER STATESMAN

The difference between being an elder
statesman 2160

ELECT

you have to put up with the man you elect 448

(Democrats) can't get elected unless things get
worse 516

A rayformer thinks he was ilicted because he was
a rayformer 710

What is the use of being elected ... unless you
stand for something? 2082

The trouble with practical jokes is that very often
they get elected. 2588

Before you can become a statesman you first have
to get elected 2641

to be elected you have to be a politician pledging support   2641

More men have been elected between Sundown and Sunup   2742

but he may be elected without it   2988

I am acutely aware that you have not elected me as your president   3017

ELECTION

Democracy substitutes election by the incompetent many   374

a small technical detail: the conduct of elections   399

they do not forfeit through elections the rights   483

We are no longer interested in elections except as a means   624

We cannot have free government without elections;   704

if the rebellion could force us to forego or postpone a national election   704

An election is coming.   705

I know nothing grander ... than a well-contested American national election.   707

"free and honest elections"   708

Elections are won ... chiefly because most people vote against somebody   713

An election is a bet on the future   725

This election is not about ideology;   727

th' supreme coort follows th' iliction returns   1730

a politician thinks of the next election   2058

more important than winning the election is governing the nation   2499

at stated intervals through an honest and free system of elections   2871

The process of election ... affords a moral certainty   2951

but the president says one thing during the election   3034

ELECTORATE

how to fascinate ... or otherwise strike the fancy of the electorate   2564

ELECTRIFICATION

Socialism is Soviet power plus ... electrification   132

ELEPHANT

Call an elephant a rabbit only if it gives you comfort   2894

The elephant has a thick skin, a head full of ivory   3173

ELIMINATION

Work for elimination of concrete evils   3486

ELITE

Communism is governed by an elite   168

Democracy represents the disbelief ... in all elite societies: 362

few elites which will put up with the bother of it   1151

an elite that accomplishes mediocrity for the public good   2650

ELITIST

but it is an elitist democracy—and becoming more so every year   628

ELOQUENCE

immunity to eloquence is of the utmost importance   23

men possessed of much more eloquence than I   2036

ELOQUENT

"We, the people." It is a very eloquent beginning.   255

EMANCIPATE

all nations desirous of emancipating themselves from a foreign yoke   3204

EMANCIPATION

We shall never secure emancipation from the tyranny of the white oppressor   596

emancipation will be a proclamation—but it will not be a fact   3362

EMBRACE

I supposed they only wanted to know what was good in order to embrace it.   3093

EMERGENCY

emergencies may arise when a resort to arms can alone save it from dishonor   3747

It must ... in existence when the emergency arises   3769

EMINENCE

If men of eminence are exposed to censure on one hand   2004

our real eminence as a nation lies in the victories of peace   3754

EMINENT

Censure is the tax a man pays to the public for being eminent.   2522

EMOTIONAL

90 percent of any decision is emotional   1742

EMPEROR

Emperors ... little people—at the bottom we are all alike   757

EMPHASIS

criticism, even when, for the sake of emphasis, it parts ... with reality   2133

EMPIRE

Great Britain has lost an Empire and has not yet found a role.   1676

Law's empire is defined by attitude   1960

EMPLOY

authority is very seldom resisted when it is well employed   1488

EMPLOYMENT

Faced with the alternative of saying good-bye to ... his own employment   2585

I will undoubtedly have to seek what is happily known as gainful employment   2606

EMPTY

He whose belly is full believes not him whose is empty.   38

retiring with hands as clean as they are empty   780

ENCOUNTER

most exciting thing you encounter in government is competence   1572

ENCOURAGE

kill an admiral ... in order to encourage the others   3690

ENCROACHMENT

the best security against ... encroachments on the public liberty   673

by gradual and silent encroachments of those in power   1236

The greatest dangers to liberty lurk in insidious encroachment   1361

excites the public odium ... to conceal its own abuses and encroachments   2854

END

Power is an end in itself   160

This is the beginning of the end.   854

not the end. ... it is, perhaps the end of the beginning   973

first sign of corruption ... is that the end justifies the means   1005

Freedom of the press is not an end in itself   1184

Liberty is not a means to a higher political end.   1310

The free way of life proposes ends   1448

no other rule possible than ... the end justifies the means   2757

Justice is the end of government. It is the end of society.   3422

final end of government is not to exert restraint   3445

Government should not be made an end in itself;   3468

ENDANGER

bites with keener fangs than freedom never endangered   1199

ENDEAVOR

in foreign policy we are all engaged in a common national endeavor   1705

ENDLESS

Foreign relations are ... endless.   1693

ENEMY

comes to regard the public as its enemy   7

English laborer does not find his worst enemy in the nobility   48

what their enemies have done in the name of defending us   166

The enemies of democracy take advantage of this   417

as well as he that goes over to the enemy   776

remain as trophies unto the enemies of truth   830

They love him most for the enemies he has made.   912

A man cannot be too careful in the choice of his enemies.   913

Life'd not be worth livin' if we didn't keep our inimies.   921

Instead of loving your enemy, treat your friend a little better.   936

We have met the enemy and he is us.   1059

has not done all he could deserves to be counted as an enemy to it   1247

make his own liberty secure, must guard even his enemy from oppression   1248

After you get your freedom, your enemy will respect you.   1453

we have no perpetual enemies   1619

an enemy who was universal, an enemy whose acts ... trouble the entire world   1696

I am going to fight Your Majesty's enemies ... I leave you in the midst of mine   2011

being a good patriot often means being the enemy of the rest of mankind   2391

never attempt to buy the favor of your enemies   2493

My worst enemies couldn't say that.   2652

To rule with the help of one's enemies   2704

support whatever the enemy opposes and oppose whatever the enemy supports   2755

the worst enemies of civil freedom   3218

The main enemy is at home.   3773

No sane enemy ... would destroy the War Office.   3784

liquidating enemies is one of the most alarming developments of modern war   3851

I do not approve the extermination of the enemy;   3851

One needs the enemy.   3851

They were all enemy. They were all to be destroyed.   3946

ENERGY

Energy in a nation is like sap in a tree;   87

there is compensation for them in the spirit and energy it awakens   338

Our decision about energy will test the character of the American people   1071

Energy in government is essential to that security   1505

Governments destitute of energy, will ever produce anarchy.   1506

one party devotes its chief energies ... to prove that the other ... is unfit   2500

Power when wielded by abnormal energy is the most serious of facts.   2863

ENFEEBLE

The spirit of party serves always to ... enfeeble the public administration.   2459

ENFORCE

A wise government knows how to enforce with temper   1491

the right both of making and enforcing the laws, is vested in one ... man   3505

ENFRANCHISEMENT

"Liberty, freedom, and enfranchisement."   270

the natural outcome of political enfranchisement   1320

we expected a great deal from our enfranchisement   3337

ENGINEER

Hoover was the greatest engineer in the world   954

ENGLAND

England is the mother of parliaments.   901

the watchful eye and the strong arm of England will protect him   1621

England has been offered a choice between war and shame.   3819

ENGLISHMAN

nothing so bad or so good that you will not find Englishmen doing it;   789

ENIGMA

a riddle wrapped in a mystery inside an enigma   959

ENJOY

Next to enjoying ourselves ... preventing others from enjoying themselves   2868

ENJOYMENT

to maintain all in the secure and tranquil enjoyment of the rights   1512

ENLARGE

A man cannot gradually enlarge his mind as he does his house.   2046

ENLIGHTEN

Enlighten the people generally   669

if we think them not enlightened enough to exercise their control   672

ENOUGH

When do any of us ever do enough?   1073

There are not enough jails, not enough policemen   1940

ENSLAVE

Man alone can enslave man.   613

easy to govern, but impossible to enslave   676

he enslaves you on imperial principles   789

such an individual can never be enslaved   1405

when one man is enslaved, all are not free   1447

having enslaved us, it is natural ... to prove us unfit for freedom   2900

ENSLAVEMENT

whereas enslavement is a certainty of the worse   1186

ENSNARE

if anything small falls into them they ensnare it   1828

ENTANGLE

entangling alliances with none   1612

ENTERTAINER

I think he is an entertainer.   1096

ENTHUSIASM

Trust nothing to the enthusiasm of the people.   1521

considering that enthusiasm moves the world   2108

ENVIRONMENT

imposes his will and his ideas on his environment   2614

ENVY

The instinctive appeal of every successful political movement is to envy   2738

the envy which makes revolutionaries   3221

EPIGRAM

France was long a despotism tempered by epigrams.   558

EPITAPH

the saddest epitaph which can be carved in memory of a vanished liberty   1373

the greatest epitaph in the country is here in Arizona   2144

EQUAL

it is when people who are equal have not got equal shares   35

had the earth been divided into equal portions among all its inhabitants   39 with all our boasted "free and equal" superiority 79

For equal division of unequal earnings 114

However energetically society in general may strive to make all citizens equal 323

principle of our Government is that of equal laws 345

everybody is everybody's equal 362

erected on the premise that all men are created equal 435

we now practically read it, all men are created equal except Negroes 566

we began by declaring that all men are created equal 566

every American man and woman stands as the equal of every other American 712

because men are equally free, they claim to be absolutely equal 737

the notion that those who are equal in any respect are equal in all respects 737

every individual ... has an equal right to the protection of government 742

Equal laws protecting equal rights 743

that all men and women are created equal 747

The founder of the Democratic party declared that all men were created equal. 749

they did not intend to declare all men equal in all respects 750

all men equal—equal with "certain inalienable rights" 750

we shall once more stand up declaring that all men are created equal 751

Join the union, girls, and together say Equal Pay for Equal Work. 752

some respects in which men are obviously not equal 758

All animals are equal/But some animals are more equal 761

there is no greater inequality than the equal treatment of unequals 762

the principle of equal pay for equal work without discrimination 764

men shall be free today—but shall be equal a little later 767

A government ... dedicated to the purpose that all men are born free and equal 767

The guarantee of equal protection cannot mean one thing 769

If both are not accorded the same protection, then it is not equal. 769

True liberty ... defends the equal rights of all men 1275

an America which practices what it preaches about equal rights 1683

This home iv opporchunity where ivry man is th' equal iv ivry other man 1796

the poor are our equals in every sense except that of being equal to us 2275

The minority possess their equal rights, which equal laws must protect 2283

debar them in any way from equal privileges and equal rights 2310

where all are declared equal an ostracised class of half of the people 2903

many "created equal" have been treated within our lifetimes as inferior 2946

In respect of civil rights, all citizens are equal before the law. 3323

the doctrine of "separate but equal" has no place 3347

a strong America requires the assurance of full and equal rights 3355

It was founded on the principle that all men are created equal 3358

talked long enough in this country about equal rights 3359

that all men are created equal 3363

a universal society founded on equal justice for all 3563

Only a peace between equals can last. 3779

EQUALITY

Equality of talents, of education, or of wealth can not be produced 43

dispensing a sort of equality to equals and unequals alike 263

If liberty and equality ... are chiefly to be found in democracy 264

what people have always sought is equality before the law 738

which would be the case in a general state of equality 740

The foundation ... is the natural equality of man. 741

Democracy and socialism have nothing in common but one word: equality. 746

democracy seeks equality in liberty, socialism seeks equality in restraint 746

We wish, in a word, equality - equality in fact 753

Choose equality. 754

Equality—the informing soul of Freedom! 755

at least an approximate equality in the conditions 758

an equality of self-respect and of mutual respect, an equality of rights 758

Liberty without equality is a name of noble sound and squalid result. 759

We clamor for equality 763

very hard in military or personal life to assure complete equality 765

To live anywhere in the world today and be against equality because of race 768

then he labors in vain ... in the vineyards of equality 2936

As man seeks justice in equality, so society seeks order in anarchy. 3443

There never can be equality of awards or possessions   3527

Socialism means equality of income or nothing.   3562

a system of taxation that would operate with perfect equality   3593

EQUALIZER

Education ... is the great equalizer of the conditions of men   679

EQUALLY

by distributing equally the benefits and burdens of the Union   865

To know how to be free is not given equally to all men and all nations.   1365

EQUILIBRIUM

real guarantee of freedom is an equilibrium of social forces   1419

Order is ... an equilibrium which is set up from within.   1555

Peace is an unstable equilibrium   3931

EQUITY

an act against natural equity is void   228

EQUIVOCATE

I am in earnest—I will not equivocate —I will not excuse   1256

ERA

(This is) an era of violent peace.   3969

ERR

The most may err as grossly as the few.   274

Freedom is not worth having if it does not connote freedom to err.   1429

ERROR

the function of the citizen to keep the Government from falling into error   26

not the function of our Government to keep the citizen from ... error   26

with an earnest supplication that whatever errors it may be my lot to commit   316

as you multiply judgements, you reduce the incidence of errors   488

This Administration intends to be candid about its errors;   806

"An error doesn't become a mistake until you refuse to correct it."   806

Many ... have too rashly charged the troops of error   830

Delay is preferable to error.   848

I shall try to correct errors when shown to be errors   893

Error moves with quick feet   909

a righteous cause, is stronger than all the hosts of error   917

I wish we might have less condemnation of error   943

Reason and free inquiry are the only effectual agents against error.   1108

error alone which needs the support of government   1499

no greater error than to expect ... real favors from nation to nation   1610

Most of the errors of public life ... come, not because men are morally bad   2573

The commonest error in politics is sticking to the carcass of dead policies.   2714

Politics ... hold up torches of martyrdom to the reformers of error.   3088

ESCAPE

but large things break through and escape   1828

ESSENCE

Power is an end in itself and the essence of contemporary Communism.   160

The essence of a republican government is not command.   455

the essence of politics; all the rest is speculation   2237

The essence of Government is power;   2851

ESSENTIAL

Diplomats are just as essential to starting a war as Soldiers   3859

ESTABLISHMENT

nothing more agreeable ... than to make peace with the Establishment   2150

today's Establishment is the new George III   3282

ESTATE

there sat a Fourth Estate, more important by far   1169

Burke said there were Three Estates in Parliament;   1169

ETERNAL

Eternal truths will be neither true nor eternal   968

The price of eternal vigilance is indifference.   1040

The condition upon which God hath given liberty to men is eternal vigilance.   1241

Eternal vigilance is the price of liberty.   1272

man's eternal desire to be free and independent   1425

We have no eternal allies   1619

Our interests are eternal and perpetual   1619

ETERNITY

Its foundation lays hold upon eternity.   384

everything changes, there is no eternity here   1545

Keyword Index

ETHICAL

confidence is endangered when ethical standards falter   807

ethical bankruptcy of those who preach a right to life   1952

retreat is ... shameful if even suggested for ethical reasons   2792

ETHICS

"Put yourself in his place" strikes the keynote of ethics.   203

In civilized life, law floats in a sea of ethics.   1933

EUROPE

The lamps are going out all over Europe   930

EVENT

exercised so powerful and enduring an influence over ... the events of history   137

much better policy to prophesy after the event   975

I claim not to have controlled events ... events have controlled me   2072

EVERY

Legislation is not changed every day.   2226

if any thing is to be hoped, every thing ought to be tried   3703

EVERYBODY

Why Democracy means/ Everybody but me   431

EVERYONE

a condition of war of everyone against everyone   3679

EVERYTHING

What is the Third Estate? Everything.   300

Winning isn't everything.   1082

He knows nothing and he thinks he knows everything.   2565

it's everything he wants, and nothing you want   2697

Public opinion in this country is everything.   3049

In revolutions those who want everything always get the better   3201

EVIDENCE

they cannot alter the state of facts and evidence   839

Don't think you are going to conceal faults by concealing evidence   1135

any statement he does make may be used as evidence   1941

any reason for suspending the power of courts to get evidence   3019

EVIL

The most grinding poverty is a trifling evil compared with ... inequality   72

Conservative, n. A statesman who is enamored of existing evils   207

The evils of popular government appear greater than they are;   338

One of the evils of democracy is, you have to put up with the man you elect   448

evil that a single man should crush the herd   606

vanish like the evil spirits at the dawn of day   669

prefer to be defeated than to defeat injustice by evil means   772

No man is justified in doing evil on the ground of expediency.   791

just as evil as those who steal from the public purse   805

Every political good carried to the extreme must be productive of evil.   849

There is no evil in the atom; only in men's souls.   993

In battling evil, excess is good;   1023

and if we are sure, stifling it would be an evil still   1116

it is necessary to submit to the inevitable evils that it creates   1167

but every good in this life has its alloy of evil   1208

must in the course of human events produce one or other of two evils   1242

There is only one cure for the evils which newly acquired freedom produces   1255

government, even in its best state is but a necessary evil;   1497

Since government, even in its best state is an evil   1511

no necessary evils in government ... evils exist only in its abuses   1527

if it blurs decency and kindness ... it is an evil government   1565

All punishment in itself is evil.   1772

less evil that some criminals should escape   1803

Obscures the show of evil   1840

they generally cure an evil by a lesser or a passing evil   1890

a thousand hacking at the branches of evil   2060

secondly, that it be not the probable source of greater evils   2222

pervading evil of democracy is the tyranny of the majority   2298

Party divisions, whether on the whole operating for good or evil   2450

We cannot cure the evils of politics with politics.   2803

Carter, Ford and Nixon—See No Evil, Hear No Evil and Evil   3030

that which is most likely to prevent the greatest sum of evil   3424

We are now suffering the evils of a long peace.   3663

Among other evils which being unarmed brings you   3668

War is an unmitigated evil.   3855

EVILNESS

solely on the evilness of a dictatorship   631

EVOLVE
continuing evolving process to higher and higher
levels 3380

EX-PRESIDENT
"What shall be done with our ex-
Presidents?" 2962
Oh, that lovely title, ex-president. 2991
en route to the blessed condition of being an ex-
President 3002
the reunion ... of three ex-presidents 3030

EXACT
Politics is not an exact science. 2700

EXAMINATION
A decent and manly examination of the acts of
Government 1532

EXAMPLE
George the Third ... may profit by their
example 3637

EXASPERATION
Exhaustion and exasperation are ... the
handmaidens of legislative decision 2262

EXCELLENCE
in matters in which we ourselves cannot hope to
obtain excellence 763

EXCEPTION
No rule is so general, which admits not some
exception. 1843

EXCESS
Excess of wealth is cause of covetousness. 37
Excess of severity is not the path to order. 587
the supply has always been in excess of the
demand 900
In battling evil, excess is good; 1023
Every reform ... will by weak minds be carried to
an excess 3089

EXCESSIVE
Wherever there is excessive wealth, there is also ...
excessive poverty 59

EXCITEMENT
no excitement ... to match the excitement of an
American presidential campaign 2438
Politics is motion and excitement. 2813
all the excitement the most restless spirits can
desire 3566
not merely cruelty that leads men to love war, it is
excitement 3753

EXCLUSION
absorb ten million Negro Americans ... at less cost
than their ... exclusion 2908

EXCOMMUNICATION
Anyone today who speaks of class ... runs the risk
of excommunication 113

EXCUSE
Any excuse will serve a tyrant. 517
Ignorance of the law is no excuse in any
country. 1869
Difficulty is the excuse history never
accepts. 2162

EXECUTE
too severe, seldom executed 1859

EXECUTION
men will not adopt and carry into execution
measures ... for their own good 1500
execution of the laws is more important than the
making 1871
no method to secure the repeal of bad ... laws as
their stringent execution 1889

EXECUTIONER
History is the judge;—its executioner, the
proletarian. 125

EXECUTIVE
The executive of the modern state is but a
committee 56
to rescue Liberty from the grasp of executive
power 1258
the action an executive must take when he has
information so incomplete 2159
The great executives have given inspiration and
push 2254
become the pliant instrument of the Executive
will 2544
when the legislative power is nominated by the
executive 3509
his assigned executive powers is not subject to ...
another branch 3512
no technique for ... free government except that
the executive be under the law 3513
but in war, to the executive solely 3710

EXEMPTION
that which arises from a fancied exemption from
all prejudice 2895

EXERCISE
a just and honourable war is the true
exercise 3676
No body can be healthful without exercise, neither
natural body or politic; 3676

EXERTION
not an exertion that has a foreseeable end 1708
what the people have attained with such
exertions 3711

EXHAUSTED
once all other alternatives have been
exhausted 1692
in the rain late at night when he's
exhausted 2432

EXHAUSTION

Exhaustion ... frequently the handmaidens of legislative decision   2262

EXILE

one is head of state and the other is in exile   1046

EXIST

A government is not legitimate merely because it exists.   1575

republics ... which have never been ... known to exist   2673

They don't really exist.   3560

EXISTENCE

government not too strong ... can be strong enough to maintain its existence   1542

EXPEDIENCY

No man is justified in doing evil on the ground of expediency.   791

lawyer's truth is not Truth, but ... a consistent expediency   1886

EXPEDIENT

Decision by majorities is ... an expedient   334

The true danger is when liberty is nibbled away, for expedients   1230

Government is at best but an expedient;   1535

only actual states of peace which ... are mere expedients   3805

EXPEL

Communist countries never expel correspondents for telling lies.   178

EXPENSE

Expense, and great expense, may be an essential part of true economy.   3584

EXPENSIVE

Politics has got so expensive that it takes lots of money to ... get beat   2748

EXPERIENCE

primarily a mode of associated living, of conjoint communicated experience   382

Experience is the name everyone gives to their mistakes.   915

The experience may have been costly, but it was also priceless.   1061

Experience has taught us that men will not adopt and carry into execution   1500

The law is the last result of human wisdom acting upon human experience   1867

the worst I wish the law is that his eye may be opened by experience   1881

Law is experience developed by reason and applied ... to further experience.   1937

A statesman who too far outruns the experience of his people will fail   2194

a statesman who limits his policies to the experience of his people   2194

The statesman's duty is to bridge the gap between his nation's experience   2210

too many politicians who believe, with a conviction based on experience   2597

experience enough of the conduct of governments   2682

Experience suggests that the first rule of politics is never to say never.   2794

Experience has two things to teach: 3099

EXPERIMENT

Democracy is only an experiment in government   371

making a great experiment and taking a leap in the dark   902

principles at the root of all government--stability and experiment   2464

EXPLAIN

Never complain and never explain.   2761

EXPLANATION

A little inaccuracy sometimes saves tons of explanation.   945

EXPLOIT

To exploit and to govern mean the same thing.   2708

EXPLOITATION

The law is simply ... made for the exploitation   1915

EXPOSE

probing journalism that first exposed most of the serious scandals   1192

EXPOSURE

Nothing checks all the bad practices of politics as public exposure.   795

EXPRESS

not do something to people either for the views they have or ... express   1144

EXPRESSION

but it must be after a full, fair, and candid expression   364

EXPROPRIATE

who expropriates the property of his subjects   532

EXTERIOR

Beneath that cold, harsh, impersonal exterior   1944

EXTERMINATION

I do not approve the extermination of the enemy;   3851

EXTERNAL
When internal and external forces which are
hostile to Socialism   174
Freedom is an internal achievement rather than an
external judgment.   1460

EXTINCTION
It will be a slow extinction from apathy   458

EXTINGUISH
If our house be on fire ... we must try to
extinguish it   851

EXTOLL
Hardly a day passes without its being
extolled   1131

EXTORTION
such exaction becomes ruthless extortion   3603

EXTRAVAGANCE
supplying the invented wants of courtly
extravagance   3426

EXTREME
Every political good carried to the extreme must
be productive of evil.   849
Any plan ... must fail when the circumstances are
set in extremes   858
Extreme justice is often unjust.   1760
Extreme law is often extreme injustice.   1823

EXTREMISM
extremism in the defense of liberty is no
vice   1042
Political extremism involves two prime
ingredients: 2795
Extremism in the pursuit of the Presidency is an
unpardonable vice   3000
I loathe all manifestations of extremism   3390

EXTREMIST
what is dangerous about extremists is not that
they are extreme   1041
You show me a black man who isn't an
extremist   1048

EYE
If a man destroy the eye of another man, they
shall destroy his eye.   1747
As President, I have no eyes but constitutional
eyes;   2959

EYEBALL
We were eyeball-to-eyeball and the other fellow
just blinked.   1033

EYELASH
You win or lose, live or die—and the difference is
just an eyelash.   3918

FACADE
a sort of facade behind which candidates sneak
into power   2430

FACE
Never corner an opponent, and always assist him
to save his face.   2167
I'm surprised that they even dare to show their
face.   2520
a war that knows no borders or seldom has a
face   3972

FACT
a movement ... further removed from the facts
than Marxism   163
behind them in knowledge of the facts because the
facts have not been given   472
Facts are stubborn things;   839
no longer an allegation ... an established
fact   1022
It could probably be shown by facts and
figures   2240
very few facts, at least ascertainable facts, in
politics   2693
Practical politics consists in ignoring facts.   2727
injustice no longer; it is an accomplished fact of
life   2914

FACTION
where the Government is too feeble to withstand
the enterprises of faction   1512
impossible that the whisper of a faction shall
prevail against the ... nation   2286
When a faction in a state attempts to nullify a
constitutional law   2287
party degenerates into faction, and faction is
reduced to self   2449
The most common and durable source of
faction   2453
By a faction, I understand a number of
citizens   2454
Liberty is to faction what air is to fire   2455
Moderation is fatal to factions   3206

FACULTY
From each according to his faculties, to each
according to his needs;   753
only those withdrawn into a brooding imagination
have the faculty for it   2061
Yours for the unshackled exercise of every
faculty   3313

FADE AWAY
old soldiers never die; they just fade away   989

FAIL
We shall not fail or falter;   969
no real freedom without the freedom to fail   1449
With public sentiment, nothing can fail;   2063

FAILURE
You show me a good and gracious loser, and I'll
show you a failure!   2119
the key to failure is trying to please
everybody   2198

FAIR

every individual, has a right to expect from his
  government a Fair Deal   977

Diplomats are useful only in fair weather.   1677

He never wants anything but what's right and
  fair;   2697

Politics can be relatively fair in the breathing
  spaces of history;   2757

fair to judge peoples by the rights they will
  sacrifice most for   3334

"A fair day's wages for a fair day's work"   3447

FAIRNESS

Fairness is what justice really is.   1806

FAITH

My faith in the constitution is whole.   253

Both absolute power and absolute faith are
  instruments of dehumanization.   622

absolute faith corrupts as absolutely as absolute
  power   622

the triumphant result of faith in human kind   707

The core of our defense is the faith we have in the
  institutions we defend.   963

My faith in the proposition that each man should
  do ... as he pleases   1276

Faith is necessary to victory.   2045

It is at night that faith in light is
  admirable.   2091

Patriotism is in political life what faith is in
  religion.   2403

does not matter how small you are if you have
  faith   3269

FALLACY

effect in restraining a powerful military nation ...
  has been a ... fallacy   3778

FALSE

apt to be deluded into false security by political
  catch-words   2710

FALSE-FACE

almost always only a false-face for the urge to rule
  it   2877

FALSEHOOD

he whose mind is filled with falsehoods and
  errors   1164

by the falsehoods which interest dictates, and
  credulity encourages   3689

Everyone ... learns to live in a new element:
  falsehood   3810

FAME

Men in great places are ... servants of fame   1990

Fame usually comes to those who are thinking
  about something else.   2064

Blessed is he whose fame does not outshine his
  truth.   2106

when the love of fame shall cease to be the ...
  passion of our public men   2554

The love of fame is consistent with the steadiest
  attachment to principle   2846

FAMILY

If it is too much to have to take care of a
  family   2336

FAMOUS

the orders you disobey that make you
  famous   2201

FANATIC

tired of the effort of willing they become fanatics
  about conversatism   210

fanatic is one who can't change his mind   998

FANATICISM

From fanaticism to barbarism is only one
  step.   836

FANCY

or otherwise strike the fancy of the
  electorate   2564

FANG

Freedom suppressed and again regained bites with
  keener fangs   1199

FAR

those who are far off are attracted   1476

FARM

Burn down your cities and leave our farms   639

destroy our farms and the grass will grow in the
  streets   639

FARMER

farmer is the only man in our economy who buys
  everything at retail   656

difference between a pigeon and the American
  farmer   1600

FARMING

Farming looks mighty easy when your plow is a
  pencil   9

FASCINATING

the terrible fascinating power of the hope of
  freedom   1386

FASCINATION

The curious fascination in this job   2654

FASCISM

Fascism is Capitalism plus Murder.   591

Under the species of Syndicalism and
  Fascism   595

Fascism is not defined by the number of its
  victims   609

Fascism was a counter-revolution against a
  revolution that never took place.   3255

Social Democracy is the moderate wing of
  fascism   3558

The great corruption of Socialism ... calls itself
Fascism in Italy   3565

We are the first victims of America fascism.   3642

FASCIST

It is much more likely to present fascist
features.   146

FASHION

will not cut my conscience to fit this year's
fashions   804

the fashion to style the present moment an
extraordinary crisis   871

(Law is) vulnerable to the winds of ... moral
fashion   1958

FAT

Lean liberty is better than fat slavery.   1207

Be sure not to get too fat, because you'll have to
sit there in the back seat.   2995

Better a lean peace than a fat victory.   3685

FATAL

fatal to the existence of American liberty   1242

fatal to enter any war without the will to win
it   3874

FATE

Upon the education of the people ... the fate of
this country depends.   681

The fate of America cannot depend on any one
man.   2124

What a man thinks of himself, that is which
determines ... his fate   3047

FATHER

Our fathers waged a bloody conflict with
England   557

As always, victory finds a hundred fathers   974

My father always told me that all business men
were sons of bitches   1595

Not war but peace is the father of all
things.   3949

FATHERLAND

When it is a question of saving the
fatherland   1834

Everything belongs to the fatherland when the
fatherland is in danger.   2395

Living ... For one's fatherland, is sweet.   3723

FATIGUE

to reap the blessing of freedom must ... undergo
the fatigue of supporting it   1226

FAULT

Most faults are not in our Constitution, but in
ourselves.   247

FAVOR

no greater error than to expect ... real favors from
nation to nation   1610

The favor of princes does not exclude merit   2675

FBI

The man who walks alone is soon trailed by the
F.B.I.   3375

FEAR

They wanted us to be afraid of the tanks ... and
instead we don't fear them   183

to face all problems frankly and meet all dangers
free from panic or fear   471

Let them hate me, so they but fear me.   522

People tolerate those they fear further than those
they love.   584

When men are ruled by fear   619

The only thing we have to fear is fear itself   953

to think sanely under the influence of a great
fear   986

Fear ... cannot alone justify suppression of free
speech   1127

No government can be maintained without the
principle of fear   1523

Let us never negotiate out of fear, but let us never
fear to negotiate.   1672

since love and fear can hardly exist together, it is
far safer to be feared   1974

whether it is better to be loved rather than
feared   1974

Charismatic leadership is hungered for, but ... we
fear it   2196

Conservatism is distrust of the people tempered by
fear.   2267

Fear finds its great moral revelation in
patriotism.   2423

when power is wedded to chronic fear that it
becomes formidable   2874

"Freedom from fear" could be said to sum up ...
human rights   3348

The ultimate aim of government is not to rule, or
restrain, by fear   3410

Better beans and bacon in peace than cakes and
ale in fear.   3645

the Kingdom that is not always prepared has
much to fear   3682

It drives away fear and brings bravery to the
surface.   3855

FEARFUL

we are not descended from fearful men, not from
men who feared to write   2153

FEATHER BED

not to expect to be translated from despotism to
liberty in a feather bed   1239

FEDERAL

We do many things at the federal level that would
be considered dishonest   822

The first ladyship is the only federal office ... can
neither be fired   3031

If we get the federal government out of the
classroom   3163

The Federal Government is the people   3620

everything is under federal control nowadays except the federal budget   3624

FEELING

Men have feelings but the law does not.   1875

FEET

They are men with feet of clay   172

It expects its idols to have feet of clay   2170

Better to die on one's feet than to live on one's knees.   3340

FELON

in the same felon category as the man who strikes his brother in anger   3767

FEMALE

being female put many more obstacles in my path than being black   4002

FEROCITY

All laws are an attempt to domesticate the natural ferocity of the species.   1949

FERTILIZE

only the blood of the oppressors can fertilize the soil   3229

FERVOR

It is action that puts fervor to work.   2157

FESTIVAL

Revolution is the festival of the oppressed.   3283

FETTER

To allow it to be fettered is to be fettered ourselves.   1177

resolves that he will no longer be a slave, his fetters fall   1398

authorized whenever they can to rise and break their fetters   3196

True, the movement for women's rights has broken many old fetters   3991

FEW

an oligarchy when control lies with the rich and better-born, these being few   267

The most may err as grossly as the few.   274

election by the incompetent many for appointment by the corrupt few   374

or we can have great wealth concentrated in the hands of a few   425

that inclination from the few persons who may happen to approach them   2024

I hear many condemn these men because they were so few.   2065

Party-spirit ... is but the madness of many for the gain of a few.   2446

Every social war is a battle between the very few on both sides   3265

not only the legitimate interests of the few are protected   3477

a system by which the many are exploited by the few   3846

partial success had crowned the faith ... of the few   3986

FIBRE

If the moral and physical fibre of its manhood ... is not a state concern   3474

FICKLE

democracies are at least contemporarily fickle and heartless   390

FIDELITY

The fidelity of the United States to security treaties   1715

good government implies ... fidelity to the object of government   3421

FIFTEEN

A revolution only lasts fifteen years   3249

FIFTEENTH AMENDMENT

The (Fifteenth) Amendment nullifies sophisticated ... discrimination   2913

FIFTH AMENDMENT

The 5th Amendment is an old friend and a good friend   1417

FIFTY-FIFTY

There can be no fifty-fifty Americanism in this country.   2376

FIGHT

To fight against the government with any means is a basic right   356

There is nothing I love as much as a good fight.   927

that Britain would fight on alone whatever they did   970

often easier to fight for principles than to live up to them   991

not ... the size of the dog in the fight ... the size of the fight in the dog   1016

Don't fight the problem, decide it.   1100

The fight must go on.   1281

A man who has nothing which he is willing to fight for   1298

worthy thing to fight for one's freedom ... finer to fight for another man's   1325

Freedom is not worth fighting for if it means no more than license   1375

such a thing as man being too proud to fight   1639

not possible to fight beyond your strength, even if you strive   1967

I am going to fight Your Majesty's enemies   2011

And I will not stop fighting.   2130

I am fighting, as I have always fought, for the rights of the little man   2130

not interested in fighting persons ... but in fighting things. 2488
never wear your best trousers when you go out to fight for freedom 3103
A right is worth fighting for only when it can be put into operation. 3326
We are not fighting for integration, nor are we fighting for separation. 3366
We are fighting for ... human rights. 3366
There is a time to fight, and that time has now come. 3694
I propose to fight it out on this line, if it takes all summer. 3735
You cannot fight hard unless you think you are fighting to win. 3772
We shall fight in France, we shall fight on the seas 3829
we shall fight on the beaches, we shall fight on the landing grounds 3829
going to have peace even if we have to fight for it 3843
A war regarded as inevitable ... has a very good chance of being fought 3953
If they've been put there to fight, there are far too few. 3962

FILIBUSTER
A little group of willful men representing no opinion 2243

FINAL
we are infallible only because we are final 1735
but most often it manages to deal it the final blow 2855

FINALITY
Finality is not the language of politics. 2698

FINEST
"This was their finest hour." 967

FIRE
follow the right side even to the fire, but excluding the fire if I can 828
If our house be on fire, without inquiring whether it was fired from within 851
free speech would not protect a man in falsely shouting fire in a theatre 1122
light up in distant lands the fire of freedom 1260
a glorious fire has been lighted upon the altar of liberty 1260
if they are ready to fight a fire, should be able to count on us 1702

FIRST
He who would be free must strike the first blow. 1278

FIRST AMENDMENT
what I consider to be the minimum guarantee of the First Amendment 1145
If the 1st Amendment means anything 1148

That's the new gloss on the 1st Amendment. 1153
The First Amendment gives newspapermen a status and a mandate 1195
parents have a 1st Amendment right to send their children to ... institutions 3385

FIRST LADY
The first lady is ... an unpaid public servant 3005
Being first lady is the hardest unpaid job in the world. 3014
The first ladyship is the only federal office 3031

FIRST MINISTER
not become the King's First Minister in order to preside over the liquidation 2136

FISCAL
liberal governments have been wrecked on rocks of loose fiscal policy 3612

FIST
You cannot shake hands with a clenched fist. 1087

FIT
the British public in one of its periodical fits of morality 867
a fit country for heroes to live in 935

FIX
but they are more fixed than all the written laws 1826
As soon as the people fix one Shame of the World 3118

FIXITY
therefore laws have no fixity 1899

FLAG
two American flags ... one for the rich and one for the poor 99
Not for the flag/ Of any land because myself was born there 1418
The things that the flag stands for were created by the experiences 2412
wrap yourself up in the American flag and talk about the Constitution 2557
We shall not flag or fail. We shall go on to the end. 3829

FLAIR
a mixture of having a flair for the thing that you are doing 2217

FLAME
Though the flame of liberty may sometimes cease to shine 1227
I would jump off the cliff with the flag flying 2820

FLATTER
men usually flatter themselves on their great deeds 1999

FLATTERY

they are as much liable to flattery on the other 2004

called a mediocre man; but this is unwarranted flattery 2561

FLOOD

The flood of money that gushes into politics 820

When a just cause reaches its flood tide 3327

FLOW

thinks he is guiding the log, but it's ... just going with the flow 2648

FLOWER

Democracy is not a fragile flower; 493

FLY

Laws are like cobwebs, which may catch small flies 1849

Politics, which ... are the fly in the amber 2739

FOE

The foes from whom we pray to be delivered are our own passions 924

FOLLOW

The people may be made to follow a path of action 664

cannot ... ask other people to follow you, unless you know how to follow 2169

FOLLOWER

The king presupposes subjects; the leader, followers. 2128

FOLLY

Tyrants never perish from tyranny, but always from folly. 564

A law can be both economic folly and constitutional. 1965

The history of the world's great leaders is often the story of human folly. 2010

It is a folly second to none,/ To try to improve the world. 3083

War contains so much folly, as well as wickedness 3703

FONCTIONNAIRE

less than that which the smallest fonctionnaire possesses 5

FOND

well that war is so terrible—we should grow too fond of it 3731

FOOD

The Master said, "Give them enough food 1477

FOOL

Vote, n. The instrument ... of a freeman's power to make a fool of himself 709

but that is nothing compared with the fools 840

You can fool some of the people all of the time 886

The wisest thing to do with a fool is to encourage him to hire a hall 1119

For forms of government let fools contest; 1485

A patriot is a fool in ev'ry age. 2390

the court fool ... whom the king can least afford to lose 2574

that you can fool all the people all of the time 2597

It makes a fool of a man and a worse fool of a fool. 2720

Anti-semitism is the socialism of fools. 2906

I am not nonviolent, but I'm not a fool either 3131

FOOLISH

He never said a foolish thing,/ Nor ever did a wise one. 2332

FORCE

The use of force alone is temporary. 537

Force is the vital principle ... of despotism 548

The one means that wins the easiest victory over reason: terror and force. 588

Force is not a remedy. 907

most powerful single force ... is neither Communism nor capitalism 1425

Governments only keep their word when they are forced to 1525

justice means force as well as virtue 1779

in ways that enable society to achieve its goals with a minimum of force 1947

If by the mere force of numbers a majority should deprive a minority 2294

politician's first duty is to appeal to the forces that unite 2627

Modern politics is ... a struggle not of men but of forces 2728

In the field of politics, force and consent are correlative terms 2744

Some people draw a comforting distinction between "force" and "violence". 2894

no group ... that can withstand the force of an aroused public opinion 3070

can be directed only by reason and conviction, not by force 3140

effect radical reforms in their ... institutions, by force 3235

must rest upon an implied willingness ... to use force 3238

no such force as the force of a man determined to rise 3325

international public opinion, unbacked by force 3778

FORE-SHOULDER

Politicians are like the bones of a horse's fore-shoulder 2552

FOREIGN

The language of the law must not be foreign 1916

As home his footsteps he hath turn'd,/ From wandering on a foreign strand! 2396

the true method of warfare for ... emancipating themselves from a foreign yoke 3204

A foreign war is a lot milder than a civil war. 3671

FOREIGN AFFAIRS

What we call foreign affairs is no longer foreign affairs. 1669

the devilish thing about foreign affairs: they are foreign 1684

Watching foreign affairs is sometimes like watching a magician; 1722

FOREIGN MINISTER

If any foreign minister begins to defend to the death a "peace conference" 3878

FOREIGN OFFICE

Time is the ... commodity which the Foreign Office is expected to provide 1651

a Foreign Office joke that I could never make a speech 1709

The politician who will refuse the Foreign Office is not yet born. 2651

FOREIGN POLICY

The foreign policy adopted by our government is to do justice to all 1614

The foreign policy of the noble Earl ... "meddle" and "muddle" 1624

The foreign policy of America can best be described by one word--peace. 1644

Our foreign policy has one primary object ... peace 1645

In the field of foreign policy I would dedicate this nation 1649

My (foreign) policy is to be able to ... go anywhere I damn well please 1657

Foreign policy must be clear, consistent and confident. 1658

a political society does not live to conduct foreign policy 1660

finding a balance between means and ends that is the heart of foreign policy 1661

A foreign policy is not difficult to state. 1665

purpose of foreign policy is not to provide an outlet for our own sentiments 1678

you can get killed by one made in foreign policy 1685

We are handicapped by (foreign) policies based on old myths 1687

No foreign policy ... has any chance of success ... born in the minds of a few 1703

Making foreign policy is a little bit like making pornographic movies. 1704

Our greatest foreign policy problem is our divisions at home. 1705

in foreign policy we are all engaged in a common national endeavor 1705

Human rights is the soul of our foreign policy 3389

My foreign policy? I wage war. 3786

FOREIGN RELATIONS

in the management of our foreign relations ... of speaking plainly 1616

our foreign relations ... a careful respect for the rights of other nations 1618

In foreign relations ... a policy has been formed 1654

Foreign relations are like human relations. 1693

There can be only one voice ... in the field of foreign relations 2985

FOREIGN SECRETARY

A Foreign Secretary ... always faced with this cruel dilemma. 1663

FOREIGNER

How much better to make it so ... foreigners want to come 1490

the nation that has absorbed ten million foreigners 2908

reject all value systems that seek to make him a foreigner 3384

FOREVER

the Supreme Court, through its decisions, goes on forever 1741

FORGIVE

Forgive us for pretending to care for the poor 111

The motto should not be: Forgive one another 928

he neither forgives you nor allows you to forgive yourself 2722

FORGIVENESS

I believe in the forgiveness of sin and the redemption of ignorance. 1037

God, at least, has a degree of forgiveness. 2649

FORM

For forms of government let fools contest; 1485

not interested too much in the form of government 1569

the delusion that a change in form is a change in substance 2740

FORMALITY

In statesmanship get formalities right, never mind about the moralities. 2084

FORMIDABLE

when power is wedded to chronic fear ... it becomes formidable 2874

FORTITUDE
no higher fortitude than stubbornness in the face of overwhelming odds   2174

FORTNIGHT
In politics ... no use looking beyond the next fortnight   2718

FORTUNATE
fortunate who are born at a time when a great struggle for human freedom   1347

FORTUNE
all the increased wealth ... goes but to build up great fortunes   67

the consolation of having added nothing to my private fortune   780

nothing so disastrous for a small fortune as a large tax   1530

you can still make a small fortune in agriculture   1599

nothing so subject to the inconstancy of fortune as war   3673

FORWARD
A conservative is a man who ... has never learned how to walk forward   216

but the new view must come, the world must roll forward   217

yet not go forward fast enough to wreck the country's cause   2070

FOUNDATION
foundation of a free society is the binding tie of cohesive sentiment   424

Political institutions are a superstructure resting on an economic foundation.   641

Good order is the foundation of all things.   845

chief foundations of all states ... are good laws and good arms   1836

Moral principle is the foundation of law.   1961

Its foundations are laid far back.   3214

The health of the people is really the foundation   3457

FOUNDER
the Founders wisely provided the means for that endurance   250

the newspapers nobly did precisely that which the Founders hoped   1190

FOUNDING FATHERS
commended for serving the purpose that the Founding Fathers saw   1191

(Congress is) functioning the way the Founding Fathers intended   2261

FOUNDLING
A politician ought to be born a foundling and remain a bachelor.   2643

FOUNTAIN
free people, the purest source and original fountain of all power   285

There are in nature certain fountains of justice   1759

FOUR
can very seriously injure the government in ... four years   342

more interested in four sandwiches than four freedoms   1420

FOURTH
the fourth will be fought with bows and arrows   3950

FOURTH AMENDMENT
The 4th Amendment and the personal rights it secures   3354

The 4th Amendment protects the individual's privacy   3392

FOURTH ESTATE
there sat a Fourth Estate, more important by far   1169

FOURTH OF JULY
Republicans believe every day is the Fourth of July   3182

FOX
the foxes have a sincere interest in prolonging the lives of the poultry   705

One must therefore be a fox to recognize traps   1977

FOXHOLE
there are no "white" or "colored" signs on the foxholes   2929

FRANCE
France was long a despotism tempered by epigrams.   558

France cannot be France without greatness.   1003

When I want to know what France thinks, I ask myself.   2182

All my life I have held on to a certain idea of France.   2383

FRANCHISE
I hope that no American ... will waste his franchise   3160

the duty of the women of this country to secure ... the elective franchise   3980

FRATERNITY
We did not win ... by appealing to reason but by developing ... fraternity   3285

FRAUD

as easily discovered at the first view as fraud is surely detected at last   1495

then a good many great men must have been frauds   2093

(politics) is a beautiful fraud   2798

FREE

who would protect the rights and privileges of free people   27

If a free society cannot help the many who are poor   104

Democracy is the form of government in which the free are rulers.   265

Any government is free to the people under it where the laws rule   275

Men being ... by Nature, all free, equal and independent   277

The only maxim of a free government ought to be to trust no man living   283

That all men are by nature equally free and independent   286

essence of a free government consists in an effectual control of rivalries   299

"For a nation to be free, it is only necessary that she will it."   307

His merciful providence for the maintenance of our free institutions   316

Democracy ... is a covenant among free men   416

foundation of a free society is the binding tie of cohesive sentiment   424

A free society is one where it is safe to be unpopular.   461

The history of free men is never really written by chance   466

Commerce ... also helped to make them free   632

Free trade, one of the greatest blessings which a government can confer   636

Social prosperity means man happy, the citizen free   637

If a nation expects to be ignorant and free   670

The free man cannot be long an ignorant man.   684

we must be free to follow wherever that search may lead us   693

We cannot have free government without elections;   704

to suggest that men shall be free today—but shall be equal a little later   767

dedicated to the purpose that all men are born free and equal   767

Free Discussion is the only necessary Constitution   1111

never so likely to settle a question rightly as when they discuss it freely   1112

Free speech, exercised both individually and through a free press   1121

protection of free speech would not protect a man in falsely shouting fire   1122

Free speech is about as good a cause as the world has ever known.   1124

"I'm in favor of free speech."   1125

Fear of serious injury cannot alone justify suppression of free speech   1127

the function of free speech to free men from the bondage of ... fears   1127

the principle of free thought—not free thought for those who agree with us   1128

Free speech does not live ... after free industry and free commerce die   1129

Everyone is in favour of free speech.   1131

Free speech is not to be regulated like diseased cattle and impure butter.   1137

The censor's sword pierces deeply into the heart of free expression.   1140

It is part of the right of free speech.   1141

The first principle of a free society is an untrammeled flow of words   1142

a threat of censorship that by its very existence chills free speech   1150

no nation so poor that it cannot afford free speech   1151

Free speech carries with it some freedom to listen.   1154

A free press stands as one of the great interpreters   1177

Freedom of the press is ... a means to the end of a free society   1184

A free press can of course be good or bad   1186

Paramount among the responsibilities of a free press   1189

Man is born free; and everywhere he is in chains.   1212

not because we have been free, but because we have a right to be free   1245

A people are free in proportion as they form their own opinions.   1249

No one can be perfectly free till all are free;   1271

Our own free institutions were not the offspring of our Revolution.   1274

He who would be free must strike the first blow.   1278

A person should be free to do as he likes   1291

Your huddled masses yearning to breathe free   1315

No man can be just who is not free.   1337

while there is a soul in prison, I am not free   1351

Only free peoples can hold their purpose and their honor steady   1352

When we lose the right to be different, we lose the privilege to be free.   1357

end of the State was to make men free to develop their faculties   1359

The truth is found when men are free to pursue it.   1369

the constitutional rights of free speech, free press and free assembly   1371

Human kindness has never weakened the stamina ... of a free people. 1377

None who have always been free can understand 1386

Men would rather be starving and free than fed in bonds. 1387

Diversity of opinion within the framework of loyalty to our free society 1400

true that an inherently free ... person may be destroyed 1405

Neither does he know where he is not free; 1407

The American feels so rich in his opportunities for free expression 1407

Man in Society is not free where there is no law; 1409

A hungry man is not a free man. 1411

But I will love that land where man is free 1418

He is free ... who knows how to keep in his own hands the power to decide 1424

man's eternal desire to be free and independent 1425

We have confused the free with the free and easy. 1431

The free way of life proposes ends 1448

maintain a free society only if we recognize that in a free society 1465

If you are tempted to brandish the word "free" 1466

The essence of a free life is being able to choose 1468

Only free men can negotiate; 1472

man is not free unless government is limited 1475

totalitarianism ... will threaten free nations and free institutions 1699

Permissive legislation is the characteristic of a free people. 2238

most certain test by which we judge whether a country is really free 2297

government is free in proportion to the rights it guarantees to the minority 2311

Men are not born free 2334

Martyred many times must be/ Who would keep his country free. 2416

Party divisions ... are things inseparable from free government. 2450

Parties must ever exist in a free country. 2452

All free governments are party government. 2483

all men are equally entitled to the free exercise of religion 3140

The day that this country ceases to be free for irreligion 3159

it will cease to be free for religion 3159

to claim our rights as women, not only to be free 3328

The freer that women become, the freer will men be. 3383

the most important social service ... is to keep them alive and free 3479

A free people ought not only to be armed, but disciplined; 3701

if we allow it a free hand to corrupt democratic societies 3971

FREEDOM

The Constitution is the sole source and guaranty of national freedom. 241

If political freedom is more advantageous for the development of wealth 309

that this nation, under God, shall have a new birth of freedom 344

We are inclined to confuse freedom and democracy 475

Necessity is the plea for every infringement of human freedom. 541

True individual freedom cannot exist without economic security 653

freedom of action without freed capacity of thought behind it is only chaos 685

Equality—the informing soul of Freedom! 755

When people talk of the freedom of writing, speaking or thinking 1110

Freedom of expression is the matrix ... of nearly every other form of freedom. 1130

The problem of freedom ... is ... maintaining a competition of ideas 1132

Laws alone cannot secure freedom of expression; 1133

freedom of speech means you shall not do something ... for the views they have 1144

freedom of the individual is not just the luxury of one intellectual 1152

if he permits his freedom of expression to be abolished 1152

The freedom of the press is one of the great bulwarks of liberty 1158

Sovereignty of the people and freedom of the press are each necessary 1168

Freedom of conscience ... among the very fundamentals of democracy 1178

I ... will die for the freedom of the press 1180

Freedom from something is not enough. It should also be freedom for something. 1182

Freedom of the press is not an end in itself but a means to the end 1184

Freedom is nothing else but a chance to be better 1186

Freedom of the press belongs to those who own one. 1194

Freedom ... regained bites with keener fangs than freedom never endangered 1199

Freedom can't be kept for nothing. 1200

Without Freedom of Thought ... no such Thing as Wisdom; 1205

no such Thing as publick Liberty, without Freedom of Speech 1205

The jaws of power are always open to devour ... freedom 1214

Freedom and not servitude is the cure of
anarchy; 1222

Those who expect to reap the blessing of
freedom 1226

how much it cost the present generation to
preserve your freedom 1231

Freedom of religion ... press ... person ... form the
bright constellation 1251

the nation which enjoys the most freedom must be
... the most powerful 1254

one cure for the evils ... freedom produces, and
that cure is freedom 1255

The history of the world is ... the progress of the
consciousness of freedom 1257

True freedom is to share/ All the chains our
brothers wear 1263

revolutions do not always establish freedom 1274

The only freedom which deserves the name, is that
of pursuing our own good 1283

In giving freedom to the slave, we assure freedom
to the free. 1299

For what avail the plow or sail,/ Or land or life, if
freedom fail? 1305

The spirit of truth and the spirit of freedom ... the
pillars of society 1311

oscillation ... between anarchy and despotism is to
be replaced by ... freedom 1313

what is freedom? ... the will to be responsible to
ourselves 1319

freedom of speech, freedom of conscience, and the
prudence never to practice 1324

worthy ... to fight for one's freedom; it is ... finer
to fight for another 1325

Freedom remains still the wisest cure for
freedom's temporary inconveniences. 1326

The distinction between freedom and liberty is not
accurately known; 1331

The only freedom consists in the people taking
care of the government. 1339

Most men, after a little freedom, have preferred
authority 1344

two good things in life—freedom of thought and
freedom of action 1348

While the state exists there is no freedom; when
there is freedom ... no state 1350

Radicalism is ... always applied to people who are
endeavoring to get freedom 1355

necessary to grow accustomed to freedom before
one may walk ... sure-footedly 1358

Men born to freedom are naturally alert to repel
invasion of their liberty 1361

Freedom is a very great reality. But it means ...
freedom from lies. 1363

Freedom belongs to the strong. 1368

Freedom to learn is the first necessity 1374

Freedom is not worth fighting for if it means no
more than license 1375

the ideal of freedom which is the political
expression of morality 1376

We have learned that freedom in itself is not
enough. 1378

Freedom of speech is of no use to a man who has
nothing to say. 1378

If a nation values anything more than freedom, it
will lose its freedom; 1381

dagger plunged in the name of Freedom is
plunged into the breast of Freedom 1382

Freedom is an indivisible word. 1385

Freedom has its life in the hearts ... of men 1390

The winning of freedom is not to be compared to
the winning of a game 1390

The ruling class or race must share their freedom
with everyone 1391

I wish that every human life might be pure
transparent freedom. 1394

No man is entitled to the blessings of freedom
unless he be vigilant 1397

Freedom and slavery are mental states. 1398

not enough merely to realize how freedom has
been won 1399

Freedom always entails danger. 1402

A Country can get more real joy out of just
hollering for their Freedom 1404

they lose their social freedom ... in seeking to
become like each other 1406

Everything that is really great and inspiring is
created by ... freedom 1408

The right to be let alone is indeed the beginning of
all freedoms. 1414

The real guarantee of freedom is an equilibrium of
social forces 1419

We cannot choose freedom established on a
hierarchy of degrees of freedom 1423

Freedom has been defined as the opportunity for
self-discipline. 1426

you can't ... allow freedom to be pushed back to
the ... United States 1427

Freedom is a hard-bought thing. 1428

Freedom is not worth having if it does not
connote freedom to err. 1429

If men ... are in chains, anywhere in the world,
then freedom is endangered 1430

only a few generations have been granted the role
of defending freedom 1433

Conformity is the jailer of freedom and the enemy
of growth. 1434

Freedom is not something ... given; freedom is
something people take 1435

We stand for freedom. 1436

then the peril to freedom will continue to
rise 1437

The best road to progress is freedom's road. 1438

The cost of freedom is always high 1439

capitalism is a necessary condition for political
freedom 1440

competitive capitalism, also promotes political
freedom 1441

Freedom in economic arrangements is a component of freedom broadly understood 1442

Economic freedom is also an indispensable means toward ... political freedom 1442

Economic freedom is also an indispensable means toward ... political freedom 1442

Today, in the world of freedom, the proudest boast is "Ich bin ein Berliner." 1444

the cause of freedom versus tyranny 1446

Freedom is indivisible, and when one man is enslaved, all are not free. 1447

There can be no real freedom without the freedom to fail. 1449

Freedom is the understanding of necessity and the transformation of necessity. 1451

After you get your freedom, your enemy will respect you. 1453

Freedom to many means immediate betterment 1454

less a matter of horror than the curtailment of the freedom to profit 1455

You can't separate peace from freedom 1456

Freedom is sweet fat, and that's for me. 1457

Freedom is sweet, on the beat 1457

Freedom is an internal achievement rather than an external judgment. 1460

In the act of resistance the rudiments of freedom are already present. 1461

We know that the road to freedom has always been stalked by death. 1467

The biggest menace to American freedom is the intelligence community. 1470

We know what works: Freedom works. We know what's right: Freedom 1474

either the people must have freedom based on law 1487

Man is about the same ... whether with freedom 1544

The freedom of the city is not negotiable. 1674

in the highest position ... the least freedom of action 1972

the duty of the liberal ... to extend the basic democratic freedoms 2272

Nor do men ... enjoy any greater share of this freedom in a pure commonwealth 2331

No free Country ... without parties ... a natural offspring of Freedom 2456

Power in defense of freedom is greater than power in behalf of tyranny 2883

never wear your best trousers when you go out to fight for freedom 3103

it wants more freedom to graze on its own 3133

"Freedom from fear" could be said to sum up ... human rights 3348

as the Negro plunges deeper into the quest for freedom and justice 3350

The Negro revolt is not aimed at winning friends but at winning freedom 3372

freedom ... includes the freedom to buy whatever a white man can buy 3377

Freedom is never granted; it is won. 3380

Freedom and justice must be struggled for by the oppressed of all lands 3380

for freedom is never a final fact 3380

a celebration of individual freedom, not of homosexuality 3394

the freedom ... of man ... the sole objects of all legitimate government 3434

If freedom makes social progress possible, so social progress enlarges freedom 3546

essential to freedom ... that no taxes be imposed ... but with ... consent 3579

History does not long entrust the care of freedom to the weak 3876

Peace and freedom do not come cheap 3906

a struggle for freedom on every front of human activity 3920

When man ... enjoys his natural freedom, let him despise woman 3978

with the same freedom to express herself in the religion and government 3988

FREEMAN

Vote, n. The instrument ... of a freeman's power to make a fool of himself 709

No freeman shall be taken, or imprisoned 1829

FREETHINKING

The freethinking of one age is the common sense of the next. 906

FREIGHT

The farmer is the only man ... who ... pays the freight both ways 656

FRESH

Eternal truths will be neither true nor eternal unless they have fresh meaning 968

FREUD

Fifty years ago if we had gone the way of Freud 2803

FRICTION

inevitable friction incident to the distribution of the governmental powers 3510

FRIEND

I am a good friend to Communists abroad 165

that he that holds it does not trust his friends 518

Abuse a man unjustly, and you will make friends for him. 926

Instead of loving your enemy, treat your friend a little better. 936

Let the word go forth from this time and place, to friend and foe alike 1025

The 5th Amendment is an old friend and a good friend 1417

No ... friend of the American people which is not a friend of American business 1596

A state worthy of the name has no friends 1675

Whenever you put a man on the Supreme Court he ceases to be your friend. 1736

that friend shall be down inside me 2071

I have lost every friend on earth, I shall at least have one friend left 2071

the king was the only monarch on earth who had a friend 2340

when they talk of supporting their party, mean serving their friends 2449

never attempt to buy the favor of your enemies at the expense of your friends 2493

Let no man be put ... out or in merely because he is our friend. 2555

it brings nothing but ... daily loss of friends 2955

But my damn friends, my god-damn friends 2979

The Negro revolt is not aimed at winning friends 3372

If I had to choose between betraying my country and betraying my friend 3641

FRIENDLESS
to be Omnipotent but friendless is to reign 2035

FRIENDSHIP
Peace, commerce, and honest friendship with all nations 1612

to allow the friendship between nations to rest upon deep and permanent things 1631

The friendships of nations, built on common interests 1643

passion for politics stems usually from an insatiable need ... for friendship 2642

FROG
become like the log that was given to the frogs to be their king 1842

FRONT
A leader should not get too far in front of his troops 2207

however extreme may seem to be the men who sit on the Front Bench 2583

FRUGAL
A wise and frugal Government, which shall restrain men 1517

FRUSTRATING
He'll find it very frustrating. 2993

FRUSTRATION
Absolute frustration is a dangerous emotion to run a world with. 2889

FUEL
The problem isn't a shortage of fuel, it's a surplus of government. 1574

if there be fuel prepared, it is hard to tell whence the spark shall come 3186

FULCRUM
sentiment gives you the fulcrum and the place to stand on 2076

FULL
He whose belly is full believes not him whose is empty. 38

FULLNESS
bitter ... when the fullness of democracy is denied 447

FUN
It's more fun doing it than watching it. 1704

FUNCTION
not the function of our Government to keep the citizen from falling into error 26

The function of parliamentary democracy ... is to expose wealth-privilege 467

distributing to every one exactly the functions he is competent to perform 1524

I don't think it's the function of Congress to function well. 2263

The function ... of the President is to set before the American people 2994

All of the functions it carries out are not noble ones. 3462

FUNCTIONARY
The functionaries of every government have propensities to command at will 1166

to keep the public functionaries within the bounds of law and duty 2466

FUND
among the mass of our people a fund of wisdom 291

FUNDAMENTAL
This policy rests upon the fundamental law 731

among the very fundamentals of democracy 1178

one thing solid and fundamental in politics 2802

all revolutions must be social revolutions, based upon fundamental changes 3248

FUNERAL
its funeral bell is already rung 201

FURROW
I must plough my own furrow alone, but before I get to the end of that furrow 2089

FUTILITY
Herein lies the futility of war. 3794

FUTURE
I have been over into the future, and it works. 130

in Russia they are slaves to the future 139

makes no preparation for the Future 194

An election is a bet on the future 725

in dealing with the present, thought is steadily
taken for the future   731

With our eyes fixed on the future, but recognizing
the realities of today   1080

I will collect the evidence of your future conduct
from ... your opinions   1238

Men are powerless to secure the future;   1522

In the White House, the future rapidly becomes
the past;   2999

men of narrow vision who are afraid of the
future   3179

a future in which our country will match its
military strength   3488

GALLOP
Democracy has arrived at a gallop in
England   690

GALLUP POLL
Nothing is more dangerous in wartime than ... a
Gallup Poll   3073

GAME
Defeat ... was part ... of the great gambling game
of politics   2778

You find you can't stop playing the game   2808

War is a game in which princes seldom win   3715

GAMING
All voting is a sort of gaming   701

GANGSTERISM
Totalitarianism is bad, gangsterism is worse   1068

GAP
The statesman's duty is to bridge the gap between
his nation's experience   2210

GARAGE
The slogan of progress is changing ... to the full
garage   645

GARDEN
the center of gravity might shift ... and tilt
everybody into the garden   2203

GARMENT
Non-violence is not a garment to be put on and
off   984

GAS-MASK
that we should be digging trenches and trying on
gas-masks   3818

GATE
We did not choose to be the guardians of the
gate   3924

GAUNTLET
toss the gauntlet before the feet of tyranny   2940

GEAR
the lie with so many tiny gears and fragile
connecting rods   2617

GENERAL
Amid the pressure of great events, a general
principle gives no help.   869

The general has dedicated himself so many
times   994

no such thing as liberty in general   1367

Politicians have the same occupational hazard as
generals   2664

A victorious general has no faults in the eye of the
public   3688

War is much too serious a matter to be left to
generals.   3785

A general and a bit of shooting makes you forget
your troubles   3896

GENERAL MOTORS
What is good for the country is good for General
Motors   1594

GENERATION
which has furnished leaders to the nation ... for
generations   379

The earth belongs always to the living
generation   728

assets which it must turn over to the next
generation increased   730

For this generation ... life is nuclear survival   736

not of the generation that regards honesty as the
best policy   819

how much it cost the present generation to
preserve your freedom   1231

The ideals of liberty cannot be fixed from
generation to generation   1333

There will be no greater burden in our
generation   1338

only a few generations have been granted the role
of defending freedom   1433

laws have no fixity, but shift from generation to
generation   1899

a statesman thinks of the next generation   2058

American political situation is about the same
from generation to generation   2773

fifteen years ... which coincides with the
effectiveness of a generation   3249

Each generation should be made to bear the
burden of its own wars   3704

GENEROUS
Be just before you're generous.   1767

GENIUS
Herein lies political genius   2025

GENTLE
to make kinder the face of the nation and gentler
the face of the world   1105

GENTLEMAN

objection to a Communist always resolves itself ... he is not a gentleman 155

that call me everything that is a good deal less than ... a gentleman 1180

Nominee, n. A modest gentleman shrinking from the distinction of private life 2567

the noble toga that political gentlemen drape over the will to power 2625

GEOMETRIC

to tax the higher portions of property in geometric progression 3582

GEORGE III

We must realize that today's Establishment is the new George III. 3282

George the Third ... may profit by their example 3637

GESTAPO

would have to fall back on some form of Gestapo 3567

GET

If you want to get along, go along. 1018

GEWGAW

with each new gewgaw of a revolution or new constitution that it finds 3209

GIANT

the world's most powerful nation ... acts like a pitiful, helpless giant 1699

The war of the giants is over and the pigmies will now start to squabble. 3842

GIRL

Treaties are like roses and young girls. 3913

GIVE

Never give in, never give in, never 971

Give me your tired, your poor 1315

A right is not what someone gives you; 3386

A government that is big enough to give you all 3489

GLAD

People are glad to be defended, but they are not glad about paying 3599

GLASNOST

Without glasnost there is not, and there cannot be, democratism 185

GLASS

Get thee glass eyes;/ And, like a scurvy politician 2517

GLOBALONEY

what Mr. Wallace calls his global thinking is ... still globaloney 1653

GLORIFICATION

Stalin himself ... supported the glorification of his own person 158

GLORY

everything ... must be done in their interest ... and for their glory 308

Great ambition, unchecked by ... the love of glory, is an unruly tyrant. 549

To win without risk is to triumph without glory. 829

There was such a glory over everything. 1308

yet this I count the glory of my crown: 1981

One is not born for glory unless he is aware of the pace of time. 2008

Glory is only given to those who have always dreamed of it. 2131

its glory is to lead them not where they want to go but where they should go 2691

"Why would anyone want to be President today?" the answer is not one of glory 3003

war as all glory, but, boys, it is all hell 3744

Who would prefer peace to the glory of hunger and thirst 3802

GO

Be always sure you are right—then go ahead. 872

If you want to get along, go along. 1018

discover a problem and then throw money at it, hoping it will somehow go away 3483

GOAL

If Negroes secure their goals ... they must win them 3341

If our air forces are never used, they have achieved their finest goal. 3890

GOBBLEDYGOOK

complicated, unfair, cluttered with gobbledygook 3631

GOD

"The voice of the people is the voice of God" 268

Were there a people of gods, their government would be democratic. 280

You have the God-given right to kick the government around 477

the negation of God erected into a system of Government 562

it is said that God is always on the side of the big battalions 840

The march of God in the world, that is what the state is. 852

stronger governments than hers have been shattered by the bolts of a just God 879

God reigns and the government at Washington still lives. 898

knowing that here on earth God's work must truly be our own 1030

363

I just want to do God's will.   1043

God grants liberty only·to those who love
it   1259

under a just God, cannot long retain it   1293

by the goodness of God ... we have those three
unspeakably precious things   1324

Freedom of worship is of no use to a man who has
lost his God.   1378

the soul, which belongs to God and must be let
alone by government   1412

May God prevent us from becoming "right-
thinking men"   1462

Property is a god. This god already has its
theology   1582

God and history will remember your
judgment.   1652

Though God hath raised me high, yet this I count
the glory of my crown: 1981

I am one of those whose heart God hath drawn
out   1994

I cannot but think that God is beginning of
them   1994

You cannot choose your battlefield,/ The gods do
that for you   2114

We're in the hands of the state legislature and
God   2265

Kings are justly called Gods   2328

God has given you your country as cradle, and
humanity as mother;   2402

God, at least, has a degree of forgiveness.   2649

I'd rather keep my promises to other politicians
than to God.   2649

God does not take sides in American
politics   2827

assumes that it has the means as well as the duty
to do God's work   2886

peculiarly susceptible to the idea that its power is
a sign of God's favor   2886

I ask for your help—and God's.   2998

Some think it is the voice of God.   3060

If men think that a ruler is religious and has a
reverence for the gods   3135

and unto God the things that are God's   3136

It does me no injury for my neighbor to say there
are twenty gods, or no God.   3142

maybe we'll get God back in   3163

I tremble for my country when I reflect that God
is just;   3291

Wherever there is a human being, I see God-given
rights   3320

The gods sent not/ Corn for the rich men
only.   3515

for they shall be called the children of God   3660

The gods are on the side of the stronger.   3662

living in peace, they should serve God   3669

"My God, what have we done?"   3886

the first woman God ever made was strong
enough to turn the world upside down   3981

GOLD

you shall not crucify mankind upon a cross of
gold   81

the alternative of saying good-bye to the gold
standard   2585

GOLDEN

I lift my lamp beside the golden door.   1315

GOLF

Politics, like music and golf, is best learned at an
early age.   2805

GOOD

but for the appalling silence of the good
people   30

they therefore will ever maintain good
government   40

The good sense of the people is the strongest
army   294

No government can continue good but under the
control of the people.   310

No man is good enough to govern another man
without that other's consent.   333

Democracy ... may be rationally defended, not as
being good   389

if the masses really knew what was good for
them   408

Popular government has not yet been proved to
guarantee ... good government.   463

Democracy is good.   470

Democracy, the profoundly good, is also the
profoundly productive.   499

not always the same thing to be a good man and a
good citizen   771

When bad men combine, the good must
associate;   838

Every political good carried to the extreme must
be productive of evil.   849

most of our people have never had it so
good   1013

not that we were so good, but those who followed
us were so bad   1060

They want an America as good as its
promise.   1072

but we have to take the good with the bad   1172

he can bet there are good men in jail   1193

newspapers filled with nothing but good
news   1193

let all lovers of liberty everywhere join in the great
and good work   1277

The only freedom ... is that of pursuing our own
good in our own way   1283

two good things in life—freedom of thought and
freedom of action   1348

Good government obtains when those who are
near are made happy   1476

at least see that it competes with the public
good   1486

Good men will obey the last, but bad ones the former only. 1523

What is good for the country is good for General Motors 1594

dedicate this nation to the policy of the good neighbor 1649

Justice and good will will outlast passion. 1791

Good laws if they are not obeyed, do not constitute good government. 1822

The good of the people is the supreme law. 1824

The law is good, if a man use it lawfully. 1827

The chief foundations of all states ... are good laws and good arms; 1836

Good and evil, reward and punishment, are the only motives 1848

Good laws lead to the making of better ones; 1861

to break a bad law, thereby authorizes everyone else to break the good ones 1874

Good men must not obey the laws too well. 1883

The best use of good laws is to teach men to trample bad laws 1887

Great and good are seldom the same man. 2005

The internal satisfaction of a good conscience is always present 2017

You cannot accomplish good for the people unless you face up to the weak 2027

A great man's greatest good luck is to die at the right time. 2152

far more easy to point out what will do harm than what will do good 2230

There is good news from Washington today. 2248

The Senate is a place filled with goodwill and good intentions 2260

Party divisions, whether on the whole operating for good or evil 2450

an elite that accomplishes mediocrity for the public good 2650

The wicked are always surprised to find ability in the good. 2676

More power than any good man should want 2869

The good neighbor looks beyond the external accidents 2930

no more good must be attempted than the nation can bear 3087

The good and happiness of the members ... is the great standard 3417

A good government implies two things: 3421

the first and only legitimate object of good government 3433

The final end of government is not to exert restraint but to do good. 3445

Good government ... has for its objects the protection of every person 3459

There never was a good war or a bad peace. 3692

GOODNESS
We do not base a choice on the goodness of democracy 631

GOODWILL
to multiply whatever of geniune good-will may exist 2745

GORILLA
a little like makin' love to a gorilla ... you quit when the gorilla's tired 1079

GOVERN
not that a particular class is unfit to govern 69

Governments ... deriv(e) their just powers from the consent of the governed. 288

Mobs will never do to govern states 296

The only legitimate right to govern is an express grant of power 326

for men to choose whether they will govern themselves or be governed 361

man has the moral and intellectual capacity ... to govern himself 450

a nation is not governed which is perpetually conquered 537

Whoever puts his hand on me to govern me is a usurper 561

easy to govern, but impossible to enslave 676

Let the people think they govern and they will be governed. 1482

the science of those who govern is to at least see that it competes 1486

To be governed is to be watched over, inspected 1537

times when one must govern liberally 1545

To govern is always to choose among disadvantages. 1571

the governed must be convinced that it is right 1776

He that would govern others, first should be Master of himself. 1992

not with ... explanations of theory that nations are governed 2032

To govern you do not follow any more or less good theory 2037

The Right Divine of Kings to govern wrong. 2339

Even more important than winning the election is governing the nation. 2499

The great art of governing consists in not letting men grow old in their jobs. 2533

The art of governing is a great metier, requiring the whole man 2541

the degree of ability among the governed and the lack of it among the governing 2543

it is as just a demand as governed men ever made of governing 3447

GOVERNMENT

Governments may come and governments may go 4

Oligarchy: A government resting on a valuation of property 33

The freest government, if it could exist, would not be long acceptable 42

The government ... is a device for maintaining the rights 91

A government which robs Peter to pay Paul 98

skepticism of the powers of government agencies to do good 221

Democracy ... is a charming form of government 263

when all persons alike share in the government to the utmost 264

Governments will never be awed by the voice of the people 282

happiness of the people is the sole end of government 284

Governments ... deriv(e) their just powers from the consent of the governed. 288

a free government is ... what the people think so 290

Every government degenerates when trusted to the rulers of the people alone. 293

good sense of the people is the strongest army our government can have 294

If government be founded in the consent of the people 302

the right of the people to establish Government 304

That government is the strongest of which every man feels himself a part. 306

No government can continue good but under the control of the people. 310

Government is a trust, and the officers of the government are trustees; 315

The people's government, made for the people 317

Our government ... was made for the people—not the people for the Government 346

free governments are managed by ... combined wisdom and folly 355

To fight against the government with any means is a basic right 356

Democracy is only an experiment in government 371

The government is us; we are the government 375

something to be said for government by a great aristocracy 379

Democracy is the most difficult form of government 381

a people are responsible for the acts of their government 388

There is one thing better than good government 396

that is government in which all people have a part 396

In the hands of a people's Government this power is wholesome and proper. 407

government is ourselves and not an alien power over us 414

Democracy is the superior form of government 419

Many forms of Government have been tried 441

democracy is the worst form of Government except all those other 441

a kind of balance between the will of the people and the government 451

governments have been mainly engaged in kicking people around 462

You have the God-given right to kick the government around 477

That problem is making Government sufficiently responsive to the people. 480

A government is not in power; 492

"We the People" tell the government what to do 500

"We the people" are the driver—the government is the car. 500

It is not having a share in government; 526

Whatever government is not a government of laws, is a despotism, 555

the negation of God erected into a system of Government 562

dictatorships do not grow out of strong and successful governments 600

A popular government without popular information 675

basis of effective government is public confidence 807

Secrecy in government has become synonymous ... with deception 814

God reigns and the government at Washington still lives 898

A great writer is ... a second government in his country. 1044

The Liberals talk about a stable government 1047

better for a Government to be hard of hearing 1113

basis of our government being the opinion of the people 1160

whether we should have a government without newspapers 1160

We live under a government of men and morning newspapers. 1170

Without criticism ... the government cannot govern 1188

natural progress of things is for ... government to gain ground 1237

See to the government. See that the government does not acquire too much power. 1261

man is not free unless government is limited 1475

certain inherently governmental actions which ... are lawful 1950

He who exercises government by means of his virtue 1968

public is interested more in government than in politics 2129

great problem of legislation is, so to organize the civil government 2232

government will never be able to restrain a ... discontented majority 2292

Governments exist to protect the rights of minorities. 2293

Government is ... controlled by powerful minorities 2305

government is free in proportion to the rights it guarantees to the minority 2311

No government can be long secure without ... opposition 2469

A politician is a man who understands government 2615

No government is better than the men who compose it. 2621

When the Government ... and the Opposition ... take the same side 2734

Good government cannot exist ... with bad politics: 2777

the best government is the best politics 2777

Truth is the glue that holds governments together. 2801

Compromise is the oil that makes governments go. 2801

The essence of Government is power; 2851

Public opinion sets bounds to every government 3040

A government is based on public opinion 3041

Whoever can change public opinion can change the government 3048

Government ... is organized opinion 3068

A government can be no better than the public opinion that sustains it. 3071

religions united with government are more or less inimical to liberty 3145

government ought to stay out of the prayer business 3164

A great revolution is never the fault of the people, but of the government. 3197

Old forms of government finally grow so oppressive 3216

otherwise it is not revolution, but merely a change of government 3248

easier to run a revolution than a government 3287

The true aim of government is liberty. 3409

ultimate aim of government is not to rule ... by fear 3410

Government has no other end but the preservation of Property. 3412

Government is ... instituted for the common benefit 3418

Government is instituted no less for protection of the property 3423

The aggregate happiness of society ... is ... the end of all government 3425

Government is a contrivance of human wisdom to provide for human wants. 3427

a just government, which impartially secures to every man, whatever is his own 3428

Government is instituted to protect property of every sort; 3428

Government was intended to suppress injustice 3429

And having looked to the Government for bread 3430

freedom and happiness ... the sole objects of all legitimate government 3434

The office of government is not to confer happiness 3438

business of government is not ... to make the people rich 3439

Governments do not and cannot support the people. 3439

The whole duty of government is to prevent crime 3442

end of government is not to exert restraint 3445

A government never loses anything by mildness 3446

The less government we have, the better 3448

these are rather the proper duties of a government 3449

government, is to do for ... people, whatever they need to have done 3452

In all that people can individually do ... government ought not to interfere 3452

The government is not an almoner of gifts among the people 3460

the people should patriotically and cheerfully support their Government 3463

That government is not best which best secures mere life and property 3464

Government should not be made an end in itself; 3468

the ideal of government was for every man to be left alone 3469

the best government was the government that did as little governing as possible 3469

Government has the ... duty to use all its power 3478

most important ... service that a government can do ... is to keep them alive 3479

The government must be the trustee for the little man 3480

Government should be concerned with anti-social conduct 3482

business of government is the business of the people 3485

A government that is big enough to give you all 3489

where there are no secrets from
government   3491

government big enough to give you everything you
want   3495

skeptical about the ability of government to solve
problems   3497

the government can do it worse   3500

the moral test of government is how that
government treats ... the children   3501

the whole of what is meant and understood by
government   3504

Under a government which imprisons any
unjustly   3518

his original means devoured by interest ... so must
it be with a government   3596

a good revenue system is the life of an organized
government   3600

the money we do spend on Government   3611

Government expands to absorb revenue and then
some.   3621

The government will ... go on ... conscripting
American manhood   3782

A government needs one hundred soldiers for
every guerrilla it faces.   3897

people ... are going to do more to promote peace
than our governments   3898

GOVERNOR

Our supreme governors, the mob.   279

Men ... could never have the liberty to choose
either Governors   2334

the first inroads upon the laws have been made by
the governors   3198

GRACIOUS

being seasoned with a gracious voice,/ Obscures
the show of evil?   1840

You show me a ... gracious loser, and I'll show
you a failure   2119

GRAIN

If one man offers you democracy and another
offers you a bag of grain   468

A police state finds it cannot command the grain
to grow.   615

You have to be like the pebble in the stream,
keeping the grain   2051

GRANITE

If there ever existed a monarchy strong as
granite   635

GRANT

only legitimate right to govern is an express grant
of power   326

GRASS-ROOTS

politicians will not stick their necks out unless ...
grass-roots support   2653

GRATEFUL

grateful for even the sharpest criticism   905

GRATITUDE

Gratitude is not an active sentiment in
politics.   2690

GRAVE-DIGGER

the bourgeoisie ... produces ... its own grave-
diggers   58

GRAVITY

center of gravity might shift, and the whole room
might tilt   2203

Religion ... is ... the centre of gravity in a
realm   3147

GRAY

you realize that gray isn't such a bad color   2779

It's between two horrible shades of gray.   2811

GRAZE

it wants more freedom to graze on its own   3133

GREASY POLE

I have climbed to the top of the greasy pole.   903

GREAT

the greatest happiness of the greatest number   289

they are great when these numbers ... are
employed in the service of an ideal   354

A great democracy must be progressive   378

all the great work of the world is done through
me   452

with small men no great thing can really be
accomplished   568

Social prosperity means man happy ... the nation
great   637

The poorest he ... hath a life to live as the greatest
he   739

Amid the pressure of great events, a general
principle gives no help.   869

Everything ... great ... is created by the individual
who can labor in freedom   1408

no nation which is greater than any other   1652

Great cases like hard cases make bad law.   1905

Even though men usually flatter themselves on
their great deeds   1999

qualities that go into the making of a great
ruler   2001

Great and good are seldom the same man.   2005

No man was ever great by imitation.   2013

Great men are the guide-posts and landmarks in
the state.   2018

Great offices will have great talents.   2020

No man is truly great who is great only in his
lifetime.   2038

the great man is he who in the midst of the crowd
keeps ... independence   2047

To be great is to be misunderstood.   2049

history of the world is but the biography of great
men   2050

Man is only truly great when he acts from the
passions.   2053

Great events make me quiet and calm;   2056

To do great things is difficult; but to command great things is more difficult.   2079

great men are like great mountains   2088

A great man's failures to understand define him.   2090

then a good many great men must have been frauds   2093

Great men are but life-sized.   2110

privilege of the great is to see catastrophes from the terrace   2127

No man is great enough ... for any of us to surrender our destiny to   2134

I distrust Great Men.   2148

A great man's greatest good luck is to die at the right time.   2152

Few great men could pass Personnel.   2165

His crimes are the only great things about him   2528

The voice of great events is proclaiming to us, Reform   3094

which procures the greatest happiness for the greatest numbers   3414

those means which will give the greatest good to the greatest number   3453

GREAT BRITAIN

Great Britain has lost an Empire and has not yet found a role.   1676

GREAT SOCIETY

If this is a Great Society, I'd hate to see a bad one.   1067

The great society ... where men are more concerned with the ... their goals   3490

but upward to the Great Society   3544

GREATNESS

people have always some champion whom they ... nurse into greatness   521

The abuse of greatness is when it disjoins/ Remorse from power.   525

France cannot be France without greatness.   1003

Be not afraid of greatness: 1982

some are born great ... and some have greatness thrust upon them   1982

He who comes up to his own idea of greatness   2041

men owe most of their greatness   2087

salvation can only come through greatness   2154

We have ... confused power with greatness   2885

GREED

We have earned the hatred of entrenched greed.   955

GREEN-BAIZE

The field of combat was a ... green-baize covered table   3872

GRIEF

A man who wishes to act virtuously in every way necessarily comes to grief   1978

GRIEVANCE

A grievance is most poignant when almost redressed.   988

no grievance that is a fit object of redress by mob law   3207

GROUND

The first man who, having enclosed a piece of ground   837

When the ground shakes under governments   3199

GROW

Every man who takes office in Washington either grows or swells.   2575

GROWN-UP

If we are to regard ourselves as a grown-up nation   2171

GROWTH

maximum growth of government plus zero economic growth   661

GUARANTEE

basic guarantees of our Constitution are warrants for the here and now   244

Controversy over the meaning of our nation's most majestic guarantees   252

Popular government has not yet been proved to guarantee ... good government   463

real guarantee of freedom is an equilibrium of social forces   1419

No one can guarantee success in war   3856

GUARANTY

Constitution is the ... guaranty of national freedom   241

private property is the most important guaranty of freedom   1392

It is the surest guaranty of peace.   3759

GUARD

But who is to guard the guards themselves?   773

The subject's love is the king's best guard.   2007

GUARDIAN

legislatures are ultimate guardians of the liberties   2241

We did not choose to be the guardians of the gate   3924

GUERRILLA

Guerrilla warfare is to peasant uprisings what Marx is to Sorel.   173

Insurrection—by means of guerrilla bands   3204

A government needs one hundred soldiers for every guerrilla it faces.   3897

Keyword Index

GUIDE
Each one thinks he is guiding the log   2648

GUIDE-POSTS
Great men are the guide-posts ... in the
state   2018

GUILT
it cannot be absolved from the faults due to the
guilt of the regime   605

GUILTLESS
No one can rule guiltlessly.   2023

GUILTY
A guilty man punished is an example for the
mob;   1763
better that ten guilty persons escape, than that one
innocent suffer   1768
better 100 guilty Persons should escape   1770
better to risk saving a guilty man than to condemn
an innocent one   1852
more dangerous that even a guilty person should
be punished   1870
some people are a little bit guilty, while other
people are guilty as hell   1954

GUINEA
I would not give half a guinea to live under one
form of government   1492

GUN
"Political power grows out of the barrel of a
gun."   142
the Party commands the gun, and the gun must
never be allowed to command   143
We can do without butter, but ... not without
guns.   3813
Guns will make us powerful;   3814
to get rid of the gun it is necessary to take up the
gun   3822

GUNFIRE
they should march their troops towards the sound
of gunfire   1036

GUNPOWDER
since the invention of gunpowder ... I continually
tremble   3684

GUTS
In politics, guts is all.   2806
I hope I should have the guts to betray my
country   3641

GUTTER
all in the gutter, but some of us are looking at the
stars   2083
people who go to the gutter on either the right or
the left   2784

GYMNASIUM
It is life's gymnasium, not of good only, but of
all.   351

HABEAS CORPUS
freedom of person under the protection of habeas
corpus   1251

HABIT
Tyranny is a habit;   570
I'm not a politician and my other habits are
good.   2549
In politics habits ... rule humanity   2735
Nothing so needs reforming as other people's
habits.   3105

HABITUAL
only when government has become habitual can
we ... make it democratic   1559

HACK
a thousand hacking at the branches of evil   2060

HAILSTORM
Being president is like being a jackass in a
hailstorm.   3009

HAIR
the people who know how to run the country are
.. . cutting hair   2202

HALF
Democracy is the recurrent suspicion that more
than half ... are right   440
this government cannot endure, permanently half
slave and half free   885
Half-heartedness never won a battle.   920
He conceals the other half out of fear of the
people's wrath   1023
Compromise used to mean that half a loaf was
better than no bread.   2732
We're half the people; we should be half the
Congress.   3996

HALL
wisest thing to do with a fool is to encourage him
to hire a hall   1119

HAMMER
Communism is a hammer which we use to crush
the enemy.   152

HAMSTRING
the party that prevents the Government from
running amuck by hamstringing it   2730

HAND
Whoever puts his hand on me to govern me is a ...
tyrant;   561
our task ... to hand down undiminished ... the
natural wealth   734
retiring with hands as clean as they are
empty   780
it's a tool in the killer's hand   825
You cannot shake hands with a clenched
fist.   1087

The hand that rules the press ... rules the country   1179

failed to stretch forth a saving hand   1373

Civilization and profits go hand in hand.   1589

the eye is drawn to the hand performing the dramatic flourishes   1722

You can only make them change hands.   2849

Certain rights ... must be kept in the hands of the people   3345

they will turn and bite the hand that fed them   3430

before long they will be wringing their hands   3686

HANDICAP

Of my two "handicaps," being female put many more obstacles in my path   4002

HANDMAIDEN

the handmaidens of legislative decision   2262

HANDOUT

If we take the route of the permanent handout   3494

HANDSHAKING

Handshaking is friendly until your hands bleed.   2433

HANG

We must all hang together, or assuredly we shall all hang separately.   843

the support that the rope gives to a hanged man   1015

I think we ought to let him hang there   1062

We are reforming, not the hanged man   1757

Men are not hanged for stealing Horses, but that Horses may not be stolen.   1847

HAPPEN

Everything that happened once can happen again.   1085

Nothing just happens in politics.   2750

HAPPINESS

the happiness of the people is the sole end of government   284

pursuing and obtaining happiness and safety   286

the greatest happiness of the greatest number   289

among the ... people a fund of wisdom ... which will preserve their happiness   291

Those who have given ... the most concern about the happiness of peoples   908

Liberty is the means in the pursuit of happiness.   1334

of no moment to the happiness of an individual   1492

their greatest happiness is having good government   1533

Power is not happiness.   2844

white man's happiness cannot be purchased by the black man's misery   2899

That action is best, which procures the greatest happiness   3414

The good and happiness of the members ... the great standard   3417

capable of producing the greatest degree of happiness and safety   3418

happiness ... are the objects at which all political institutions aim   3420

The aggregate happiness of society ... is ... the end of all government   3425

happiness of man ... the sole objects of all legitimate government   3434

The office of government is not to confer happiness   3438

the foundation upon which all their happiness ... depend   3457

Do not aim at establishing happiness by political means.   3486

HAPPY

Social prosperity means man happy   637

better that some should be unhappy than that none should be happy   740

no one can be perfectly happy till all are happy   1271

Good government obtains when those who are near are made happy   1476

What a happy country this will be, if the whites will listen.   2896

a group of people who will never be happy   3574

HARD

Freedom is a hard-bought thing.   1428

Great cases like hard cases make bad law.   1905

I do not know anyone who has got to the top without hard work.   2216

HARDSHIP

to be a poor race in a land of dollars is the very bottom of hardships   83

it will make two hardships to cure one   2709

HARE

just as a sporting dog is the intermedium between the sportsman and the hare   44

HARLOT

power without responsibility—the prerogative of the harlot throughout the ages   1176

HARM

How can we best avoid situations in which a bad ruler causes too much harm?   498

only purpose for which power can be ... exercised is to prevent harm to others   1289

far more easy to point out what will do harm   2230

HARMONY

these two classes should dwell in harmony and agreement   78

socialism cannot be brought into harmony with ... the Catholic Church   3561

HARSH
Every ruler is harsh whose rule is new. 1969

HARVARD
Every Harvard class should have one
Democrat 509

If Moses had gone to Harvard Law School 2258

HAT
She went to the ballot-box touching her hat. 412

My hat's in the ring. 2733

take care to do it in a very smart hat 3253

HATCHET
Nobuddy ever fergits where he buried a
hatchet. 2746

HATE
Let them hate me, so they but fear me. 522

put these instruments in the hands of men of
hate 612

Authority is never without hate. 824

Those who hate you don't win unless you hate
them. 1063

but freedom for the thought that we hate 1128

For the white man to ask the black man if he
hates him 2934

the same constitutional bundle as those of the
most hated member 3388

HATRED
We have earned the hatred of entrenched
greed. 955

foremost art of kings is the power to endure
hatred 1973

Whom hatred frights,/ Let him not dream on
sovereignty. 1983

I have an invincible hatred of words and empty
phrases 2040

national hatred is something peculiar 2366

I must have no hatred or bitterness towards
anyone. 2411

Politics ... has always been the systematic
organization of hatreds. 2723

HAVEN
nor should this court ... be thought of as a general
haven for reform movements 245

HAWK
between a hawk and a dove the hawk has a great
advantage 3928

HE
The poorest he ... hath a life to live as the greatest
he 739

HEAD
though counting heads is not an ideal way to
govern 401

The mob has many heads but no brains. 835

the simple reasoning of the head of the
house 1857

The heart of a statesman must be in his
head. 2034

many accuse me of conducting public affairs with
my heart instead of my head 2189

Uneasy lies the head that wears a crown. 2327

I ain't never seen no head so level 2720

HEADACHE
Those who see and observe kings ... discover that
they have headaches 2009

this king business has given me personally nothing
but headaches 2362

HEALTH
The health of any democracy ... depends on a
small technical detail: 399

first consideration ... should be the health of the
people 3455

The health of the people is really the
foundation 3457

HEAR
In that hearing, we didn't hear anything. 1102

our need as a self-governing people to hear
everything relevant 1139

Parliament will train you ... to hear ... foolish
talk 2234

HEARD
The right to be heard does not ... include the right
to be taken seriously 1147

AND I WILL BE HEARD 1256

HEART
the soundness of heart of its average men and
women 460

Among men, Hinnissy, wet eye manes dhry
heart. 922

To wear your heart on your sleeve isn't a very
good plan; 1101

Liberty lies in the hearts of men and
women; 1389

must first come to pass in the heart 1659

if it is born in the minds of a few and carried in
the hearts of none 1703

They have a Right to censure, that have a Heart
to help: 1764

passion must ever sway the heart of man 1821

you cannot change people's hearts merely by
laws 1923

Judicial decrees may not change the heart, but
they can restrain the heartless. 1935

Beneath that cold ... exterior there beats a cold,
harsh, impersonal heart 1944

The heart of a statesman must be in his
head. 2034

must never be mistakes which result from
faintness of heart 2141

Those who don't know how to weep with their whole heart   2189

In the majority beat many hearts, but it has no heart.   2300

the issue raised by this case touches the heart of what makes individuals   2322

So long as the human heart is strong and the human reason weak   2353

I am fain to explore the ... purity of its heart   2400

In your heart, you know he's right.   2431

Socialism must come down from the brain and reach the heart.   3557

HEAT

The thing to be supplied is light, not heat.   2105

"If you can't stand the heat, get out of the kitchen."   2164

HEAVEN

man has tried to make it his heaven   550

it stands as much in need of heaven as of earth   870

It isn't created to take you to heaven.   1000

heavens will not fall and you will not be thrown out   1143

I shall repent it in Heaven   1231

Princes are like to heavenly bodies   2330

If I could not go to heaven but with a party   2457

easier for a ... rich man to enter the kingdom of heaven   2526

every man must go to heaven in his own way   3139

HEEL

It should drag its heels on the way to decision.   2263

HELL

Tyranny, like hell, is not easily conquered;   539

What has always made the state a hell on earth   550

I never did give anybody hell ... they thought it was hell   985

If Hitler invaded hell   987

the United Nations is created to prevent you from going to hell   1000

if the road to hell is paved with them, then it's a pretty good detour   2260

It is hell to belong to a suppressed minority.   2312

For the first six months you wonder how the hell you ever got here.   2639

My God, this is a hell of a job!   2979

Kansas had better stop raising corn and begin raising hell.   3107

"To hell with you."   3277

the author of a war lets loose the whole contagion of hell   3698

but, boys, it is all hell   3744

HELP

A lie is an abomination unto the Lord, and a very present help in trouble.   803

If you don't know what ... men are up against how are you going to help   1549

"I'm from the government and I'm here to help."   1576

HENROOST

So we defend ourselves and our henroosts, and maintain slavery.   3519

HERD

reducing everything unique to the level of the herd   427

it is evil that a single man should crush the herd   606

HERE

"Henry, why are you here?" "Waldo, why are you not here?"   2054

HERESY

worse to suppress dissent than to run the risk of heresy   1138

no worse heresy than that the office sanctifies the holder   2558

HERETIC

Every revolutionary ends by becoming either an oppressor or a heretic.   3262

HERITAGE

I survived an Ice Age and helped to keep this heritage intact   1195

HERO

make Britain a fit country for heroes to live in   935

Heroes are created by popular demand   2138

Unlucky the country that needs a hero.   2139

We like to think that heroes can emerge from obscurity   2816

We pray for the wisdom that this hero be America's last unknown.   3965

HEROICS

America's present need is not heroics, but healing;   939

HEROISM

The greatest height of heroism ... is to know how to face ridicule   2102

HIDE

a hide two feet thick, and no apparent interest in politics   2660

the taxidermist leaves the hide   3619

HIERARCHY

We cannot choose freedom established on a hierarchy of degrees   1423

HIGH

There is a higher law than the Constitution.   235

To die for an idea is to place a pretty high price upon conjectures.   931

in the highest position there is the least freedom of action   1972

It yields a short-term high but does long-term damage   2264

to make them capable ... of the highest degree of culture   2347

one of the privileges of high office   2640

a chance to play for higher stakes and perform at a higher level   2815

If you rebel against high-heeled shoes   3253

HILL

If Moses had ... spent three years working on the Hill   2258

HIROSHIMA

As the bomb fell over Hiroshima and exploded   3886

HISS

All he has to do to be hissed is to live long enough.   2612

HISTORIAN

I am speaking as an historian.   3169

HISTORY

The history of ... society is the history of class struggles.   55

You who have read the history of nations   62

History is the judge;   125

history is on our side   156

to the history of the time of framing and to ... history of interpretation   258

upward course of a nation's history is due ... to the soundness of heart   460

history of free men is never really written by chance but by choice   466

History proves that dictatorships do not grow out of strong ... governments   600

Human history ... a race between education and catastrophe   688

great results of history are brought about by discreditable means   785

Assassination has never changed the history of the world.   899

History knows no resting places and no plateaus.   1084

history of the world is ... the progress of the consciousness of freedom   1257

The whole history of the progress of human liberty   1280

The history of liberty is a history of resistance.   1340

History suggests that capitalism is a necessary condition for political freedom   1440

governments never have learned anything from history   1528

history of the world's great leaders is often the story of human folly   2010

The test of greatness is the page of history.   2038

Politics are vulgar when they are not liberalised by history   2716

History has taught me that rulers are much the same   2845

History shows that no Administration ... has been free from ... mistakes   2961

History buffs probably noted the reunion ...of three ex-presidents   3030

it forms popular instincts which are the result of history   3222

History shows that wars are divided into two kinds   3821

History does not long entrust the care of freedom to the weak   3876

HIT

The unforgivable crime is soft hitting. Do not hit at all   2099

HITLER

If Hitler invaded hell I would make ... a favorable reference to the devil   987

Even Hitler and Mussolini were, according to themselves.   3849

HOBGOBLIN

A foolish consistency is the hobgoblin of little minds   2048

menacing it with an endless series of hobgoblins   2737

HOKUM

elections do matter, even though the process is at least part hokum   2816

HOLE

The hole and the patch should be commensurate.   3084

HOLLER

A Country can get more real joy out of just hollering for their Freedom   1404

HOLLOW

A marciful Providunce fashioned us holler   782

HOLY

Christian socialism is but the holy water   3150

If ever ... a holy war, it was that which saved our liberties   3712

HOMAGE

not to be won by trifling favors, but by lavish homage   1879

HOME

Without a home their çan be no good citizen. 21

when we do not like poor people and do not want them in our homes 111

We shall be judged more by what we do at home 1679

A nation can be no stronger abroad than she is at home. 1683

At home, you always have to be a politician; 2161

He who loves not his home and country ... how shall he love humanity 2413

I make up for lost time when I come home. 2765

the right of a man to retreat into his own home 3354

right ... to conduct intimate relationships in the intimacy of ... her own home 3401

the foundation of American life rests upon the home 3473

The main enemy is at home. 3773

HOMELESS

The hungry and the homeless don't care about liberty 1370

HOMOSEXUAL

Homosexual behavior between consenting adults 3351

HOMOSEXUALITY

a celebration of individual freedom, not of homosexuality 3394

(Disapproval of homosexuality cannot justify) invading the houses 3402

HONEST

To request an honest man to vote according to his conscience is superfluous. 699

even a politician who is honest in the highest sense 797

conception of an "honest" politician is not ... a simple one 798

You cannot adopt politics as a profession and remain honest. 801

Most of us are honest at all time, and all of us are honest most of the time. 811

An ambassador is an honest man sent to lie abroad 1603

that of an honest broker who means to do business 1626

an innocent man convicted is the business of every honest person 1763

The life of the nation is secure only while the nation is honest 2370

An honest politician is one who ... will stay bought. 2551

In politics nothing is just save what is honest; 2683

my fellow citizens who are ... honest cease to believe that I represent them 2967

HONESTY

while honesty in Public Men is generally attributed to Dumbness 802

intellectual honesty is not the coin of the realm in politics 818

not of the generation that regards honesty as the best policy 819

HONEYED

to have the art of honeyed words but not to seem neutral 2591

HONOR

difference between a moral man and a man of honor 799

When there is a lack of honor in government 809

never give in except to convictions of honor and good sense 971

we mutually pledge ... our Lives, our Fortunes, and our sacred Honor 1228

have brought you back peace—but a peace ... with honour 1627

but with this shield ... we march always in the ranks of honor 2132

A nation reveals itself ... also by the men it honors 2176

Honor is not the exclusive property of any political party. 2508

not for the honor of the thing, he would much rather walk 2958

When you get to be President, there are all those things, the honors 3016

When neither their property not their honor is touched 3406

If peace cannot be maintained with honor, it is no longer peace. 3724

prosperity which is bought at the price of national honor 3766

the second time that there has come back ... peace with honour 3817

yield every honor which has been accorded by war 3925

The greatest honor history can bestow is the title of peacemaker. 3939

We must not treat her differently from a man, except to honor her more. 3997

HONORABLE

It is sweet and honorable to die for your country. 3658

It is the object only of war that makes it honorable. 3697

HOPE

Is there any better or equal hope in the world? 341

A poor man with nothing in his belly needs hope 956

Keep hope alive. 1103

We shall nobly save or meanly lose the last, best hope of earth. 1299

the terrible fascinating power of the hope of
freedom   1386

When hopes and dreams are loose in the
streets   3263

the hope of better things incites people to
revolt   3276

spending the sweat of its labourers ... the hopes of
its children   3877

no hope even that woman ... will ever purify
politics   3992

HORRIBLE
How horrible ... that we should be digging
trenches   3818

HORSE
not best to swap horses while crossing the
river   896

Men are not hanged for stealing Horses, but that
Horses may not be stolen.   1847

difference of opinion that makes horse races   2719

HOSE
should be able to count on us to furnish the hose
and water   1702

HOSTILE
to take up the notion that class is naturally hostile
to class   78

HOSTILITY
the hostility of one nation to another will come to
an end   54

eternal hostility against every form of
tyranny   547

but seldom that any one overt act produces
hostilities   1613

HOT
If you let me write $200 billion worth of hot
checks every year   663

HOT AIR
A straw vote only shows which way the hot air
blows.   3063

HOUSE
the contrast between the House of Have and the
House of Want   67

a house divided against itself cannot stand   80

If a house be divided against itself, that house
cannot stand.   826

If our house be on fire ... we must try to
extinguish it   851

"A house divided against itself cannot
stand."   885

A man's house is his castle.   1844

One thing the House will NEVER forgive   2252

He is like a good prewar house—solidly
built.   2634

the right of the people to be secure in their ...
houses   3392

(Disapproval of homosexuality cannot justify)
invading the houses   3402

Let not him who is homeless pull down the house
of another   3521

HOUSE OF COMMONS
I am a child of the House of Commons.   426

The leap which the House of Commons is
taking   891

The House of Commons allows itself to be
led   2235

the House of Commons is the most
unrepresentative of ... assemblies   2255

HOUSELESS
Houseless, adj. Having paid all taxes on household
goods.   3605

HOUSEWIFE
the American housewife ... a lot better
economists   3495

HUMAN
they acquiesced in the pre-eminence of economic
forces over human welfare   50

Give socialism back its human face.   175

When, in the course of human events   287

Human dignity, economic freedom ...
characteristics that distinguish democracy   442

indispensable to a good condition of human
affairs   1284

but a value that is fundamentally and universally
human   1376

to calculate on the weaker springs of the human
character   1507

Foreign relations are like human relations.   1693

One can't be just if one is not human at the same
time.   1766

men, who ... lead the activity of the human
race   2067

will be remembered ... for our contribution to the
human spirit   2172

to create resentment oppositions attribute them to
human causes   2494

those inner qualities that make all men
human   2930

whites must be made to realize that they are only
human   2944

to recognize that we are humans   2948

Civil liberty can be established on no foundation
of human reason   3146

black man must reject all value systems that
...reduce his human dignity   3384

The state is like the human body.   3462

But none of them must take precedence over
human needs.   3623

War is an invention of the human mind. The
human mind can invent peace   3875

Women—one half the human race at least   3984

HUMAN BEING

Always human beings will live and progress to ... fuller life   1014

No problem of human destiny is beyond human beings.   1039

like any other sensible human being, always learns more from his opponents   2754

Human beings have rights, because they are moral beings   3301

Yours for the unshackled exercise of every faculty by every human being.   3313

Wherever there is a human being, I see God-given rights   3320

We are fighting for recognition as human beings.   3366

the indispensable condition of the liberation of the human being   3559

HUMAN LIFE

I wish that every human life might be pure transparent freedom.   1394

something that governments care far more for than human life   3237

care of human life and happiness ... object of good government   3433

Prolong human life only when you can shorten its miseries.   3493

Hungry men have no respect for law, authority or human life.   3529

HUMAN NATURE

the highest type of human nature—a type nowhere ... existing   368

human nature that rules the world, not governments   1090

you see the whole gamut of human nature   1739

Every so often, we pass laws repealing human nature.   1922

The sad knowledge of human nature, that always comes too late   2525

A political career brings out the basest qualities in human nature.   2579

Politicians, who have not time to become acquainted with human nature   2586

Knowledge of human nature is the beginning and end of political education.   2726

Power is always charged with the impulse to eliminate human nature   2888

HUMAN RIGHTS

who wrongly holds that every human right is secondary to his profit   1585

human rights and property rights are fundamentally ... identical   3324

human rights must have the upper hand;   3324

having the government ... more concerned about human rights   3329

when they espouse human rights, make their own mental reservations   3335

out of the shadow of states' rights and into the sunlight of human rights   3344

"Freedom from fear" ... the whole philosophy of human rights   3348

Where ... do universal human rights begin?   3352

America stands for progress in human rights   3355

We are fighting for human rights   3366

I don't know of any human right that is more important than a job   3387

Human rights is the soul of our foreign policy   3389

we should strive ... for the dignity and human rights of mankind   3390

America did not invent human rights ... human rights invented America   3393

HUMAN SOCIETY

have as little of it as the general peace of human society will permit   1511

great executives have given ... push to the advancement of human society   2254

end of human society is ... living in peace, they should serve God   3669

HUMANITARIAN

A man may have strong humanitarian and democratic principles;   3531

HUMANITY

more misery among the lower classes than ... humanity in the higher   64

Humanity is only I writ large   904

all humanity shares the common hunger for peace   996

That government which thinks in terms of humanity will continue.   1558

what humanity, reason, and justice tell me I ought to do   1864

Be ashamed to die until you have won some victory for humanity.   2066

no idea so uplifting as the idea of the service of humanity   2095

how shall he love humanity in general which he has not seen   2413

In politics habits ... rule humanity   2735

friend of humanity cannot recognize a distinction between what is political   2741

urge to save humanity ... a false-face for the urge to rule it   2877

After all there is but one race—humanity.   2907

Property is an instrument of humanity;   3329

The State ... is the most flagrant negation ... of humanity   3454

I am for Socialism because I am for humanity.   3556

not by the principles of humanity that man lives   3799

not going to have a society that understands its humanity   4007

HUMANKIND
Of all the tyrannies on humankind ... worst is that which persecutes the mind   528

HUMBLE
It is sometimes well to be humble.   2553

HUMBUG
Vox populi, vox humbug.   343
Talking of patriotism, what humbug it is;   2409

HUMILIATE
a few kind words better than ... dollars given in a humiliating way   1057

HUMORIST
you've got to be a humorist to stay one   507

HUNDRED
Letting a hundred flowers blossom   161
will not be finished in the first hundred days   1026
It usually takes a hundred years to make a law   1893

HUNGER
all humanity shares the common hunger for peace   996
Hunger does not breed reform;   3117
a war against hunger and pestilence and disease   3873
Every gun that is fired ... a theft from those who hunger   3877

HUNGRY
And the tigers are getting hungry.   598
Give a hungry man a stone and tell him what beautiful houses are made of it;   678
The hungry and the homeless don't care about liberty   1370
A hungry man is not a free man.   1411
a hungry man is more interested in four sandwiches than four freedoms   1420
Hungry men have no respect for law, authority   3529

HURRAH
The Last Hurrah.   1008

HURT
Nothing doth more hurt ... than that cunning men pass for wise   1989

HUSBAND
The first lady ... an unpaid public servant elected by ... her husband   3005

HUSK
been paid with the husks—and bidden to thank God they had the husks   86

HYPERBOLE
the Democratic Way ... via hyperbole, sham   512
Hyperbole was to Lyndon Johnson what oxygen is to life.   2632

HYPOCRISY
A conservative government is an organized hypocrisy.   196
where despotism can be pure, and without the base alloy of hypocrisy   566
I don't like hypocrisy—even in international relations.   1701

HYPOCRITE
hypocrites, called priests, have put crowns upon the heads of thieves   3153

HYPOCRITICAL
whose speeches, hypocritical, unctuous and slovenly   808

I
Humanity is only I writ large   904
I am alone with the masses.   2195

ICE AGE
I survived an Ice Age and helped to keep this heritage intact   1195

IDEA
ruling ideas of each age have ever been the ideas of its ruling class   53
It is ideas ... which are dangerous for good or evil   649
an idea whose time has come   880
To die for an idea is to place a pretty high price upon conjectures.   931
Nothing is more dangerous than an idea   949
Every idea is an incitement.   1123
All my life I have held on to a certain idea of France.   2383
when a politician does get an idea he usually gets it all wrong   2592
I don't think ideas are incompatible with political reality.   2776
Ideas are great arrows, but there has to be a bow.   2788
when certain historic ideas in the life of the nation had to be clarified   2974
the Republican party ... has not had a new idea in 30 years   3169
A revolutionary idea is revolutionary, vital, real   3222

IDEAL
when these numbers ... are employed in an ideal   354
their concept of the ideal republic   394
The ideals of liberty cannot be fixed from generation to generation;   1333
The ideal is when a man receives the seals of office   2562

Politics ... are shaped by men without
ideals   2759
the ideal of government was for every man to be
left alone   3469

IDEALISM
Idealism is the noble toga that ... gentlemen drape
over the will to power   2625
Idealism is the despot of thought   2707

IDENTIFICATION
political genius ... the identification of an
individual with a principle   2025

IDEOLOGICAL
the great ideological wars of our time   2918

IDEOLOGY
This election is not about ideology;   727
Politics without ideology ... equals
Liberalism   2278
opinions adopted by parties ... are
ideologies   2513
States do not prosper through ideology.   3431

IDIOT
the law is a ass—a idiot   1881

IDOL
To kick over an idol, you must first get off your
knees.   2495

IGNOBLE
a less evil ... than that the government should play
an ignoble part   1803
No one can expect a majority to be stirred by
motives other than ignoble.   2306

IGNORANCE
The ignorance of one voter in a democracy
impairs the security of all.   29
Tyrants are but the spawn of Ignorance   559
If ignorance paid dividends, most Americans could
make a fortune   658
Poverty has many roots, but the tap root is
ignorance.   697
Ignorance of the law is no excuse in any
country.   1869
never found ... that criticism is ever inhibited by
ignorance   2785
Prejudice is the child of ignorance.   2897
ignorance ... of the majority of women ... is not
remarkable   3986

IGNORANT
If a nation expects to be ignorant and free   670
The free man cannot be long an ignorant
man.   684
One is to be completely ignorant.   2923
ignorant and violent men will write it on the
soil   3213

ILL
ills of democracy can be cured by more
democracy   403
because a possibility remains of their doing
ill   1503
Ill can he rule the great that cannot reach the
small.   1980
optimist ... assumes that there must be some
remedy for every political ill   2709
I see one-third of a nation ill-housed, ill-
clad   3532

ILLEGAL
Despotism accomplishes great things
illegally;   318
Nothing is illegal if one hundred businessmen
decide to do it   1597
Life and liberty can be as much endangered from
illegal methods   1929
When the President does it, that means that it is
not illegal.   3026

ILLITERATE
No amount of charters ... will make a democracy
out of an illiterate people   687

ILLOGICAL
a doctrine so illogical ... can have exercised so
powerful ... an influence   137

ILLUSION
I could give you an illusion of prosperity,
too   663
under no illusion that the Russian people are
fighting for the Communist party   2381
the illusion that either you are being useful   2654

IMAGINATION
Conservatism ... is mainly due to want of
imagination   202
The nose of a mob is its imagination.   560
all the stupidities they can think of, plus some that
are beyond imagination   1049
Liberty, n. One of Imagination's most precious
possessions.   1332
it spreads wherever it can capture the imagination
of men   1432
only those withdrawn into a brooding imagination
have the faculty for it   2061

IMAGINE
a mind that is able to imagine itself believing
anything   2270

IMBALANCE
Social imbalance reflects itself in inability to
enforce laws   3537

IMITATE
many a public figure has come to imitate the
journalism which describes him   2572

380

IMITATION
No man was ever great by imitation.   2013

IMMORAL
they regard the whole thing as somewhat
 immoral   3502

IMMORALITY
To buy and sell land is an immorality   117
public immorality to ... lead an opposition on a
 certain plea   783

IMMORTALITY
nearest approach to immortality ... is a
 government bureau   6

IMMUNITY
immunity to eloquence is of the utmost
 importance to ... a democracy   23

IMPARTIAL
We must be impartial in thought as well as in
 action.   1638
There are only two ways to be quite unprejudiced
 and impartial.   2923
government ... which impartially secures to every
 man, whatever is his own.   3428
Inexorable as to principles, tolerant and impartial
 as to persons.   3450
the selective brutality of terrorism or the impartial
 horrors of war   3958

IMPATIENCE
Impatience is fatal in politics.   3226

IMPEACH
the only federal office in which the holder can
 neither be fired nor impeached   3031

IMPEACHMENT
if the system can stand impeachment   3013

IMPERATIVE
only one categorical imperative   1866

IMPERFECT
Decide on some imperfect Somebody and you will
 win   2829

IMPERFECTION
very easy to accuse a government of
 imperfection   1480

IMPERIALISM
By its economic essence imperialism is monopolist
 capitalism.   128
really universal enemy is ... Yankee
 imperialism   1696

IMPORTANT
ambitious not to make important decisions but to
 say important things   2598

IMPOSE
simply shows himself resolved to impose his
 opinions   595

IMPOSSIBLE
may make acceptable tomorrow what seems
 outrageous or impossible today   2794

IMPOSTUMATION
he that turneth the humours back ... endangereth
 ... pernicious impostumations   3082

IMPOTENCE
only equaled by their incurable impotence in
 exercising it   1093

IMPOVERISH
A reasonable internal debt will not impoverish our
 children   3614

IMPRISON
if two men, or a number of men imprison you,
 that is freedom   347
destroying the terrible walls which imprison
 men   720
No freeman shall be taken, or imprisoned   1829
Under a government which imprisons any
 unjustly   3518

IMPRISONMENT
willingly accepts ... imprisonment in order to
 arouse ... the community   1938

IMPROVE
A disposition to preserve, and an ability to
 improve   2021
It is a folly second to none,/ To try to improve
 the world.   3083

IMPROVEMENT
one cannot leave too large a space for
 improvements   230
The spirit of improvement is not always a spirit of
 liberty   1292

IMPRUDENCE
Nothing but a permanent body can check the
 imprudence of democracy.   297

INACCURACY
A little inaccuracy sometimes saves tons of
 explanation.   945

INACTIVITY
were confusing the duty of preservation with
 inactivity   191
The Commons ... remained in a wise and masterly
 inactivity.   2223
to abstain—to observe a wise and masterly
 inactivity   2231

INCAPABLE
When a people shall have become incapable of
 governing themselves   543

INCEST
Nationalism is our form of incest   2384

INCH
The ground of liberty is to be gained in
  inches.   1240
Ay, every inch a king.   1986

INCIDENT
Martyrs are needed to create incidents.   3258

INCITEMENT
Every idea is an incitement.   1123

INCLINATION
business of ministers ... to consult the inclinations
  of the people   2024

INCLUDE
I was not included in that "We, the people"   255

INCOGNITO
A sect or party is an elegant incognito   2463

INCOHERENT
if the laws be ... so incoherent that they cannot be
  understood   1917

INCOME
whose political actions are not ... to increase his
  own income   798
Socialism means equality of income or
  nothing.   3562

INCOME TAX
When there is an income tax, the just man will
  pay more   3576
Income Tax has made more Liars   3607

INCOMPARABLE
All nations have ... reasons for thinking
  themselves incomparable   2385

INCOMPATIBILITY
Incompatibility in the laws ... must render ... this
  great Country weak   3419

INCOMPATIBLE
I don't think ideas are incompatible with political
  reality.   2776

INCOMPLETE
the action an executive must take when he has
  information so incomplete   2159

INCONVENIENCE
the inconveniencies attending too much
  liberty   1243
Freedom remains still the wisest cure for
  freedom's temporary inconveniences.   1326

INCREASE
assets which it must turn over to the next
  generation increased   730

INCREDIBLE
One cannot fashion a credible deterrent out of an
  incredible action.   3933

INDEFENSIBLE
political speech ... largely the defense of the
  indefensible   2767

INDEPENDENCE
Liberty can no more exist without virtue and
  independence   1220
Those who won our independence believed that
  the final end of the State   1359
he who in the midst of the crowd keeps ... the
  independence of solitude   2047
Those who won our independence by revolution
  were not cowards.   3246
preserve their independence, we must not let our
  rulers load us with ... debt   3587
a holy war ... that which saved our liberties and
  gave us independence   3712

INDEPENDENT
Colonies do not cease to be colonies because they
  are independent.   1623
A judiciary independent of a king or executive
  alone, is a good thing;   1727
An independent is the guy who wants to take the
  politics out of politics.   2791
No country without an atom bomb could properly
  consider itself independent.   3937

INDIA
people thought that India was shaking   2212

INDICTMENT
I do not know the method of drawing up an
  indictment against a whole people.   842

INDIFFERENCE
The price of eternal vigilance is
  indifference.   1040
All politics are based on the indifference of the
  majority.   2793

INDIFFERENT
Communists have committed great crimes, but
  they have not ... been indifferent   169
Judges ... should be totally indifferent to pressures
  of the times   1963
The other is to be completely indifferent.   2923

INDIGNATION
the civil rights movement ... has restored the
  dignity of indignation   3373

INDISCRETION
forever poised between the cliche and the
  indiscretion   1663

INDISPENSABLE
no indispensable man in a democracy   438

INDIVIDUAL

The cult of the individual acquired such monstrous size   158

We must abolish the cult of the individual   159

Nations are not great ... because the individuals composing them are numerous   354

that every individual ... has an equal right to the protection of government   742

equal protection cannot mean one thing when applied to one individual   769

limit to ... interference of collective opinion with individual independence   1284

individual is not accountable to society for his actions   1286

The liberty of the individual must be thus far limited;   1287

An individual who breaks a law that conscience tells him is unjust   1938

The liberal, emphasizing the ... rights of the individual   2273

this case touches the heart of what makes individuals what they are   2322

The worth of a State ... is the worth of the individuals composing it   2367

not that you set the individual apart from society   3343

Yet they are the world of the individual person: 3352

fundamental interest all individuals have in ... their intimate associations   3403

whatever they ... can not do ... in their ... individual capacities   3452

As an individual who undertakes to live by borrowing   3596

individual beings are condemned by the monstrous conventions of politics   3816

INDIVIDUALISM

If the nineteenth century was a century of individualism   597

INDIVIDUALITY

Whatever crushes individuality is despotism   567

Individualities may form communities   2368

INDIVISIBLE

Freedom is an indivisible word.   1385

Freedom is indivisible   1447

Peace is indivisible.   3809

INDOLENT

having denounced us as indolent   2900

INDULGE

they are apt to indulge themselves excessively   3976

INDUSTRIALIST

to extend the political importance of the industrialists   1579

INDUSTRY

The other classes decay and finally disappear in the face of modern industry;   57

The principle of our Government is that of equal laws and freedom of industry.   345

Free speech does not live ... after free industry and free commerce die   1129

not justify our taxing industry ... to accumulate treasure for wars   3585

INEFFICIENCY

The only thing that saves us from the bureaucracy is inefficiency.   12

INEQUALITY

Inequality has the natural ... effect ... of materializing our upper class   66

The most grinding poverty is a trifling evil compared with inequality   72

Communism is inequality, but not as property is.   116

to form somewhere an inequality to their own advantage   323

no greater inequality than the equal treatment of unequals   762

INEQUITY

There is always inequity in life.   765

INEVITABLE

A war regarded as inevitable ... has a very good chance of ... being fought   3953

INEXACTITUDE

The politician is ... trained in the art of inexactitude.   2618

INEXORABLE

Inexorable as to principles, tolerant ... as to persons   3450

INEXPEDIENT

all governments are sometimes, inexpedient   1535

INFALLIBLE

we know that we are infallible only because we are final   1735

INFANCY

the moral obligation of providing for old age, helpless infancy   3426

INFANTILE

Nationalism is an infantile disease.   2377

INFERIOR

therefore they must be placed in an inferior position   751

No one can make you feel inferior without your consent.   2912

They must be made to realize that they are also human, not inferior.   2944

have been treated ... as inferior both by law and by
their fellow citizens   2946

I am the inferior of any man whose rights I
trample under foot.   3317

INFERIORITY

the lie of their inferiority is accepted as
truth   2938

INFERNO

an oasis amid the inferno of world
capitalism   138

INFIRMITY

A declining political class has all the infirmities of
old age   2756

INFLATION

Inflation is a great conservatizing issue.   225

Nothing so weakens government as persistent
inflation.   654

effects of inflation eat away at ties that bind us
together   660

maximum growth of government ... plus runaway
inflation   661

nothing wrong with the Republican Party that
double-digit inflation won't cure   3178

There's only one place where inflation is
made: 3627

INFLEXIBLE

Important principles may and must be
inflexible.   2073

INFLUENCE

chief justices have probably had more ... lasting
influence   1738

guard against the acquisition of unwarranted
influence   3904

INFLUENTIAL

If I have anything special that makes me
"influential"   2192

INFORMATION

A popular government without popular
information   675

nor can they be safe with them without
information   1166

INFRINGEMENT

Necessity is the plea for every infringement of
human freedom.   541

INGRATE

"Every time I fill a vacancy, I create a hundred
malcontents and one ingrate."   2525

INGRATITUDE

Power takes as ingratitude the writhing of its
victims.   2866

INGREDIENT

If I knew the ingredients I would bottle
them   2192

Political extremism involves two prime
ingredients: 2795

INHABITANT

Proclaim liberty throughout all the land unto all
the inhabitants thereof.   1198

INHERENT

the inherent right of the Government to lie to save
itself   1567

Of all the inherent duties of an American
President   3038

The right of revolution is the inherent right of a
people   3235

INHERIT

it is youth who must inherit the tribulation   3840

INHERITANCE

we cannot escape the burden of our
inheritance   366

INHIBITION

When you put on a uniform, there are certain
inhibitions   3867

INIMICAL

religions united with government are more or less
inimical to liberty   3145

INITIATIVE

unfortunately there can be government without
initiative   1562

INJUNCTION

not even protect a man from an injunction against
uttering words   1122

INJURY

It does me no injury for my neighbor to say there
are twenty gods   3142

INJUSTICE

true conservative ... has a real concern for
injustices   213

most powerful instrument ever devised by man for
breaking down injustice   720

A good man would prefer to be defeated than to
defeat injustice by evil means.   772

Mankind censures injustice, fearing that they may
be victims of it   1748

the source of justice was the fear of
injustice   1754

the laws of justice ... cannot subsist without
mixture of injustice   1758

love of justice ... is simply the fear of suffering
injustice   1761

Rigid justice is the greatest injustice.   1765

the feeling of injustice that is insupportable   1781

As long as justice and injustice have not
  terminated their ... fight   1786
National injustice is the surest road to national
  downfall.   1790
Justice is the sanction used to support established
  injustices.   1795
Injustice is whatever prevents my doing so.   1797
long after the sense of injustice in others has been
  thoroughly aroused   1801
Injustice is relatively easy to bear;   1802
Injustice anywhere is a threat to justice
  everywhere.   1811
Extreme law is often extreme injustice.   1823
majority of the people are often for injustice ...
  against the minority   2281
Injustice which lasts for three long
  centuries   2914
they are less afraid of suffering injustice at his
  hands   3135
they are pushed towards it by intolerable
  injustices   3244
They are not yet freed from the bonds of
  injustice;   3361
Government was intended to suppress
  injustice   3429
Where there is no property there is no
  injustice.   3516
An unrectified case of injustice has a terrible way
  of lingering   3538
Injustice ... displayed in the hour of
  triumph   3788
better to have a war for justice than peace in
  injustice   3839

INNOCENT
The willing sacrifice of the innocents   592
an innocent man convicted is the business of every
  honest person   1763
better that ten guilty persons escape, than that one
  innocent suffer   1768
better 100 guilty Persons should escape than that
  one innocent ... should suffer   1770
better to risk saving a guilty man than to condemn
  an innocent   1852
One can't reign and be innocent.   2022
Now and then an innocent man is sent to the
  legislature.   2244

INNOVATION
two parties ... the party of Conservatism and that
  of Innovation   2465

INSECURE
Successful democratic politicians are
  insecure   2608

INSEPARABLE
Liberty and Union ... one and inseparable   866

INSIGHT
Government is a matter of insight and of
  sympathy.   1549

INSOLENT
Power is so apt to be insolent   2835

INSPIRE
to inspire their souls with the conviction that filled
  me   2166
I have never accepted ... that I inspired the
  nation   3882

INSPIRING
Everything that is really great and inspiring   1408

INSTINCT
The instinct of the people is right.   339
I believe that justice is instinct and innate   1780
my instinct is always towards action   2040
War is not an instinct but an invention.   3815

INSTITUTION
worthy institutions can be conserved only by
  adjusting them   214
One can change human institutions but not
  man.   323
Democratic institutions are ... always a-
  making   366
Political institutions are a superstructure resting
  on an economic foundation.   641
core of our defense is the faith we have in the
  institutions we defend   963
end of our institutions ... that we may ... say what
  we think   1117
test of political institutions is the condition of the
  country   1543
Laws and institutions must go ... with the progress
  of the human mind   1876
institutions alone that can create a nation   2368
does not follow that ... excluding racial minorities
  from such institutions   3385
happiness of society are the objects at which all
  political institutions aim   3420
War challenges virtually every other
  institution   3831

INSTITUTIONALIZE
limited as law is as the institutionalized medium of
  reason   1930

INSTRUCTION
liberty can never be safe but in the hands of
  people with ... instruction   666

INSTRUMENT
the old instrument would be lost sight of
  altogether in a short time   239
A State which dwarfs its men ...that they may be
  more docile instruments   568
So efficient are the available instruments of
  slavery   612
The vote is the most powerful instrument ever
  devised   720

INSUPPORTABLE
the feeling of injustice that is insupportable   1781

INSURRECTION

Insurrection is the most sacred of duties.   3191

Insurrection ... warfare for all nations desirous of emancipating themselves   3204

Insurrection, n. An unsuccessful revolution.   3231

INTEGRATION

The myth of integration as propounded under the ... liberal ideology   2941

We are not fighting for integration   3366

INTEGRITY

One cannot be a Communist and preserve an iota of one's personal integrity.   181

the independence of party that you can maintain the integrity of public men   2471

dare to dispute the integrity of the President   2978

INTELLECTUAL

who believe themselves to be quite exempt from any intellectual influences   649

intellectual honesty is not the coin of the realm in politics   818

not just the luxury of one intellectual to write what he likes   1152

INTELLIGENCE

promote intelligence among the people as the means of preserving our liberties   671

Military intelligence is a contradiction in terms.   1077

The biggest menace to American freedom is the intelligence community.   1470

no inherent Constitutional authority for ... any intelligence agency   3024

It isn't wisdom or intelligence that influences a President   3027

the intelligence of public opinion is the ... condition of social progress   3051

We cannot allow the intelligence services ... to be dismantled   3496

Americans have always had an ambivalent attitude toward intelligence   3502

INTELLIGENT

If Napoleon had been as intelligent as Spinoza   2086

They may be just as intelligent as you say.   2623

INTEMPERATE

men of intemperate minds cannot be free   1244

INTENTION

Plain good intention ... is no mean force in the government of mankind   1495

INTERCOURSE

Two nations between whom there is no intercourse   51

friendly intercourse with all nations are ... the desire of our Government   1615

Courtesy ... and self-restraint should mark international ... intercourse   1633

INTERDEPENDENCE

There's too much interdependence in the world.   1427

INTEREST

A true natural aristocracy is not a separate interest   41

everything without exception, must be done in their interest   308

Commerce is the greatest of all political interests.   640

interest ... that education of the greatest number should be scientific   677

Compromise, n. Such an adjustment of conflicting interests   925

insofar as these concern the interests of no person but himself   1286

Only free peoples ... prefer the interests of mankind   1352

in no one's interest to overturn a government   1516

Government is more than the sum of all the interests;   1561

interests of those who govern ... to extend ... importance of industrialists   1579

Our interests are eternal ... and those interests it is our duty to follow   1619

friendships of nations ... cannot survive the mutability of those interests   1643

A state worthy of the name has no friends—only interests.   1675

every nation determines its policies in terms of its own interests   1682

Nations are linked only by interests.   1694

Justice is the great interest of man on earth.   1784

One person with a belief is ... equal to ninety-nine who have only interests   2069

Parliament is not a congress of ambassadors from different ... interests;   2221

scarcely any men more sour than those ... forced to be nice out of interest   2524

here to consult the interests ... of the people   2540

(The representative's) duty is to represent the interests of all those people   2671

Politics, n. A strife of interests   2724

the science of the adjustment of conflicting group interests   2751

for the very best interests of the whole people   2961

look out after the interests of the hundred and fifty million that are left   2983

interest all ... have in controlling the nature of their intimate associations   3403

finds his original means devoured by interest   3596

our interest is in concord not in conflict   3754

INTERFERE

Don't interfere with anything in the
 Constitution.   237

warranted ... in interfering with the liberty of
 action   1285

the less government interferes with private
 pursuits the better   3440

the ideal of government was for every man to be
 ... not interfered with   3469

INTERMEDDLE

no nation had a right to intermeddle in the
 internal concerns of another   1611

to do the labor not of an officious inter-meddler in
 the affairs of men   3449

INTERMEDIUM

Nobility ... is the intermedium between the king
 and the people   44

INTERNAL

Freedom is an internal achievement rather than an
 external judgment.   1460

Our national debt ... is an internal debt owed ... to
 the Nation   3614

INTERNATIONAL

so long as the sovereign state ... remains the basis
 of international life   1673

INTERPRET

The philosophers have only interpreted the world
 differently   2055

INTERPRETATION

We look ... to intervening history of
 interpretation   258

INTOLERABLE

in its worst state, an intolerable one   1497

INTOLERANCE

intolerance involves a certainty that unity will be
 destroyed   2919

INTOLERANT

what is dangerous about extremists is ... that they
 are intolerant   1041

INTRIGUE

the public business in Congress now connects itself
 with intrigues   2227

INVASION

invasion of armies can be resisted, but not an
 idea   880

behoves every man who values liberty of
 conscience ... to resist invasions   3143

INVENT

this very imperfect procedure is the best so far
 invented   498

a function of government to invent
 philosophies   1568

proud of the fact that I never invented weapons to
 kill   3776

INVENTION

War is not an instinct but an invention.   3815

INVESTIGATIVE

then serious investigative reporting will simply dry
 up   1192

INVISIBLE

led by an invisible hand to make nearly the same
 distribution   39

IRIDESCENT

The purification of politics is an iridescent
 dream.   1547

IRON

Not by speech-making ... but by iron and
 blood   894

then you have to have a touch of iron about
 you   2215

IRON CURTAIN

An iron curtain is drawn down upon their
 front.   149

From Stettin in the Baltic ... an iron curtain has
 descended   150

From behind the Iron Curtain, there are signs that
 tyranny is in trouble   610

IRONY

the irony of it is that if it is comfort or money
 that it values more   1381

IRRATIONAL

one can never legislate against the irrational
 itself   1942

IRRATIONALITY

politics consists in directing rationally the
 irrationalities of men   2799

IRRELIGION

The day that this country ceases to be free for
 irreligion   3159

IRRESPONSIBLE

the more power is divided the more irresponsible
 it becomes   2861

IRREVERENCE

Irreverence is the champion of liberty and its only
 sure defense.   1327

ISRAEL

Israel is not an aviary.   1052

387

ISSUE

Voters don't decide issues, they decide who will decide issues.   723

tempt one to believe that an issue deferred is a problem avoided   2204

the issue raised by this case touches the heart of what makes individuals   2322

our obligation to resolve issues—not to create them   2627

talk about huge issues in 30 seconds in a field somewhere   2670

ITCH

knowing every politician in the state and remembering where he itches   2604

JACKASS

Being president is like being a jackass in a hailstorm.   3009

Any jackass can draw up a balanced budget on paper.   3628

JAIL

he can bet there are good men in jail   1193

There are not enough jails, not enough policemen   1940

Mr. Emerson visited Thoreau at the jail   2054

Ye can't be sint to jail f'r it, but it's a kind iv a disgrace.   2965

people wud rather be wrong an' comfortable thin right in jail   3110

JAILER

Conformity is the jailer of freedom and the enemy of growth.   1434

JAW

The jaws of power are always open to devour   1214

To jaw-jaw always is better than to war-war.   3881

JEALOUS

Liberty is the most jealous and exacting mistress   1328

JEFFERSON

with the possible exception of when Thomas Jefferson dined alone   1032

Jefferson ... was a master politician   2987

Jefferson's Declaration of Independence is a practical document   3236

JEW

Then they came for the Jews, and I didn't speak up because I wasn't a Jew.   3342

JOB

Give us the tools and we will finish the job.   969

not by whining that one carries out the job of king   2031

the job is so vast and the need for wise judgment is so urgent   2147

fascination in this job is the illusion that ... you are being useful   2654

My God, this is a hell of a job!   2979

Any man who has had the job I've had   2982

I don't know of any human right that is more important than a job   3387

entitled to say, "Give me a job!" and the state is obliged to find a job   3458

a terribly hard job to spend a billion dollars   3617

(My job is) to give the president ... military advice   3966

JOIN

If you can't lick 'em, jine 'em.   950

JOKE

But history sometimes indulges in jokes of questionable taste.   146

The trouble with practical jokes is that very often they get elected.   2588

JOURNALISM

Responsible journalism is journalism responsible ... to the editor's conviction   1187

Journalism governs for ever and ever   2963

JOY

A Country can get more real joy out of just hollering for their Freedom   1404

You shall have joy, or you shall have power   2858

correctness of the path that women take is joy in the struggle   3283

JUDGE

The American aristocracy can be found in ... the judge's bench.   47

History is the judge;—its executioner, the proletarian.   125

Constitution was not written ... to be washed away by each wave of new judges   249

they, and not I, are the natural, lawful, and competent judges   290

rather trust twelve jurors ... than I would a judge   488

we are all able to judge it   496

Men are the best judges of the consequences of their own opinions   1238

We shall be judged more by what we do at home   1679

Judges must beware of hard constructions and strained inferences   1723

The duty of judges is to render justice;   1724

but the Constitution is what the judges say it is   1731

But even judges sometimes progress.   1732

when it deals with judge-made ... law having little or no cognizable roots   1746

too lazy ... to think for themselves and be their own judges 1911

Judges ... rule on the basis of law, not public opinion 1963

The most certain test by which we judge whether a country is really free 2297

"you mustn't judge us by our politicians" 2568

fair to judge peoples by the rights they will sacrifice most for 3334

JUDGMENT

We hold the view that the people make the best judgment in the long run. 469

the reason democracy works is because as you multiply judgements 488

but no one complains about his judgement 832

One cool judgment is worth a thousand hasty counsels. 2105

the job is so vast and the need for wise judgment is so urgent 2147

There cannot be a greater Judgement befall a Country 2445

Your representative owes you, not his industry only, but his judgment; 2527

Power-worship blurs political judgment 2770

JUDICIAL

the ... duty of the judicial department to say what the law is 1726

hardly a political question ... which does not ... turn into a judicial one 1729

judicial system is the most expensive machine ever invented 1740

Judicial decrees may not change the heart 1935

JUDICIARY

The judiciary ... is the subtle corps of sappers 1727

the judiciary is the safeguard of our liberty 1731

(The judiciary is) the least dangerous branch 1744

JUICE

They don't know what Washington juice is made of. 2768

JUNGLE

not a jungle war, but a struggle for freedom 3920

JUNKET

Give a member of Congress a junket 2659

JUROR

rather trust twelve jurors with all their prejudices and biases 488

JUST

No man can be just who is not free. 1337

All virtue is summed up in dealing justly. 1750

unable to make what is just strong, we have made what is strong just 1762

One can't be just if one is not human at the same time. 1766

Be just before you're generous. 1767

To be just is not simply doing right 1776

Once the laws are just, then men will be just. 1793

the just can be strong in the defense of justice 1810

In politics nothing is just save what is honest; 2683

I tremble for my country when I reflect that God is just; 3291

When there is an income tax, the just man will pay more 3576

In order for a war to be just, three things are necessary. 3665

And if there was ever a just war since the world began 3697

History shows that wars are divided into two kinds, just and unjust. 3821

JUSTICE

Where justice is denied ... neither persons nor property will be safe 75

Communism is the corruption of a dream of justice. 153

We current Justices read the Constitution in the only way we can 259

a patient confidence in the ultimate justice of the people 341

Man's capacity for justice makes democracy possible 434

The slave begins by demanding justice 608

moderation in the pursuit of justice is no virtue 1042

Justice and liberty have neither birth nor race, youth nor age. 1245

lies at the foundation of the sense of justice there is in me 1276

The foreign policy adopted by our government is to do justice to all 1614

Equal and exact justice should characterize all our intercourse 1618

The duty of judges is to render justice; 1724

Let justice be done, though the sky falls. 1725

chief justices have probably had more profound ... influence 1738

it involves justice. That's what is important. 1739

Everywhere ... one principle of justice ... the interest of the stronger 1749

no such thing as justice in the abstract 1751

More law, less justice. 1753

that the source of justice was the fear of injustice 1754

Justice is that virtue that assigns to every man his due. 1755

there is no right where there is no justice 1756

One of the uses of our system of justice is to warn others. 1757

laws of justice ... cannot subsist without mixture of injustice   1758

Extreme justice is often unjust.   1760

love of justice in most men is simply the fear of suffering injustice   1761

Justice without strength is powerless, strength without justice is tyrannical   1762

the rest is Cruelty, not Justice   1764

Rigid justice is the greatest injustice.   1765

attaining a civil society which can administer justice universally   1769

administration of justice is the firmest pillar of Government.   1771

Justice is itself the great standing policy of civil society;   1773

justice, not charity, that is wanting in the world   1774

Equal and exact justice to all men of whatever state or persuasion   1775

There is no authority without justice.   1777

justice means force as well as virtue   1779

I believe that justice is instinct and innate   1780

Justice is truth in action.   1783

Justice is the great interest of man on earth.   1784

Sir, I say that justice is truth in action.   1785

justice and injustice have not terminated their ... fight for ascendancy   1786

severest justice may not always be the best policy   1787

mercy bears richer fruits than strict justice   1789

Justice and good will will outlast passion.   1791

Justice should remove the bandage from her eyes   1792

r-right when he says: "Justice is blind."   1794

Justice is the sanction used to support established injustices.   1795

Justice is my being allowed to do whatever I like.   1797

The firm basis of government is justice, not pity.   1798

men who decide all cases with impartial justice   1799

that justice and judgment lie often a world apart   1800

our sense of justice never turns in its sleep   1801

what stings is justice   1802

Thou shall not ration justice.   1804

Peace and justice are two sides of the same coin.   1805

not be satified until justice rolls down like waters   1808

Justice is like a train that's nearly always late.   1809

Injustice anywhere is a threat to justice everywhere.   1811

Justice delayed is democracy denied.   1812

Get out of the way of justice. She is blind.   1813

The price you pay for peace is justice.   1814

the scales of American justice are out of balance   1815

to none deny or delay, right or justice   1830

When kings the sword of justice first lay down   2338

sad duty of politics is to establish justice in a sinful world   2804

To me, the black man, it is a place where justice is dispensed with.   2931

a courthouse ... is a place where justice is dispensed   2931

If powerful men will not write justice with black ink   3213

Until justice is blind to color ... emancipation ... will not be a fact   3362

Justice is never given; it is exacted.   3380

Justice is the end of government.   3422

As man seeks justice in equality   3443

The administration of justice lies at the foundation of government.   3467

a world opinion made ready to grant justice precisely as it exacts it   3793

justice is better served in conferences of peace than in conflicts at arms   3793

The only true and lasting peace (is) based on justice and right.   3795

better to have a war for justice than peace in injustice   3839

The human man can invent peace with justice.   3875

JUSTIFY

Only he deserves power who every day justifies it.   2181

Disapproval of homosexuality cannot justify invading the houses   3402

KANSAS

When Kansas and Colorado have a quarrel ... in the Arkansas River   1656

Kansas had better stop raising corn and begin raising hell.   3107

KENNEDY

The Kennedy organization doesn't run, it purrs.   2434

Senator, you're no Jack Kennedy.   2441

Kennedy said that if we had nuclear war we'd kill 300 million people   3935

KEY

the key to failure is trying to please everybody   2198

it is the key to that era   3208

Here's the key, there's the Treasury   3630

KHRUSHCHEV

Khrushchev reminds me of the tiger hunter   1027

Keyword Index

KITCHEN

"If you can't stand the heat, get out of the kitchen." 2164

KLANSMAN

any more than a Klansman with a sheet on his back 3370

KNEE

To kick over an idol, you must first get off your knees. 2495

Better to die on one's feet than to live on one's knees. 3340

KNIGHT

our knight wins by no clean thrust of lance or sword 495

KNOCK

You knock over the first one 999

KNOT

When you get to the end of your rope, tie a knot and hang on. 962

Battle, n. A method of untying with the teeth a political knot 3765

KNOW

He who knows only his own side of the case, knows little of that. 1115

but I know it when I see it 1939

The leader must know, must know he knows 2179

He knows nothing and he thinks he knows everything. 2565

What did the president know and when did he know it? 3015

KNOWLEDGE

Liberty cannot be preserved without general knowledge among the people. 665

Knowledge ... is our best protection against unreasoning prejudice 691

If we value the pursuit of knowledge, we must be free to follow wherever 693

to make use of this knowledge or not according to his need 1978

Knowledge of human nature is the beginning and end of political education. 2726

the bitterest pain among men, to have much knowledge but no power 2832

Knowledge is power. 2833

a knowledge of the means by which that object can be best attained 3421

KREMLIN

Until we stop pushing the Kremlin against a closed door 1667

KU KLUX KLAN

The Ku Klux Klan never dies. They just stop wearing sheets 2945

LABEL

Radicalism ... is always applied to people who are endeavoring to get freedom 1355

LABOR

a convenient belief to those who live on the labor of others 74

If capital an' labor ever do git t'gether it's good night fer th' rest of us. 89

Vote Labor and you build castles in the air. 219

characteristics of a free ... nation that it have free ... labor unions 421

the totalitarian or closed society ... brutish direction of labor 616

Labour ... is the only universal ... measure of value 633

The demand of the Labour party is for economic freedom. 1320

shall not take from the mouth of labor the bread it has earned 1517

If there is a free contract, in open market, between capital and labour 2239

When we (Labor) get into trouble, we start blaming each other 2501

Labor ... cannot be free so long as labor in a black skin is branded 2905

the labour of those who would ameliorate the conditions of the working classes 3101

What is said by great employers of labour against agitators is ... true 3104

Property is the fruit of labor. 3521

I am weary seeing our laboring classes so wretchedly housed 3522

Labor may be likened to a man who ... is waylaid by a series of robbers 3555

If the Labour Party is not going to be a Socialist Party 3571

The two most important emotions of the Labour Party 3573

LABORER

The English laborer does not find his worst enemy in the nobility 48

Man exists for his own sake and not to add a laborer to the State. 3441

LACK

Lack of money is the root of all evil. 3524

LADY

If particular care is not paid to the ladies 3977

LAISSER FAIRE

Socialism and laisser faire are like the north and south poles. 3560

LAME DUCK

how many swan songs can a lame duck deliver? 1069

LAMP

The lamps are going out all over Europe 930

LAND

Proclaim liberty throughout all the land   1198

But I will love that land where man is free,/ And that will I defend.   1418

Peace is much more precious than a piece of land.   3955

LANDMARK

one of the great landmarks in men's struggle to be free   1417

LANDSCAPE

The landscape should belong to the people who see it all the time.   3548

LANGUAGE

The language of laws should be simple;   1856

The language of the law must not be foreign   1916

No one has a finer command of language than the person who keeps his mouth shut   2163

Political language ... is designed to make lies sound truthful   2498

no greater liability than a command of language   2616

Finality is not the language of politics.   2698

LARCENY

taxes which are not absolutely required ... is ... a species of ... larceny   3609

LAST

The Last Hurrah.   1008

LATE

Justice is like a train that's nearly always late.   1809

But what in hell have you done for me lately?   2774

It is never too late to give up our prejudices.   2901

LATITUDE

Liberty is so much latitude as the powerful choose to accord   1364

LAUGH

it hurt too bad to laugh, and he was too big to cry   884

LAUREL

Whether in chains or in laurels, liberty knows nothing but victories.   1290

Let arms yield to the toga, the laurel crown to praise.   3653

LAW

There is a higher law than the Constitution.   235

Our great republic is a government of laws   254

free ... where the laws rule and the people are a party to the laws   275

or Restraint of any Law, but what the Legislative shall enact   278

the rights to have the law ... applied to every citizen   483

The laws can't be enforced against the man who is the laws' master.   523

Where law ends, tyranny begins.   536

Whatever government is not a government of laws, is a despotism   555

For what people have always sought is equality before the law.   738

Free Discussion is the ... only necessary Law of the Constitution   1111

Laws alone cannot secure freedom of expression;   1133

Liberty is the right of doing whatever the laws permit.   1209

wise see in it ... the potent Law of Laws   1314

The shallow consider liberty a release from all law   1314

when it can not take a long breath, laws are girdled too tight   1318

Liberty fixed in unalterable law would be no liberty at all   1333

Man in Society is not free where there is no law;   1409

A government of laws, and not of men.   1493

confine each member of society within the limits prescribed by the law   1512

corporation ... must be held to strict compliance with the ... fundamental law   1584

no worse torture than the torture of laws   1723

duty of the judicial department to say what the law is   1726

What five members of the Supreme Court say the law is   1733

not our job to apply laws that have not yet been written   1743

nearest to illegitimacy when it deals with judge-made constitutional law   1746

More law, less justice.   1753

laws of justice ... cannot subsist without mixture of injustice   1758

For the law holds, that it is better that ten guilty persons escape   1768

When I refuse to obey an unjust law   1782

Once the laws are just, then men will be just.   1793

th' equal iv ivry other man befure th' law   1796

Law is order, and good law is good order.   1819

Even when laws have been written down, they ought not always remain unaltered   1820

Whereas the law is passionless, passion must ever sway the heart of man.   1821

Good laws if they are not obeyed   1822

Extreme law is often extreme injustice.   1823

The good of the people is the supreme law.   1824

No law is quite appropriate for all.   1825

Certain laws have not been written, but they are more fixed   1826

The law is good, if a man use it lawfully.   1827

Laws are like spider's webs 1828

except by the legal judgment of his peers or by the law of the land 1829

Law: an ordinance of reason for the common good 1831

Whoever desires to found a state and give it laws 1833

good morals ... have need of the laws, so the laws ... have need of good morals 1835

If we insist ... that sovereign power means exemption from all law 1837

Nothing is more subject to change than the laws. 1838

In law, what plea so tainted and corrupt 1840

We must not make a scarecrow of the law 1841

Laws that only threaten, and are not kept 1842

Where-ever Law ends, Tyranny begins. 1845

Laws are like cobwebs, which may catch small flies 1849

The more laws, the more offenders. 1850

Law cannot persuade where it cannot punish. 1851

The wording of laws should mean the same thing to all men. 1853

Care must be taken that laws do not offend against nature. 1854

Laws should not be changed without good reason. 1855

The language of laws should be simple; 1856

Laws should not be subtle; 1857

useless laws weaken necessary ones 1858

Laws too gentle are seldom obeyed; 1859

The first of all laws is to respect the laws: 1860

Laws grind the poor, and rich men rule the law. 1862

Laws made by common consent must not be trampled on by individuals. 1865

The law is the last result of human wisdom acting upon human experience 1867

Government implies the power of making laws. 1868

dangerous that even a guilty person should be punished without the forms of law 1870

The execution of the laws is more important than the making of them. 1871

but one law for all ... that law which governs all law, the law of our Creator 1872

The mass of the people have nothing to do with the laws but to obey them. 1873

Men have feelings but the law does not. 1875

Laws ... must go hand in hand with the progress of the human mind 1876

Laws are made for men of ordinary understanding 1877

victim to too severe a law is considered as a martyr 1878

"The Law will admit of no rival" 1879

If a law commands me to sin I will break it; 1880

the worst I wish the law is that his eye may be opened by experience 1881

"If the law supposes that ... the law is a ass—a idiot 1881

Our written law is often difficult to understand 1882

Good men must not obey the laws too well. 1883

The law is only a memorandum. 1884

Many laws as certainly make bad men, as bad men make many laws. 1888

I know no method to secure the repeal of bad or obnoxious laws 1889

Laws are like medicine; 1890

Coercion is the basis of every law in the universe 1891

The law embodies the story of a nation's development 1892

It usually takes a hundred years to make a law 1893

Riches without law are more dangerous than is poverty without law. 1894

Law will never be strong ... unless ... the sentiment of the people behind it 1895

To the law we bow with reverence. 1896

the exceptional liberty we enjoy within the law ... and by the law 1898

Law is merely the expression of the will of the strongest 1899

Law is largely crystallized custom 1900

Every new time will give its law. 1902

Today there's law and order in everything. 1903

No man is above the law and no man is below it; 1904

Laws are sand, customs are rock. Laws can be evaded 1906

It cannot be helped ... that the law is behind the times 1907

that is what laws are for, to be made and unmade. 1908

As in law so in war, the longest purse finally wins. 1910

Those who are too lazy ... obey the laws 1911

One with the law is a majority. 1912

The law must be stable, but it must not stand still. 1913

In a government of laws ... imperilled if it fails to observe the law 1914

The law is ... made for the exploitation of those who do not understand it 1915

The language of the law must not be foreign 1916

if the laws be so voluminous that they cannot be read 1917

of little avail ... that the laws are made by men of their own choice 1917

Nobody has a more sacred obligation to obey the law 1918

If one man can be allowed to determine ... what is law, every man can 1919

An unjust law is itself a species of violence. 1920

Government can ... exist without law, but law cannot exist without government 1921

Every so often, we pass laws repealing human nature. 1922

Laws presumably express the conscience of a nation 1923

you cannot change people's hearts merely by laws 1923

whether we obey the law only when we approve of it 1924

Common sense often makes good law. 1925

We have never stopped sin by passing laws; 1927

We have never stopped sin by passing laws; 1927

The police must obey the law while enforcing the law. 1928

Fragile as reason is and limited as law is 1930

The law is a causeway upon which ... a citizen may walk safely 1931

defiance of the law is the surest road to tyranny 1932

observance of the law is the eternal safeguard of liberty 1932

In civilized life, law floats in a sea of ethics. 1933

It may be true that the law cannot make man love me 1934

Law alone cannot make men see right. 1936

Law is experience developed by reason 1937

not enough courts to enforce a law not supported by the people 1940

If there isn't a law, there will be. 1943

This is what has to be remembered about the law: 1944

The rule of law can be wiped out in one misguided ... generation. 1945

Law is a reflection and a source of prejudice. 1946

men of law have been persistently concerned with the resolution of disputes 1947

laws are an attempt to domesticate the natural ferocity of the species 1949

times when national interest is more important than the law 1951

Things in law tend to be black and white. 1954

We have the means to change the laws we find unjust 1956

far too much law for those who can afford it 1957

(Law is) vulnerable to the winds of intellectual or moral fashion 1958

under the law everything is prohibited except that which is permitted 1959

Law's empire is defined by attitude 1960

Moral principle is the foundation of law. 1961

The law ... is constantly based on notions of morality 1962

Judges ... rule on the basis of law 1963

A taxpaying public that doesn't understand the law ... can't comply 1964

that he found law dear and left it cheap 2042

Only make wise and moderate laws. 2225

cannot be right that one of the ... parties should have the making of the laws 2239

If you love the law and you love good sausage 2259

A good king will frame his actions to be according to the Law 2326

Loyalty is a sentiment, not a law. 2372

to execute the laws which the people have made 2556

Power politics is the diplomatic name for the law of the jungle. 2764

Law not served by power is an illusion; but power not ruled by law is a menace 2887

law ... permitting discrimination in public education must yield 2922

far deeper than any law for or against discrimination 2925

a besetting disposition to make publick opinion stronger than the law 3044

No written law has ever been more binding than unwritten custom 3061

There must be public opinion back of the laws 3062

wealth has a wholesome respect for the law 3065

Laws do not make reforms, reforms make laws. 3119

Let the law be ruthless and order will be restored. 3194

the first inroads upon the laws have been made by the governors 3198

Human law may know no distinction among men in respect of rights 3316

where ... any rights existed ... until ... a duly promulgated body of laws 3333

to write the next chapter—and to write it in books of law 3359

will not deny the equal protection of the law to the unwashed 3376

The less government we have, the better—the fewer laws 3448

preserving free government except that the executive be under the law 3513

Hungry men have no respect for law 3529

Not one cent should be raised unless it is in accord with the law. 3586

Laws are silent in time of war. 3652

will not hold ourselves bound by any laws in which we have no voice 3977

When man, governed by reasonable laws, enjoys his natural freedom 3978

LAW AND ORDER

a vast conspiracy against the forces of law and order 105

respect for law and order ... in precise relationship to ... his paycheck 108

When law and order prevail in the land, a man may be bold in speech 1106

LAWBREAKER

more or less what the law declares them:
  lawbreakers 3370
We are here, not because we are
  lawbreakers; 3990

LAWFUL

The law is good, if a man use it lawfully. 1827
one should not stop for a moment to consider
  whether something is lawful 1834
certain inherently governmental actions which ...
  are lawful 1950

LAWGIVER

you are the rulers and the ruled, the lawgivers and
  the law-abiding 457

LAWLESSNESS

No good cause can be promoted upon the lines of
  lawlessness. 1897

LAWMAKER

What the lawmaker has to ascertain is not the true
  belief 3078
we are here in our efforts to become lawmakers 3990

LAWYER

The American aristocracy can be found in the
  lawyer's bar 47
The first thing we do, let's kill all the
  lawyers. 1839
It is not, what a lawyer tells me I may do; 1864
The lawyer's truth is not Truth 1886
act ... where no contrary opinion of a lawyer can
  be had, we should never act 2030
That 150 lawyers should do business together is
  not to be expected. 2229
And who benefits most? The lawyers. 2798

LAZY

Those who are too lazy ... obey the laws 1911

LEAD

Education makes a people easy to lead 676
the beaten path doesn't seem to be leading
  anywhere 2191
its glory is to lead them not where they want to
  go 2691
to lead by reason and a gift of cooperation 2864

LEADER

he is always stirring up some war ... that the
  people may require a leader 520
our best protection against ... panic-stricken
  leaders 691
history of the world's great leaders is often the
  story of human folly 2010
A leader of whom it is said, "he's a nice man," is
  lost. 2029
To be a leader of men one must turn one's back
  on men. 2078

harder for a leader to be born in a palace 2097
The great leaders have always stage-managed their
  effects. 2126
The king presupposes subjects; the leader,
  followers. 2128
The real leader has no need to lead—he is content
  to point the way. 2135
final test of a leader is that he leaves behind ... the
  will to carry on 2142
The leader is always alone in times of
  doom. 2155
You cannot be a leader ... unless you know how to
  follow 2169
The leader must know, must know he
  knows 2179
A political leader must keep looking over his
  shoulder 2180
If an individual wants to be a leader and isn't
  controversial 2199
A leader should not get too far in front of his
  troops 2207
I am a leader by default 2214
A boss is a political leader who is on somebody
  else's side. 2645
not of the stuff of which leaders are made 2778
Jefferson ... was a master politician, and this
  helped make him a great leader 2987
a time when leaders should keep their ears to the
  ground 3074
so simple as to take literally ... the things their
  leaders tell them 3075
never be happy unless they ... are about to be
  betrayed by their leaders 3574

LEADERSHIP

Leadership and learning are indispensable to each
  other. 696
You know what makes leadership? 2146
Charismatic leadership is hungered for 2196
So long as the people ... place hopes of political
  salvation in leadership 2546
It is right and wrong, and leadership ... that make
  ... history 3076

LEAN

Liberty & Learning, each leaning on the
  other 674
Lean liberty is better than fat slavery. 1207
Better a lean peace than a fat victory. 3685

LEAP

the House of Commons is taking ... a leap
  absolutely in the dark 891
No doubt we are making a great experiment and
  taking a leap in the dark. 902

LEARN

prevail on our future masters to learn their
  letters 680
Freedom to learn is the first necessity 1374

LEARNED

Learned Institutions ought to be favorite objects with every free people.   673

LEARNING

indirectly because it is more favorable to learning   309

What spectacle can be more edifying ... than that of Liberty & Learning   674

the want of learning is a calamity to any people   683

A little learning ... may be a dangerous thing   683

always those with little learning who overthrow those with much learning   694

Liberty without learning is always in peril   695

Leadership and learning are indispensable to each other.   696

LEAST

Yet it is the opinion of the least able.   273

Vote for the man who promises least; he'll be the least disappointing.   716

LEAVE

This country is so bad ... that we can't let anyone leave   1490

LEFT

A sharp Right turn ... is likely to be followed by an even sharper Left turn.   227

I felt somehow ... that Washington and Hamilton, just left me out by mistake   255

the Right and the Left, and in the middle is the Swamp.   2729

The definition of the Left   3574

LEGAL

a society with no other scale but the legal one is not quite worthy of man   1953

LEGISLATE

Morality cannot be legislated, but behavior can be regulated.   1935

One can always legislate against specific acts of human wickedness;   1942

one can never legislate against the irrational itself   1942

You cannot legislate for virtue.   3112

not until then ... will he be able to legislate as wisely   3988

LEGISLATION

Legislation is not changed every day.   2226

The science of legislation is like that of medicine   2230

The great problem of legislation is, so to organize the civil government   2232

Nearly all legislation is the result of compromise.   2245

illuminate their rude legislation with burning castles   3213

LEGISLATIVE

The Liberty of Man ... is to be under no other Legislative Power   278

when the legislative power is nominated by the executive   3509

LEGISLATOR

Poets and philosophers are the unacknowledged legislators of the world.   857

obstacles which legislators are continually putting in their way   1581

it is the legislator who has given stability and continuity   2254

Legislators represent people, not trees or acres.   2257

a great deal easier ... to use one's influence with the legislators   2968

LEGISLATURE

we have some legislatures that bring higher prices than any in the world   786

No man's life ... are safe while the Legislature is in session   2236

legislatures are ultimate guardians of the liberties   2241

Now and then an innocent man is sent to the legislature.   2244

The legislature ... has ceased to be even the creature of the people   2249

Public opinion is stronger than the legislature   3052

LEGITIMATE

only legitimate right to govern is an express grant of power from the governed   326

A government is not legitimate merely because it exists.   1575

power is legitimate only when it is under contract   2876

LENIN

The working class is for a Lenin what ore is for a metal worker.   129

Lenin had a revolution to practice on and Marx had not   162

LENINISM

Leninism is a combination of two things   140

LEPROSY

clung to them like an hereditary leprosy   2845

LESS

Democracy is ... less bad than any other   389

The less government we have, the better   3448

LESSON

the most important lesson that a man can learn   2496

LET

the right to be let alone—the most comprehensive of rights   3339

LETTER

you should prevail on our future masters to learn
their letters   680

LEVEL

not that every man shall be on a level with every
other man   360

a chance to play for higher stakes and perform at
a higher level   2815

LIABILITY

American newspapers as one of its assets--liability
would be a better term   1174

no greater liability than a command of
language   2616

LIAR

The Income Tax has made more Liars   3607

LIBEL

Political truth is a libel—religious truth
blasphemy.   856

LIBERAL

distinguished from the Liberal, who wishes to
replace them with others   207

Somehow liberals have been unable to acquire
from life   221

A conservative is a liberal who was mugged the
night before.   223

The Liberals talk about a stable
government   1047

There are times when one must govern
liberally   1545

criticism of the criminal justice system ... was so
much liberal bleating   1817

I am a moderate liberal, as all rational people
are   2266

Liberal institutions straightway cease from being
liberal   2268

A liberal mind is a mind that is able to imagine
itself believing anything.   2270

A Liberal is a man who uses his legs ... at the
behest ... of his head   2271

duty of the liberal to protect ... the basic
democratic freedoms   2272

essence of the Liberal outlook lies not in what
opinions are held   2274

We who are liberal ... know that the poor are our
equals   2275

a liberal is a man who tells other people what to
do with their money   2276

The liberals in the House strongly resemble
liberals I have known   2277

There are no more liberals. ... They've all been
mugged.   2279

Is either a little Liberal/ Or else a little
Conservative!   2486

liberal ideology ... makes people believe that
something is being achieved   2941

The Negro revolution is controlled by foxy white
liberals   3273

liberal governments have been wrecked on rocks
of loose fiscal policy   3612

LIBERALISM

Liberalism is trust of the people tempered by
prudence;   2267

The main principle ... of liberalism is the rejection
of the divine law   2269

Political liberalism should also be defined in terms
of objectives.   2273

Politics without ideology ... equals
Liberalism   2278

LIBERATE

We have to talk about liberating minds as well as
liberating society.   1463

it's men who must be liberated in this
country   4009

LIBERATION

first step toward liberation ... is to use the power
in hand   721

Liberation is not deliverance.   1300

liberation of the diverse energies of free nations
and free men   1443

True liberation can be acquired ... only when the
Negro people possess power   2872

the indispensable condition of the liberation of the
human being   3559

LIBERTY

An efficient bureaucracy is the greatest threat to
liberty.   12

If liberty and equality ... are chiefly to be found in
democracy   264

The basis of a democratic state is liberty.   266

"Liberty, freedom, and enfranchisement."   270

The Liberty of Man ... is to be under no other
Legislative Power   278

trust no man living with power to endanger the
public liberty   283

Real liberty is neither found in despotism or the
extremes of democracy   295

liberty doesn't even go to the trouble of
accomplishing small things legally   318

but that every man shall have liberty to be what
God made him   360

peace must be planted on the ... foundations of
political liberty   386

retain all personal liberty which does not adversely
affect their neighbors   410

foundation of democratic liberty is a willingness to
believe   445

For the people, I desire their liberty and
freedom   526

The more a regime claims to be the embodiment
of liberty   627

Liberty cannot be preserved without general
knowledge   665

warranted ... in interfering with liberty ... is self-protection 1285

The liberty of the individual must be thus far limited; 1287

Liberty consists in doing what one desires. 1288

liberty knows nothing but victories 1290

I am the son of Liberty and to her I owe all that I am. 1296

Liberty ... we understand as the faculty of choosing 1297

Human liberty, the only true foundation of human government. 1301

Where Slavery is, there Liberty cannot be; 1302

the wolf denounces him for the same act, as the destroyer of liberty 1303

Where the State begins, individual liberty ceases 1306

I should fight for my liberty as long as my strength lasted 1309

one of two things I had a right to, liberty or death 1309

Liberty is not a means to a higher political end. 1310

Liberty, next to religion, has been ... the common pretext of crime 1312

The shallow consider liberty a release from all law 1314

Liberty cannot live apart from constitutional principle. 1316

When liberty becomes license 1317

Liberty is the soul's right to breathe 1318

Liberty recast the old forms of government into the Republic 1321

Liberty produces wealth and wealth destroys liberty. 1322

Liberty and monopoly cannot live together. 1323

Irreverence is the champion of liberty 1327

Liberty is the most jealous and exacting mistress 1328

Liberty means responsibility. 1329

distinction between freedom and liberty is not accurately known 1331

Liberty, n. One of Imagination's most precious possessions. 1332

The ideals of liberty cannot be fixed from generation to generation; 1333

Liberty is the means in the pursuit of happiness. 1334

Liberty trains for liberty. 1335

The cost of liberty is less than the price of repression. 1336

The history of liberty is a history of limitations of governmental power 1340

Liberty has never come from the government. 1340

Liberty is its own reward. 1341

You cannot ... safely plant the tree of liberty in soil that is not native 1342

than to a rich nation that had ceased to be in love with liberty 1343

Liberty does not consist ... in mere general declarations of the rights of man 1346

Liberty is often a fierce and intractable thing 1349

We do not profess to be the champions of liberty 1353

Liberty is not collective, it is personal. 1356

All liberty is individual liberty. 1356

They valued liberty both as an end and as a means. 1359

They believed liberty to be the secret of happiness 1359

Liberty don't work as good in practice as it does in Speech. 1360

greatest dangers to liberty lurk in insidious encroachment 1361

Liberty is so much latitude as the powerful choose 1364

liberty is the hardest test that one can inflict on a people 1365

a rarer thing to give liberty to others who do not agree with us 1366

Liberty is not just an idea, an abstract principle. 1367

saddest epitaph which can be carved in memory of a vanished liberty 1373

you cannot create liberty when it has gone 1380

If liberty has any meaning it means freedom to improve. 1383

liberty has largely been ... the observance of procedural safeguards 1384

Liberty lies in the hearts of men and women; 1389

spirit of liberty is ... not too sure it is right 1393

Political liberty is nothing else but the diffusion of power. 1395

The cause of liberty becomes a mockery 1401

Too little liberty brings stagnation 1403

Liberty is the possibility of doubting 1410

We can afford no liberties with liberty itself. 1415

We can afford no liberties with liberty itself. 1415

Liberty is always unfinished business. 1422

Liberty is never out of bounds or off limits; 1432

There is no "slippery slope" toward loss of liberties 1471

(American liberty) is premised on the accountability of free men 1473

as government expands, liberty contracts 1475

(Liberty) is indeed little less than a name 1512

we shall pay any price ... to assure the survival and the success of liberty 1670

the judiciary is the safeguard of our liberty and of our property 1731

Liberty, my fellow citizens, is responsibilty 1898

representatives of the people are not defenders of
  liberty　2228
legislatures are the ultimate guardians of the
  liberties ... of the people　2241
Liberty is to faction what air is to fire　2455
Liberty to be saucy　2835
and Liberty but its satellite　2843
then liberty will soon be dead in this nation　3029
To give moderate liberty for griefs and
  discontentments to evaporate　3082
It behoves every man who values liberty of
  conscience for himself　3143
All religions united with government are ...
  inimical to liberty　3145
tree of liberty grows only when watered by the
  blood of tyrants　3193
The spirit of revolution ... is a spirit radically
  opposed to liberty　3200
a nation which has undertaken to be the refuge of
  liberty　3210
They did not exalt order at the cost of
  liberty.　3246
This country should be agitated ... till the battle of
  liberty is won　3319
Next to the right of liberty, the right of property
  is the most important　3330
the personal right to liberty and the personal right
  in property　3382
The true aim of government is liberty.　3409
wherever these two powers are united together,
  there can be no public liberty　3505
Peace is liberty in tranquility;　3656
Women have, or ought to have, but little
  liberty;　3976

LIBRARY
I heard his library burned down and that both
  books were destroyed　2665

LICENSE
License of the press is no proof of liberty.　1157
the tendency of its liberty to degenerate into
  license　1171
When liberty becomes license　1317

LICK
If you can't lick 'em, jine 'em.　950
I believe that we could ... single-handed lick any
  nation in the world.　1646
In politics women ... type the letters, lick the
  stamps　4006

LIE
Communist countries never expel correspondents
  for telling lies.　178
A lie is an abomination unto the Lord　803
Repetition does not transform a lie into a
  truth.　958
But it means, above all things, freedom from
  lies.　1363

the inherent right of the Government to lie to save
  itself　1567
an honest man sent to lie abroad for the good of
  his country　1603
Then he doesn't lie.　2432
All political parties die at last of swallowing their
  own lies.　2448
Political language ... is designed to make lies
  sound truthful　2498
McCarthy invented the multi Lie—the lie with so
  many tiny gears　2617
if they stop telling lies about us, we would stop
  telling the truth　3172

LIEUTENANT
The most terrible warfare is to be a second
  lieutenant leading a platoon　3884

LIFE
namely, the enjoyment of life and liberty　286
experience of democracy is like the experience of
  life itself　489
The poorest he ... hath a life to live as the greatest
  he　739
Life'd not be worth livin' if we didn't keep our
  inimies.　921
Believe in life!　1014
Is life so dear, or peace so sweet　1219
For what avail the plow or sail,/ Or land or life, if
  freedom fail?　1305
There are two good things in life—freedom of
  thought and freedom of action.　1348
Freedom has its life in the hearts　1390
Government and co-operation are in all things the
  laws of life;　1541
Life and liberty can be as much endangered from
  illegal methods　1929
Only those engaged in the jar of life have the
  material for it;　2061
as soon as men are not afraid to risk their
  lives　2107
There is something better ... that a man can give
  than his life.　2109
I only regret that I have but one life to lose for
  my country.　2393
worst thing that can be said of the most powerful
  ... they can take your life　2847
among these are Life, Liberty and the pursuit of
  happiness　3290
Every dollar that we waste means that their life
  will be ... the more meager　3608

LIFE-SIZED
Great men are but life-sized.　2110

LIFETIME
we shall not see them lit again in our
  lifetime　930
No man is truly great who is great only in his
  lifetime.　2038
Of the four wars in my lifetime　3956

LIGHT

They throw that light over the public mind 673
only town in the world where sound travels faster than light 1076
light up in distant lands the fire of freedom 1260
It is at night that faith in light is admirable. 2091
The thing to be supplied is light, not heat. 2105

LIKE

If you don't like me, 90 cents. 1095
A person should be free to do as he likes 1291
Justice is my being allowed to do whatever I like. 1797
the ability to get men to do what they don't want to do, and like it 2146

LIMIT

Liberty must be limited in order to be possessed. 1229
a limit to the legitimate interference of collective opinion 1284
Nations, like individuals, have to limit their objectives 1695

LIMITATION

It surely runs a poor second to the statute of limitations. 815
The history of liberty is a history of limitations of governmental power 1340

LINCOLN

Our aim is to recognize what Lincoln pointed out: 758
They all start competing against Lincoln as the greatest president. 3032
One hundred years of delay have passed since ... Lincoln freed the slaves 3361

LINE

When I found I had crossed that line 1308
I propose to fight it out on this line 3735
but a line a century hence crediting a contribution to the advance of peace 3925

LION

One must therefore be ... a lion to frighten wolves 1977
It was the nation ... that had the lion's heart 3882

LIP

Read my lips: no new taxes. 3635

LIQUIDATION

in order to preside over the liquidation of the British Empire 2136

LISTEN

Free speech carries with it some freedom to listen. 1154
they will listen today, they will listen tomorrow 3277

LITERAL

no surer way to misread any document than to read it literally 1029

LITTLE

"Yes; the little ones does." 1630
A foolish consistency is the hobgoblin of little minds 2048
by the time he wins them, they are no longer little things 2048
I am fighting ... for the rights of the little man 2130
The government must be the trustee for the little man 3480
whether we provide enough for those who have too little 3532

LITTLENESS

these are contrasted by the littleness of his motives 2528
He was a politician of monumental littleness. 2561

LIVABLE

Government does not go beyond its sphere ... to make life livable for them 3472

LIVE

Life'd not be worth livin' if we didn't keep our inimies. 921
often easier to fight for principles than to live up to them 991
being with one mind resolved to die free rather than live slaves 1223
greater gainers by suffering each other to live as seems good to themselves 1294
it conducts foreign policy in order to live 1660
something that he will die for, he isn't fit to live 2175
now we realize that we know where it lives, that it is inside ourselves 3838
win or lose, live or die—and the difference is just an eyelash 3918

LIVING

it is primarily a mode of associated living 382
Government is for the living, and not for the dead 1510
the struggle everybody is engaged in to get better living conditions 1569
Living, just as much as dying 3723

LOAF

Compromise used to mean that half a loaf was better 2732

LOBBY

Everyone else is represented in Washington by a rich and powerful lobby 479

LOBBYIST

A Lobbyist is ... supposed to help a
Politician   2600

President is the only lobbyist that ... Americans
have   2983

he's the only lobbyist that all the ... people in this
country have   2992

LOBSTER

A man that'd expict to thrain lobsters to fly   3108

LOCOMOTIVE

Revolutions are the locomotives of history.   3267

LOFTY

Democratic institutions generally give men a lofty
notion   322

LOG

log that was given to the frogs to be their
king   1842

Each one thinks he is guiding the log   2648

LOG-ROLLING

it has not become great by political log-
rolling   2749

LOGIC

Laws ... are not exercises in the art of logic   1857

LOGICAL

the notion that political beliefs are logically
determined collapses   2571

LONELY

To be President of the United States is to be
lonely   2986

LONG RUN

the people make the best judgment in the long
run   469

People don't eat in the long run   952

LOP

That man's the true Conservative/ Who lops the
moulder'd branch away.   200

LORD

I swear to the Lord/ I still can't see   431

when the time came ... the Lord would let them
take me   1309

The Lord so constituted everybody   3534

LOSE

tragedy of life is not that man loses   2112

LOSER

show me a good ... loser, and I'll show you a
failure   2119

no losers in peace and no victors in war   3915

LOST

A leader of whom it is said, "he's a nice man," is
lost.   2029

Nothing except a battle lost can be half so
melancholy as a battle won.   3713

LOVE

Mankind in the mass is not moved ... by love of
what is right   82

Communism is not love.   152

I love the Democratic Party; but I love America
... more   503

People tolerate those they fear further than those
they love.   584

They love him most for the enemies he has
made.   912

There is nothing I love as much as a good
fight.   927

Instead of loving your enemy, treat your friend a
little better.   936

the love of power is the love of ourselves   1252

The love of liberty is the love of others;   1252

like the word "love" in the mouth of a
courtesan   1270

But I will love that land where man is free   1418

true that the law cannot make man love me   1934

whether it is better to be loved rather than
feared   1974

love and fear can hardly exist together   1974

glory of my crown: that I have reigned with your
loves   1981

The subject's love is the king's best guard.   2007

The love of country is the first virtue   2397

Whenever you hear a man speak of his love for his
country   2417

they are simply men who want to be loved   2619

love of fame is consistent with the steadiest
attachment to principle   2846

whereas the love of power ... requires the sacrifice
of principle   2846

it even makes women love old men   2857

No government has the right to tell its citizens
when or whom to love.   3394

The only queer people are those who don't love
anybody.   3394

You don't have to love them.   3400

to love and to be wise, is not given to men   3580

LOWBROW

One has to be a lowbrow ... to be a
politician   2628

LOWER CLASS

more misery among the lower classes than ...
humanity in the higher   64

While there is a lower class I am in it   1351

LOYALTY

loyalty more valuable than either   2103

An ounce of loyalty is worth a pound of
cleverness.   2117

Loyalty is a sentiment, not a law. 2372

My kind of loyalty was loyalty to one's country 2407

Party loyalty lowers the greatest men to the level of the masses. 2443

Sometimes party loyalty asks too much. 2506

loyalties are tested far more severely; 2918

LUNATIC FRINGE

Every reform movement has a lunatic fringe. 3115

sometimes find something good in the lunatic fringe 3124

LUST

Their insatiable lust for power 1093

LUXURY

politics in the presence of social dangers to be a luxury 2695

Luxury, more deadly than war 3663

LYING

rulers of the state ... should have the privilege of lying 1601

The patriotic art of lying for one's country. 1634

LYNCH

it can keep him from lynching me 1934

MACHIAVELLI

much beholden to Machiavel ... that write what men do 2674

MACHINE

judicial system is the most expensive machine ever invented 1740

how difficult it is to move ... the great machine of society 3087

The mass of men serve the state ... as machines 3451

MACHINERY

our whole political machinery pre-supposes a people so fundamentally at one 397

we reared giant machinery which made it impossible 3470

MACKEREL

He shines and stinks like rotten mackerel by moonlight. 781

MAD

Oppression makes a wise man mad. 563

If you fear making anyone mad 3134

MADE

that is what laws are for, to be made and unmade 1908

MADNESS

the madness of many for the gain of a few 2447

Hunger does not breed reform; it breeds madness 3117

they have not so much madness left in their brains 3750

MAGIC

the political magic ... in the president's vision 3973

MAGICIAN

Watching foreign affairs is ... like watching a magician 1722

Budgeting is a black art practiced by bureaucratic magicians. 3625

MAGISTRACY

In all tyrannical governments the supreme magistracy ... is vested in one man 3505

MAGISTRATE

A man cannot ... convey it by compact to the magistrate 1203

the function of the Magistrate to risk even this outward peace 3669

MAGNIFICENT

It is magnificent, but it is not war. 3727

MAJORITY

For them majority rule is a device. 226

The majority is the best way 273

puts himself under an obligation to ... the majority 276

Decision by majorities is as much an expedient as lighting by gas. 334

The bottom principle ... is ... control by the majority 363

The majority voice should be controlling 364

we do not say the majority vote will always be right 498

A majority is always the best repartee. 700

I do not contest the right of the majority to command 1782

One with the law is a majority. 1912

Any man more right than his neighbors constitutes a majority of one. 2057

When were the good and the brave ever in a majority? 2065

interest of the majority is the political standard of right and wrong 2280

the majority of the people are often for injustice 2281

the majority, trampling on the rights of the minority 2282

the will of the majority is in all cases to prevail 2283

the majority may not ... respect the rights of the minority 2284

American people are too well schooled in ... submitting to the ... majority   2285

The tyranny of the majority.   2288

blessings of Liberty ... may be enjoyed alike by minorities and majorities   2289

A wise man will not leave the right to ... the power of the majority   2291

your government will never be able to restrain a distressed ... majority   2292

If ... a majority should deprive a minority of any ... right   2294

The majority rules.   2295

pervading evil of democracy is the tyranny of the majority   2298

In the majority beat many hearts, but it has no heart.   2300

Desperate courage makes One a majority.   2301

So long as a minority conforms to the majority   2302

unless the majority exercise the self-restraint   2303

Constitutions are checks upon the hasty action of the majority.   2304

No one can expect a majority to be stirred by motives other than ignoble.   2306

when great principles are involved, as a rule the majority are wrong   2307

A majority can do anything.   2308

A resolute minority has usually prevailed over an easygoing ... majority   2314

no assumption that today's majority is "right"   2317

the rights of those whose choices upset the majority   2322

I borrowed the Duke of Newcastle's majority   2678

All politics are based on the indifference of the majority.   2793

President has to be a politician ... to get the majority to go along   2987

the majority of men live content   3406

good ... of the majority of the members of any state   3417

MAKE-BELIEVE

the comfortable pre-war world of make-believe   2247

MAKING

It's a little like makin' love to a gorilla.   1079

execution of the laws is more important than the making   1871

the supreme magistracy, or the right both of making and enforcing the laws   3505

MALADMINISTRATION

best which ... is most effectually secured against ... maladministration   3418

MALCONTENT

Every time I fill a vacancy, I create a hundred malcontents   2525

To ask malcontents to be moderate   3206

MALE

the equivalent of closing male eyes to female facts   3999

MALICE

With malice toward none; with charity for all;   3736

MAN

Before Man made us citizens, great Nature made us men.   19

confrontation between a man ... and Communism is always over in two rounds   177

The man for whom law exists—the man of forms ... is a tame man   197

A conservative is a man with two perfectly good legs   216

Men being ... by Nature, all free, equal   277

No man is good enough to be another man's master.   582

the worst form of slavery ... when the herd crushes out the man   606

evil that a single man should crush the herd   606

Man alone can enslave man.   613

not always the same thing to be a good man and a good citizen   771

A man cannot be too careful in the choice of his enemies.   913

everywhere man, the heir of nature, is poor   916

A man always has two reasons for what he does   948

Man does not live by words alone   1002

Our problems are man-made, therefore they may be solved by man.   1039

Mix a conviction with a man and something happens.   1051

Man is born free; and everywhere he is in chains.   1212

A man who has nothing which he is willing to fight for   1298

the social world is certainly the work of man   1483

The test of every ... system, is the man which it forms   1538

Man is about the same ... whether with despotism   1544

No man is above the law and no man is below it;   1904

If one man can be allowed to determine for himself what is law, every man can.   1919

man who commands efficiently must have obeyed others   1971

A man ain't got no right to be a public man   2547

Man is by nature a political animal.   2672

It makes a fool of a man and a worse fool of a fool. 2720

That ... man ... says women can't have as much rights as man 3305

Man had nothing to do with it. 3305

the word man defines all rights 3322

for property belongs to man and not man to property 3324

Man seeketh in society comfort, use, and protection. 3407

Man exists for his own sake and not to add a laborer to the State. 3441

A man who is good enough to shed his blood for his country 3466

More than that no man is entitled to, and less than that no man shall have. 3466

Man is not like other animals 3622

Victory shifts from man to man. 3644

The condition of man ... is a condition of war 3679

War ... brings men into ... collision in critical moments that man measures man 3751

man and not materials that counts 3823

Great is the hand that holds dominion over/ Man by scribbled name. 3879

terrible dangers which man has created can only be controlled by man 3899

nothing worse than a man-governed world 3995

In politics if you want anything said, ask a man. 4008

MANHOOD

not going around looking for opportunities to prove our manhood 2190

there is a more valuable thing—manhood 3464

If the moral and physical fibre of its manhood ...is not a state concern 3474

Peace hath higher tests of manhood 3725

induce the young manhood ... to do the fighting for them 3781

highly democratic method of conscripting American manhood 3782

MANIFESTO

said that this manifesto is more than a theory, that it was an incitement 1123

MANIPULATE

If you can manipulate news, a judge can manipulate the law. 1197

They advance politically only as they ... manage to manipulate 2608

MANKIND

Mankind in the mass is not moved by hatred 82

nine-tenths of mankind have been grinding the corn 86

They who study mankind with a whip in their hands will always go wrong. 569

My country is the world; my countrymen are mankind. 864

Our true nationality is mankind. 938

mankind would be no more justified in silencing that one person 1114

sole end for which mankind are warranted ... in interfering with ... liberty 1285

Mankind are greater gainers by suffering each other to live as seems good 1294

Only free peoples can ... prefer the interests of mankind 1352

Mankind needs government 1559

never make a speech of any length without using the word "mankind" 1709

Mankind censures injustice, fearing that they may be victim 1748

If we do not lay out ourselves in the service of mankind 2019

being a good patriot often means being the enemy of the rest of mankind 2391

What difference does party make when mankind is involved? 2491

fate of mankind, are shaped by men without ideals 2759

a generall inclination of all mankind, a perpetuall ... desire of Power 2834

Unless man is committed to the belief that all of mankind are his brothers 2936

unless I identified myself with the whole of mankind 3158

we should strive ... for the dignity ... of mankind 3390

Mankind has grown strong in eternal struggles 3797

We must call into action the ... moral forces of mankind 3798

MANNERS

in a democracy manners are the only effective weapons against the bowie-knife 352

MANURE

It is its natural manure. 1234

MANY

Democracy substitutes election by the incompetent many 374

tyranny of the many would be when one body takes over the rights of the others 531

I would prefer the tyranny of one to that of the many 533

Party-spirit, which at best is but the madness of many 2446

that the welfare and the rights of the many are conserved 3477

a system by which the many are exploited by the few 3846

MARCH

Democracy is ... an everlasting march 405

MARGIN

margin is narrow, but the responsibility is clear 718

MARK
take an aim much higher than their mark   1975

MARRIAGE
Women ... care fifty times more for a
marriage   3984

MARRIED
A married woman has the same right to control
her own body   3396

What has the women's movement learned ...?
Never get married.   4014

MARTYR
victim to too severe a law is considered as a
martyr   1878

Martyred many times must be/ Who would keep
his country free   2416

Martyrs are needed to create incidents.   3258

MARTYRDOM
Politics ... hold up torches of martyrdom to the
reformers of error.   3088

The Negro was willing to risk martyrdom   3368

MARX
the revelation of the secret of capitalistic
production ... we owe to Marx   127

difference between Marx and Lenin is that Lenin
had a revolution to practice on   162

Guerrilla warfare is to peasant uprisings what
Marx is to Sorel.   173

Fifty years ago if we had gone the way of Freud ...
instead of Marx   2803

Marx will have come true willy-nilly, so let's get
on with it   4001

MARXIAN
Marxian Socialism must always remain a
portent   137

He who places his trust in the Marxian
synthesis   145

MARXISM
Marxism is essentially a product of the bourgeois
mind.   147

a movement ... further removed from the facts
than Marxism   163

Marxism is too uncertain of its grounds to be a
science.   163

There may be thousands of principles of
Marxism   171

MASOCHISM
A spirit of national masochism prevails   1056

MASS
The first are the rich ... the other the mass of the
people   40

to render the great mass of the population
dependent and penniless   42

Having behind us the producing masses of the
nation   81

We must have faith in the masses   154

among the mass of our people a fund of
wisdom   291

best form of Government ... is one where the
masses have little power   336

I will back the masses against the classes   348

mass of the English people are politically
contented   349

What the masses vote or do not vote for is not
important   408

great masses of the people ... will more easily fall
victims to a big lie   589

The mass of men lead lives of quiet
desperation.   882

Civilization exists precisely so that there may be
no masses   1421

he who must make articulate the wants ... of the
masses   2149

I am alone with the masses.   2195

an interest distinct from that of the mass of the
people   2305

a dynamic interaction of two factors: minorities
and the masses   2309

sensitive to the vehemence and passion of mass
sentiment   2610

A mass movement attracts and holds a
following   3125

Mass movements can rise and spread without
belief in a God   3126

The revolutionary war is a war of the
masses;   3250

MASSACRE
bourgeoisie ... looks complacently upon the
wholesale massacre   65

MASSES
Party loyalty lowers the greatest men to the level
of the masses.   2443

MASTER
As I would not be a slave, so I would not be a
master.   335

the people are the rightful masters   337

laws can't be enforced against the man who is the
laws' master   523

When a people shall have become ... fit for a
master   543

No man is good enough to be another man's
master.   582

You kill one dog, the master buys another   583

prevail on our future masters to learn their
letters   680

the poor change nothing beyond the change of
their master   1479

We cannot all be masters, nor all masters /
Cannot be truly followed.   1985

He that would govern others, first should be/
    Master of himself. 1992
strongest is never strong enough to be always the
    master 2014
officers of the government are ... never the
    masters 2594
picking up crumbs ... from the table of someone
    who considers himself my master 3398
state is the servant of the citizen, and not his
    master 3484
Socialism is a ... society in which ... neither master
    nor master's man 3554

MATCH
the story of an ape playing with a box of
    matches 3903

MATERIAL
Its cause is altogether a material one. 793
you build with the materials you have at
    hand; 2037
Heroes are created ... sometimes out of the
    scantiest materials 2138
achieved first in the moral, and afterwards in the
    material sphere 3203

MATERIALIST
Liberty, misunderstood by materialists 1297

MATERIALISTIC
the materialistic conception of history ... we owe
    to Marx 127
They wanted us to be materialistic and incapable
    of sacrifices: 183

MATRIX
Freedom of expression is the matrix ... of nearly
    every other form of freedom 1130

MAXIM
the sacred principles of liberty, which are
    embodied in one maxim 93
those who would govern kingdoms with maxims
    found in books 833
Nothing is so useless as a general maxim. 862
that maxim by which you can ... will that it
    should become a universal law 1866
an old maxim that there are other ways of killing
    a cat 2968

MAXIMUM
a society with a minimum of compulsion, a
    maximum of individual freedom 491

MCCARTHYISM
whatever is illiberal ... or merely swinish will
    hereafter be McCarthyism 1017

MEANING
If liberty has any meaning it means freedom to
    improve. 1383
Unless these rights have meaning there, they have
    little meaning anywhere. 3352

MEANNESS
always a certain meanness in the argument of
    conservatism 192

MEANS
taking possession of the means of production in
    the name of society 126
great results of history are brought about by
    discreditable means 785
first sign of corruption in a society ... is that the
    end justifies the means 1005
Freedom of the press is not an end in itself but a
    means 1184
The free way of life proposes ends, but it does not
    prescribe means. 1448
the nation's purposes always exceed its
    means 1661
renown of great men should be measured by the
    means ... used to acquire it 1995
Politics are now nothing more than a means of
    rising in the world. 2680
Politics is not an art, but a means. 2743
for those means which will give the greatest good
    to the greatest number 3453
Government should not be made an end in itself;
    it is a means only 3468
War is ... the continuation of state policy with
    other means 3718

MEASLES
Nationalism ... is the measles of mankind 2377

MEASURE
"I understand: Tory men and Whig
    measures." 193
peculiar circumstances ... may render a measure
    more or less wise 234
you cannot pick it up; you cannot measure
    it 2387

MEDDLE
summed up in two short homely but expressive
    words, "meddle" and "muddle" 1624

MEDICINE
Like medicine, the test of its value is ... its
    effects 1459
Laws are like medicine; 1890
science of legislation is like that of medicine 2230
we ought to throw in no medicine at all—to
    abstain 2231
a medicine for the sound health of
    government 3190

MEDIOCRE
great human advances have not been brought
    about by mediocre men 2145
He (John Tyler) has been called a mediocre
    man; 2561

MEDIOCRITY
an elite that accomplishes mediocrity for the
    public good 2650

MEDIUM

gives the advertisers a certain hold over the medium   1181

MEEK

anybody ... who ... believes that the meek shall inherit the earth   944

MELANCHOLY

Nothing except a battle lost can be half so melancholy as a battle won.   3713

MELODRAMA

one is sometimes tempted to define it practically as ... melodrama   395

MELTING POT

I hear that melting pot stuff a lot, ... we haven't melted   2315

melting pot failed to bring a minority into the full stream of American life   2924

MEMBERSHIP

dues that we pay for the privileges of membership in an organized society   3613

MEMORANDUM

Bureaucrats write memoranda ... because they appear to be busy   13

The law is only a memorandum.   1884

MEMORIAL

building becomes the symbol, the memorial to that dream   3032

MEMORY

We can make this thing into a Party, instead of a Memory.   505

Everyone complains about his memory   832

proper memory for a politician is one that knows what to remember   2576

how often men are ruined by having too good a memory   2696

Washington has no memory.   2812

Nothing is so admirable in politics as a short memory.   2819

MEN

Before Man made us citizens, great Nature made us men.   19

"I understand: Tory men and Whig measures."   193

Not thrones and crowns, but men!   314

with small men no great thing can really be accomplished   568

did not intend to declare all men equal in all respects   750

but that men know so little of men   923

Governments, like clocks, go from the motions men give them   1481

Wherefore governments rather depend upon men than men upon governments   1481

A government of laws, and not of men.   1493

To be governed is to be watched over ... by men who have neither the right   1537

Men and nations do behave wisely   1692

Men may be linked in friendship.   1694

Men have feelings but the law does not.   1875

we should be men first, and subjects afterward   1885

not only by the men it produces but also by the men it honors   2176

Treat us like men, and ... we will all live in peace   2896

so did men when they fought for theirs   3337

the State, and that alone, makes them men   3436

mass of men serve the state thus, not as men   3451

a nation of men who have risen to that height of moral cultivation   3750

in the minds of men that the defences of peace must be constructed   3847

men are not a reasoned or reasonable sex   4004

Men get elected.   4006

it's men who must be liberated in this country   4009

aren't many women now I'd like to see as President--but ... fewer men   4010

MEND

it destroys what it loves, because it will not mend it   190

MENDACITY

the Democratic Way ... via ... public-spirited mendacity   512

MENTAL

Freedom and slavery are mental states.   1398

MENTALITY

far more difficult to change the mentality   3079

MENU

I want the full menu of rights.   3398

MERCHANTMAN

A monarchy is a merchantman which sails well   2345

MERCY

We shall show mercy, but we shall not ask for it.   966

I have always found that mercy bears richer fruits than strict justice.   1789

Become them with one half so good a grace/ As mercy does   1984

mercy of princes is often just a way of gaining the affection of the people   1997

MERIT

Persistence in one opinion has never been considered a merit   2515

The favor of princes does not exclude merit   2675

To delight in war is a merit in the soldier   3764

METIER

not the metier of a Tory to have a policy   198
The art of governing is a great metier   2541

METRO

for me, only the people who take the Metro   2183

MEXICO

In Mexico an air conditioner is called a
politician   2662
Mexico is unjustly overrun and conquered   3210

MICE

doesn't matter if a cat is black or white, so long as
it catches mice   184

MIDDLE

The middle man governs   2583
in politics the middle way is none at all   2681
There is no working middle course in
wartime.   3836

MIDDLE CLASS

best political community is formed by citizens of
the middle class   34
laborer does not find his worst enemy in the
nobility, but in the middling class   48
right of the middle classes to exploit the
workers   50
Keep up the middle class; ... let the middle class ...
have the power   60
government by the middle classes would seem to
be the most economical   1530
middle-class reformers will find ... the populace is
going ... to bite the hand   3133

MIGHT

Let us have faith that right makes might   890
all matters of right, are at bottom only questions
of might   2705

MIGHTY

risks reprisal from the mightiest nation   1707
People who think the mighty in Washington can
be persuaded   2768

MILD

The face of tyranny / Is always mild at first.   527

MILITANCY

militancy of men ... has drenched the world with
blood   3994

MILITANT

no substitute for a militant freedom   1354
our privilege ... to take some part in this militant
movement   3328

MILITARISM

cannot organize civilization around the core of
militarism   601
the slogan of all-powerful militarism in every
belligerent nation   3790

MILITARIST

We want to get rid of the militarist   3792

MILITARY

military policy is dependent on public
opinion   430
trouble with military rule is that every ... general
is soon full of ambition   621
Military intelligence is a contradiction in
terms.   1077
retreat is honorable if dictated by military
considerations   2792
The military should be no exception.   3391
a future in which our country will match its
military strength   3488
for that very reason it is the most military of
instruments   3721
a man ... who has not been raised in the military
services   3887
acquisition of unwarranted influence ... by the
military-industrial complex   3904
We don't thrive on military acts.   3942

MILLIONAIRE

power which a multiple millionaire ... has over me
is very much less   5

MIND

The worst is that which persecutes the mind.   528
most potent weapon in the hands of the oppressor
is the mind of the oppressed   623
They throw that light over the public mind which
is the best security   673
Men are ... only prisoners of their own
minds   960
A fanatic is one who can't change his mind   998
We have produced a world of ... discontented
minds   1053
The mind is the expression of the soul   1412
We have to talk about liberating minds   1463
Laws and institutions must go ... with the progress
of the human mind   1876
he laid an exaggerated stress on not changing
one's mind   2104
A liberal mind is a mind that is able to imagine
itself believing anything.   2270
Lobbyist is a person ... supposed to help a
Politician to make up his mind   2600
Unlimited power is apt to corrupt the minds of
those who possess it.   2837
I don't mind not being president. I just mind that
someone else is.   3035
in the minds of men that the defences of peace
must be constructed   3847
The major deterrent (to war) is in a man's
mind.   3902

MINDLESS

when things become "unthinkable," ... action
becomes mindless   1450

MINIMUM

(Our goal is) a society with a minimum of compulsion   491

MINION

The arts of power and its minions are the same   2854

MINISTER

the business of ministers very much to consult ... the people   2024

One thing the House will NEVER forgive and that is if a Minister misleads it   2252

for my words are my own, and my actions are my ministers'   2333

A fellow once came to me to ask for an appointment as a minister abroad.   2553

No minister ever stood ... against public opinion   3043

MINISTRY

the action and reaction between the Ministry and the Parliament   2703

Women ... care fifty times more for a marriage than a ministry   3984

MINOR

no regime has ever loved great writers, only minor ones   1044

MINORITY

democracy ... recognizes the subjection of the minority to the majority   385

Knowledge ... is our best protection against ... illiberal minorities   691

majority of the people are often for injustice ... against the minority   2281

the majority, trampling on the rights of the minority   2282

The minority possess their equal rights   2283

the majority may not sufficiently respect the rights of the minority   2284

blessings of Liberty ... may be enjoyed alike by minorities and majorities   2289

the rich, who are always a minority, absolutely at its mercy   2292

Governments exist to protect the rights of minorities.   2293

If by the mere force of numbers a majority should deprive a minority   2294

most certain test ... is the amount of security enjoyed by minorities   2297

The minority is always right.   2299

So long as a minority conforms to the majority, it is not even a minority.   2302

to secure ... a respect for the rights of the minority   2304

Government is everywhere to a great extent controlled by powerful minorities   2305

a dynamic interaction of two factors: minorities and the masses   2309

moment a numerical superiority proceeds to ignore the needs ... of the minority   2310

A government is free in proportion to the rights it guarantees to the minority.   2311

hell to belong to a suppressed minority   2312

the recognition of the rights of minorities   2313

A resolute minority has usually prevailed over an easygoing ... majority   2314

we are all minorities now—indeed, some more than others   2318

role of a minority party is to hammer out a program   2507

failed to bring a minority into the full stream of American life   2924

MINUET

We didn't have to do the minuets of diplomacy.   1714

MIRACLE

they are no longer little things: they are miracles   2920

to believe that the miracle is going to happen   3337

MISCHIEF

bind him down from mischief by the chains of the Constitution   232

All punishment is mischief.   1772

MISCHIEVOUS

his position on almost every public question was ... mischievous   918

MISERABLE

Caesars and Napoleons will duly rise and make them miserable   599

Those ... have made their neighbors very miserable   908

MISERY

always more misery among the lower classes than ... humanity in the higher   64

a right to life that means ... utter misery   1952

ambitions are lawful except those which climb upward on miseries   2094

white man's happiness cannot be purchased by the black man's misery   2899

Prolong human life only when you can shorten its miseries.   3493

inherent virtue of socialism is the equal sharing of miseries   3569

MISFORTUNE

A war ... is a national misfortune   3745

MISGOVERN

This country is ... so misgoverned that we can't let anyone leave   1490

MISGOVERNMENT

appellatives which have been commonly employed
as cloaks for misgovernment 554

Revolution, n. In politics, an abrupt change in the
form of misgovernment. 3230

MISLEAD

One thing the House will NEVER forgive and
that is if a Minister misleads it. 2252

MISMANAGEMENT

Great Depression ... was produced by government
mismanagement 657

MISREAD

no surer way to misread any document than to
read it literally 1029

MISRULE

Disaffection's failure to substitute misrule for bad
government 3231

Rebel, n. A proponent of a new misrule who has
failed to establish it. 3232

MISSION

imbued with the idea of a mission, a great nation
... assumes it has the means 2886

MISTAKE

folly to argue that the people cannot make
political mistakes 393

hard ... to construct a constitution that safeguards
against mistakes 497

"An error doesn't become a mistake until you
refuse to correct it." 806

Experience is the name everyone gives to their
mistakes. 915

Liberty is the possibility of ... making a
mistake 1410

You can always survive a mistake in domestic
affairs 1685

may make mistakes—but they must never be
mistakes ... from faintness of heart 2141

Anyone would make mistakes with the problems
that lie ahead of us. 2168

enough mistakes of the Democrats for the
Republicans to criticize 2509

If I make a mistake it doesn't merely affect me, or
you, but the country. 2960

the 22nd Amendment was a mistake 3037

MISTRESS

Liberty is the most ... exacting mistress 1328

The Law ...is a jealous mistress 1879

No lover is ever satisfied with the first smile of his
mistress. 2856

MISUNDERSTOOD

To be great is to be misunderstood. 2049

MOB

turbulence of the mob is always close to
insanity 268

Our supreme governors, the mob. 279

Mobs will never do to govern states 296

I am the people—the mob—the crowd—the
mass. 452

The nose of a mob is its imagination. 560

The mob has many heads but no brains. 835

A guilty man punished is an example for the
mob; 1763

Mobs do not discriminate 1897

When I hear a man applauded by the mob 2612

is no grievance that is a fit object of redress by
mob law 3207

an easy and a vulgar thing to please the
mob 3437

MOCKERY

Democracy: a mockery that mouths the
words 413

The cause of liberty becomes a mockery 1401

MODERATE

Real liberty is ... found ... in moderate
governments 295

Only make wise and moderate laws. 2225

I am a moderate liberal, as all rational people
are 2266

no such thing as a moderate in the civil rights
movement 3379

Every reasonable human being should be a
moderate Socialist. 3568

MODERATION

plan conceived in moderation must fail when the
circumstances are ... extremes 858

moderation in the pursuit of justice is no
virtue 1042

Moderation in the affairs of the nation is the
highest virtue 3000

Moderation is fatal to factions 3206

MODERN

tragedy of modern democracies is ... not yet
succeeded in effecting democracy 428

modern world is not given to uncritical
admiration 2170

MODEST

if you make a modest contribution you are told
you are only tinkering 3122

MOISTURE

Power and Liberty are like Heat and
Moisture; 2836

MOLOTOV COCKTAIL

A rioter with a Molotov cocktail in his
hands 3370

MONARCH

Adam was an absolute Monarch, and so are all
Princes   2334

A monarch frequently represents his subjects
better   2359

No medieval monarch ... ever had such
power   2363

Public opinion is the most potent monarch   3059

MONARCHY

Parliament has joined the monarchy as a ...
element in the Constitution   2256

a commonwealth ... can hardly be established
except in a monarchy   2324

A monarchy is a merchantman which sails
well   2345

Monarchy is only the string which ties the
robbers' bundle.   2346

Monarchy alone tends to bring men
together   2347

sovereign has, under a constitutional monarchy ...
three rights   2352

An absolute monarchy is one in which the
sovereign does as he pleases   2357

Something as curious as the monarchy won't
survive   2364

monarchies of Europe were really destroyed by
their ... supporters   2365

You are apprehensive of monarchy; I, of
aristocracy.   2950

MONEY

I've got money so I'm a Conservative.   224

When a fellow says it hain't the money ... it's th'
money   800

flood of money that gushes into politics   820

money ... comes into the world with a congenital
bloodstain   910

Money is ... the vital principle of the body
politic   1578

An organised money market has many
advantages.   1592

a liberal ... tells other people what to do with their
money   2276

it takes lots of money to even get beat with   2748

more time than you'd like to spend asking people
for more money   2826

money is like muck, not good except it be
spread   3408

Lack of money is the root of all evil.   3524

That most delicious of all privileges—spending
other people's money.   3592

Everywhere they think they get their money's
worth   3597

not because I wish to save money, but because I
wish to save people   3608

Lord, the money we do spend on
Government   3611

the government we got for one-third the money
twenty years ago   3611

Endless money forms the sinews of war.   3654

The world in arms is not spending money
alone.   3877

MONIED

To erect and concentrate and perpetuate a large
monied interest   1242

MONOPOLIST

By its economic essence imperialism is monopolist
capitalism.   128

MONOPOLY

Liberty and monopoly cannot live together.   1323

MONROE DOCTRINE

the Monroe Doctrine will go far   1632

MONSTER

Whoever fights monsters should see to it that ... he
does not become a monster   2080

MONUMENTAL

He was a politician of monumental
littleness.   2561

MOON

where a candidate can promise the moon and
mean it   1028

I'd rather be a dog and bay at the moon   2246

MORAL

something which does not exist ... a complete
moral code   144

moral strength of democracy ... alone can give any
meaning to ... security   449

when its moral convictions weaken it becomes
easy prey for the demagogue   454

confuse freedom and democracy, which we regard
as moral principles   475

moral way of government is the practical
way   499

Moral principle is a looser bond than pecuniary
interest.   784

The difference between a moral man and a man of
honor   799

This difficult effort will be the "moral equivalent
of war"   1071

never wholly herself unless ... engaged in high
moral principle   1105

no one can be perfectly moral till all are
moral   1271

the moral sense is as much a part of our
constitution   1780

we are not going to take a great moral ideal and
achieve it merely by law   1927

Moral principle is the foundation of law.   1961

never be mistakes which result from ...
abandonment of moral principle   2141

Public officials ... inevitably reflect the moral tone
of the society   2622

The Presidency ... is pre-eminently a place of moral leadership   2974

Great revolutions ... are achieved first in the moral ... sphere   3203

Human beings have rights, because they are moral beings: 3301

moral obligation of providing for old age   3426

moral test of government is how that government treats ... the needy   3501

There must be a moral bond first.   3640

MORALISTIC
a strong moralistic strain in the civil rights movement   2882

MORALITY
the creed of modern morality that all labor is good in itself   74

principles of public morality are as definite as ... morality of private life   788

When morality comes up against profit   813

no spectacle so ridiculous as the public in one of its ... fits of morality   867

Morality, and the ideal of freedom which is the political expression of morality   1376

its morality ... "That man is worth so much!"   1582

Morality cannot be legislated   1935

The law ... is constantly based on notions of morality   1962

In statesmanship ... never mind about the moralities   2084

people who treat politics and morality separately will never understand   2679

Those who would treat politics and morality apart will never understand   2713

Morality is contraband in war.   3853

MORALS
always known that heedless self-interest was bad morals   650

Corruption of politics has nothing to do with the morals of ... personalities   793

just as good morals ... have need of the laws   1835

by improving the mind and morals of society, to lessen the disposition to war   3714

MORE
The more laws, the more offenders.   1850

MORES
can't ... try to change the mores faster than people can accept it   3127

MORTAL
easy to accuse a government of imperfection ... mortal things are full of it   1480

MOSES
the history of nations, from Moses down   62

If Moses had gone to Harvard Law School   2258

MOST
The most may err as grossly as the few.   274

MOTHER
England is the mother of parliaments.   901

God has given you your country as cradle, and humanity as mother;   2402

MOTION
Politics is motion and excitement.   2813

so in the case of the body politic, when motion ceases, the body dies   3090

MOTIVE
The people ... are the motive force   980

the moment that man inquires into the motives which govern ... his sovereign   1262

the motive which impels them—the desire to do right   2404

contrasted by the littleness of his motives   2528

in politics ... you are much exposed to the attribution of false motives   2761

treaties that ought to count ... effect a settlement between ulterior motives   3806

MOTTO
The motto should not be: Forgive one another   928

MOULD
to have moulded a public personality out of so amorphous an identity   2211

MOUNTAIN
And He's allowed me to go up to the mountain.   1043

MOUTH
No one has a finer command of language than the person who keeps his mouth shut   2163

MOVE
wipe the dew off your spectacles, and see that the world is moving   204

MOVEMENT
I do not know a movement ... further removed from the facts than Marxism   163

When the people are in movement   3187

Without a revolutionary theory there can be no revolutionary movement.   3227

the movement for women's rights has broken many old fetters   3991

What has the women's movement learned from (Geraldine Ferraro's) candidacy   4014

MUCK
only if they know when to stop raking the muck   792

money is like muck, not good except it be spread   3408

MUDDLE
two short homely but expressive words, "meddle" and "muddle" 1624

MUFFLED
He rowed to his object with muffled oars. 2039

MUG
A conservative is a liberal who was mugged the night before. 223
no more liberals ... They've all been mugged. 2279
The current tax code is a daily mugging. 3632

MULE
The Democratic Party is like a mule. 501
The government's like a mule, it's slow 1548

MULTILATERAL
no limitation of armaments on a multilateral scale can be effected 3947

MULTIPLICATION
multiplication table ... distinguishes right from wrong in the government 347

MULTIPLY
to multiply whatever of geniune good-will may exist 2745

MULTITUDE
error that multitude is divine because it is multitude 2296
A multitude of rulers is not a good thing. 2323
Politics is the art of knowing and leading a multitude 2691

MUNICH
The pact of Munich was a greater blow to humanity 3861

MURDER
Fascism is Capitalism plus Murder. 591
whin business gets above sellin' ... nails ... hard to tell it fr'm murther 1583
condemned by the monstrous conventions of politics to murder 3816
to kill in war is not a whit better than to commit ordinary murder 3871

MUSIC
Politics, like music ... is best learned at an early age 2805

MUTABILITY
friendships of nations ... cannot survive the mutability of those interests 1643

MYOPIA
myopia which masks the reality that many "created equal" 2946

MYSELF
When I want to know what France thinks, I ask myself. 2182

MYTH
myth of integration as propounded under ... the liberal ideology 2941

NABOB
the nattering nabobs of negativism 1058

NAME
The Democratic Party is a party in name only 513
McCarthy stamped with his name a tendency 1017
O liberty! O liberty! what crimes are committed in thy name! 1246

NAPOLEON
So long as men worship the Caesars and Napoleons 599
If Napoleon had been as intelligent as Spinoza 2086

NARROW
In a narrow sphere great men are blunderers. 2026

NASTY
Diplomacy is to do and say the nastiest thing in the nicest way. 1647

NATION
Two nations between whom there is no intercourse 51
the Privileged and the People formed two nations 52
Numerous cross-divisions favour peace within a nation 100
Not kings and lords, but nations! 314
Nations are not ... great ... because individuals composing them are numerous 354
As a nation, we began by declaring that all men are created equal. 566
No nation was ever ruined by trade. 634
If a nation expects to be ignorant and free 670
Righteousness exalteth a nation. 770
no nation so poor that it cannot afford free speech 1151
nation which enjoys the most freedom must ... be ... the most powerful nation 1254
A nation does not have to be cruel to be tough. 1377
If a nation values anything more than freedom 1381
A nation which makes the final sacrifice for ... freedom 1388
every nation has a right to establish that form of government 1607
Peace with all nations ... are our object 1608
no greater error than to expect ... favors from nation to nation 1610
no nation had a right to intermeddle 1611
no nation which is greater than any other 1652

415

Let every nation know ... that we shall pay any price, bear any burden 1670

any nation that seeks peace—and hates war 1680

every nation determines its policies in terms of its own interests 1682

A nation can be no stronger abroad than she is at home. 1683

Nations are linked only by interests. 1694

Nations, like individuals, have to limit their objectives 1695

that law which governs all law ... the law of nature, and of nations 1872

not with ... theory that nations are governed 2032

There are men, who ... carry nations with them 2067

things a man must not do even to save a nation 2177

We are of course a nation of differences. 2319

Kings are ... Born to sustain and prop the Nations weight 2335

institutions alone that can create a nation 2368

Size is not grandeur, and territory does not make a nation. 2369

nation is secure only while the nation is honest 2370

good for a nation to know that it must sacrifice 2373

Nations are formed ... by the fact that they have a program for tomorrow 2378

All nations have ... reasons for thinking themselves incomparable 2385

To me the nation is the ultimate political reality. 2387

Neither philosophy, nor religion ... will ever govern nations 2841

the nation that has absorbed ten million foreigners 2908

A nation cannot live ... if its refugees are among its citizens 2915

not healthy when a nation lives within a nation 2915

The nation is a power hard to rouse 3056

This Nation was founded by men of many nations 3358

To have a nation with a government that is as good ... as are the ... people 3499

strongest bond ... should be one uniting all working people of all nations 3520

nation shall not lift up sword against nation 3650

From hence, let fierce contending nations know 3683

A nation will not count the sacrifice it makes 3728

do all which may achieve ... a lasting peace ... with all nations 3736

when a nation that lifts up the sword against a nation 3767

As long as there are ... nations possessing great power 3844

NATIONAL

Let no one think ... that national debate means national division 476

Though a revolution may call itself "national" 3256

NATIONAL DEBT

A national debt ... will be to us a national blessing 3581

I ... do not believe that a national debt is a national blessing 3591

Our national debt after all is an internal debt 3614

NATIONAL INTEREST

That key is Russian national interest. 959

times when national interest is more important than the law 1951

NATIONALISM

Nationalism is an infantile disease. 2377

a wind of nationalism and freedom blowing round the world 2379

Nationalism has two fatal charms for its devotees 2382

Nationalism is our form of incest, is our idolatry 2384

nationalism, when the hate for people other than your own comes first 2386

Nationalism is a silly cock crowing on its own dunghill. 2415

NATIONALIST

The nationalist has a broad hatred and a narrow love. 2375

NATIONALITY

Our true nationality is mankind. 938

separation between one nationality and the other ... is a reactionary idea 2371

NATIONALIZATION

a doctrinaire faith in nationalization, without knowing what it means 3573

NATIONHOOD

nationhood is not achieved otherwise than in arms 1345

human rights is the very soul of our sense of nationhood 3389

NATIVE LAND

Who never to himself hath said,/ This is my own, my native land! 2396

NATURAL

ever any domination which did not appear natural to those who possessed it 572

To waste, to destroy, our natural resources, to skin and exhaust the land 729

The nation behaves well if it treats the natural resources as assets 730

our task ... to hand down undiminished ... the
natural wealth 734

To prevent resentment, governments attribute
misfortunes to natural causes; 2494

NATURE

Before Man made us citizens, great Nature made
us men. 19

Nature is rich; but everywhere man, the heir of
nature, is poor. 916

Nature is neutral. Man has wrested from nature
the power to make ... a desert 993

Liberty ... ought to be maintained in a manner
suitable to her nature 1216

Governments must be conformable to the nature
of the governed; 1484

There are in nature certain fountains of
justice 1759

Care must be taken that laws do not offend
against nature. 1854

Man is by nature a political animal. 2672

nature will not allow it 3199

NAUSEOUS

The nauseous sham goodfellowship our ... public
men get up 2580

NAVIGATE

As the master politician navigates the ship of
state 2626

NAVY

If the American Nation will ... build ... a
thoroughly efficient navy 1632

A good navy is not a provocative of war. 3759

A modern navy can not be improvised. 3769

The navy ... is the right arm of the United
States 3774

NAZISM

the referendum, which has only too often been the
instrument of Nazism 714

NEAR

Good government obtains when those who are
near are made happy 1476

NECESSARY

When it is not necessary to change, it is necessary
not to change. 187

"For a nation to be free, it is only necessary that
she will it." 307

do what is necessary and make the best of
it 2037

Politics ... only profession for which no
preparation is thought necessary 2775

But to many the superfluous is the
necessary 3472

NECESSITY

Necessity is the plea for every infringement of
human freedom. 541

Free speech ... is a necessity in any country where
people are ... free 1121

Freedom is the understanding of necessity and the
transformation of necessity. 1451

First, that the necessity of the times requires
it; 2222

NECK

Some chicken! Some neck! 970

without ... finding the other end fastened about his
own neck 3315

NEED

From each according to his abilities, to each
according to his needs. 115

The greatest need a people have is for
government; 1533

the exploitation of those ... who out of naked need,
cannot obey it 1915

we have an obligation to those in need 3503

Understanding human needs is half the job 3536

the budget is a reflection of their need 3620

NEGATION

the negation of God erected into a system of
Government 562

State ... is the most flagrant negation ... of
humanity 3454

NEGATIVISM

the nattering nabobs of negativism 1058

NEGLECT

too long neglected to nourish its heart—the court
systems 1816

NEGLIGIBLE

difference between being an elder statesman/ And
posing ... Is negligible 2160

NEGOTIABLE

The freedom of the city is not negotiable. 1674

NEGOTIATE

Only free men can negotiate; 1472

If we are to negotiate peace ... I imagine an
essentially modest role 1626

Let us never negotiate out of fear 1672

NEGRO

We now practically read it, all men are created
equal except Negroes. 566

we hear the loudest yelps for liberty among the
drivers of negroes 1225

True liberation can be acquired ... only when the
Negro people possess power 2872

Cannot the nation ... absorb ten million Negro
Americans into ... political life 2908

417

the Negro's circumstance that ... smallest things ... take him so very long   2920

Only in the case of the Negro has the melting pot failed   2924

To be a Negro is to participate in a culture of poverty and fear   2925

the Negro remains in bondage to the color of his skin   2928

Discrimination is a hellhound that gnaws at Negroes   2938

Nonviolent action, the Negro saw, was the way to supplement ... change   3128

The Negro revolution is controlled by foxy white liberals   3273

If Negroes secure their goals ... they must win them   3341

as the Negro plunges deeper into the quest for freedom and justice   3350

The Negro was willing to risk martyrdom   3368

The Negro revolt is not aimed at winning friends   3372

NEIGHBOR

have made their neighbors very miserable   908

allow every man in America to look his neighbor in the face and see a man   2933

It does me no injury for my neighbor to say there are twenty gods   3142

World peace ... does not require that each man love his neighbor   3914

NEIGHBORLINESS

A democracy ... is bound together by the ties of neighborliness   404

NERO

a possible Nero in the gentlest human creature that walks   581

NERVOUS BREAKDOWN

making remarkable progress toward an agreement--and ... a nervous breakdown   1065

NEUTRAL

The Constitution is not neutral.   256

Nature is neutral.   993

The United States must be neutral in fact as well as in name.   1638

NEUTRALITY

Even to observe neutrality you must have a strong government.   1606

if this country could ... maintain strict neutrality   1611

government must pursue a course of complete neutrality toward religion   3165

NEVER

Never give in, never give in, never, never   971

Never complain and never explain.   2761

first rule of politics is never to say never   2794

NEW

I called a New World into existence   860

I pledge you, I pledge myself, to a new deal   951

We stand today on the edge of a new frontier   1021

to make conquest of a new freedom for America   1338

Every new time will give its law.   1902

Every ruler is harsh whose rule is new.   1969

to take the lead in the introduction of a new order of things   1976

the new wine of ... equal rights ... into the old bottle of privilege   3245

NEWSPAPER

whether we should have a government without newspapers   1160

man who never looks into a newspaper is better informed   1164

We live under a government of men and morning newspapers.   1170

even if we have to include the American newspapers   1174

not newspapers in the ordinary acceptance of the term   1176

even for the freedom of newspapers that call me everything   1180

newspapers nobly did precisely that which the Founders hoped   1190

newspapers should be commended   1191

their newspapers filled with nothing but good news   1193

a Parliament with Newspaper Reporters ... cannot do work   2233

NEWSPAPERMAN

The First Amendment gives newspapermen a status   1195

NIBBLE

The true danger is when liberty is nibbled away   1230

NICE

Diplomacy is to do and say the nastiest thing in the nicest way.   1647

A leader of whom it is said, "he's a nice man," is lost.   2029

any men more sour than those who are forced to be nice out of interest   2524

NIGHT

It is at night that faith in light is admirable.   2091

NIGHTMARE

My fellow Americans, our long national nightmare is over.   1064

NIP

Nip the shoots of arbitrary power in the bud   1224

NIXON

Nixon is not of the generation that regards honesty as the best policy 819

You won't have Nixon to kick around anymore 2173

Nixon is like a good prewar house—solidly built 2634

If Nixon is not forced to turn over tapes of his conversations 3029

NO

To think is to say no. 1126

Liberty is ... the possibility of saying "No" 1410

the duty to say no on matters of principle 3038

NO ONE

Bureaucracy, the rule of no one, has become the modern form of despotism. 10

I know that I can save this country and that no one else can. 2012

Then they came for me and by that time no one was left 3342

NOAH

Noah must have taken into the Ark two taxes 3615

NOBILITY

Nobility ... is the intermedium between the king and the people 44

The English laborer does not find his worst enemy in the nobility 48

NOBLE

The noblest of all forms of government is self-government; 376

No matter how noble the objectives of a government 1565

Every noble crown is ... a crown of thorns 2348

American politics is one of the noblest arts 2790

Political society exists for the sake of noble actions 3404

All of the functions it carries out are not noble 3462

NOBODY

Almost nobody means precisely what he says 1125

You can't beat Somebody with Nobody. 2829

Nobody can overthrow me—I have the power. 2892

NOISE

When I am picking up noise from ... the left and right 2178

NOMINATE

I will not accept if nominated 911

NOMINEE

Nominee, n. A modest gentleman shrinking from the distinction of private life 2567

NON-POLITICS

toleration of the Conservative Party because it is the party of non-politics 220

NONPOLITICAL

no such thing as a nonpolitical speech by a politician 2609

NONSENSE

Nothing chills nonsense like exposure to the air. 1119

Mr. Wallace's warp of sense and his woof of nonsense 1653

We said nonsense but it was important nonsense. 1719

NONVIOLENCE

This can never happen except through non-violence. 444

Non-violence is not a garment to be put on and off at will. 984

he will plunge even deeper into the philosophy of non-violence 3350

Nonviolence is the answer to the crucial ... questions 3369

NONVIOLENT

Nonviolent action ... was the way to supplement ... change 3128

Personally, I am not nonviolent, but I'm not a fool 3131

A non-violent revolution is not a program of seizure of power. 3261

In a nonviolent movement there must be a latent threat of eruption 3278

Nonviolent resistance paralyzed and confused the power structures 3368

NORMAL

Government ... ought to be a very normal and deliberate proceeding 1552

NORMALCY

America's present need is not ... nostrums, but normalcy 939

NORTHERN

Washington is a city of Southern efficiency and Northern charm. 1035

NOTHING

Nothing is more dangerous than an idea 949

Freedom can't be kept for nothing. 1200

Freedom of speech is of no use to a man who has nothing to say. 1378

He knows nothing and he thinks he knows everything. 2565

he'll say, "Do this! Do that!" And nothing will happen. 2993

That doesn't mean you do nothing 3127

NOTION

how impossible to advance the notions of a whole
people   3087

NOTORIOUS

The abuses of the press are notorious.   1157

NOURISHMENT

a planet whose resources are devoted to the ...
nourishment of its inhabitants   736

you require the same amount of
nourishment   3534

NOWHERE

All dressed up, with nowhere to go.   933

NUCLEAR

right of the Government to lie to save itself when
faced with nuclear disaster   1567

A world without nuclear weapons would be less
stable   1721

power not ruled by law is a menace which our
nuclear age cannot afford   2887

If the Third World War is fought with nuclear
weapons   3950

It's the nuclear age, and war can annihilate us
all.   3952

NUISANCE

he must not make himself a nuisance to other
people   1287

NULLIFY

When a faction in a state attempts to nullify a
constitutional law   2287

NUMBER

the greatest happiness of the greatest number   289

he is as big as the number of persons who believe
in him   2096

None of us really understands what's going on
with all these numbers.   3629

number itself in armies importeth not much   3674

OAK

A revolution is as natural a growth as an
oak.   3214

OASIS

impossible to build a socialist paradise as an
oasis   138

OBEDIENCE

The doctrine of blind obedience ... to any human
power   1880

We owe subjection and obedience to all our
kings   1979

Obedience to the laws and to the Sovereign, is
obedience to a higher Power   2350

OBEY

the duty of every individual to obey the
established Government   304

Good laws if they are not obeyed   1822

Laws too gentle are seldom obeyed;   1859

people have nothing to do with the laws but to
obey them   1873

Good men must not obey the laws too well.   1883

nor do we ask any man's permission when we ask
him to obey it   1904

law is ... made for ... those ... who out of naked
need, cannot obey it   1915

whether we obey the law only when we approve of
it   1924

the man who obeys dutifully is worthy of being
some day a commander   1971

If you command wisely, you'll be obeyed
cheerfully.   2006

OBJECT

The care of human life ... is the only legitimate
object of good government   3433

OBJECTION

objections ... brought against a standing
army   1536

OBJECTIONABLE

What is objectionable ... is ... that they are
intolerant   1041

OBJECTIVE

no longer interested in elections except as a means
to reach our objectives   624

Nations ... have to limit their objectives   1695

Political liberalism should also be defined in terms
of objectives.   2273

the great objective which Church and State are
both demanding   3156

war can no longer be considered ... as a means of
attaining ... a ...objective   3807

OBLIGATION

The laws of necessity, of self-preservation ... are of
higher obligation   17

those lands to which we have obligations ... should
be able to count on us   1702

Nobody has a more sacred obligation to obey the
law   1918

obligation of the federal government ... to restore
... constitutional rights   3395

we have an obligation to those in need   3503

those who vote for a tax can escape the obligation
to pay it   3595

OBLITERATION

declaring that one or other ... is lagging ... in
potential for obliteration   3954

OBLIVION

Every Harvard class should have one Democrat to
rescue it from oblivion.   509

OBNOXIOUS

no method to secure the repeal of ... obnoxious laws so effective   1889

OBSCENE

creations which yesterday were ... the obscene become the classics of today   1146

OBSCURITY

Nominee, n. A modest gentleman ... seeking the ... obscurity of public office   2567

OBSERVANCE

strict observance of the laws is ... one of the virtues of a good citizen   17

observance of the law is the eternal safeguard of liberty   1932

OBSOLETE

religions are obsolete when the reforms do not proceed from them   3152

OBSTACLE

Trade and commerce ... would never manage to bounce over the obstacles   1581

OBSTRUCT

Democracy: a mockery that ... obstructs every effort   413

not just obstruct the work of the majority party   2507

when the legal ... methods ... are so obstructed   3235

OCCUPATION

no occupation ... which belongs either to women or to men   3974

ODDS

If a person ... figures out the odds   821

ODIUM

It marks its victim ... and excites the public odium   2854

OFF LIMITS

Liberty is never out of bounds or off limits;   1432

OFFEND

Care must be taken that laws do not offend against nature.   1854

OFFENDER

The more laws, the more offenders.   1850

OFFENSE

Let the punishment match the offense.   1752

Princes are more sensitive to any offense   2052

OFFICE

a free government consists in considering offices as public trusts   321

it is in office, put there by the will of the people   492

Great offices will have great talents.   2020

High office teaches decision making, not substance.   2205

one higher office than president   2424

men want to be always in office   2514

In the appointments to the great offices of the government   2532

Offices are as acceptable here as elsewhere   2534

Every man who has been in office a few years   2539

passion for office among members of Congress   2548

no worse heresy than that the office sanctifies the holder of it   2558

Every man who takes office in Washington either grows or swells.   2575

tired of an office where I can do no more good   2955

To leave office before my term is completed   3018

They ... have a right to vote and a right to run for office   4003

OFFICEHOLDER

My kind of loyalty was loyalty to one's country, not to its ... officeholders   2407

OFFICER

Never ... an officer of the people ... become the instrument of the Executive   2544

OFFICIAL

By placing discretion in the hands of an official to grant or deny a license   1150

government officials shall be subjected to the same rules of conduct   1914

OIL

Compromise is the oil that makes governments go.   2801

OLD

our people have the most enormous appetite for Old World titles   79

old soldiers never die; they just fade away   989

Of course it's the same old story. Truth usually is the same old story.   1086

handicapped by policies based on old myths   1687

Old age is a shipwreck.   2156

governing consists in not letting men grow old in their jobs   2533

The older you get the more you realize that gray isn't such a bad color.   2779

Power makes you attractive; it even makes women love old men.   2857

Old men running for the Presidency ... are like old men who take young brides   3028

Old forms of government finally grow so oppressive   3216

the moral obligation of providing for old age   3426

Older men declare war.   3840

OLIGARCHY

Oligarchy: A government resting on a valuation of property   33

does not rest, like many oligarchies, on the cruelty of the rich to the poor   84

an elite as steadfast ... to maintain its prerogatives as any oligarchy   168

an oligarchy when control lies with the rich and better-born   267

What we have done ... is to broaden the basis of oligarchy   398

place us under the despotism of an oligarchy   1728

OMNIPOTENT

to be Omnipotent but friendless is to reign   2035

ON-THE-JOB

The Presidency is no place for on-the-job training.   3022

ONCE

That we can die but once to save our country!   2389

ONE

prefer the tyranny of one to that of the many   533

One country, one constitution, one destiny.   874

When liberty becomes license, some form of one-man power is not far distant.   1317

One with the law is a majority.   1912

One must be something, in order to do something.   2043

The fate of America cannot depend on any one man.   2124

Desperate courage makes One a majority.   2301

The Soviet Union would remain a one-party nation   2512

ONE-THIRD

I see one-third of a nation ill-housed, ill-clad   3532

ONESELF

To rule over oneself is the first condition   2111

ONLOOKER

A Communist has no right to be a mere onlooker.   157

ONLY

It is the only thing.   1082

OPEN

It is living in the open space.   794

first principle ... is an untrammeled flow of words in an open forum   1142

One wonders when able rascals will discover this open door   2577

An open mind is considered irresponsible   2605

An open convention is when your delegates are in control.   2787

OPERATION

A right is worth fighting for only when it can be put into operation.   3326

OPINION

a decent respect to the opinions of mankind   287

Most people's opinions are of no value at all.   490

I'll tell you what his 'pinions is.   790

opinions ... held with passion are those for which no good ground exists   1024

Opinions become dangerous to a state   1109

If all mankind, minus one, were of one opinion   1114

never be sure that the opinion ... is a false opinion   1116

the most stringent censorships ... give credibility to the opinions they attack   1156

The basis of our government being the opinion of the people   1160

He that complies against his will is of his opinion still.   1204

A people are free in proportion as they form their own opinions.   1249

the opinions of men change also   1510

where no contrary opinion of a lawyer can be had   2030

easy in the world to live after the world's opinion   2047

A little group of willful men representing no opinion but their own   2243

essence of the Liberal outlook lies not in what opinions are held   2274

Party is organised opinion.   2478

opinions are nothing but the mere result of chance   2496

opinions adopted by parties ... not to be identified with ordinary human opinions   2513

Persistence in one opinion has never been considered a merit   2515

in choosing men to serve ... takes no notice of their opinions   2518

he betrays ... if he sacrifices it to your opinion   2527

basis of our government (is) the opinion of the people   3039

Government must always be in advance of public opinion   3045

though a different opinion prevails in the country   3297

OPIUM

It is the opium of the people.   3149

OPPONENT

One must, if one can, kill one's opponent   876

The evil is ... what they say about their opponents   1041

handles gently the property ... even while his opponents are its tenants   2460

learn to respect sincerity of conviction in our opponents   2701

OPPORTUNITY

all of us should have an equal opportunity to develop our talents   766

no security on this earth; there is only opportunity   1006

This home iv opporchunity where ivry man is th' equal iv ivry other man   1796

includes the opportunity to rise to leadership, to be uncommon   2145

We believe in equal opportunity for all   2145

not going around looking for opportunities to prove our manhood   2190

Our task is to help replace their despair with opportunity.   2932

isn't wisdom or intelligence that influences a President, it's opportunity   3027

Such an opportunity ... is a right which must be made available to all   3346

The office of government is ... to give men opportunity   3438

riches will avail us little if we do not use them to expand ... opportunities   3487

the additional burden of being deprived of the opportunity for an education   3549

OPPOSE

conservatives define themselves in terms of what they oppose   222

We should support whatever the enemy opposes   2755

OPPOSITE

He keeps his balance by saying the opposite of what he does.   2581

OPPOSITION

to form ... an opposition on a certain plea ... and then ... to abandon it   783

duty of an Opposition was ... to oppose everything   2467

No government can be long secure without formidable opposition.   2469

not exactly the mode of acquiring influence ... particularly in opposition   2472

Don't say in Power what you say in Opposition;   2590

A good politician with nerve ... can win in the face of the stiffest opposition   2613

Opposition, n. ... the party that prevents the Government from running amuck   2730

When the Government ... and the Opposition ... take the same side   2734

The opposition is indispensable.   2754

OPPRESS

merely the organized power of one class for oppressing another   2860

OPPRESSED

The most potent weapon ... of the oppressor is the mind of the oppressed.   623

No oppressed people have ever secured their liberty without resistance.   1264

Oppressed people cannot remain oppressed forever.   1445

Truth is on the side of the oppressed.   1452

Time is on the side of the oppressed today   1458

Religion is the sigh of the oppressed creatures   3149

An oppressed people are authorized ... to rise   3196

Freedom and justice must be struggled for by the oppressed   3380

the masses of all oppressed classes ... have been stolid   3986

OPPRESSION

The state is nothing but an instrument of oppression   77

Oppression makes a wise man mad.   563

Oppression costs the oppressor too much if the oppressed stand up   586

oppressions of body and mind will vanish like the evil spirits   669

To the press ... for all the triumphs ... over error and oppression   1161

but that men should fly from oppression   1202

make his own liberty secure, must guard even his enemy from oppression   1248

minority possess their equal rights ... to violate which would be oppression   2283

Secession ... may be morally justified by the extremity of oppression   3205

contempt is due to those people who ask us to submit to unmerited oppression   3328

the need for man to overcome oppression ... without resorting to oppression   3369

OPPRESSIVE

democracy in which everybody had an equal responsibility ... would be oppressive   446

OPPRESSOR

emancipation from the ...oppressor until we have achieved it in our own souls   596

most potent weapon ... of the oppressor is the mind of the oppressed   623

Only on the bones of the oppressors can the people's freedom be founded   3229

Every revolutionary ends ... either an oppressor or a heretic   3262

OPTIMIST

You've got to be (an) optimist to be a Democrat   507

For myself I am an optimist   997

optimist view of politics assumes that there must be some remedy   2709

OPULENCE

atmosphere of private opulence and public
squalor 655

ORATORY

rarity of great political oratory 2061

ORDER

Watch out for the fellow who talks about putting
things in order! 545

none more conspicuous in this atmosphere of
illusion than the word Order 554

Good order is the foundation of all things. 845

Order is not pressure which is imposed on
society 1555

Law is order, and good law is good order. 1819

If you do beat anyone, it's got to be for the sake
of order. 1903

It's the orders you disobey that make you
famous. 2201

A party of order or stability, and a party of
progress ... are both necessary 2477

Let the law be ruthless and order will be
restored. 3194

They did not exalt order at the cost of
liberty. 3246

Revolt and terror pay a price. / Order and law
have a cost. 3251

the purpose of political order: which is simply
peace and security of life 3411

so society seeks order in anarchy 3443

the greatest liberty consistent with the good
order 3459

That was the order of the day. 3945

To promote a Woman to bear rule ... is the
subversion of good Order 3975

ORE

The working class is for a Lenin what ore is for a
metal worker. 129

ORGANIC LAW

no government ... had a provision in its organic
law for its own termination 1539

ORGANIZATION

This organization is created to prevent you from
going to hell. 1000

power is the product and flower of
organization 2872

Party organization matters. 4012

ORGANIZE

I am not a member of any organized party—I am
a Democrat. 508

There must be ... not organized rivalries, but an
organized common peace 1640

ORGY

Political campaigns are designedly made into
emotional orgies 2428

ORNITHOLOGICAL

not conscious of falling under any of those
ornithological divisions 1054

ORPHAN

victory finds a hundred fathers but defeat is an
orphan 974

OSCILLATION

If the perpetual oscillation of nations between
anarchy and despotism 1313

OSTRACIZE

an ostracised class of half of the people 2903

OUGHT

what humanity ... and justice tell me I ought to
do 1864

he who abandons what is done for what ought to
be done 2673

beholden to Machiavel ... that write what men do,
and not what they ought 2674

OURSELVES

Most faults are not in our Constitution, but in
ourselves. 247

we know where it lives, that it is inside
ourselves 3838

OUST

isn't a foot of land in the world which doesn't
represent the ousting 2409

OUT

When more and more people are thrown out of
work, unemployment results. 644

The one that's out always looks the best. 2492

If power corrupts, being out of power corrupts
absolutely. 2893

OUTCAST

those who start out as outcasts can wind up as
being part of the system 3550

OUTCOME

outcome of the greatest events is always
determined by a trifle 850

Of war men ask the outcome, not the
cause. 3659

OUTDOOR RELIEF

a gigantic system of outdoor relief for the
aristocracy of Great Britain 887

OUTLOOK

essence of the Liberal outlook lies not in what
opinions are held 2274

OUTRAGE

if anyone says anything back, that is an
outrage 1131

OUTSKIRTS

many Americans live on the outskirts of
hope 2932

OUTSTRIP
No man in public life thinks of the many he has
    outstripped;   2516

OUTWARD
No prince is so Great, as not ... to give an
    outward ... worship to the laws   1846

OVAL OFFICE
the feeling of being with the president in the Oval
    Office ... Ovalitis   3021

OVERREACT
focusing on the last battle and overreacting to
    that   2664

OVERTHROW
ends can be obtained only be forcible overthrow of
    existing social conditions   120
not to overthrow the Constitution, but to
    overthrow the men who pervert it   337
Nobody can overthrow me—I have the
    power.   2892

OVERTURN
no one's interest to overturn a government in
    which everyone with ability   1516

OWE
Never in the field of human conflict was so much
    owed by so many to so few.   3827

OWN
He who knows only his own side of the
    case   1115
Freedom of the press belongs to those who own
    one.   1194

OWNER
represent the ousting and re-ousting of a long line
    of successive owners   2409

PACIFIC
nation which has gradations of class ... likely to be
    more ... pacific   100
Our institutions are essentially pacific.   1615

PACIFISM
a doctrinaire faith in pacifism   3573

PAGEANT
In the pageant of unity ... a Whitmanesque litany
    of races and classes   515

PAIN
that there are no gains without pains   995
This is the bitterest pain among men, to have
    much knowledge but no power.   2832
To know the pains of power, we must go to those
    who have it   2848
if he have a pain in his bowels ... he forthwith sets
    about reforming the world   3097

PALACE
harder for a leader to be born in a palace   2097

PALESTINE
Pilate's paramount duty was to preserve the peace
    in Palestine   1118

PANACEA
The Constitution is not a panacea for every blot
    upon the public welfare   245

PANDA
Our debates have been like the mating of pandas
    in the zoo   2440

PANTHER
use the panther as our symbol and call our
    political vehicle the Black Panther   3284

PAPER
All reactionaries are paper tigers.   982
Any jackass can draw up a balanced budget on
    paper.   3628

PAPERWORK
all the damned paperwork this was going to
    mean   3927

PARADISE
impossible to build a socialist paradise as an
    oasis   138

PARADOX
Politicians fascinate because they constitute such a
    paradox   2650
the fundamental paradox of the welfare
    state   3542

PARALYZE
unjustified terror which paralyzes needed
    efforts   953
all government ... is a dead weight that paralyzes
    the free spirit   1554

PARAPHERNALIA
The whole paraphernalia of the criminal law   110

PARIAH
of Woman, the pariah of humanity   3982

PARLEY
I hold that we should rearm in order to
    parley.   3866

PARLIAMENT
under a system in which men are sent to
    Parliament to serve themselves   699
England is the mother of parliaments.   901
Parliament is not a congress of ambassadors from
    different ... interests   2221
a Parliament with Newspaper Reporters ... cannot
    do work   2233
Parliament will train you to talk;   2234
When not realities but words are to be discussed
    Parliament wakes up.   2247
For us parliament is not an end in itself   2250

Parliament has joined the monarchy as a dignified ... element in the Constitution   2256

When I first came into parliament   2467

you can maintain ... the power and influence of Parliament itself   2471

"Don't teach my boy poetry; he is going to stand for Parliament."   2611

English politics is the action ... between the Ministry and the Parliament   2703

The British Parliament has no right to tax the Americans.   3578

PARLIAMENTARY

function of parliamentary democracy ... is to expose wealth-privilege   467

cannot choose between party government and Parliamentary government   2473

In our Parliamentary government, connections are absolutely necessary;   2677

PARROT

the parrots will now begin to chatter   3842

PARSIMONY

Mere parsimony is not economy.   3584

PARTNER

inseparable partners in the great adventure of humanity   3546

PARTY

One can be right only with the party, and through the party   135

The party in the last instance is always right   135

Party commands the gun, and the gun must never be allowed to command the Party   143

We must have faith in the masses and we must have faith in the Party.   154

No right to disregard it belongs to a party till released by ... other parties   319

Th' dimmycratic party ain't on speakin' terms with itsilf.   502

We can make this thing into a Party, instead of a Memory.   505

the task of our party to break with foolish traditions   506

I am not a member of any organized party—I am a Democrat.   508

The dictator ... is held in the grip of his party   602

No political party can be a friend ... which is not a friend of ... business   1596

the tyranny of ... that party ... that succeeds ... in carrying elections   2298

Those who think that all virtue is to be found in their own party principles   2442

Party loyalty lowers the greatest men to the level of the masses.   2443

The best Party is but a kind of Conspiracy   2444

Party-spirit, which at best is but the madness of many for the gain of a few.   2446

a total end of all the unhappy divisions of mankind by party-spirit   2447

All political parties die at last of swallowing their own lies.   2448

principles are fitted to party, party degenerates into faction   2449

Party divisions ... are things inseparable from free government   2450

Party is a body of men united, for promoting ... the national interest   2451

Parties must ever exist in a free country.   2452

No free Country has ever been without parties   2456

If I could not go to heaven but with a party   2457

warn you ... against the baneful effects of the spirit of party   2458

The spirit of party serves always to distract the public councils   2459

Your party man ... is always opposed to any limitation of sovereignty   2460

Party is in England a stronger passion than love   2461

party attachments ... are in the first class of a statesman's duties   2462

A sect or party is an elegant incognito   2463

The two parties which divide the state   2465

If parties in a republic are necessary to secure a degree of vigilance   2466

political parties were like snakes   2468

things must be done by parties, not by persons using parties as tools   2470

only by maintaining the independence of party   2471

maintain the line of demarcation between parties   2471

not exactly the mode of acquiring influence in a political party   2472

cannot choose between party government and Parliamentary government   2473

We have a country as well as a party to obey.   2474

All parties ... are varieties of absolutism   2475

can be but two great political parties   2476

A party of order or stability, and a party of progress ... are ... necessary   2477

Party is organised opinion.   2478

parties are formed more with reference to controversies that are gone by   2479

I had to prepare the mind of the country, and to educate ... our Party   2480

So long as we have government by party   2481

He serves his party best who serves his country best.   2482

All free governments are party government.   2483

what was best for the entire country was going to help both political parties   2484

a real, democratic party is impossible unless it be a working man's party   2485

You cannot influence a Political Party to do
Right   2487

I wish that party battles could be fought with less
personal passion   2488

I believe in party tradition   2489

party means little except when the Nation is using
the party for a ... purpose   2490

What difference does party make when mankind is
involved?   2491

each party is worse than the other   2492

remember in politics to stick to your party   2493

that no party is on the whole better than
another   2496

quite competent to judge a political party   2497

one party ... trying to prove that the other party is
unfit   2500

in the strip poker of American politics, the parties
are weak   2503

Sometimes party loyalty asks too much.   2506

Honor is not the exclusive property of any
political party.   2508

opinions adopted by parties ... not to be identifed
with ordinary human opinions   2513

political party whose leaders knew a little
psychology could sweep the country   2586

a hundred things ... for promotion in party politics
besides ability   2603

Opposition, n. ... the party that prevents the
Government from running amuck   2730

the party that wants to see an America in which
people can still get rich   3181

A revolutionary party is a contradiction in
terms.   3254

it always marks the victory of a single
party   3256

Party organization matters.   4012

PASSION

the appeal to the passions of the many   189

most of their passions either end in the love of
riches   325

opinions ... held with passion are always those for
which no good ground exists   1024

Their passions forge their fetters.   1244

Because the passions of men will not
conform   1501

Justice and good will will outlast passion.   1791

Whereas the law is passionless, passion must ever
sway the heart of man.   1821

Man is only truly great when he acts from the
passions.   2053

a number of citizens ... who are united ... by some
common ... passion   2454

Party is in England a stronger passion than
love   2461

I wish that party battles could be fought with less
personal passion   2488

The passion for office among members of
Congress   2548

when the love of fame shall cease to be the
sovereign passion of our public men   2554

A passion for politics stems usually from an
insatiable need   2642

amiable passions in human nature, are the most
dangerous guides in politics   2682

The agents that move politicks, are the popular
passions   2684

PASSIVE

If we remain passive, they will surely win.   2653

Passive resistance is a sport for gentlemen   3957

PASSIVITY

way to divest himself of passivity without arraying
himself in vindictive force   3128

PAST

the problems a President has to face have their
roots in the past   2984

PASTIME

Indeed this is quite a popular pastime.   1075

PATCH

The hole and the patch should be
commensurate.   3084

PATERNALISM

The lessons of paternalism ought to be
unlearned   3463

PATHWAY

Our "pathway" is straight to the ballot box   706

PATIENCE

Patience! the first, and last ... virtue of a
politician   2529

PATRIARCHAL

Women's liberation, if it abolishes the patriarchal
family   4001

PATRIOT

A patriot is a fool in ev'ry age.   2390

being a good patriot often means being the enemy
of the rest of mankind   2391

When his cause succeeds ... then it costs nothing
to be a patriot   2410

In the beginning ... the patriot is a scarce man,
and brave   2410

The military caste did not originate as a party of
patriots   2420

one higher office than president and I would call
that patriot   2424

A politician will do anything to keep his job--even
become a patriot.   2593

In time of war the loudest patriots are the greatest
profiteers.   3740

PATRIOTISM

"Patriotism" is its cult.   2384

Patriotism is when love of your own people comes first;   2386

Patriotism is the last refuge of the scoundrel.   2392

Patriotism itself is a necessary link in the golden chains of our affections   2399

When a whole nation is roaring Patriotism at the top of its voice   2400

Patriotism is in political life what faith is in religion.   2403

True patriotism sometimes requires of men to act exactly contrary   2404

I think patriotism is like charity   2405

Talking of patriotism, what humbug it is;   2409

I realize that patriotism is not enough.   2411

Patriotism is easy to understand in America.   2414

Patriotism is a lively sense of responsibility.   2415

Patriotism is not a short ... outburst of emotion   2418

To strike freedom of the mind with the fist of patriotism   2419

to be so blind with patriotism that you can't face reality   2421

only because of a patriotism that stands for love of country   2422

Fear finds its great moral revelation in patriotism.   2423

the stainless patriotism of those who suffered its scars   3964

PATRONAGE

Congress ... spotted also with the gravy of political patronage   808

PAUL

government which robs Peter to pay Paul can always depend on support of Paul   98

PAY

hear a man speak of his love for his country ... he expects to be paid   2417

to help a Politician to make up his mind, not only help him but pay him   2600

People are glad to be defended, but they are not glad about paying for it.   3599

PAYCHECK

respect for law and order exists in relationship to the size of his paycheck   108

PEACE

democracy constitute the most important guarantee of international peace   411

Pilate's paramount duty was to preserve the peace in Palestine   1118

Is life so dear, or peace so sweet   1219

You can't separate peace from freedom   1456

as little of it as the general peace of human society will permit   1511

vigor maintains peace and prosperity in a state   1515

Among them are peace, honor, charity, and idealism.   1590

Peace with all nations ... are our object   1608

Peace, commerce, and honest friendship with all nations   1612

speaking plainly, dealing justly ... (are) the best conservatives of the peace   1616

brought you back peace—but a peace, I hope, with honour   1627

not organized rivalries, but an organized common peace   1640

Open covenants of peace, openly arrived at   1641

foreign policy of America can best be described by one word--peace   1644

Our foreign policy has one primary object, and that is peace.   1645

We are for peace ... for very simple reasons   1665

You don't promote the cause of peace by talking ... to people with whom you agree.   1666

As long as any ... cannot enjoy the blessings of peace with justice   1669

any nation that seeks peace ... will find the United States by their side   1680

We keep a vigil of peace around the world.   1681

Peace and justice are two sides of the same coin.   1805

White folks don't want peace; they want quiet.   1814

Until there is justice, there will be no peace   1814

We do not admire a man of timid peace.   2085

American people ... believe that peace should rest upon the rights of peoples   3331

the purpose of political order: which is simply peace and security of life   3411

Prepare for war in time of peace.   3461

to set up a universal society founded on ... equal peace for all nations   3563

Better beans and bacon in peace than cakes and ale in fear.   3645

We make war that we may live in peace.   3649

between peace and slavery there is the greatest difference   3655

Peace is liberty in tranquility;   3656

Certain peace is better and safer than anticipated victory.   3657

Where they make a desert, they call it peace.   3661

We are now suffering the evils of a long peace.   3663

Let him who desires peace prepare for war.   3664

most disadvantageous peace is better than the most just war   3666

live together in peace, but that, living in peace, they should serve God   3669

PEACEFUL

A nation without dregs and malcontents, is ...
peaceful 990

a ... transformation of relationships, ending in a
peaceful transfer of power 3261

Those who make peaceful revolution
impossible 3271

Revolutions are never peaceful. 3274

PEACEMAKER

Blessed are the peacemakers 3660

The navy of the United States ... is emphatically
the peacemaker 3774

The greatest honor history can bestow is the title
of peacemaker. 3939

PEASANT

Guerrilla warfare is to peasant uprisings what
Marx is to Sorel. 173

That a peasant may become king does not render
the kingdom democratic. 2358

PEBBLE

You have to be like the pebble in the
stream 2051

PECULIAR

We Americans are a peculiar people. 1066

PECUNIARY

Moral principle is a looser bond than pecuniary
interest. 784

PEER

humblest is the peer of the most powerful 3323

PEN

May the pens of the diplomats not ruin
again 3711

PENCIL

Farming looks mighty easy when your plow is a
pencil 9

PENDULUM

The pendulum will swing back. 942

The pendulum swung furiously to the left 2689

PENT-UP

it is pent-up feelings that are dangerous 3233

PEOPLE

people who think that a democratic State is
scarcely distinguishable from the people 3

the Privileged and the People formed two
nations 52

The people are the safest ... lodgement of
power 60

He mocks the people who proposes that the
Government shall protect the rich 76

most unfortunate people are those who must do
the same thing over and over 107

I was not included in that "We, the people." 255

What is the city but the people? 271

power of Kings ... is ... what is ... committed to
them ... from the People 272

where ... the people are a party to the laws 275

free people, the purest source and original fountain
of all power 285

what a free government is ... it is what the people
think so 290

The people themselves ... are its only safe
depositories 293

a government which derives all its powers ... from
the great body of the people 298

but one element of government, and that is the
people 307

Sovereignty resides in the French People 308

No government can continue good but under the
control of the people. 310

The people made the Constitution, and the people
can unmake it. 311

from the people, and for the people, all
springs 313

The people's government, made for the
people 317

Where the people possess no authority, their rights
obtain no respect. 320

The American idea ... is a democracy, that is a
government of all the people 330

the people are the rightful masters of both
congresses and courts 337

that government of the people ... shall not perish
from the earth 344

Our government springs from and was made for
the people 346

The people themselves must think, because the
people alone can act. 358

Democracy means simply the bludgeoning of the
people by the people 367

My plan cannot fail if the people are with us 369

no better or safer human tribunal than the
people 370

the people must either go on or go under 387

a people are responsible for the acts of their
government 388

folly to argue that the people cannot make
political mistakes 393

government in which all people have a part 396

our whole political machinery pre-supposes a
people so fundamentally at one 397

I do not want the voice of the people shut
out. 400

"Trust the people"—that was his message. 426

from the people and the people alone flows the
authority of government 433

believe that other people may perhaps be wiser
than oneself 445

I am the people—the mob—the crowd—the
mass. 452

to expose wealth-privilege to the attacks of the
people 467

the people make the best judgment in the long run 469

But there is no lobby for the people. 479

People are not an interruption of our business. People are our business. 481

"We the people" are the driver 500

When a people shall have become incapable of governing themselves 543

The people are always in the wrong when they are faced by the armed forces. 551

The third is called the People. 578

The people may be made to follow a path of action 664

Education makes a people easy to lead, but difficult to drive; 676

drawing up an indictment against a whole people. 842

cannot fool all of the people all of the time 886

People don't eat in the long run 952

The people, and the people alone, are the motive force 980

No people on earth can be held, as a people, to be an enemy 996

When people ... stop thinking of the United Nations as a weird Picasso 1004

most of our people have never had it so good 1013

Rarely have so many people been so wrong about so much. 1094

Where the people rule, discussion is necessary. 1120

way to make sure people you agree with can speak 1149

The people never give up their liberties but under some delusion. 1232

No people will be truly free till all are free. 1376

freedom is something people take and people are as free as they want to be 1435

Let the people think they govern and they will be governed. 1482

Governments arise either out of the people or over the people. 1509

See that government ... does not unnecessarily burden the people 1519

Peoples ... never have learned anything from history 1528

Like People like Government 1534

Government cannot be stronger or more tough-minded than its people. 1564

Governments got in the way of the dreams of the people. 1711

if the republic is the weal of the people 1756

The good of the people is the supreme law. 1824

The mass of the people have nothing to do with the laws but to obey them. 1873

no man can take the place of a whole people 2166

You cannot be a leader, and ask other people to follow you 2169

some people ... think the way to be a big man is to shout 2187

People tend to want to follow the beaten path. 2191

legislatures are ultimate guardians of the liberties ... of the people 2241

The legislature ... has ceased to be even the creature of the people 2249

Legislators represent people, not trees or acres. 2257

if people don't want it, they won't have it 2364

but a patriotism that stands for love of people 2422

While people and their opinions always deserve the greatest respect 2513

So long as the people of any country place their hopes of political salvation 2546

Public officers are the servants ... of the people 2556

people who treat politics and morality separately will never understand either 2679

The people of this country are a straightforward people. 2731

People who think ... Washington can be persuaded ... by anything less than votes 2768

People never move towards revolution; 3244

We did not win the People over by appealing to reason 3285

A bill of rights is what the people are entitled to 3294

The people know their rights, and they are never slow to assert ... them 3302

Most people ... when they espouse human rights 3335

Two things only the people anxiously desire, bread and the circus games. 3405

its functions do not include the support of the people 3463

landscape should belong to the people who see it 3548

The Federal Government is the people 3620

May the pens of the diplomats not ruin again what the people have attained 3711

War is a game in which princes seldom win, the people never. 3715

The wars of the people will be more terrible 3757

A really great people ... would face all the disasters of war 3766

in a faraway country between people of whom we know nothing 3818

People who are ... brutal often find war enjoyable 3863

people want peace so much that ... governments had better get out of the way 3898

People do not want words 3941

PERCENT

If you treat people right they will treat you right 961

PERFECT

So perfect a government is not for men. 280

the more liberty is given ... the more perfect it will become 1217

PERFORMANCE

audience ... that hissed yesterday may applaud ... for the same performance 1137

My strong point ... is performance 2188

PERFORMER

I would prefer if he were a performer. 1096

PERIL

A love for tradition has ... strengthened nations in their hour of peril 217

then the peril to freedom will continue to rise 1437

which statesmen will henceforth ignore at their peril 2374

PERILOUS

In these perilous hours ... the American people are ahead of their leaders 472

PERISH

Better to perish with the revolution 3211

PERMANENT

our true policy to steer clear of permanent alliance 1609

to allow the friendship between nations to rest upon deep and permanent things 1631

PERMISSION

nor do we ask any man's permission when we ask him to obey it 1904

PERMISSIVE

Permissive legislation is the characteristic of a free people. 2238

PERMIT

under the law everything is prohibited except that which is permitted 1959

PERPETUAL

We have no eternal allies, and we have no perpetual enemies. 1619

PERPETUITY

Perpetuity is implied ... in the fundamental law 1540

PERSECUTION

Persecution was at least a sign of personal interest. 2910

objects of fear or derision and targets of persecution for either side 2918

where plots ... are hatched for the persecution ... of other human beings 2937

persecution for cause of conscience is ... contrary to the doctrine of Christ 3137

Rather it condemns the ... persecution of others 3161

PERSISTENCE

Persistence in one opinion has never been considered a merit 2515

PERSON

better 100 guilty Persons should escape than that one innocent Person ... suffer 1770

One person with a belief is a social power equal to ninety-nine 2069

when the person interested is himself able ... to stand up for them 3307

PERSONAL

A Presidential campaign may easily degenerate into a mere personal contest 2426

if they attack one personally ... they have not a single political argument 2823

PERSONALITY

to have moulded a public personality out of so amorphous an identity 2211

PERSONNEL

Few great men could pass Personnel. 2165

PERSUADE

under which you have to persuade the largest number of persons 381

Law cannot persuade where it cannot punish. 1851

PERVERSION

What a perversion of the normal order of things! 2843

PERVERT

not to overthrow the Constitution, but to overthrow the men who pervert it 337

PESSIMISTIC

no need to feel pessimistic about this country 112

PETER

government which robs Peter to pay Paul can depend on the support of Paul 98

PETTICOAT

which might thus be said to be under petticoat government 3979

PH.D.

Where there are two PhDs in a developing country 1046

PHILANTHROPY

to realise the condition of the unfortunate is the beginning of philanthropy 203

PHILOSOPHER

The philosophers have only interpreted the world differently 2055

PHILOSOPHY

my political philosophy ... Trust the people   465

a function of government to invent philosophies   1568

Neither philosophy, nor religion ... will ever govern nations   2841

PHRASE

Such phrases have always been ... of those who have vested interests   3825

PHRASEOLOGY

a habit of comparing the phraseology of communiques   1712

PHYSICS

predictable as a law of physics: as government expands, liberty contracts   1475

indeed a law of politicks as well as of physicks   2685

PICASSO

When people ... stop thinking of the United Nations as a weird Picasso   1004

PICK

They pick a president and then for four years they pick on him.   2981

PIECE OF CAKE

It's a piece of cake until you get to the top.   2808

PIGEON

a pigeon can still make a deposit on a John Deere   1600

PIGMIES

the pigmies will now start to squabble   3842

PILATE

I would rather have blood on my hands than water like Pilate.   169

Was Pilate right in crucifying Christ?   1118

PILLARS

spirit of truth and the spirit of freedom—they are the pillars of society   1311

Kings are the publick Pillars of the State   2335

PINCH

the system that functions in the pinches that survives   1560

PINPRICK

nations should avoid the pinpricks that precede cannon shots   3708

PISTOL

One who brandishes a pistol must be prepared to shoot.   2122

PLACE

the need of the upper class to keep the lower class in its place   110

a certain personal superiority by reason of one's belonging to a place   2382

PLAIN

Nothing astonishes men so much as common sense and plain dealing.   875

A faithful observance ... of speaking plainly, dealing justly   1616

PLAN

planned ... economic system could ... bring about distributive justice   144

My plan cannot fail if the people are with us   369

plan conceived in moderation must fail when circumstances are set in extremes   858

If something happens you can be sure it was planned that way.   2750

to which end a uniform and well-digested plan is requisite   3701

PLANET

as if they were ... inhabitants of different planets   51

a planet whose resources are devoted to the ... nourishment of its inhabitants   736

superpowers have the privilege of being able to destroy our planet   3954

PLATEAU

History knows no resting places and no plateaus.   1084

PLATFORM

some cynics who think that a Platform is just a list of platitudes   2430

party platforms are contracts with the people   2502

If you have a weak ... platform, wrap yourself up in the ... flag   2557

But when at last woman stands on an even platform with man   3988

PLATITUDE

Platitudes are there because they are true.   1089

perfection of Parliamentary style is to utter cruel platitudes   2570

PLEA

In law, what plea so tainted and corrupt ... Obscures the show of evil?   1840

PLEASE

but the key to failure is trying to please everybody   2198

but to tax and to please ... is not given to men   3580

PLEASURE

An honest man can feel no pleasure in the exercise of power 2536

The real pleasure comes when he hands them back. 2562

Power is pleasure; and pleasure sweetens pain. 2850

next greatest pleasure ... preventing others from enjoying themselves 2868

PLEDGE

I pledge you, I pledge myself, to a new deal 951

we mutually pledge to each other our Lives 1228

PLIANT

Never ... shall an officer of the people ... become the pliant instrument 2544

PLOW

Farming looks mighty easy when your plow is a pencil 9

I must plough my own furrow alone 2089

PLOWSHARE

they shall beat their swords into plowshares 3650

PLUCKING

so plucking the goose as to obtain the largest possible amount of feathers 3577

PLUNDER

it everywhere constitutes a system of plunder 3523

To tax the community for the advantage of a class ... is plunder 3598

PLUNGE

dagger plunged in the name of Freedom is plunged into the breast of Freedom 1382

PLUTOCRACY

the social habits and mentality of the oldest and toughest plutocracy 412

PLUTOCRATIC

that a people half democratic and half plutocratic cannot permanently endure 80

POEM

something about a bureaucrat that does not like a poem 11

When poems stop talking about the moon and begin to mention poverty 1396

POET

Poets and philosophers are the unacknowledged legislators of the world. 857

POETRY

You can campaign in poetry. You govern in prose. 2437

" Don't teach my boy poetry; he is going to stand for Parliament." 2611

When power corrupts, poetry cleanses 2879

POIGNANT

A grievance is most poignant when almost redressed. 988

POINT

grateful for even the sharpest criticism, as long as it sticks to the point 905

The real leader has no need to lead—he is content to point the way. 2135

POISON

the morals of the whole people are poisoned 809

covert follies that warp and poison the mind 3233

POLE

to keep power divided, to prevent a small core from either pole 486

Socialism and laisser faire are like the north and south poles. 3560

POLEMICS

better to discuss things, to argue and engage in polemics 1720

POLICE

For the urban poor the police are those who arrest you. 105

A police state finds it cannot command the grain to grow. 615

When poems stop talking about the moon ... somebody tells the police 1396

men who agree perfectly with their own police 1462

We Americans have no commission from God to police the world. 1629

The police must obey the law while enforcing the law. 1928

No socialist system can be established without a political police. 3567

POLICEMAN

Can you imagine a policeman being required to secure the assent of parties 1718

POLICING

art of policing is, in order not to punish often 1778

POLICY

It is not the metier of a Tory to have a policy 198

I shall on all subjects have a policy to recommend 350

Although only a few may originate a policy, we are all able to judge it. 496

Kings will be tyrants from policy 544

They misjudge individual speeches for public policy. 620

They mistake restlessness for a rejection of policy. 620

not of the generation that regards honesty as the best policy   819

the only good policy is to pursue no policy   861

A policy is a temporary creed liable to be changed   941

Refined policy ever had been the parent of confusion   1495

The really basic thing in government is policy.   1563

our true policy to steer clear of permanent alliance   1609

peaceful relations abroad constitute the true permanent policy of our country   1620

Whenever our policy in the West has run aground   1642

a policy ... only when commitments and power have been brought into balance   1654

Justice is itself the great standing policy of civil society;   1773

severest justice may not always be the best policy   1787

Government includes the art of formulating a policy   2123

To render legislation agreeable to good policy   2222

commonest error in politics is sticking to the carcass of dead policies   2714

They are the vital process of policy among free men.   2769

Never forget posterity when devising a policy.   2797

happiness of society ... is best promoted by the practice of a virtuous policy   3425

My home policy? I wage war. My foreign policy? I wage war.   3786

War is not the continuation of policy. It is the breakdown of policy.   3801

You ask, what is our policy?   3828

I want to make a policy statement.   3998

POLITIC

What is right must unavoidably be politic.   2686

POLITICAL

best political community is formed by citizens of the middle class   34

enough political economy for me to know that the idle rich class is rich   73

What has it hitherto been in the political order?   300

basis of our political system is the right of the people to make ... constitutions   303

not supported by democratic institutions ... is not political freedom   329

Democracy is a political method   429

political ones are insoluble and the economic ones are incomprehensible   1045

Intellectual slavery ... always have as a natural result ... political slavery   1307

because men will ... deal with with political, as ... with scientific questions   1313

To model our political system upon speculations of lasting tranquility   1507

the fundamental problem of a rational political theory   1577

true end of political action is ... to affect the deeper convictions of men   1668

hardly a political question ... which does not ... turn into a judicial one   1729

political leaders who realize the great public is interested more in government   2129

both necessary elements of a healthy state of political life   2477

Persistence in one opinion has never been considered a merit in political leaders.   2515

when life-long professional soldiers abstain from seeking high political office   2599

Man is by nature a political animal.   2672

political spirit is the great force in throwing ... truth ... into a secondary place   2712

There is nothing that is not political.   2741

A declining political class has all the infirmities of old age   2756

tragedy of all political action is that some problems have no solution   2781

All political structures are based on power.   2867

than it is to change a country's political order   3079

If the abuse be enormous, nature will ... overturn a corrupt political system   3188

They did not fear political change.   3246

as long as the political problems are not tackled   3947

POLITICIAN

We cannot safely leave politics to politicians   358

Bad politicians are sent to Washington by good people who don't vote.   726

When I want to buy up any politician   787

even a politician who is honest in the highest sense may be very harmful   797

politician wouldn't dream of being allowed to call a columnist the things   1183

politician thinks of the next election   2058

At home, you always have to be a politician;   2161

best time to listen to a politician is when he's on a stump ... late at night   2432

like a scurvy politician, seem/ To see the things thou dost not   2517

No man can be a politician, except he be first a historian or a traveller;   2519

than for a politician to lay aside disguise   2526

to be a sound politician ... must be governed by higher ... considerations   2538

politicians think much more about the security of their seats   2545

I'm not a politician and my other habits are good.   2549

Politicians are like the bones of a horse's fore-shoulder   2552

The politician who once had to learn to flatter Kings   2564

Politician, n. An eel in the fundamental mud   2566

"you must judge us by our politicians"   2568

Politicians are to serve the people, not to direct them.   2569

Politicians tend to live "in character"   2572

I am a Virginian, so naturally I am a politician.   2578

The politician is an acrobat.   2581

Politicians ... are peculiarly ignorant of the desires that move ordinary men   2586

when a politician does get an idea he usually gets it all wrong   2592

A politician will do anything to keep his job   2593

if we could consult the veteran instead of the politician   2595

too many politicians who believe ... that you can fool all the people   2597

Politicians are ambitious not to make important decisions   2598

A Lobbyist is ... supposed to help a Politician   2600

Politicians ... are not over a year behind Public Opinion   2601

knowing every politician in the state and remembering where he itches   2604

politicians are shocked by those who ... let their thinking reach any conclusion   2605

Successful democratic politicians are insecure and intimidated men.   2608

no such thing as a nonpolitical speech by a politician   2609

but if more politicians knew poetry   2611

A good politician with nerve ... can win in the face of the stiffest opposition   2613

distinction between a statesman and a politician is that the former imposes his will   2614

A politician is a man who understands government   2615

A statesman is a politician who's been dead 10 or 15 years.   2615

The politician is ... trained in the art of inexactitude   2618

The politician in my country seeks votes   2619

Politicians are the same all over.   2620

Since a politician never believes what he says   2624

As the master politician navigates the ship of state   2626

professional politician's first duty is to appeal to the forces that unite   2627

One has to be a lowbrow ... to be a politician   2628

danger for a politician is to shake hands with a man who is ... stronger   2629

the kind of politician who would cut down a redwood tree   2630

once said cynically of a politician, "He'll double-cross that bridge   2631

distinctive characteristic of the successful politician is selective cowardice   2633

certainly not get it from their politicians   2635

Politicians trim and tack in their quest for power   2636

to get elected you have to be a politician   2641

A politician ought to be born a foundling   2643

Most politicians have a right to feel morally superior   2644

I'd rather keep my promises to other politicians   2649

Politicians fascinate because they constitute such a paradox: 2650

The politician who will refuse the Foreign Office is not yet born.   2651

populist politician ... who says things because he believes them to be popular   2652

Most politicians will not stick their necks out   2653

people who say worse things about politicians than reporters are ... politicians   2655

He loved politicians—even Republicans.   2658

average politician goes through a sentence like a man exploring a ... mine   2663

Politicians have the same occupational hazard as generals   2664

A President has to be a politician ... to get the majority to go along   2987

I am not speaking as a politician;   3169

POLITICKING

In writing and politicking, it's best not to think about it   2818

POLITICS

Politics ought to be the part-time profession of every citizen   27

We cannot safely leave politics to politicians   358

Politics and law are ... merely results   359

Conscience has no more to do with gallantry than it has with politics.   778

You cannot adopt politics as a profession and remain honest.   801

The Army will hear nothing of politics from me   929

Opinions in politics ... are almost always held passionately   1024

the very existence of politics, the cause of freedom versus tyranny   1446

The purification of politics is an iridescent dream.   1547

Politics is the reflex of the business and industrial world.   1586

In public politics ... character is better than brains 2103

public is interested more in government than in politics 2129

The more you read and observe about this Politics thing 2492

remember in politics to stick to your party 2493

an animal with a hide two feet thick, and no apparent interest in politics 2660

people who treat politics and morality separately 2679

Politics are ... a means of rising in the world 2680

in politics the middle way is none at all 2681

In politics nothing is just save what is honest 2683

The agents that move politicks, are the popular passions; 2684

a law of politicks ... that a body in action must overcome a ... body at rest 2685

In politics ... we have less charity for those who believe half of our creed 2687

Gratitude is not an active sentiment in politics. 2690

Politics is the art of knowing and leading a multitude 2691

In politics you should always leave an old bone behind 2692

very few facts ... in politics 2693

politics in the presence of social dangers to be a luxury 2695

in politics how often men are ruined by having too good a memory 2696

My pollertics ... being of an exceeding' accommodatin' character 2699

Politics is not an exact science. 2700

Politics is the art of the possible. 2702

politics is the action and reaction between the Ministry and the Parliament 2703

Politics makes strange bed-fellows. 2706

just as politics is the despot of will 2707

Exploitation and government are ... what is called politics. 2708

optimist view of politics assumes ... some remedy for every political ill 2709

In politics one must take nothing tragically 2711

Those who would treat politics and morality apart 2713

Politics are vulgar when they are not liberalised by history 2716

Politics is not a science ... but an art 2717

In politics there is no use looking beyond the next fortnight. 2718

Politics ... has always been the systematic organization of hatreds 2723

Politics, n. A strife of interests masquerading as a contest of principles. 2724

Administration, n. An ingenious abstraction in politics 2725

Practical politics consists in ignoring facts. 2727

Modern politics is ... a struggle not of men but of force 2728

In politics habits ... rule humanity 2735

Politics are almost as exciting as war 2736

aim of practical politics is to keep the populace alarmed 2737

Politics, which, the planet over, are the fly in the amber 2739

Politics ... the delusion that a change in form is a change in substance 2740

Politics is not an art, but a means. 2743

In the field of politics, force and consent are correlative terms 2744

The more cant there is in politics the better. 2745

Politics has got so expensive 2748

Nothing just happens in politics. 2750

The science of politics ... the adjustment of conflicting group interests 2751

Politics: Who Gets What, When, How. 2752

Politics is war without bloodshed 2753

Politics can be relatively fair in the breathing spaces of history 2757

politics seem like provincial struggles for booty 2758

Politics ... are shaped by men without ideals 2759

Politics is the art of preventing people from taking part in affairs 2760

Politics is the science of who gets what, when, and why. 2762

In politics ... no such thing as one getting something for nothing 2763

If you ever injected truth into politics you have no politics. 2766

What is politics but persuading the public to vote for this 2771

Politics is the only profession for which no preparation is thought necessary 2775

the best government is the best politics 2777

Defeat ... was part ... of the great gambling game of politics 2778

And in politics you work with it or you don't work 2779

Politics is a systematic effort to move other men 2783

If you're in politics and you can't tell ... who's for you 2786

And politics is the bow of idealism. 2788

American politics is one of the noblest arts of mankind; 2790

An independent ... wants to take the politics out of politics 2791

In politics ... retreat is honorable if dictated by military considerations 2792

All politics are based on the indifference of the majority. 2793

politics consists in directing rationally the
irrationalities of men   2799
Politics is the skilled use of blunt objects.   2800
one thing solid and fundamental in politics—the
law of change   2802
We cannot cure the evils of politics with
politics.   2803
sad duty of politics is to establish justice in a
sinful world   2804
Politics ... is best learned at an early age   2805
In politics, guts is all.   2806
Politics is the art of looking for trouble   2807
Politics I supposed to be the second-oldest
profession.   2809
If you're in politics, you're a whore
anyhow.   2810
choice in politics isn't usually between black and
white   2811
Politics is motion and excitement.   2813
The best politics is no politics.   2814
through politics we can change our society   2816
he never did get it through his head that's what
politics is all about   2817
Nothing is so admirable in politics as a short
memory.   2819
I seldom think of politics more than 18 hours a
day.   2821
Politics in America is the binding secular
religion.   2822
Politics, where fat, bald, disagreeable men ... teach
a president how to act   2825
God does not take sides in American
politics.   2827
I care not who governs its politics   2878
What we won ... must not be lost in ...
politics   3004
Politics ... hold up torches of martyrdom   3088
Politics would become an utter blank to me   3151
that I could not do unless I took part in
politics   3158
the black man should control the politics ... in his
own community   3367
being in politics has taught me is that men are not
a ... reasonable sex   4004
In politics women ... type the letters   4006
In politics if you want anything said, ask a
man.   4008

POLL

It isn't polls or public opinion alone of the
moment that counts.   3076

POLLING

Inside the polling booth every American ... stands
as equal   712
Polling is merely an instrument for gauging public
opinion.   3080

POLLUTION

flood of money that gushes into politics today is a
pollution of democracy   820

POMPOSITY

if a little pomposity be superadded   2570

POOR

the rich have power and the poor man is deprived
of it   33
directed to the purpose of making the rich richer
and the poor poorer   49
The rich rob the poor and poor rob one
another.   61
the rich are rich because they rob the poor   73
protect the rich and ...they in turn will care for
the laboring poor   76
To be a poor man is hard, but to be a poor race in
a land of dollars   83
the perennial and unfailing kindness of the poor to
the rich   84
It's no disgrace t' be poor, but it might as well
be.   88
when the poor fly it it means danger,
revolution   99
When the rich wage war it's the poor who
die.   101
If a free society cannot help the many who are
poor   104
For the urban poor the police are those who arrest
you.   105
ask of the poor that they get up and act just like
everyone else   106
the poor in America are sick, dirty,
disorganized   109
Forgive us for pretending to care for the
poor   111
You don't make the poor richer by making the
rich poorer.   659
poorest he that is in England hath a life to
live   739
but everywhere man, the heir of nature, is
poor   916
A poor man with nothing in his belly needs
hope   956
But, like the poor, it is always with us   1124
no nation so poor that it cannot afford free
speech   1151
I would rather belong to a poor nation that was
free   1343
poor change nothing beyond the change of their
master   1479
criticism of the criminal justice system for its
treatment of the poor   1817
Laws grind the poor, and rich men rule the
law.   1862
the poor are our equals in every sense except that
of being equal   2275
A decent provision for the poor is the true test of
civilization.   3517
No poor ... person should ... be... deprived of the
opportunity for an education   3549
a condition of society in which there should be
neither rich nor poor   3554

when lawmaking falls exclusively to the lot of the poor   3594

POPE
The Pope! How many divisions has he got?   3157

POPULACE
aim of practical politics is to keep the populace alarmed   2737

The populace doesn't want to be fed;   3133

three ways for the populace to escape its wretched lot   3224

POPULAR
evils of popular government appear greater   338

Popular government has not yet been proved to guarantee ... good government   463

A popular government without popular information or the means of acquiring it   675

Heroes are created by popular demand   2138

A President cannot always be popular.   2989

POPULARITY
never will (I hope) do anything for the sake of popularity   2537

POPULATION
the expression of what cultivation exists in the population   1884

POPULIST
populist politician ... says things because he believes them to be popular   2652

PORK BARREL
Our nation was not founded on the pork barrel   2749

PORNOGRAPHIC
Making foreign policy is a little bit like making pornographic movies.   1704

POSITION
his position on almost every public question was either mischievous   918

people in positions of this kind ... manage without ... any acting experience   2661

official position ... is defined by decisions ...of the President   2985

POSSESS
Liberty must be limited in order to be possessed.   1229

POSSESSION
most valuable of human possessions ... is the reputation of being well to do   392

in the peaceful possession of what belongs to him   3416

POSSESSOR
because its possessors failed to stretch forth a saving hand   1373

POSSIBILITY
Liberty is the possibility of doubting   1410

POSSIBLE
Politics is the art of the possible.   2702

Politics is not the art of the possible.   2796

POSTERITY
Constitution of the United States was made ... for posterity   236

Posterity! You will never know how much it cost   1231

Never forget posterity when devising a policy.   2797

POSTURE
very hard to look up to leaders who are ... in that somewhat ungainly posture   3074

POTOMAC RIVER
as easily bail out the Potomac River with a teaspoon   895

POULTRY
the foxes have a sincere interest in prolonging the lives of the poultry   705

POVERTY
not easy for men to rise whose qualities are thwarted by poverty   36

Wherever there is excessive wealth, there is also ... excessive poverty   59

most grinding poverty is a trifling evil compared with ... inequality   72

where poverty is enforced ... neither persons nor property will be safe   75

How can wealth persuade poverty ... to keep wealth in power?   218

either poverty will use democracy to win the struggle against property   456

Poverty has many roots   697

Riches without law are more dangerous than is poverty without law.   1894

To be a Negro is to participate in a culture of poverty   2925

live on the outskirts of hope—some because of their poverty   2932

the moral obligation of providing for ... poverty   3426

aim at the elimination of poverty by direct means   3486

ours ought to be a country free from the great blotches of distressed poverty   3527

For every talent that poverty has stimulated   3539

Political sovereignty is but a mockery without the means of meeting poverty   3540

administration ... declares unconditional war on poverty   3543

POWDER
only take the ideas of the economists to reduce it to powder   635

439

Keyword Index

441

POWERFUL

If ... the world's most powerful nation ... acts like a pitiful, helpless giant   1699

Every country is renewed out of unknown ranks and not out of the ... powerful   2098

worst ... that can be said of the most powerful is that they can take your life   2847

The powerful can usually help themselves   3480

POWERLESSNESS

Powerlessness frustrates; absolute powerlessness frustrates absolutely.   2889

PRACTICAL

Practical men, who believe themselves ... exempt from intellectual influences   649

The most practical kind of politics is the politics of decency.   2721

Practical politics consists in ignoring facts.   2727

Declaration of Independence is a practical document for the use of practical men   3236

PRACTICE

not moral principles, but simply the accepted practices   475

Liberty don't work as good in practice   1360

not because we claim freedom, but because we practice it   1423

Human law may know no distinction ... but human practice may   3316

PRAISE

Let arms yield to the toga, the laurel crown to praise.   3653

those who praise it without participating in it   3775

PRAY

"No, I look at the Senators and pray for the country."   2251

a time to preach and a time to pray   3694

PRAYER

so I ask you to confirm me with your prayers   3017

no longer be satisfied to represent only the Conservative Party at prayer   3155

the government ought to stay out of the prayer business   3164

PRECEDENT

Mere precedent is a dangerous source of authority.   868

nothing ... more obscure ... than a legal system based on precedent   1882

One precedent in favor of power is stronger than an hundred against it.   2840

PREDECESSOR

The elephant ... proceeds best by grasping the tail of his predecessor   3173

PREDISPOSITION

there exists, more commonly ... a predisposition to take offense   1613

PREGNANCY

The states are not free ... to intimidate women into continuing pregnancies   1948

PREJUDICE

I ... decry the appeal to the passions of the many or the prejudices of the few   189

Knowledge ... is our best protection against unreasoning prejudice   691

No man is prejudiced in favor of a thing knowing it to be wrong.   846

Law is a reflection and a source of prejudice.   1946

even those at present the most prejudiced against us   2017

no prejudice so strong as ... from a fancied exemption from all prejudice   2895

Prejudice is the child of ignorance.   2897

Prejudice is never easy unless it can pass itself off for reason.   2898

never too late to give up our prejudices   2901

prejudice against color ... is no stronger than that against sex   2902

Race prejudice decreases values both real estate and human;   2909

tendency ... is to pick out ... a sample which supports ... its prejudices   2911

No one can eliminate prejudices—just recognize them.   2921

PREMIER

And what makes a man Premier?   2077

PREPARE

so too the Kingdom that is not always prepared has much to fear   3682

To be prepared for War is one of the most effectual means of preserving peace.   3700

preserve peace when it is well understood that we are prepared for war   3719

Wars occur because people prepare for conflict   3850

not to proceed by the dubious indirection of preparing for it   3858

PREPAREDNESS

a better preparedness in a public mind ... made ready to grant justice   3793

PREROGATIVE

an elite as steadfast in its determination to maintain its prerogatives   168

PRESENCE

one provision was conspicuous by its presence   888

PRESERVATION

confusing the duty of preservation with
   inactivity   191

the only sure reliance for the preservation of our
   liberty   667

Government has no other end but the preservation
   of Property.   3412

PRESERVE

"to preserve is to act", has always served me   191

Liberty cannot be preserved without general
   knowledge   665

to their interest to preserve peace and order   667

Our Union: It must be preserved.   863

if its rulers are not warned ... that people preserve
   the spirit of resistance   1235

harder to preserve than to obtain liberty   1268

whatever resolve will ... preserve the freedom of
   one's country   1834

A disposition to preserve, and an ability to
   improve   2021

Reform, that you may preserve   3094

PRESIDE

to preside over the liquidation of the British
   Empire   2136

PRESIDENCY

always get the truth ... after he has ... given up all
   hope of the Presidency   2550

No man will ever carry out of the Presidency the
   reputation   2954

Presidency, n. The greased pig in ... American
   politics   2964

Th' prisidincy is th' highest office   2965

The Presidency is not merely an administrative
   office.   2974

Extremism in the pursuit of the Presidency is an
   unpardonable vice   3000

American Presidency ... a way station en route to
   ... being an ex-President   3002

The presidency has made every man who occupied
   it ... bigger   3006

that there was a cancer growing on the
   presidency   3008

The presidency has many problems, but boredom
   is the least of them.   3011

I shall resign the presidency effective at noon
   tomorrow   3018

The Presidency is no place for on-the-job
   training.   3022

Old men running for the Presidency   3028

the presidency is an institution over which you
   have temporary custody   3036

PRESIDENT

getting caught doing what the two presidents
   before him got away with   817

If you don't like the president, it costs you 90
   bucks to fly to Washington   1095

Presidents come and go, but the Supreme Court ...
   goes on forever   1741

that is what your President has been trying to
   do   2144

Nor does any American President have power
   approaching this.   2363

one higher office than president   2424

Administration, n. ... designed to receive the kicks
   ... due to the president   2725

where fat, bald, disagreeable men ... teach a
   president how to act   2825

I would ... have given more power to the President
   and less to the Senate   2950

President will never fall to ... any man who is not
   in an eminent degree endowed   2951

I had rather be right than be President.   2956

As President, I have no eyes but constitutional
   eyes;   2959

In America the President reigns for four
   years   2963

President is at liberty ... to be as big a man as he
   can   2966

The President can exercise no power ...not ...
   traced to some specific grant   2969

public wants a solemn ass as a President   2970

Presidents who have served eight years   2972

The President cannot ... constantly appeal to the
   country   2973

the President has become increasingly the
   depository of all national ills   2975

"sometimes I wish I could be President and
   Congress too."   2976

President ... is neither an absolute monarch   2978

dispute the integrity of the President   2978

In America any boy may become President ... one
   of the risks he takes   2980

They pick a president and then for four years they
   pick on him.   2981

The President is the only lobbyist ... Americans
   have   2983

the problems a President has to face have their
   roots in the past   2984

official position ... is defined by decisions ... of the
   President   2985

To be President of the United States is to be
   lonely   2986

A President needs political understanding   2988

A President cannot always be popular.   2989

The President is the representative of the whole
   nation   2992

the President is to set before the ... people the
   unfinished business   2994

No easy problems ever come to the
   President   2996

when things don't go well they like to blame the
   Presidents   2997

A President's hardest task is not to do what is
   right   3001

443

not because the President offers a chance to be somebody 3003

"Why would anyone want to be President today?" 3003

I shall not seek ... the nomination of my party for another term as president 3004

the confidentiality of the office of the president would always be suspect 3007

Being president is like being a jackass in a hailstorm. 3009

nothing ... authorizes ... president to have anything to do with criminal activities 3012

When people ask if the United States can afford to place on trial the president 3013

What did the president know and when did he know it? 3015

it isn't for you. It's for the Presidency. 3016

you have not elected me as your president 3017

as president I must put the interests of America first 3018

simply because it is the president ... who holds the evidence 3019

The president's need for complete candor 3020

the feeling of being with the president in the Oval Office ... Ovalitis 3021

President is the only person who can change the direction 3023

no inherent Constitutional authority for the President ... to violate the law 3024

When the President does it, that means that it is not illegal. 3026

It isn't wisdom ... that influences a President, it's opportunity 3027

Once a president gets to the White House, only audience ... left ... is history 3032

I said I didn't want to run for president 3033

the president says one thing during the election 3034

Frankly, I don't mind not being president. 3035

Of all the inherent duties of an American President, the duty to say no 3038

When a president ... pays attention to poll results 3080

the duty of the President to propose and ... of the Congress to dispose 3511

the manner in which the president personally exercises his ... powers 3512

cannot be left to a President ... to decide what must be kept secret 3514

Certainly in the next 50 years we shall see a woman president 4000

aren't many women now I'd like to see as President 4010

PRESS

press may be made an engine to complete their ruin 1157

abuses of the press are notorious ... License of the press is no proof of liberty 1157

To the press alone ... the world is indebted for all the triumphs 1161

let me have but an unfettered Press 1165

chief danger which threatens the influence and honor of the press 1171

all of us at times suffered from the liberty of the press 1172

In old days men had the rack. Now they have the press. 1173

liberty of the press ... approved when it takes liberties with the other fellow 1175

The hand that rules the press ... rules the country 1179

very difficult to have a free, fair and honest press anywhere 1181

Freedom ought to be a means to enable the press to serve the proper functions 1182

Whenever the press quits abusing me 1185

Freedom of the press belongs to those who own one. 1194

reasonably sure that press and camera will report 2170

we start blaming each other and rushing to the press 2501

Never lose your temper with the Press 2780

The press is not public opinion. 3050

PRESSURE

Order is not pressure which is imposed on society 1555

Competing pressures tempt one to believe that an issue deferred 2204

The legislature ... is the creature of pressure groups 2249

PRESTIGE

Authority must be accompanied by prestige 2125

many expensive national projects may add to our prestige 3623

PRESUMPTION

an object lesson of the limits of human presumption 2211

PRETEND

Ignorance of the law ... can be always pretended 1869

PREVENT

Politics is the art of preventing people from taking part in affairs 2760

best frame of government is that which is most likely to prevent ... evil 3424

The way to prevent war is to bend every energy toward preventing it 3858

You don't "prevent" anything by war except peace. 3892

PREVENTIVE

Democracy ... is the best preventive of such jealousies 383

PRICE

some legislatures that bring higher prices than any
in the world   786

A man who knows the price of everything, and
the value of nothing.   914

The price of eternal vigilance is
indifference.   1040

Eternal vigilance is the price of liberty.   1272

cost of liberty is less than the price of
repression   1336

we shall pay any price, bear any burden   1670

price of running ... is spending more time ...
asking people for more money   2826

Revolt and terror pay a price.   3251

a price which is too great to pay for peace   3777

One cannot pay the price of self-respect.   3777

PRICELESS

The experience may have been costly, but it was
also priceless.   1061

PRIDE

personal pride of individuals will always seek to
rise above the common level   323

PRIEST

holy water ... the priest consecrates the heart-
burnings of the aristocrat   3150

hypocrites, called priests, have put crowns upon
the heads of thieves   3153

PRIME MINISTER

would you rather be a country gentleman than a
Prime Minister?   2120

ever had such power as ... modern British Prime
Minister   2363

essentials of a successful prime minister   2646

The Prime Minister wins debate after debate and
loses battle after battle.   3835

PRINCE

necessary for a prince ... to learn how not to be
good   775

the princes of the earth are subject to the laws of
God   1837

No prince is so Great, as not ... to give an
outward ... worship to the laws   1846

A prince ... must imitate the fox and the
lion   1977

Many punishments ... discredit a prince   1993

mercy of princes is often just a way of gaining
affection   1997

Princes are more sensitive to any offense   2052

Princes are like to heavenly bodies   2330

The prince is the first servant of his state.   2341

A prince is a gr-reat man in th' ol'
counthry   2356

The favor of princes does not exclude merit   2675

A prince should therefore have no other aim ...
but war   3667

War is a game in which princes seldom win   3715

PRINCETON

CIA is made up of boys whose families sent them
to Princeton   2669

PRINCIPLE

If we doubt these principles, we shall accomplish
nothing.   154

Conservatism ... shrinks from Principle   194

The bottom principle ... is the principle of control
by the majority.   363

Democracy is not so much a form of government
as a set of principles.   372

when subjects are rebels from principle   544

Force is the vital principle ... of despotism   548

O' purpose thet we might our princerples
swaller   782

He fights you on patriotic principles; he robs you
on business principles   789

When a fellow says it hain't the money but the
principle   800

citizen is influenced by principle in direct
proportion to his distance   810

easier to fight for principles than to live up to
them   991

any principle ... calls for attachment ... it is the
principle of free thought   1128

first principle of a free society is an untrammeled
flow of words   1142

If this country cannot be saved without giving up
the principle   1295

Liberty cannot live apart from constitutional
principle.   1316

Peoples and governments never have ... acted on
principles   1528

Important principles may and must be
inflexible.   2073

anyone being woefully violated personally or in
terms of his principles   2192

when great principles are involved, as a rule the
majority are wrong   2307

must sacrifice ... to vindicate the principles   2373

By this gradation, principles are fitted to
party   2449

Party is a body of men united ... upon some
particular principle   2451

two great antagonistic principles at the root of all
government   2464

party tradition ... as it is founded upon eternal
principles   2489

Politics, n. A strife of interests masquerading as a
contest of principles.   2724

Political principles resemble military
tactics;   2747

first principle ... is that power is legitimate only
when it is under contract   2876

Great revolutions are the work rather of
principles   3203

Inexorable as to principles   3450

A man may have strong humanitarian and
democratic principles;   3531

Sound principles will not justify our taxing ... for wars 3585

Those who in principle oppose birth control   3800

we'd have to admit that our glorious principles were wrong   3833

PRINT

Print is the sharpest and the strongest weapon   134

separates the wheat from the chaff and then prints the chaff   1001

Everything I say, you know, goes into print.   2960

PRIORITY

do the things that need to be done according to priority   3127

PRISON

imprison a person or keep him in prison because he is unpopular   432

while there is a soul in prison, I am not free   1351

respect public opinion ... as necessary to ... to keep out of prison   3069

the true place for a just man is also a prison   3518

PRISONER

Men are not prisoners of fate, but only prisoners of their own minds.   960

prisoners cannot enter into contracts   1472

Everyone is a prisoner of his own experiences.   2921

soldier's pack is not so heavy ... as a prisoner's chains   3880

PRISTINE

If ... public life be reserved for those whose personal history is pristine   2656

PRIVACY

Constitution sometimes insulates criminality ... to protect the privacy of us all   262

a right of privacy older than the Bill of Rights   3371

The 4th Amendment protects the individual's privacy   3392

the heart of the Constitution's protection of privacy   3401

We are rapidly entering the age of no privacy   3491

PRIVATE

Private ownership of land is the nether millstone.   68

an atmosphere of private opulence and public squalor   655

principles of public morality are as definite as those of ... private life   788

No human government has a right to enquire into private opinions   1238

but which if undertaken by private citizens are not   1950

never to turn aside in public affairs through views of private interest   2016

A private Life is to be preferr'd;   2521

He that puts on a public gown must put off a private person.   2523

his life, public or private, becomes the fair subject of ... discussion   2531

No man has a right to pry into his neighbour's private concerns;   2531

No public character has ever stood the revelation of private utterance   2559

Homosexual behavior between consenting adults in private   3351

Anything that the private sector can do   3500

should not be the provider ... for things that the private sector can produce   3503

PRIVATE PROPERTY

Abolition of private property.   119

The system of private property is the most important guaranty of freedom   1392

If we women are wrong in destroying private property   3993

PRIVILEGE

to have those privileges of citizenship regardless of race   31

the Privileged and the People formed two nations   52

with the ultimate extinction of all privileged classes   91

only the business that thrives on special privilege   1587

privilege of the great is to see catastrophes from the terrace   2127

a social shock absorber placed between privilege and ... popular discontent   2255

when the privilege depends solely on the broad ... claim of public interest   3020

they poured the new wine ... into the old bottle of privilege for some   3245

What men value in this world is not rights but privileges.   3349

I don't believe in government for special privilege.   3535

That most delicious of all privileges—spending other people's money.   3592

PRIZE

The only prize much cared for by the powerful is power.   2865

In war there is no second prize for the runner-up.   3862

PROBABILITY

and lastly, that it have a probability of success   2222

PROBLEM

willingness of a free and determined people ... to face all problems frankly　471

Our problems are man-made, therefore they may be solved by man.　1039

No problem of human destiny is beyond human beings.　1039

There are two problems in my life.　1045

You're either part of the solution or part of the problem.　1055

Each success only buys an admission ticket to a more difficult problem.　1081

The chief cause of problems is solutions.　1083

Don't fight the problem, decide it.　1100

I believe that government is the problem　1573

An entirely new problem should be recognised as the fundamental problem　1577

solution of one problem usually leads to another　1693

greatest problem for the human species ...is that of attaining a civil society　1769

Anyone would make mistakes with the problems that lie ahead of us.　2168

tempt one to believe that an issue deferred is a problem avoided　2204

The problems seem so easy out there on the stump.　2435

tragedy of all political action is that some problems have no solution　2781

problem of power is how to achieve its responsible use　2880

No easy problems ever come to the President　2996

man ... disturbed about the condition of humanity either has no problems　3123

skeptical about the ability of government to solve problems　3497

problems of victory are more agreeable　3834

PROCEEDINGS

These proceedings are closed.　979

PROCESS

Legal process is an essential part of the democratic process.　1919

Politics ... is not a product, but a process　2743

PROCLIVITY

Where sexual proclivity does not relate to job function　3399

PRODUCTION

Socialist production and Unsocialist distribution.　3565

PRODUCTIVE

Democracy ... is also the profoundly productive　499

PROFESSION

Politics ought to be the part-time profession of every citizen　27

You cannot adopt politics as a profession and remain honest.　801

Politics ... the only profession for which no preparation is thought necessary　2775

Politics I supposed to be the second-oldest profession.　2809

PROFESSIONALISM

It was sheer professionalism and inspiration　2218

PROFESSOR

Politics is not a science, as many professors imagine　2717

PROFIT

When morality comes up against profit, it is seldom that profit loses.　813

to many less a matter of horror than the curtailment of the freedom to profit　1455

every human right is secondary to his profit　1585

Civilization and profits go hand in hand.　1589

PROFITEER

the loudest patriots are the greatest profiteers　3740

PROFUSION

We must make our election between ... profusion and servitude　3587

PROGRAM

Nations are formed ... by the fact that they have a program for tomorrow　2378

role of a minority party is to hammer out a program　2507

not a theory of government, but a program of action　3236

World War II was the last government program that really worked.　3498

PROGRESS

Material progress is the upper millstone.　68

Economic progress, in capitalist society, means turmoil.　651

Always human beings will live and progress to ... fuller life　1014

All progress is precarious　1038

making remarkable progress toward an agreement　1065

natural progress of things is for liberty to yield　1237

If there is no struggle there is no progress.　1279

The whole history of the progress of human liberty　1280

The best road to progress is freedom's road.　1438

But even judges sometimes progress.　1732

Laws and institutions must go hand in hand with the progress of the human mind.　1876

Every step of progress the world has made has
been from scaffold to scaffold   2059

A party of order ... a party of progress ... are both
necessary   2477

the two great engines of progress   3121

Would you realize what Revolution is, call it
Progress;   3219

all wars that impede progress are unjust   3821

PROGRESSIVE

A great democracy must be progressive   378

Sound business need have no fear of progressive
government.   1587

PROHIBIT

Whatever is contra bonos mores et decorum ... our
laws prohibit   1863

In Germany, under the law everything is
prohibited   1959

PROHIBITION

Communism is like Prohibition   151

PROLETARIAN

History is the judge;—its executioner, the
proletarian.   125

What the proletarian lacks is capital   3444

PROLETARIAT

the proletariat alone is a really revolutionary
class   57

Its fall and the victory of the proletariat are
equally inevitable.   58

Civilization cannot survive if it rests upon a
propertyless proletariat.   96

class struggle necessarily leads to the dictatorship
of the proletariat   124

what can victory bring to the proletariat?   3790

PROLIFIC

taxes must have been the most prolific
animals   3615

PROMINENT

Men prominent in life are mostly hard to converse
with.   2143

PROMISE

so many candidates ... there were not enough
promises to go around   514

Vote for the man who promises least; he'll be the
least disappointing.   716

They want an America as good as its
promise.   1072

When I have made a promise as a man I try to
keep it   1637

according to those promises that He hath held
forth   1994

Here lies our sovereign lord the King,/ Whose
promise none relies on;   2332

They promise to build a bridge even where there is
no river.   2620

I can promise nothing but purity of
intentions   2952

then, the 13th Amendment made a promise it
cannot keep   3377

PROMISED LAND

And I've looked over, and I've seen the Promised
Land.   1043

PROMOTE

Party is a body of men united, for promoting ...
the national interest   2451

PROMOTION

a hundred things to single you out for promotion
in ... politics besides ability   2603

PROPAGANDA

In dealing with the Communists ... what is public
is merely propaganda   170

They are engines of propaganda   1176

Give me the writing of a nation's advertising and
propaganda   2878

PROPAGATION

to compel a man to furnish contributions ... for
the propagation of opinions   3141

PROPERTY

Oligarchy: A government resting on a valuation of
property   33

if the ... laws were to create a rapid accumulation
of property in few hands   42

I seek to preserve property and to respect
order   189

So much property, widely distributed ... is the ...
basis of democracy   331

or property, in fear of poverty, will destroy
democracy   456

Morality ... are not the property of a given
party   1376

private property is the most important guaranty of
freedom   1392

Property is a god.   1582

every man holds his property subject to the
general right of the community   1585

source of faction has been the ... unequal
distribution of property   2453

Honor is not the exclusive property of any
political party.   2508

You cannot divorce property from power.   2849

governments care far more for ... the security of
property   3237

a man is said to have a right to his
property   3296

right to acquire property ... gives to property ... a
right to protection   3298

for property belongs to man and not man to
property   3324

property rights must be carefully
safeguarded   3324

government ... more concerned about human
rights than about property rights   3329
the right of property is the most important
individual right   3330
Property does not have rights . People have
rights.   3381
interdependence exists between ... liberty and the
personal right in property   3382
When neither their property not their honor is
touched   3406
Government has no other end but the preservation
of Property.   3412
the foundation of the social contract is
property   3416
Government is instituted to protect
property   3428
first end of government is to give security to life
and property   3456
while property may be regulated to a certain
extent   3471
Where there is no property there is no
injustice.   3516
Property is the fruit of labor.   3521
Property is theft.   3552
transformation of the regime of property   3559

PROPHESY
I always avoid prophesying beforehand   975

PROPOSAL
tempted to make a proposal to our Republican
friends   3172

PROPOSE
the duty of an Opposition was ... to ... propose
nothing   2467
It is the duty of the President to propose   3511

PROPRIETORSHIP
what he gains is civil liberty and the
proprietorship of all he possesses   1211

PROSE
You can campaign in poetry. You govern in
prose.   2437

PROSPER
neither man nor nation can prosper unless ...
thought is ... taken for the future   731
States do not prosper through ideology.   3431

PROSPERITY
Social prosperity means man happy, the citizen
free   637
Prosperity is only an instrument to be used   646
I could give you an illusion of prosperity,
too   663
undermining in the days of our children the very
prosperity   729
that America can prosper as we have known
prosperity   1665
Prosperity is necessarily the first theme of a
political campaign.   2425

PROSTRATE
then claim the right of trampling on them forever,
because they are prostrate   3300

PROSTRATION
the prostration of agriculture at the feet of
commerce   1242

PROTECT
the strong arm of England will protect him   1621
To protect the weak and the minority   3449
not only the legitimate interests of the few are
protected   3477

PROTECTION
Everyone who receives the protection of society
owes a return   20
every individual ... has an equal right to the
protection of government   742
every man is equally entitled to protection by
law   745
If the government would confine itself to equal
protection   1529
not deny the equal protection of the law to the
unwashed   3376
Man seeketh in society comfort, use, and
protection   3407
Good government ... has for its object the
protection of every person   3459
Women must not depend upon the protection of
man   3985

PROTECTOR
the root from which a tyrant springs; when he
first appears he is a protector   521

PROTEST
Oppression costs the oppressor too much if the
oppressed ... protest   586
One who comes to the Court must come to adore,
not to protest.   1153

PROUD
such a thing as a man being too proud to
fight   1639
proud of the fact that I never invented weapons to
kill   3776

PROVIDENCE
A marciful Providunce fashioned us holler   782
with a firm reliance on the protection of Divine
Providence   1228
doing what appears to me right ... leaving the
consequences with Providence   2016

PROVIDER
government should not be the provider of first
resort   3503

PROVOCATIVE
To apply the latter was provocative and
useless.   3909

PROXIMITY
It is a question of proximity and degree.   1122

PRUDENCE
the prudence never to practice either   1324

contracts ... habits of prudence and
   restraint   2046

Liberalism is trust of the people tempered by
   prudence;   2267

PSYCHIATRIC
I'll show you one who needs psychiatric
   attention   1048

PSYCHIATRY
believe that foreign policy is a subdivision of
   psychiatry   1713

PUBLIC
Bureaucracies are designed to perform public
   business.   7

In dealing with the Communists ... what is public
   is merely propaganda   170

things on which the public thinks long   292

we have built up new instruments of public
   power   407

where public services have failed to keep
   abreast   655

Public life is a situation of power and
   energy;   776

synonymous, in the public mind, with
   deception   814

as the ... public in one of its periodical fits of
   morality   867

An unconditional right to say what one pleases
   about public affairs   1145

things can get terribly confused in the public
   mind   1196

diplomacy shall proceed always frankly and in the
   public view   1641

The law is the last result of human wisdom ... for
   the benefit of the public   1867

never to turn aside in public affairs through views
   of private interest   2016

We must not in the course of public life expect
   immediate approbation   2017

he who molds public sentiment goes deeper   2063

With public sentiment, nothing can fail;   2063

Public men are bees working in a glass
   hive;   2081

public is interested more in government   2129

When statesmen forsake ... private conscience for
   the sake of their public duties   2186

No man in public life thinks of the many he has
   outstripped;   2516

the Honour ... of publick Posts, bearing no
   proportion with the Comfort of it   2521

He that puts on a public gown must put off a
   private person.   2523

his life, public or private, becomes the fair subject
   of public discussion   2531

When a man assumes a public trust, he should
   consider himself as public property.   2535

opinions of public men ... must not be curiously
   contrasted   2542

A man ain't got no right to be a public man,
   unless he meets the public views.   2547

love of fame ... the sovereign passion of our public
   men   2554

No public character has ever stood the revelation
   of private utterance   2559

many a public figure has come to imitate the
   journalism which describes him   2572

Public office is the last refuge of the
   scoundrel.   2589

The public official must pick his way nicely   2591

does not describe holding public office   2606

Public officials are not a group apart.   2622

Every public official should be recycled
   occasionally.   2647

If ... public life be reserved for those whose
   personal history is pristine   2656

I borrowed the Duke of Newcastle's majority to
   carry on the public business.   2678

Great public measures cannot be carried by the
   influence of mere reason.   2694

persuading the public to vote for this and support
   that   2771

how to get men of power to live for the public
   rather than off the public   2880

no undefined residuum of power ... because it
   seems to be in the public interest   2969

Public sentiment is to public officers what water is
   to the wheel   3058

anything, that is, except public office   3170

The public must and will be served.   3413

whenever the public mind is to be diverted ... a
   crusade is inaugurated   3526

public debt as the greatest of the dangers to be
   feared   3588

public ... ask their Congressmen to enact goodies
   in the form of spending   3627

A victorious general has no faults in the eye of the
   public   3688

PUBLIC OPINION
where small groups control rather than the great
   body of public opinion   383

military policy is dependent on public
   opinion   430

tides of public opinion which lap at the courtroom
   door   1745

Judges ... rule on the basis of law, not public
   opinion   1963

Politicians ... are not over a year behind Public
   Opinion   2601

the master politician ... both creates and responds
   to public opinion   2626

Public opinion sets bounds to every
   government   3040

A government is based on public opinion   3041

Public opinion is the mixed result of the intellect of the community   3042

No minister ever stood ... against public opinion   3043

a besetting disposition to make publick opinion stronger than the law   3044

Public opinion is a weak tyrant   3047

Whoever can change public opinion can change the government   3048

Public opinion in this country is everything.   3049

The press is not public opinion.   3050

intelligence of public opinion is the indispensable condition of ... progress   3051

Public opinion is stronger than the legislature   3052

Public opinion, the fear of losing public confidence   3053

What we call public opinion is generally public sentiment.   3054

that he wanted "to take a bath in public opinion."   3055

nothing that makes more cowards and feeble men than public opinion   3057

Public opinion is the most potent monarch   3059

Its name is Public Opinion. It is held in reverence.   3060

There must be public opinion back of the laws   3062

Where public opinion is free and uncontrolled   3065

Public opinion, a vulgar ... tyrant   3066

We are ruled by Public Opinion, not by Statute-law.   3067

Where there is little or no public opinion   3068

One should respect public opinion ... as is necessary to avoid starvation   3069

no group in America that can withstand the force of an aroused public opinion   3070

A government can be no better than the public opinion that sustains it.   3071

structure of democracy rests on public opinion   3072

It isn't polls or public opinion alone of the moment that counts.   3076

Polling is merely an instrument for gauging public opinion.   3080

The belief that public opinion ... had the slightest effect   3778

PUBLIC SERVANT
I think not a useful public servant   2537
Your public servants serve you right;   2607
The first lady is ... an unpaid public servant   3005

PUBLICITY
Publicity is one of the purifying elements of politics.   795

PULPIT
Some to the common pulpits, and cry out, "Liberty   270

PULSE
always feeling one's pulse and taking one's temperature   3073

PUNISH
in order not to punish often, to punish severely   1778
Law cannot persuade where it cannot punish.   1851

PUNISHMENT
Pure despotism is the punishment for men's bad conduct.   535
Let the punishment match the offense.   1752
All punishment is mischief. All punishment in itself is evil.   1772
reward and punishment, are the only motives to a rational creature   1848
a sanction ... a penalty or punishment   1868
but an openly transgressed custom brings sure punishment   1906
Many punishments ... as much discredit a prince as many funerals a physician   1993

PUPPET
in the hands of political puppets of an economic autocracy   407

PURCHASABLE
I always find the anti-monopolists the most purchasable   787

PURIFICATION
The purification of politics is an iridescent dream.   1547

PURPOSE
The deeper purpose of democratic government   410
If people want a sense of purpose they should get it from their archbishop.   2635
They like honesty and straightforwardness of purpose.   2731
purpose of the government to see that ... welfare ... of the many are conserved   3477

PURR
The Kennedy organization doesn't run, it purrs.   2434

PURSE
As in law so in war, the longest purse finally wins.   1910

PURSUIT
Politics is a systematic effort to move other men in the pursuit of some design.   2783
Life, Liberty and the pursuit of happiness   3290

QUALIFY
Minorities are individuals ... especially qualified   2309

Keyword Index

QUALITY

Not the least of the qualities ... is the ability of
letting others serve him   2001
more concerned with the quality of their
goals   3490

QUARREL

when there is a quarrel between two states   1622
Once blood is shed in a national quarrel
reason   3812

QUEEN

America cannot always sit as a queen in
peace   879
I would not be a queen/ For all the world.   1988
The queens in history compare favorably   3987

QUEER

The only queer people are those who don't
love   3394

QUEST

Democracy ... is a quest   402

QUESTION

never so likely to settle a question rightly   1112
All political questions ... are at bottom only
questions of might   2705
Nonviolence is the answer to the crucial political
and moral questions   3369
injustice has a terrible way of lingering ... like an
unfinished question   3538

QUESTIONING

Prior to any questioning, the person must be
warned   1941

QUIBBLING

discard all this quibbling about this man   751

QUICK

The quickest way of ending a war is to lose
it.   3864
you should win as quick as you can   3932

QUIET

When a country is tolerably quiet   1113

QUILT

America is more like a quilt   2320

QUIT

you quit when the gorilla's tired   1079

QUITTER

I have never been a quitter.   3018

QUOTE

a regime in which people quote instead of
thinking   603

RABBIT

comfort to feel that you are about to be trampled
to death by a rabbit   2894

RACE

to have those privileges of citizenship regardless of
race   31
to be a poor race in a land of dollars is the very
bottom of hardships   83
a race between education and catastrophe   688
a race to see which will be achieved first   1065
no matter what their race or the color of their
skin   1385
After all there is but one race—humanity.   2907
Race prejudice is ... a shadow over all of us   2916
No one has been barred on account of his race
from fighting or dying   2929
If discrimination based on race is constitutionally
permissible   2943
The race problem is a moral one.   3318
no special right because they belong to one
race   3322
equal rights to all its citizens, of any race   3355
until education is unaware of race   3362

RACISM

If we practice racism then it is racism that we
teach.   2917

RACIST

The American economy, the American society ...
are all racist   2926

RACK

In old days men had the rack.   1173

RADICAL

a Radical to remove all that is bad   189
The radical invents the views.   205
radical of one century is the conservative of the
next   206
Few radicals have good digestions.   208
I never dared to be radical when young   215
If we wish a change to be as radical as
possible   3102
effect radical reforms in their system of
government   3235
The most radical revolutionary will become a
conservative   3281
no such thing as a moderate in the civil rights
movement; everyone is a radical   3379

RADICALISM

Those who worry about radicalism in our
schools   443
Radicalism itself ceases to be radical   611
Radicalism ... always applied to people
endeavoring to get freedom   1355
Radicalism, n. The conservatism of tomorrow   3111

RAFT

a republic is a raft which will never sink   2345
the Titanic voyage was a success because a few
people survived on life rafts   2510

RAGE

reason and right are swept aside by the rage of angry men 3812

RAIN

best time to listen to a politician is when he's ... in the rain 2432

RAINBOW

but our nation is a rainbow 2321

RAISE

A man who raises himself by degrees to wealth 2046

One cannot raise the bottom of a society 3541

RAKE

only if they know when to stop raking the muck 792

RANK

I cannot conceive a rank more honorable 285

Every country is renewed out of the unknown ranks 2098

RAPIST

just like the rapist asking the raped 2934

RAPSCALLION

All kings is mostly rapscallions. 2354

RARE

competence, because it's so rare 1572

RASCAL

when able rascals will discover this open door 2577

RASH

That is quite different from being rash. 2140

RATIONAL

The rational part of us supplies the reasons 1742

I am a moderate liberal, as all rational people are 2266

politics consists in directing rationally the irrationalities of man 2799

RATIONALE

sovereign state, with its supremely self-centered rationale 1673

RATIONING

Communism because it hands out wealth through rationing books 179

RE-ELECT

If you think too much about being re-elected 2100

REACTION

the action and reaction between the Ministry and the Parliament 2703

than to seek refuge in the almshouse of reaction 3211

REACTIONARY

reactionaries who themselves do not bear allegiance to the ... principles 443

All reactionaries are paper tigers. 982

It was the most reactionary people who tried to hold onto something 2365

separation between one nationality and the other ... is a reactionary idea 2371

the men who sit on the Front Bench, in their reactionary ... opinions 2583

Everything reactionary is the same; 3259

Women have been and are prejudiced, narrowminded, reactionary 4003

READ

every man should receive those papers, and be capable of reading them 1160

Men of power have no time to read; 2208

Reading about one's failings in the daily papers 2640

Read my lips: no new taxes. 3635

but Peace is poor reading 3768

REAL

A man always has two reasons for what he does 948

You never hear a real American talk like that. 1372

it is to shape real events in a real world 1678

The real war will never get into the books. 3749

REALITY

Freedom is a very great reality. 1363

to act wisely and creatively upon the new realities of our time 1450

do not resent criticism, even when ... it parts for the time with reality 2133

When not realities but words are to be discussed 2247

the nation is the ultimate political reality 2387

imagined republics ... which have never been ... known to exist in reality 2673

I don't think ideas are incompatible with political reality. 2776

When the reality of power has been surrendered 2855

REALIZATION

only limit to our realization of tomorrow 981

REAP

Were we directed from Washington when to ... reap, we should soon want bread 3435

REARM

I hold that we should rearm in order to parley. 3866

REASON

The one means that wins the easiest victory over reason: 588

a type of man who does not want to give reasons   595

A man always has two reasons for what he does   948

Reason and free inquiry are the only effectual agents against error.   1108

reason is not the subversion but the salvation of freedom   1416

Because the passions of men will not conform to the dictates of reason   1501

Law: an ordinance of reason for the common good   1831

Laws should not be changed without good reason.   1855

Fragile as reason is   1930

enable society to achieve its goals with a ... maximum of reason   1947

Reason may be the lever   2076

men are beginning to reason upon the facts   2489

Great public measures cannot be carried by the influence of mere reason.   2694

Prejudice is never easy unless it can pass itself off for reason.   2898

That religion ... can be directed only by reason and conviction   3140

We did not win the People over by appealing to reason   3285

reason and right are swept aside by the rage of angry men   3812

REASONABLE

Democracy ... is based on a respect for man as a reasonable being   419

Every reasonable human being should be a moderate Socialist.   3568

men are not a reasoned or reasonable sex   4004

REASONING

the great force in throwing ... accurate reasoning into a secondary place   2712

REBEL

when subjects are rebels from principle   544

we are descended ... in spirit from ... rebels   1136

not too soon for honest men to rebel and revolutionize   3210

Rebel, n. A proponent of a new misrule   3232

If you rebel against high-heeled shoes   3253

The rebel is careful to preserve the abuses   3260

REBELLION

Rebellion is justified.   171

if the rebellion could force us to forego or postpone a national election   704

if rebellion was the certain consequence   1725

Rebellion is as the sin of witchcraft.   3183

I like a little rebellion now and then.   3189

a little rebellion now and then, is a good thing   3190

and every unsuccessful one a rebellion   3192

To despise legitimate authority ... is as a rebellion against the Divine Will   3225

As a dimension of man, rebellion actually defines him.   3266

we are determined to foment a rebellion   3977

RECANTATION

not let oneself in for the shameful act of recantation   181

RECESSION

Recession is when your neighbor loses his job.   662

RECIPE

hard work ... is the recipe   2216

RECOGNIZE

I recognize no rights but human rights   3148

RECONCILIATION

as it represents a genuine reconciliation of differences   2789

RECOVERY

And recovery is when Jummy Carter loses his.   662

RECYCLE

Every public official should be recycled   2647

RED

"That man is a Red, that man is a Communist".   1372

RED TAPE

entire Civil Service is like a fortress made of ... red tape   1

REDEMPTION

I believe in the forgiveness of sin and the redemption of ignorance.   1037

REDRESS

I called a New World into existence to redress the balance of the Old.   860

A grievance is most poignant when almost redressed.   988

there will be increasing pressure on government to redress the failure   1426

REDWOOD

Once you've seen one redwood, you've seen them all.   735

the kind of politician who would cut down a redwood tree   2630

REFERENDUM

a device so alien to all our traditions as the referendum   714

REFINED

it cannot be so refined, so leisurely and gentle 3247

REFLECTION

what is government ... but the greatest of all reflections on human nature 1504

REFLEX

Politics is the reflex of the business and industrial world. 1586

REFORM

nor should this court ... be thought of as a general haven for reform movements 245

What we have done in all the progress of reform 398

they will, besides having a sense of shame, reform themselves 1478

We are reforming, not the hanged man, but everyone else. 1757

that sentiment of responsibility which is the first step to reform 1895

A slender reform amuses and lulls the people: 3086

Every reform ... will by weak minds be carried to an excess 3089

Attempts at reform, when they fail, strengthen despotism 3092

but never suspected that the people in power were against reform 3093

Reform, that you may preserve 3094

Conservatism goes for comfort, reform for truth. 3096

if he have a pain in his bowels ... he ... sets about reforming the world 3097

Cautious, careful people ... never can bring about a reform 3098

Nothing so needs reforming as other people's habits. 3105

Reform must come from within, not without. 3112

the men who stand against reform are standing against nature 3114

Every reform movement has a lunatic fringe. 3115

Hunger does not breed reform; 3117

Laws do not make reforms, reforms make laws. 3119

The desire to understand the world and the desire to reform it 3121

try to make a big reform you are told you are doing too much 3122

To give up the task of reforming society is to give up one's responsibility 3129

To achieve reforms, you have sometimes to try to make the revolution. 3130

The religions are obsolete when the reforms do not proceed from them. 3152

A reform is a correction of abuses; 3220

REFORMATION

Was it not an individual ... who produced the reformation? 3091

can do nothing effectual for the permanent reformation of the world 3148

REFORMER

A rayformer thinks he was ilicted because he was a rayformer 710

Reformers can be as bigoted and sectarian 3100

Reformers who are always compromising 3106

is called a rayformer an' remains at large 3108

All reformers are bachelors. 3109

Th' rayformer don't undherstand that people wud rather be wrong 3110

Every man is a reformer until reform tramps on his toes. 3113

Unless the reformer can invent something which substitutes attractive virtues 3116

Nobody expects to find comfort ... in reformers 3120

Many middle-class reformers will find to their surprise 3133

REFORMIST

I was ... a great reformist 3093

REFUGE

A technical objection is the first refuge of a scoundrel. 957

Patriotism is the last refuge of the scoundrel. 2392

Public office is the last refuge of the scoundrel. 2589

REFUGEE

A nation cannot live ... if its refugees are among its citizens 2915

REFUSE

it can have no power over any individual by whom that consent is refused 302

The wretched refuse of your teeming shore 1315

When I refuse to obey an unjust law 1782

REGIME

When a nation has allowed itself to fall under a tyrannical regime 605

The more a regime claims to be the embodiment of liberty 627

A regime ... is rarely overthrown by a revolutionary movement 3268

REGRESSIVE

dictatorship of the proletetariat is an historically regressive idea 182

REGRET

acknowledge it at once and express your regret 2252

I only regret that I have but one life to lose for my country. 2393

REGULATE
Free speech is not to be regulated like diseased cattle   1137

REGULATION
if regulation goes too far it will be recognized as a taking   3471

REIGN
One can't reign and be innocent.   2022
to be Omnipotent but friendless is to reign   2035
must be thrown off even at the risk of reigns of terror   3216

REINS
reins whereby all mankind are ... guided   1848
when I come to lay down the reins of power   2071

RELATION
democracy, which is a mental and moral relation of man to man   715

RELATIONSHIP
the problem of a law-governed external relationship with other states   1605
a program of transformation of relationships   3261

RELEVANT
our need as a self-governing people to hear everything relevant   1139

RELIGION
in different compartments of their soul—religion and business   140
as religion, and not atheism, is the true remedy for superstition   1222
Liberty, next to religion, has been the motive of good deeds   1312
Patriotism is in political life what faith is in religion.   2403
as in religion ... we have less charity for those who believe half of our creed   2687
Politics in America is the binding secular religion.   2822
Politics, like religion, hold up torches of martyrdom   3088
All religions must be tolerated   3139
religion, or the duty which we owe to our Creator   3140
Are not Religion & Politics the Same Thing? Brotherhood is Religion.   3144
All religions united with government are more or less inimical to liberty.   3145
Religion ... is and ever has been the centre of gravity in a realm   3147
Religion is the sigh of the oppressed creatures   3149
that we were mistaken in maintaining their association with religion   3151

religions are obsolete when the reforms do not proceed from them   3152
government must pursue a course of complete neutrality toward religion   3165

RELIGIOUS
If men think that a ruler is religious   3135
which will not at the same time demonstrate the right to religious freedom   3146
not be leading a religious life unless I identified myself with ... mankind   3158
for me or against me solely on account of my religious affiliation   3160

REMEDY
find a remedy in the harmony and wisdom of your counsels   316
Force is not a remedy.   907
Politics is the art of ... applying the wrong remedies   2807
A desperate disease requires a dangerous remedy.   3185

REMEMBER
If the row comes, REMEMBER THE MAINE   919
Then you'll never have to remember what you said   1019
proper memory for a politician is one that knows what to remember   2576

REMORSE
The abuse of greatness is when it disjoins/ Remorse from power.   525

REMOULD
Liberty ... must remould our institutions of wealth   1321

REND
dreadful Spirit of Division as rends a Government into two distinct People   2445

RENDER
Render therefore unto Caesar the things which are Caesar's   3136

RENEW
Every country is renewed out of the unknown ranks   2098

RENOUNCE
To renounce liberty is to renounce being a man   1213

RENOWN
renown of great men ... measured by the means which they have used to acquire it   1995

REPAINT
He's also been repainted several times.   2634

REPARTEE
A majority is always the best repartee.   700

REPEAL
to secure the repeal of bad ... laws so effective as
    their stringent execution   1889
Every so often, we pass laws repealing human
    nature.   1922

REPENT
We will have to repent in this generation   30

REPETITION
Repetition does not transform a lie into a
    truth.   958

REPORTER
in the Reporters' Gallery yonder, there sat a
    Fourth Estate   1169
if reporters should ever lose the right to protect ...
    confidentiality   1192
The only people who say worse things about
    politicians than reporters   2655

REPOSE
the very notion of repose must be foreign to
    English politics   2481

REPRESENT
A monarch frequently represents his subjects
    better   2359

REPRESENTATION
Taxation and representation are inseparably
    united.   3578
will not hold ourselves bound by any laws in
    which we have no ... representation   3977

REPRESENTATIVE
The benefits of the Representative system are
    lost   312
popular conscience that sears the conscience of the
    people's representatives   473
The right of voting for representatives is the
    primary right   698
representatives of the people are not defenders of
    liberty   2228
Your representative owes you ... but his
    judgment;   2527
representative's duty is to represent the interests of
    all   2671
then to make it the representative of a whole
    class   2911
The President is the representative of the whole
    nation   2992
but with their own consent, given personally or by
    their representatives   3579
In times of peace the people look most to their
    representatives   3710

REPRESSION
cost of liberty is less than the price of
    repression   1336
ready to support repression as long as it is done
    with a quiet voice   1464
The seed of revolution is repression.   3241

REPRISAL
He who tugs Uncle Sam's beard too hard risks
    reprisal   1707

REPTILE
Toryism ... ever remains the same reptile   211

REPUBLIC
a republic ... derives all its powers ... from the
    great body of the people   298
the republic is the weal of the people   1756
This Republic was not established by
    cowards;   2151
a republic is a raft that will never sink   2345
Republics weak because they appeal to the
    understanding   2353
Many have imagined republics ... which have
    never been seen or known   2673
The true Republic: men their rights and nothing
    more;   3304
The life of a republic lies certainly in the energy ...
    of its citizens   3600

REPUBLICAN
We are now forming a republican
    government.   295
republican ... only government which is not at ...
    war with the rights of mankind   301
The Republican form of government is the highest
    form of government: 368
The essence of a republican government is not
    command.   455
Republicans believe that the moneyed
    "aristocracy" ... should rule   504
Let us not seek the Republican answer or the
    Democratic answer   2504
no Democratic or Republican way of cleaning the
    streets   2505
He loved politicians—even Republicans.   2658
some Republicans I would trust with
    anything   3170
tempted to make a proposal to our Republican
    friends   3172
to vote Republican ... is the same as a chicken
    voting for Colonel Sanders   3176
I spent three years in Washington under a
    Republican administration   3177
(Republicans are) men of narrow vision   3179
Thou shalt not criticize other Republicans.   3180
Republicians believe every day is the Fourth of
    July   3182

REPUBLICAN PARTY
better for the country than the Republican Party
    at its best   510
however bad the Republican party was   3166
the Republican party as the sheet anchor of the
    colored man's political hopes   3167
Th' raypublican party broke ye   3168
the Republican Party ... has not had a new idea in
    30 years   3169

the Republican Party is an ancient political
vehicle   3171

Brains ... are suspect in the Republican
Party   3174

Republican Party is only going to be an effective
party   3175

nothing wrong with the Republican Party that
double-digit inflation won't cure   3178

REPUGNANCE

he will have to overcome certain physical
repugnances   3531

REPUGNANT

To promote a Woman to bear rule ... is
repugnant   3975

REPUTATION

most valuable of ... possessions ... is the reputation
of being well to do   392

a smart reporter could ruin your reputation--
unfairly   1197

No man will ever carry out of the Presidency the
reputation   2954

careful people, always casting about to preserve
their reputation   3098

REQUISITE

requisite of a good citizen ... be able ... to pull his
weight   22

RESCUE

But emperor and kings and popes will come to its
rescue.   3824

RESEMBLANCE

it bears a very close resemblance to the first   2809

RESENTMENT

To prevent resentment, governments attribute
misfortunes to natural causes;   2494

RESIDUUM

no undefined residuum of power which he can
exercise   2969

RESIGN

but from which he cannot resign   2990

RESIST

I rejoice that America has resisted.   1215

to resist counsels that are hard to resist   2109

I respect only those who resist me   2185

RESISTANCE

Let your motto be resistance ...
RESISTANCE!   1264

In the act of resistance the rudiments of freedom
are already present.   1461

spirit of resistance to government is so
valuable   3189

simplest truths often meet the sternest
resistance   3311

RESOLUTION

men of law have been persistently concerned with
the resolution of disputes   1947

In War: Resolution. In Defeat: Defiance.   3852

RESOLVE

highly resolve ... that this nation ... shall have a
new birth of freedom   344

RESOURCE

use all its ... resources to meet new social
problems   3478

Our resources should be used for the benefit of
all   3535

RESPECT

respect for law and order ... in precise relationship
to ... his paycheck   108

Where the people possess no authority, their rights
obtain no respect.   320

Democracy ... is a covenant among free men to
respect the rights   416

After you get your freedom, your enemy will
respect you.   1453

The first of all laws is to respect the laws   1860

in reality expressing the highest respect for the
law   1938

Let us learn to respect sincerity of conviction in
our opponents.   2701

wealth has a wholesome respect for the law   3065

You just have to respect their rights.   3400

a healthy respect for the ability of people to solve
problems   3497

Hungry men have no respect for law   3529

RESPONSE

After a time he will get no response.   2973

RESPONSIBILITY

a classic example of power without
responsibility   4

the man who manages to make no decisions and
escape all responsibility   8

A democracy in which everyone had an equal
responsibility   446

because a dictator ... would rob all others of their
responsibility   631

The margin is narrow, but the responsibility is
clear.   718

Most of them come down to this: Deny your
responsibility.   812

Paramount among the responsibilities of a free
press   1189

Liberty means responsibility.   1329

Responsibility is the first step in
responsibility.   1335

I do not shrink from this responsibility   1433

a big appetite at one end and no sense of
responsibility at the other   1570

Liberty ... is responsibilty, and responsibilty is
duty   1898

A chief is a man who assumes
responsibility. 2137

To give up the task of reforming society is to give
up one's responsibility 3129

RESPONSIBLE

a people are responsible for the acts of their
government 388

because I do not want to be responsible for
whatever they may say 1163

It is the will to be responsible to ourselves. 1319

He is personally responsible to persons. 2671

RESPONSIVE

That problem is making Government sufficiently
responsive to the people. 480

RESTING PLACE

History knows no resting places and no
plateaus. 1084

RESTORATION

not revolution, but restoration 939

RESTRAIN

government will never be able to restrain a
distressed ... majority 2292

Nothing but force ... can restrain them 2841

RESTRAINT

Liberty exists in proportion to wholesome
restraint. 1267

self-imposed restraints of a whole people 2304

It rests on love, not on restraint. 2372

The final end of government is not to exert
restraint but to do good. 3445

Progress is born ... not from government
restraints 3475

our country will match its military strength with
our moral restraint 3488

the obligation to match national strength with
national restraint 3915

RESULT

A statesman is judged by results. 4

great results of history are brought about by
discreditable means 785

but there's never any kind of result 2440

Violence seldom accomplishes permanent and
desired results. 3794

RETREAT

In the Soviet Army it takes more courage to
retreat than to advance. 3832

REVEAL

In revealing the workings of government 1190

REVELATION

No public character has ever stood the revelation
of private utterance 2559

REVENUE

for the sake of the advantage which is to be gained
from the public revenues 2514

a good revenue system is the life of an organized
government 3600

Government expands to absorb revenue and then
some. 3621

REVERENCE

Its name is Public Opinion. It is held in
reverence. 3060

REVERSAL

the most revolutionary reversal of his
record 3845

REVOLT

at that moment man revolts 1262

Every successful revolt is termed a
revolution 3192

Revolt and terror pay a price. 3251

the hope of better things incites people to
revolt 3276

The Negro revolt is not aimed at winning
friends 3372

interests which they want to preserve against those
in revolt 3825

REVOLUTION

when the poor fly it it means danger,
revolution 99

Lenin had a revolution to practice on and Marx
had not 162

revolutions most disastrous to freedom are effected
without shedding of blood 571

Revolutions do not go backward. 749

revolutions do not always establish freedom 1274

it might, in a moral point of view, justify
revolution 2294

In Prussia it is only kings who make
revolutions. 2351

To achieve reforms, you have sometimes to try to
make the revolution. 3130

revolution always starts from the outbreak of
internal dissension 3184

Every successful revolt is termed a
revolution 3192

A great revolution is never the fault of the
people 3197

If we trace the history of most revolutions 3198

The spirit of revolution ... is a spirit radically
opposed to liberty 3200

In revolutions those who want everything always
get the better 3201

Great revolutions are the work rather of
principles 3203

Every revolution was first a thought in one man's
mind 3208

with each new gewgaw of a revolution 3209

Better to perish with the revolution 3211

All men recognize the right of revolution; 3212

Revolutions are not made; they come. A revolution is as natural ... as an oak   3214

Revolutions never go backward.   3215

worst enemies of civil freedom are the absolute monarchy and the revolution   3218

Would you realize what Revolution is, call it Progress;   3219

a revolution is a transfer of power   3220

People's revolutions are born from the course of events.   3223

the third is by that of the social revolution   3224

Revolution or dictatorship can sometimes abolish bad things   3226

Revolution, n. ... an abrupt change in the form of misgovernment   3230

Insurrection, n. An unsuccessful revolution.   3231

can never have a revolution in order to establish a democracy   3234

The revolution is incapable either of regretting ... its dead   3239

Thinkers prepare the revolution;   3240

The seed of revolution is repression.   3241

revolutions always destroy themselves   3242

Revolutions are as a rule not made arbitrarily.   3243

Revolution is an expression of the impossibility of reconstructing class society   3243

People never move towards revolution;   3244

A revolution is not a dinner party   3247

all revolutions must be social revolutions   3248

A revolution only lasts fifteen years   3249

Though a revolution may call itself "national"   3256

Revolutions are needed to create progress.   3258

A non-violent revolution is not a program of seizure of power.   3261

The time to stop a revolution is at the beginning   3264

Revolutions are the locomotives of history.   3267

I began revolution with 82 men.   3269

A revolution that does not ... grow deeper is a revolution that is retreating   3270

who make peaceful revolution impossible will make violent revolution inevitable   3271

the Black Revolution is controlled only by God   3273

Revolutions are never peaceful.   3274

Revolutions are based upon bloodshed.   3275

Revolutions are never waged singing "We Shall Overcome".   3275

We used to think that revolutions are the cause of change.   3279

change prepares the ground for revolution   3279

the redress, honored in tradition, is also revolution   3282

Revolution is the festival of the oppressed.   3283

Revolution is a drama of passion.   3285

It takes a revolution to make a solution.   3286

easier to run a revolution than a government   3287

only successful revolution of this century is totalitarianism   3288

REVOLUTIONARY

they can exercise their ... revolutionary right to ... overthrow it   340

the envy which makes revolutionaries   3221

A revolutionary idea is revolutionary, vital   3222

Without a revolutionary theory there can be no revolutionary movement.   3227

We have learned that it is ... whispered purposes that are revolutionary   3233

The revolutionary war is a war of the masses;   3250

A revolutionary party is a contradiction in terms.   3254

The successful revolutionary is a statesman   3257

The revolutionary wants to change the world;   3260

Every revolutionary ends by becoming either an oppressor or a heretic.   3262

A regime ... is rarely overthrown by a revolutionary movement;   3268

The duty of every revolutionary is to make a revolution.   3280

The most radical revolutionary will become a conservative   3281

end of all revolutionary social change is ... the sanctity of human life   3530

revolutionary transformation of the regime of property ... is not an end   3559

REVOLUTIONISING

a horror of revolutionising any country for a political object   3202

REVOLUTIONIST

Here in America we are descended ... from revolutionists   1136

person under the age of thirty who ... is not a revolutionist, is an inferior   3228

The revolutionists did not succeed in establishing human freedom;   3245

REWARD

With a good conscience our only sure reward   1030

Liberty is its own reward.   1341

The world usually rewards the appearance of ability   1996

RHETORIC

My strong point is not rhetoric   2188

The difference is whether or not one is all rhetoric   3379

RHETORICAL

Deficits shrink with a rhetorical flourish.   2435

RHINOCEROS

Here is an animal (the rhinoceros) with a hide two
feet thick   2660

RICH

all the measures of the government are directed to
... making the rich richer   49

Two nations ... the rich and the poor   51

The rich rob the poor and poor rob one
another.   61

the rich are rich because they rob the poor   73

He mocks the people who proposes that the
Government shall protect the rich   76

the perennial ... kindness of the poor to the
rich   84

two American flags always; one for the rich and
one for the poor   99

When the rich wage war it's the poor who
die.   101

The forces of a capitalist society ... tend to make
the rich richer   103

it cannot save the few who are rich   104

The Democrats today trust in the people ... neither
superlatively rich   504

Commerce ... has made the citizens of England
rich   632

You don't make the poor richer by making the
rich poorer.   659

the rich ... all too often bend the acts of
government   745

Nature is rich; but everywhere man, the heir of
nature, is poor.   916

a rich nation that had ceased to be in love with
liberty   1343

Laws grind the poor, and rich men rule the
law.   1862

has the rich, who are always a minority, absolutely
at its mercy   2292

The loved and the rich need no protection   2293

the very rich, who contract out the messy things
of life;   2656

the party that wants to see an America in which
people can still get rich   3181

The business of government is not directly to
make the people rich   3439

no nation is rich enough to pay for both war and
civilization   3476

The gods sent not/ Corn for the rich men
only.   3515

RICHES

most of their passions either end in the love of
riches   325

Riches without law are more dangerous than is
poverty without law.   1894

All our material riches will avail us little   3487

RIDDLE

Communism is the solution of the riddle of
history   118

a riddle wrapped in a mystery inside an
enigma   959

RIDICULE

height of heroism ... is to know how to face
ridicule   2102

RIDICULOUS

no spectacle so ridiculous as the ... public in one
of its ... fits of morality   867

his position on ... every public question was either
mischievous or ridiculous   918

RIGGED

A rigged convention is one with the other man's
delegates in control.   2787

RIGHT

Because all Americans just must have the right to
vote.   31

The party in the last instance is always right   135

A sharp Right turn ... is likely to be followed by
an even sharper Left turn.   227

the right of the people to make ...
constitutions   303

right of the people to establish Government,
presupposes the duty ... to obey   304

The only legitimate right to govern is an express
grant of power   326

The instinct of the people is right.   339

the essential test that distinguishes right from
wrong   347

Democracy ... more than half of the people are
right more than half of the time   440

right of voting ... is the primary right by which
other rights are protected   698

follow the right side even to the fire   828

He is attached to it on the belief of its being
right.   846

may our country be always successful, but ...
always right   855

We uniformly applaud what is right   859

Be always sure you are right—then go
ahead.   872

The assailant is often in the right; the assailed is
always.   881

Let us have faith that right makes might   890

I wish we might have ... more commendation of
right   943

If you treat people right they will treat you
right   961

no man has the right to strangle democracy with a
single set of vocal cords   1134

not so much concerned with the right of everyone
to say anything he pleases   1139

An unconditional right to say what one
pleases   1145

right to be heard does not ... include the right to be taken seriously 1147

but because we have a right to be free ... we ought to demand freedom 1245

They are slaves who dare not be/ In the right with two or three. 1265

When we lose the right to be different 1357

spirit of liberty is the spirit which is not too sure it is right 1393

right to be let alone is indeed the beginning of all freedoms 1414

May God prevent us from becoming "right-thinking men" 1462

We know what's right: Freedom is right. 1474

being so right that it does not need to convince ... by force that it is right 1639

no right where there is no justice 1756

They have a Right to censure, that have a Heart to help: 1764

not simply doing right, the governed must be convinced that it is right 1776

not desirable to cultivate a respect for the law, so much as for the right 1885

Law alone cannot make man see right. 1936

person must be warned that he has a right to remain silent 1941

a right to life that means a bare existence in utter misery 1952

unless he transforms strength into right 2014

Any man more right than his neighbors constitutes a majority of one. 2057

if we have a right to prevent it, it is our duty 2092

Those who believe that they are exclusively in the right 2118

never the right time to take a particular stand 2184

the interest of the majority is the political standard of right and wrong 2280

A wise man will not leave the right to ... chance 2291

If they want anything not right, they get it, too. 2295

The minority is always right. 2299

A way of life that is odd ... but interferes with no right 2317

can be no assumption that today's majority is "right" 2317

The Right Divine of Kings to govern wrong. 2339

may she always be in the right; but our country, right or wrong. 2398

Our country, right or wrong. When right, to be kept right; 2408

In your heart, you know he's right. 2431

You cannot influence a Political Party to do Right 2487

What is right must unavoidably be politic. 2686

He never wants anything but what's right and fair; 2697

all matters of right, are at bottom only questions of might 2705

There are the Right and the Left, and in the middle is the Swamp. 2729

I had rather be right than be President. 2956

that's all right, it's the exercise of the right of petition 2983

President's hardest task is not to do what is right, but to know what is right 3001

Shouldn't the people have the right to vote for someone 3037

rather be wrong an' comfortable thin right in jail 3110

All men recognize the right of revolution 3212

right of revolution is the inherent right 3235

right ... to do whatever is necessary to defend our own people right here 3272

As a man is said to have a right to his property 3296

The personal right to acquire property, which is a natural right 3298

the assertion of the natural right of all to the ballot; 3312

till ... every man in the land is guaranteed fully every civil ... right 3319

Men have no special right because they belong to one race 3322

A right is worth fighting for only when it can be put into operation. 3326

Next to the right of liberty, the right of property is the most important 3330

no right to strike against the public safety 3332

only one right in the world and that right is one's own strength 3338

the right to be let alone—the most comprehensive of rights 3339

education ... is a right which must be made available to all on equal terms 3346

Every American ought to have the right to be treated as he would wish 3364

interdependence ... between ... right to liberty and ... right in property 3382

A right is not what someone gives you; 3386

A married woman has the same right to control her own body 3396

right of an individual to conduct intimate relationships 3401

to strengthen his natural right to exist and work 3410

"A fair day's wages for a fair day's work": ... is the everlasting right of man 3447

the right of every human being to liberty and well-being 3530

most important power entrusted to the government is the right to tax 3590

The fear of doing right is the grand treason in times of danger. 3639

right of conquest has no foundation other than the right of the strongest　3691

with firmness in the right, as God gives us to see the right　3736

The right is more precious than peace.　3783

only true and lasting peace (is) based on justice and right　3795

RIGHTEOUS

a great help in persuading people that wars are righteous　3863

RIGHTEOUSNESS

Righteousness exalteth a nation.　770

the fundamental confusion that government ... can also create righteousness　1556

not be satisfied until ... righteousness like a mighty stream　1808

Generally peace tells for righteousness;　3761

our fealty is first due to the cause of righteousness　3761

those who fought the battle of righteousness　3994

RIGHTS

a device for maintaining in perpetuity the rights of the people　91

only form of government ... not eternally at ... war with the rights of mankind　301

Where the people possess no authority, their rights obtain no respect.　320

For rights that were not open to all alike would be no rights.　738

equal with "certain inalienable rights　750

only be preserved by respecting the rights of the States　865

support the rights of people you don't agree with　1149

to surrender the rights of humanity and even its duties　1213

Liberty does not consist ... in ... declarations of the rights of man　1346

We hear about constitutional rights, free speech and the free press.　1372

In anarchy it's not just the king who loses his rights　1551

my aim to observe a careful respect for the rights of other nations　1618

The liberal, emphasizing the civil and property rights of the individual　2273

violence ... by the majority, trampling on the rights of the minority　2282

that the majority may not ... respect the rights of the minority　2284

government is free in proportion to the rights it guarantees to the minority　2311

sovereign has ... three rights　2352

I recognize no rights but human rights—I know nothing of men's rights　3148

nature will rise up ... claiming her original rights　3188

they are endowed by their creator with certain inalienable Rights　3290

The public good is in ...the protection of every individual's private rights　3292

If we cannot secure all our rights, let us secure what we can.　3293

Man did not enter into society to ... have fewer rights than he had before　3295

If the abstract rights of man will bear discussion　3297

the miserable sophism of the Rights of Man　3299

Rights! There are no rights whatever without corresponding duties　3299

Human beings have rights, because they are moral beings:　3301

people know their rights, and they are never slow to assert ... them　3302

They have rights who dare maintain them.　3303

men their rights and nothing more; women: their rights and nothing less　3304

That ... man ... says women can't have as much rights as man　3305

rights ... of every ... person are only secure　3307

stir about colored men getting their rights, but not a word about colored women　3310

Human law may know no distinction among men in respect of rights　3316

I am the inferior of any man whose rights I trample under foot.　3317

Wherever there is a human being, I see God-given rights　3320

no security for the personal or political rights of any man　3321

The word man defines all rights　3322

We are here to claim our rights as women　3328

peace should rest upon the rights of peoples, not the rights of governments　3331

Men speak of natural rights　3333

fair to judge peoples by the rights they will sacrifice most for　3334

Rights that depend on the sufferance of the State are of uncertain tenure.　3336

the individual must have rights that are guarded　3343

Certain rights can never be granted to the government　3345

What men value in this world is not rights but privileges.　3349

I want every American free to stand up for his rights　3353

In giving rights to others ... we give rights to ourselves　3357

rights of every man are diminished when the rights of one man are threatened　3358

Property does not have rights. People have rights.　3381

rights of all persons are wrapped in the same constitutional bundle   3388

wherever ... any individual's constitutional rights are being unjustly denied   3395

You just have to respect their rights.   3400

all the fanatical ... theories about the rights of man   3507

During war we imprison the rights of man.   3811

RIGID

Rigid justice is the greatest injustice.   1765

RING

My hat's in the ring.   2733

RIOT

A riot is a spontaneous outburst.   3929

RIOTER

A rioter with a Molotov cocktail ... is not fighting for civil rights   3370

RISE

if they rise of themselves, well and good   3202

RISING

All rising to great place is by a winding stair.   1991

RISK

When you stop a dictator there are always risks.   629

To win without risk is to triumph without glory.   829

better to risk saving a guilty man than to condemn an innocent one   1852

Take calculated risks.   2140

any boy may become President ... it's just one of the risks he takes   2980

RIVALRY

free government consists in an effectual control of rivalries   299

the seed of war in the modern world is industrial and commercial rivalry   3791

RIVER

not best to swap horses while crossing the river   896

RIVIERA

If the unemployed could eat plans ... would be able to ... winter on the Riviera   647

ROAD

The best road to progress is freedom's road.   1438

A Congressman is never any better than his roads   2602

These are the white man's roads.   2935

ROAR

I had the luck to be called upon to give the roar.   3882

ROBBER

Monarchy is only the string which ties the robbers' bundle.   2346

the robber that takes all that is left, is private property in land   3555

ROBOT

You cannot ... ask him to accept the status of a political robot outside   607

ROCK

on either the right or the left and hurl rocks at those in the center   2784

liberal governments have been wrecked on rocks of loose fiscal policy   3612

ROLE

an essentially modest role ... that of an honest broker   1626

Great Britain has lost an Empire and has not yet found a role.   1676

ROLLS ROYCE

all right to have a Rolls Royce ego   2220

ROOM

if you ... can't tell when you walk into a room who's for you   2786

The more bombers, the less room for doves of peace.   3894

ROOT

a thousand hacking at the branches of evil to one who is striking at the root   2060

Lack of money is the root of all evil.   3524

ROOTAGE

You cannot tear up ancient rootages and safely plant the tree of liberty   1342

ROPE

When you get to the end of your rope, tie a knot and hang on.   962

rather in the nature of the support that the rope gives to a hanged man   1015

ROSE

Treaties are like roses and young girls.   3913

ROTATION

It is a rotation in office that will perpetuate our liberty.   2539

ROTTENNESS

a rottenness begins in his conduct   2534

ROUSE

nation is a power hard to rouse, but when roused harder still ... to resist   3056

ROW

He rowed to his object with muffled oars.   2039

ROYALTY

Royalty will be strong because it appeals to
diffused feeling   2353

RUDIMENT

In the act of resistance the rudiments of freedom
are already present.   1461

RUGGER

When you join a team in the expectation that you
are going to play rugger   3571

RUIN

some things which seem virtues would ... lead to
one's ruin   774

who abandons what is done for what ought to be
... will bring about his ruin   2673

RULE

It's a poor rule that won't work both ways.   748

No rule is so general, which admits not some
exception.   1843

government officials shall be subjected to the same
rules of conduct   1914

rule of law can be wiped out in one misguided ...
generation.   1945

They should rule who are able to rule best.   1970

Ill can he rule the great that cannot reach the
small.   1980

No one can rule guiltlessly.   2023

To rule over oneself is the first condition for one
who would rule over others   2111

The truth is that you don't rule with the
fist.   2121

just one rule for politicians all over the
world   2590

To rule with the help of one's enemies is ever the
worst kind of policy.   2704

where the one rules absolutely, the other is
absent   2891

Where the state is weak, the army rules.   3432

To promote a Woman to bear rule ... is repugnant
to Nature;   3975

RULER

Every government degenerates when trusted to the
rulers ... alone   293

naturally alert to repel invasion of their liberty by
evil-minded rulers   1361

rulers of the state are the only ones who should
have the privilege of lying   1601

Every ruler is harsh whose rule is new.   1969

A multitude of rulers is not a good thing. Let
there be one ruler, one king.   2323

not well for a ruler to have too strong tendencies
for other affairs   2541

History has taught me that rulers are much the
same in all ages   2845

If men think that a ruler is religious ... less afraid
of suffering injustice   3135

RULING CLASS

The ruling ideas of each age have ever been the
ideas of its ruling class.   53

Let the ruling classes tremble at a communist
revolution.   122

The ruling class or race must share their freedom
with everyone   1391

revolution always starts from ... internal dissension
in the ruling class   3184

a heroic enterprise for the ruling classes but a
grievous burden on the rest   3957

RUMOR

Rumor travels faster, but it don't stay put as long
as truth.   946

RUN

I do not choose to run.   947

easier to run a revolution than a
government   3287

RUNNER-UP

In war there is no second prize for the runner-
up.   3862

RUSSIA

in Russia they are slaves to the future   139

What is to happen about Russia? ... An iron
curtain is drawn down   149

to some country where they make no pretense of
loving liberty--to Russia   566

I cannot forecast to you the action of
Russia.   959

Russia ... has demonstrated that all government ...
is a dead weight   1554

They are fighting for Mother Russia.   2381

RUTHLESS

Let the law be ruthless and order will be
restored.   3194

SACRAMENT

Voting is a civic sacrament.   724

SACRED

Some men look at constitutions with ... reverence
... too sacred to be touched   233

no cause half so sacred as the cause of a
people   2095

SACRIFICE

willing sacrifice of the innocents is the most
powerful retort to ... tyranny   592

an unpitied sacrifice in a contemptible
struggle   838

A nation which makes the final sacrifice for ...
freedom does not get beaten   1388

good for a nation to know that it must
sacrifice   2373

fair to judge peoples by the rights they will
sacrifice most for   3334

happiness of society ... to which all such institutions must be sacrificed   3420

A nation will not count the sacrifice it makes   3728

SAFE

The people are the safest ... reliable lodgement of power   60

Where justice is denied ... neither persons nor property will be safe   75

The world must be made safe for democracy.   386

A free society is one where it is safe to be unpopular.   461

In crises the most daring course is often safest.   1088

Where the press is free ... all is safe   1166

The law is a causeway upon which ... a citizen may walk safely.   1931

To give moderate liberty for griefs ... to evaporate ... is a safe way   3082

SAFEGUARD

it is the only safeguard of our liberties   237

hard ... to construct a constitution that safeguards against mistakes   497

importance of safeguarding the community from incitements   1371

history of liberty has largely been ... observance of procedural safeguards   1384

observance of the law is the eternal safeguard of liberty   1932

SAFETY

Those who would give up essential Liberty, to purchase ... temporary Safety   1210

no right to strike against the public safety   3332

The purpose is clear. It is safety with solvency.   3618

SAIL

Your Constitution is all sail and no anchor.   238

(Constitutional law is) a ship with a great deal of sail   260

they do so in order to get the wind of votes in their sails   2636

SAKE

Man exists for his own sake and not to add a laborer   3441

SALVATION

salvation can only come through greatness   2154

SAME

Constitution ... is changing ... even when its words remain the same   240

Of course it's the same old story. Truth usually is the same old story.   1086

SAMPLE

tendency ... is to pick out ... a sample which supports ... its prejudices   2911

SANCTIFY

no worse heresy than that the office sanctifies the holder   2558

SANCTIMONIOUS

A sanctimonious man is one who under an atheist king would be atheist.   3138

SANCTION

suicidal nature of this weapon renders it unsuitable ... as a sanction   1668

Justice is the sanction used to support established injustices.   1795

essential to the idea of a law, that it be attended with a sanction   1868

two kinds of sanctions, effective and ineffective   3909

SANCTITY

end of all revolutionary social change is ... the sanctity of human life   3530

I hear the same talk about "sanctity of treaties"   3825

SANCTUARY

Criticism of government finds sanctuary in ... the 1st Amendment   1141

but disorder will give them but an incommodious sanctuary   1202

SAND

Our Constitution was not written in the sands   249

Laws are sand, customs are rock.   1906

SANDWICH

a hungry man is more interested in four sandwiches than four freedoms   1420

SAP

Energy in a nation is like sap in a tree;   87

SAUSAGE

If you love the law and ... good sausage   2259

SAVE

When it is a question of saving the fatherland   1834

I know that I can save this country   2012

things a man must not do even to save a nation   2177

not because I wish to save money, but because I wish to save people   3608

SAWDUST

Have you ever tried to split sawdust?   511

SAY

that we may think what we like and say what we think   1117

not so much concerned with the right of everyone to say anything   1139

In politics if you want anything said, ask a man.   4008

SCAFFOLD
Every step of progress the world has made has
 been from scaffold to scaffold   2059

SCALE
the scales of American justice are out of
 balance   1815
a society with no other scale but the legal one is
 not quite worthy of man   1953

SCANDAL
The prince must not mind incurring the scandal of
 those vices   774

SCARCITY
on the very first scarcity they will turn   3430

SCARECROW
We must not make a scarecrow of the law   1841

SCENERY
Not one cent for scenery.   732

SCHEDULE
There cannot be a crisis next week. My schedule is
 already full.   1070

SCHOOL
Letting ... a hundred schools of thought
 contend   161
Political democracy ... supplies a training school
 for making first-class men   351
But it is not a school of social ethics or of political
 responsibility.   1592
American people are too well schooled in ...
 submitting to the ... majority   2285

SCIENCE
With these discoveries socialism becomes a
 science.   127
You need neither art nor science to be a
 tyrant.   529
Politics is not an exact science.   2700
Politics is not a science ... but an art   2717
science of politics ... the science of the adjustment
 of ... group interests   2751
Politics is the science of who gets what, when, and
 why.   2762
many expensive national projects may add to our
 prestige or serve science   3623

SCIENTIFIC
in democratic societies ... education ... should be in
 scientific ... subjects   677

SCIENTIST
Statesmen must learn to live with scientists   2115

SCOUNDREL
A technical objection is the first refuge of a
 scoundrel.   957
Patriotism is the last refuge of the
 scoundrel.   2392

Public office is the last refuge of the
 scoundrel.   2589

SCREAM
Sometimes a scream is better than a thesis.   873
A crush of screaming women is flattering until
 they tear your clothes.   2433

SCRIBBLE
Great is the hand that holds dominion over/ Man
 by scribbled name.   3879

SCRIMMAGE
Football strategy does not originate in a
 scrimmage   2427

SCRUPULOUS
While it is true that an inherently ... scrupulous
 person may be destroyed   1405

SCURVY
like a scurvy politician, seem/ To see the things
 thou dost not.   2517

SEA
boisterous sea of liberty is never without a
 wave   1253
In civilized life, law floats in a sea of ethics.   1933
He that commands the sea is at great
 liberty   3675

SEAL
ideal is when a man receives the seals of
 office   2562

SEARCH
what the Constitution forbids is not all searches
 and seizures   243

SEAT
Actually, ruling is staying seated.   2121

SECESSION
Secession, like any other revolutionary act, may be
 morally justified   3205

SECOND
Politics I supposed to be the second-oldest
 profession.   2809

SECONDARY
the great force in throwing love of truth ... into a
 secondary place   2712

SECRECY
Secrecy and a free, democratic government don't
 mix.   484
Secrecy in government has become synonymous ...
 with deception   814
There are more secrets, but there is not more
 secrecy.   1097
necessary for the people to communicate their
 ideas under the bond of secrecy   1109

SECRET

what is secret is serious, and what is public is
merely propaganda   170
There are more secrets, but there is not more
secrecy.   1097
The secret of success is constancy to
purpose.   2075
The secret of power is the will.   2852
it cannot be left to a President ... alone to decide
what must be kept secret   3514
lest men should ... uncover some secret ... of
abolishing mankind   3684

SECRETARY

call in a secretary or a staff man and chew him
out   2668

SECRETARY OF STATE

Give a member of Congress a junket ... and he
thinks he is secretary of state   2659

SECT

A sect or party is an elegant incognito   2463

SECULAR

Politics in America is the binding secular
religion.   2822

SECURE

No kingdom can be secure in its independence ...
that is not free in its spirit   305
If we cannot secure all our rights, let us secure
what we can.   3293
The rights of ... any person are only secure from
being disregarded   3307

SECURITY

ignorance of one voter in a democracy impairs the
security of all   29
the best security against ... encroachments   673
some others which appear vices result in one's
greater security   774
no security on this earth; there is only
opportunity   1006
Therein lies the security of the Republic   1371
no governments ought to interfere ... except for
the security of what is due   1607
whether a country is ... free is the amount of
security enjoyed by minorities   2297
more about the security of their seats than about
the security of their country   2545
no security for ... political rights of any man ...
where any man is deprived   3321
except when the Nation's security is at
stake   3374
to free every man from fear, that he may live in all
possible security   3410
purpose of political order: which is simply peace
and security of life   3411
first end of government is to give security to life
and property   3456
Security, the chief pretence of civilization   3525

SEDITION

surest way to prevent seditions ... is to take away
the matter of them   3186

SEED

We Communists are like seeds and the people are
like the soil.   148
perhaps without the seed of things to come   990
The seed of revolution is repression.   3241
the seed of war in the modern world is ...
commercial rivalry   3791

SEGREGATION

I say segregation now ... segregation forever   2940

SELF

good points about all ... wars. People forget
self.   3730

SELF-

a movement more self-centered ... than
Marxism   163
the type of all the objections raised to the
extension of self-government   357
The noblest of all forms of government is self-
government;   376
Democracy, the practice of self-government, is a
covenant among free men   416
When the white man governs himself, that is self-
government;   565
always known that heedless self-interest was bad
morals   650
inherent in the capitalist system a tendency toward
self-destruction   652
Capitalists are no more capable of self-
sacrifice   934
Man's drive for self-expression ... does not stay
within set bounds   1146
warranted ... in interfering with ... liberty of action
... is self-protection   1285
guaranteeing that man himself shall be self-
reliant   1374
If the self-discipline of the free cannot match the
iron discipline of the fist   1437
We can afford to exercise the self-restraint of a
really great nation   1636
Avoid self-righteousness like the devil—nothing so
self-blinding.   2167
among these childish things the first to go ...
should be self-idealization   2171
self-love and social may be made the same   2232
unless the majority exercise the self-
restraint   2303
Self-determinism is not a mere phrase.   2374
it presupposes local self-sufficiency   2382
because it can satisfy the passion for self-
renunciation   3125
We hold these truths to be self-evident   3290
Self-determination is but a slogan if the future
holds no hope.   3540
One cannot pay the price of self-respect.   3777

SELFISH
powerful all too often bend the acts of government to their selfish purpose   745

SELFISHNESS
Conservatism ... is a euphemism for selfishness   202

SELL
farmer ... sells everything he sells at wholesale   656
To none will we sell ... right or justice   1830

SENATE
Th' Sinit is ruled be courtesy, like th' longshoreman's union.   2242
only way to do anything in the American government is to bypass the Senate   2253
The Senate is a place filled with goodwill and good intentions   2260
price of running for the Senate today   2826
given more power to the President and less to the Senate   2950

SENATOR
"No, I look at the Senators and pray for the country."   2251

SENSE
Let's talk sense to the American people.   995
our sense of justice never turns in its sleep   1801
hard work and a certain sense of purpose   2217
they have a grand sense for where the votes are   2511
main essentials of a successful prime minister ... and a sense of history   2646
Any man who has had the job I've had and didn't have a sense of humor   2982

SENSITIVE
Princes are more sensitive to any offense   2052
Being black has made me sensitive to any group   2316

SENTENCE
"No, no!" said the Queen. "Sentence first—verdict afterwards."   1788
average politician goes through a sentence like a man exploring a disused mine   2663

SENTIMENT
ultimate foundation of a free society is the binding tie of cohesive sentiment   424
when it costs us nothing but the sentiment   859
not to provide an outlet for our own sentiments of hope   1678
sentiment gives you the fulcrum and the place to stand on   2076
What we call public opinion is generally public sentiment.   3054
Public sentiment is to public officers what water is to the wheel   3058

SENTIMENTAL
We're a sentimental people.   1057

SEPARATE
two societies, one black, one white—separate and unequal   2939
Separate educational facilities are inherently unequal.   3346
the doctrine of "separate but equal" has no place   3347

SEPARATION
separation between one nationality and the other ... is a reactionary idea   2371
Under the doctrine of separation of powers   3512

SERFDOM
Better to abolish serfdom from above   883

SERGEANT
The sergeant is the Army.   3948

SERIOUS
right to be heard does not ... include the right to be taken seriously   1147
In politics one must take nothing tragically and everything seriously.   2711
War is much too serious a matter to be left to generals.   3785

SERPENT
Toryism ... like the serpent sheds its skin   211

SERVANT
Men in great places are thrice servants: 1990
The prince is the first servant of his state.   2341
Public officers are the servants and agents of the people   2556
The best servants of the people, like the best valets   2574
In our democracy officers of the government are the servants   2594
I am a public servant doing my best against the odds.   2657
The state is the servant of the citizen   3484

SERVE
I will not accept if nominated and will not serve if elected.   911
the ability of letting others serve him   2001
Politicians are to serve the people   2569
Your public servants serve you right;   2607
The public must and will be served.   3413

SERVICE
If we do not lay out ourselves in the service of mankind whom should we serve?   2019
Princes are more sensitive to any offense ... than to any service   2052
without them he must be incapable of performing any useful service   2462

469

There never was a bad man that had ability for good service. 2530

failure to maintain and improve essential service 3537

Who would prefer peace to ... dying in the service of one's country 3802

SERVITUDE

Freedom and not servitude is the cure of anarchy; 1222

SESSION

No man's life ... or property are safe while the Legislature is in session 2236

SETTLE

never so likely to settle a question rightly as when they discuss it freely 1112

SETTLEMENT

achieved by negotiated settlements of conditional surrender 3889

submitting their disputes to a just and peaceful settlement 3914

SEVENTY

always get the truth from an American statesman after he has turned seventy 2550

SEVERE

The art of policing is, in order not to punish often, to punish severely. 1778

The victim to too severe a law is considered as a martyr 1878

SEX

equal pay for equal work without discrimination because of sex 764

prejudice against color ... is no stronger than that against sex 2902

God-given rights inherent in that being whatever may be the sex 3320

by the union of the working classes of both sexes to organize labor 3983

SHACKLE

such power would provide the shackles for the liberties of the people 407

tyranny will bankrupt itself in making shackles 576

SHADOW

Race prejudice is not only a shadow over the colored 2916

the time has come to walk out of the shadow of states' rights 3344

those who are in the shadows of life 3501

We kill because we're afraid of our own shadow 3833

SHAKE

You cannot shake hands with a clenched fist. 1087

people thought that India was shaking 2212

SHALLOW

(Constitutional law) a ship with a great deal of sail but a very shallow keel. 260

The shallow consider liberty a release from all law 1314

SHAM

nauseous sham goodfellowship our ... public men get up for shop use 2580

socialist democracy may eventually turn out to be more of a sham 3564

SHAME

As soon as the people fix one Shame of the World 3118

a choice between war and shame. She has chosen shame and will get war. 3819

SHEATH

One sword keeps another in the sheath. 3678

SHEEP

"It never troubles the wolf how many the sheep be." 3674

SHEET

They just stop wearing sheets because sheets cost too much. 2945

SHEET ANCHOR

the Republican party as the sheet anchor of the colored man's political hopes 3167

SHELTER

not the shelter of the incompetent and the corrupt 1561

SHEPHERD

for which the sheep thanks the shepherd as his liberator 1303

SHERIFF

I'd feel a helluva lot better if just one of them had ever run for sheriff 2623

SHIELD

the only shield to his memory is the ... sincerity of his actions 2132

SHINING CITY

our destiny to be as a shining city on a hill 1080

SHIP

a ship with a great deal of sail but a very shallow keel 260

SHIPWRECK

Old age is a shipwreck. 2156

SHOCK ABSORBER

a social shock absorber placed between privilege and ... popular discontent 2255

SHOOT

One who brandishes a pistol must be prepared to shoot. 2122

"Take them out and shoot them" 2962

whose leaders are inclined to shoot from the hip 3179

SHORT

Constitutions should be short and vague. 231

Most of them, indeed, are rather short. 2110

SHORTAGE

The problem isn't a shortage of fuel 1574

SHOULDER

A political leader must keep looking over his shoulder 2180

now that ye're down we'll not turn a cold shoulder to ye 3168

SHOUTING

Shouting is not a substitute for thinking 1416

SHOVEL

Of course we will not bury you with a shovel. 167

SHOWMANSHIP

must get the American public to look ... beyond the showmanship 3081

SHREWDNESS

Shrewdness in Public Life all over the World is always honored 802

SHUDDER

I shudder to think of what could happen in this country 3887

SICKLY

The sickly, weakly, timid man fears the people 188

SICKNESS

a sickness rooted and inherent/ in the nature of a tyranny 518

SIDE

When it comes time to show on which side they will be counted 2277

A boss is a political leader who is on somebody else's side. 2645

God does not take sides in American politics. 2827

SIGNIFICANCE

false excuse that ... one in one hundred forty million has no significance 439

SILENCE

You have not converted a man because you have silenced him. 573

mankind would be no more justified in silencing that one person 1114

not achieve that by silencing one brand of idea 1132

SILENT

the great silent majority of my fellow Americans 478

person must be warned that he has a right to remain silent 1941

Laws are silent in time of war. 3652

Silent, mournful, abandoned, broken, Czechoslovakia recedes into darkness 3820

SIMILARITY

and noting a certain similarity of words 1712

SIMPLE

What the people want is very simple. 1072

SIMPLE-MINDED

People on the whole are very simple-minded 3075

SIMPLIFICATION

Totalitarianism spells simplification: 618

Power ... is partial to simplification 2881

SIN

If you're going to sin, sin against God, not the bureaucracy 14

waste of public money is like the sin against the Holy Ghost 796

If a law commands me to sin I will break it; 1880

We have never stopped sin by passing laws; 1927

SINEW

Endless money forms the sinews of war. 3654

SINFUL

The sad duty of politics is to establish justice in a sinful world. 2804

SING

Revolutions are never waged singing "We Shall Overcome". 3275

SIT

free to stand up for his rights, even if he has to sit down 3353

SKEPTICAL

skeptical about the ability of government to solve problems 3497

SKEPTICISM

a healthy skepticism of the powers of government agencies to do good 221

SKILLED

Politics is the skilled use of blunt objects. 2800

SKY

"Let justice be done, though the sky falls." 1725

SLANDER
Truth is generally the best vindication against slander.   897

SLAVE
a people who are slaves to market-tyrants ... come to be their slaves in all   80

in Britain we are slaves to the past, in Russia they are slaves to the future   139

For a nation to be a slave, it is only necessary that she will it.   307

As I would not be a slave, so I would not be a master.   335

It is the argument of tyrants, it is the creed of slaves.   541

Power ... Makes slaves of men   552

Begotten by the slaves they trample on   559

The slave begins by demanding justice   608

Under a pure despotism, a people may be contented, because all are slaves   744

so dead to all the feelings of liberty, as voluntarily to submit to be slaves   1215

I am tired of ruling over slaves.   1233

They are slaves who dare not be/ In the right with two or three.   1265

didn't know I was a slave until I found out I couldn't do the things I wanted   1266

he who would be no slave must consent to have no slave   1293

In giving freedom to the slave, we assure freedom to the free.   1299

The moment the slave resolves that he will no longer be a slave   1398

The slave has only one master;   2002

One hundred years ago, the slave was freed.   2928

When a sixth of the population of a nation ... are slaves   3210

years of delay have passed since President Lincoln freed the slaves   3361

SLAVERY
an immorality surpassed only by the immorality of selling oneself into slavery   117

Slavery they can have anywhere.   538

Slavery always has, and always will, produce insurrections   556

The prolonged slavery of women is the darkest page in human history.   575

the worst form of slavery, which is when the herd crushes out the man   606

So efficient are the available instruments of slavery   612

To take away this right is to reduce a man to slavery   698

But this is slavery, not to speak one's thought.   1107

Lean liberty is better than fat slavery.   1207

Where Slavery is, there Liberty cannot be;   1302

Whenever (I) hear any one, arguing for slavery   1304

Intellectual slavery ... will ... result both political and social slavery   1307

many things more horrible than bloodshed; and slavery is one of them   1345

If slavery is not wrong, nothing is wrong.   3309

So we defend ourselves and our henroosts, and maintain slavery.   3519

All socialism involves slavery.   3553

between peace and slavery there is the greatest difference   3655

SLEEP
The main essentials of a successful prime minister (are) sleep   2646

It doesn't make any difference who you sleep with.   2810

SLEEVE
To wear your heart on your sleeve isn't a very good plan;   1101

SLICK
We were told our campaign wasn't sufficiently slick.   2439

SLIPPERY SLOPE
There is no "slippery slope" toward loss of liberties   1471

SLOGAN
If you feed the people just with revolutionary slogans   3277

SLOW
The government's like a mule, it's slow   1548

SMALL
more easily fall victims to a big lie than to a small one   589

Small nations are like indecently dressed women.   1688

Ill can he rule the great that cannot reach the small.   1980

who spend their time on small things usually become incapable of large ones   1998

They lack small-talk   2143

presidency has made every man who occupied it, no matter how small, bigger   3006

SMEAR
enough mistakes ... to criticize constructively without ... political smears   2509

SMITH
We Smiths want peace so bad we're prepared to kill every one of the Joneses   3857

SNAKE
political parties were like snakes, guided not by their heads but by their tails   2468

SNOB
an effete corps of impudent snobs   1056

SOCIAL

by forcible overthrow of all existing social conditions   120

In a social system in which power is open to all   415

What man loses by the social contract is his natural liberty   1211

The real guarantee of freedom is an equilibrium of social forces   1419

the social world is certainly the work of man   1483

intelligence of public opinion ... indispensable condition of social progress   3051

Social movements are at once the symptoms and the instruments of progress.   3064

the foundation of the social contract is property   3416

Government has the duty ... to meet new social problems with new social controls   3478

most important social service ... is to keep them alive and free   3479

Capitalism ... educates and subsidizes a vested interest in social unrest   3533

inability to enforce laws ... which protect and advance basic social justice   3537

Social imbalance reflects itself in inability to enforce laws   3537

If freedom makes social progress possible   3546

Objectively, Social Democracy is the moderate wing of fascism.   3558

only way ... seems to be for the different social systems to coexist   3952

SOCIALISM

With these discoveries socialism becomes a science.   127

Socialism is Soviet power plus ... electrification   132

little reason to believe that socialism will mean the advent of the civilization   146

When ... forces which are hostile to Socialism   174

Give socialism back its human face.   175

Democracy and socialism have nothing in common but one word: equality.   746

Anti-semitism is the socialism of fools.   2906

Christian socialism is but the holy water   3150

All socialism involves slavery.   3553

Socialism is a condition ...in which there should be neither rich nor poor   3554

I am for Socialism because I am for humanity.   3556

Socialism must come down from the brain   3557

the liberation of the human being, which is ... the final goal of socialism   3559

Socialism and laisser faire are like the north and south poles.   3560

socialism ... cannot be brought into harmony with the ... Catholic Church   3561

Religious socialism, Christian socialism, are ... contradictions in terms   3561

Socialism means equality of income or nothing.   3562

aim of Socialism is to set up a universal society founded on equal justice   3563

The great corruption of Socialism which threatens us at present   3565

Unimaginative people disparage Socialism   3566

the inherent virtue of socialism is the equal sharing of miseries   3569

Between the barbarity of capitalism ... and the barbarity of socialism   3575

SOCIALIST

A Bolshevik ... is nothing but a socialist who wants to do something about it.   131

Socialists believe in making the Government the people's master   504

socialist democracy may ... turn out to be more of a sham than capitalist   3564

Socialist production and Unsocialist distribution   3565

No socialist system can be established without a political police.   3567

Every reasonable human being should be a moderate Socialist.   3568

If the Labour Party is not going to be Socialist ... I don't want to lead it   3571

SOCIETY

Everyone who receives the protection of society owes a return   20

Society is composed of two classes: 45

A society without an aristocracy ... is not a society   90

Every Man ... puts himself under an obligation to every one of that Society   276

when they enter into a state of society, they cannot ... divest their posterity   286

Society in every state is a blessing   1497

Society is produced by our wants   1498

Order is not pressure which is imposed on society   1555

Society is always a dynamic interaction of two factors   2309

Our nation is moving toward two societies   2939

Man did not enter into society to become worse   3295

A state is not a mere society   3404

Political society exists for the sake of noble actions   3404

Man seeketh in society comfort, use, and protection.   3407

The aggregate happiness of society ... is ... the end of all government   3425

As man seeks justice in equality, so society seeks order in anarchy.   3443

The State exists for the sake of Society, not Society for the sake of the State.   3468

One cannot raise the bottom of a society without benefiting everyone above. 3541

the dues that we pay for the privileges of membership in an organized society 3613

To conclude that women are unfitted to the task of our historic society 3999

SOFT

Speak softly and carry a big stick 1632

SOIL

We Communists are like seeds and the people are like the soil. 148

Our soil belongs also to unborn generations. 733

You cannot ... plant the tree of liberty in soil that is not native to it 1342

To call war the soil of courage ... is like calling debauchery the soil of love 3763

SOLDIER

when life-long professional soldiers abstain from seeking high political office 2599

Just as with the soldier who does not carry his sword at all times 3682

No soldier starts a war—they only give their lives to it. 3804

a soldier's pack is not so heavy a burden as a prisoner's chains 3880

A government needs one hundred soldiers for every guerrilla it faces. 3897

The soldier ... prays for peace 3910

"Bad war, good soldier." 3961

SOLECISM

a judiciary ... independent of the will of the nation is a solecism 1727

SOLIDARITY

only by the power of association based on solidarity 3983

SOLITUDE

the great man is he who ... keeps ... the independence of solitude 2047

The person who wants to fight senses his solitude 2423

SOLUTION

Communism is the solution of the riddle of history 118

the solution of one problem brings us face to face with another problem 1038

You're either part of the solution or part of the problem. 1055

The chief cause of problems is solutions. 1083

useless to expect solutions in a political campaign 2427

some problems have no solution 2781

It takes a revolution to make a solution. 3286

If man does find the solution for world peace 3845

SOLVENCY

The purpose is clear. It is safety with solvency. 3618

SOMEBODY

best classified by ... the "somebodies" they are ... endeavoring to satisfy 1557

You can't beat Somebody with Nobody. 2829

SOMEONE

The world is divided into those who want to become someone 2206

SOMETHING

Do something. It it doesn't work, do something else. 1099

Freedom from something is not enough. It should also be freedom for something. 1182

One must be something, in order to do something. 2043

Fame usually comes to those who are thinking about something else. 2064

What is the use of being elected ... unless you stand for something? 2082

If you don't stand for something, you will stand for anything. 2200

no such thing as one getting something for nothing 2763

SON

I am the son of Liberty and to her I owe all that I am. 1296

I have a dream that one day ... sons of former slaves 3363

SONG

The song that nerves a nation's heart / Is in itself a deed. 2406

SONS OF BITCHES

My father always told me that all business men were sons of bitches 1595

SOPHISM

you will find nowhere ... the miserable sophism of the Rights of Man 3299

SOPORIFIC

artificially integrated circles are a soporific to the blacks 2941

SORE

a conference was held for one reason ... to give everybody a chance to get sore 1650

SOUL

our souls contain exactly the contrary of what they wanted 183

the despot who tyrannizes over soul and body alike 578

never secure emancipation ... until we have achieved it in our own souls 596

Equality—the informing soul of Freedom! 755

the wearing of striped pants in the soul that I object to   1050

but every subject's soul is his own   1201

Liberty of thought is the life of the soul.   1206

than the body can live and move without a soul   1220

Liberty is the soul's right to breathe   1318

The mind is the expression of the soul   1412

These are the times that try men's souls.   2394

Breathes there the man, with soul so dead   2396

The human soul cannot be permanently chained.   3325

SOUND

Washington is the only town ... where sound travels faster than light   1076

People do not want words—they want the sound of battle   3941

SOUR

scarcely any men more sour than those who are forced to be nice   2524

SOURCE

The Constitution is the sole source and guaranty of national freedom.   241

if reporters should ever lose ... the confidentiality of their sources   1192

the source of justice was the fear of injustice   1754

SOUTH

I have heard something said about allegiance to the South.   2401

SOUTHERN

Washington is a city of Southern efficiency and Northern charm.   1035

SOVEREIGN

A subject and a sovereign are clean different things.   526

At the moment that man inquires into the motives ... of his sovereign   1262

or the sovereign must be all-powerful   1487

If we insist ... that sovereign power means exemption from all law whatsoever   1837

common law is ... the articulate voice of some sovereign or quasi sovereign   1909

if undertaken by the sovereign ... are lawful   1950

how much nobler will be the sovereign's boast   2042

principal mark of a commonwealth ... existence of a sovereign power   2324

Obedience to the laws and to the Sovereign, is obedience to a higher Power   2350

The sovereign has ... three rights   2352

Public opinion ... is the real sovereign in every free one   3040

SOVEREIGNTY

Sovereignty resides in the French People   308

Sovereignty remains all times with the people   483

Sovereignty of the people and freedom of the press are each necessary   1168

I ... appeal from the sovereignty of the people to the sovereignty of mankind   1782

Whom hatred frights,/ Let him not dream on sovereignty.   1983

Your party man ... is always opposed to any limitation of sovereignty.   2460

Political sovereignty is but a mockery without the means of meeting poverty   3540

SOVIET

Socialism is Soviet power plus the electrification of the whole country.   132

The Soviet Union would remain a one-party nation   2512

In the Soviet Army it takes more courage to retreat than to advance.   3832

SOW

Were we directed from Washington when to sow ... we should soon want bread   3435

SPACE

one cannot leave too large a space for improvements   230

SPACE AGE

This is the first convention of the space age   1028

SPARK

let the sparks that continually go up from it fall on other altars   1260

hard to tell whence the spark shall come that shall set it on fire   3186

SPEAK

Th' dimmycratic party ain't on speakin' terms with itsilf.   502

But this is slavery, not to speak one's thought.   1107

Let other people speak out.   1143

The only way to make sure people you agree with can speak   1149

"Speak softly and carry a big stick; you will go far."   1632

I didn't speak up because I wasn't a Communist   3342

SPEAKER

allowing a speaker in a public hall to express his views   1155

To be both a speaker of words and a doer of deeds.   1966

the House will instinctively recognize the speaker as a Statesman   2570

SPECIMEN

naturalists have never been able to find a living specimen of either   1331

SPECTACLE

What spectacle can be more edifying or more seasonable   674

SPECTATOR

stakes ... are too high for government to be a spectator sport   487

curious spectators enjoy themselves in watching every secret movement   2081

who fire their shots across a crowd of spectators   3265

SPECTRE

A spectre is haunting Europe—the spectre of Communism.   121

SPECULATION

This is the essence of politics; all the rest is speculation.   2237

SPECULATIVE

that makes it such a speculative, uncertain business   1661

SPEECH

Not by speech-making ... will the great questions of the day be settled   894

When law and order prevail in the land, a man may be bold in speech   1106

Liberty don't work as good in practice as it does in Speech.   1360

no such thing as a nonpolitical speech by a politician   2609

political speech and writing are largely the defense of the indefensible   2767

Never think of posterity when making a speech.   2797

as with speeches that bring people to their senses   3081

SPENDING

ask their Congressmen to enact goodies in the form of spending   3627

The world in arms is not spending money alone.   3877

SPIDER'S WEBS

Laws are like spider's webs   1828

SPINOZA

If Napoleon had been as intelligent as Spinoza   2086

SPIRIT

The spirit of improvement is not always a spirit of liberty   1292

The spirit of truth and the spirit of freedom--they are the pillars of society   1311

spirit of liberty is the spirit which is not too sure it is right   1393

his living spirit to a service that is not easy   2109

in this spirit that I have tried to act throughout a long life   2266

Let me now ... warn you ... against the baneful effects of the spirit of party   2458

Our sense of power is more vivid when we break a man's spirit   2875

spirit of revolution, the spirit of insurrection is ... opposed to liberty   3200

SPIRITUAL

The driving force of a nation lies in its spiritual purpose   2380

SPLIT

Have you ever tried to split sawdust?   511

SPORT

To fight against the government with any means is a basic right and sport   356

Passive resistance is a sport for gentlemen   3957

SQUALOR

in an atmosphere of private opulence and public squalor   655

SQUARE DEAL

We demand that big business give the people a square deal;   1588

to shed his blood for his country is good enough to be given a square deal   3466

STABILITY

the legislator who has given stability and continuity   2254

two great ... principles at the root of government-- stability and experiment   2464

STABLE

a stable government, but we don't know how bad the stable is   1047

A world without nuclear weapons would be less stable   1721

The law must be stable, but it must not stand still.   1913

STAGE-MANAGE

The great leaders have always stage-managed their effects.   2126

STAGNATION

Too little liberty brings stagnation   1403

STAIRCASE

There is no "slippery slope" toward loss of liberties, only a long staircase   1471

STAKE

stakes ... are too high for government to be a
  spectator sport   487
Every step of progress the world has made has
  been ... from stake to stake   2059
All you get is a chance to play for higher
  stakes   2815

STALIN

because Stalin himself ... supported the
  glorification of his own person   158

STALINISM

Stalinism is the essence of Communism.   176

STALWART

so long as ... its stalwarts sit up and beg for sugar-
  plums   2495

STAMINA

Human kindness has never weakened the stamina
  ... of a free people.   1377

STAND

I hope to "stand firm" enough not to go
  backward   2070
never the right time to take a particular
  stand   2184
If you don't stand for something, you will stand
  for anything.   2200
the men who stand against reform are standing
  against nature   3114
when the person interested is himself able ... to
  stand up for them   3307
I want every American free to stand up for his
  rights   3353

STANDARD

He who comes up to his own idea of greatness
  must ... have a very low standard   2041
But you can plant a standard/ Where a standard
  never flew   2114
that the interest of the majority is the political
  standard of right   2280

STANDING

may ... be brought against a standing
  government   1536
objections ... against a standing army ... deserve to
  prevail   1536

STANDPATISM

Standpatism is ... impossible in modern
  conditions   3114

STANDPATTER

Expect to be called a standpatter, but don't be a
  standpatter.   209

STAR

who exercises government by ... virtue may be
  compared to the north polar star   1968
all in the gutter, but some ... are looking at the
  stars   2083

START

I am not sure I should have dared to start;   1011

STARVATION

One should respect public opinion ... as is
  necessary to avoid starvation   3069

STATE

some people who think that a democratic State is
  ... the people   3
The State is a collection of officials   3
The state is nothing but an instrument of
  oppression of one class by another   77
State interference in social relations becomes ...
  superfluous   126
The first act by virtue of which the State really
  constitutes itself   126
The states' role in our system of government   261
What has always made the state a hell on
  earth   550
A State which dwarfs its men   568
The State is still ... a collective despot   580
The state is the divine idea as it exists on
  earth.   852
therefore worship the state as the manifestation of
  the divine on earth   852
only be preserved by respecting the rights of the
  States   865
the more liberty is given to everything which is in
  a state of growth   1217
Where the State begins, individual liberty
  ceases   1306
While the state exists there is no freedom;   1350
the final end of the State was to make men
  free   1359
the exercise of free will unhampered by the
  state   1474
For a state to be strong   1487
in its worst state, an intolerable one   1497
Society in every state is a blessing   1497
government, even in its best state is but a
  necessary evil;   1497
how is the state to be constituted so that bad
  rulers can be got rid of   1577
the problem of a law-governed external
  relationship with other states   1605
A state worthy of the name has no friends   1675
Whoever desires to found a state and give it
  laws   1833
The states are not free ... to intimidate women into
  continuing pregnancies   1948
Men in great places are thrice servants: servants of
  the ... state   1990
at the moment, the state legislature has more to
  say than God   2265
Kings are the publick Pillars of the State   2335
The worth of a State ... is the worth of the
  individuals   2367
The State, in choosing men to serve it, takes no
  notice of their opinions.   2518

477

A state without some means of change   3085

not the master òr the servant of the state, but ... the conscience of the state   3162

Rights that depend on the sufferance of the State are of uncertain tenure.   3336

A state is not a mere society   3404

that the treasure and monies in a state be not gathered into a few hands   3408

the great standard by which every thing relating to that state   3417

The primary cause of all our disorders lies in the different State Governments   3419

States do not prosper through ideology.   3431

Where the state is weak, the army rules.   3432

neither ... have men made the State; but that the State ... makes them men   3436

What the proletarian lacks is capital ... the state is to see that he gets it   3444

the state ... think of it as the poor man's bank   3444

The mass of men serve the state ... but as machines   3451

The State ... is the most flagrant negation ... of humanity   3454

the state is obliged to find a job for him   3458

The state is like the human body.   3462

If the state has the power to send the flower of its manhood to die   3465

The State exists for the sake of Society, not Society for ... the State   3468

If the moral and physical fibre of its manhood ... is not a state concern   3474

The state is the servant of the citizen   3484

War is regarded as nothing but the continuation of state policy   3718

Every State must conquer or be conquered.   3739

The word state is identical with the word war.   3752

Without war no state could exist.   3758

War ... will endure ... as long as there is a multiplicity of states   3758

while we still have the state of tension that now exists   3887

STATES' RIGHTS
out of the shadow of states' rights   3344

STATESMAN
A statesman is judged by results.   4

A disposition to preserve ... would be my standard of a statesman   2021

The heart of a statesman must be in his head.   2034

A statesman should be possessed of good sense   2044

difference between a politician and a statesman   2058

a statesman thinks of the next generation   2058

A constitutional statesman is in general a man of common opinions   2062

A great statesman is he who knows when to depart from traditions   2068

Statesmen must learn to live with scientists   2115

the greatest duty of any statesman is to educate   2123

when you're abroad, you almost feel yourself a statesman   2161

When statesmen forsake their own private conscience   2186

A statesman who too far outruns the experience of his people will fail   2194

party attachments ... are in the first class of a statesman's duties   2462

You ... get the truth from an American statesman after he has turned seventy   2550

As compared with the statesman, he suffers the disadvantage of being alive.   2566

a statesman ... imposes his will and his ideas on his environment   2614

A statesman is a politician who's been dead 10 or 15 years.   2615

Before you can become a statesman you first have to get elected   2641

A good statesman ... always learns more from his opponents   2754

The successful revolutionary is a statesman   3257

They bust her, and they become statesmen and heroes.   3638

a dangerous quality in the captain and a positive crime in the statesman   3764

STATESMANSHIP
In statesmanship get formalities right   2084

We lost the American colonies because we lacked the statesmanship   2197

Ignore them and statesmanship is irrelevant;   3064

That's statesmanship of the highest order.   3616

STATIC
Democracy is not a static thing. It is an everlasting march.   405

STATUE
while thousands of dollars are wasted every year over unsightly statues   3522

STATUS QUO
The only alteration they are likely to desire in the status quo   3

STATUTE-LAW
We are ruled by Public Opinion, not by Statute-law.   3067

STEP
Power never takes a back step   2884

STERILITY
a statesman who limits his policies ... is doomed to sterility   2194

STETTIN

From Stettin in the Baltic to Trieste ... an iron
curtain has descended   150

STIFLE

the opinion we are endeavoring to stifle is a false
opinion   1116

STILL

when the ground shakes under governments ... no
good their trying to sit still   3199

STING

Injustice is relatively easy to bear; what stings is
justice.   1802

STIR

if they rise of themselves, well and good, but do
not stir them up   3202

a great stir about colored men getting their
rights   3310

STOCK IN TRADE

the stock in trade of those who have vested
interests ... they want to preserve   3825

STOMACH

The healthy stomach is nothing if not
conservative.   208

STOP

but I am sure I should not have dared to
stop   1011

The time to stop a revolution is at the
beginning   3264

STORM

like a storm in the atmosphere   3189

as necessary in the political world as storms in the
physical   3190

STRAIGHT

fight for what is straight and honest   2967

STRAIN

It is always a strain when people are being
killed.   3936

STRANGER

If a man be ... courteous to strangers, it shows he
is a citizen of the world   1604

STRANGLE

no man has the right to strangle democracy with a
single set of vocal cords   1134

STRATEGY

Football strategy does not originate in a
scrimmage;   2427

STRAW VOTE

A straw vote only shows which way the hot air
blows.   3063

STREAM

certain fountains of justice, whence all civil laws
are derived but as streams   1759

until justice rolls down like waters and
righteousness like a mighty stream   1808

You have to be like the pebble in the
stream   2051

The man who is swimming against the stream
knows the strength of it.   2101

STREET

Whoever can conquer the street will one day
conquer the state   593

a policeman being required to secure the assent of
parties to a street fight   1718

competent to judge a political party that works
both sides of a street   2497

no Democratic or Republican way of cleaning the
streets   2505

When hopes and dreams are loose in the
streets   3263

STRENGTH

strength in the union even of very sorry men   823

the self-restraint of a really great nation which
realizes its own strength   1636

our will that is being tried and not our
strength   1697

Justice without strength is powerless, strength
without justice is tyrannical.   1762

not possible to fight beyond your strength, even if
you strive   1967

detecting in those they destine for their tools the
exact quality of strength   2087

The man who is swimming against the stream
knows the strength of it   2101

They're the source of our strength.   2319

only one right in the world and that right is one's
own strength   3338

Our strength is a contented and intelligent
community.   3461

To insist on strength ... is not war-
mongering.   3922

STRIKE

If trade unionists failed to register their protest by
striking   50

no right to strike against the public safety by
anybody   3332

STRING

Monarchy is only the string which ties the
robbers' bundle.   2346

STRINGENT

no method to secure the repeal of bad ... laws ...
as their stringent execution   1889

STRIP POKER

in the strip poker of American politics, the parties
are weak   2503

STRIPED PANTS

the wearing of striped pants in the soul that I
object to   1050

STRIVE

in the seeking ... and the striving for them there
are many roads to follow   402

not possible to fight beyond your strength, even if
you strive   1967

STRONG

Communism is exploitation of the strong by the
weak   116

Property is exploitation of the weak by the
strong.   116

Don't expect to build up the weak by pulling
down the strong.   209

That government is the strongest of which every
man feels himself a part.   306

Make men large and strong, and tyranny will
bankrupt itself   576

All strong without, he is all-weak within.   602

The ballot is stronger than the bullet.   702

Freedom belongs to the strong.   1368

Give them a strong and ... a good, government;
but, above all, a strong one   1521

whether any government not too strong for the
liberties of its people   1542

Government cannot be stronger or more tough-
minded than its people.   1564

Even to observe neutrality you must have a strong
government.   1606

one principle of justice, which is the interest of the
stronger   1749

unable to make what is just strong, we have made
what is strong just   1762

the just can be strong in the defense of
justice   1810

the strong can be just in the use of strength   1810

Law is merely the expression of the will of the
strongest   1899

The strongest is never strong enough to be always
the master   2014

Keep strong, if possible. In any case, keep
cool.   2167

The most important thing is to be strong.   2193

The gods are on the side of the stronger.   3662

The right of conquest has no foundation other
than the right of the strongest.   3691

The battle, sir, is not to the strong alone;   3693

Of the four wars ... none came about because the
U.S. was too strong   3956

STRUCTURE

The whole structure of democracy rests on public
opinion.   3072

Peace is ... quietly building new structures   3917

STRUGGLE

The struggle is confused;   495

an unpitied sacrifice in a contemptible
struggle   838

This struggle may be a moral one   1279

If there is no struggle there is no progress.   1279

progress of ... liberty shows that concessions ...
have been born of struggle   1280

The struggle between liberty and authority is the
most conspicuous feature   1282

at a time when a great struggle for human
freedom is in progress   1347

the struggle everybody is engaged in to get better
living conditions   1569

Modern politics is ... a struggle not of men but of
forces   2728

all politics seem like provincial struggles for booty
between dusky tribes   2758

he that struggles tightens those cords he does not
succeed in breaking   3092

if it supposes it is engaged in a struggle for its
fame   3728

Mankind has grown strong in eternal
struggles   3797

Struggle is the father of all things.   3799

STUBBORN

Facts are stubborn things;   839

STUBBORNNESS

no higher fortitude than stubbornness in the face
of overwhelming odds   2174

STUFF

each man obtains the chance to show the stuff that
is in him   758

STUMP

The best time to listen to a politician is when he's
on a stump   2432

The problems seem so easy out there on the
stump.   2435

cut ... a redwood tree, then mount the stump and
make a speech for conservation   2630

STUPID

Stupid people can only see their own side to a
question: 203

If democracy is so stupid as to give us free
tickets   594

the West would say we were either stupid or
weak   1010

Against war it may be said that it makes the
victor stupid   3743

STUPIDITY

Stupidity and unconscious bias often work more
damage than venality.   797

the Americans will commit all the stupidities they
can think of   1049

STYLE

I've always advocated the politics of substance, not the politics of style. 3022

SUBDUE

may subdue for a moment ... it does not remove the necessity of subduing again 537

SUBJECT

A subject and a sovereign are clean different things. 526

for slavery consists in being subject to the will of another 698

A fanatic is one who can't change his mind and won't change the subject. 998

Every subject's duty is the king's; but every subject's soul is his own. 1201

we should be men first, and subjects afterward 1885

The subject's love is the king's best guard. 2007

The king presupposes subjects; 2128

The good of subjects is the end of kings. 2338

SUBJECTION

A democracy ... recognizes the subjection of the minority to the majority 385

intended to be in subjection to the white Saxon man 2902

SUBJUNCTIVE

cracking his shins on a subordinate clause or a nasty bit of subjunctive 2663

SUBLIME

The way ... Christ keeps aloof from politics, is truly sublime 3154

SUBMARINE

I like to operate like a submarine on sonar. 2178

SUBMISSION

anything that goes beyond ... is voluntary submission to ... tyranny 3069

SUBMISSIVENESS

The benevolent despot ... demands from others the submissiveness of sheep 617

SUBORDINATION

The necessary ... subordination of the military to civil power 2599

SUBSISTENCE

the state's obligation, which owes to every citizen an assured subsistence 3415

SUBSTANCE

The substance of government may be taken away, while ... the shadow remain 571

High office teaches decision making, not substance. 2205

the delusion that a change in form is a change in substance 2740

I've always advocated the politics of substance, not the politics of style. 3022

We must get the American public to look ... to the reality, the hard substance 3081

SUBSTITUTE

There is no substitute for a militant freedom. 1354

In war there is no substitute for victory. 3865

SUBTLE

Laws should not be subtle; 1857

SUBTLETY

To strike freedom of the mind with ... patriotism is an old ... subtlety 2419

SUBVERSION

what their enemies have done in the name of defending us against subversion 166

As their heirs, we may never confuse honest dissent with disloyal subversion. 1136

finally it is the subversion of good Order, of all equity and justice 3975

SUCCEED

public sentiment ... without it, nothing can succeed 2063

Some men succeed by what they know; 2116

SUCCESS

Success makes men rigid 210

Each success only buys an admission ticket to a more difficult problem. 1081

has any chance of success if it is born in the minds of a few 1703

The secret of success is constancy to purpose. 2075

I don't know the key to success 2198

What is success? 2217

success of a party means little except when ... for a large ... purpose 2490

like saying the Titanic voyage was a success because a few people survived 2510

if prudently formed ... the success of them is infallible 2677

No one can guarantee success in war 3856

SUCCESSFUL

may our country be always successful, but whether successful ... right 855

SUCCESSION

No communist country has solved the problem of succession. 180

He regards himself as the next in succession 2460

SUCK

Capital is dead labor that ... lives only by sucking living labor 71

SUFFER

The bureaucracy is what we all suffer from.   2

If the people of a state make bad laws, they will suffer for it.   1895

We will soon wear you down by pure capacity to suffer.   3350

SUFFERANCE

Rights that depend on the sufferance of the State are of uncertain tenure.   3336

SUFFERING

Not actual suffering but the hope of better things incites people   3276

SUFFRAGE

Liberty can be safe only when Suffrage is illuminated by Education.   682

We demand in the Reconstruction suffrage for all the citizens of the Republic.   706

if only they have secured the suffrages of the members of a large union   2577

SUICIDAL

The suicidal nature of this weapon renders it unsuitable   1668

SUIT

Toughness doesn't have to come in a pinstripe suit.   4013

SUMMER SOLDIER

The summer soldier and the sunshine patriot will ... shrink from ... service   2394

SUMMIT

Nations touch at their summits.   1625

similarity of optimism in the reports which followed the summit meetings   1712

SUN

The sun never sets upon the interests of this country.   1617

SUNDOWN

More men have been elected between Sundown and Sunup   2742

SUNLIGHT

Sunlight remains the world's best disinfectant.   816

SUNSHINE

The summer soldier and the sunshine patriot will ... shrink from service   2394

SUNUP

More men have been elected between Sundown and Sunup   2742

SUPERFICIAL

not that it engage in gestures of superficial equality   257

SUPERFLUOUS

to many the superfluous is the necessary   3472

SUPERIOR

There they have no superiors.   712

politicians have a right to feel morally superior to their constituencies   2644

whites must be made to realize that they are only human, not superior   2944

SUPERIORITY

certain meanness in ... conservatism, joined with a certain superiority   192

it suggests ... a certain personal superiority   2382

for that discipline ... gives one army the superiority over another   3695

SUPERLEGISLATURE

We do not sit as a superlegislature to weigh the wisdom of legislation.   1734

SUPERMAN

They (communists) are not supermen at all.   172

Democracy cannot be saved by supermen   464

But, alas, there are no supermen.   2147

SUPERPOWER

The superpowers have the privilege of being able to destroy our planet   3954

SUPERSTITION

as religion, and not atheism, is the true remedy for superstition   1222

SUPERSTRUCTURE

Political institutions are a superstructure resting on an economic foundation.   641

SUPPLY

As scarce as truth is, the supply has always been in excess of the demand.   900

supply American boys to do the job that Asian boys should do   3921

SUPPORT

Liberty & Learning, each leaning on the other for their mutual ... support   674

the support that the rope gives to a hanged man   1015

a power over a man's support is a power over his will   2842

Governments do not and cannot support the people.   3439

while the people should patriotically ... support their Government   3463

its functions do not include the support of the people   3463

SUPPORTER

the monarchies of Europe were destroyed by their ... most ardent supporters   2365

A good statesman ... learns more from his opponents   2754

SUPPRESS
In the end it is worse to suppress dissent   1138
Freedom suppressed and again regained bites with keener fangs   1199

SUPREMACY
an unstable equilibrium, which can be preserved only by acknowledged supremacy   3931

SUPREME COURT
th' supreme coort follows th' iliction returns   1730
What five members of the Supreme Court say the law is   1733
Whenever you put a man on the Supreme Court he ceases to be your friend.   1736
the Supreme Court, through its decisions, goes on forever   1741

SURFACE
the more smoothly all things move on the surface   574

SURPLUS
Democracy is ... appropriate for countries which enjoy an economic surplus   459
The problem isn't a shortage of fuel, it's a surplus of government.   1574

SURPLUS-VALUE
the revelation of the secret of capitalistic production through surplus-value   127

SURPRISE
Whoever can surprize well must Conquer.   844
When we got into office, the thing that surprised me most   1031

SURRENDER
No terms except an unconditional and immediate surrender can be accepted.   3733
we shall fight in the hills; we shall never surrender   3829

SURVEILLANCE
the age of no privacy, where everyone is open to surveillance   3491

SURVIVAL
for without victory there is no survival   3826
from the point of view of those who desire the survival of culture   3851

SUSPICION
Democracy is the ... suspicion that more than half of the people are right   440

SUSTAIN
A government can be no better than the public opinion that sustains it.   3071

SUSTENANCE
When more ... is exacted through ... taxation than is necessary   3603

SWAMP
the Right and the Left, and in the middle is the Swamp   2729

SWAN SONGS
how many swan songs can a lame duck deliver?   1069

SWAP
not best to swap horses while crossing the river   896

SWEAT
I have nothing to offer but blood, toil, tears and sweat.   965
The more you sweat in peace, the less you bleed in war.   3970

SWEEP
This is also like sweeping the floor;   3259

SWEET
Freedom is sweet, on the beat/ Freedom is sweet to the reet complete   1457
The name of peace is sweet and the thing itself good   3655
Living ... For one's fatherland, is sweet   3723

SWELL
Every man who takes office in Washington either grows or swells.   2575

SWIFT
Swift justice demands more than just swiftness.   1807

SWIM
the man who would not go into the water until he had learned to swim   357

SWORD
A sword never kills anybody;   825
The censor's sword pierces deeply into the heart of free expression.   1140
nation shall not lift up sword against nation   3650
One sword keeps another in the sheath.   3678
Just as with the soldier who does not carry his sword at all times   3682
a Union that can only be maintained by swords ... has no charm for me   3729
we must have a great deal more than the power of the sword   3798

SYMBOL
I suggested that we use the panther as our symbol   3284

SYMPATHY
The strongest bond of human sympathy ... one uniting all working people   3520

SYNDICALISM
Under the species of Syndicalism and Fascism   595

SYNTAX
A candidate for office can have no greater advantage than muddled syntax; 2616

SYNTHESIS
He who places his trust in the Marxian synthesis as a whole 145

SYSTEM
systems have their root ... in the innate conservatism of the human mind 212

Democracy is good ... because other systems are worse 470

The test of every religious, political, or educational system 1538

Any system of government will work when everything is going well. 1560

the system that functions in the pinches that survives 1560

beneficiaries of a system cannot be expected to destroy it 3528

Most (tax revisions) didn't improve the system 3631

TACK
Adept at tacking with the wind 2626

Politicians trim and tack in their quest for power 2636

TAIL
political parties were like snakes, guided ... by their tails 2468

TAKE
wasting the labors of the people, under the pretence of taking care of them 1518

if regulation goes too far it will be recognized as a taking 3471

government that is big enough to give ... is big enough to take 3489

TALENT
All of us do not have equal talent 766

Great offices will have great talents. 2020

The grounds of this are virtue and talent. 2033

For every talent that poverty has stimulated it has blighted a hundred. 3539

TALK
a Parliament ... is an entity which ... can do talk only 2233

Parliament will train you to talk; and ... to hear ... foolish talk 2234

Talk is nauseous without practice. 2495

We have talked long enough ... about equal rights 3359

For it isn't enough to talk about peace. 3868

the talk may be boring ... it is preferable to war 3967

TAME
The man for whom law exists ... is a tame man 197

TAPE
If I were to make public these tapes 3007

If Nixon is not forced to turn over tapes 3029

TARGET
far more important to be able to hit the target 3895

TASK
A President's hardest task is not to do what is right 3001

To give up the task of reforming society 3129

To conclude that women are unfitted to the task of our historic society 3999

TASTE
The taste of democracy becomes a bitter taste 447

TAX
because they were taxed without being represented 557

nothing so disastrous for a small fortune as a large tax 1530

Censure is the tax a man pays to the public for being eminent. 2522

The British Parliament has no right to tax the Americans. 3578

no taxes be imposed on them but with their own consent 3579

to tax and to please ... is not given to men 3580

to tax the higher proportions of property in geometric progression 3582

nothing in this world is certain but death and taxes 3583

the power to tax involves the power to destroy 3589

the most important power entrusted to the government is the right to tax 3590

the only one in which those who vote for a tax can escape the obligation 3595

Of all debts men are least willing to pay the taxes. 3597

To tax the community for the advantage of a class is not protection 3598

taxes should be so distributed as to not fall unduly on the poor 3601

The thing generally raised on city land is taxes. 3602

Taxes are what we pay for civilized society. 3604

Houseless, adj. Having paid all taxes on household goods. 3605

The power to tax is the power to destroy. 3606

A government which lays taxes on the people not required by ... necessity 3606

any taxes which are not absolutely required 3609

The power to tax is not the power to destroy while this Court sits. 3610

Taxes, after all, are the dues that we pay 3613

Noah must have taken into the Ark two taxes 3615

When everybody has got money they cut
taxes   3616

difference between a tax collector and a
taxidermist   3619

animals have instincts, we have taxes   3622

Tax reform means "Don't tax you, don't tax me,
tax that fellow   3626

they are unhappy about having taxes raised to pay
for those goodies   3627

The current tax code is a daily mugging.   3632

(A tax loophole is) something that benefits the
other guy.   3634

If it benefits you, it is tax reform.   3634

Read my lips: no new taxes.   3635

It has but one thing certain, and that is to increase
taxes.   3699

Give women the vote ... there will be a crushing
tax on bachelors   3989

TAXATION

they work ceaselessly to limit power and to
decrease taxation   1579

The art of taxation consists in so plucking the
goose   3577

Taxation and representation are inseparably
united.   3578

to exempt all from taxation below a certain
point   3582

man never yet contrived ... taxation that would
operate with ... equality   3593

When more ... is exacted through the form of
taxation than is necessary   3603

TAXICAB

Too bad ... all the people who know how to run
the country are driving taxicabs   2202

TAXIDERMIST

the taxidermist leaves the hide   3619

TAXPAYING

A taxpaying public that doesn't understand the
law   1964

TEACH

you can only teach the things that you are   2917

TEASPOON

as easily bail out the Potomac River with a
teaspoon   895

TECHNICAL

A technical objection is the first refuge of a
scoundrel.   957

TECHNICALITY

Wrong must not win by technicalities.   1818

TECHNOLOGY

efficient government equipped with ... a highly
developed technology   3481

TEETH

Battle, n. A method of untying with the teeth a
political knot   3765

this is what a hound has teeth for—to bite when
he feels like it   3893

TELEVISION

Television is democracy at its ugliest.   485

TELL

Tell a man whose house is on fire, to give a
moderate alarm;   1256

TEMPER

Never lose your temper with the Press or the
public   2780

TEMPERATURE

a Gallup Poll, always feeling one's pulse and
taking one's temperature   3073

TEMPESTUOUS

Timid men who prefer the calm of despotism to
the tempestuous sea of liberty.   546

TEMPT

Small nations are like indecently dressed women.
They tempt the evil-minded.   1688

TEN

You will kill 10 of our men, and we will kill 1 of
yours   3943

TEN COMMANDMENTS

he would have written the Ten Commandments
with three exceptions   2258

Public opinion is ... nearly as strong as the ten
commandments   3052

TENDENCY

McCarthy stamped with his name a tendency, a
whole cluster of tendencies   1017

tendency of the casual mind is to pick out ... a
sample   2911

TENSION

armaments are a function and not a cause of
political tensions   3947

TENT

The prize of the general is not a bigger tent   2865

TERMINATION

no government ever had a provision in its organic
law for its own termination   1539

no other procedure involves the purposeful
termination of a potential life   1955

TERRACE

The privilege of the great is to see catastrophes
from the terrace.   2127

TERRIBLE

well that war is so terrible—we should grow too
fond of it   3731

TERRIFIC
the cost to the oppressor is terrific 586

TERRITORY
you really cannot have people marching into other people's territory 2218

Size is not grandeur, and territory does not make a nation. 2369

TERROR
The one means that wins the easiest victory over reason: terror and force. 588

The only thing we have to fear is fear itself-- nameless ... terror 953

till custom make it/ Their perch, and not their terror 1841

invented by little minds in order to substitute terror 1860

Let us make terror the order of the day. 3195

Let us call a truce to terror. 3905

TERRORISM
through the selective brutality of terrorism 3958

Terrorism (takes) us back to ages we thought were long gone 3971

Terrorism has become the systematic weapon of a war that knows no borders 3972

TEST
liberty is the hardest test that one can inflict 1365

The test of every ... educational system, is the man which it forms 1538

The test of political institutions is the condition of the country 1543

final test of a leader is that he leaves behind him ... the will to carry on 2142

To act coolly ... in perilous circumstances is the test of a man 2158

The most certain test by which we judge whether a country is really free 2297

those of woman ... will not shrink from the same test 3297

Peace hath higher tests of manhood/ Than battle ever knew. 3725

TEXT
what do the words of the text mean in our time 258

THEFT
Property is theft. 3552

Every gun that is fired ... a theft from those who hunger 3877

THEME
one doesn't like to confront them with their own great themes 2143

Prosperity is necessarily the first theme of a political campaign. 2425

THEORY
that this manifesto is more than a theory 1123

The experience of Russia, more than any theories 1554

not with the words ... of theory that nations are governed 2032

To govern you do not follow any more or less good theory 2037

Without a revolutionary theory there can be no revolutionary movement. 3227

With all the fanatical and preposterous theories about the rights of man 3507

THESIS
Sometimes a scream is better than a thesis. 873

THIEF
the reasons why the workers get so little is that ... thieves get so much 70

hypocrites, called priests, have put crowns upon the heads of thieves 3153

All wars are wars among thieves 3781

THING
things a man must not do even to save a nation. 2177

THINK
things on which the public thinks long it commonly attains to think right 292

that we may think what we like and say what we think 1117

To think is to say no. 1126

If you think too much about being re-elected 2100

THINKER
Thinkers prepare the revolution; 3240

THINKING
an elegant incognito devised to save a man from the vexation of thinking 2463

Political thinking consists in deciding upon the conclusion first 2605

THIRD ESTATE
What is the Third Estate? Everything. 300

THIRD WORLD WAR
If the Third World War is fought with nuclear weapons 3950

THIRTY
Any person under the age of thirty who ... is not a revolutionist 3228

THORN
Every noble crown is ... a crown of thorns. 2348

THOU
Thou shalt not criticize other Republicans. 3180

THOUGHT

freedom of action without freed capacity of thought behind it is only chaos   685

Without Freedom of Thought, there can be no such Thing as Wisdom;   1205

Liberty of thought is the life of the soul.   1206

What we need is a synthesis of practical thoughts and idealistic aspirations.   2782

Every revolution was first a thought in one man's mind   3208

Our thought has been "Let every man look out for himself   3470

THOUSAND

a thousand hacking at the branches of evil   2060

THREAT

An efficient bureaucracy is the greatest threat to liberty.   12

THREATEN

Laws that only threaten, and are not kept   1842

THREE

but three ways for the populace to escape its wretched lot   3224

THRONE

A man may build himself a throne of bayonets   579

Even on the highest throne in the world, we are still sitting on our ass.   827

THROW

discover a problem and then throw money at it   3483

TICKBIRD

my head will roll just as surely as the tickbird follows the rhino   1454

TICKET

an admission ticket to a more difficult problem.   1081

TIDDLY-WINKS

you can't be ... enthusiastic if you are asked to play tiddly-winks   3571

TIDEWAITER

Finally, he asked to be made a tidewaiter.   2553

TIES

effects of inflation eat away at ties that bind us   660

TIGER

And the tigers are getting hungry.   598

Dictators ride to and fro upon tigers which they dare not dismount.   598

the tiger hunter who has picked a place on the wall to hang the tiger's skin   1027

TILT

the whole room might tilt everybody into the garden   2203

TIME

what do the words of the text mean in our time   258

an idea whose time has come   880

you'll never have to remember what you said the last time   1019

Time is on the side of the oppressed today   1458

times when one must govern liberally and times when one must be dictatorial   1545

Time is the ... commodity which the Foreign Office is expected to provide   1651

Every new time will give its law.   1902

the law is behind the times   1907

not born for glory unless he is aware of the pace of time   2008

Princes are like to heavenly bodies, which cause good or evil times   2330

These are the times that try men's souls.   2394

Always be on time.   2995

a time for all things, a time to preach and a time to pray   3694

a time to fight, and that time has now come   3694

I believe it is peace for our time.   3817

TIMID

Timid men who prefer the calm of despotism   546

We do not admire a man of timid peace.   2085

When his cause succeeds, the timid join him   2410

TINHORN

Tinhorn politicians.   2563

TINKER

(if) continually tinkered with it would lose all its prestige   239

if you make a modest contribution you are told you are only tinkering   3122

TIRE

I am tired of ruling over slaves.   1233

Give me your tired, your poor   1315

in the end it will be you who tire of it   3943

TITANIC

like saying the Titanic voyage was a success   2510

TITLE

our people have the most enormous appetite for Old World titles   79

TOAST

Now it's time for you to send it back to me-- toasted and buttered   1091

TODAY

Today there's law and order in everything.   1903

TOE

like the boy that stumped his toe   884

TOGA

the noble toga that political gentlemen drape over the will to power   2625

Let arms yield to the toga   3653

TOLERANCE

Democracy is not tolerance.   435

The highest result of education is tolerance.   686

there must be a spirit of tolerance in the entire population   1133

Tolerance is composed of nine parts of apathy   2910

If tolerance of diversity involves an admitted element of risk   2919

Tolerance implies no lack of commitment to one's own beliefs.   3161

it requires only that they live together with mutual tolerance   3914

TOLERANT

Inexorable as to principles, tolerant and impartial as to persons.   3450

TOLERATE

I respect only those who resist me, but I cannot tolerate them.   2185

All religions must be tolerated   3139

TOLERATION

I am driven to grudging toleration of the Conservative Party   220

TOMORROW

tomorrow speak what tomorrow thinks in hard words again   2048

Nations are formed ... by the fact that they have a program for tomorrow.   2378

would you realize what Progress is, call it Tomorrow   3219

TOOL

Give us the tools and we will finish the job.   969

the ability of detecting in those they destine for their tools   2087

TOP

The defeats and victories of the fellows at the top   95

It will not always get you to the top   2216

TORCH

that the torch has been passed to a new generation of Americans   1025

TORTURE

there is no worse torture than the torture of laws   1723

TORY

The sickly, weakly, timid man fears the people, and is a Tory by nature.   188

not the metier of a Tory to have a policy   198

stability and experiment. The former is Tory, and the latter Whig: 2464

When the Tories are in trouble, they bunch together   2501

TORYISM

Toryism ... like the serpent sheds its skin, but ... remains the same reptile   211

TOTALITARIAN

Nothing more exactly identifies the totalitarian or closed society   616

totalitarian regimes ... cannot really understand the nature of our democracy   620

The totalitarian state is not power unchained   626

Ours is not yet a totalitarian government   628

TOTALITARIANIAM

in our loathing of totalitarianism, there is ... admiration for its efficiency   604

TOTALITARIANISM

Totalitarianism spells simplification   618

Totalitarianism is bad, gangsterism is worse   1068

the forces of totalitarianism and anarchy will threaten free nations   1699

The only successful revolution of this century is totalitarianism.   3288

whether the mad destruction is wrought under the name of totalitarianism   3854

TOUCH

What touches all shall be approved by all.   269

TOUCH-STONE

the basic human truths which must serve as the touch-stone of our judgment   2879

TOUGH

A nation does not have to be cruel to be tough.   1377

TOUGHNESS

Toughness doesn't have to come in a pinstripe suit.   4013

TOURNAMENT

It bears the same relation to governing that tournaments did to fighting.   2077

TRADE

To make it an object of trade was ... making human beings an object of trade   117

No nation was ever ruined by trade.   634

Trade and commerce, if they were not made of Indian rubber   1581

TRADITION

A love for tradition has never weakened a
  nation   217

Let it be ... the task of our party to break with
  foolish traditions   506

A great statesman is he who knows when to
  depart from traditions   2068

TRAGEDY

but a prologue to a farce or a tragedy   675

Herein lies the tragedy of the age: not that men
  are poor   923

The tragedy of life is not that man loses   2112

The tragedy of all political action is that some
  problems have no solution;   2781

TRAGICAL

In politics one must take nothing tragically and
  everything seriously.   2711

TRAIN

I train troops to defend democracy.   494

Justice is like a train that's nearly always
  late.   1809

TRAITOR

They conspire to bust up a country—they fail, and
  they're traters.   3638

TRAMP

Every man is a reformer until reform tramps on
  his toes.   3113

TRAMPLE

Laws made by common consent must not be
  trampled on by individuals.   1865

The best use of good laws is to teach men to
  trample bad laws   1887

then claim the right of trampling on them
  forever   3300

I am the inferior of any man whose rights I
  trample under foot.   3317

TRANQUILITY

To model our political system upon speculations
  of lasting tranquility   1507

Tranquility at home and peaceful relations
  abroad   1620

No important political improvement was ever
  obtained in ... tranquility   3086

Peace is liberty in tranquility;   3656

TRANSCEND

he transcends it and moves toward the
  future   3260

TRANSLATION

the translation of those declarations into definite
  action   1346

TRANSPARENT

I wish that every human life might be pure
  transparent freedom.   1394

TREASON

For if it prosper, none dare call it treason.   3636

Treason doth never prosper: what's the
  reason?   3636

If this be treason, make the most of it.   3637

The fear of doing right is the grand treason in
  times of danger.   3639

TREASURE

policy is to be used that the treasure ... be not
  gathered into a few hands   3408

Sound principles will not justify our taxing ... to
  accumulate treasure for war   3585

TREASURY

Here's the key, there's the Treasury   3630

TREAT

If you treat people right they will treat you right--
  90 percent of the time.   961

Every American ought ... to be treated as he
  would wish to be treated   3364

TREATY

fidelity of the United States to security treaties is
  not just an empty matter   1715

The first object of a treaty of peace should be to
  make future war improbable.   3741

The only treaties that ought to count   3806

The hand that signed the treaty bred a
  fever   3879

Treaties are like roses and young girls.   3913

TREE

The body politic is like a tree;   870

The tree of liberty must be refreshed from time to
  time   1234

You cannot tear up ancient rootages and safely
  plant the tree of liberty   1342

always tremors when a great tree falls   2212

Legislators represent people, not trees or
  acres.   2257

The tree of liberty grows only when watered by
  the blood of tyrants.   3193

"Don't tax you, don't tax me, tax that fellow
  behind the tree."   3626

TREMBLE

Let the ruling classes tremble at a communist
  revolution.   122

I tremble for my country when I reflect that God
  is just;   3291

TREMOR

But there are always tremors when a great tree
  falls.   2212

TRENCH

How horrible ... that we should be digging
  trenches   3818

TRIAL

people ask if the United States can afford to place on trial the president   3013

TRIBE

all politics seem like provincial struggles for booty between dusky tribes   2758

TRIBUNAL

no better or safer human tribunal than the people   370

TRIBUTE

The citizen who criticizes his country is paying it an implied tribute.   32

TRIED

What is conservatism? Is it not adherence to the old and tried   199

Many forms of Government have been tried, and will be tried in this world   441

TRIFLE

The outcome of the greatest events is always determined by a trifle.   850

it is only trifles that irritate my nerves   2056

TRILLION

we want to know what you've done with the trillion you've got   3633

TRIM

Politicians trim and tack in their quest for power   2636

TRIUMPH

the harder the conflict, the more glorious the triumph   539

To win without risk is to triumph without glory.   829

the world is indebted for all the triumphs which have been gained by reason   1161

Injustice, arrogance, displayed in the hour of triumph   3788

TROOP

I deplore ... the use of troops anywhere to get ... citizens to obey ... courts   28

Many ... have too rashly charged the troops of error   830

they should march their troops towards the sound of gunfire   1036

A leader should not get too far in front of his troops   2207

The possession of battle-ready troops   3687

TROPHY

trophies unto the enemies of truth   830

TROUBLE

A lie is an abomination unto the Lord, and a very present help in trouble.   803

plenty of recommendations on how to get out of trouble cheaply and fast   812

When the Tories are in trouble, they bunch together   2501

The trouble with this country is that there are too many politicians   2597

Politics is the art of looking for trouble   2807

A general and a bit of shooting makes you forget your troubles   3896

TROUSERS

he asked me for an old pair of trousers   2553

never wear your best trousers when you go out to fight for freedom   3103

TRUCE

Let us call a truce to terror.   3905

TRUDEAU

In ... Trudeau Canada has at last produced a ... leader worthy of assassination   2637

TRUE

a true democracy has never existed   281

TRUISM

the truest truism in politics is: You can't beat Somebody with Nobody.   2829

TRUST

I repeat ... that all power is a trust;   313

Government is a trust, and the officers of the government are trustees;   315

free government consists in considering offices as public trusts   321

Trust the people.   465

"Give them enough food ... and the common people will have trust in you."   1477

Trust nothing to the enthusiasm of the people.   1521

some Republicans I would trust with anything   3170

TRUSTEE

The government must be the trustee for the little man   3480

TRUTH

Truth no more relies for success on ballot boxes   327

The totalitarian state is not power unchained it is truth chained.   626

When young people grasp a truth they are invincible   694

We hold these truths to be self-evident ... all men and women are created equal   747

a place where truth is not necessarily the best defense   815

remain as trophies unto the enemies of truth   830

Political truth is a libel—religious truth
  blasphemy. 856
Truth is generally the best vindication against
  slander. 897
As scarce as truth is, the supply has always been
  in excess of the demand. 900
Error moves with quick feet ... and truth must
  never be lagging behind 909
Not that men are ignorant—what is truth? 923
Rumor travels faster, but it don't stay put as long
  as truth. 946
Repetition does not transform a lie into a
  truth. 958
Eternal truths will be neither true nor
  eternal 968
I just told the truth, and they thought it was
  hell. 985
Son, always tell the truth. 1019
The Assembly has witnessed ... how historical
  truth is established; 1022
Truth usually is the same old story. 1086
he who knows nothing is nearer the truth 1164
The spirit of truth and the spirit of freedom--they
  are the pillars of society. 1311
The truth is found when men are free to pursue
  it. 1369
Truth is on the side of the oppressed. 1452
Truth is on the side of the oppressed today 1458
Truth can stand by itself. 1499
Justice is truth in action. 1783
Sir, I say that justice is truth in action. 1785
The lawyer's truth is not Truth 1886
Blessed is he whose fame does not outshine his
  truth. 2106
so few enthusiasts can be trusted to speak the
  truth 2108
the misfortune of kings that they will not listen to
  the truth 2349
You can always get the truth from an American
  statesman 2550
The political spirit is ... throwing love of truth ...
  into a secondary place 2712
If you ever injected truth into politics you have no
  politics. 2766
Truth is the glue that holds governments
  together. 2801
Conservatism goes for comfort, reform for
  truth. 3096
never wear your best trousers when you go out to
  fight for freedom and truth 3103
truth is the only safe ground to stand upon 3106
we would stop telling the truth about them 3172
We hold these truths to be self-evident, that all
  men are created equal 3290
The simplest truths often meet the sternest
  resistance 3311
it is to be fought out with the weapons of
  truth 3318
Among the calamities of war ... diminution of the
  love of truth 3689

TRUTHFUL
The life of the nation is secure only while the
  nation is honest, truthful 2370

TUBERCULOSIS
The cure for bad politics is the same as the cure
  for tuberculosis. 794

TURBULENCE
The cause of Liberty is a cause of too much
  dignity to be sullied by turbulence 1216

TURMOIL
Economic progress ... means turmoil 651
men ... who do not respect dissent, who cannot
  cope with turmoil 1464

TURN
The lady's not turning. 2209

TURNING POINT
at its critical turning points ... no other rule
  possible than the old one 2757

TWENTY
It takes twenty years or more of peace to make a
  man 3900

TWILIGHT
those who are in the twilight of life, the
  elderly; 3501

TWIST
let him twist slowly, slowly in the wind 1062

TWO
Two Cheers for Democracy ... Two cheers are
  quite enough 453
There can be but two great political parties in this
  country. 2476
The two-party system has given this country the
  war of Lyndon Johnson 2510

TYPHUS
War is not an adventure. It is a disease. It is like
  typhus. 3837

TYRANNICAL
When a nation has allowed itself to fall under a
  tyrannical regime 605
The more a regime claims ... liberty the more
  tyrannical it is likely to be 627
give them a tyrannical Prince ... and let me have
  but an unfettered Press 1165
most unnatural and tyrannical to say, "As you
  think, so must you act" 1238
money for the propagation of opinions which he ...
  abhors, is ... tyrannical 3141
In all tyrannical governments the supreme
  magistracy ... is vested in one man 3505

TYRANNIZE
There is the despot who tyrannizes over the
  body. 578

TYRANNY

The fortunate must not be restrained in the exercise of tyranny   93

If one man imprisons you, that is tyranny   347

a kind of balance ... which prevents its degeneration into tyranny   451

Tyranny and oppression ... become the order of the day   454

a sickness rooted and inherent/ in the nature of a tyranny   518

Death is better, a milder fate than tyranny.   519

The face of tyranny/ Is always mild at first.   527

Of all the tyrannies on humankind   528

The tyranny of the many ... when one body takes over the rights of the others   531

Under which kind of tyranny would you rather live?   533

Where law ends, tyranny begins.   536

Tyranny, like hell, is not easily conquered;   539

eternal hostility against every form of tyranny   547

Tyranny is a habit;   570

tyranny will bankrupt itself in making shackles   576

willing sacrifice ... is the most powerful retort to insolent tyranny   592

there are signs that tyranny is in trouble   610

tyranny and oppressions of body and mind will vanish   669

Where-ever Law ends, Tyranny begins.   1845

all we have standing between us and the tyranny of mere will   1930

defiance of the law is the surest road to tyranny   1932

not defenders of liberty but candidates for tyranny   2228

The tyranny of the majority.   2288

The one pervading evil of democracy is the tyranny of the majority   2298

in the most liberal State as in the most oppressive tyranny   2744

Power in defense of freedom is greater than power in behalf of tyranny   2883

I draw the line in the dust and toss the gauntlet before the feet of tyranny   2940

the particular form in which tyranny exhibits itself   3044

anything that goes beyond this is voluntary submission to ... tyranny   3069

the right to ... resist ... when its tyranny ... are great   3212

And yet Revolutions have never lightened the burden of tyranny   3228

that the efforts in human nature towards tyranny can alone be checked   3504

may justly be pronounced the very definition of tyranny   3506

one of the most powerful barriers ... ever been devised against the tyranny   3508

Neither you nor I are willing to accept the tyranny of poverty   3547

not a protector of liberty, but an instrument of tyranny   3606

TYRANT

"The consent of the governed" is more than a safeguard against ... tyrants   380

Any excuse will serve a tyrant.   517

When the tyrant has disposed of foreign enemies by conquest or treaty   520

the root from which a tyrant springs   521

For how can tyrants safely govern home   524

You need neither art nor science to be a tyrant.   529

All men would be tyrants if they could.   530

We call a tyrant the leader whose only law is that of his own whim   532

It is the argument of tyrants, it is the creed of slaves.   541

Kings will be tyrants from policy, when subjects are rebels from principle.   544

Great ambition ... is an unruly tyrant.   549

Tyrants are but the spawn of Ignorance   559

Whoever puts his hand on me to govern me is a usurper and a tyrant;   561

Tyrants never perish from tyranny, but always from folly.   564

those personal appeals which have sometimes moved ...tyrants to pity   580

The tree of liberty must be refreshed ... with the blood of ... tyrants   1234

Public opinion is a weak tyrant compared with our own private opinion.   3047

Public opinion, a vulgar ... tyrant   3066

The tree of liberty grows only when watered by the blood of tyrants.   3193

U-TURN

waiting with bated breath for that favourite media catch-phrase, the U-turn   2209

U.S.

Of the four wars in my lifetime, none came ... because the U.S. was too strong   3956

UGLY

Television is democracy at its ugliest.   485

War is an ugly thing, but not the ugliest of things: 3732

ULCER

I'm not the type to get ulcers. I give them.   1092

UNARMED

Among other evils which being unarmed brings you   3668

Rendering oneself unarmed when one had been the best-armed   3746

UNCERTAINTY

It increases the uncertainty of every
   circumstance   3716
to live out most if not all of our lives in
   uncertainty   3906

UNCLE SAM

He who tugs Uncle Sam's beard too hard   1707

UNCOMMON

in general a man of common opinions and
   uncommon abilities   2062

UNCONDITIONAL

No terms except an unconditional and immediate
   surrender can be accepted.   3733
Unconditional war can no longer lead to
   unconditional victory.   3907

UNCONSTITUTIONAL

The layman's ... view is that ... which he doesn't
   like is unconstitutional   251
Where sexual proclivity does not relate ... it seems
   clearly unconstitutional   3399
the power ... of pronouncing a statute to be
   unconstitutional   3508

UNCONTROLLED

Where public opinion is free and
   uncontrolled   3065

UNDERDOG

for the underdog no matter how much of a dog he
   is   1066

UNDERESTIMATED

I have been underestimated for decades.   2219

UNDERMINE

miners constantly working under ground to
   undermine the foundations   1727

UNDERSTAND

who places his trust in the Marxian synthesis ... to
   understand present problems   145
The people may be made to follow ... but they
   may not be made to understand   664
rather, Understand one another   928
The law is ... made for the exploitation of those
   who do not understand it   1915
A great man's failures to understand define
   him.   2090
None of us really understands what's going on
   with all these numbers.   3629

UNDERSTANDING

Freedom is the understanding of necessity and the
   transformation of necessity.   1451
Laws are made for men of ordinary
   understanding   1877
A President needs political understanding to run
   the government   2988
Understanding human needs is half the job of
   meeting them.   3536

UNDERWEAR

You're still the king—even in your
   underwear.   2355

UNEASY

Uneasy lies the head that wears a crown.   2327

UNEMPLOYED

If the unemployed could eat plans and
   promises   647
Or should I go downtown and talk about ... jobs
   for unemployed Negroes?   3132

UNEMPLOYMENT

When more and more people are thrown out of
   work, unemployment results.   644
like most other periods of severe unemployment,
   was produced by government   657

UNEQUAL

For equal division of unequal earnings   114
because men are unequal that they have that much
   more need to be brothers   760
no greater inequality than the equal treatment of
   unequals   762
source of faction has been the ... unequal
   distribution of property   2453
Our nation is moving toward two societies ...
   separate and unequal   2939
Separate educational facilities are inherently
   unequal.   3346

UNFAIR

Life is unfair.   765

UNFETTERED

let me have but an unfettered Press   1165

UNFINISHED

Liberty is always unfinished business.   1422

UNFIT

not that a particular class is unfit to govern. Every
   class is unfit to govern   69
devotes its chief energies to trying to prove that
   the other party is unfit   2500

UNFORTUNATE

the most unfortunate people are those who must
   do the same thing over and over   107
Justice should remove the bandage ... to
   distinguish ... the unfortunate   1792

UNHAPPY

better that some should be unhappy than that
   none should be happy   740

UNIFORM

When you put on a uniform, there are certain
   inhibitions that you accept.   3867

UNIFORMITY

Every central government worships
   uniformity   1531

UNIMAGINATIVE
Unimaginative people disparage Socialism 3566

UNINSTRUCTED
To lead an uninstructed people to war is to throw them away. 3647

UNION
Join the union, girls, and together say Equal Pay for Equal Work. 752
There is strength in the union even of very sorry men. 823
Our Union: It must be preserved. 863
The Union, next to our liberty, most dear. 865
Liberty and Union, now and forever, one and inseparable. 866
I do not expect the Union to be dissolved 885
If we do this, we shall not only save the Union 1277
When a faction in a state attempts to ... destroy the union 2287
The Union, sir, is my country. 2401
But I'm a Union man. 2549
The Trade Union Movement has become ... an avenue to political power 2577
a Union that can only be maintained by swords ... has no charm for me 3729

UNIONISM
Unionism seldom ... uses such power as it has to insure better work 643

UNIONIST
If trade unionists failed to register their protest by striking 50

UNITE
Working men of all countries, unite! 122
Let us discard all these things and unite as one people throughout this land 751
What we won when all of our people united ... must not be lost 3004

UNITED NATIONS
When people ... stop thinking of the United Nations as a weird Picasso 1004
After four years at the United Nations I sometimes yearn for the peace 1689
appeal to the United Nations in the ...certainty that it will let you down 1716
If the United Nations is a country unto itself, then ... it exports ... words 1717

UNITED STATES
you can't ... allow freedom ... to be pushed back to ... the United States 1427
North Vietnam cannot defeat ... the United States 3938

UNITY
May we know unity - without conformity. 1012
intolerance involves a certainty that unity will be destroyed 2919

UNIVERSAL
The function of parliamentary democracy, under universal suffrage 467
Universal peace is declared 705
censorship and universal suffrage are contradictory 1168
really universal enemy is precisely Yankee imperialism 1696
that it should become a universal law 1866
A universal feeling ... cannot be safely disregarded 3046
aim of Socialism is to set up a universal society 3563

UNIVERSE
would be a citizen of the universe 16

UNIVERSITY
Diversity of opinion ... is not only basic to a university 1400

UNJUST
Abuse a man unjustly, and you will make friends for him. 926
Extreme justice is often unjust. 1760
An unjust law is itself a species of violence. 1920
We have the means to change the laws we find unjust 1956
When there is an income tax, the just man will pay more 3576
War is a dreadful thing, and unjust war is a crime against humanity. 3770
But it is such a crime because it is unjust, not because it is war. 3770

UNLIMITED
Unlimited power is apt to corrupt the minds of those who possess it. 2837

UNLUCKY
Unlucky the country that needs a hero. 2139

UNMADE
what laws are for, to be made and unmade 1908

UNPAID
Being first lady is the hardest unpaid job in the world. 3014

UNPALATABLE
choosing between the disastrous and the unpalatable 2796

UNPOPULAR
A free society is one where it is safe to be unpopular. 461
Free trade ... is in almost every country unpopular. 636
not from men who feared ... defend causes which were, for the moment unpopular 2153

UNPREJUDICED
only two ways to be quite unprejudiced and impartial 2923

UNPROFITABLE
Make wars unprofitable and you make them impossible. 3789

UNQUALIFIED
when unqualified blacks, browns and women join the unqualified men 4005

UNREASON
We will not be driven by fear into an age of unreason 2153

UNREASONABLE
not all searches and seizures, but unreasonable searches and seizures 243

UNRECTIFIED
An unrectified case of injustice has a terrible way of lingering 3538

UNREST
The way in which, amid ... unrest ... Christ keeps aloof from politics 3154

UNSHACKLED
Yours for the unshackled exercise of every faculty 3313

UNSOCIALIST
it means the same thing: Socialist production and Unsocialist distribution 3565

UNTHINKABLE
We must dare to think about "unthinkable things" 1450

UNTRAMMELED
The first principle of a free society is an untrammeled flow of words 1142

UNTRIED
Is it not adherence to the old and tried against the new and untried? 199

UNWASHED
This court will not deny the equal protection of the law to the unwashed 3376

UNWISE
What is constitutional may still be unwise. 242

UP
What's up today is down tomorrow. 2802

UPPER
only the upper echelons who are licked 112

UPPER CLASS
the need of the upper class to keep the lower class in its place 110

UPSIDE DOWN
Communism is a Russian autocracy turned upside down. 123

the first woman God ever made was strong enough to turn the world upside down 3981

URINATE
trying to make sure cows don't urinate on our shoes 2670

US
The government is us; we are the government 375

We have met the enemy and he is us. 1059

USEFUL
The only kinds of courage and honesty which are permanently useful 1799

USELESS
Nothing is so useless as a general maxim. 862

useless laws weaken necessary ones 1858

USUFRUCT
they may manage it, then ... during their usufruct 728

USURPATION
more instances of the abridgment of freedom ... than by ... sudden usurpations 1236

USURPER
Whoever puts his hand on me to govern me is a usurper 561

UTOPIA
are not now the right sign-posts to the socialist Utopia 3572

UTTERANCE
Government should be concerned with anti-social conduct, not with utterances. 3482

VACANCY
"Every time I fill a vacancy, I create a hundred malcontents and one ingrate." 2525

VACANT
a revolutionary movement ... takes over the powers that have become vacant 3268

VACILLATION
Vacillation and inconsistency are as incompatible with successful diplomacy 1628

VACUUM
I am a leader by default, only because nature does not allow a vacuum. 2214

VAGUE
Constitutions should be short and vague. 231

VAIN
No great man lives in vain. 2050

so vain that he wants to figure ... as the settler of all the great questions 2470

A quarter of a century of peace does not pass over a nation in vain. 3720

VALUE

Most people's opinions are of no value at all. 490

Labour ... is the only universal ... measure of value 633

A man who knows the price of everything, and the value of nothing. 914

If a nation values anything more than freedom 1381

Race prejudice decreases values both real estate and human; 2909

What men value in this world is not rights but privileges. 3349

VAMPIRE

Capital is dead labor that, vampire-like, lives only by sucking living labor 71

VANITY

I first of all subtract the man's vanity from his other qualities 2074

"Vanity of vanities, all is vanity" 3455

VEHICLE

Republican Party is an ancient political vehicle 3171

VEIL

If it is necessary to veil her statue it is not for me to do it. 1296

VENAL

Give them a corrupt House of Lords, give them a venal House of Commons 1165

VENERATION

Princes are like to heavenly bodies ... which have much veneration but no rest 2330

VERDICT

"Sentence first—verdict afterwards." 1788

VERGE

The ability to get to the verge of war 3888

VERTEBRAE

Congressmen with vertebrae of putty 3804

VESTRYMAN

not a single crowned head ... would entitle him to be elected a vestryman 2344

VESUVIUS

We live as in a villa on Vesuvius. 3252

VETERAN

How different the new order would be if we could consult the veteran 2595

Within the soul of each Vietnam veteran 3961

VETO

to wait until they do pass and then veto them 2968

VEXATION

an elegant incognito devised to save a man from the vexation of thinking 2463

VICE

the American vice ... reducing everything unique to the level of the herd 427

all such plans nourish some of the meanest vices of human nature 756

some others which appear vices result in one's greater security 774

The prince must not mind incurring the scandal of those vices 774

extremism in the defense of liberty is no vice 1042

it's true that you can't abolish vice 1486

the latter negatively by restraining our vices 1498

Extremism in the pursuit of the Presidency is an unpardonable vice 3000

I am against vice in every form, including the Vice Presidency. 3025

The inherent vice of capitalism is the unequal sharing of blessings 3569

VICE PRESIDENT

contrived for me the most insignificant office (the vice-presidency) 2953

Th' vice-prisidincy is th' next highest an' the lowest. 2965

I am against vice in every form, including the Vice Presidency. 3025

learned from (Geraldine Ferraro's) candidacy for vice president 4014

VICIOUS

remove the bandage ... to distinguish between the vicious and the unfortunate 1792

VICTIM

made the nation sound like an immense ingathering of victims 515

Fascism is not defined by the number of its victims 609

Mankind censures injustice, fearing that they may be victims 1748

victim to too severe a law is considered as a martyr 1878

It marks its victim: denounces it; 2854

just enough to enable the victim to maintain life 3555

We are the first victims of America fascism. 3642

Youth is the first victim of war; 3900

VICTOR

In this age ... can be no losers in peace and no victors in war 3915

VICTORIA STATION

to be able to take a ticket at Victoria Station and go anywhere 1657

VICTORIOUS

A victorious general has no faults in the eye of the public 3688

A war, even the most victorious, is a national misfortune. 3745

VICTORY

The defeats and victories of the fellows at the top 95

I glory in conflict, that I may hereafter exult in victory. 878

Victory attained by violence is tantamount to a defeat 937

As always, victory finds a hundred fathers 974

Whether in chains or in laurels, liberty knows nothing but victories. 1290

with the victory recorded forever in history 1390

Faith is necessary to victory. 2045

Be ashamed to die until you have won some victory for humanity. 2066

be remembered not for victories or defeats 2172

Victory shifts from man to man. 3644

Dead men have no victory. 3648

Certain peace is better and safer than anticipated victory. 3657

It's not victory if it doesn't end the war. 3672

Peace hath her victories no less renowned than war. 3680

Better a lean peace than a fat victory. 3685

Victory or defeat? It is the slogan of all-powerful militarism 3790

And yet, what can victory bring to the proletariat? 3790

spirit ... of the man who leads that gains the victory 3808

for without victory there is no survival 3826

Victory at all costs, victory in spite of all terror 3826

The problems of victory are more agreeable than those of defeat 3834

victory required a mighty manifestation of the most ennobling of the virtues 3848

In Victory: Magnanimity. 3852

In war there is no substitute for victory. 3865

VIETNAM

In revealing the workings of government that led to the Vietnam War 1190

Vietnam was the first war ever fought without any censorship. 1196

VIEW

I shall adopt new views so fast as they shall appear to be true views. 893

not do something to people ... for the views they have or views they express 1144

VIGIL

We keep a vigil of peace around the world. 1681

VIGILANCE

Eternal vigilance is the price of liberty. 1272

VIGILANT

No man is entitled to the blessings of freedom unless he be vigilant 1397

not to the strong alone; it is to the vigilant 3693

VIGOR

vigor maintains peace and prosperity in a state 1515

But have them carried out with force and vigor. 2225

Power vegetates with more vigour after these gentle prunings. 3086

VIGOROUS

Men are conservatives when they are least vigorous 195

VILLAIN

a conviction that there are identifiable villains 2795

VINEYARD

then he labors in vain ... in the vineyards of equality 2936

VIOLATE

no inherent Constitutional authority for the President ... to violate the law 3024

VIOLATION

a violation of the natural order of things 556

VIOLENCE

The dictatorship of the Communist Party is maintained by ... violence 136

an organization for the systematic use of violence by one class 385

Victory attained by violence is tantamount to a defeat 937

An unjust law is itself a species of violence. 1920

Power and violence are opposites; 2891

Some people draw a comforting distinction between "force" and "violence". 2894

If violence is wrong in America, violence is wrong abroad. 3272

War therefore is an act of violence intended to compel our opponents 3717

Violence seldom accomplishes permanent and desired results. 3794

the use of violence for political gain has become more, not less widespread 3963

VIOLENT

If I die a violent death, as ... a few are plotting 2213

I have invariably objected to all violent and extreme measures 2472

who make peaceful revolution impossible ... make violent revolution inevitable 3271

(This is) an era of violent peace. 3969

VIRGIL
as Virgil saith, "It never troubles the wolf how
many the sheep be." 3674

VIRGINIAN
I am a Virginian, so naturally I am a
politician. 2578

VIRTUE
observance of the written laws is ... one of the
high virtues 17
While the people retain their virtue and
vigilance 342
Liberty can no more exist without virtue 1220
Guide them by virtue, keep them in line with the
rites 1478
All virtue is summed up in dealing justly. 1750
Justice is that virtue that assigns to every man his
due. 1755
justice means force as well as virtue 1779
He who exercises government by means of his
virtue 1968
The grounds of this are virtue and talent. 2033
With strength, one can conquer others, and to
conquer others gives one virtue. 2193
but little virtue in the action of masses of
men 2291
The love of country is the first virtue 2397
Those who think that all virtue is to be found in
their own party principles 2442
Patience! the first, and last ... virtue of a
politician 2529
The highest proof of virtue is to possess boundless
power without abusing it. 2859
Power tends to confuse itself with virtue 2886
Moderation in the affairs of the nation is the
highest virtue. 3000
You cannot legislate for virtue. 3112
economy among the ... most important of
republican virtues 3588
Peace is ... a virtue based on strength of
character 3681
a mighty manifestation of the most ennobling of
the virtues of man 3848

VIRTUOUS
necessarily comes to grief among so many who are
not virtuous 1978
he must learn how not to be virtuous 1978
The life of the nation is secure only while the
nation is ... virtuous. 2370

VISION
bridge the gap between his nation's experience and
his vision 2210
(Republicans are) men of narrow vision 3179
that goal that supplies the political magic ... in the
president's vision 3973

VISITOR
You have to stand three or four hours a day of
visitors 2971

VITRIOLIC
to repent ... not merely for the vitriolic words 30

VOCAL CORD
no man has the right to strangle democracy with a
single set of vocal cords 1134

VOICE
"The voice of the people is the voice of
God" 268
so long as it is a mere voice, without overt
acts 282
Governments will never be awed by the voice of
the people 282
The majority voice should be controlling 364
I do not want the voice of the people shut
out. 400
not willing to be governed by laws which they had
no voice in making 557
he has abolished their freedom to find in his voice
a voice for their wrongs 1152
his being a voice which can speak for those who
are silent 1152
only one voice in stating the position of this
country 2985

VOID
An act against the Constitution is void; an act
against natural equity is void. 228

VOLCANO
as it is impossible ... to keep its place above the
force of a volcano 3114

VOLUMINOUS
if the laws be so voluminous that they cannot be
read 1917

VOTE
Vote Labor and you build castles in the air. 219
the obvious disadvantage of merely counting
votes 371
What the masses vote ... for is not important 408
at what stage of starvation will you prefer the
grain to the vote 468
To request an honest man to vote according to his
conscience is superfluous. 699
"Vote early and vote often" 703
Vote, n. The instrument and symbol of a
freeman's power 709
We'd all like t'vote fer th' best man 711
because most people vote against somebody 713
Vote for the man who promises least; 716
A whore's vote is just as good as a
debutante's. 717
The vote is the most powerful instrument ever
devised by man 720
And the power in hand is the vote. 721
Bad politicians are sent to Washington by good
people who don't vote. 726

they have a grand sense for where the votes
are   2511

in order to get the wind of votes in their
sails   2636

the mighty in Washington can be persuaded ... by
anything less than votes   2768

the most valuable thing their victims own, their
votes   2798

to vote Republican ... is the same as a chicken
voting for Colonel Sanders   3176

I want to stand by my country, but I cannot vote
for war. I vote no.   3780

Give women the vote, and ... there will be a
crushing tax on bachelors.   3989

no hope even that woman, with her right to vote,
will ever purify politics   3992

They, of course, have a right to vote   4003

VOTER

The ignorance of one voter in a democracy
impairs the security of all.   29

Democracy, which requires a whole population of
capable voters   373

The ultimate rulers of our democracy are ... the
voters of this country   414

The voters are the people who have spoken—the
bastards.   722

Voters don't decide issues, they decide who will
decide issues.   723

Legislators are elected by voters, not farms   2257

a Platform is just a list of platitudes to lure the
naive voter   2430

"Every intelligent voter" ... everybody who is
going to vote for them   2596

VOTING

The right of voting for representatives is the
primary right   698

All voting is a sort of gaming, like chequers   701

Voting is merely a handy device;   715

Voting is a civic sacrament.   724

"How can you think of voting for my
opponent?"   2774

VOX

Vox populi, vox humbug.   343

VULGAR

It is an easy and a vulgar thing to please the
mob   3437

When it is looked upon as vulgar, it will cease to
be popular.   3755

WAGE

"A fair day's wages for a fair day's work"   3447

The American wage earner ... are a lot better
economists   3495

WALK

willing to walk with them—walk with them every
step of the way   1680

The man who walks alone is soon trailed by the
F.B.I.   3375

WALL

strange that ... people build walls to keep an
enemy out   186

WALLET

We have more will than wallet;   1104

WANT

but the want of learning is a calamity to any
people   683

Society is produced by our wants   1498

We want wealth, but there are many other things
we want very much more.   1590

Government is a contrivance of human wisdom to
provide for human wants.   3427

WAR

When the rich wage war it's the poor who
die.   101

the only form of government which is not ... at
open or secret war   301

Only governments and not people initiate
wars.   383

then he is always stirring up some war   520

there is always need that we should war   924

This difficult effort will be the "moral equivalent
of war"   1071

Vietnam was the first war fought without any
censorship.   1196

If you are going to try to go to war, or to prepare
for war   1593

We never lost a war and we never won a
conference   1646

Sometimes it takes two or three conferences to
scare up a war   1650

they don't call out the National Guard in each
state and go to war over it   1656

diplomacy is a continuation of war by other
means   1662

Our ultimate goal is a world without war.   1686

As in law so in war, the longest purse finally
wins.   1910

In war you can only be killed once, but in politics
many times.   2736

Politics are almost as exciting as war   2736

they are usually designed for a war which is
over   2747

Politics is war without bloodshed while war is
politics with bloodshed.   2753

The revolutionary war is a war of the
masses;   3250

Every social war is a battle between the very
few   3265

Prepare for war in time of peace.   3461

no nation is rich enough to pay for both war and civilization 3476

Nations have recently been led to borrow billions for war; 3476

This administration today ... declares unconditional war on poverty 3543

To lead an uninstructed people to war is to throw them away. 3647

We make war that we may live in peace. 3649

neither shall they learn war any more 3650

He is wise who tries everything before arms. 3651

Laws are silent in time of war. 3652

Of war men ask the outcome, not the cause. 3659

Luxury, more deadly than war, broods over the city 3663

Let him who desires peace prepare for war. 3664

for a war to be just, three things are necessary 3665

The most disadvantageous peace is better than the most just war. 3666

A prince should therefore have no other aim or thought ... but war 3667

Accurst be he that first invented war. 3670

It's not victory if it doesn't end the war. 3672

nothing so subject to the inconstancy of fortune as war 3673

He that commands the sea ... may take as much and as little of the war 3675

to a kingdom ... a just and honourable war is the true exercise 3676

A just fear of an imminent danger ... is a lawful cause of war. 3677

a condition of war of everyone against everyone 3679

Peace hath her victories no less renowned than war. 3680

Peace is not the mere absence of war, but a virtue 3681

the real reasons which moved me to war 3687

Among the calamities of war ... the diminution of the love of truth 3689

if there was ever a just war since the world began, it is this 3697

It is the object only of war that makes it honorable. 3697

War involves in its progress such a train of unforeseen ... circumstances 3699

To be prepared for War is one of the most effectual means of preserving peace. 3700

Whatever enables us to go to war, secures our peace. 3702

War contains so much folly, as well as wickedness 3703

Each generation should be made to bear the burden of its own wars 3704

To make war upon those who trade with us 3705

no war can be long carried on against the will of the people 3707

My views and feelings (are) in favor of the abolition of war 3714

War is a game in which princes seldom win 3715

War is the province of chance. 3716

War ... is an act of violence intended to compel our opponents 3717

War is regarded as nothing but the continuation of state policy 3718

War is a blessing compared with national degradation. 3722

the pretence for war will never be wanting 3726

It is magnificent, but it is not war. 3727

There are good points about all ... wars. 3730

well that war is so terrible—we should grow too fond of it 3731

War is an ugly thing, but not the ugliest of things: 3732

War is cruelty, and you cannot refine it. 3734

The legitimate object of war is a more perfect peace. 3737

All wars are boyish, and are fought by boys. 3738

In time of war the loudest patriots are the greatest profiteers. 3740

object of a treaty of peace should be to make future war improbable 3741

will think twice before beginning a war 3742

Against war it may be said that it makes the victor stupid 3743

many a boy here to-day who looks on war as all glory 3744

A war, even the most victorious, is a national misfortune. 3745

War is not the normal state of the human family 3748

The real war will never get into the books. 3749

they will not declare war or carry arms 3750

War educates the senses, calls into action the will 3751

The word state is identical with the word war. 3752

not merely cruelty that leads men to love war, it is excitement 3753

As long as war is regarded as wicked, it will always have its fascination. 3755

The wars of the people will be more terrible than those of the kings. 3757

Without war no state could exist. All those we know of arose through war. 3758

War, therefore, will endure to the end of history 3758

Capitalism carries within itself war 3760

War, n. A by-product of the arts of peace. 3762

To call war the soil of courage and virtue 3763

To delight in war is a merit in the soldier 3764

A really great people ... would face all the disasters of war 3766

War makes rattling good history; 3768

War is a dreadful thing, and unjust war is a crime against humanity. 3770

I find war detestable but those who praise it ... even more so 3775

I want to stand by my country, but I cannot vote for war. 3780

All wars are wars among thieves who are too cowardly to fight 3781

No sane enemy ... would destroy the War Office 3784

War is much too serious a matter to be left to generals. 3785

My home policy? I wage war. My foreign policy? I wage war. 3786

far easier to make war than to make peace 3787

Make wars unprofitable and you make them impossible. 3789

the seed of war in the modern world is industrial and commercial rivalry 3791

Herein lies the futility of war. 3794

either incapable of arithmetic or else in favour of war 3800

War is not the continuation of policy. 3801

There are only actual states of peace which, like wars, are mere expedients. 3805

Everyone knows that war can no longer be considered 3807

war can no longer be considered ... a means of attaining ... a ... objective 3807

Wars may be fought with weapons, but they are won by men. 3808

Everyone, when there's war in the air 3810

During war we imprison the rights of man. 3811

War is not an instinct but an invention. 3815

The most shocking fact about war 3816

offered a choice between war and shame ... chosen shame and will get war 3819

We have sustained a defeat without a war. 3820

All wars that are progressive are just ... wars that impede progress are unjust 3821

History shows that wars are divided into two kinds, just and unjust. 3821

War can be abolished only through war 3822

nothing to stop war from going on forever 3824

You ask, what is our policy? ... to wage war 3828

cannot accept the doctrine that war must be ... man's destiny 3830

War challenges virtually every other institution 3831

he fights debates like a war and a war like a debate 3835

War is not an adventure. It is a disease. 3837

We used to wonder where war lived 3838

better to have a war for justice than peace in injustice 3839

Older men declare war. 3840

Peace, like war, can succeed only where there is a will to enforce it 3841

The war of the giants is over 3842

As long as there are ... nations possessing great power, war is inevitable. 3844

war is the ultimate sanction of that exploitation 3846

Since wars begin in the minds of men 3847

I hate war as only a soldier who has lived it can 3848

I have never met anybody who wasn't against war. 3849

Wars occur because people prepare for conflict, rather than for peace. 3850

In War: Resolution. In Defeat: Defiance. 3852

War is an unmitigated evil. 3855

No one can guarantee success in war 3856

The way to prevent war is to bend every energy toward preventing it 3858

You take Diplomacy out of war and the thing would fall flat 3859

Diplomats are ... essential to starting a war 3859

In war there is no second prize for the runner-up. 3862

People who are vigorous and brutal often find war enjoyable 3863

a great help in persuading people that wars are righteous 3863

The quickest way of ending a war is to lose it. 3864

In war there is no substitute for victory. 3865

After each war there is a little less democracy to save. 3869

War is both the product of an earlier corruption 3870

to kill in war is not a whit better than to commit ... murder 3871

I hate war. War destroys individuals and whole generations. 3873

fatal to enter any war without the will to win it 3874

War is an invention of the human mind. 3875

To jaw-jaw always is better than to war-war. 3881

The war has started incredibly badly. 3885

The ability to get to the verge of war without getting into the war 3888

You have to take chances for peace, just as you must take chances in war. 3888

nothing more foolish than to think that war can be stopped by war 3892

opposed even to the thought of fighting a "preventive war" 3892

You don't "prevent" anything by war except peace. 3892

it takes only twenty seconds of war to destroy him 3900

Youth is the first victim of war; 3900

we can secure peace only by preparing for
war   3901

let us join in dismantling the national capacity to
wage war   3905

Unconditional war can no longer lead to
unconditional victory.   3907

Mankind must put an end to war or war will put
an end to mankind.   3907

If we were to apply the former, we ran the risk of
war   3909

Aggressive conduct ... ultimately leads to
war.   3912

The mere absence of war is not peace.   3916

That's the way it is in war.   3918

This is not a jungle war, but a struggle for
freedom   3920

all of a sudden I thought, "War can't be this
bad"   3923

War is a poor chisel to carve out
tomorrows.   3926

little basis for confidence that reason can prevail in
... mounting war fever   3928

A war is subject to advance planning.   3929

when you get in a war, get everything you need
and win it   3932

I say when you get into a war, you should win as
quick as you can   3932

in our war with the Arabs we had a secret
weapon--no alternative   3940

Not war but peace is the father of all
things.   3949

A war regarded as inevitable or even
probable   3953

Of the four wars in my lifetime, none came ...
because the U.S. was too strong   3956

War is just like bush-clearing   3959

"Bad war, good soldier"   3961

(It is time to) separate the war from the
warrior.   3961

should not cause us to forget the fact that it is
preferable to war   3967

WAR-MONGERING

To insist on strength ... is not war-
mongering.   3922

WARFARE

No man can sit down and withhold his hands
from the warfare against wrong   3771

The most terrible warfare is to be a second
lieutenant leading a platoon   3884

Warfare ... is a means to an end   3889

WARRANT

His own good, either physical or moral, is not a
sufficient warrant.   1289

WARRIOR

He who has once gazed into the glazed eye of a
dying warrior   3742

(It is time to) separate the war from the
warrior.   3961

WARTIME

Nothing is more dangerous in wartime than ... a
Gallup Poll   3073

There is no working middle course in
wartime.   3836

WASHINGTON

the bitter experience of all public men from
George Washington down   390

Bad politicians are sent to Washington by good
people who don't vote.   726

Washington is a place where the truth is not
necessarily the best defense.   815

The more I observed Washington ... I understood
how prophetic L'Enfant was   1009

Washington is a city of Southern efficiency and
Northern charm.   1035

Washington is the only town in the world where
sound travels faster than light.   1076

I remember when I first came to
Washington.   2639

Washington has no memory.   2812

Nothing ever gets settled in this town
(Washington)   2824

Were we directed from Washington when to
sow   3435

our Washington reflex is to discover a problem
and then throw money at it   3483

only one place where inflation is made ...
Washington   3627

If you had to work in the environment of
Washington, D.C. as I do   4009

WASP

Laws are like cobwebs, which may catch small
flies, but let wasps ... through   1849

WASTE

The very essence of competitive commerce is
waste   638

waste of public money is like the sin against the
Holy Ghost   796

If we can prevent the government from wasting
the labors of the people   1518

What a waste.   2660

WATCH

he trespasses against his duty who sleeps over his
watch   776

If you love the law and you love good sausage,
don't watch ... them being made   2259

WATER

the man who would not go into the water until he
had learned to swim   357

greatest domestic problem ... is saving our soil and
water   733

Not all the water in the rough rude sea   2325

Leave it perfectly still, and the water will remain
uncongealed;   3091

The tree of liberty grows only when watered by
the blood of tyrants.   3193

WATERGATE

(Watergate) was worse than a crime, it was a blunder. 1078

WAVE

The boisterous sea of liberty is never without a wave. 1253

The wave of the future is not the conquest of the world 1443

WAY

Fascism is not defined by the number of its victims, but by the way it kills 609

The free way of life proposes ends, but it does not prescribe means. 1448

WAYSIDE

if they are, some of us will fall by the wayside 3572

WEAK

Communism is exploitation of the strong by the weak. 116

Property is exploitation of the weak by the strong. 116

Don't expect to build up the weak by pulling down the strong. 209

democracy is that ... the weakest should have the same opportunity 444

If we let things take their course the West would say we were ... weak 1010

You cannot accomplish good for the people unless you face up to the weak 2027

Like all weak men he laid an exaggerated stress on not changing one's mind. 2104

but the same thing can be said of the most weak 2847

fail to use them and it is weak 3064

Where the state is weak, the army rules. 3432

WEAKEN

Nothing so weakens government as persistent inflation. 654

WEAKNESS

Don't forget that weakness produces civil wars 1515

I know only too well my limits and weaknesses 2166

usually a regime collapses of its own weakness and corruption 3268

WEAL

I will govern according to the common weal 2329

WEALTH

Excess of wealth is cause of covetousness. 37

Wherever there is excessive wealth, there is also ... excessive poverty; 59

So long as all the increased wealth which modern progress brings 67

three ways by which an individual can get wealth 70

How can wealth persuade poverty ... to keep wealth in power? 218

If political freedom is more advantageous for the development of wealth 309

We can have democracy ... or we can have great wealth concentrated 425

True wealth is not a static thing. 648

it must remould our institutions of wealth into the Commonwealth 1321

Liberty produces wealth and wealth destroys liberty. 1322

You can easily rebuild wealth, but you cannot create liberty 1380

We want wealth, but ... other things we want very much more 1590

As wealth is power, so all power will infallibly draw wealth to itself 2839

Where public opinion is free and uncontrolled, wealth has a wholesome respect 3065

Wealth is the means, and people are the ends. 3487

taxes should ... fall ... on the accumulated wealth 3601

WEALTH-PRIVILEGE

The function of parliamentary democracy ... is to expose wealth-privilege 467

WEAPON

Print is the ... strongest weapon of our party 134

The most potent weapon in the hands of the oppressor 623

Wisdom is better than weapons of war. 1602

proud of the fact that I never invented weapons to kill 3776

Wars may be fought with weapons, but they are won by men. 3808

Weapons are an important factor in war 3823

Terrorism has become the systematic weapon of a war that knows no borders 3972

WEAR

To wear your heart on your sleeve isn't a very good plan; 1101

WEED

It is a weed that grows in every soil. 538

WEEK

There cannot be a crisis next week. 1070

WEIGH

it has the ... disadvantage of merely counting votes instead of weighing them 371

See that government weighs as little as possible 1519

WEIGHT

a good citizen ... shall be able and willing to pull his weight   22

They must throw in their whole weight in the opposite direction.   2302

think of the weight ... of a whole kingdom   2336

WELCOME

I do not shrink from this responsibility—I welcome it.   1433

WELFARE

effort ... to establish a government for the welfare of the people   413

Welfare is hated by those who administer it   1074

profit must now give way to the advocate of human welfare   1585

unceasing concern for the welfare ... for every individual   2942

that the welfare and the rights of the many are conserved   3477

the fundamental paradox of the welfare state   3542

WELL-BEING

The taste for well-being is the ... indelible feature of democratic times   324

WEST

If we let things take their course the West would say we were either stupid   1010

Whenever our policy in the West has run aground   1642

WEST POINT

The world has turned over many times since I took the oath ... at West Point   989

WET

Among men, Hinnissy, wet eye manes dhry heart.   922

WHEAT

An editor is someone who separates the wheat from the chaff   1001

WHEEL

Public sentiment is to public officers what water is to the wheel of the mill.   3058

WHIG

stability and experiment. The former is Tory, and the latter Whig   2464

WHIM

We call a tyrant the leader whose only law is that of his own whim   532

they are foreign and will not always conform to our whim   1684

WHINE

not by whining that one carries out the job of king   2031

WHIP

They who study mankind with a whip in their hands will always go wrong.   569

WHISPER

impossible that the whisper of a faction shall prevail against ... a nation   2286

WHITE

When the white man governs himself, that is self-government;   565

White folks don't want peace; they want quiet.   1814

The choice in politics isn't usually between black and white.   2811

What a happy country this will be, if the whites will listen.   2896

The white man's happiness cannot be purchased by the black man's misery.   2899

Labor in a white skin cannot be free   2905

To the average white man, a courthouse ... is ... where justice is dispensed.   2931

For the white man to ask the black man if he hates him   2934

These are the white man's roads.   2935

whites must be made to realize that they are only human   2944

will white people hear what we are trying to say?   2948

includes the freedom ... to live wherever a white man can live   3377

WHITE HOUSE

Divine right ... doesn't belong to the White House aides.   482

You have to stand three or four hours a day of visitors (to the White House).   2971

In the White House, the future rapidly becomes the past;   2999

Once a president gets to the White House, the only audience ... is history.   3032

WHITEY

Should I ... stand on 125th Street cussing out Whitey   3132

WHO

Politics: Who Gets What, When, How.   2752

WHOLE

My faith in the constitution is whole.   253

Democrats believe that the whole people should govern   504

WHORE

A whore's vote is just as good as a debutante's.   717

If you're in politics, you're a whore anyhow.   2810

WHY

You see things; and you say, "Why?" 940

But I dream things that never were; and I say "Why not?" 940

WICKED

The wicked are always surprised to find ability in the good. 2676

As long as war is regarded as wicked, it will always have its fascination. 3755

WICKEDNESS

no administration, by any extreme of wickedness or folly 342

Society is produced by our wants, and government by our wickedness; 1498

One can always legislate against specific acts of human wickedness; 1942

WIDESPREAD

the use of violence for political gain has become more, not less widespread 3963

WIFE

a traditional prerogative of the political wife 2667

His wife "ruled the roast" 3979

WILL

the creature of their own will, and lives only by their will 311

a policy to recommend, but none to enforce against the will of the people 350

a kind of balance between the will of the people and the government 451

The man who is born to be a dictator is not compelled; he wills it. 590

We have more will than wallet; but will is what we need. 1104

He that complies against his will is of his opinion still. 1204

it is on this ... that the true will of the people can develop 1269

only purpose for which power can be rightfully exercised ... against his will 1289

the will to be responsible to ourselves 1319

corporation ... must be held to strict compliance with the will of the people 1584

our will that is being tried and not our strength 1697

a test of wills and ideas—a trial of spiritual resolve 1710

Law is merely the expression of the will of the strongest 1899

every one which in their turns determine their wills 2009

govern according to the common weal, but not according to the common will 2329

spiritual purpose, made effective by free, tolerant ... national will 2380

here to consult the interests and not to obey the will of the people 2540

the noble toga that political gentlemen drape over the will to power 2625

a power over a man's support is a power over his will 2842

The secret of power is the will. 2852

no war can be long carried on against the will of the people 3707

an act of violence intended to compel our opponents to fulfil our will 3717

War educates the senses, calls into action the will 3751

fatal to enter any war without the will to win it 3874

Their will was resolute and remorseless 3882

WIN

Winning isn't everything. It is the only thing. 1082

not enough merely to realize how freedom has been won 1399

If you think you can win, you can win. 2045

tragedy of life is not that man loses but that he almost wins 2112

Even more important than winning the election 2499

Whoever is winning at the moment will always seem to be invincible. 2770

You never really win anything in politics. 2815

That is where the Republican Party has won. 3175

Nothing except a battle lost can be half so melancholy as a battle won. 3713

You cannot fight hard unless you think you are fighting to win. 3772

fatal to enter any war without the will to win 3874

You win or lose, live or die—and the difference is just an eyelash. 3918

when you get into a war, you should win as quick as you can 3932

WIND

The wind of change is blowing through the continent. 1020

let him twist slowly, slowly in the wind 1062

a wind of nationalism and freedom blowing round the world 2379

WINDING STAIR

All rising to great place is by a winding stair. 1991

WIREPULLER

In a pure democracy the ruling men will be the wirepullers 353

WISDOM

free governments are managed by the combined wisdom and folly of the people   355

Without Freedom of Thought, there can be no such Thing as Wisdom;   1205

Wisdom is better than weapons of war.   1602

We do not sit as a superlegislature to weigh the wisdom of legislation.   1734

The law is the last result of human wisdom acting upon human experience   1867

We thought, because we had power, we had wisdom.   2870

My country has in its wisdom contrived for me the most insignificant office   2953

It isn't wisdom or intelligence that influences a President   3027

Government is a contrivance of human wisdom to provide for human wants.   3427

whether we have the wisdom to use wealth to ... elevate our national life   3544

We pray for the wisdom that this hero be America's last unknown.   3965

WISE

Wise and prudent men—intelligent conservatives   214

peculiar circumstances ... may render a measure more or less wise   234

Oppression makes a wise man mad.   563

The number of wise men will always be small.   840

A wise government knows how to enforce with temper   1491

Nothing doth more hurt ... than that cunning men pass for wise   1989

Only make wise and moderate laws.   2225

A wise man will not leave the right to the mercy of chance   2291

He never said a foolish thing,/ Nor ever did a wise one.   2332

no more than to love and to be wise   3580

He is wise who tries everything before arms.   3651

wise to kill an admiral ... to encourage the others   3690

WISELY

Men and nations do behave wisely   1692

If you command wisely, you'll be obeyed cheerfully.   2006

WITCH

Men feared witches and burned women.   1127

WITCHCRAFT

Rebellion is as the sin of witchcraft.   3183

WITHER

like a flower cut from its life-giving roots, it will wither and die   1390

WOLF

The shepherd drives the wolf from the sheep's throat   1303

"It never troubles the wolf how many the sheep be."   3674

WOMAN

the way in which women are governed in this Republic   557

The prolonged slavery of women is the darkest page in human history.   575

all men and women are created equal   747

The states are not free ... to intimidate women into continuing pregnancies.   1948

woman feels the invidious distinctions of sex   2904

those of woman ... will not shrink from the same test   3297

women: their rights and nothing less   3304

man ... says women can't have as much rights as man   3305

From God and a woman. Man had nothing to do with it.   3305

Many Abolitionists have yet to learn the ABC of woman's rights.   3306

stir about colored men getting ... rights, but not a word about ... women   3310

here to claim our rights as women, not only to be free   3328

The freer that women become, the freer will men be.   3383

women are now providing all types of skills in every profession   3391

no occupation ... which belongs either to women or to men   3974

To promote a Woman to bear rule ... above any Realm   3975

Women have, or ought to have, but little liberty;   3976

let him despise woman, if she do not share it with him   3978

the duty of the women of this country to secure ... the franchise   3980

the first woman God ever made was strong enough to turn the world upside down   3981

the chain of the most oppressed of all—of Woman, the pariah of humanity   3982

the civil and political equality of women   3983

Women ... care fifty times more for a marriage than a ministry   3984

Women must not depend upon the protection of man   3985

when at last woman stands on an even platform with man   3988

Give women the vote, and ... there will be a crushing tax on bachelors.   3989

True, the movement for women's rights has broken many old fetters   3991

no hope even that woman ... will ever purify politics.   3992

Keyword Index

WORLD

To live anywhere in the world today and be
against equality   768

My country is the world; my countrymen are
mankind.   864

Whatever America hopes to bring to pass in the
world   1659

Our ultimate goal is a world without war. A world
made safe for diversity.   1686

I would not be a queen/ For all the world.   1988

The world usually rewards the appearance of
ability   1996

easy in the world to live after the world's
opinion   2047

world is divided into those who want to become
someone   2206

The desire to understand the world and the desire
to reform it   3121

in this world no such force as ... a man
determined to rise   3325

Yet they are the world of the individual
person: 3352

If man does find the solution for world
peace   3845

WORLD WAR II

World War II was the last government program
that really worked.   3498

WORM

Politics, which, the planet over, are ... the worm in
the bud   2739

WORRY

In government, you don't have to worry about
that.   1598

WORSE

(Democrats) can't get elected unless things get
worse   516

Man did not enter into society to become
worse   3295

Anything that the private sector can do, the
government can do it worse.   3500

WORSHIP

We must therefore worship the state   852

With what deep worship I have still adored   1250

when he refuseth a real, worship to the
laws   1846

WORST

democracy is the worst form of Government
except all those other   441

The worst thing in this world, next to anarchy, is
government.   1546

worst thing that can be said of the most
powerful   2847

WORTH

Freedom is not worth having if it does not
connote freedom to err.   1429

"That man is worth so much!"   1582

very difficult to be worth re-electing   2100

The worth of a State ... is the worth of the
individuals composing it.   2367

state of moral ... feeling which thinks nothing
worth a war   3732

WOUND

if they have a cutting edge they may later ...
wound him   2618

for he must suffer and bear the deepest wounds
and scars of war   3910

WRATH

He conceals the other half out of fear of the
people's wrath.   1023

When hopes ... are loose in the streets ... lie low
until the wrath has passed   3263

WRECK

Vote, n. ... a freeman's power to make a ... wreck
of his country   709

WRING

before long they will be wringing their
hands   3686

WRITE

not our job to apply laws that have not yet been
written   1743

Even when laws have been written down, they
ought not ... remain unaltered.   1820

Certain laws have not been written, but they are
more fixed   1826

Our written law is often difficult to
understand   1882

I cannot do anything else but write about
it.   2790

In writing and politicking, it's best not to think
about it   2818

time now to write the next chapter—and to write
it in books of law   3359

WRITER

A great writer is ... a second government in his
country   1044

no regime has ever loved great writers   1044

WRITHING

Power takes as ingratitude the writhing of its
victims.   2866

WRONG

Decisions arrived at democratically ... may be
wrong   497

people are always in the wrong when they are
faced by the armed forces   551

No man is prejudiced in favor of a thing knowing
it to be wrong.   846

We uniformly applaud what is right and condemn what is wrong 859

Rarely have so many people been so wrong about so much. 1094

Whenever the press quits abusing me I know I'm in the wrong pew. 1185

Wrong must not win by technicalities. 1818

when great principles are involved, as a rule the majority are wrong 2307

That the king can do no wrong 2343

but our country, right or wrong 2398

Our country, right or wrong ... when wrong, to be put right 2408

Wrong is wrong, no matter who does it 2421

cannot influence a Political Party ... if you stick to it when it does wrong 2487

when a politician does get an idea he usually gets it all wrong 2592

one can be almost sure that some great wrong is at hand 2734

people wud rather be wrong an' comfortable thin right in jail 3110

If slavery is not wrong, nothing is wrong. 3309

began by asking to have certain wrongs redressed 3314

America's view of apartheid ... We believe it is wrong 3397

whenever the public mind is to be diverted from a great social wrong 3526

No man can ... withhold his hands from the warfare against wrong 3771

YANKEE
really universal enemy is precisely Yankee imperialism 1696

YEAR
Politicians ... are not over a year behind Public Opinion 2601

YEARNING
yearning after equality is the offspring of covetousness 756

YELP
the loudest yelps for liberty among the drivers of negroes 1225

YIELD
the right time and the manner of yielding what is impossible to keep 2197

YOLKS
you have nothing to lose but your yolks 1007

YOUNG
When a nation's young men are conservative 201

I never dared to be radical when young 215

When young people grasp a truth they are invincible 694

YOUNGSTER
youngsters yelling in the streets ... are the ones who pay the price 3804

YOURSELF
looking out for yourself by looking out for your country 2414

YOUTH
But it is youth that must fight and die. 3840

Youth is the first victim of war; the first fruit of peace. 3900

ZEAL
it has got to be pursued with apostolic zeal 941

greatest dangers to liberty lurk in insidious encroachment by men of zeal 1361

ZERO
zero defects in products plus zero pollution plus zero risk on the job

Keyword Index

509